REVIVING THE ANCIENT FAITH

Reviving the Ancient Faith

The Story of Churches of Christ in America

Richard T. Hughes

WILLIAM B. EERDMANS PUBLISHING COMPANY
GRAND RAPIDS, MICHIGAN / CAMBRIDGE, U.K.

© 1996 Wm. B. Eerdmans Publishing Co.
255 Jefferson Ave. S.E., Grand Rapids, Michigan 49503 /
P.O. Box 163, Cambridge CB3 9PU U.K.

Printed in the United States of America

00 99 98 97 96 95   7 6 5 4 3 2 1

Library of Congress Cataloging-in-Publication Data

Hughes, Richard T. (Richard Thomas) 1943-
Reviving the ancient faith: the story of Churches of Christ in
- America / Richard T. Hughes.
p.   cm.
Includes index.
ISBN 0-8028-4086-8 (paper: alk. paper)
1. Churches of Christ — History. 2. United States — Church history.
BX7075.H84   1996
286.6′3 — dc20   95-47321
CIP

Portions of this book appeared in a different form in Richard T. Hughes, "The Apocalyptic
Origins of Churches of Christ and the Triumph of Modernism," *Religion and American
Culture* 2 (1992): 181-214. The author and publisher are grateful to the editor of this
journal for permission to incorporate the material in this volume.

For Jan and Andy

Contents

Preface

Fourteen years ago, in 1981, Greenwood Press asked me to write a history of Churches of Christ for their "Denominations in America" series. Greenwood intends for that series to be a collection of reference volumes in which the narrative of each volume will be a summary and overview of central themes in the history of a given tradition. The book I finally produced, however, was a monograph, much longer than Greenwood wanted. Greenwood therefore granted the William B. Eerdmans Publishing Company permission to publish this monograph in a paperbound edition, and I agreed to furnish Greenwood with the reference volume they want at a later date. The narrative of that volume will be roughly half the size of this book, and it will be joined to an extensive section of biographical sketches authored by R. L. Roberts.

I mention this because the original agreement with Greenwood has determined to a great extent the nature of the present volume. I never set out to write a history of Churches of Christ the centerpiece of which would be an abundance of facts — names, dates, and places. Instead, from the beginning I sought to produce a book that would explain the character of Churches of Christ — who they are and why, and how they have changed over the years from one stage to another. That objective has remained constant over the past fourteen years.

Writing this book has not been an easy task. I am a lifelong member of Churches of Christ but also an historian of American religion. Those two commitments have pulled at one another in a variety of ways over the years that this book has been in production. One's allegiance to one's own tradition always prompts one to tell only the good, to negate the bad, and to make the story look better than perhaps it really is. As a historian, however, I had to resist that temptation. I have tried in this book to tell the truth as I see it. The book is not without interpretations, though I have sought to inform those interpretations by seriously engaging the extensive literature produced by Churches of Christ for almost two hundred years.

I owe a great debt of gratitude to many people who have contributed to this volume in a variety of ways over the years. When I first signed the contract with Greenwood Press in 1981, I was teaching at Southwest Missouri State University in Springfield. My dean, Holt V. Spicer, and department chair, Gerrit J. tenZythoff, graciously offered to grant me a leave of absence to launch this project if I could raise financial support for a year. A number of people contributed to that support, including Mr. and Mrs. Bill H. Branch of Roanoke, Virginia; Dr. and Mrs. Quinton Dickerson and Mr. and Mrs. J. C. Redd of Jackson, Mississippi; Mr. and Mrs. Dwain Evans, Mr. and Mrs. Robert Fitts, Mr. and Mrs. Joe Foy, Dr. and Mrs. Norman Garner, Mr. and Mrs. David S. Holland, Dr. and Mrs. Terry Koonce, Dr. and Mrs. Bill Love, and Mr. and Mrs. Robert Norris, all of Houston, Texas; Dr. and Mrs. Claude Hocott of Austin, Texas; Mr. and Mrs. Ray McGlothlin of Abilene, Texas; and the Church of Christ of Chapel Hill, North Carolina.

I owe a special debt of gratitude to Dr. William J. Teague, then president of Abilene Christian University, who graciously offered to name me Scholar-in-Residence at ACU for the 1982-83 academic year, thereby making me eligible for a library office and other support services at that institution. I therefore undertook this project in the bowels of the Herman and Margaret Brown Library at Abilene Christian University. The following year I accepted an offer to teach at Abilene Christian. President Teague extended the Scholar-in-Residence designation on a half-time basis for the 1983-84 and 1986-88 academic years, thereby enabling me to make even further progress on this book.

In the fall of 1988, my family and I left Texas for California and returned to the institution where I began my teaching career in 1971, Pepperdine University. I took up my old position there as professor of the history of Christianity. I am grateful to four Pepperdine University students, Chad Huddleston, Ron Cox, Margaret Smith, and Carl Flynn, who helped in a variety of ways on this project. I am also grateful to Pepperdine University for a grant that freed me from teaching responsibilities for the summer of 1990 and to the Pew Charitable Trusts for a grant in 1990 that freed me from teaching responsibilities for an additional semester, thereby enabling me to move this history even further toward completion.

I am especially grateful to the following persons for their skillful photographic reproduction: Ron Hall of Pepperdine University, David England of David Lipscomb University, and Jami West of Abilene Christian University.

Terry and Beverly Koonce have supported my work financially from the beginning, making possible extended research over several summers both at Abilene Christian University and the Harding University Graduate School of Bible and Religion in Memphis, Tennessee. Words cannot express my gratitude to the staffs of those two libraries. I am especially indebted in that regard to

R. L. Roberts, retired archivist in the Center for Restoration Studies at the ACU library, and to Don Meredith, director of the library at the Harding Graduate School.

R. L. Roberts, in particular, has been my mentor for all these years, guiding me into the proper sources and suggesting helpful interpretations. When I took a year's leave of absence from Southwest Missouri State University in 1982-83, I seriously thought I would research and write the book in that one year. I shall never forget Roberts's words the first day I encountered him in the ACU library and explained to him my zealous intentions. "Not so fast," he said. Indeed, it has not been fast. Fourteen years has been a very long time, but the task has been rewarding.

Many people have read portions of the manuscript at various stages along the way and made extremely helpful comments and suggestions, many of which have been incorporated into the final manuscript. These people include Leonard Allen, Dan Anders, Judy Anders, Molefe Kete Asante, David Baird, Calvin Bowers, Walter Burch, Fran Carver, Michael Casey, John Allen Chalk, Dan Danner, Dwain Evans, Harry Robert Fox, Anne Frashier, Loyd Frashier, Edward Fudge, Leroy Garrett, Fred Gray, Andrew Hairston, David Edwin Harrell Jr., Don Haymes, Samuel S. Hill, Bill Jenkins, David Jones, Eugene Lawton, Steven Lemley, Hubert G. Locke, Bill Love, William Martin, Martin Marty, Lester McAllister, Rob McRay, Lynn Mitchell, Tom Olbricht, Roy Osborne, Kathy Pulley, Robert M. Randolph, R. L. Roberts, Jerry Rushford, J. Harold Thomas, Grant Wacker, and Dewayne Winrow.

In particular, I would like to thank my editor at William B. Eerdmans Publishing Company, Tim Straayer, who made innumerable excellent suggestions regarding the composition of the text; Charles Van Hof, managing editor at Eerdmans, who made the process of publication extraordinarily pleasant from beginning to end; and Henry Bowden, general editor of the Greenwood Press "Denominations in America" series, who has encouraged me regarding this project at every step along the way.

In the end, however, only I am responsible for the shortcomings of this volume.

I am especially grateful to my wife, Janice, and my son, Andy, who have borne with this project for fourteen years. It has altered the shape of our lives in a variety of ways for all those years. It has meant upheaval in the form of two moves, taking us halfway across the United States, and it has meant certain summer months away from home and long hours in the office.

Jan, however, has not only borne with this project but participated at every step along the way as I have shared with her my ideas and interpretations and as she, in turn, has shared with me insights that have consistently proven helpful and productive.

Glossary

NOTE: This glossary seeks to provide the reader with a brief definition of technical terms and concepts important to this book.

Apocalyptic worldview An outlook on life whereby the believer gives his or her allegiance to the kingdom of God, not to the kingdoms of this world, and lives as if the final rule of the kingdom of God were present in the here and now. Such a perspective inevitably generates a countercultural lifestyle.

Baconianism An eighteenth-century philosophical perspective based on the assumption that human beings, by exercising their common sense, can know reality precisely as it is, with full confidence in the accuracy of their knowledge. Because this school of thought originated in Scotland and emphasized the knowledge of reality through common sense, it is more accurately designated Scottish Common Sense Realism. However, because it insisted on the scientific method of induction (as opposed to deduction), it often went by the label "Baconianism," after the founder of the scientific method, Francis Bacon. In antebellum America, many Christians embraced the *Baconian* perspective, insisting that the scientific method could unlock even biblical truths with scientific precision. *See* Scottish Common Sense Realism.

Denomination In the American context, a church that recognizes it is only a part of the universal body of Christ. A denomination has typically made its peace with the dominant culture in which it exists. *See* Sect.

Dispensational premillennialism A version of premillennial thinking popular among American fundamentalists in the early twentieth century. Dispensationalism divides human history into several periods, or dispensations, in which God used unique means to bring his rule to bear on the earth. New dispensations became necessary as God's plans were frustrated. For example, God sought to set up his kingdom or universal reign through the ministry of Christ, but when human beings rejected Christ, God settled for the church as second best. Little wonder that many among Churches of Christ felt that dispensational premillennialism belittled the church. Dispensationalists held that in the final dispensation, God's complete rule over the earth would become a reality. *See* Millennial; Premillennial.

Eschatology The body of learning that pertains to the final age and the second coming of Christ. The various theories regarding the final age color this body of learning in different ways; thus, we can speak of premillennial eschatology, postmillennial eschatology, and the like. See Millennial; Postmillennial; Premillennial.

Millennial Having to do with the final, golden age of human history. Largely based on Revelation 20:1-9, which describes an angel casting Satan into "the bottomless pit" for a thousand years (millennium), this perspective anticipates a period characterized by peace, justice, and righteousness. *See* Dispensational premillennialism; Postmillennial; Premillennial.

Postmillennial An outlook that suggests that human beings will usher in the millennium, or the final golden age, by virtue of human progress. In this scenario, Christ's second coming will occur only at the conclusion of the millennium and will therefore be "postmillennial." Many Christians embraced this perspective following the eighteenth-century Enlightenment with its emphasis on progress through science and human rationality. *See* Dispensational premillennialism; Millennial; Premillennial.

Primitivism An effort to model the contemporary church on the primitive church described in the New Testament or to reproduce the behavior and practices of the primitive (earliest) Christians. *See* Restoration.

Premillennial An outlook that suggests that Christ, at his second coming, will usher in the millennium, or the final golden age on earth, and will rule with his saints on earth for a thousand years. In contrast to the postmillennial perspective, the premillennial position emphasizes that God alone is capable of inaugurating the millennial age. *See* Dispensational premillenialism; Millennial; Postmillennial.

Restoration The attempt to restore or recreate primitive Christianity in the modern world. *See* Primitivism.

Scottish Common Sense Realism A philosophical orientation that originated in Scotland in the late eighteenth century based on the assumption that human beings can know reality precisely as it is, especially if they utilize the scientific method. *See* Baconianism.

Sect A religious organization that insists that it — and it alone — constitutes the entirety of the kingdom of God. Typically, a sect stands in judgment both on other religious organizations and on the larger culture in which it exists. *See* Denomination.

CHAPTER 1

Introduction:
The Character of Churches of Christ

This book is a history of Churches of Christ in the United States, but that statement requires qualification. Over the years, Churches of Christ have divided and subdivided to such an extent that *The Encyclopedia of American Religions* lists eight major wings of this tradition.[1] Together, the various wings of Churches of Christ embraced roughly 1,700,000 members in 1990.[2]

Through that maze of division, I seek in this volume to follow the majority, mainstream tradition of the movement. While I do take seriously, for example, the Pre-millennial Churches of Christ, the Non-Class Churches of Christ, the One-Cup Churches of Christ, the Anti-Institutional Churches of Christ, and the International (Boston) Churches of Christ, as well as those congregations that are predominantly African American, none of these traditions stands at the heart of this volume. Instead, this book is principally about the white mainstream of Churches of Christ that traces its American heritage to Barton W. Stone and Alexander Campbell in the early nineteenth century and that, in the twentieth century, has thrived especially in a region running from Middle Tennessee to West Texas. At the same time, particularly when dealing with the twentieth century, I attempt to tell the story of mainline Churches of Christ from the viewpoint of various dissenting streams of this tradition — a point clarified later in this introduction.

It is my contention in this book that four major themes have shaped the character of this tradition from its nineteenth-century beginnings.

First, the defining characteristic of Churches of Christ throughout their history, until late in the twentieth century, was the notion of the restoration of primitive Christianity — the attempt to recover in the modern age the Christian faith as it was believed and practiced in the first century. This vision flourished especially in the heady, utopian climate of the early nineteenth century when

1

Churches of Christ in America first began. Many Americans of that period, deeply impressed with the glories of the new nation and of the land it occupied, imagined that a golden age was near, perhaps even the final triumph of the kingdom of God. In that context, a number of religious movements dedicated themselves to recovering primitive Christianity in all its purity and perfection. The two most notable manifestations of that impulse in the antebellum period were the Churches of Christ and the Latter-day Saints, though these two traditions took that impulse in very different directions.[3] Throughout this book, I use the term *primitivism* to refer to this attempt to recover the ancient Christian faith.

Second, Churches of Christ began as a sect in the early nineteenth century and evolved into a denomination during the course of the twentieth century.[4] This fact would hardly be striking, or even very interesting, were it not for the fact that Churches of Christ have passionately rejected the labels *sect* and *denomination* as pertinent to their own identity. Indeed, their resolute rejection of these labels has been central to what Churches of Christ have been about for almost two hundred years. Since their denial of these categories flies in the face of social reality, their story is one of deep irony and absorbing interest.

Often, these people have argued that they have restored the primitive church of the apostolic age and are therefore nothing more or less than the true, original church described in the New Testament. For this reason, Churches of Christ generally have denied that they had a defining history other than the Bible itself and have expressed little or no interest in their particular history in the United States. Many members of Churches of Christ remain to this day virtually ignorant of Alexander Campbell, the early nineteenth-century leader who helped give shape and texture to this movement in its founding years. What is more, many of these same people studiously avoid learning about Campbell or any other important leader from their past: they fear that to acknowledge dependence on any human leader would make them a denomination with a human founder rather than the true, primitive church founded by Christ. This unique self-understanding has served to create institutional identity out of a denial of institutional identity, and it has shaped the history and character of Churches of Christ in countless and often paradoxical ways. The material I present in this book substantiates the assertion a colleague and I have made elsewhere that churches that root their identity in efforts to restore ancient Christianity are susceptible to the illusion that they have escaped the influence of history and culture altogether.[5]

Third, this book will argue that the nineteenth-century sectarian character of Churches of Christ drew from two first-generation leaders, not one. To the extent that scholars and members of Churches of Christ have acknowledged their history, most have assumed that the tradition is indebted mainly to Alexander Campbell. While acknowledging Campbell's significance, I will argue that Barton W. Stone was equally important for shaping this tradition. It is my contention that one cannot understand the history and character of Churches of Christ unless one understands the thought and contributions of both of these men.

Fourth, I will argue that Campbell and Stone understood the Christian message and oriented themselves to the world in which they lived in very different ways. These differences contributed not only to the character of Churches of Christ but also to divisions that ruptured this movement, both in the nineteenth and in the twentieth centuries. Three terms are pertinent in this context: *apocalypticism, postmillennialism,* and *premillennialism.*

Since Alexander Campbell embraced a highly optimistic view of the world, we will refer to his outlook as *postmillennial.* Like many Americans living in the early nineteenth century, Campbell imagined that human progress would usher in the kingdom or rule of God (the millennium) and that Jesus would return only at the conclusion of that golden age. Thus, he believed that Jesus' second coming would be *postmillennial.*

Barton Stone, on the other hand, embraced a pessimistic understanding of the world. We will refer to Stone's perspective as *apocalyptic.* Apocalypticism in this context does not involve millennial theories or speculation regarding the time of the second coming. Instead, it signifies an outlook on life whereby Stone and many of his people lived their lives as if the final rule of the kingdom of God were present in the here and now. Stone and many who looked to him for leadership denied that human progress could contribute anything at all to the creation of the kingdom of God on this earth. They gave their unqualified allegiance to God's rule and rejected allegiance to human governments and to the popular values of the culture in which they lived. This outlook gave their activities a radical, even countercultural dimension.

While I do not use the term *apocalypticism* in reference to any particular theory about the millennium or the final golden age, it is nonetheless true that Stone and many of his people embraced a decidedly *premillennial* reading of human history. They believed that this world could not become the kingdom of God unless and until God himself ordained it. Many therefore held that the world could not be renewed until Christ himself returned to establish his millennial rule on earth. Thus they believed the second coming of Christ would be *premillennial,* or prior to the final golden age.

A caution, however, is in order at this point. The reader should not confuse my use of the term *apocalyptic* with *premillennial* perspectives. While apocalyptic thinking has often given rise to premillennial perspectives, the two are not the same. I use the phrase *apocalyptic worldview* in this book to refer to the kind of piety that led Stone and many of his followers to place themselves directly under the rule of God and to refuse to conform themselves to the values of the world.

Understanding the "Nondenominational" Ideal

In addition to these key terms, we must also attempt to understand at the outset of this book what it means to say that Churches of Christ began as a sect and evolved into a denomination but denied that they were either. This is a critical consideration, since the transition from sect to denomination, along with the persistent refusal of Churches of Christ to acknowledge and come to terms with that transition, is one of the central stories in the history of this tradition. In fact, the conviction of its members that Churches of Christ constituted no denomination at all, but had recovered instead the purity of the primitive Christian communities, has been, until very recent years, its most important defining characteristic.

During the 1960s, Churches of Christ promoted a tract entitled "Neither Catholic, Protestant, Nor Jew" that illustrates this point well. Translated into French, German, and Arabic, and arguably the most widely distributed tract ever published by Churches of Christ or anyone associated with that tradition, it proclaimed that

> the church of Christ is neither Catholic, Protestant, nor Jewish. We are unique and different for we are endeavoring to go all the way back to the original New Testament church. Using the New Testament as our blueprint we have re-established in the twentieth century Christ's church. It fits no modern label. It is not just another denomination.[6]

We need to be clear, therefore, about what we mean by the terms *sect* and *denomination* and about what Churches of Christ have meant when they have spoken of "nondenominational Christianity."

According to common understanding in the broad Christian context, the term *sect* refers to any segment of the universal body of Christ that regards itself as the total body of Christ. This understanding of the term is pertinent in this regard, since Churches of Christ for most of their history have regarded themselves as the whole of the body of Christ. On the other hand, the term *denomination* is commonly used to refer to a segment of the universal body of Christ that recognizes itself as a segment and confesses itself to be a segment. When applied to Churches of Christ, this understanding of *denomination* can be deceptive, since Churches of Christ have always verbally denied denominational status, but for most of the twentieth century they have behaved as though they were a part of the larger whole.

To unravel this knotty situation, we need to explore these terms from a sociological perspective. When used in their classic, sociological sense, the terms *church, denomination,* and *sect* signify social realities, not theological ideals. Sociologically speaking, the term *church* refers to a legally established ecclesiastical institution. In that sense, there is no "church" in the United States at all:

the First Amendment to the Constitution places all religious communities on an equal footing before the law and leaves them with only two options — to exist either as *sect* or as *denomination.*

A *sect* stands over against the dominant culture for the simple reason that it views itself as the exclusive domain of both truth and salvation, from which it maintains that other religious bodies and the culture at large have departed. Moreover, it is often bellicose in the prophetic judgments it hurls against the culture and its handmaidens, the popular denominations. This was precisely the way Churches of Christ understood themselves and behaved in the nineteenth century.

A *denomination,* on the other hand, has typically made its peace with the dominant culture, abandoned its exclusivist rhetoric, muted its prophetic voice, and come to behave as a well-mannered, compliant member of the larger culture and of the larger Christian community. Churches of Christ began moving unmistakably toward such a position during the World War I era; now, in the waning years of the twentieth century, they have, with a few notable exceptions, practically completed their sect-to-denomination transition.

The point, again, is that in sociological terms every Christian tradition in America must exist as either sect or denomination. That is social reality, and Churches of Christ were — and are — no exception.

Throughout the history of Churches of Christ, there have been some — albeit a distinct minority — who understood this fact and who therefore viewed the notion of "nondenominational Christianity" not as something Churches of Christ could actually achieve but rather as a biblical ideal to which they might aspire. These people argued that the New Testament knows one church only, which implies that the denominational arrangement is wrong, but they refused to argue that they themselves did not partake of this sin. Among these people one finds the highest and noblest conception of the "nondenominational" ideal as it was understood by Churches of Christ.

Perhaps no one in the history of this tradition represents this perspective more clearly than did F. D. Srygley, a turn-of-the-century preacher and staff writer for the Nashville-based *Gospel Advocate,* the single most influential journal among Churches of Christ in his time. Srygley published a book in 1910 consisting of articles he had written for the *Advocate* over the years. This volume, entitled *The New Testament Church,* contains the essence of his perspective.

Srygley flatly rejected the notion that the Churches of Christ in the United States constituted the one, true, primitive church while all others were false and therefore denominations. When the editor of the Texas-based *Firm Foundation* argued that "the law of Christ is a wall of separation between the church of Christ and all other religious bodies of whatever name or faith," Srygley took serious exception. He based his rebuttal on his simple conviction that Christians make mistakes. Accepting in principle the nondenominational ideal, he countered that "in the midst of all the denominations that beset this age and country, it would be absolutely miraculous if some Christians did not get into some of them occasionally. If there are no Christians in any denomination, it is the only place except hell they have all kept out of." He asserted, for example, that there were Christians "in saloons, on the race track, at the theater, in the ballroom, around the gambling tables, in the calaboose, behind the jail doors, in the penitentiary, and on the gallows." Why, then, should it be surprising "if a few of the meanest specimens of them should occasionally be found tem-porarily in the most respectable and pious religious denominations of this desperate and God-forsaken country?"[7]

When the Cincinnati-based *Christian Standard* affirmed that the church of Christ was larger than "the current Reformation," Srygley reported that the statement created "a great commotion" among his more sectarian brothers and sisters, and again he entered the fray, affirming that "there are many who have been scripturally baptized and are living godly lives who are not counted with us." Further, he said, "No church is at any time wholly free from apostasy. . . . From this point of view, therefore, it would be impossible to say 'we as a people' compose the church of Christ."[8]

Syrgley's alliance on this point with the *Christian Standard* was all the more remarkable because, in the late nineteenth century, the *Standard* and Srygley's own *Gospel Advocate* stood opposed on most issues. Further, these two papers represented the two factions that would, by 1906, be formally recognized by the federal government as two separate denominations: the Disciples of Christ (the *Standard*) and the Churches of Christ (the *Advocate*). While people continued to advocate Srygley's views throughout the twentieth century, as we shall see, they constituted a diminishing minority within the larger Churches of Christ, which more and more confused the nondenominational ideal with their own particular tradition.

The difficulty in defining the notion of nondenominational Christianity can be seen most clearly in the thought of Alexander Campbell, who time and again sought to define what the movement he led was all about without ever succeeding in fully clarifying the issue. The concept remained a two-edged sword.

On the one hand, the notion of nondenominational Christianity pointed to the ideal I just described. In this connection, Campbell wrote that

> the *true* Christian church . . . is composed of all those in every place that do publicly acknowledge Jesus of Nazareth as the true Messiah, and the only Saviour of men; and, building themselves upon the foundation of the Apostles and Prophets, associate under the constitution which he himself has granted and authorized in the New Testament, and are walking in his ordinances and commandments — and of none else.[9]

Accordingly, Campbell never doubted that there were "New Testament Chris-tians" scattered throughout the various denominations, and he refused to identify nondenominational Christianity with any particular sect or movement, his own included.

On the other hand, Campbell himself was not an idealized abstraction but a human being who belonged to human history. He could not avoid defining "New Testament Christianity" in concrete terms, laying out its terms of admission, its organizational structure, and its order of worship. And when he did this, many of his followers inevitably identified nondenominational Christianity with the particular movement that, in the early days, they called "Churches of Christ" or "Disciples of Christ."

More than anything else, Campbell's insistence on immersion for the forgiveness of sins and salvation encouraged that identification.[10] While Campbell waffled on this question throughout his career,[11] many of his opponents understood Campbell to be arguing that only those in his own movement were saved, and they ridiculed his position with sarcastic outbursts like the following:

> Ho, every mother's son and daughter,
> Here's the "gospel in the water,"
> Here's the ancient gospel way,
> Here's the road to endless day,
> Here begins the reign of heaven,
> Here your sins shall be forgiven.
> Every mother's son and daughter,
> Here's the "gospel in the water."[12]

More to the point, it was not just Campbell's enemies who understood him to claim that only those in his own movement were saved; many of his followers believed it as well.

This was the two-edged sword of nondenominational Christianity, and the dilemma it created plagued Churches of Christ for two centuries. On the one hand, in their best moments Churches of Christ were committed only to the *ideal* of nondenominational Christianity and admitted, on that basis, that there were genuine Christians scattered throughout the denominational world. But inevitably, members and leaders alike confused the ideal with their own particular movement and argued that the Church of Christ in America was not a denomination but the true church of the apostolic era. All others, according to this logic, were simply not Christians.[13] In this way they created a nondenominational sect.

But because they refused to accept the notion of a nondenominational denomination, they found themselves caught in the trap of belonging to a very particular denomination, all the while denying its denominational dimensions. The only way to resolve this dilemma was to reaffirm the original, idealized vision according to which "New Testament Christians" were scattered throughout the sects. Some, indeed, took this step, but they thereby robbed the flesh-and-blood reality called the Church of Christ of its exclusive character, which, as we shall see, served from the early nineteenth century as a central feature of the church's self-identification.

Accordingly, Churches of Christ developed a peculiar vocabulary which reinforced the conviction that the Church of Christ was not a denomination but simply the one true church of the apostolic age. Churches of Christ therefore spoke of themselves as the "church of Christ" with a small "c," signifying thereby the church universal. They routinely spoke of themselves as "New Testament Christians," as opposed to "the denominations." And they refused even to use the phrase "*other* denominations." All this became orthodoxy from an early date. Already in 1860, the old Kentucky preacher John Rogers, for example, admonished his people not to speak of "other denominations": "When we speak of other *denominations,* we place ourselves *among them,* as one of *them.* This, however, we can never do, unless we abandon the distinctive ground — the apostolic ground — the anti-sectarian ground, we have taken."[14]

By the 1960s — a hundred years later — the notion that the flesh and blood Church of Christ was not a denomination was seldom questioned; it was simply assumed. One dissident from this orthodoxy complained that "this central dogma of our brotherhood so thoroughly permeate[s] the area that its source cannot be discovered. Like the myth of white supremacy, or the sacredness of the Bible, or the existence of God, it is taken for granted and never questioned." He went on to complain of "the tricky logic used to defend it."[15] Indeed, that "tricky logic" has, in many ways, stood at the heart of Churches of Christ for almost two full centuries.

Methodology

There are other important dimensions of this book that the reader should understand from the outset. First, I intend this book to be a descriptive and historical analysis of the *character* of Churches of Christ. It therefore asks, "Who are these people?"; "What made/makes them tick?"; and "What are the forces that have shaped them and made them who they are?"

Second, in keeping with the intent to analyze the character of Churches of Christ, I have made the book primarily an intellectual history — that is, a history of the ideas that have molded and shaped the tradition. At the same time, a variety of social and cultural factors — wars, economics, religious pluralism, and democratic culture, for example — also helped shape Churches of Christ and their theology and therefore helped define the terms for many of their internecine quarrels and debates. For this reason, I have also sought to pay serious attention to the social setting in which Churches of Christ have lived and moved and had their being.

Further, since this book focuses chiefly on the intellectual character of Churches of Christ, readers should not expect it to serve as an exhaustive history of the tradition, replete with every name, date, and event that has been in any way significant to the tradition. I provide this sort of detail only insofar as it relates to the book's central, overarching themes.[16] Some leaders typically regarded as key personalities in the movement do not appear in these pages at all. Some controversies long regarded as defining issues for Churches of Christ (e.g., concerning instrumental music and missionary societies) receive scant attention here, simply because they reflected rather than defined the basic character of the tradition.

This book not only focuses on the nondenominational self-identity of Churches of Christ but also seeks to explore the intellectual history of Churches of Christ by utilizing two distinct methodologies — one in Part I ("The Churches of Christ: The Making of a Sect"), which explores the nineteenth-century story, and another in Part II ("The Churches of Christ: The Making of a Denomination"), which explores the twentieth-century story.

Two points should be made regarding the nineteenth-century story. First, when this book was but a conception and not yet on paper, various friends and colleagues advised me to "forget the nineteenth century. The real story of Churches of Christ," they said, "is a twentieth-century story." There is a sense, of course, in which that is true, since there was no recognized Church of Christ separate from the Disciples of Christ prior to 1906, when the United States Census listed the two denominations separately for the first time.

But to argue for the irrelevance of the nineteenth century is to miss one very fundamental reality — namely, that the Church of Christ is not simply a denomination but a powerful ideal around which a denomination finally built a separate and distinct identity. This powerful ideal is the vision of primitive Christianity and, in the context of the religious culture of the United States, the corresponding myth of nondenominational Christianity. The earliest nineteenth-century roots of this ideal lie in the work of Barton W. Stone and in Alexander Campbell's first publication, the *Christian Baptist*. But one finds partisans of this ideal utilizing it in a variety of ways to define Churches of Christ as a separate and peculiar people as early as the 1830s. The burden of the entire nineteenth-century story, therefore, rests with defining and clarifying this ideal as *the* defining characteristic of this people. Because this ideal in many ways *became* the Church of Christ, to ignore the nineteenth century would be to ignore the very heart and soul of the tradition and to render the twentieth-century story of Churches of Christ essentially absurd.

Because the nineteenth-century story is one of defining the ideal and hammering out a separate identity for Churches of Christ, it is appropriate to focus in the first part of the book on those who were most influential in carrying out those tasks. But who were these people? Certainly not the clerics and bishops. Because Churches of Christ believed so strongly in the notion of democratic governance, they routinely claimed that they had no clergy, no power structure other than elders in local congregations, and no organizational reality above those congregations. To some extent, this was just one more aspect of their claim to be nondenominational. To a great extent, however, their democratic governance reflected the radical democratic sentiment that pervaded antebellum America.

If those who defined the ideal and shaped the identity of the emerging Churches of Christ were not clerics and bishops, who were they? W. T. Moore answered that question quite effectively when he wrote in 1909 that "the Disciples of Christ do not have bishops, they have editors."[17] Moore pointed here to the truth that those who wielded intellectual power in this tradition were those who wielded the pen. Further, editors were, in a very real sense, democratically chosen by the people, for their power was only as great as the length of their circulation lists. This means that editors both reflected and shaped the popular orthodoxy at any given time. For this reason, in exploring the nineteenth-century story, it is altogether appropriate to focus on the thought of the most significant editors — and writers — in the movement.

My treatment of the story in the twentieth century focuses on the evolution of Churches of Christ from sect to denomination. Because no one more accurately perceived that transition than those who were still committed to the old sectarian identity, in Part II I seek to tell the story of Churches of Christ in the twentieth century not from the perspective of mainstream editors but from the perspective of those sectarians who dissented from the emerging denominational mainstream. These dissenters included people active in the premillennial movement, the anti-institutional movement, African American Churches of Christ, and the youth counterculture of the 1960s.

My intent in employing this methodology is not to criticize mainstream Churches of Christ but rather to make certain that the dissenting traditions are taken seriously. But I also believe that this approach can shed new light on the mainstream tradition in that it avoids mainstream triumphalism and entertains alternate perspectives.

Finally, though many personalities appear within these pages, this book does not provide a definitive biography of any individual. More often than not, I introduce individuals into the narrative only insofar as they contribute to a particular story and to a particular context. For that reason, readers will gain only partial — and sometimes extremely partial — glimpses of most of the people who are discussed.

Brief Introductory History

All this, however, should be set within the broader context of the history of Churches of Christ. Thus far I have offered some brief glimpses of that history, but for purposes of orientation, it will be useful to undertake a thumbnail sketch of the larger picture.

Churches of Christ trace their American origins to two principal nineteenth-century leaders, Barton W. Stone and Alexander Campbell. Stone's leadership dates from the famous Cane Ridge Revival of 1801, at Cane Ridge, Kentucky. Chastised by the Presbyterian Church for his participation in that revival but claiming for religion the same freedoms he enjoyed in the civic sphere, Stone and five others completely broke from the Synod of Kentucky and organized the separatist "Springfield Presbytery." By 1804, in the name of freedom from human institutions, they dissolved even that presbytery, declaring their intentions in an important document, "The Last Will and Testament of the Springfield Presbytery."[18] Having divorced themselves from Presbyterianism altogether, they then constituted themselves simply as a community of Christians. Over the next forty years, Stone attracted a sizable following, especially in southern Ohio, Kentucky, Tennessee, and northern Alabama.

His leadership was characterized by several themes, and surely one of the most important of these was his insistence on freedom from human traditions in religion. Like Alexander Campbell, he actively promoted the restoration of primitive Christianity as the means of uniting all Christians. But if Alexander Campbell was essentially a rationalist, Stone was essentially a pietist. In addition, as we shall see in Chapter 5, Stone held to a profoundly apocalyptic worldview which drove him to advocate simple, ethical living, to separate himself from the prevailing values of his culture, and to hold himself aloof from militarism and even from politics. From 1804 to 1826, Stone solidified the movement he led principally through preaching, but from 1826 through 1844 he also edited an influential journal which he called the *Christian Messenger*.

Alexander Campbell came to America from Northern Ireland in 1809, two years after his father, Thomas, had arrived in southwest Pennsylvania. Because of efforts on the part of his Seceder Presbyterian denomination to control his preaching, Thomas already had withdrawn from that body and drafted the well-known "Declaration and Address."[19] This document, which calls for Christian unity through a return to the clear and unambiguous teachings of the New Testament, in many ways charted the course for the movement the Campbells led.

But it was Alexander who emerged as the pivotal leader of the movement his father had begun. Gripped by the postmillennial anticipation of his time, Alexander reshaped his father's agenda in the interest of the millennial age.[20] It was his belief that the restoration of primitive Christianity would bring Christian unity, which, in turn, would bring the millennial dawn.

Especially important for Churches of Christ was the *Christian Baptist*, which Campbell edited from 1823 to 1830. In the pages of that publication Campbell regularly assaulted creeds, clerics, and denominational systems that he believed must collapse before the millennium would dawn. He especially attacked missionary societies and any ecclesiastical institutions that he thought detracted from the glory of the local congregation. Though his chief interest, even in the *Christian Baptist,* was ecumenical, his rhetoric often sounded both sectarian and legalistic. This dimension of the early Campbell exerted a tremendous influence on the emerging Churches of Christ — a point developed more fully in Chapters 3 and 4.

It should be emphasized at this point that both the Stone and the Campbell movements were profoundly American in several respects. First, their discomfort over religious pluralism on the American frontier (i.e., the diversity of religious sects and denominations) provided both with their motivation for Christian unity. Second, both addressed the problem of religious pluralism in a way that was common on the American frontier: they sought to escape pluralism by returning to primitive Christianity. One finds that approach not only in Stone and Campbell but also in the closely allied movements of James O'Kelley in Virginia and Elias Smith and Abner Jones in New England and even in Joseph Smith's Latter-day Saints. Third, reflecting the democratic impulse so prominent in their time, both Stone and Campbell were driven by a passion for freedom from creeds, clerics, and ecclesiastical control. With so much in common, the Stone and Campbell movements formally united in Lexington, Kentucky, in 1832.

But there were differences as well. The most notable of these differences was the fact that while Stone was a pietist who insisted that a return to apostolic holiness was the surest means to Christian union, Campbell was a rationalist who based Christian union on adherence to the New Testament as a kind of scientific blueprint for the church. Central to Campbell's thought was his dependence on Enlightenment philosophy, especially the thought of John Locke and the perspectives of the "Baconian" school of Scottish Common Sense Realism. The impact that these philosophic traditions had on his thought and behavior is spelled out in more detail in Chapter 2.

More than this, while Stone held to an apocalyptic worldview that rendered him pessimistic about his culture and his age, Campbell entertained an optimistic, postmillennial perspective that rendered him an apostle not only for primitive Christianity but also for science, technology, and American civilization. His optimism regarding American civilization became especially apparent in 1837, when he undertook a defense of American Protestantism — and in doing so began his own transition from sect to denomination.

This shift, however, alienated many who had followed Campbell since the *Christian Baptist* period — followers who well remembered Campbell's earlier denunciation of all Protestant parties. Increasingly estranged from Campbell's latter-day moderation, these people formed an early nucleus of Churches of Christ. In Chapters 3 and 4 we shall explore who some of these people were, what they taught, and why.

Within a few short years, the Stone-Campbell unity movement was pulling apart, and by 1906 the religious census of the United States government recognized two denominations instead of just one: the Churches of Christ and the Disciples of Christ.

Several factors precipitated the division. In the first place, there were those who failed to see the close relation between restoration and unity that was so apparent to Campbell and who therefore tended to coalesce around one or the other of these two themes. Those who principally served the restoration ideal, and who therefore worked for the recovery of primitive Christianity, would become known exclusively as Churches of Christ. Those whose interest was chiefly ecumenical, and who therefore worked for the unity of all Christians, would increasingly wear the label Disciples of Christ. Second, the Civil War played an important role in helping to sectionalize the movement; when all was said and done, the restorationist Churches of Christ centered predominantly in the Upper South, while the ecumenical Disciples centered predominantly in the old Campbell heartland of Kentucky and the Middle West. Third, undergirding the division were the differences between Campbell and Barton W. Stone. Campbell's Disciples, especially following the Civil War, increasingly reflected Campbell's commitment to progress and American civilization. But the Churches of Christ, which centered especially in Middle Tennessee, often reflected the sectarian, Stoneite commitment to the kingdom of God that would finally triumph over human progress and civilization.

This latter theme, however, should not be overplayed, because, to a significant extent, Campbell's outlook tended to overshadow Stone's from the time Campbell first visited Kentucky in 1823. From that time on, many who came out of the old Stone tradition blended Stone's apocalypticism with the rationalism, legalism, and sectarianism they perceived in Campbell's *Christian Baptist*. More than anything else, an unequal fusion of these two traditions — that of the early Campbell and that of Barton W. Stone — came to define the emerging Churches of Christ.

In many ways typical of this emerging tradition were the principal second- and third-generation leaders of the movement in Middle Tennessee — Tolbert Fanning and David Lipscomb, respectively. Both men were committed to a profoundly sectarian vision, informed both by the early Campbell and by Stone.

By World War I, however, leaders among Churches of Christ renounced at least the Stoneite side of their sectarian agenda and began the slow transition from sect to denomination. This transition, which occupied a full half-century, generated three especially notable controversies between the emerging mainstream and the sectarian dissenters. Significantly, each of these controversies corresponded in certain ways to one of America's twentieth-century wars.

The first of the controversies, triggered in part by World War I, involved premillennialism and raged from 1915 to roughly 1940, when the mainstream finally succeeded in expelling the premillennial dissidents. Since the premillennial faction perpetuated the apocalyptic perspectives of Barton W. Stone to a significant extent, their expulsion symbolized not only the rejection of apocalypticism by mainstream Churches of Christ but also the rejection of any sectarian identity that might be rooted in an apocalyptic worldview. This story will be traced in Chapter 7.

The second controversy, triggered in part by World War II, involved efforts to promote congregational cooperation and to create various sorts of institutions, mainly to expedite mission work in the aftermath of the war. Fought mainly in the late 1940s and 1950s, this battle once again resulted in the withdrawal/expulsion of the sectarians. Though mainstream Churches of Christ time and again characterized those who opposed institutionalization as unfaithful to the heritage, the truth is that these dissenters stood squarely in one set of footprints of the nineteenth-century Churches of Christ. And by the time the battle over institutions was complete, it was the mainstream — not the dissenters — that had removed itself almost entirely from its nineteenth-century roots. In place of those roots, what remained among mainstream Churches of Christ was, for the most part, an ingrained exclusivism unconnected with any serious theological tradition from the nineteenth century. I explore these developments especially in Chapter 10.

By the 1960s — the era of the controversial Vietnam war — Churches of Christ faced the third major wave of dissent, this time from disaffected and alienated youth who strongly objected both to the lingering exclusivism among Churches of Christ on the one hand and to the peace that Churches of Christ had now made with the values of the surrounding culture on the other. The struggle between the mainstream and the dissidents involved a host of issues — race, war, gender, generational differences, the Holy Spirit, and the nature of the Bible, to name a few. But to the new denominational mainstream and to the sectarian right-wing minority that still persisted, the struggle was over one thing only: liberalism. All of this we will explore in Chapters 12 and 13.

Reflections on Historiography

The history of Churches of Christ, as a history separate from that of the Disciples, has — with few exceptions — been ignored.[21] There are two good reasons why this is true. First, with their profoundly primitivist identification with first-century Christianity, Churches of Christ have ignored, and often even rejected, their own history in the United States. This rejection is closely related to their insistence that they do not constitute a denomination: if they took seriously their American history and identity, it might detract from their identification with the first Christian age and mark them simply as another American denomination.

Second — for the very reasons indicated above — Churches of Christ have essentially abdicated the writing of their story to historians representing the Disciples of Christ. And Disciples historians, naturally enough, have been interested in telling their own particular story, not the story of Churches of

Christ. It is little wonder, then, that Churches of Christ emerge in Disciples' historiography essentially as a footnote — and a twentieth-century footnote at that.

Central to Disciples' historiography has been their treatment of the division that resulted in the two separate denominations listed by the United States Bureau of the Census in 1906. Until 1964, most historians rooted this division in a late nineteenth-century dispute over missionary societies and instrumental music in worship, with the emerging Churches of Christ coalescing around the negative position on both these issues. According to this view, the Disciples represented the mainstream of this tradition throughout the nineteenth century and even into the twentieth, and Churches of Christ amounted to little more than a splinter group with little theological identity apart from their resistance to the "innovations" of the parent denomination — and hence possessed no serious history of their own until the twentieth century.[22]

Most major histories of American religion rely precisely on this interpretation. Sydney Ahlstrom, for example, portrays Churches of Christ as a splinter off the "parent denomination" near the dawn of the twentieth century. Edwin Gaustad concurs that "early in the twentieth century, the conservatives who resisted many aspects of the creeping liberalism . . . withdrew to form a new denomination: the Churches of Christ." And Winthrop Hudson recognizes Churches of Christ only — and literally — in a footnote, an afterthought as it were to the mainstream of Disciples history: "By 1906 the rigidly biblicistic wing of the Disciples — the 'Churches of Christ' of the middle South — had gone its separate way." Though Richard Wentz recognizes that perspectives characteristic of Churches of Christ were present "in the early decades of the Disciples movement," he nonetheless argues that people who held these views "eventually separated from the Disciples movement and formed themselves into Churches of Christ."[23]

Such judgments are inadequate for a number of reasons. Most important, they reflect the bias of denominational historiography rather than the actual record. Moreover, Churches of Christ, far more than Disciples, are distinctly a product of the primitivist impulse that abounded in the early national period of American history, and by relegating the origins of Churches of Christ to the late nineteenth century (or early twentieth), such interpretations essentially obscure the centrality of the primitivist impulse in the early Republic.

The work that until recently constituted the only comprehensive history of Churches of Christ — Earl I. West's *Search for the Ancient Order* — employs the same interpretive assumptions, but for opposite reasons. Thus, West argues that "by 1906, . . . the 'Christian Churches' or 'Disciples of Christ,' as they preferred to be called, took their instruments and their missionary society and walked a new course."[24]

In 1964, however, David Edwin Harrell Jr. took sharp exception to these interpretations and pushed the division back a half-century to the Civil War era. In fact, Harrell suggested that the fundamental incompatibility of the unity and restoration ideals provided the early ideological seeds of the division.[25] But he was even more impressed with the sectional alignments of the division. Noting that Churches of Christ in the early twentieth century resided over-whelmingly in the Upper South and that Disciples in the same period centered in the Midwest, he concluded that the genesis of Churches of Christ as a denomination separate from the Disciples must have been sectional. "The most likely place to look for the sectional origins of a church in the nineteenth century," he wrote, "is in the wake of the bitter struggle centering around slavery and culminating in the Civil War." Further, he argued, the forces that most profoundly shaped the character and identity of Churches of Christ were social forces related to that conflict. Harrell concluded that "the twentieth-century Churches of Christ are the spirited offspring of the religious rednecks of the post bellum South."[26]

While there is considerable truth in these interpretations, Harrell did not fully discern the nature of the theological issues that gave Churches of Christ their peculiar theological identity and that predated the Civil War by many years.[27] Further, even when writing of nineteenth-century Churches of Christ, Harrell typically couched his analyses under the supposedly broader rubric "Disciples of Christ,"[28] implying yet again that Churches of Christ are but a johnny-come-lately stepchild of the parent denomination.

The truth is that historians have fully as much warrant to speak of the larger history of this movement as "Churches of Christ" as they do to speak of it as "Disciples of Christ." After all, for most of the nineteenth century, the terms "Church of Christ," "Disciples of Christ," and "Christian Church" were used more or less interchangeably.

And yet there is at least one notable exception to this pattern: in Middle Tennessee, a region long dominated by the work of Barton Stone, the common designation from a very early date was "Church of Christ." This is due to the fact, no doubt, that Stone vehemently opposed the term "Disciples of Christ" as a designation for this movement and strongly favored the labels "Christian" when applied to individuals and "Churches of Christ" when applied to congre-gations. On the masthead of virtually every issue of the *Christian Messenger,* which Stone published from 1826 through 1844, he identified himself as "an elder in the Church of Christ." Likewise, when R. L. Roberts counted the dif-ferent designations used in a single volume of Stone's *Christian Messenger,* he found that " 'church of Christ' (or with capital 'C') occurs 30 times (including 'congregations of Christ' once), while 'C. Church,' 'a Christian church,' and 'a Christian assembly' each appears one time only, a ratio of ten to one in a total of 288 pages."[29]

It is certainly true that Campbell's influence was felt in this region as well, as we shall see. There were also instances in which leaders in this region used Campbell's preferred terminology, "Disciples of Christ." But by the 1840s,

Stone's preferred label, "Church of Christ," was becoming the standard designation for churches in this region. This explains, for example, why John R. Howard, in defending the "true church" in 1848 (see Chap. 3), referred to it simply as the "Church of Christ."

Further, the designation "Church of Christ" rapidly became the standard designation for the sectarian wing of the Stone/Campbell movement throughout the South. In this connection, the testimony of the dentist-evangelist B. F. Hall is important. Hall identified himself with the Stone movement in 1820, when, in the shadow of the Cane Ridge meetinghouse, he responded to the preaching of the influential Kentucky preacher John Rogers.[30] He shifted his allegiance to Campbell in 1826, however, when he read Campbell's debate with W. L. McCalla (see Chap. 5). Nonetheless, Hall continued to use the designation "Church of Christ" wherever he preached for the remainder of his life. As early as 1829, for example, Hall agreed to join a Baptist congregation, "provided the church would agree to adopt the title Church of Christ instead of the name Baptist." Again, Hall reports that when he first established the Stone/Campbell movement in Little Rock, Arkansas, in the early 1830s, "nearly every Methodist and Presbyterian in the place [meetinghouse] united with the Church of Christ." Later Hall preached near Benton, Arkansas, "and fully organized the Church of Christ there."[31]

The fundamental point, then, is this: by the 1840s, if not before, we can trace the beginnings of an emerging sect called the "Church of Christ." This sect was still linked to Campbell's "Disciples," to be sure, but it was far more concerned with questions regarding "the true church" and "the ancient order" than it was with ecumenicity or human progress. Increasingly, therefore, it was embarking on paths fundamentally different from those charted by Alexander Campbell.

The Disciples of Christ essentially are the flesh-and-blood embodiment of a *denominational* ideal that was present in the mind of Alexander Campbell from the beginning of his reform — an ideal found especially in his emphasis on Christian unity and in his optimistic, postmillennial assessment of human progress and American culture. On the other hand, Churches of Christ essentially are the flesh-and-blood embodiment of a *sectarian* ideal that was present not only in the mind of Alexander Campbell but perhaps even more fully in the mind of Barton W. Stone.

It is true that it took fifty or more years for other Americans — and even for many within the movement — to discover that by 1906 there were two denominations where earlier there had seemed to be only one. But to argue that Churches of Christ were simply a sectarian spin-off from the Disciples at some point in the late nineteenth or early twentieth century is to distort the record badly. By the late nineteenth century, Churches of Christ were devoted to perpetuating a primitivist, sectarian tradition to which they had given their allegiance for almost one hundred years. It is not at all difficult to trace the leaders who embraced and furthered that sectarian tradition from the beginnings of the movement. Those leaders, and the people who followed them, constituted the earliest Churches of Christ, though it is true that they continued to share considerable intellectual ground with the Disciples for a half century and more.

Who were those leaders, and how did they frame their sectarian vision? This is the story I now seek to tell.

A final note is in order, however, before I begin the story. Although members in this tradition routinely employed the term "Church of Christ" throughout the nineteenth century, the label "Churches of Christ" gradually became the standard designation in the twentieth century. This latter term is appropriate because it reflects the truth that there is — and was — no formal organizational structure that one can identify as the "Church of Christ" beyond a single local congregation. At the same time, this term is deceptive because it implicitly denies the informal organizational structure that binds this tradition into a cohesive denomination. Still, because there has never been an acknowledged power structure higher than the local congregation and because the term "Churches of Christ" was both common in the twentieth century and not unknown in the nineteenth, this will be the term normally employed throughout this book.

PART I

CHURCHES OF CHRIST:
THE MAKING OF A SECT

CHAPTER 2

The Enduring Influence of Alexander Campbell's *Christian Baptist*

In molding the enduring character of Churches of Christ, nothing compares with Alexander Campbell's magazine the *Christian Baptist,* which he edited and distributed throughout the country between 1823 and 1830.[1] Though Campbell began a new journal in 1830, which he called the *Millennial Harbinger,* the spirit

Especially through his magazine, the *Christian Baptist,* which he edited from 1823 to 1830, Alexander Campbell (1788-1866) contributed to Churches of Christ a perspective that was at once rational, legal, and exclusive. Ironically, many who formed the vanguard of Churches of Christ in the early nineteenth century never fully understood Campbell's ecumenical intent.
(Photo courtesy Disciples of Christ Historical Society)

and outlook of the *Christian Baptist* dominated even the *Harbinger* through 1836. We are therefore justified in speaking of the *Christian Baptist* not simply as a magazine but as a mind-set, a perspective on reality and on the Christian faith that dominated the thinking of Campbell throughout the 1820s and the first half of the 1830s. During these years, the *Christian Baptist* decisively shaped the emerging Churches of Christ, which continued to bear its imprint well into the middle of the twentieth century.[2]

In one sense, the message of that magazine was very direct: the restoration of primitive Christianity was the only means to the unity of all Christians, which, in turn, would usher in the millennial age on earth.

But in another sense, the message was thoroughly ambiguous. In fact, the ambiguities appeared first when Campbell paired restoration (or primitivism) with the ideal of Christian unity and second when he paired restoration with his fervent postmillennial expectations.

Tension between Restoration and Unity

In the first place, Campbell seemed not to grasp, at least during the years of the *Christian Baptist* when he was still young and brash, that restoration and unity were, in many respects, mutually exclusive terms. He seemed quite oblivious to the fact that the restoration ideal, at least as he defined it, was a radically sectarian vision, hardly suited to an ecumenical enterprise. From his platform of primitive Christianity, in fact, he launched a devastating attack on everything and everyone who did not agree with his vision of the ancient Christian faith. As L. C. Rudolph aptly put it,

> The *Christian Baptist* castigated creeds, confessions of faith, synods, associations, Bible and missionary societies, religious experiences and testimonies, mourning benches and anxious seats, religious ranks and titles, preaching on isolated texts, clergy and the training programs which produced them, and every variation from the paradigm of New Testament practice as Alexander discerned it. No church organization was spared.[3]

Campbell was convinced that institutional Christianity was thoroughly bankrupt, right across the board. Catholicism was apostate, and neither Luther, Calvin, nor Wesley had moved much beyond the spirit of Rome. All, he argued, had "given employment to taxgatherers, jail-keepers, and grave-diggers," because all had relied on human invention and tradition rather than on the clear word of God. Even in the early 1830s, he still was sounding the same theme: "The christian religion has been for ages interred in the rubbish of human invention and tradition."[4]

On the other hand, Campbell did not hesitate to announce that the movement he led was the first in the entire history of Christendom that sought to "unite and build upon the *Bible* alone." In fact, he imagined that "there is not one voice heard in all the world outside of the boundaries of the present reformation, calling upon the people to return to the *original gospel and order of things*." For this reason, he suggested, "The *era of Restoration* will as far transcend . . . [the era of Reformation] . . . as the New Testament transcends . . . the dogmas . . . of Westminster and the canons of the Assembly's Digest." Not only this, but his confidence in the judgments of the *Christian Baptist* was so bold that in 1830 he remarked that "no seven years of the last ten centuries" had contributed more to the dawn of millennial bliss than had "the last seven" when he had produced that paper.[5]

It was one thing for Campbell to argue that his movement was the first in the history of Christendom to *seek* to build on the Bible alone. It was something else entirely for him to claim that his movement had, in fact, recovered primitive Christianity in its entirety. Following 1837, Campbell resolutely refused to make such a claim,[6] but in the earlier years of his reform, such claims abounded. As late as 1835, he wrote in his *Christian System* that while Christianity had "been buried under the rubbish of human traditions for hundreds of years," it "has never been, till recently, disinterred." He went on to say, "Various efforts have been made, and considerable progress attended them; but since the Grand Apostasy was completed, till the present generation, the gospel of Jesus Christ has not been laid open to mankind in its original plainness, simplicity, and majesty." In his preface to the *Christian System*, he made this point unmistakably clear:

> We flatter ourselves that the principles . . . on which the church of Christ — all believers in Jesus as the Messiah — can be united . . . ; on which the gospel and its ordinances can be restored in all their primitive simplicity, excellency, and power . . . : — I say, *the principles* by which these things can be done are now developed, as well as the *principles themselves*, which together constitute *the original gospel* and *order of things* established by the Apostles.[7]

It is little wonder that Campbell's printer, much to Campbell's chagrin in his later years, published the *Christian System* in 1835 under the title *Christianity Restored*.[8] It is also little wonder that many Christians in the historic Protestant churches viewed Campbell's claims in this regard as sheer, unabashed sectarianism. One of his Baptist critics, Jeremiah Jeter, for example, argued that Campbell's attitude during the *Christian Baptist* period "was eminently sectarian."

> What is sectarianism, but an undue confidence in the soundness of our views of Scripture truth, an excessive partiality for the party concurring with us in these views, and the lack of candor, tenderness, and forbearance towards those who dissent from them? When tried by this standard, no enlightened and

unbiased reader of the *Christian Baptist* can doubt that Mr. Campbell's sectarianism was unmitigated.[9]

Campbell's thought was rich and complex and embraced far more than mere sectarianism, as we shall see. But there were those who found most compelling, of all he wrote and thought, this sectarian vision so characteristic of the *Christian Baptist* and of the early years of the *Millennial Harbinger*. Thus one of Alexander Campbell's chief contributions to Churches of Christ was a mind-set — a worldview — that focused on restoring and maintaining the true church and that prized a profoundly sectarian spirit. The "unmitigated" sectarian spirit of which Jeremiah Jeter spoke would become, by the 1840s, the virtual substance of the movement increasingly known in those days as "the Church of Christ."

But during the *Christian Baptist* period Campbell also provided clear and lucid descriptions of precisely what shape the true church of the apostolic era should take. Central to that vision was immersion of adults for the forgiveness of sins. Beyond that, Campbell argued that the true, apostolic church would celebrate the Lord's supper every first day of the week; that the supper was a simple memorial feast; that each congregation would be strictly independent, governed by a plurality of elders, with deacons serving in various capacities; and that worship would consist essentially of five basic acts — preaching, praying, singing, giving to the weekly contribution, and sharing in the Lord's supper.[10]

But there is more. Campbell not only fathered a sectarian spirit. He also fathered, in defense of his restoration, a hard, combative style that prized verbal assault on the positions of opponents and enemies. John Rogers, a devout follower of Campbell after 1823 and preacher for the Church of Christ in Carlisle, Kentucky, made this point clear. During the entire *Christian Baptist* period, he wrote,

> All religious parties were more or less agitated by his powerful, argumentative, scriptural, & sometimes terribly sarcastic pen. He was regarded as a sort of religious Ishmaelite — his hand against every Sect, & the hand of every Sect against him. He raised against himself a fearful storm, by his scathing onslaught upon the "Kingdom of the Clergy." They were about his ears as thick as wasps or hornets, whose nests had been rudely disturbed.[11]

Jeremiah Jeter concurred. "The publication of the Christian Baptist," he wrote, "was an open, formal declaration of war against all the religious sects and parties in the country."[12]

Of course, such a style was by no means foreign to religious discussions on the American frontier in Campbell's day. But Campbell employed this style and extolled its virtues so regularly that it became, in time, central to the identity and character of the emerging Churches of Christ.

Accordingly, Campbell wrote in January 1830 that "no man ever achieved any great good to mankind who did not wrest it with violence through ranks of opponents." He cited several models in this connection: John the Baptist "lost his head, the Apostles were slaughtered, the Saviour was crucified, the ancient confessors were slain." Campbell concluded that he would be an unworthy advocate of the Christian faith if he were not "traduced, slandered, and misrepresented." That same month, Campbell expanded on this theme. "In proportion as a person is intelligent and benevolent, he will be controversial," he proclaimed. "Hence the Prince of Peace never sheathed the sword of the Spirit while he lived. He drew it on the banks of the Jordan and threw the scabbard away." With that example in mind, he exhorted his followers, "To your posts, then, O Israel! Remember . . . you have vowed allegiance during the war." He used similar rhetoric on many other occasions. In 1834, for example, he wrote to his followers,

> There are no winter quarters in the good fight of faith, neither is there a truce nor an armistice in the war between truth and error. . . . As respects the faith formerly delivered to the saints, the allied sects, like the ancient Philistines, are still sounding new defiances against the armies of the God of Israel. . . . Much has been done — much is doing — but more is yet to be done before the victory is won. But our motto is, *"Glory to the victor, and victory to the brave!"*[13]

From the days of Campbell until very recent years, militaristic metaphors — warfare, battles, verbal guns and bullets, bastions, assaulting error, defending truth, and the like — were common parlance in large segments of the Churches of Christ. This was so much the case that anyone wishing to sketch the character of Churches of Christ from the *Christian Baptist* era down to, say, 1960 would have to acknowledge that the identity of this tradition lay not only in a set of beliefs and doctrines but also in a mind-set and demeanor that, with some notable exceptions that we will examine later, tended to be highly combative. The point here is that the pugnacious young Alexander Campbell of the *Christian Baptist* period was himself the fountainhead of this perspective.

But more than this, in the hands of Campbell, this perspective became the basis for a vigorous debating tradition that also became part and parcel of the heritage of Churches of Christ. Campbell held five particularly notable debates — with the Seceder Presbyterian John Walker in 1820, with the Presbyterian W. L. McCalla in 1823, with the social reformer Robert Owen in 1829, with the Roman Catholic Bishop of Cincinnati John Purcell in 1837, and with the Presbyterian Nathan L. Rice in 1843. Following the McCalla debate, Campbell triumphantly concluded that "a week's debating is worth a year's preaching . . . for the purpose of disseminating truth and putting error out of countenance."[14]

It must be acknowledged that debating was a common part of religious life and served even as a major source of entertainment on the American frontier. That Campbell embraced the debating tradition, therefore, is hardly surprising or even noteworthy. But it is noteworthy that debating remained a standard means of religious discourse among Churches of Christ for well over a century — in large part because those who composed the emerging Churches of Christ in the 1830s increasingly centered their focus on the sectarian side of Alexander Campbell.

Roots of Campbell's Sectarian Vision

Ironically, however, Campbell never intended to adopt a sectarian posture, even in the days of the *Christian Baptist.* Quite the opposite. Campbell pointedly viewed himself as an ecumenist. This seemingly inconsistent posture can be resolved if we keep in mind three things: (1) the nature of the Old World religious establishments, (2) the formula that emerged from the eighteenth-century Age of Reason (Enlightenment) for undermining those religious establishments and securing religious unity for all people, and (3) Campbell's use of this Enlightenment formula in his own movement.

Campbell's searing denunciations of the various denominations and their clergy can best be understood when one keeps in mind the fact that Campbell, as a first-generation Scotch-Irish immigrant to America, knew firsthand the power of the European religious establishments. Further, though the First Amendment — which made any federally supported church illegal — was law before Campbell ever arrived in this country, the dismantling of state-supported churches was not completed in all of the states until 1833. Campbell thus imagined — with some justification, to be sure — that many of the denominations of his day were committed in principle to the old state-church ideal and were therefore still chiefly interested in maintaining power and privilege.

Nathan Hatch has argued persuasively that Campbell sought to counteract these denominations by democratizing Christianity, placing power in the hands of the people. He urged people to reject the authority and traditions of their churches and to read and interpret the Bible for themselves.[15] Further, thanks to his Baconian outlook, which assured him that all Christians could read and understand the Bible alike, Campbell imagined that once the people took matters into their own hands, Christian unity could not be far away.

But the story is more complex than this, for Campbell, like his father before him, embraced an Enlightenment model for achieving that unity. This model was mediated to Campbell through John Locke, who had somewhat Christianized the thought of the father of the English Enlightenment, Lord Herbert of Cherbury.

Herbert first outlined that model in his book *De Veritate* in 1624. Writing during the Thirty Years' War (1618-1648), which saw various Christian establishments locked in mortal combat, Herbert sought to undermine any rationale for religious warfare by reducing religion to a set of essentials upon which all reasonable people could agree. He reasoned that, once agreed upon, these few essentials, drawn from God's "second book of nature," would bring unity to Christendom on a voluntary basis and undermine the power of the various state churches to coerce the consciences of the faithful.

Thomas Jefferson employed this model in the Declaration of Independence in an effort to render irrelevant to the public sphere the various creeds and power structures of the traditional churches. He focused the Declaration, so far as religion was concerned, on two essential items of belief upon which he imagined all reasonable people could agree: (1) the notion of God ("Nature and Nature's God") and (2) the notion of a self-evident moral order ("unalienable rights"). Jefferson envisioned these two themes forming the core of an American civic faith, binding all Americans together regardless of denominational differences.

The ecumenical intentions of both Herbert and Jefferson are obvious. At the same time, however, both were sectarian. Jefferson, for example, seriously thought that the various denominational structures would soon crumble into the dust and that all Americans would turn to embrace the Unitarian faith, simply affirming the notion of God and the notion of a moral order.[16]

Seen in this light, Campbell was surely no more sectarian than the civic ecumenist Thomas Jefferson. Campbell imagined that once Christians abandoned their creeds and traditions and turned to the Bible and the Bible alone, the denominational structures would fall and all Christians would be united in the primitive Christian faith. But Campbell, like Jefferson, inevitably particularized that ostensibly universal and ecumenical faith, sketching out for his followers what seemed to him the clear, self-evident essentials of the true Church of Christ. In this way, sectarianism was simply implicit in Campbell's ecumenism.

There is a sense in which later Churches of Christ, who made that implicit sectarian vision their very reason for being, staked their identity on a situation that ceased to exist in America after 1833. For Campbell's scathing denunciation of sects, clerics, creeds, and ecclesiastical machinery of all kinds had a great deal to do with his fear of a Protestant establishment in America. By 1833, however, when Massachusetts became the last state in the Union to abolish a state church, the grounds for that fear had vanished. Further, within a few short years, Campbell no longer opposed the Protestants in America but effectively joined them, as we shall see shortly. In the meantime, however, those among Churches of Christ who continued their strong and strident attacks against other sects and denominations were acting out a script that Campbell himself had abandoned.

This point should not be overplayed, however, for Campbell did not confine his interests to disestablishment alone. He also keenly felt, during the *Christian Baptist* period especially, that the various denominations had genuinely departed from the religion of the New Testament which his movement was restoring. Later Churches of Christ shared that perspective.

Campbell and Legalism

But there is more to the complexity of Alexander Campbell even than this. Campbell's sectarian rhetoric often suggested, even to his followers, that he had little sense of the grace of God and conceived the Christian faith principally in legal terms. For example, he labeled the doctrine of justification by faith alone as "unscriptural" and "unreasonable" and published articles that assailed the notion as "*absurd* in *theory,* and *false* in *fact.* It is an unwholesome doctrine and very full of misery. It is a doctrine of darkness and doubts!"[17]

Yet Campbell held unwaveringly to the principle of God's sovereign grace. He maintained that grace manifests itself especially in God's commands — a point we shall examine in Chapter 8. Suffice it to say for now that those who composed the emerging Churches of Christ increasingly focused their attention on God's commands as a principal locus of his grace. Further, Campbell often spoke of the New Testament not so much as a theological document but as a veritable constitution for the church. He argued that "the constitution and law of the primitive church shall be the constitution and law of the restored church."[18] And he recalled in 1835 that "the principle which was inscribed upon our banners when we withdrew from the ranks of the sects was, '*Faith in Jesus as the true Messiah, and obedience to him as our Lawgiver and King.* . . .'"[19] Not surprisingly, those most impressed with the sectarian side of his rhetoric were also often impressed with the legalistic connotations of his thought. As a result, Churches of Christ, as they evolved from the *Christian Baptist* emphasis, often reflected a legalistic approach to the Christian faith — a theme we also shall explore further in Chapter 8.

Campbell imagined that the Protestant world had largely accepted such notions as justification by grace through faith, and so he felt that there was little compelling reason to make these themes a central dimension of his reform. He was convinced that the greatest need of American religion in the early nineteenth century was for unity, and so he committed his life to articulating a principle that he felt would achieve that goal. In time, however, it became apparent even to Campbell that a restoration vision so susceptible to sectarian emphases and misunderstandings could hardly sustain an ecumenical program. Campbell's movement began to fracture as early as the late 1830s into two discernible intellectual traditions, one committed primarily to unity and the other committed primarily to the restoration of the ancient order. Those whose chief interest was ecumenism became known, certainly by the late nineteenth century, as Disciples of Christ. Those whose chief interest was the restoration of the ancient order became known as Churches of Christ.

Tension between Restoration and Postmillennial Eschatology

There was another tension in Campbell's thought, this one between the principle of restoration and his postmillennial eschatology.[20] Campbell imagined these two themes completely compatible and thought that restoration of primitive Christianity would lead directly to the millennial age. Restoration was the means; the millennium was the end. He made this point on any number of occasions during the *Christian Baptist* period. For example, in 1825 he proclaimed that "just in so far as the ancient order of things, or the religion of the New Testament, is restored, just so far has the Millennium commenced." And in 1829, when he debated the socialist Robert Owen, Campbell told the audience that "a restoration of ancient christianity, and a cordial reception of it" would "fill the world with all the happiness, physical, intellectual, and moral, which beings like us in this state of trial could endure."[21]

The problem, which Campbell failed to see at the time but which became abundantly apparent as the years went by, was that primitivism and postmillennialism, as Campbell employed those concepts, pointed in two fundamentally opposite directions. Primitivism pointed backward, not forward. It was a tool for regression, not for progression. It prized the past, not the future. Primitivism, as Campbell defined the concept (though he never used the term), stood fundamentally opposed to human progress as progress generally was understood in the eighteenth and nineteenth centuries in Europe and America.

Campbell's postmillennial expectations, on the other hand, were progressive. They anticipated a glorious future, not a primitive past. There would have been no problem whatever if Campbell, like the Puritans of New England, had defined progress specifically in terms of progress into the past. But Campbell was too much a child of the eighteenth-century Enlightenment for that. When he described the means that would introduce the final, golden age, Campbell increasingly spoke not only of primitive Christianity but also of science, technology, education, and republican institutions.

This emphasis in Campbell's thought became especially apparent in the 1830s and grew in intensity for most of the rest of his life. For example, in 1833-34, Samuel M. McCorkle, a preacher in the Stone-Campbell movement from Rockville, Indiana, directly challenged Campbell's contention that a recovery of primitive Christianity would launch the millennial dawn. McCorkle was convinced that humanity was impotent to renovate and transform this world in any fundamental sense. "The present cannot be renovated," he complained. "No means on earth can bring or restore the administration back to primitive rectitude; it grows worse yearly in despite of all the efforts that can be made to heal."[22]

Writing under the pseudonym "A Reformed Clergyman," Campbell was incredulous. Had not Bacon, Locke, and Newton inspired tremendous progress in politics and science? And what of the noble contributions of Luther, Calvin, and Zwingli? Beyond this, "the invention of gunpowder, the mariner's compass, the printing press, the discovery of America, the American Revolution — what have they wrought!!" Even his own religious movement, Campbell affirmed, would launch "a restoration" that would "bless the world in ten thousand ways." A millennium would dawn, to be sure, and its driving force would be "knowledge, scientific, political, and religious." To Campbell, the conclusion of the entire matter was clear: "This is, of all ages and of all generations, the most unpropitious for the assertion of the dogma that moral and intellectual means can benefit society in no very valuable nor permanent way. Almost every common newspaper presents insuperable difficulties to such a preposterous opinion."[23]

Campbell made this point again in 1858, in response to claims that the revival of that year was the harbinger of the golden age. In rebutting this claim, Campbell argued for the "incomparably paramount" consideration that "it was but yesterday that the mariner's compass was discovered, that printing was shown to be practicable, that steam power was laughed at as an absurdity, and the electric telegraph ridiculed as the hobby of a vagarian's brain. . . . We have too much faith in progress . . . to subscribe to the doctrines of these theological gentlemen who hint the last days are at hand."[24]

Campbell's phrase "too much faith in progress" says it all. While he was a restorationist of sorts who sought to rebuild the ancient order, Campbell was also a protomodernist who leaned downwind into the future. For this reason, Campbell was hardly a classical primitivist at all, if we take as the model of classical Christian primitivism, say, the Puritans of New England or even the evangelical Anabaptists of the sixteenth century.[25] He sensed no radical discontinuity between the first age of the Christian faith and his own period, dominated as it was by Enlightenment thinking, science, and technology. Infatuated with modernity, he even advocated scuttling the study of Greek and Roman classics as staples in American university learning, except insofar as those classics illumined the biblical message. Campbell focused instead on such moderns as Newton, Leibnitz, Locke, Butler, Bacon, Milton, Shakespeare, and others.[26] For all these reasons, we might best characterize Campbell's position as *rational progressive primitivism*.

Campbell and the Bible

To grasp Campbell's primitivism even better, we should note that he focused his restorationist lens only on the New Testament. In fact, he narrowed the focus further even than that. He divided the Bible into three dispensations: the patriarchal (from Adam to Moses), the Mosaic (from Moses to Peter's sermon on the Day of Pentecost, recorded in Acts 2), and the Christian (from Pentecost to the last judgment). Since he maintained that the Christian dispensation alone provided the pattern for the primitive church, Campbell essentially held that neither the Old Testament nor the four Gospels carried normative weight for the church in his day.[27] This judgment crippled the ethical witness of Churches of Christ, but that is a story for Chapter 12.

How, then, did Campbell reconcile his devotion to primitive Christianity with his devotion to the modern? The answer is closely connected with his passion for Christian unity. Campbell thought that divisions among Christians could be traced directly to human opinions *about* the Christian faith, codified and formalized in the various creeds. He sought, therefore, to eliminate the defining importance of opinions in religion. He was most impressed in this regard with the unanimity in the scientific community, which he believed was a result of that community's determination to focus on hard, indisputable facts rather than on opinions or theories. If focusing on "facts" could bring unanimity to the world of science, he reasoned, why could such an approach not also bring unity to Christendom?

Consequently, Campbell's reconstruction of primitive Christianity was shaped by early modern, Enlightenment presuppositions, and especially by Scottish Common Sense Realism and the method it espoused, popularly known in those days as "Baconianism." This philosophical perspective, immensely popular in antebellum America, emphasized induction — as opposed to deduction — as the way to truth and knowledge. According to this method, one simply collects all the pertinent facts on a given topic and then draws the proper conclusions on the basis of those facts. We recognize this procedure as the scientific method, and Campbell's faith in this method of inquiry underscores the extent to which he viewed study of the Bible as a kind of scientific enterprise. For example, he argued that the "inductive style of inquiring and reasoning, is to be as rigidly carried out in reading and teaching the Bible facts and documents, as in the analysis and synthesis of physical nature."[28]

The important point here, however, is how the inductive method helped join, in the minds of Campbell and his followers, the primitive and the modern. Admittedly, Baconianism was a modern method, but to its proponents it also seemed a primitive method, simply because it seemed so natural and so free from contrivance, bias, or presupposition. In their view, its genius lay in its ability to open up truths of nature that were as old as the creation itself.

Christian primitivists like Campbell and his followers believed that Baconianism could also open up the truths of primitive Christianity. Robert Richardson, a longtime colleague of Campbell at Bethany College and Campbell's personal physician, exulted that even the apostles "began with facts and drew from these by induction the proper inferences and rules of action."[29]

Fascinated as he was with scientific facts, it is hardly surprising that Campbell would view the Bible precisely in these terms. "The Bible is a book of facts," he declared, "not of opinions, theories, abstract generalities, nor of verbal definitions. . . . The meaning of the Bible facts is the true biblical doctrine." Further, in good Baconian fashion, Campbell considered the meaning of these facts to be self-evident, requiring no human interpretation. For this reason, he chastised "religious philosophers of the Bible" — singling out Calvin, Arminius, and Wesley — for having developed a theological vocabulary that had little to do with "Bible facts" and everything to do with human theories and speculation. Time and again Campbell advised Christians discussing biblical themes to employ only biblical language which conveyed the self-evident meaning of the biblical facts. To do otherwise, he warned, would open the door to disputation and division over human opinions. "We choose," he wrote, "to speak of Bible things by Bible words, because we are always suspicious that if the word is not in the Bible the idea which it represents is not there. . . . There is nothing more essential to the union of the disciples of Christ than purity of speech."[30]

In Campbell's view, the Bible was not so much a book of theology as a kind of scientific manual or technical blueprint, laying out in precise, factual detail the outlines both of primitive theology (what he called "the ancient gospel") and the primitive church (what he called "the ancient order"). It was in this way that Campbell reconciled and fused the modern and the primitive.

But the fusion of these themes was no more satisfactory than the fusion of restoration and unity. The theme of restoration and the postmillennial fascination with the modern finally pulled apart and went their separate ways. In due time, restoration of primitive Christianity became the almost exclusive focus of Churches of Christ, while Disciples of Christ increasingly identified themselves both with ecumenism and with human progress in the modern world.

The Cause of Campbell's Change:
Defending Protestantism

The separation of the ideals that composed Campbell's original agenda took place, first, in the mind and actions of Campbell himself. The process by which this occurred essentially developed out of two factors: (1) Campbell's growing fears of Catholic control of the United States, which led to a growing identification with American Protestantism, and (2) his growing disillusionment with those within his own movement who focused on the sectarian rather than on the ecumenical dimensions of his rhetoric. We should take a closer look at each factor in turn.

Anti-Catholicism was implicit in Campbell's version of Christian primitivism.[31] He believed that the church had fallen from its purity and simplicity with the emergence of the papacy and the development of Roman Catholic tradition. Yet, from the beginning of his career until the early 1830s, Campbell seldom attacked the Catholic faith. Instead, he regularly and persistently lambasted what to him was the far greater threat: the "little popes" of Protestantism.

In Campbell's view, the "little popes" of the Protestant churches differed hardly at all from the pope in Rome. Indeed, he maintained that they descended from Rome and, like the pontiff himself, represented a corrupted form of the Christian faith that Campbell labeled "Babylon." With nothing to commend themselves but their human traditions, he said, these "little popes" had relied for centuries on the state to coerce conformity to their traditions.

The American experiment had changed all that, however, by placing all the sects on an equal footing before the law and forcing them to rely on persuasion rather than on coercion. But Campbell feared that the "little popes," now shorn of established status, would attempt to reassert their power and to control the nation through cooperative interdenominational societies. He was convinced that the Bible societies, missionary societies, and tract societies constituted a grand conspiracy, led especially by Presbyterians and Congregationalists, to control the West and, in so doing, to control the nation.

This fear at least partly explains Campbell's stinging attacks on the Protestant clergy throughout the *Christian Baptist* period. He regularly branded them as wolves in sheep's clothing, as men who sought only wealth and power and who milked naive and gullible Christians to achieve their sordid ends. It also helps explain his rabid opposition during the 1820s to missionary societies, tract societies, Sunday school societies, Bible societies, and in fact to every ecclesiastical organization over and above the local congregation. The most effective antidote to the sinister designs of the "little popes," Campbell believed, was the primacy of the local congregation patterned, as one might expect, after the primitive church. Thus he argued in 1823 that the primitive churches "were not fractured into missionary societies, Bible societies, educational societies; nor did they dream of organizing such. . . . They knew nothing of the *hobbies* of modern times. *In their church capacity alone they moved.*"[32]

Campbell was not alone, however, either in his diagnosis of the problem or in the solution he proposed. Indeed, he joined a host of Deists, Baptists, Quakers, Universalists, and Stoneite Christians in opposing efforts of the "little popes" to foist a religious establishment on the American people. Byron Cecil Lambert has demonstrated the existence of an informal but sizable network of alarmed Christians throughout the new nation who took up this cause. At the center of this movement was New York–based Theophilus Ransom Gates and his publication *Reformer,* which served as a veritable clearinghouse for propaganda decrying Christian societies. Gates occasionally plundered Campbell's *Christian Baptist* for anticlerical and antisociety copy, and Campbell occasionally plundered Gates's *Reformer* for the same purposes.[33]

Nor was Campbell's solution unusual or unique. He proposed to rob the "little popes" of credibility by locating their authority solely in history and tradition while, at the same time, rooting his own authority in Scripture as it revealed the primitive church. If the primitive church knew no societies or organizations above the local congregation, then all such societies were *ipso facto* illegitimate. Strikingly, this was the appeal of practically all the sects who rejected the power and authority of the former Christian establishments. The titles of various journals associated with the antisociety coalition attest to the diffusion of the primitivist appeal: *Plain Truth, Gospel Advocate, Priestcraft Unmasked, The Evangelical Restorationist,* and *Priestcraft Exposed and Primitive Christianity Defended.*[34] Indeed, even Deists such as Thomas Jefferson roundly condemned the machinations of the clergy for power and control and compared their efforts unfavorably with the simple religion of Jesus Christ, and Mormons sought to escape the power and control of the "little popes" by claiming to have restored in 1830 the primitive "Church of Christ."

In a word, Campbell and others in this antisociety coalition were full-fledged participants in what Nathan Hatch has called "the democratization of American Christianity." That is to say, they committed themselves to the struggle to defrock the power brokers of the older, established churches and to place power and authority squarely where, in their view, it belonged: in the hands of the people. In the context of Churches of Christ, this point is extremely significant. Ironically, the democratization impulse finally hardened into a virtual orthodoxy, which became, by the mid-twentieth century, the basis for one of the major schisms within Churches of Christ, as we shall see in Chapter 10.

By the early 1830s, however, the focus of Campbell's battle had changed. Whatever designs the "little popes" may have had upon America, their failure was apparent by 1833, when Massachusetts became the last state in the Union to disestablish and to accept in law the principle of church-state separation. At that point he was satisfied that not only the national government but the states as well were fully protected from the Protestant conspiracy.

At just this point, however, Campbell began to voice his suspicions of a conspiracy on the part of the Roman pope to gain control in America. In 1833 Campbell noted that while he had to that point been largely silent respecting the political aims of the pope, he was now ready to speak out on the issue: "There is, on the part of the Roman See, a settled determination, accompanied with a lively expectation of success — a fixed purpose, from which 'His Holiness' is never to depart, to bring these United States into the bosom of the Catholic Church, and to add all America, North and South, to the territory of its dominions."[35] From time to time during the next several years, Campbell continued to write about a Catholic threat to American liberties in the pages of his *Millennial Harbinger.* Things finally came to a head in a session of the fifth annual convention of the Western Literary Institute and College of Professional Teachers meeting in Cincinnati, October 3, 1836.

That meeting set in motion a series of events that would alter the course of Campbell's reform — a story that Don Haymes has told in detail.[36] The College of Teachers was not a school at all, but a group of leading citizens dedicated to the extension of public education in the West. This group included among its number, from time to time, such luminaries as William Holmes McGuffey of *McGuffey Reader* fame, Calvin Stowe (husband of Harriett Beecher Stowe), Lyman Beecher, Bishop John Baptist Purcell, and Alexander Campbell.[37]

On October 3, 1836, Campbell delivered a speech to the College in which he argued that the genius of the English-speaking peoples lay in their acceptance of the fundamentally Protestant notion that every individual should "think for himself."[38] When Bishop Purcell objected, the two men agreed to meet for public discussion, though not for formal debate, the following week.

Before this discussion was ended, Campbell received from the citizens of Cincinnati a communication that would change the course of his career, foster division in the movement he led, and put him on a course significantly different from that of the Churches of Christ. Signed by fifty-seven of Cincinnati's leading citizens, but containing assurances that the signatures of "one half of the city could be obtained, would time permit," the note read,

> Dear Sir — The undersigned, citizens of Cincinnati, having listened with much pleasure to your exposure and illustrations of the absurd claims and usages of the Roman Catholic Church, would respectfully and earnestly request you to proceed immediately to establish before this community the six propositions announced at the close of your lecture, last evening. This request is made under the conviction that the present state of feeling in this city and the critical state of the country, with reference to Romanism, demand this and will fully justify such a course, and also with the expectation that it may result in much good to the cause of Protestantism in the West.[39]

In effect, Campbell had been invited to champion the interests of American Protestantism against the interests of Rome. Significantly, he accepted the invitation and met Purcell in debate in Cincinnati from January 13 through January 21, 1837.

In his work in progress on the confrontation with Purcell, Don Haymes has argued convincingly that this debate was the turning point in Campbell's religious development; from that time on, Campbell acted and spoke far more as a mainstream American Protestant than as a simple, primitive Christian.[40] Should anyone wonder how such a transition could be possible, especially in light of Campbell's undisguised antipathy for the "little popes" of Protestantism some years before, the answer is not without irony.

Haymes has also explored the dynamics of that irony. He contends that one first must realize that "evangelical" Protestants in the Ohio Valley saw Campbell as something less than a true Christian: in their eyes he was the father of a heretical cult that despised the historic creeds, required immersion in water for regeneration, and stole sheep from their pastures by the thousands.[41] Bishop Purcell saw immediately that Campbell lacked credibility as a "Protestant" spokesperson, and he made the most of it.

In an effort to affirm his "Protestant" credentials, Campbell appealed, quite naturally, to the Reformation principle of *sola Scriptura* — despite the fact that he had repeatedly and eloquently accused all Protestants of having effectively abandoned it. The new menace of Catholicism, personified in the articulate, learned, and youthful Bishop of Cincinnati, brought Campbell and his erstwhile antagonists together in principle even as they continued to diverge in practice.

So it was that these newfound allies confronted the specter of Rome. For Campbell, this was a crucial step. As in his earlier discussion with Robert Owen, Campbell now emphasized his affinities with the dominant culture rather than his differences from it. In so doing, he began a metamorphosis, of which he was perhaps only partly conscious, from militant sectarian to irenic ecumenist.

The story of Campbell's subtle shift from primitivism to Protestantism only began with the Purcell debate, however. The second phase of the story involved Campbell's increasing identification of the principles of Protestantism with the principles of the American nation. In his preliminary discussion with Bishop Purcell, Campbell defended the proposition that "the declaration of free thinking made by Martin Luther . . . [led] in the progress of the reformation to the declaration of American independence."[42] While Campbell rejected the notion of Protestant establishment out of hand, he candidly proclaimed that the American nation was the first political fruit of the principles of the Protestant Reformation.

Having asserted that the nation was the fruit of Protestantism, Campbell increasingly attributed to Protestant America the results he once had attributed to the primitive church alone. He affirmed that Protestantism already had brought a fundamental underlying unity to the American people. "Notwithstanding all our sectarian differences," Campbell proclaimed in 1841,

> we yet have something called a *common* Christianity; — that there are certain great fundamental matters — indeed, every thing elementary in what is properly called piety and morality — in which all good men of all denominations are agreed; and that these great common principles and views form a common ground on which all Christian people can unite, harmonize and co-operate in one great system of moral and Christian education.[43]

And since Protestant America had brought unity to a widely diversified and pluralistic people, it was reasonable to assume, thought Campbell, that Protestant America might introduce the millennium as well. In 1849, he heralded his view that the Lord God would extend the power and influence of the Protestant Anglo-Saxon peoples around the globe, from north to south, "as they have already from east to west." When that process was complete, Campbell jubilantly proclaimed, "Then will 'they hang their trumpet in the hall, and study war no more.' Peace and universal amity will reign triumphant. For over all the earth there will be but one Lord, one faith, one hope and one language."[44]

Campbell had come a long way. The man who earlier had predicated on restoring the primitive church (1) the destruction of the Protestant sects and (2) the millennial reign of Christ — this same man now heralded Protestant America as God's chosen vessel for uniting humankind and inaugurating the millennial dawn. Significantly, he maintained that this millennium would see God as its Lord, Protestantism as its universal faith, and English as its universal language.

While Campbell had come far, in another sense he had not come far at all. He remained committed throughout his life to the goal of restoring the primitive church. He frequently wrote and spoke of his dedication to this ideal until his death in 1866. His change, therefore, was not so much a matter of moving from primitivism to ecumenism but rather of discovering the seeds of primitive Christianity within the highest ideals of Protestantism. Campbell refused to champion the Protestant *denominations*, but he gladly championed the Protestant *faith*.

The Cause of Campbell's Change: Sectarianism among His Followers

The threat to American liberties that Campbell thought he saw in the Catholic Church was not the only factor that nudged him toward an alliance with Protestantism. The fact that many of his own followers had missed his ecumenical intent and sectarianized his vision pushed him in that direction as well. As early as 1826, Campbell expressed his frustration with the sectarians in his movement:

> This plan of making our own nest, and fluttering over our own brood; of building our own tent, and of confining all goodness and grace to our noble selves and the "elect few" who are like us, is the quintessence of sublimated pharisaism. . . . To lock ourselves up in the bandbox of our own little circle; to associate with a few units, tens, or hundreds, as the pure church, as the elect, is real Protestant monkery, it is evangelical nunnery.[45]

In spite of these admonitions, however, more and more of Campbell's followers confused the ideals of primitive Christianity with the particular movement that Campbell led. Many of these people became leaders in the embryonic Churches of Christ, and we will explore the identities and thinking of some of these people in the following two chapters.

It is important here, however, to take note of one of the early sectarians of the movement who finally brought upon himself the wrath of Campbell, who then left the Campbell movement altogether, and who finally became the founder of the Christadelphians. This man was Dr. John Thomas, an English physician who became a follower of Campbell in 1833. Campbell opposed Thomas not only because of Thomas's sectarian teachings but also because of his dogmatic speculations regarding the resurrection, the nature of the human soul, and the afterlife, which he routinely published in his own periodical, the *Apostolic Advocate*. Thomas's heterodoxy on these latter topics, which within the context of the Campbell movement were nothing short of bizarre, made him an especially convenient target for Campbell's strictures on sectarianism and exclusivism.

Central to Thomas's sectarianism was his contention that Baptists could not become members of the Church of Christ until they had been reimmersed, since Baptist immersion was nothing more than immersion into Antichrist. More than this, said Campbell, Thomas relegated the entire Protestant movement to perdition: "To Calvin's honors he has superadded that of 'the Arch Perverter of the Faith of Christ.' . . . Some of the Methodistic clergy he has dubbed 'Draconic Lambs,' in honor of the Old Serpent, I presume. And all the Protestant churches and sects are elevated to the rank of 'Synagogues of Satan.'" Not surprisingly, Thomas admonished Campbell for "the sinfulness of defending Protestantism."

It may well be that Campbell saw in Thomas's extreme rhetoric a reflection of his own scathing attacks on Protestantism and the Protestant clergy during the *Christian Baptist* period. At any rate, Campbell was in the midst of change and now came down hard on Thomas, ranking him with "these infallible dogmatists, so supremely devoted to his own opinions," and calling him to repentance.[46]

Almost twenty years later, another of Campbell's opponents, the Baptist preacher Jeremiah Jeter, noted the positive changes in Campbell's outlook that had become evident since 1837. "He has been a careless observer of Campbellism who has not perceived its effort to get rid of the *odium theologicum* by comforming its teachings, more and more, to the popular views," Jeter wrote. Moreover, Jeter viewed the John Thomas affair as the watershed in Campbell's thought. "From the rise of Thomasism may be dated the decline of the vaunting, pugnacious spirit of the Reformation."[47] Jeter was right. But he failed to see that the Thomas affair was symbolic of a much larger complex of ideas and events. Thomas was simply the wrong man in the wrong place at the wrong time, symbolizing for Campbell the sectarian spirit that he now sought to counteract.

Campbell made it abundantly clear that the growing sectarianism in his movement was precisely what finally drove him into the Protestant alliance. "Some of our brethren," he confessed, "were too much addicted to denouncing the sects and representing them *en masse* as wholly aliens from the possibility of salvation — as wholly antichristian and corrupt. . . . [Therefore], we have been always accused of aspiring to build up and head a party. . . . On this account I consented the more readily to defend Protestantism."[48]

The Fruit of Campbell's Change

The change was thoroughgoing enough that in 1849 Campbell — the man who, during the *Christian Baptist* period, had vehemently opposed missionary societies, Bible societies, and all extracongregational organizations of any kind — became the president of the American Christian Missionary Society. By then he was determined to promote that "common Christianity . . . in which all good men of all denominations are agreed." If opponents of his latter-day moderation thought missionary societies the chief point at issue, they were badly mistaken. Campbell's involvement in societies was but a symbol of a much deeper shift. Campbell had moved from a primitivist posture that many construed as sectarian to the more cosmopolitan and ecumenical primitivism implicit in the Protestant faith that Campbell thought to be the soul of the American Republic. In a word, Campbell, along with many of his followers, was making the classic American transition from sect to denomination.

Perhaps nothing suggests more clearly Campbell's transition from a sectarian to a denominational mentality than his judgment in 1839 that his movement needed fewer converts and fewer baptisms and more nurture of the converts it already had or that he himself now sought "fewer controversies" and greater efforts toward edification.[49]

Accordingly, in 1837 — the very year that Campbell debated the Roman Catholic Bishop Purcell and emerged as champion of Protestants in the West — in that very year he rejected immersion as absolutely essential to one's status as Christian. This judgment had been prompted by a woman in Lunenburg, Virginia, who had been "very much surprised . . . , while reading in the Harbinger, to see that you . . . say, you 'find in all Protestant parties Christians.'" The woman was astonished that Campbell had not confined the name "Christian" only to "those who believe the *gospel*, repent, and are buried by baptism into the death of Christ."

In his response, Campbell did not mince words. Among other things, he wrote,

> Should I find a Pedobaptist more intelligent in the Christian Scriptures, more spiritually-minded and more devoted to the Lord than a Baptist, or one immersed on a profession of the ancient faith, I would not hesitate a moment in giving the preference of my heart to him that loveth most. . . . I cannot be a perfect Christian without a right understanding and a cordial reception of

immersion in its true and scriptural meaning and design. But he that thence infers that none are Christians but the immersed, as greatly errs as he who affirms that none are alive but those of clear and full vision.

Significantly, Campbell later wrote that he responded to the Lunenburg querist as he did because he detected the influence of John Thomas's *Apostolic Advocate* in her questions "and answered them accordingly."[50]

In 1840, Campbell established Bethany College as an institution that would serve the society in which he lived rather than the interests of any particular sect, even his own. At the very heart of the Bethany curriculum stood the Bible — not a Bible prostrated to sectarian interests but a Bible to be studied for its literary, historic, and especially its moral qualities.[51] In part because the Virginia Assembly refused to charter institutions organized around specific theological perspectives, Bethany never developed a theological school. For the same reason — though one can assume Campbell agreed with the provision — the Bethany charter stipulated that particularistic theologies or doctrines of any kind would never be taught in the Bethany general curriculum.[52] Campbell made no requirements that the institution's trustees be aligned with his own movement, and indeed they came from a wide variety of Protestant persuasions. College Hall resounded each Sunday with worship and instruction "performed by respectable ministers of various denominations."[53] It is clear that Campbell committed Bethany College to the cause of that "*common* Christianity . . . in which all good men of all denominations are agreed."

Campbell's discovery of primitive Christianity in the principles of Protestantism went largely unperceived by many in the church. In the first place, the rhetoric of primitive and undenominational Christianity persisted in the very midst of Campbell's shift and obscured the fundamental changes occurring at a very substantive level. In the second place, Campbell's followers were extraordinarily reluctant to perceive anything amiss in his thinking or behavior. By the late 1830s, Campbell's stature in the movement was so great that his integrity had to be preserved at almost any price. There developed in this way a substantial though largely unrecognized rift between the reality of the older Alexander Campbell and the myths and images of Campbell drawn from his earlier *Christian Baptist* career.

The Conservative Response

Gradually, however, the fact of Campbell's change became increasingly apparent to those whose firm allegiance was to the early Campbell and the principles of the *Christian Baptist*. By his own account, Campbell received an avalanche of criticism for his response to the "Lunenburg Letter." The protests were sufficiently numerous to fill an entire volume, he said, and the vigor of the response convinced him "that there are but few 'Campbellites' in the country."[54] Three years later in a letter to John Allen Gano, T. M. Allen wrote of Campbell, "I wish he would cease the duties of an editor. He is through with every thing important to this reformation, & now I fear he is to do harm by speculating, & going deep into the 'language of Ashdod,' — there is plenty of it in his 'Christian System' — on account of which I would not purchase it."[55]

Four years later, in 1844, Tolbert Fanning, the recognized leader of the emerging Churches of Christ in Tennessee and a protégé of Campbell, thought he heard the sounds of compromise coming from the hills of Bethany. When Robert Richardson of Bethany wrote that the ancient-gospel movement had originated in southwest Pennsylvania in 1810, Fanning was incensed. "If this be a fair representation of the disciples," he asked, "why not confess ourselves a sect or heresy in fact, and recognize all our heretical neighbors, as fully authorized by the Bible as ourselves?" In Fanning's view, the Church of Christ originated in Jerusalem under apostolic auspices, not in southwest Pennsylvania in 1810.

In October of 1845, Fanning attacked the spirit of compromise that he perceived in the "greatest reformers." He singled out neither Campbell nor Bethany by name, but it is clear whom he had in mind.

> When reformers begin to boast of their *respectability*, they have started to the city of confusion, — when they court the smiles of corrupt denominations, they are at the very gates, and when they shake hands with the sects, they are in the midst of "Babylon the Great." The charge has been made, that the disciples are inclining to the *denominations*, and judging from the tone and spirit of some of the periodicals, whose editors stood forth first to advocate the cause of primitive Christianity, I fear there is more sober truth than poetry in the allegation.[56]

In 1906, David Lipscomb, recognized by his contemporaries as perhaps the most influential third-generation leader of Churches of Christ, also denounced Campbell's change. Many persons break away from sterile orthodoxy in their youth, Lipscomb commented, but then, "when the conservatism of age comes upon them, turn back to their early faith and undo much of the reformatory work of their vigorous manhood. Alexander Campbell was thus circumstanced."[57]

No one, however, more explicitly denounced Campbell's change than did that cantankerous old Kentuckian Jacob Creath Jr. Born in 1799 and a close friend of Alexander Campbell especially during the *Christian Baptist* period, Creath recalled during his seventy-eighth year the profound changes he had seen in the patriarch from Bethany. In an article appropriately entitled "Old and New Things Contrasted," Creath challenged his readers to "compare the Alexander Campbell of the Christian Baptist, and first 20 years of the Harbinger with . . . the A. Campbell of organs, big suppers, conventions and all the other human inventions." With a keen sense for the facts of the matter, Creath was concerned to show that the emerging Disciples of Christ, with their organs and conventions, were children of the late Campbell and had nothing in common with the Campbell of the *Christian Baptist.* "That the human inventions now practiced by those who claim to be the Reformation . . . are not in the Bible nor the Christian Baptist," he asserted, "is as clear as a sunbeam, and therefore no part nor parcel of it."

As early as 1850, Creath had objected to the newly formed American Christian Missionary Society of which Campbell served as president. He appealed especially to the memory and tradition of Barton W. Stone to argue his case. Pointing to the fact that Francis Palmer, Joel Haden, and other pioneers of the Stone movement had not joined the society, Creath affirmed that "these, and other men . . . , would not go into it from the regard they have to the name, the memory, and virtues of that venerated man, Barton W. Stone."[58] Stone having died and Campbell having moved away from his original position, George E. Taylor of Missouri looked to Creath to carry the banner of the Churches of Christ: "Bro. Stone is out of the way and I fear that many things will be attempted now that was not thought off [*sic*] during his stay. It is to you then Bro. Creath that we must look as to a sentinel to guard from the evils which now threaten us, and which are likely to create divisions amongst us."[59]

Creath himself was clearly despondent over the changes that Campbell's assumption of the presidency of the missionary society symbolized, and he complained directly to Campbell: "If you were right in the *Christian Baptist,* you are wrong now. If you are right now, you were wrong then." When an "aged and experienced Judge" warned Creath that the Christians had "departed from your platform, you are becoming as sectarian as other people, you will henceforth be a divided people, and will go down," Creath could only respond that "it was even so. I could not deny it."[60]

In 1878, James L. Thornberry, now an old man living in Texas, complained bitterly of the changes the older Campbell had introduced. Significantly, Thornberry had been "immersed by B. W. Stone, in 1833" and had been "raised near Georgetown, Ky.," where he was "constantly under the influence of such men as Stone, the Smiths, Creaths, Ryers, et al." In spite of his early allegiance to Stone, Thornberry rejoiced that "Bro. A. Campbell in his Christian Baptist, exposed the clerical order, the church of the clergy, councils, conventions and sectism generally." But by 1850, Thornberry complained, Campbell had changed. Attending a state meeting of the movement in Lexington, Kentucky, that year, Thornberry heard Campbell say that "it was not enough, to hand a man the New Testament and say, That is my creed. We would have to explain a little. Also that the name Christian would not do now; if we say we are the Christian church, we are saying others are not; and that we must now have an educated ministry, who could pronounce the language properly. . . . I was vexed." In consequence of such pronouncements, said Thornberry, the meetings of the Christians "were turned into business meetings, and money-raising organizations, and preacher-making was introduced." It was "a pity," he concluded, that Campbell had "built a college, [and] sanctioned and called for conventions, to decide 'prudential matters.'"[61]

The Myth of the Singular Campbell

By and large, however, leaders of Churches of Christ have been extraordinarily reluctant to trace to Campbell the origins either of apostasy or of division in the movement. They have depicted Campbell instead as singular in purpose so long as his mind was strong and clear, wavering only under the influence of senility. When changes in Campbell's emphasis could not be denied, partisans of the early Campbell and his *Christian Baptist* began suggesting that Campbell had been seduced, cajoled, or manipulated by various conspiratorial agents who had gained control over the old man's mind and over the institutions he had established.

Jacob Creath charged that the change occurred when "a certain man went to the rich oil men of Pennsylvania, and obtained large subscriptions of money for Bethany College, and by that means that man obtained influence over the Harbinger and Bethany College." Admitting the unfounded nature of this report, Creath nonetheless contended that if it were true, it would account "in part for the change that took place in the Christian Baptist and the first and best days of the Harbinger and its last days." Clearly the change had occurred, but, as Creath observed, "*How* the change was effected, and *who* effected it, are different matters."[62] So far as Creath was concerned, Campbell was wholly free from blame.

Tolbert Fanning attributed Campbell's change to senility — an allegation that circulated widely among the churches in the South. Fanning, the founding editor of the Nashville-based *Gospel Advocate* (1855-), became embroiled in 1857 in a bitter controversy with Robert Richardson, Campbell's colleague and physician, over the nature of the Bible — a story related in detail in Chapter 4. In the course of the dispute, Fanning traveled to Bethany to convince Campbell to stand against Richardson. In 1884, David Lipscomb, Fanning's successor as editor of the *Advocate,* recalled the story.

> Brother Fanning, distressed at the course A. Campbell was pursuing on these subjects, so utterly at variance with his life-long principles, made a visit to Bethany, to talk with him on the subject. I remember well, on his return he stated that he was shocked to find his mind was so shaken that he could, with difficulty, keep it on one subject; that he could converse in general terms on things he had studied in the past, but that all power of close, connected

reasoning was gone; that he had to be continually prompted to keep up an ordinary conversation. He said while A. Campbell, while his mind was directed to it, would reiterate and agree to his former positions, that he was merely a child in the hands of his friends.[63]

Jacob Creath typified those who picked up on this story. He claimed that Richardson "laid the foundation for the great change that came over the Harbinger" when he published his "German Neology and French Philosophy in the *Harbinger*" in 1857.

Lipscomb, however, enlarged the story considerably, suggesting that Campbell's mental decline had begun already in the 1840s.[64] Indeed, he wrote that Campbell had "failed in his mental and will power early in life. His later years were years of a second childhood." The decline began, Lipscomb claimed, in 1847, a year in which his favorite son, Wyckliffe, drowned and Campbell was imprisoned in Scotland.[65] From that time on, said Lipscomb, he was "credulous, trusting, and was mainly controlled by his friends," and in this condition he "violated his own principles, built again the [missionary] society he destroyed and destroyed that supreme and undivided respect for the word of God, and his [God's] appointments which he [Campbell] had vindicated."[66] In 1886, John F. Rowe, editor of the Cincinnati-based *American Christian Review,* also charged that Campbell had abandoned the truths of the *Christian Baptist* because of his mental deterioration: "Alexander Campbell, while he had complete possession of his mental faculties, never wrote a syllable in favor of such ecclesiasticism."[67]

It is difficult to know how to evaluate such reports of Campbell's failing mental powers. Even Richardson, whose denial of this report would have greatly enhanced his case against Fanning, nonetheless concurred. "Unfortunately," he wrote, "Bro. Campbell is now advanced in years and too susceptible of the influence of designing and selfish persons who want to make use of the college for their own purposes. He ceases to know his own true friends and the true friends of the reformation and of the college."[68] On the other hand, Benjamin Franklin, a strategic leader among the emerging Churches of Christ (see Chap. 4), indicated just the reverse. After hearing Campbell speak in 1856 (before Fanning began circulating his story in 1857), Franklin reported that "his intellect is as clear, vigorous and giant-like as ever."[69] One must add, however, that Franklin's intense veneration of Campbell renders his judgment somewhat suspect.

Whether Campbell had failed in his mental powers or not, however, is to some extent beside the point.[70] Many leaders in Churches of Christ believed that he had, and they sought in this way to preserve the memory of a man who was single-minded in his commitment to the principles of the *Christian Baptist.*

The Millennium: The Constant in Campbell's Thought

This portrait of the single-minded, unswerving Alexander Campbell whose capitulation occurred only when his mind grew weak and his friends grew strong is the basis for a great deal of misunderstanding of the movement he led. According to this view, apostasy came late in Campbell's life and was singularly un-Campbellian when it came. Further, this view suggests that outright division between Churches of Christ and Disciples of Christ occurred only when that apostasy had gathered sufficient momentum to divide churches over the very concrete issues of missionary societies and musical instruments in worship and that these developments occurred only after Campbell was dead. Laying claim to a uniformity that simply did not exist, Moses Lard announced immediately following the Civil War that *"we can never divide."*[71] Lard was blind to the fact that the movement had ruptured ideologically, though not geographically, long before the War. He also failed to see that this rupture resulted, to a very great degree, from ambiguities in Alexander Campbell's own theology and ecclesiology.

The failure to perceive the shift in Campbell's emphasis also reflects a failure to perceive the substance of the Campbell reform. Partisans of the *Christian Baptist* and of the Churches of Christ have long argued that the heart of Campbell's concern was for recovery of primitive Christianity. On the other hand, partisans of the Disciples of Christ have claimed that Campbell ultimately was concerned for the unity of Christendom. Actually, neither of these views finally is correct. Campbell's ultimate concern was for the kingdom of God, the millennium on earth. In Campbell's mind, unity was merely a means to the millennial dawn, and restoration a basis for unity. When recovery of the New Testament Church of Christ failed to bring the unity he sought, he increasingly embraced a broader vision to achieve his objective — namely, a Protestant *"common* Christianity . . . in which all good men of all denominations are agreed," and an American republic the ideals of which were inspired by that common faith. Thus, Campbell's millennial dream was one of the constant factors upon which his other, penultimate commitments shifted and changed.

The other constant factor, very much related to his millennial dream, was his firm and unchanging conviction that there were Christians scattered throughout the various sects. Following his response to the "Lunenburg Letter," he defended himself against charges of change by pointing to his consistency on this point. "Why should we so often have quoted and applied to apostate Christendom what the Spirit saith to saints in Babylon — 'Come out of her, my people, that you partake not of her sins, and that you receive not of her plagues' — had we imagined that the Lord had no people beyond the pale of our communion!"[72] At one time Campbell had thought "of our own community, that it is a *nucleus* around which may one day congregate all the children of God."[73] But by 1837 he was not so sure. It seemed to him that his "community" had grown far too narrow to accommodate "all the children of God," and he had therefore turned to Protestant America as a fuller embodiment of the primitive faith and as the basis for the final realization of the millennial kingdom on earth. By 1851, he candidly acknowledged that "among them all [i.e., the various Protestant sects], we thank the grace of God that there are many who believe in, and love the Saviour, and that, though we may not have Christian churches [i.e., churches built on the primitive pattern], we have many Christians."[74] The mere fact that there were "many Christians" scattered throughout the nation was enough to nourish Campbell's dream of the millennial kingdom on earth through most of his life.

It is significant that Campbell never edited a journal called the *Unity Harbinger* or one called the *Restoration Harbinger*. Instead, he provided the world with a clear statement of his major concern when he named his second periodical the *Millennial Harbinger*. But by the 1840s and certainly by the 1850s, America's millennial vision was growing dim. The debate over slavery was growing increasingly rancorous, and few by 1850 were contending that America would be the site of "the most glorious renovation of the world," as Jonathan Edwards had predicted in 1742. With the loss of the postmillennial vision in the broader culture, it was inevitable that Campbell's followers would lose that vision as well and seize instead on his penultimate concerns — unity and restoration — and then divide into hostile camps around those banners. Not surprisingly, each camp claimed for its banner the place of honor in the legacy of the Sage of Bethany.

To a significant degree, the ambiguity in the thought of Alexander Campbell accounts for the major nineteenth-century rupture in the movement he led. By the dawn of the twentieth century, when the Disciples of Christ and Churches of Christ were physically separating from one another and court battles were determining which group would retain possession of church buildings, appeals were often made to the "earlier" or "later" teachings of Alexander Campbell. In the 1906 legal battle between conservatives and progressives in Sand Creek, Illinois, for example, the court "urged . . . that the plaintiffs . . . are in accord with the spirit of a more enlightened age than the defendants . . . , and that their practices are in harmony with the later teachings of Alexander Campbell himself."[75] Campbell resolved those ambiguities, to the extent that he did, only by refocusing his energies in his later years on the "*common* Christianity" of Protestant America. The Disciples of Christ are the legitimate offspring of this later Campbell. But it is to the young, brash, and swashbuckling Alexander Campbell of the *Christian Baptist* era that Churches of Christ principally belong.

CHAPTER 3

The True Church and the Hard Style:
Radicalizing Alexander Campbell (Part I)

Jeremiah B. Jeter, a Baptist preacher from Richmond, Virginia, proved to be among Campbell's most formidable opponents in the later years of Campbell's career. In his stinging attack in 1855, Jeter characterized Campbell's earliest disciples during the *Christian Baptist* period as "for the most part, restive, contentious, and factious." But, asked Jeter,

> How could they be otherwise? They read the Christian Baptist, had strong confidence in the wisdom and piety of its editor, imbibed its spirit, adopted its principles, clothed themselves with the armor which it furnished, entered heartily into all the schemes which it advocated for the destruction of creeds, the overthrow of the clergy, the arrest of benevolent operations, and, in short, the "restoration of the ancient order of things" set up, or brought to light at Bethany.[1]

While Jeter unquestionably wrote from a prejudiced point of view and sought to discredit Campbell and his movement, he was nonetheless correct in asserting that many of the rational sectarians of the movement had learned their lessons directly from Alexander Campbell and the ideas he proclaimed in the *Christian Baptist*.

Jeter failed, however, to observe that the ideology of the *Christian Baptist* era had given birth to a radical tradition that was flourishing even as Jeter wrote his book in 1855. This radical tradition, in fact, provided the foundational program of Churches of Christ which were defining their identity in the middle years of the nineteenth century.

Most historians have defined the theological identity of Churches of Christ in terms of their refusal either to use instrumental music in worship or to participate in missionary societies. Neither of these issues defined the intellectual core of the tradition, however. This core was defined by a potent mix of traditional Christian primitivism combined with Scottish Common Sense Realism and Lockean epistemology, which in turn produced powerful strains of biblical literalism, sectarianism, and exclusivism. Once in place, this core thoroughly radicalized the agenda Alexander Campbell had proclaimed in the *Christian Baptist* era.

Instrumental music and missionary societies became divisive issues only after it became apparent that the Stone-Campbell movement had produced two irreconcilable traditions — one defined by ecumenical progressivism and the other by sectarian primitivism — and that the movement was in fact dividing along those lines. These two issues, therefore, functioned chiefly not as defining themes in their own right but rather as symbolic banners around which those who embraced these differing intellectual traditions might rally. As David Edwin Harrell Jr. aptly observed, if these people "had not disagreed over instrumental music and missionary societies, they would have divided over something else."[2] In this book, I am more concerned to investigate the theological core of Churches of Christ than the more visible and immediate issues of music and societies.

In this chapter and the one following, we will explore the ways in which the theological core of Churches of Christ evolved. More specifically, we will look at some of the radicals who helped develop that core from the early years through the middle of the nineteenth century, considering who they were, how they depended on Alexander Campbell and the ideology of the *Christian Baptist,* and how they took Campbell's early teachings in directions that Campbell himself in time came to reject.

Walter Scott

Unquestionably, the person who stood at the fountainhead of the radical Campbell tradition — and therefore of Churches of Christ, in many respects — was Walter Scott (1796-1861).[3] Reared a Presbyterian in Scotland, Scott emigrated to America in 1818 and made his way to Pittsburgh the following year. There he found employment in an academy run by George Forrester, a man who had been influenced by the restorationist teachings of the Scottish separatists Robert Sandeman and Robert and James Haldane.[4]

Forrester's church was thoroughly enamored of the vision of primitive Christianity that its members had picked up from Sandeman and the Haldanes — so much so that they insisted on baptism by immersion, foot washing, and the "holy kiss," they exercised stringent church discipline, and they maintained a rigid wall of separation between themselves and other Christians. Deeply impressed by this brand of restorationist Christianity, Scott abandoned his

Walter Scott (1796-1861) helped to radicalize Alexander Campbell's agenda when he claimed that, through his preaching on the Western Reserve, he had restored the ancient gospel for the first time since the days of the apostles.
(Photo courtesy Disciples of Christ Historical Society)

native Church of Scotland and was baptized by immersion into this primitive "Church of Christ."

In addition, the Scottish school of "Baconian" Common Sense Realism exercised a great influence over the imagination of Walter Scott. In 1836 he helped establish in Georgetown, Kentucky, the movement's first college, which bore the name Bacon College "in honor of Lord Francis Bacon, father of the inductive method of reasoning and the new science." Scott became the institution's first president, and his inaugural address extolled the virtues of Bacon's *Novum Organum.*[5]

The British philosopher John Locke shaped Scott's thinking even further.[6] Scott was especially taken with Locke's book *The Reasonableness of Christianity,* in which he discovered that the heart and soul of the Christian faith is the single fact that Jesus is the Messiah, a proposition Locke thought amply proved by miracles and fulfilled prophecies. In the very first volume of the *Christian Baptist,* Scott offered the first in a series of articles arguing this very point.[7]

Scott also fervently anticipated the union of all Christians and the consequent dawn of the millennial age, both of which he tied directly to the progress of the primitive gospel. Like Campbell, Scott felt certain that Christians would unite and the millennium would become reality to the extent that the primitive gospel triumphed in the hearts of humankind.

Scott met Alexander Campbell in 1821 in the home of Robert Richardson, one of Scott's students in the Pittsburgh academy. The two men recognized one another as kindred spirits, and Scott soon became one of Campbell's closest friends and most trusted colleagues. Campbell consulted with Scott before he announced in 1823, in his celebrated debate with W. L. McCalla, that the purpose of baptism is the forgiveness of sins — a theme that would become a central plank in the doctrinal structure of Churches of Christ. And it was Scott who convinced Campbell to call his new journal not simply the *Christian,* as Campbell had proposed, but the *Christian Baptist,* a name that might allay Baptist prejudice. From the very beginning of the *Christian Baptist* in 1823, Scott was a regular contributor. Writing under the pen name "Philip," Scott clearly thought that his relation to Campbell was analogous to Philip Melanchthon's relation to Martin Luther. Scott's death in 1861 moved Campbell to write that "no death in my horizon, out of my own family, came more unexpectedly or more ungratefully to my ears than this of . . . Walter Scott; and none awoke more tender sympathies and regrets. . . . I knew him well. I knew him long. I loved him much."[8] In spite of this warm relationship, however, Scott took Campbell's thought to extremes of which Campbell himself finally disapproved.

Scott's radicalism focused especially on what he often called "the ancient gospel," as distinct from "the ancient order" (e.g., organization and worship of the primitive church), the development of which he left to Campbell.[9] Accordingly, in the very first volume of the *Christian Baptist,* Scott began to explain, in thoroughly Lockean and Baconian terms, how he had discovered what he called the "one uniform and universal plan of teaching the [Christian] religion." He claimed that this plan differed dramatically from "the various stupid schemes, all different and all wrong, pursued by Roman Catholics, Socinians, Arians, Covenanters, Seceders, Presbyterians, High-Churchmen, Baptists, Independents, and so forth," for this plan had been "pursued by God — by the Lord Jesus Christ — by the Holy Spirit, . . . and by the apostles." The plan was very simple, consisting solely in the proposition that "Jesus is the Christ."[10] Indeed, Scott found the clarity of this primitive plan so dazzling that he could hardly understand why the various Christian denominations continued in their "voluminous confessions of faith, and their ecclesiastical constitutions." In his zeal for the primitive order, he un-Christianized them all: they "are not churches of Jesus Christ," he trumpeted, "but the legitimate daughters of that Mother of Harlots, the Church of Rome."[11]

In the context of the emerging character and theological development of Churches of Christ, Scott's emphasis on "the plan" is worth underscoring. The notion of a rationally conceived "plan of salvation" has long been central to

Church of Christ thought and undoubtedly owes its origin to Scott himself. "The plan" did go through several stages of development, however.

The first change in "the plan" took place in 1827, while Scott was serving as evangelist to the Western Reserve on behalf of the Mahoning Baptist Association — the organization with which the fledgling Campbell movement was at that time affiliated. By then, Scott had enlarged "the plan" from the simple proposition that "Jesus is the Christ" to a covenantal conception involving human responsibilities and God's gracious response. The human duties were three — believing the fact that Jesus is the Messiah, repenting of one's sins, and submitting to immersion for the forgiveness of sins. In return, Scott taught, God's gracious response involves the forgiveness of sins, the gift of the Holy Spirit, and eternal life.[12]

It is important that we grasp the Baconian dimensions of this "plan." The Baconian method — essentially the scientific method as we understand it today — called for the investigator to elicit from the mass of potential data all the relevant facts and then to support those facts with proper evidence. The relevant facts of Christianity, in Scott's view, were those mentioned above: belief, repentance, immersion, forgiveness, the gift of the Holy Spirit, and eternal life. The evidence consisted of miracles and fulfillment of prophecy.

Though Scott rigorously insisted that the Holy Spirit dwelled within the believer,[13] he nonetheless described the process of conversion in strictly rational terms. He defined the gospel as "a rational advocacy . . . [that] pleads the faith in its saving proposition from evidence," and he argued that "the Christian faith . . . belongs to the science of inference — reason — logic, and depends for its reception in society on proof." In this connection he argued that the task of the Spirit is not to "enter the soul of the sinner" but rather to convince "us as we convince one another — by truth and argument."[14]

Further, the Baconian dimensions of Scott's scheme were intimately connected to his Christian primitivist cast of mind. Indeed, one of the fundamental purposes of Scottish Common Sense Realism was to uncover the natural order of things — that is, the way things were meant to be from the beginning. Put another way, Baconianism revealed the primitive order of things, the way things were when they came from the hand of God. Viewed in this way, Baconianism obviously had the potential to harmonize beautifully with Christian primitivism, and in Scott's hands this potential was realized. Nowhere, perhaps, in the entire literature of the movement was this intimate connection demonstrated more clearly than in the title of Scott's book *The Gospel Restored: A Discourse of the True Gospel of Jesus Christ, in Which the Facts, Principles, Duties, and Privileges of Christianity Are Arranged, Defined, and Discussed.*[15]

Scott was absolutely convinced that he was proclaiming "the ancient gospel" when he made this six-point "plan" the burden of his preaching in the Western Reserve in 1827. In the interest of publicizing his meetings, however, he reduced the six points to five, so that he could use the mnemonic device of five fingers. He accomplished this reduction by collapsing the last two points into one — the gift of the Holy Spirit. He routinely spoke to children on their way home from school and taught them what he called the "five-finger exercise." He placed one of his five points on each of the five fingers, and then told the children to make a fist and keep it closed until they arrived home. Then they should open their fists, show their parents what was "on their fingers," and explain that the man who taught them that exercise would be preaching that very evening.

Scott's "five-finger exercise" brand of preaching produced two significant results. First, the legalistic tendencies inherent in the primitivism and rationalism of both Scott and Campbell came in due time to dominate Churches of Christ. When that happened, Scott's heirs transformed the five-point plan from one that emphasized both the work of humankind and the gracious response of God to one that featured only the work of humankind. By the twentieth century, this five-point plan of salvation had become commonplace and was routinely featured in Church of Christ preaching. It featured five human tasks: hear the gospel (i.e., Jesus is the Messiah), believe the gospel, repent of one's sins, confess the name of Jesus, and be baptized for the forgiveness of sins. Even more startling is the fact that this more legalistic form of Scott's "plan" was heralded as orthodoxy as early as the 1840s. For example, in 1848 John R. Howard characterized a plan almost precisely like this one as the "terms for admission" into the true Church of Christ, as we shortly shall see.

The other result of Scott's preaching in the Western Reserve was his astounding success: from the fall of 1827 through the summer of 1828, he won close to a thousand new converts. At this point, Scott had hardly radicalized Alexander Campbell. Campbell's father, Thomas, visited the Western Reserve to hear Scott's preaching for himself and was on the whole pleased with what he found. He wrote to Alexander that while "we have long . . . spoken and published many things 'correctly concerning' the ancient gospel, . . . I am at present for the first time upon the ground where the thing has appeared to be 'practically exhibited' to the proper purpose."[16]

Scott may have allowed himself to take Thomas's phrase "for the first time" far too literally. In a report he made the following year to the Mahoning Association, which had sponsored his work, Scott made the bold and startling claim that in his own preaching he had restored the true, ancient method of proclaiming the gospel to this earth. Scott could hardly believe that "it remained for any so late as 1827, to restore to the world the manner — the primitive manner — of administering to mankind the gospel of our Lord Jesus Christ! . . . Yet these things have actually occurred." He was therefore convinced that the millennium could not be far away. Waxing rapturous and eloquent, Scott envisioned the nineteenth century as "a sublime eminence" from which one could detect "the whole train of events leading to the *Millennium*." Indeed, "the ancient gospel and ancient order of the church must prevail," he proclaimed, "to the certain abolition of all those contumacious sects which now so woefully afflict mankind," and he closed his report with the confident affirmation that "the Millennium — the Millennium described in Scripture — will doubtless be a wonder, a terrible wonder to ALL."[17]

In years to come, Scott would wax even bolder, claiming that he had restored not only the true *method* of proclaiming the gospel but the true, ancient gospel itself.[18] He summarized his contention in the preface to his *magnum opus, The Gospel Restored:*

> The present century . . . is characterized by . . . three successive steps, which the lovers of our Lord Jesus have been enabled to make, in their return to the original institution. First the Bible was adopted as sole authority in our assemblies, to the exclusion of all other books. Next the Apostolic order was proposed. Finally the True Gospel was restored.[19]

In Scott's view, Thomas Campbell had restored the Bible as authoritative, Alexander Campbell had restored the "ancient order" (worship and organization of the church) through his articles in the *Christian Baptist,* and he himself had restored the ancient gospel by means of the five-point plan of salvation.

There is little evidence that Alexander Campbell resisted such extravagant claims throughout the entire *Christian Baptist* era. To the contrary, there is evidence that Campbell lent encouragement. In fact, in 1832 Campbell spoke of Scott as "the first successful proclaimer of this ancient gospel."[20]

But by 1838 Campbell had identified himself with American Protestantism and had come to find such claims appalling. He made this clear when Francis Emmons suggested that both Campbell and Scott claimed to have restored the ancient gospel — Campbell in 1823 and Scott in 1827. Not one to be outranked in this regard, even by Alexander Campbell, Scott admitted that Campbell had taught immersion for the forgiveness of sins as early as 1823, but he insisted that "the restoration of the whole gospel in 1827, can never be confounded with the definition of a single one of its terms in 1823, or in any year preceding it." Campbell stood appalled and amazed. He denied ever claiming that he had restored the gospel in 1823. He admitted that the first edition of his *Christian System,* which appeared in 1835, bore the title *Christianity Restored,* but he claimed that the choice of title had been made by his printer, not himself. Severely rebuking Scott, Campbell pointed out that "*to restore the gospel* is really a great matter, and implies that the persons who are the subjects of such a favor once had it and lost it." In the Protestant phase of his career, this was a judgment Campbell refused to make.[21]

This much said, we should also note that Scott, like Campbell, held within his soul a deep antipathy toward arid, sectarian systems, in spite of the contributions he made to creating the very sort of system he deplored. As early as 1832, he complained of the *"bare-bone proclaimers"* within the movement, "theoretical to a hair-breadth, and proclaimers of water rather than of Christ," individuals who "talk of baptism for the remission of sins, until every body is sick of it."[22]

This more conciliar side of Scott rendered him, by 1840, far less ecstatic about the future of the movement than he had been in 1828. In fact, he became subdued and disappointed. The primitive ship that he once had thought would carry all Christians to the millennial shore had, in fact, run aground on the shoals of religious pluralism in the United States. The unity of all Christians was still an elusive goal, the millennium seemed far, far away, and the Church of Christ, to which he had given his life, seemed now, in so many ways, only another Protestant sect. In a letter to Philip Fall, a preacher for the Church of Christ in Nashville, Tennessee, he wrote, "When you express your doubts of the matters connected with the recent Reformation, I sympathize with you, for the thing has not been what I hoped it would be by a thousand miles. We are indeed 'a sect' differing but little, of anything that is good, from the parties around us. Alas! my soul is grieved every day."[23]

Religious Pluralism and the Radical Campbell Tradition

It is difficult to understand the full-blown emergence of the radical Campbell tradition apart from the stubborn fact of religious pluralism in the United States. Put another way, America was a nation in which many religious traditions competed with one another in the great free market of souls. Yet, one should recall that Campbell — and many of his followers — originally envisioned a millennial age in which religious diversity would simply cease to exist. Campbell thought that Christians from all denominations would find the restored primitive church so compelling that they would abandon their human-made sects and flow like a mighty horde into the one universal ark of God's salvation. That was the original vision. But, as Walter Scott learned from bitter experience, it proved illusory.

There were other radicals, however — younger men who had learned their lessons in sectarian theology both from Scott and from the early Campbell — who refused either to resign themselves to the realities of religious pluralism or to move, like Campbell, toward mainstream American Protestantism. These younger men bowed their backs in resistance to religious pluralism, and in their hands the original Campbellian vision changed dramatically. They promoted the idea of the primitive church not as an ecumenical ark for all Christians but as the one true church in a sea of false and apostate denominations.

This change in vision was prompted by the rapid institutionalization of the movement, well advanced already by the 1840s. Robert Richardson estimated in 1849 that the Disciples/Church of Christ movement fell "but little short of 200,000" communicants.[24] With this kind of presence, outsiders no longer viewed the movement as an experiment in ecumenicity (if, indeed, they ever had) but rather as a denomination, pure and simple, competing against all the others in the great American religious marketplace. It is hardly surprising, then, that outsiders increasingly challenged preachers in Churches of Christ to justify, through hard-nosed debate, their very right to exist. Not at all bashful about debating, Church of Christ preachers eagerly rose to the challenge. Standing in the venerable debating tradition of Alexander Campbell, armed with the sword of logic and panoplied with hundreds of biblical texts committed to memory, these preachers hurled the challenge back at their accusers and denied that any religious organization had any right to exist other than the Church of Christ. By 1863, Moses Lard surmised that "in no denomination of Christendom, we venture to think, . . . can an equal number of discriminating critics, accomplished logicians, and skillful debatants be found."[25]

In addition, by the early 1840s, members of Churches of Christ increasingly behaved like a separate denomination, counting members and tallying the totals for the true church of God in every community. Hundreds of reports like the following now appeared in virtually all the periodicals associated with the movement.

> There are seven congregations of Christ in this county. One of 20 members, one of 22, one of 35, one of 45, one of 65, one of 100 and one of 135. And I should have planted the eighth . . . had my health permitted, with eight members; making in all, the No. of *four hundred and thirty* members who have united with the church of God in this county.[26]

In passages like this, one finds telltale evidence that the very engine that had powered the Campbell side of this movement in the teens, twenties, and thirties had now died — at least for those who formed the vanguard of the emerging Churches of Christ. That engine was the Campbellian, postmillennial faith that serious Christians could restore the ancient gospel, unite the church, and usher in the kingdom of God. By the late 1830s and early 1840s, it was clear to practically everyone in the movement that the original postmillennial vision was either flawed or dead and that religious pluralism in America — unshaken by the primitive gospel — was here to stay.

Partisans of the Campbell movement responded in two ways to this growing realization and, perhaps more than anything else, those two responses prompted the incipient division in the movement. It should be quickly stated, however, that it took years and, in some instances, even decades for these two responses to disengage themselves from one another. Further, these two divergent responses would define the character of the two denominations that would evolve out of this movement in the nineteenth century: the Disciples of Christ and the Churches of Christ.

Those who formed the vanguard of the emerging Disciples maintained their postmillennial faith in human progress but, like Alexander Campbell, increasingly defined the object of their faith as Protestant American civilization. On the other hand, those who formed the vanguard of the emerging Churches of Christ abandoned postmillennial optimism altogether and, along with it, the original ecumenical vision. That left them with only one plank from the original Campbellian platform: the vision of the primitive church. With neither postmillennial optimism nor ecumenical vision to sustain them, these people increasingly identified the primitive church of the New Testament age with the Church of Christ movement to which they belonged, and they defended that church against all comers. In this way, ironically, they built a sect on the foundation of the original vision of "nondenominational" Christianity.

John R. Howard: Defining Church of Christ Orthodoxy

John R. Howard was a well-known and influential preacher/editor in Tennessee in the 1830s and 1840s who launched the *Bible Advocate,* "perhaps the first paper published in the state [Tennessee] for the avowed purpose of advocating a return to primitive Christianity."[27] More important, Howard contributed perhaps as much as anyone in the movement's early years toward defining the Church of Christ in America as the "true church" and toward denominationalizing the concept of nondenominational Christianity. He did this by writing numerous articles for the *Bible Advocate* but especially by offering a classic sermon, which went through numerous reprintings: "The Beginning Corner; or, The Church of Christ Identified," first published in 1848.[28]

Howard was troubled by a question associated with religious pluralism in America, a question that stood at the very root and core of the emerging identity of the earliest Churches of Christ: In the midst of the denominational diversity in the new nation, "*where* is the true church *now* to be *found?* — and how shall we be enabled to know it? — to *identify* and recognize it?"

In formulating his answer to this question, Howard noted how the early pioneers in the "western country" had established their claims to land. Each pioneer would find a tree to mark the beginning corner of the land he wished to claim. He would then make three marks on that tree, each mark facing one of the other three corners of the tract. In this fashion, he could line out his entire claim from the beginning corner.

Howard told of an old revolutionary soldier in Virginia who had claimed a tract of land in the western country in this way and then returned to Virginia. After several years, he went back to the western country to settle on his land only to find that in the meantime vines and undergrowth had covered up his "beginning corner" so that he could not locate it. Even worse, others had settled on and around his tract of land. The old soldier was about to despair until he found a man who knew the location of his original "beginning corner." This man located the tree, cleared the underbrush, and found the three marks the old settler had made years ago. The later settlers fought the old soldier's attempts to take possession of the land, but in the end the courts upheld the validity of his original claims.

Then Howard made the application in which he acknowledged his dependence, first and foremost, on Alexander Campbell. The old soldier's "beginning corner" was the "old Jerusalem" gospel, he said. Later settlers — Catholics, Episcopalians, Presbyterians, Methodists, Baptists, and the like — had staked out claims as the vines and underbrush of human tradition had covered over the "old Jerusalem trunk." But Alexander Campbell

> exposed and tore away the human additions and appendages, the traditions, mysticism, and error with which the marks on the Jerusalem trunk — the corner of primitive Christianity — had been covered over, obscured, and hidden from the view of men; and *identified* it, by the *original* marks, to be the *same one* made by Peter. And this is the reason why . . . Alexander Campbell . . . is so much opposed and abused by the various religious parties, who have made their new corners, and run out their tracts on the old survey![29]

Then Howard listed the "original marks" that would always identify the true Church of Christ.

   I. The Church of Christ originated . . . in the days of the Apostles, and was founded by them. . . .

  II. The Church of Christ is known and recognized in the New Testament, by such appellations as . . . "Church of God," and "Churches of Christ." . . . Hence we may with propriety call it the "CHRISTIAN CHURCH," or "CHURCH OF CHRIST." . . .

 III. The Church now which has no creed but the *Bible* . . . is, all things else being equal, the true Church of Christ. . . .

 IV. The Church of Christ is *catholic*. . . . The word catholic means *universal*, and the Church of Christ is the only true *catholic* or universal Church; all others are only sectarian parties. . . .

  V. A fifth mark of the true church of Christ, is its TERMS OF ADMISSION. These are *Faith, Repentance, Confession,* and *Baptism,* in the order here presented, and in their Biblical import and application. . . .

 VI. Another mark of the true church of Christ is its ORGANIZATION and [congregational] INDEPENDENCE . . . [with] certain officers [including] . . . 1. *Bishops,* or elders; 2. *Deacons* and *deaconesses;* 3. *Evangelists.*

VII. The congregations thus organized met together every Lord's day, to . . . partake of the Lord's supper, and to attend to the *public* worship of God. . . . The GOVERNMENT of these congregations, was strictly that of the

New Testament form. . . . The church now having this *worship* and this
government, is, all things else being equal, or having all the other marks,
the true church of Christ.[30]

It seems legitimate to quote so liberally from this statement because it is
such a remarkable document from a relatively early date — the late 1840s. It
reveals already a hardening Church of Christ orthodoxy in the midst of the
religious pluralism of the United States, including the persistent use of the label
"Church of Christ."

Howard did not so much define this orthodoxy as reflect and summarize
an orthodoxy already taking shape around him. Further, the ideas he presented
crystallized from an early date into an informal creed around which this non-
creedal, nondenominational church would rally. In retrospect, it is remarkable
how much the ideas Howard presented in 1848 still characterize traditional,
mainstream congregations of Churches of Christ in the waning years of the
twentieth century. Indeed, most of the traditional congregations still hold as
fundamental everything Howard wrote, with one exception: his inclusion of the
office of deaconess (see Chap. 14).

Since there were some in the movement who still used the term "Church
of Christ" in the sense of a nondenominational ideal, it is important to make
one final clarification. Lest one think that Howard used the term "Church of
Christ" to refer only to an ideal and not to a particular ecclesiastical organization, it is important to hear his conclusion:

> And it may . . . be said to us; "You have unchristianized every church in the
> land but one — but your own — and consigned them all alike to the disap-
> probation of God, disownment by the Lord Jesus Christ, and utter extinction
> and annihilation!" If so . . . it is not *we* who have done it, but it has been
> done by the New Testament — by the WORD OF GOD.[31]

By 1843, having abandoned the postmillennial, ecumenical vision of Alexander Campbell, Howard discovered a useful alternative. William Miller of New
York had predicted for that year the imminent second coming of Christ, and
this prediction created enormous excitement throughout the United States.
Capitalizing on that excitement, Howard urged "sectarians," as he called them,

> to cast away all your unscriptural names, forms and practices; and return
> back to the true faith — the pure, original Gospel. . . . The coming of the
> Lord, in vengeance to destroy his enemies, cannot . . . be very far off. . . . And
> should *you* not be found among his true people — his genuine disciples —
> but arrayed in opposition against them, he will "destroy" you "with the *breath*
> of his *mouth*, and with the *brightness* of his *coming*."[32]

Arthur Crihfield: Heretic Detector

If John R. Howard contributed to defining an emerging Church of Christ orthodoxy, Arthur Crihfield simply took that orthodoxy as axiomatic and devoted
his career to identifying and exposing heretics. Crihfield was one of the earliest
in the history of Churches of Christ to take up this particular task, but in so
doing he prefigured a theological/rhetorical tradition that became increasingly
central to Churches of Christ from his time until the mid-twentieth century.

In 1837 Crihfield launched a publication from Middleburgh, Ohio, that
he named, appropriately enough, the *Heretic Detector.* It continued to appear
through 1842. When some of the more moderate followers of Campbell criticized this title, Crihfield admitted that it "was not the most soft and pleasing"
but was one that "gave scope to the unbiased operations of my own mind,"
since "I dislike milk-and-water publications."

Crihfield apparently believed that the task of restoration centered on detecting heretics. "Any effort to reinstate the Apostles upon their thrones, and the gospel
to its honors, is an effort to detect heresy," he trumpeted, "since by heresy all the
mischief to be repaired, has been brought about."[33] And so, in the columns of the
Heretic Detector, Crihfield regularly engaged in onslaughts on Presbyterians,
Methodists, Baptists, Episcopalians, Universalists, Deists, and anyone else not of
his tribe. He argued that all denominationalism was simply a species of unbelief
and infidelity. Not surprisingly, his paper attracted articles by a variety of radicals
who suggested, for example, that all who would not unite with the Church of
Christ had rejected Christ and that no sectarian — including Methodists, Baptists,
Presbyterians, Quakers, and others — could possibly be saved.[34]

Crihfield and John R. Howard both exerted a substantial influence in the
old Southwest, where Churches of Christ were hammering out their identity.
In fact, Crihfield became so popular in that region that members of Churches
of Christ in Kentucky invited him to leave his home in Ohio and settle in
Harrodsburg, bringing his *Heretic Detector* with him.[35]

Crihfield's fundamental dependence on Alexander Campbell is beyond
dispute, and he praised Campbell for having "restored the gospel."[36] Still, one
would think that by 1837, when Crihfield launched the *Heretic Detector,* Campbell
would have shunned him and his paper. But Campbell seemed aware of the diverse
impulses in his movement, and he did what he could to conciliate the various
factions. Accordingly, he commended Crihfield's *Heretic Detector* in 1837 for "its
spirited defence of the gospel, and many excellent and fundamental views of
Christian truth."[37] And in 1839 Crihfield persuaded Campbell to make a contribution to the paper. The piece, entitled "Essay on Heresy," was clearly intended
by Campbell to serve as a two-edged sword: he praised Crihfield for exposing
heretics and sects but warned him to "be cautious that we form not a new one."[38]

As religious pluralism in the United States expanded, however, Crihfield
grew correspondingly narrow in his outlook. By 1843 he had abandoned the

Heretic Detector, had edited the *Christian Family Library* for a year, and had begun to edit the *Orthodox Preacher*. In despair over the growing diversity of denominations, he abandoned Campbell's ecumenical vision and postmillennial optimism altogether, complaining that only "slight topical ameliorations will be effected by the reproclamation of the gospel; a few from the different parties will be induced to leave; but the Sects, as such, will never become extinct till 'the sign of the Son of Man is seen in the heavens.'" He flatly rejected the prospect of "a millennium brought about by science and theology, while money without stint is appropriated to sectarian purposes."[39] Campbell had only scorn and ridicule for such views, noting that "from being a *Heretic Detector* and a *Christian Family Library* keeper, our versatile brother Crihfield has become all at once an ORTHODOX PREACHER; and has taken up his abode . . . under the banners of the much exciting subject of the immediate second advent of Messiah."[40]

By 1846, relations between Crihfield and Campbell had worsened. Increasingly critical of Campbell's high level of comfort with Protestantism, American progress, and the world, Crihfield charged that Bethany College "may turn out a great many white-fingered and pretty dapper preachers, whose voices will be cultivated to the most scientific squeak, whose sentences will be framed with the most punctilious regard to both rhetoric and logic, and whose gestures will be most gracefully mechanical; but such lads will be found unfit for pioneers in this wilderness of sin." Clearly unhappy, Campbell urged Crihfield to "make honorable amends for this assault against myself and Bethany College."[41] By 1847, however, Crihfield had deserted Campbell and had become an Episcopalian (though he later returned to the Campbellian fold).[42]

Moses Lard: Rationalist Par Excellence

While John R. Howard typified a generation increasingly devoted to Church of Christ orthodoxy in the middle years of the nineteenth century, and while Arthur Crihfield typified those who prosecuted all who deviated from "the truth" during that same period, Moses Lard typified those who sought to undergird Church of Christ orthodoxy with an unassailable framework of rationality.[43]

We have already noted that in 1855 Jeremiah Jeter launched a scathing attack on the religious principles of Alexander Campbell. Among other things, Jeter accused Campbell of confining all Christians to his own movement, and he ridiculed Campbell's claim that he based his movement on the Bible alone, apart from human judgment or interpretation.[44] A graduate of Bethany College, Moses Lard took up the task of responding to Jeter at Campbell's invitation and on Campbell's behalf. Regarding the charge that Campbell thought his movement the true church, Lard shot back, "Mr. Campbell does not claim for himself and his brethren that they, as a body, exhaust the meaning of the term *the church*." But Lard was quick to add, "so far as the body of Christ has on earth *a denominational* existence, they are that body."[45]

But it was Jeter's other charge that struck directly at the heart of the emerging Churches of Christ. When Jeter claimed that Campbell and his followers interpreted the Bible rather than just taking the Bible at face value, he undermined the very philosophical premise of the movement. Lard therefore returned to this issue again and again as one of prime importance. In 1863, for example, he published a classic article in the literature of Church of Christ ideology entitled "The Reformation for Which We Are Pleading — What Is It?" Central to Lard's understanding was the Baconian common sense principle that all persons can know a thing precisely as it is without any differences in perception whatever. Like Campbell, Lard applied this Baconian epistemology directly to Scripture. "The Bible, then, being assumed true," Lard declared, "we hold that its contents may be so apprehended that the mind has . . . the highest possible assurance that its knowledge is correct." This was Lard's starting point and, indeed, the philosophical starting point for the sectarian vision of Churches of Christ.

Moses Lard (1818-1880) made substantial contributions to the rational mind-set of Churches of Christ. He argued that the Campbell movement embraced "the exact meaning of Holy Writ as our religious theory" and conformed itself "to the revealed will of Christ" with absolute precision.
(Photo courtesy Disciples of Christ Historical Society)

With this foundation, Lard was "prepared to answer more definitely" the question regarding "our plea." "The reformation for which we are pleading consists," he wrote, "1st. *In accepting the exact meaning of Holy Writ as our religious theory. . . .* 2d. *In the minute conformity of our practice to the revealed will of Christ. . . .* Hence all practices having their origin in tradition, human reason, or expediency, are utterly eschewed. . . . Thus it is proposed continually to construct the body of Christ after the Divine model."[46]

Several months later, Lard elaborated on these arguments in another key article, "Have We Not Become a Sect?" There he argued that all Christians can see the Bible alike. "It is a humiliating fact [therefore] . . . that they *will* not see alike, . . . [and] a grand lie that they cannot." He admitted in principle that there were individual Christians within the denominations,[47] but he effectively read these Christians out of the true church when he argued that "if a man knowingly holds one false doctrine, or one which with reasonable effort he might know to be false . . . , it is simply certain that he cannot be saved if he remains in this condition." At the same time, he claimed that the Churches of Christ of the Campbell movement had been absolutely successful in conforming their doctrine and practice precisely to the Bible at every point. "Have we introduced into the church any foreign element or doctrine unsanctioned by the Bible . . . ? If so, I shall only say that forty years watching and labor upon the part of our opponents who have lacked neither ability nor industry, have been wholly insufficient . . . to detect that element." Lard concluded that "we accept as the matter of our faith precisely and only what the Bible teaches, rejecting everything else." He left no doubt, therefore, that he believed the movement fathered by Alexander Campbell to be virtually identical with the nondenominational church of the apostolic era.[48]

In spite of Lard's contention that "we accept as the matter of our faith precisely and only what the Bible teaches," he nonetheless argued that a biblical doctrine or practice might be established in one of two ways: "by being actually asserted [in the biblical text]" or "by being necessarily implied."[49] He thereby made explicit what had been implicit among Churches of Christ for many years — namely, the belief that the New Testament makes its requirements clear in one of three ways: through direct command, through example, or through necessary inference. This threefold hermeneutic has characterized Churches of Christ ever since, hardening into a virtual orthodoxy by the twentieth century (see Chap. 14).[50]

Lard also echoed what increasingly was becoming orthodoxy among Churches of Christ regarding the issue of baptism — namely, that adult immersion for the forgiveness of sins was essential for one's salvation and for one's identity as a Christian. Campbell himself had vacillated on this point throughout much of the *Christian Baptist* period, one month claiming that one could not be saved without immersion, and the next month claiming that one could. Undoubtedly, his vacillation in this regard reflected the tension that he felt between the principles of unity and restoration. But following Walter Scott's astounding success on the Western Reserve in 1827, Campbell moved toward a more consistent position of requiring immersion — except in the case of ignorance — both for salvation and for one's status as a Christian.[51]

Campbell's most conservative position on this issue quickly became the centerpiece of the most conservative wing of the movement and in time became the centerpiece of Church of Christ orthodoxy. From the late 1820s on, this issue was the line in the sand that the movement's sectarians drew between themselves and other denominations. No one, however, drew that line more clearly than did Moses Lard in 1863.

> I mean to say distinctly and emphatically that Martin Luther, if not immersed, was not a Christian. . . . If a man can be a Christian without immersion, let the fact be shown. I deny both. Immovably I stand here. But I shall be told that this is Phariseeism, that it is exclusivism. Be it so; if it be true . . . then am I so far the defendant of Phariseeism and exclusivism.

And he concluded, "I recognize no human being a Christian who is not immersed."[52]

Conclusion

It would be foolish to suggest that these four men — Walter Scott, John R. Howard, Arthur Crihfield, and Moses Lard — would have shared, had they lived into the twentieth century, in all the points of orthodoxy that finally came to characterize Churches of Christ. Moses Lard, for example, strongly opposed instrumental music, but he accepted missionary societies. Even more important, Lard published late in his life a commentary on Romans that reflects a spirit of grace largely missing from his earlier polemical works and missing, as well, from the prevailing orthodoxy of Churches of Christ through the 1950s (see Chap. 8).[53] And yet, these four helped define in significant ways the intellectual core of this evolving tradition.

Likewise, it would be foolish to suggest that these were the only persons who helped define that core. But they were central to that task and, perhaps even more important, they put into words the key sectarian ideas developing all around them. By the time of the Civil War, a sizable segment of the Stone-Campbell movement held that the true Church of Christ had at last been restored to the earth, understood the precise contours and boundaries of that church, remained convinced that they and they alone constituted that church, and grounded all these notions in a Baconian worldview.

At the same time, there were others who contributed additional dimensions to the evolving orthodox outlook of Churches of Christ. We consider two of those others in Chapter 4.

CHAPTER 4

The True Church and the Hard Style: Radicalizing Alexander Campbell (Part II)

In 1843, John R. Howard noted with considerable unhappiness the announcement that a new periodical called the *Christian Review* would begin serving the Stone-Campbell movement in the South in head-on competition with his own *Bible Advocate*. He complained that when the *Bible Advocate* began in 1842, "there was not a single periodical [serving this cause] in the south; and it has struggled its way through difficulties into existence. After risking the experiment, they [the publishers] are determined now not to give place to any other publication."[1] Little did Howard know that the *Bible Advocate* would cease publication in 1850 or that the editor of the new publication would become the most powerful and influential person in Churches of Christ in the South during the middle years of the nineteenth century.

Tolbert Fanning

The editor of the *Christian Review* was Tolbert Fanning, and he embraced all the ideas we have already encountered in Crihfield, Howard, and Lard. The new journal, issued from Nashville, began publication in 1844. It was the first of four successive, highly influential publications that Fanning circulated among Churches of Christ, especially in the South. The others included the *Christian Magazine* (1848-1853), the *Gospel Advocate* (1855-), and the *Religious Historian* (1872-1874). In addition, Fanning founded Franklin College near Nashville, the first college associated with Churches of Christ in the South, and served as president of the institution from 1845 until the eve of the Civil War.

Born in 1810, Fanning grew up in northern Alabama under the tutelage of preachers whose first allegiance was to Barton W. Stone, and he absorbed

Steeped in the thought of John Locke, Tolbert Fanning (1810-1874) did more than perhaps any other person of his age to shape the historic nondenominational self-understanding of Churches of Christ, especially in the American South. Fanning believed that Churches of Christ had faithfully reproduced the church of the apostolic age and therefore had no human creed, no human theology, and no human history.
(Photo courtesy Disciples of Christ Historical Society)

many Stoneite perspectives himself (see Chap. 6). At the same time, while still in his teen years, he also came under the influence of people devoted especially to Alexander Campbell. For example, B. F. Hall, a man devoutly loyal to the teachings of Campbell, preached the sermon that actually converted Fanning in 1826 (see Chap. 5). Significantly, the theme of that sermon was "baptism for remission of sins."[2]

By the early 1830s, two other developments led Fanning to become a devoted disciple of Alexander Campbell. First, either in the late 1820s or the early 1830s, Fanning met Campbell and was enormously impressed by him.[3] And second, Fanning enrolled in 1832 in the University of Nashville and there studied under Philip Lindsley from Princeton, a strong proponent of Baconian Common Sense rationalism. Fanning's work under Lindsley simply reinforced his devotion to the principles of Alexander Campbell.

Defining the True Church

Fanning's relationship to Campbell apparently blossomed when Campbell invited Fanning to accompany him on preaching tours in 1835 and again in 1836. In 1836, the two traveled through New England and on into Canada, but Fanning lingered in Boston, where he delivered an address that is extremely important for assessing his early development. In this address, Fanning demonstrated little if any interest in the Campbellian theme of the unity of all Christians. Instead, he revealed his enormous frustration with religious pluralism in the United States. Because so many people believed that "if you are not pleased with one religion, select another," Fanning suggested that the nineteenth century might well be regarded "as the most remarkable era, for . . . aberrations from the truth, in the annals of time."[4] Further, he sought to demonstrate to his New England audience that the true church of the apostolic age had been restored to the earth and now thrived in the American Southwest. "Do my sectarian friends ask me for an example, now in the world, of apostolic order? In the United States, there are over a hundred thousand, mostly in the western country, who have taken the Bible, untrammelled by human philosophy and scholastic extravagances, and made a bold and solemn march for primitive ground and practices."[5]

It was his concern about religious pluralism that prompted Fanning to launch the *Christian Review* in 1844. He was distressed that among the various sects, the Church of Christ was "woefully misrepresented, and perverted throughout the length and breadth of the land. . . . Publications in opposition to our teaching are constantly being issued from the sectaries around us, and something for self-defense, is absolutely required."[6] He envisioned the *Christian Review* as a platform from which he could explain the beliefs and practices of Churches of Christ to the world. Accordingly, he delineated in a lengthy series of articles the nature of the church, its organization, its worship, and its requirements for admission. And in the second periodical that he edited, the *Christian Magazine*, Fanning published John R. Howard's sermon "Identification of the Church of Christ." In all of this, Fanning, like John Howard, contributed enormously — perhaps decisively — to defining the character and theological contours of the emerging Churches of Christ.

The Spirit, the Book, and Locke

Fanning's significance went far beyond this, however. As much as any one person in the nineteenth century, he typified the historical naivete that generally has characterized Churches of Christ since the early nineteenth century. By historical naivete, I mean Fanning's deep and abiding conviction that Churches of Christ had escaped the molding and shaping influences of history, culture, and tradition and were in no way corrupted by human ideals or constructions. Fanning was convinced that Churches of Christ had authentically reproduced the primitive and apostolic church, which, in turn, was a faithful replication of an ideal revealed from the mind of God. Fanning therefore spoke often of the Church of Christ in negative rather than positive terms, asserting, for example, that it was not a denomination, that it had no creed, that it had no theology, and, indeed, that it had no human history at all, inasmuch as it was a divine rather than a human institution.

This is what Fanning meant by "primitive Christianity," and it was this understanding that informed his classic sermon "The Mission of the Church of Christ." There Fanning argued that throughout the entire history of Christianity, no predecessors — not even the Protestant Reformers — had truly sought "to return to the spiritual purity and authority of the Church of God." Instead, all had satisfied themselves, to some degree, with historic and human traditions.

This perspective typified Fanning's somber and negative cast of mind. Indeed, Fanning typically found thorns where others found roses. A speech he delivered in his debate with N. L. Rice is a case in point. William Ramsey, who attended the debate, reported Fanning's comment that "Elijah thought he was the only true worshiper, but the Lord told him that seven thousand had not bowed the knee to Baal. He [Fanning] said that was quite a minority compared to the millions who were wrong."[7]

On the other hand, Fanning's mood brightened when he described the Church of Christ and the movement that had produced it. "Early in the nineteenth century," he exulted, "great men of God" had determined to have "no denomination, party, or creed to defend, and no plans, expedients, or organizations . . . to foster." Instead, they sought simply to belong to the "body of Christ" described in the New Testament. This, Fanning suggested, was "the mission of the Church of Christ."[8]

This sort of historical and cultural naivete was not, as one might suspect, simply a function of Fanning's Christian primitivist point of view. Rather, it was a function of the *type* of primitivism Fanning espoused, which was almost entirely informed by Lockean epistemology and Scottish Baconianism. What is more, Fanning saw no difference between the two, arguing that "John Locke [was] the *real* author of the Baconian philosophy."[9]

Fanning believed that the human mind is a kind of *tabula rasa,* that human knowledge always originates outside the self, stamping the mind with its content, and hence that the human mind is incapable of originating any ideas whatsoever. Accordingly, he prized the Bible not only as the word of God but as the *only* possible source of sacred truth.[10] He also affirmed that, inasmuch as God had revealed sacred truth in a book, that truth necessarily remains static from age to age, immune to the winds of change and the relativities of time, culture, and history.

Fanning's understanding of Locke and the Scottish Baconians thus defined his understanding of the task of reading Scripture. From Locke, Fanning learned that one should simply receive on one's mind the impress of revelation, unmutilated by human opinion or tradition. From the Baconian tradition, he learned that one should read the Bible as though it were a science book, always sensitive to the facts, and that one must gather all the facts on any subject before drawing any final conclusions. On this basis, he determined that the project of restoring primitive Christianity was simply a matter of following the Book in Baconian/Lockean fashion. If one gathered all the facts and followed all the instructions of the Book in precise detail, one could rightfully claim to have no theology but the Bible, no creed but the Bible, no organizational schemes other than the biblical pattern, and, indeed, one could rightfully claim that one's church was no denomination at all but the true church of the first age.

Fanning's slavish allegiance to Lockean epistemology rendered him hostile to any suggestion that the human mind is receptive to divine illumination apart from the Bible or that divinity might in some way instruct, inspire, or edify a human being through spiritual impulses. This position inevitably sent Fanning into battle with one of the fundamental impulses of his age: romanticism.

In truth, Fanning was in many ways a period piece. As an old-time Lockean, he was steeped in eighteenth-century rationalist assumptions, but he lived in a culture in which a growing number — especially outside the South — rejected Lockean rationalism as out of step and out of style. American romantics — like romantics abroad — prized intuition, emotion, feeling, and, above all, individualism. Some American romantics, especially in New England, embraced Transcendentalism, with its rejection of dogmatic, rational, and uniform categories and its emphasis on a universal Soul that spoke directly to the individual human heart.

Spiritualism was also broadly popular at that time. Many Americans claimed to have contacted the spirit world and spoken with the dead. One man wrote to Alexander Campbell in 1856 complaining of spiritualists in his region who produced pictures of the deceased taken "from the Spirit's land, . . . which . . . we consider to be one of the greatest deceptions practised on the community."[11] Tolbert Fanning, along with most members of Churches of Christ, was inclined to view such behavior not merely as "one of the greatest deceptions" but rather as the *ultimate* deception, since it implicitly denied that the Bible was the only revelation from the Spirit to humankind.

In this context, Fanning also thought he detected fundamental errors in standard Protestant views regarding the Holy Spirit. He objected especially to the notion that the Spirit operates directly on the human heart in conversion and speaks directly to the heart following conversion, apart from the Bible. In the early 1840s, he filled the *Christian Review* with articles on the role of the Holy Spirit, and as late as 1872 he still maintained that our main controversy is with Calvinists, Armenians [sic], Quakers, Shakers and modern spiritualists regarding the work of the Holy Spirit. They unite in preaching a *direct* and *perpetual* revelation of the Spirit in conversion; and maintain that the only evidence of their pardon, regeneration and salvation, is an immediate, revelation of the Spirit in their hearts.[12]

From Fanning's point of view, there was little difference in this regard among Calvinism, Spiritualism, and Transcendentalism. All flew squarely in the face of Lockean epistemology, which, to his mind, translated into outright rejection of the Bible.

The Jesse B. Ferguson Affair

During the mid-1840s, Fanning may have confined his discussions to the Holy Spirit, but in the 1850s, events in Fanning's own congregation in Nashville propelled him into the larger arena of Spiritualism. In 1852, Jesse B. Ferguson, the polished and popular young preacher of the Nashville Church of Christ, affirmed his conviction that Jesus, along with ministering angels, continually preaches to the departed dead in the spirit world, thereby giving sinners a second chance. Opposition to Ferguson quickly mounted not only from Fanning, the spiritual leader of the congregation, but from Alexander Campbell himself, both of whom accused Ferguson of universalism. Soon the Nashville Church of Christ was deeply divided over this issue.

But Ferguson was not yet done. In 1854, he revealed that he had moved into Spiritualism, having himself received communications from the departed dead, including William Ellery Channing. When opposition intensified, Ferguson sought to defend himself:

> We desire not to tear down churches and build up other organizations, but to permeate these with the divine light now descending on all men; desire not to destroy or bring into contempt the Bible, but to free all minds from a blind reverence for the Book; to separate the human from the divine in that sacred volume, so that all may judge right from wrong by the infallible guide, planted in every breast — *Reason.*[13]

Fanning was livid. He and others in the congregation produced a document flatly stating that "the New Theology in Nashville, is, in fact and form, the misnamed Spiritualism of Theodore Parker, Francis William Newman, Henry James, Unitarians, Universalists, Spiritualists, and professedly religious Infidels generally." They further charged that Ferguson's theology was "at war with the authority of the Bible [and] subversive of the church of God."[14] In the end, Alexander Campbell himself visited Nashville for the express purpose of opposing Ferguson, and in 1856 Ferguson resigned his pulpit under pressure, leaving his congregation in shambles.

The episode involving Ferguson was the background to an even more important controversy that erupted in 1857 between Fanning and Robert Richardson, a chemistry professor at Bethany College who served as Alexander Campbell's personal physician. This controversy finally drove a wedge between Fanning and Campbell and between Nashville and Bethany, and revealed the fundamental theological differences that already were emerging between Disciples and Churches of Christ.

The Fanning/Richardson Affair

In 1856, in a series of articles in the *Millennial Harbinger,* Richardson launched a frontal attack on the rationalistic extremes that had come to characterize the Campbell movement.[15] He criticized those who viewed the Bible as a scientific blueprint, who "glory in its 'letter' [and] . . . rejoice in its facts" and who regarded it "as a system of external or outward communication, terminating upon the ordinary understanding." These people, Richardson complained, always reduce spiritual life to "a process of reasoning" and to "the simple sequence of cause and effect, as in physical science," and thereby "mistake the shadow for the substance." They altogether fail to understand, he went on, that the "Divine word . . . addresses itself to our higher spiritual nature." Then he made the really critical point that such a view does not revere the Bible so much as it reveres a philosophical perspective imposed upon the Bible, and those who revere this philosophical perspective often do so unconsciously, imagining that they are actually rejecting all philosophical systems in deference to the Bible alone.[16]

Tolbert Fanning was both astounded and incensed by this criticism. He thought he saw shades of Jesse B. Ferguson emanating, this time, not from Nashville but from Bethany. A month before Richardson published this article, the *Harbinger* had printed a commencement address delivered by a student at Bethany College emphasizing spiritual insight over and above the written word.[17] And now this. It appeared to Fanning that some, at least, on the Bethany faculty were engaged in a conspiracy to sell the birthright of the *Christian Baptist* for a bowl of Spiritualist porridge. "If we are not mad," he wrote, Richardson's teachings "fully set forth the same system" as that of Jesse B. Ferguson.[18]

In response, Fanning wrote a series of articles for the third publication that he initiated and edited, the *Gospel Advocate*. He severely criticized Richardson's efforts to elevate the Spirit above the written word and denounced Richardson as an infidel who had abandoned the Christian faith for speculative and *"Transcendental philosophy."* "The idea of becoming wise above what is written," he charged, "led men at an early date to abandon the simplicity of truth for dreams, visions, and idle fancies."[19] By implication, he even attacked Campbell's Bethany College.

> In all the schools amongst the disciples of Christ, the Bible is represented as the only foundation in morals; and still the directors have introduced the various philosophies, *mental* and *moral,* of the times. . . . We declare our solemn conviction, that no one who respects the Bible can believe in any system of philosophy in existence. Hence we think the schools generally are well calculated to make infidels.[20]

He further suggested that one of the chief reasons he had begun the *Gospel Advocate* in 1855 "was to meet some of the infidel systems of theology which are insinuating themselves into the churches." Finally, he distinguished between "speculative philosophy" and "correct thinking," the principles of which, he urged, were central to Lockean epistemology: "John Locke [was] the *real* author of the Baconian philosophy and all correct thinking in England since his day."[21]

In making this distinction, Fanning played directly into Richardson's hands, providing him with a prime example of the sort of problem he had been discussing in his articles:

> If John Locke is the author of all correct thinking in England since his day, . . . he is . . . also the author of all correct thinking in *America* during the same interval. Surely, then, unless President F. thinks *in*correctly or *not at all,* it must be admitted that John Locke is the author of *his* thinking, and that he is, however *unconscious* of it, a philosopher of the School of Locke, or, what is usually termed A SENSUALISTIC DOGMATIST.

But Richardson was not finished. He proceeded to charge Fanning with having abandoned the fundamental principles of the Campbell movement for sectarianism.

> It is when a system of philosophy is made the *basis* of religious thought; when the Scriptures must be interpreted so as to agree with it, and when the dogmas thus deduced are imposed upon men as the orthodox Christian faith, that it becomes the ground-work of sectarism [*sic*].

He professed that it was not his intention to attack Fanning, but because Fanning had "made himself so conspicuous as an opponent of philosophy, we regard him as an excellent representative of a considerable class who habitually inveigh against philosophy, yet are . . . its victims."[22]

Then Richardson turned to the issue of spirituality. Fanning had completely misunderstood his earlier articles, he said. "I look for no spiritual light . . . from other sources than the Bible. I advocate no direct spiritual communications." He explained that he simply wanted to urge his brothers and sisters to a greater openness to the spiritual dimensions of the Christian faith. But Fanning was "evidently too deeply imbued with sensualistic philosophy to receive or comprehend the spiritual things of Christianity."[23]

The problem with Fanning and his kind, he went on, was their studied attempt to equate the word with the Spirit. In this, they made

> the Bible either a rubric which prescribes forms and ordinances, or a species of mere logical machinery. . . . In the midst of their tirades against "miraculous agencies, ghosts and sights and dreams," they seem to have lost sight of the real connexion between the word and the Spirit of God, and they do not hesitate to claim for the "word ALONE," *all* power in the work of human salvation.

In taking this extreme position, said Richardson, Fanning and his kind had virtually abandoned the teachings of Alexander Campbell.[24]

Finally, Richardson suggested that Fanning and those of like mind had turned the Bible into an idol and made themselves into idolators. These people, he wrote, "need no longer trouble themselves with earnest efforts to lift themselves to the contemplation of the spiritual and the unseen, for they find all this now reduced to visible words and embodied in sensible forms, and the relief they experience is like that of the idolator when he has succeeded in embodying his conception of his divinity." These were strong words and suggested a major rift, at least from Richardson's point of view, between Bethany and Nashville. Richardson claimed that Fanning and his people had radicalized and distorted Campbell's intent beyond recognition. "They bring reproach upon the cause of the present Reformation," he charged, "by their unbecoming love of controversy, and by the crude and erroneous exhibitions which they make of the real purposes of this religious movement."[25]

When Fanning read what Richardson had written, he was simply astounded. In defending himself, however, he confirmed much that Richardson had said. Why would anyone think, he wondered, that he and his people confused the Spirit with the Bible? His true position, he said, was that the Spirit converts sinners only through the *medium* of words, that is, through the Book.

But Fanning was especially concerned to rebut the charge that he had embraced Lockean epistemology and read the Bible through that lens. And here he laid completely bare his own naivete regarding the influence of history and culture — the point with which we began this examination. Fanning simply could not believe that Richardson would "attempt to make it appear that our belief through the word is our system of philosophy." Fanning was convinced that no philosophy other than the Bible had ever shaped his thinking. But what if he did rely on Locke? Fanning wondered. Locke himself had spurned all philosophical influences and, like Fanning, had also focused on the Bible alone.

Indeed, Fanning affirmed, "John Locke denied all theories and speculations, and therefore was, strictly speaking, no philosopher."[26]

Fanning felt so strongly about all of this that he traveled to Bethany specifically to win Campbell's support in the controversy, and, for a time, he succeeded. Campbell publicly reprimanded Richardson for "placing *faith* and *philosophy* in any real or formal antagonism" and, the next month, wrote that Richardson had "been infelicitous in two respects — first in the choice of a subject, and again in his manner of treating it."[27] Finally, the attacks became personal. Richardson discovered an article in the print shop that spoke "of me in the most sarcastic and even insulting terms," but he convinced Campbell not to print it. Still, he felt that Campbell's "continuous antagonism to me deprived me of my influence for good both in the College & in the church."[28] Richardson was so devastated in fact that, after twenty-eight years of writing in the *Millennial Harbinger,* he now resigned.[29] In addition, Campbell's criticism and some other factors led Richardson to resign from Bethany College and accept a position at the new Kentucky University.[30]

Then, for reasons that have never been made clear, Campbell completely reversed his position following a trip to Kentucky in 1858.[31] He apologized to the *Harbinger* readers for his treatment of Richardson and, in the next issue, strongly rebuked Fanning. He made it clear that he considered Fanning's behavior "an outrage upon both editorial and Christian courtesy and upon the rules of church order and discipline."[32]

Further, it is clear that Campbell's long-term support and most deeply held convictions stood with Richardson and not with Fanning. By January of 1860, Campbell confided in a letter to Philip Fall,

> I have . . . ever since my late tour to Mississippi viewed Elder Fanning as intent on a war with us under some pretence or other. And I still must regard him as hostile to Bethany and indeed I know not why — or wherefore unless an unsanctified ambition lurks within him. He is a very vulnerable man, and ought not to expose himself. Unfortunately, however, such men cannot be dispossessed of that unclean spirit.[33]

What are we to make of this episode? First, it opens an extraordinarily large window on the intellectual character of the emerging Churches of Christ, for Fanning was not alone in his Lockean rationalism, his historical naivete, or the sectarianism that these qualities fostered. To the contrary, as the most powerful figure among southern Churches of Christ in his time, he reflected a mind-set that characterized an entire people. Richardson clearly recognized the existence of such a people when he cautioned that if "one [who] is of some reputation for education and intelligence" can be as historically naive as Fanning, "how much reason there is to fear that the genius of Locke holds its secret councils in the hearts of multitudes who are still less capable of detecting its presence!"[34] As we shall see, a Lockean reading of the biblical text and the historical naivete it fostered became distinguishing features of Churches of Christ well into the twentieth century.

In fact, when several of Fanning's former students from Franklin College paid him tribute in 1904/1905, they praised in Fanning precisely the characteristics described in this chapter. David Lipscomb, who succeeded Fanning as editor of the *Gospel Advocate,* recalled that Fanning "denied earnestly that man is possessed of any intuitive knowledge of God or of good and evil" and that "he is wholly dependent upon teaching from external sources to determine what is right and what is wrong." Lipscomb allowed that "this to many seems narrow. [But] it keeps man on safe ground. It ties him to God and his word in all matters of moral and religious duty and all questions of right and wrong. It clips the wings of imagination and speculation and makes the Bible the only and safest teacher of duty to man."[35] And H. R. Moore, who graduated from Franklin College in 1857, intended only the highest praise for Fanning when he recalled that "he waved no plumes, wreathed no garlands, but struck from the shoulder and at the vitals. He was destitute of poetry and barren of imagination."[36]

Second, this episode sheds light on the nature and causes of the division between Churches of Christ and Disciples of Christ — a division that the United States Bureau of the Census would belatedly recognize only in 1906. Central to that division, as we noted in Chapter 2, was the ambiguity in Campbell's own thought, which clearly came to view in the Fanning/Richardson affair. In opposing Fanning, Richardson opposed the principles of the *Christian Baptist* that had now, he thought, run amuck. He established this point in a very significant letter he wrote to Isaac Errett in July of 1857: "The philosophy of Locke with which Bro. Campbell's mind was deeply imbued in youth has insiduously mingled itself with almost all the great points in the reformation and has been all the while like an iceberg in the way — chilling the heart and numbing the hands, and impeding all progress in the right direction."[37]

For his part, Fanning had long been convinced that Campbell had departed from the bedrock principles of the *Christian Baptist.* It must be remembered that as early as 1845, Fanning had attacked the "greatest reformers" — editors who "stood forth first to advocate the cause of primitive Christianity" but who in more recent years had begun to "court the smiles of corrupt denominations." Later, as we noted in Chapter 2, Fanning announced that Campbell had fallen victim to senility and "was merely a child in the hands of his friends," who sought to shift the movement even further from those original principles. Chief among those "friends," according to Fanning, was Robert Richardson. His judgment in this regard is not surprising in light of his strongly negative response to Richardson in 1844, after Richardson had suggested that the movement Campbell led had originated in southwest Pennsylvania in 1810 rather than in Jerusalem in the first century.

Richardson was simply wrong in his contention that "this is wholly a personal matter with the Advocate" unconnected with "the true principles of the Reformation."[38] The real issue for Fanning was not Spiritualism or Transcendentalism, much less Richardson himself: it was the prospect of a departure from bedrock biblical principles — those principles that Campbell had laid down in the *Christian Baptist.* Fanning believed that even Campbell now wavered on those principles, and that Richardson was largely responsible. When Campbell suggested that Fanning was "intent on a war with us" and was "hostile to Bethany," he was absolutely correct.

This episode, then, shows that the movement had already experienced an ideological rupture. And since Fanning and the *Advocate* spoke to and for a sizable, conservative constituency, principally in the South, and Richardson wielded considerable power among the more ecumenical and progressive followers of Campbell, this rupture was very significant: in fact, it was nothing less than a prelude to outright division. Something of the severity of the breach was evident to Richardson in the midst of the dispute. He wrote to Philip Fall that he anticipated "a full exposure of the course of the Advocate. I think with you that any notice of it taken must be a thorough & searching exhibition of the base, factious & outrageous course pursued by its editor." Nonetheless, he knew the time was not right. "I have to put a strong curb upon my inclinations, I assure you, in refraining from it or even in delaying it."[39] For his part, Fanning went public with his conviction that Richardson "is not of us," and that if Richardson refused to retrace his steps, "we cannot anticipate a continuance of Christian harmony."[40]

This episode foreshadows Alexander Campbell's course in later years. For in combining such diverse and even contradictory themes into his original platform, Campbell had raised up followers who, at many points, stood diametrically opposed to one another. Tragically, he found himself related to both but estranged from both, standing in the middle of their contentions but able to do little or nothing to reconcile their disputes. By the mid-1850s, the numbers in each of the two principal groups he had spawned were legion, though they had not yet congealed into separate and recognized denominations.

Postscript: Missionary Societies

Before we take leave of the Fanning controversy, we should consider his role in opposing missionary societies, both because this opposition became such a visible symbol of the emerging identity of Churches of Christ and because Fanning was such an important leader of that opposition.

Early on, during the 1840s, Fanning was actually a strong supporter of the societies. As long as he believed that it was their intent to consult and aid local congregations, he heartily endorsed their work. But when he concluded that the national and state missionary societies were in fact seeking to legislate procedures to local congregations and supplant their work, he turned against them.

Three factors, not necessarily listed in order of importance here, help explain his opposition. The first was his commitment to the Lockean epistemology we have considered in this chapter. For Fanning, rigid adherence to Locke's principles translated into rigid adherence to the Bible alone, since the Bible was the only source of information regarding God and his law. When one began to speculate and philosophize *about* the Bible, Fanning thought, one opened the door to all sorts of human inventions that ran contrary to God's word. He eventually dismissed missionary societies as mere by-products of idle speculation and human philosophy. Fanning made this point abundantly clear in the course of his dispute with Richardson.[41] It is hardly surprising, then, that he moved from support to opposition of missionary societies precisely during the years of the Jesse Ferguson affair, though he indicated that he had had reservations about the societies long before then.[42]

Second, as an Alabama farm boy, Fanning was deeply devoted to the democratic sentiment that favored common people over the social elite in antebellum America. David Lipscomb confirmed this point when he wrote of Fanning in connection with his work with Franklin College that he "had great sympathy for the common working people, . . . but little confidence in helping or educating the children of wealth."[43] There can be little doubt that this democratic sentiment also fueled Fanning's opposition to missionary societies, inasmuch as he shifted his position on this issue when it seemed to him that the societies were seeking power and control.

But the role of the democratic sentiment in prompting Fanning's opposition to societies also was related to the Jesse Ferguson affair. For several years before Ferguson arrived to preach for the Church of Christ in Nashville in 1846, that congregation had employed no salaried preacher at all, relying instead on the talents of its members. Fanning endorsed that practice on the grounds that it conformed to the biblical model. But in 1846, Fanning found himself in the minority, and the congregation hired Ferguson as its preacher. Ferguson's striking oratorical presence in the pulpit, coupled with his "suavity of manners," enhanced his popularity throughout the city of Nashville. But the net effect of his preaching, according to Fanning and others, was "to seal the lips, if not entirely, at least measurably so, of the members of the church who could once read, exhort, preach, pray, sing and administer the Lord's ordinances acceptably in Nashville."[44] Following the Ferguson affair, Fanning spoke out even more strongly against salaried preachers, whose presence, he said, silenced the common people.[45] Doubtless Fanning saw a close parallel between salaried preachers and missionary societies, both of which he accused of preempting the work of the common people in the local congregation, and for this reason he opposed them both.

Third, Fanning's opposition to missionary societies grew from his deeply held apocalyptic conviction that the Church of Christ was more than just another organization, even an ecclesiastical organization. He believed that it was in truth the kingdom of God that would finally triumph over all the earth. For this reason, Fanning refused support not only to missionary societies but also to temperance societies. He admitted that the latter "have had a good influence in the world," but he wrote, "I beg leave to be permitted to advocate temperance from my Divine commission. If I plead temperance from human authority, I own I have not confidence in God's plan to reform the world."[46] Fanning developed these convictions not in the context of his association with Alexander Campbell but rather in the context of his early association with preachers who had been shaped and molded by Barton W. Stone. Accordingly, we shall investigate this dimension of Fanning's thought in greater detail in Chapter 6.

Benjamin Franklin

When Benjamin Franklin died in 1878, David Lipscomb wrote that "the cause loses its most able and indefatigable defender since the days of Alexander Campbell."[47] Further, he suggested that Franklin, through the periodicals he edited and through his published debates, sermons, and tracts, "has had a larger number of readers than any man that has written in the effort to restore primitive Christianity."[48] In fact, Franklin conducted some twenty-five debates,[49] six of which were published; he put out two volumes of sermons, one going through thirty-one editions and the other through nineteen editions by the end of the nineteenth century; and he was involved as editor or coeditor of four different journals, the most important of which was the *American Christian Review*, which he edited from 1856 until his death in 1878.[50]

Partisan of the Christian Baptist

Franklin was profoundly loyal to the early Alexander Campbell, and he routinely criticized his opponents on the grounds that they had departed from the teachings of the *Christian Baptist*.[51] Franklin seems not to have recognized the change that Campbell underwent in his later years. In 1850, Franklin stood in such awe of Campbell that he marveled that "one human being, seeming to differ so little, to all human appearance from the thousands of others, should be endowed with such superior powers." Six years later, he wrote of Campbell that "he has made such a defense of Christianity against the assaults of Infidels, Romanists — such an effort to separate it from everything else, and preserve it in its purity, as no other man on earth has made in the last thousand years." And as late as 1872, he resolutely identified his *American Christian Review* with the work of

Alexander Campbell: "If you want to 'undo what Alex Campbell did,' the REVIEW is not the paper for you. . . . [But] if you are for maintaining our distinctive plea and all the ground we have gained, the REVIEW is the paper you want."[52] Throughout his writings, Franklin identified "what Alex Campbell did" with his work in the *Christian Baptist.*

In addition to Campbell, Walter Scott, Arthur Crihfield, and Tolbert Fanning all helped shape Franklin's thinking. Franklin's biographers tell us that he "listened to and read after . . . [Crihfield, Scott, and Campbell] not merely to grasp their thoughts, but to learn their language" and that Fanning's *Christian Review* (1844-1847) had been "one of Mr. Franklin's favorite exchanges."[53] Franklin himself acknowledged his profound debt to Crihfield, and his first published article appeared in Crihfield's *Heretic Detector.*[54]

One should not be surprised, therefore, at Franklin's radically sectarian position. He opened his *American Christian Review,* for example, with the following statement:

Though many nineteenth-century leaders of Churches of Christ identified primitive Christianity with lower socioeconomic class prejudices, no one did so more consistently than did Benjamin Franklin (1812-1878). A poor and rustic man without formal education, Franklin believed that the true Church of Christ was democratic, plain, and poor.
(Photo courtesy Disciples of Christ Historical Society)

[Our cause] is the cause of God, and if any man proves recreant to it, he will be destroyed. . . . Better were it for a man that he had never been born, than that he should trifle with this mightiest and greatest of all causes. Men may leave one human establishment and go to another, without affecting them much; but men who leave this cause, leave Christianity, the church of God, and the Head of the church; and all such men are ruined.[55]

John F. Rowe, Franklin's associate editor on the *Review,* argued that "next to crude and coarse infidelity, we regard the support and propagation of the various denominations as the greatest and basest moral evil upon earth — in fact it is a species of infidelity itself. . . . The plea of the apostles was exclusive; *so is ours.*" Franklin concurred: "To be sincere and conscientious as a Romanist, a Methodist, or a Quaker, is one question; to be a sincere and conscientious follower of Jesus Christ is entirely another question."[56]

Franklin and his colleagues sustained their sectarian position with the same mixture of legalism and historical naivete that was characteristic of Fanning and others. "As long as we have the clear and distinct commands of Christ and his apostles to preach and enforce," wrote John F. Rowe, "what have we to do with the opinions of men?" And Franklin argued that if one could find a church "that *does all things* that . . . [the Lord] commanded, that is the body of Christ."[57]

Franklin also helped define even further what rapidly was becoming the orthodox position among Churches of Christ regarding the Holy Spirit. As early as 1850, he argued flatly that spiritual gifts had died with the apostles. Then, in the late 1850s, when Bethany graduates W. S. Russell, I. N. Carman, and others began preaching the validity of "spiritual illumination" and began praying "that we might receive the Holy Spirit," Franklin saw neglect of the plain and rational message of the Book. "You will find . . . [such teachers]," he wrote, "laboring very hard to explain their doctrine, and you laboring equally hard to understand it, and both failing." He concluded with the contention that, "as to '*personal* indwelling,' it is not New Testament language."[58]

All of this is to say that Franklin stood squarely in the *Christian Baptist* tradition, though — like Crihfield, Howard, and Fanning — he radicalized that tradition far beyond Campbell's intent.

A Plain and Democratic Gospel

Still, we have not yet discovered the heart of Benjamin Franklin or the essence of his singular contribution to Churches of Christ. These lay in his consistent blending of his vision of primitive Christianity with lower socioeconomic class prejudices. Franklin envisioned the true Church of Christ as democratic (as opposed to aristocratic), plain, and poor. We have already noted this bias in

Tolbert Fanning, and, indeed, it characterized many of those who identified themselves with Churches of Christ and the outlook of the *Christian Baptist*. In Chapter 6 we will take a closer look at the dimensions of this bias among leaders in the South.

No one exemplified this bias more graphically than Benjamin Franklin, however, particularly following the Civil War.[59] Franklin's circumstances were in many ways unique within the emerging Churches of Christ, for while those who shared the Church of Christ perspective would eventually enjoy their greatest strength in a belt running from Nashville on the east to Texas on the west, Franklin was a northerner who did most of his editorial and preaching work in Indiana and Ohio. While many southerners subscribed to Franklin's *American Christian Review* prior to the Civil War, the interruption of the mails coupled with regional animosity during the conflict increasingly estranged Franklin from his southern brothers and sisters. When the war concluded, Tolbert Fanning proposed a "consultation meeting" for southern Christians only. Hurt and disappointed, Franklin responded, "Why keep up these State lines? Have we, up here, nothing in common with brethren down there?" Fanning replied that war-related circumstances had made it important for southern Christians to work "separately for a season."[60]

In the next several years, Franklin's *American Christian Review* picked up numerous new subscriptions, but most came from the Middle West and Texas, not the Tennessee heartland of the movement.[61] Significantly, although David Lipscomb, the postwar leader of Churches of Christ in the South, admired Franklin greatly, he did not meet him personally until 1876.[62]

Following the war, Franklin found himself estranged and isolated not only from like-minded southerners but from northern church members as well. A poor and a rustic man who lacked formal education,[63] Fanning lived in a region where postwar prosperity produced an emphasis on economic progress and development, a cultured lifestyle, and educational achievement. In a word, Benjamin Franklin was a misfit.

Even before the war, many Disciples in the North had followed the mature Alexander Campbell toward a greater emphasis on wealth, ecumenicity, and postmillennial progress. A case in point was the wealthy and influential Disciples leader in Cincinnati, David Staats Burnet, with whom Franklin entered into a partnership in 1850 to publish the *Christian Age*. Franklin had to sell his small dwelling in Milton, Indiana, in order to purchase his share in this venture. He moved to Cincinnati, first taking up residence with his family in a log house that Burnet supplied for him on a farm adjacent to his own splendid estate. Later the Franklins moved into part of an unoccupied school building that Burnet offered for their use. Throughout the venture, the Franklins remained financially dependent on Burnet. Franklin's son later recalled that "the temporal surroundings of the two families were so different that free social intercourse was impossible. Mr. Franklin had always been poor, and had a large family to maintain. Their living was necessarily of the plainest kind. Mr. Burnet's family had always been accustomed to the social manners indulged in by wealthy people. . . . Mr. Franklin's family could not rise above a feeling that they were somehow subordinate and merely tributary to Mr. Burnet's splendid establishment." This disparity was symbolized each Sunday morning "when Mr. Burnet's family rolled off in a fine carriage to the city to worship, while they [the Franklins] went on foot to the village of Mt. Healthy, one mile in the opposite direction."[64]

Following the war, urban Disciples in the Middle West increasingly moved toward greater social respectability and educational attainments, embracing, even within their churches, the trappings of wealth and status. Alexander Campbell's death in 1866 seemed to remove any remaining restraint on these tendencies. Younger leaders at Bethany fostered a wholesale rejection of the principles of the *Christian Baptist,* and Disciples in city after city built lavish church buildings replete with expensive organs, established a formal clergy, adopted clerical titles, and generally launched an appeal to the refined and genteel middle and upper-middle classes. After all, this was the Gilded Age.

Essentially, these Disciples went down the same road traveled by northern, urban Methodists during the same period. Like the upwardly mobile Methodists who alienated their rural and poorer members to the point that the latter eventually abandoned Methodism altogether in favor of separate Holiness denominations, the Disciples alienated their rural and poorer members to the point that they eventually settled on Churches of Christ as the most attractive alternative. Among those rural and poorer members, none was more alienated than Benjamin Franklin.

Within a year following the war, progressive Disciples found Franklin's *American Christian Review* far too backward, sectarian, and unlettered to suit their tastes, and they established a competing journal, the *Christian Standard,* funded by the wealthy Phillips brothers of Newcastle, Pennsylvania, and edited by Isaac Errett. The introduction of this new journal alone signaled that a decisive rift had opened up between those at home with the denominational worldview of the Disciples and those at home with the sectarian worldview of Churches of Christ, though formal division still was forty years away.

In Franklin's view, Errett and those who supported the *Christian Standard* had simply abandoned biblical religion for popular tastes. All Errett had to do, he complained, was to "consult the *popular taste, the mind of the people,* the *public will,* and supply the reading it demands." He further charged that those connected with the *Standard* were rapidly displacing plain and simple Christian servants with ecclesiastical bureaucrats.[65]

No incident better symbolized Franklin's devotion to a plain and simple religion than his quarrel with the Central Christian Church of Cincinnati. In 1872, that congregation built a new building quite out of keeping with the plain and simple values that Franklin prized. Capable of seating some 2,000 people and built in French Gothic style at a cost of $140,000, the building boasted a nave some 34 feet wide, 125 feet long, and 103 feet high, a stained glass window thought to be the largest in America at the time, and an organ and choir loft behind the pulpit. At the dedication of the building, the pastor, W. T. Moore, took as his sermon topic the words of Jesus on the cross, "It is finished."[66]

Franklin was outraged and complained loudly and often in the pages of the *Review* about this "millstone they [the progressives] would hang about our necks to sink and disgrace us and the good men who now rest with Jesus!" The pastor's sermon, he lamented, ran altogether contrary to the principles of "that forsaken book, the 'Christian Baptist.'" This lavish building, in which "'the fine effect of light, warmed and tinted as it passes through the stained windows,'" stood directly at odds with the "ancient order" and "the gospel restored," wrote Franklin. Such a building would alienate not only the poor but even the Lord himself, who "is not attracted by imposing temples, worldly show, nor fine entertainments."[67]

Franklin recalled that thirty years earlier, the Disciples in Cincinnati had met in "some kind of a shop; but the brethren had bought it, papered the walls and seated it. They had procured some cheap carpet for the aisles, and the plain little platform occupied by the speaker. As near as now recollected, the house would seat about three hundred people." Those were the good old days, Franklin thought, when the "Disciples . . . [were] a plain and unpretending people . . . [and] wanted plain gospel preaching." When the Episcopalians of Cincinnati built a building for $100,000, Franklin recalled, "we talked of it as an example of extravagance beyond all endurance."[68] How things had changed!

Franklin was not the only one unhappy with the changes taking place. Like-minded believers in Pennsylvania expressed their deep appreciation to him for his stand. "In these last days in which perilous times have come," they wrote, "men being lovers of themselves, covetous, boasters, proud, *blasphemers,* etc., do we especially appreciate the worth and labors of that few, whom the Lord has kindly permitted to remain 'ancient men.'"[69]

Even Robert Richardson opposed the course of the Central Church, though for reasons significantly different from Franklin's. "I have always been highly gratified," he wrote to Franklin, "with your consistent opposition to expensive meeting-houses, artificial music in worship, church concerts, fairs, festivals and all similar worldly contrivances which minister to the flesh and not the spirit."[70]

The response to Franklin from the progressives was swift and pointed, and it revealed the great extent to which class differences now divided this fellowship. W. T. Moore's complaints were typical; he focused on Franklin's unpolished style and charged him with mean-spiritedness: "Your last reply is a curious combination of ugly epithets, irrelevant matter, evasion of the real issue, uncharitable insinuations, bad grammar, and worse rhetoric. . . . It is the dogmatic, vindictive spirit in your articles that makes your attack so unworthy."

Moore went on to charge that Franklin had not yet learned the first lesson of progress — namely, that "the *world moves.*" While the gospel remains the same, wrote Moore, methods must change. "This fact is so apparent," he insisted, that ". . . even *you* ought to understand it."[71] Younger men increasingly dismissed Franklin as an "old fogey," "a legalist," and "an alarmist."[72]

In the aftermath of the Central Church affair, no critique of Franklin was more devastating than that of Carl Crabb. It is not clear whether there actually was a real Carl Crabb or whether Franklin composed the critique himself in order to satirize the progressives. In any event, no other piece published in the *Review* during that period more clearly reflected the growing division in the movement between the primitivists and the progressivists or the way in which that division was connected to prejudices reflecting class, wealth, status, and education. Crabb entitled the piece "Franklinian Stupidity," and he explained he intended the title to describe not only Franklin but also "a large class of the brotherhood, of whom the editor of the REVIEW is almost a perfect specimen." He spoke of

> the common conclusion among the more liberal and progressive brethren that the above-named class have, for years past, been exhibiting a stubborn and perverse stupidity in reference to the progress of the age. Long since they became a real pest upon the body ecclesiastic, by standing directly in the way of those grand conceptions being realized which the more literary, refined and charitable brethren have presented from time to time for the adoption of the Christian brotherhood.

Then, in an illuminating passage, Crabb revealed his utter contempt for the principles Alexander Campbell had developed in the *Christian Baptist.* Franklin and his cohorts, he judged, "seem to be wholly incapable of appreciating anything that rises above the first plain, plodding ideas of Bro. Campbell and his co-laborers forty years ago." They refused to "admit the light of science" in religion, for instance, preferring to confine themselves to "stupidity's model" — that is, the New Testament. But "who can not see," Crabb asked, "the difference between this 'cramped, cribbed and confined' discipleship and that more liberal theology now advocated by our more advanced scribes . . . ?" He called, therefore, for a "renunciation of the old paths of stupidity, and the adoption of . . . practices more in accord with the spirit of the times" and with "the tastes and wants of the higher and more refined classes of society in our age."[73]

Franklin had stood throughout his career for a plain and simple gospel adapted to common people, and his experience with the Central Christian Church only intensified his stand. In the six years between that experience in 1872 and his death in 1878, he spoke often — and in scathing terms — of the wealthy and the powerful who, in his judgment, sought to control the church and conform it to the spirit of the Gilded Age. He turned against themselves his opponents' accusations that he and his kind were simply ignorant rustics. He recalled from his early life how "frowns and sneers" would often greet a preacher who was "poorly clad, not in style, . . . uncouth, and unaccomplished in manner." But within ten minutes, the audience would forget the man's personal appearance as it became evident that he had something meaningful to say. "On the other hand, we saw another preacher in most exquisite attire, not a hair out of place; and a beautiful cane. But when he rose before the audience to preach, it was clear that his mind had all been taken up with the *outward appearance,* a little worldly show, and the mind was vacant."[74] He contrasted well-known clerics and fashionable churches with plain preachers and simple congregations. "The idea of a modern great man," he wrote, no doubt thinking of men like Isaac Errett and W. T. Moore,

> is to get rid of the Jerusalem Church, as a model, and get Spurgeon or Beecher in view; mass the Lord's people, build a great temple; imitating Paganism more than Christianity. . . . [But] the plain and unassuming congregations of the Lord, with their humble overseers and deacons . . . does [*sic*] not suit the ambition of those who are, or would be, promoted to great popularity, distinction and power.[75]

Franklin's Jesus was a common man who refused to "identify himself with the priests, the doctors of the law, the scribes, or Pharisees, but stood aloof from them all, and rebuked them all alike." Jesus also "offended the rich," a procedure that "would have been considered very unwise by many of our great men now." But, Franklin noted, this "did not turn away the multitude. They still followed him."[76]

No wonder that Franklin, as early as 1870, wrote of the Campbell movement, "There are two elements in our midst, entirely alien to each other, at war, as much as flesh and spirit, in Paul's description." He noted that "these two elements have existed fifteen years or more, but their growth has been continuous, and is increasing of late." And then, incisively, he observed, "The different things in which they manifest themselves, at one time in this and then in that, are not the *cause,* but only the *occasion* for manifestation."[77]

Franklin's "Issues"

The "different things" to which Franklin referred were the "issues" over which the emerging Disciples of Christ and the emerging Churches of Christ now routinely quarreled — most notably, the legitimacy of instrumental music in the worship, missionary societies, and, in the minds of many, including Franklin, the legitimacy of church-related colleges and stationed "pastors." But these "issues" simply reflected the far deeper issue of whether the spirit of the age would now triumph over the plain and simple gospel bequeathed to plain and simple people by Alexander Campbell's *Christian Baptist*. Franklin's position on both instrumental music and societies must be understood in light of that larger concern.

Missionary Societies

It is important to recognize that in the 1840s, when the societies were first begun, Franklin entered into an agreement with Tolbert Fanning to oppose them on the grounds that "they were wrong." This alliance occurred, David Lipscomb informs us, when "Bro. Franklin spent a night with Bro. Fanning at his house at Franklin College." It is difficult to overemphasize the importance of this meeting, since it reveals early connections and alliances of key mid-nineteenth century leaders of the emerging Churches of Christ.

Finally, however, Franklin failed in his pledge to Fanning, Lipscomb wrote, chiefly because his "better judgment was overcome by his friends and associates."[78] One can only surmise that one of those "friends and associates" was the man Franklin so much admired, Alexander Campbell, who became president of the American Christian Missionary Society in 1849. So far as Franklin was concerned, the former editor of the *Christian Baptist* could do no wrong. Throughout the 1850s and well into the 1860s, therefore, Franklin proved one of the most outspoken advocates on behalf of the missionary societies.[79] He did not really change his tune until 1867.

Several factors precipitated the change in Franklin's position on this issue. First, and perhaps most important, was that fact that Campbell died that year. In addition, within months of Campbell's death, progressive Disciples launched the *Christian Standard* in a deliberate effort to undermine Franklin's *American Christian Review*, and the *Standard* men stood in the forefront of the missionary society movement. With Campbell gone, Franklin saw clearly what had not been so apparent to him before — namely, that the missionary societies would inevitably become centers of power that would undermine the democratic structure of the primitive church. In 1867, Franklin explicitly connected his new-found opposition to the societies with his opposition to the leaders of the *Christian Standard*, whom he charged with being far more interested in power and control than in service. "It is not *missionary work* to which we are opposed," he wrote, "but empty plans, schemes and organization, after sectarian models." Franklin praised "the missionary men" who "either go into the field and work, or contribute of their substance to support those who go," and he noted that he himself did both. Then he compared himself, by implication, to Isaac Errett, editor of the new-born *Christian Standard:* "We are not at home in a fine editorial chair, with a cigar or pipe in our mouth, opening the letters, and telling others how and where to work, but we are in the field."[80]

But Franklin most clearly revealed the democratic foundation for his opposition to missionary societies in a sermon entitled, appropriately enough, "The Simplicity of the Divine Economy." He insisted that "no matter how good the men, how honest, nor how pure their purposes — their work in any kind of aggregation, or confederation, of congregations, will result in taking away the rights and liberties of the people; oppressing and enslaving them, on the one hand, and building up a clerical aristocracy, who will tax the people and rule them with a rod of iron, on the other hand." And he made it clear that the primitive church was essentially democratic, sustaining the rights and privileges of the people. "To avoid this calamity [of clerical aristocracy] there is but one remedy, and that is to follow the model found in the first church, and admit no other form of church or rule. Stand to and maintain the congregational form of church government and management."[81]

The issue for Franklin was precisely what it had been for Campbell in the *Christian Baptist* period and for Fanning as early as the 1840s: aristocratic power must not undermine the liberty and religion of the people.

Instrumental Music

Franklin's opposition to instrumental music was rooted in similar concerns. In 1860, he wrote that he had been "pressed from several quarters to give our opinion of instrumental music in churches." His response once again reflected his bias against a social elite. Instruments, he wrote, might be appropriate "if a church only intends being a *fashionable society* [or] a mere place of amusement and secular entertainment." Further, "if a church has in it a large number of dishonest and corrupt men . . . , we have no doubt that instrumental music would be more soothing, comforting and pleasing to them than any of your old fashioned sermons on righteousness, temperance, and judgment to come." And again, "these *refined* gentlemen have *refined ears,* enjoy fine music manufactured for French theatres, interspersed with *short* prayers and *very short* sermons."[82]

That article marked the beginning of the instrumental music controversy in the movement. The following month, L. L. Pinkerton of Midway, Kentucky, complained that Franklin's criticism had been aimed at him. After all, he wrote, he was the only preacher in Kentucky who had advocated instrumental music in certain churches, and the church in Midway was "the only church that has yet made a decided effort to introduce it." It did so, Pinkerton explained, because the "singing had degenerated into a discordant bawling and screeching" that might drive away not only worshipers but even the rats.

Significantly, however, the quarrel between Franklin and Pinkerton dealt less with the merits of instrumental music than it did with the merits of middle-class propriety and style. Franklin opposed instrumental music precisely because it seemed to him to reflect the values of the rising middle class. Pinkerton was incensed by Franklin's article because it seemed to him to reflect the crudity and ignorance of lower-class rustics. "If your article on church music reflects the notions of the Reformation as to what constitutes Christian courtesy, manly literature, logic, rhetoric, religion; nay, if any considerable portion of the Reformation can even tolerate such coarse fulminations, then the sooner it is extinct the better," wrote Pinkerton. "I am ready and willing to discuss the subject of instrumental music in churches with any man who can discriminate between railing in bad grammar and Christian argumentation."[83]

Soon, however, many began to couch their resistance to instrumental music in terms of the biblical pattern. This is hardly surprising, given the powerful strains of Baconianism and biblical primitivism that characterized this movement. For example, Moses Lard appealed in 1864 to the notion that the New Testament was the only standard for "the smallest point of doctrine" and "the most trivial feature in practice."[84] In that light, he urged, there could be no defense for introducing an instrument into the worship of God. By 1870, if not before, Franklin was couching his opposition to the use of instruments in the same terms: "There is not a man anywhere who claims any [biblical] authority for the new element. . . . The worship in all its parts . . . is a matter of *revelation — divinely prescribed*. Nothing is acceptable worship, only that which the Lord ordained."[85] Franklin — and many on the conservative side of the movement — envisioned the primitive church as preeminently a church of the people, not a church of the wealthy and the privileged, and their appeals to Scripture on this issue were inevitably bound with class and social bias, at least during the nineteenth century.

The instrumental music controversy came only slowly to the South for the simple reason that southerners and southern churches were not as wealthy as their counterparts in the postbellum North and hence less likely to be able to purchase the questionable instruments. Nonetheless, the controversy occasioned comment among southerners as early as 1869, when David Lipscomb complained of efforts to stigmatize as "fools," "Pharisees," and "theological constables" those who resisted instrumental music. But as late as 1890, one could still count on one hand the number of congregations in Tennessee that had adopted instrumental music.[86]

While the movement had been moving toward division for many years for the variety of reasons we have surveyed thus far, the instrumental music controversy did more than any other factor to bring the division to a head. Fractures opened up in congregation after congregation, slowly at first during the 1870s and then at an accelerating rate during the 1880s and 1890s. The division in Springfield, Missouri, is a case in point. On February 14, 1886, the church voted 121 to 68 to bring an organ into the worship. That vote triggered increasingly acrimonious relations between the pro-organ majority and the anti-organ dissenters, among whom were the trustees of the congregation. The *Register* of the congregation records that on January 29, 1887, when the trustees sought to force their side of the issue, the pro-organ majority passed a resolution that read, in part, that if the trustees "cannot comply with the wishes of the congregation, when properly expressed, they are requested to resign, or the church will proceed to declare the offices vacant and elect others in their places."[87]

Following that entry, the church's *Register* fell silent regarding this issue, but the *St. Louis Globe Democrat* told the rest of the story in an article published on January 31, which noted the "warm and at times acrimonious warfare" that had been waged in that congregation for several weeks. "Yesterday," the story related,

> after the pastor . . . had read the opening hymn, the organist began playing and many joined in the singing, but at the same time the opponents of the organ started up another tune, and a pandemonium ensued. . . . After the sacrament, an anti-organ brother arose to smoothe matters over with a talk, but was interrupted with a lively hymn volunteered by the organ crowd. At the close of the services, Mr. Bills, having consulted a lawyer, was advised to play the organ at all hazards, and he did so, and the meeting broke up in confusion.[88]

By the spring of 1887, there were two congregations in Springfield rather than one.

Elsewhere, especially in Tennessee, the missionary society controversy contributed to the rupture. But regardless of the particular cause in particular localities, the story of division played itself out in congregation after congregation throughout the country. Finally, it became apparent to S. N. D. North, director of the 1906 Federal Census, that there were now two denominations rather than one, and he listed them separately that year as Disciples of Christ and Churches of Christ.[89] The controversy over instrumental music that Franklin sparked in 1860 ended up contributing in significant ways to the formal division of the movement.

Church-Related Colleges and "Stationed Pastors"

In addition to missionary societies and instrumental music, the emergence of a new class of stationed, salaried preachers within the movement caused Franklin (and, as we have already seen, Tolbert Fanning) great consternation. Many congregations in the South relied for their preaching on the talents of local members, supplemented by itinerant ministers, until after World War II. But in the North — especially in urban centers — more and more congregations were employing young and educated men as full-time preachers by the middle years of the nineteenth century.

As early as 1856, Franklin complained that "aged men . . . are now sneered at as 'common,' 'old fashioned,' 'fogies,' that may do to speak 'in the country,' but not in towns and cities!" He insisted that it was a great mistake to "confine our labors to cities, towns, and villages." Instead, "we must go out into the country among the people, and be one of them."[90]

What disturbed Franklin even more, however, was the growing insistence on educated preachers. Franklin attended the Ohio State Missionary Society meeting in 1863 and returned deeply troubled. Some at the meeting had suggested that preachers should have some understanding of geology and astronomy and "be versed in history, chronology and other extended fields of knowledge, or attain to some certain degree in the languages, or even English literature, before they can be accredited preachers of the gospel of Christ." Franklin was outraged. "We have no patience with this mere butterfly twaddle, toploftical, aircastle, highfalutin and empty thing," he sneered. Some of the words he heard used at the society meeting could be found, he said, in neither the dictionary nor the Bible. But that was all right, he sarcastically observed.

> We are a long ways ahead of these old books, read and admired by old fogies. These were good books in their time, and plain, old-fashioned men did their work in their day; but we are philosophers, geologists, astronomers, historians and reasoners, not going by the *Word*, but *general principles;* not confined to the *letter of Scripture*, but the *spirit*.[91]

Not surprisingly, Franklin objected to the notion that colleges could produce preachers. It was as ridiculous to imagine that one could train preachers in a theological school, he argued, as it was to suppose that one could teach "plowing, planting, sowing, reaping, threshing, &c., . . . in an agricultural school." In both cases, he insisted, the only effective training was hands-on training. Teachers had to "go out into the field and work with the young men, and show them . . . how the work is done."[92]

Still and all, for many years Franklin supported the ideal of a Christian college where the Bible was the centerpiece of the curriculum. In fact, in 1860, he praised Campbell's Bethany College "as an institution of learning [with] no superior in this country." But following the war and Campbell's death, Franklin thought he saw Bethany take a decided turn away from Campbell's teachings. He admitted that he had not foreseen, in those earlier years, that "infidels could be made professors" and that individuals "not sound in the faith . . . could get control of colleges" and turn them away from the dictates of the Bible.[93] John F. Rowe, Franklin's associate editor, complained that many of the graduates of Bethany and other colleges in the movement could "see no difference between a Methodist and a Christian."[94]

Franklin lamented that there had been "but one Alexander Campbell for the president of a college." Rowe agreed. It had taken Campbell's "master mind" to conceive "the *beau ideal* of a Christian college."[95] But lesser men now had sabotaged that ideal. In his later years, Franklin turned decidedly against Christian colleges altogether. His acrimonious stand bore substantial fruit in the early twentieth century, when Daniel Sommer, a Franklin protégé, waged the same battle against other schools founded by members of Churches of Christ — a story we shall explore in Chapter 10.

By 1871, Franklin worried that the movement Campbell had founded had lost its "distinctive plea." If that were the case, Campbell's followers owed the surrounding sects and denominations an apology. After all, they had given the sects "an immense amount of trouble and vexation of spirit; and if we have had no reason for it, . . . we should make acknowledgments." For his part, however, Franklin felt "no regret, no contrition nor remorse in view of what we have done, unless it be that we have not done more."[96]

Through it all, Franklin remained convinced that he was Campbell's man, loyal to the bedrock principles of the *Christian Baptist* from which others, sadly, had now departed. Just months before his death in 1878, Franklin portrayed Campbell as a plain, backwoods rustic who never enjoyed "the *prestige* of the great city," never climbed "on the *shoulders of rich men*," and never sought "notoriety or profit." Instead, "he went back into the hills of Brooke County, Virginia . . . , then a place of no note, and comparative obscurity," where he launched his *Christian Baptist*. Campbell never intended this publication to be "a fine pamphlet, ornamented and embellished in the finest style"; instead, he kept it a plain and simple journal, meant only to "be read and understood." In its unassuming pages, Campbell "assailed the popular clergy" and "made issue on the principal men and movements of the country, claiming to be religious." This example taught Franklin a lesson: these days, when he saw "a little, unpretending, unassuming publication, we are slow about deciding unfavorably of it. . . . It might turn out to be another *Christian Baptist*."[97] Indeed, Franklin saw his own *American Christian Review* as "another *Christian Baptist*."

How ironic, then, that Robert Richardson would confide to Philip S. Fall in 1859 that Franklin had "his own way of doing business & it is rather *a rough way*, but I hope he means well. Bro. Campbell, however, & many good brethren stand *in doubt of him*." Little wonder! By 1859, Campbell had come a very long distance from the swashbuckling ways of the editor of the *Christian Baptist* whom Franklin so much admired. Franklin never saw the change.

Conclusion

In that same letter to Fall, Richardson wrote that while Franklin stood low in the estimate of Campbell, "he has *great popularity* with a *certain class of minds* of which we have a great many in the Reformation."[98] And here lies the significance of both Franklin and Tolbert Fanning: these two men served as spiritual leaders during the middle years of the nineteenth century to a sizable body of Christians who continued to identify with the principles of the *Christian Baptist*.

By and large these Christians shared a strong commitment to the freedom of "the people" from the controlling power of the elites, a vision of Christian primitivism laced with a strong democratic bias, a philosophical worldview informed by Locke and Scottish Common Sense Realism, a strong dose of historical naivete, and a radical sectarian perspective that stood at odds with the later vision of Campbell and the Bethany community. In a word, they shared a culture increasingly alienated from the mature Campbell tradition — a culture that soon would be known exclusively as the Churches of Christ. In the middle years of the nineteenth century, no one shaped that culture more effectively than two extraordinarily powerful editors: Tolbert Fanning and Benjamin Franklin.

But Franklin's significance transcends even this, for Franklin helped father within Churches of Christ a radically primitivist and sectarian subtradition rooted in economic deprivation and estranged from the world of culture and education. Even when the mainstream of Churches of Christ in the twentieth century abandoned many of the trappings of sectarian religion and moved toward denominational status, this radically sectarian subtradition continued to keep alive the principles of Alexander Campbell's *Christian Baptist,* as we shall see in Chapters 8 and 10.

Finally, the career of Benjamin Franklin sheds considerable light on the effects of the Civil War on the growing division in the movement. The light is focused principally on the North rather than the South, and it reveals that many of the northern, postwar followers of Campbell moved with the spirit of the age and largely abandoned the principles of the *Christian Baptist*. It also reveals that this transition was in process as early as the mid-1850s, when younger, more educated city preachers relegated "old-fashioned fogies" like Franklin to the backwoods.

To explore the impact of the war on the movement in the South, we must first explore the dynamics that shaped Churches of Christ in that region. It is to that task that we turn in Chapter 5.

CHAPTER 5

The Apocalyptic Outlook
of Barton W. Stone

Readers seeking to understand the origins of Churches of Christ — and especially the sectarian perspective that dominated this tradition in the nineteenth century — can ill afford to focus exclusively on Alexander Campbell, since the early Campbell — and those who radicalized his *Christian Baptist* perspective — constitute only half the story. The other half of the story belongs to Barton W. Stone.[1]

Stone was sectarian, to be sure, but he brought to Churches of Christ a sectarian tradition that was radically different in many respects from the sectarian tradition rooted in Alexander Campbell. If those who radicalized Campbell understood his focus almost entirely in terms of the true church vis-à-vis the denominations, Stone and his successors focused their attention on the true church vis-à-vis the values of the world.

This means that whereas the Campbell reform was primarily rational and cognitive, focusing on the forms and structures of primitive Christianity, Stone's reform was primarily ethical and spiritual, focusing on inner piety and outward holiness. To understand this dimension of Stone, one must begin by recognizing the importance to his thinking of an *apocalyptic worldview*.

As I indicated in the introductory chapter, the term *apocalyptic* as I am using it in this book does not refer to millennial theories or speculation about the time of the second coming of Jesus; rather, it signifies an outlook that led Stone and many of his followers to act as though the final rule of the kingdom of God were present in the here and now. That is to say, the term as we are using it has no immediate *premillennial* associations. While apocalyptic thinking has often given rise to premillennial perspectives, the two are not necessarily connected. Stone's worldview was *apocalyptic* in the sense that it was premised on obedience to the direct rule of God. He and many of his coworkers lived their lives in the shadow

Throughout his life, Barton W. Stone (1782-1844) maintained his allegiance to the kingdom of God, which he believed would someday triumph over all the earth. In that context, he bequeathed to Churches of Christ an ethical and spiritual reform that focused on inner piety and outward holiness. (Photo courtesy Disciples of Christ Historical Society)

of the second coming[2] and thought of themselves as pilgrims who affirmed their allegiance to the kingdom of God rather than to the popular values of the world.

The idea of the kingdom of God played a critical role in the thought of Stone and those who stood in his lineage. Though Stone seldom used the exact phrase "kingdom of God," he routinely used such phrases as "God's rule," "God's reign," and "God's government," and he sought to live his life as though God's rule were complete in the present world.

He also downplayed material concerns and oriented his life toward supernatural and ethical interests. He called on his followers to open their lives to the Holy Spirit and, in the power of the Spirit, to abandon self for the sake of others, to render aid to those in need, and to stand with those who suffered. This was the sort of thing he had in mind when he called his followers to cultivate "godliness, piety, and brotherly love."

Alexander Campbell also oriented his work around the idea of the kingdom of God, but it meant something very different for him than it did for Stone. Campbell viewed the kingdom of God as a constitutional monarchy in the here and now and, for all practical purposes, equated the kingdom with the church.[3] Campbell held that the church is composed of all who "associate under the constitution which he [God] himself has granted and authorized in the New Testament, and are walking in his ordinances and commandments — and of none else."[4] Stone, on the other hand, held that the kingdom of God transcends the church on this earth. He envisioned the kingdom as God's final, triumphant rule, which will be made complete only in the last age. He granted that the church may well provide glimpses into the glories of the kingdom, but he by no means considered the two to be identical. Stone's apocalyptic and ethical understanding of God's kingdom was thus a far cry from Campbell's legal understanding of the same reality.

When one understands the apocalyptic and ethical dimensions in the thought of Stone and his followers, one can then place in perspective Stone's "moral influence" understanding of the atonement. It is well known that Stone and Campbell quarreled for many years over how the atonement should be understood. Campbell argued that Christ's death substituted for the penalty all human beings should pay apart from the grace of God. Stone argued that the death of Christ displayed first and foremost the love of God for sinners and that the atonement was intended to move human beings to repentance and holy living.[5] This notion left Stone open to charges of "works righteousness," a theme his critics played on again and again over the years. But these critics were wrong. Stone's view of the atonement actually reflected his belief in the power of the grace of God to transform a human life.

This is not to suggest that Campbell did not share these ethical emphases, for he did. But holy living was not Campbell's principal focus; nor did Campbell root his ethical concerns in an apocalyptic worldview.

Moreover, this is not to suggest that Stone was some sort of mystic who failed to value a rational approach to Scripture. In the first article of the first issue of his journal, the *Christian Messenger*, Stone wrote,

> We must believe that the Bible was addressed to rational creatures, and de-
> signed by God to be understood for their profit. When we open the Bible
> under the impression that it is a book of mysteries, understood only by a few
> learned ministers, we are at once discouraged from reading and investigating
> its contents. But believing it was written for our learning and profit, and
> therefore addressed to our understanding, we are encouraged to read and
> diligently search its sacred pages.[6]

The difference between Stone and Campbell lay in what the two men found in Scripture. Campbell primarily found models for the worship and organization of the church, whereas Stone primarily found models for holy living. Stone agreed with Campbell that Christians should separate themselves from fallen denominational structures, but he believed that denominational structures had fallen because they represented the values of this world rather than the values of the kingdom of God. In time this fundamental difference between the world-views of Barton Stone and Alexander Campbell helped produce basic theological differences between Churches of Christ and Disciples of Christ and in this way contributed to the division that finally fractured the movement later in the nineteenth century.

Throughout the nineteenth century, however, some in Churches of Christ reconciled and amalgamated the Stoneite and Campbellite points of view. Such amalgamation inevitably weakened the ethical and countercultural stance of the Stoneite tradition by slowly redefining "separation from the world" as "separation from the denominations." When that happened, the sectarian vision of Alexander Campbell finally triumphed over the sectarian vision of Barton W. Stone.

Barton W. Stone: Child of the Revivals

The first thing to be said if one is inquiring into Stone's origins is that he was not so much a product of Enlightenment rationalism as he was a product of the First and Second Great Awakenings.

Stone was born in 1772, near Port Tobacco, Maryland, some thirty years after the close of the Great Awakening. Led by George Whitefield, Jonathan Edwards, and other preachers, the Great Awakening swept the thirteen colonies into a religious ecstasy in the 1730s and early 1740s.

Stone came under the influence of that revival half a century later when, in 1790, he entered David Caldwell's "log college" in North Carolina. Caldwell had studied at Princeton when the influence of the Great Awakening there still was strong; he graduated in 1761. Little wonder, then, that he promoted revivals in his own college in the South. James McGready was conducting a revival there in 1790 when Stone enrolled as a student. The next year, Stone attended a revival led by one of Caldwell's students, William Hodge, whose fervent preaching on the love of God converted Stone to the Christian faith.[7] In 1796, when Stone received his license to preach from the Orange Presbytery of North Carolina, Henry Patillo addressed the candidates for license. Significantly, Patillo had been a student of Samuel Davies, a New Light Presbyterian who did more than anyone else to perpetuate the influence of the Great Awakening in the South. By 1801, Stone himself became a catalyst and a key player in the great Cane Ridge revival of Kentucky — an early phase of the great spiritual outpouring that historians usually call the Second Great Awakening, which convulsed the United States in religious fervor for the next quarter century.

Stone's revival background led him to embrace many of the themes important to Alexander Campbell, but he came to those themes by a very different route. One such theme was an emphasis on nondenominational Christianity, common to both the Great Awakenings. The great southern revivalist Samuel Davies had warned "against this wretched, mischievous spirit of party. . . . A Christian! a Christian! Let that be your highest distinction; let that be the name which you labor to deserve."[8] And George Whitefield, the acknowledged soul of the Great Awakening throughout the colonies, asked in one of his revivals in

Philadelphia, "Father Abraham, whom have you in heaven? Any Episcopalians? No! Any Presbyterians? No! Any Independents or Methodists? No, no, no! Whom have you there? We don't know those names here. All who are here are Christians. . . . Oh, is this the case? Then God help us to forget party names and to become Christians in deed and truth."[9]

This leveling of denominational distinctives belonged to the very essence of the revivals. Preaching in a revival context generally ignored what divided Christians and focused instead on beliefs held by all Christians — namely, that all people are sinners to whom God offers forgiveness and that the essence of Christianity is holy living, inspired by the Holy Spirit. In this way, revivalism shared some common ground with the Enlightenment. Whereas the Enlightenment sought to reduce *religion* to a set of essentials upon which all reasonable persons could agree, revivalism sought to reduce *Christianity* to a set of essentials upon which all Christians could agree. Enlightenment principles predisposed Alexander Campbell to search for a basis for the unity of all Christians, and Stone's revival experiences propelled him in the same direction — though with some important qualifications, as we shall see.

The Cane Ridge Revival

Stone experienced in the Cane Ridge Revival of 1801 what Davies and Whitefield had described in the era of the Great Awakening — the union of all Christians apart from confessional distinctives.[10] He also experienced what he judged to be the work of the Holy Spirit moving men and women alike to engage in unusual and — no doubt to some — bizarre exercises such as jerking, barking, running, and falling. In any event, Stone believed that the union of Christians at Cane Ridge grew directly out of the work of the Holy Spirit, which moved scoffers to conversion and Christians to a holy life.

Precisely at this point, Stone and five of his Presbyterian colleagues had occasion to affirm what Davies and Whitefield had affirmed some fifty years before: a vision of nondenominational Christianity. The Synod of Kentucky ruled that one of Stone's colleagues, Richard McNemar, had violated the standards of the Westminster Confession of Faith through his participation in the revivals. Because of this charge, Stone, McNemar, and four other Presbyterian ministers withdrew from the Synod's jurisdiction and formed themselves into a dissenting body, the Springfield Presbytery. That was in 1803.

By 1804, these six dissenters determined that their own Springfield Presbytery was too particularistic and therefore blocked the way to genuine Christian union. They accordingly dissolved that body on June 28, 1804, by publishing a declaration of their intention to merge into the church universal. The declaration, entitled *The Last Will and Testament of the Springfield Presbytery*, reads, in part,

We *will*, that this body die, be dissolved, and sink into union with the body of Christ at large; . . .

We *will*, that our weak brethren, who may have been wishing to make the Presbytery of Springfield their king, and wot not what is now become of it, betake themselves to the Rock of Ages, and follow Jesus for the future.

We *will*, that the Synod of Kentucky examine every member, who may be *suspected* of having departed from the Confession of Faith, and suspend every such suspected heretic immediately; in order that the oppressed may go free, and taste the sweets of gospel liberty.[11]

Here, unmistakably, was Stone's version of nondenominational Christianity, a vision inspired by the revival spirit of the First and Second Great Awakenings.

Separate Baptists

Stone's participation in the revivals did not end here. The Great Awakening of the 1730s and 1740s had moved many of the old Puritan stock in New England and elsewhere to return to the teachings of the Puritan fathers and especially to the passion of those fathers for primitive Christianity. Many who embraced this perspective became known as Separatists, and many of these, in turn, adopted believers' baptism and became Separate Baptists. In 1755, a group of Separate Baptists under the leadership of Shubal Stearns and Daniel Marshall migrated from New England to Sandy Creek, North Carolina. There they established a single congregation that, within a few short years, produced forty-two other congregations embracing literally thousands of new converts.

In the course of the westward movement, thousands of these Separate Baptists flooded into the new lands of Kentucky and the Cumberland region of Tennessee, and there they encountered the preaching of Barton W. Stone. Stone and his band of preachers urged on them his vision of nondenominational Christianity, and hundreds and thousands of Separate Baptists soon formed the core of Stone's movement. By 1811, Joseph Thomas, traveling to Kentucky for the express purpose of assessing the strength of that movement, reported that it contained over 13,000 people with well over one hundred preachers.[12] Many of these came from the ranks of the Separate Baptists.

While many Separate Baptists in Kentucky would later join the ranks of the Campbell movement, the Stone movement reaped by far the larger harvest. The point, therefore, is simply this: the revival mentality of the two Great Awakenings shaped the perspective not only of Barton W. Stone but also of hundreds and thousands who came to his movement from another revivalist heritage, that of the Separate Baptists. That is to say, the Stone movement was shaped both inside and out not by Enlightenment rationalism but by the spirit of the two Great Awakenings.

Rice Haggard

Nor did Stone's connection with the revivals end here. Shortly after the six dissidents became convinced that the Springfield Presbytery had been a mistake, a Virginian named Rice Haggard joined their deliberations. Haggard had been influenced by the New Light revivalist Samuel Davies and was convinced by reading Davies's sermons of the importance of the name *Christian* as opposed to any and all denominational labels. When James O'Kelley bolted from Francis Asbury's Methodists in 1792, it was Haggard who advised that band of Methodist dissidents that, according to the New Testament, "the disciples were called Christians, and I move that henceforth and forever the followers of Christ be known as Christians simply."[13] Haggard offered that same advice to Stone and his colleagues in 1804 in Bethel, Kentucky — advice that became pivotal in Stone's thinking for the rest of his life. In fact, Stone and his colleagues published a pamphlet by Haggard on this very point: *An Address to the Different Religious Societies, on the Sacred Import of the Christian Name.*[14]

Stone and Nondenominational Christianity

It is crucial to observe that Stone found in the nondenominational perspective of the revivals other theological emphases that would bind him closely to the outlook of Alexander Campbell. Implicit in Stone's version of nondenominational Christianity were three correlative themes: the restoration of primitive Christianity, the unity of all Christians, and the freedom of all Christians to read the Bible, understand it, and interpret it for themselves.

Primitive Christianity

With respect to the first of these themes — restoration of primitive Christianity — Stone and his colleagues imagined that they could escape denominational status if they took their stand solely and exclusively on the Bible and the first Christian age. By embracing primitive Christianity, they thought, they could escape the molding power of history, culture, and denominational tradition and proceed to affirm nothing more and nothing less than nondenominational Christianity. One early Stoneite wrote, "We are not personally acquainted with the writings of John Calvan [*sic*], nor are we certain how nearly we agree with his views of divine truth; neither do we care."[15] Another affirmed that "the primitive christian never heard of the five points of Dort, nor of Calvinism."[16] For these Christians who followed the leadership of Barton W. Stone, denominational and theological traditions were simply irrelevant to the task at hand.

Christian Unity

Stone and his colleagues believed that primitive Christianity was the only legitimate basis for Christian union on the grounds that primitive Christianity stood prior to the development of all denominational traditions. On this basis, Stone and his people continually urged Christians of all stripes to drop denominational distinctives and unite on the platform of New Testament Christianity.

The Stoneites formally united with the followers of Alexander Campbell in Lexington, Kentucky, in 1832, chiefly because the two movements shared a deep commitment to Christian union based on a restoration of primitive Christianity. Yet, in spite of the obvious similarities between the two traditions, there also were deep and far-reaching differences. One of these differences had to do with the issue of Christian freedom.

Christian Freedom

To be sure, Campbell advocated the freedom of each individual Christian to understand Scripture for him/herself. But Campbell's rational bent led him to systematize the teachings of Scripture in a way that moved inevitably toward uniformity and orthodoxy, as we have seen. The Stoneites, on the other hand, were so concerned to preserve Christian freedom that for many years they refused to develop self-consciously any definite structure, liturgy, or theological tradition whatsoever. In 1823, however, Alexander Campbell began instructing the Stoneites regarding a clear and precise vision of primitive Christianity.

One could make the case with considerable justification, therefore, that the theme of freedom constituted the very heart of the Stoneites' message, protecting their conception of nondenominational Christianity from any and all orthodox constraints. In fact, this commitment was so pronounced that many Stoneites envisioned their movement as completing the unfinished tasks of the American Revolution. One of Stone's followers wrote in 1827 that "the present conflict between the Bible and party creeds and confessions . . . is perfectly analogous to the revolutionary war between Britain and America; liberty was contended for on the one side, and dominion and power on the other."[17] Another follower employed the Jeffersonian phrase "certain inalienable rights," but focused those rights on "free investigation, [and] sober and diligent inquiry after [religious] truth."[18]

The Stoneites' insistence on radical Christian freedom was especially apparent in the positions they took regarding the Holy Spirit and baptism. The connection they made between freedom and the Holy Spirit was rooted in their conviction that the Holy Spirit, as the Spirit of the sovereign God, could and would overturn every orthodoxy devised by human imagination. For this reason, the Stoneites sought to remain open to the power of the Holy Spirit working in their midst. As early as the Cane Ridge revival, Stone himself spoke warmly of the various ecstatic exercises — jerking, running, barking, dancing, and so on — that characterized that event.[19] And when Joseph Thomas traveled among the Stoneites in Kentucky, Tennessee, and Ohio in 1810 and 1811, he reported that Spirit-led ecstatic exercises continued to characterize the worship of these people. These "Christians," Thomas wrote, "have an exercise . . . amongst them called the JIRKS. It sometimes throws them into the fire, into the mud, upon the floor, upon the benches, against the wall of the house, &c."[20]

Long after these exercises had disappeared, Stone continued to insist that Christians must be open to the power of the Holy Spirit. During the 1830s and 1840s, he grew particularly distressed by the increasingly orthodox position on the Campbell side of the movement that the gifts of the Holy Spirit had altogether ceased with the apostles — a notion that, in time, would become standard among Churches of Christ.

In the context of his disputes with Baptists over the nature of conversion, Campbell had long argued that the Spirit of God converted sinners only through the written word. He even asserted that "if the Spirit of God has spoken all its arguments" in Scripture, then "all the power of the Holy Spirit which can operate on the human mind [in conversion] is spent."[21]

Others in the emerging Churches of Christ quickly embraced this position. B. F. Hall, for example, wrote in Arthur Crihfield's *Heretic Detector* in 1837, "I believe that the Holy Spirit exerts no influence on the heart of sinners over and above the word: that his influences are in the facts he has revealed in the gospel, the evidences by which he has confirmed these facts, and in the motives to obedience presented in the Scriptures of Truth."[22] Hall's testimony is particularly important, because he began his religious career in the Stone tradition, and the change in his thinking gives some indication of the influence of Campbell's thinking among the Stoneites. Hall later recalled that in the Stone movement "we differed very little . . . from the sects in our views of spiritual influence, getting religion, the evidence of remission, and kindred subjects. Hence we practiced the mourners' bench or anxious-seat system throughout." He further observed,

> The religion of those days consisted principally of *feeling*; and those who shouted the loudest and made the greatest ado, were looked upon as the best christians. Hence our preaching, our prayers, and songs we adapted to excite the emotions. We would clap and rub our hands, stamp with our feet, slam down and tear up the Bible, speak as loud as possible and scream at the top of our voice, to get up an excitement. I often blistered my hands by clapping and rubbing them together; and my feet were made sore by repeated stamping.[23]

Though Alexander Campbell rejected these emotional displays, he never denied the indwelling of the Holy Spirit *following* conversion. In fact, as early as 1827, he flatly declared that if anyone inferred from anything he had written "that I contended for a religion in which the Holy Spirit has nothing to do, in which there is no need of prayer for the Holy Spirit; in which there is no communion of the Holy Spirit, in which there is no peace and joy in the Holy Spirit — he does me the greatest injustice." He went on to say that "a religion of which the Holy Spirit is not the author, the subject-matter and the perfecter is sheer Deism."[24]

By the late 1830s, however, many on the Campbell side of the movement — and especially those whose allegiance was to the *Christian Baptist* — increasingly found little or no place for the Holy Spirit, even following conversion. Stone had good reason in 1836 to lament that it was commonly believed within the movement that the gift of the Holy Spirit was confined to the days of the apostles.[25] A case in point was Arthur Crihfield, who scorned the doctrine of the Holy Spirit held by Stone and his followers. "These plants were merely exotics," Crihfield wrote, "and experiments have proved that they cannot be acclimated to the temperate zone of Christianity."[26]

Stone flatly disagreed with Crihfield's assessment. He quarreled with Campbell over the latter's assertion that missionaries "capable of confirming their testimony by working miracles" had ceased with the death of the apostles. "By what authority," Stone demanded to know, "have we concluded that no more such men with miraculous powers may be expected in the present dispensation or age?" He even argued that Christians might well have worked miracles through the power of the Spirit in his own day and age were it not for disbelief.[27]

The Stoneites' position on baptism also illustrates their commitment to radical Christian freedom. On the Campbell side of the movement, immersion for the forgiveness of sins rapidly became a symbol of one's status as a genuine Christian, but the Stoneites generally refused to make this matter a test of orthodoxy. When Joseph Thomas visited the Stoneites in Kentucky in 1810-1811, he found that "those that have, and those that have not been 'buried with Christ in baptism,' do not divide and contend about the subject; but they continue upon the plan which they set out upon — to let nothing divide them but Sin, and all search the scriptures for themselves, and act according to their understanding in the fear of God."[28]

Nonetheless, by the close of the 1820s, many Stoneites had embraced Campbell's notion that baptism was for the remission of sins. The key player in that transition was B. F. Hall. As we have seen, Hall's earliest religious commitments occurred in the context of the Stone tradition. Yet he remained deeply troubled by the long period of mourning that characterized most conversions, even among the followers of Stone. Hall found himself liberated, however, in 1826, when he discovered the doctrine of baptism for the remission of sins in a printed text of Campbell's debate with W. L. McCalla. There, in a crude Kentucky cabin, Hall "sprang to my feet in an ecstacy, and cried out, 'Eureka!

Eureka! I have found it! I have found it!' And I had found it. . . . I had found
the long lost link in the chain of gospel obedience. . . . I now saw the evidence
of remission, which I had never seen before."[29] Hall made this discovery en
route from Alabama to his home in Kentucky, and he later recalled, "Every
brother I met on my way from Line Creek home I told of the grand discovery."[30]
For all practical purposes, Hall became in that electric moment of discovery a
lifelong devoted follower of Alexander Campbell.

Shortly after this discovery, Hall confronted Stone himself about this
doctrine, but Stone informed him that preaching immersion for the forgiveness
of sins "was like throwing ice water on the people; that it froze all their warmth
out, and came well nigh driving vital religion out of the country." For this reason,
Stone counseled Hall "not to broach that idea in Georgetown [Kentucky]."[31]

In spite of Stone's objections, Hall won converts to this idea in the Georgetown vicinity, especially through private discourse. Then, in Alabama in 1826,
Hall preached this theme boldly. While one of his sermons converted Tolbert
Fanning, as we saw in Chapter 4, Hall also convinced James E. Matthews, who,
in turn, wrote a series of articles on that topic for Stone's *Christian Messenger*
in 1829.[32] Though Stone had embraced immersion as "a divinely instituted
means of salvation" as early as January of 1827,[33] Matthews's articles apparently
did more than anything else to convince many Stoneites that baptism was in
fact for the remission of sins.[34]

R. L. Roberts has pointed out that B. F. Hall provided a key link between
the Stone and Campbell movements on this issue. Learning immersion for the
forgiveness of sins from Campbell, Hall convinced Stone and many of his people
of the doctrine's validity. The Stone people in turn put the teaching into practice
and then convinced Campbell — for whom this idea was still only a theory —
of its practical importance. Within the Campbell movement, Walter Scott,
Jeremiah Vardeman, John Smith, Adamson Bentley, and Sidney Rigdon immersed hundreds between November 1827 and June 1828, and by the time the
Campbell and Stone movements formally united in 1832, immersion for the
forgiveness of sins appears to have become standard practice in both traditions.[35]

But while Stone and his followers increasingly recognized the importance
of baptism for the remission of sins, they typically refused to make immersion
a test of Christian fellowship. Stone criticized Campbell in 1830 for his restrictive
teachings in this regard:

> Should they make their own peculiar view of immersion a term of fellowship,
> it will be impossible for them to repel, successfully, the imputation of being
> sectarians, and of having an authoritative creed (though not written) of one
> article at least, which is formed of their own opinion of truth; and this short
> creed would exclude more christians from union than any creed with which
> I am acquainted.[36]

Stone agreed that immersion was essential for one's standing as a Christian "in the full sense of that term," but he resolutely refused to admit that those who were not immersed were therefore not Christians at all. He maintained that pious believing Christians could possess the gift of the Holy Spirit, receive remission of sins, and hold a full hope of salvation without having been immersed. Over and again he argued, "To denounce all not immersed as lost, and to cut them off from salvation however holy and pious they may be, appears to dethrone charity and forbearance from our breast." Were it otherwise, he declared, "countless millions of the fairest characters in the profession of Christianity for many centuries back, have been swept from joyful hope to gloomy despair."[37]

Even as an old man, Stone recalled how "some irresponsible zealots among the Reformers, so called [followers of Campbell] . . . rejected from Christianity all who were not baptized for the remission of sins, and who did not observe the weekly communion." This caused many, Stone complained, to represent "our religion as a spiritless, prayerless religion, and dangerous to the souls of men."[38] Nevertheless, in those later years Stone fully embraced the notion that "we must believe, repent, and be baptized before we get into Christ, and therefore before we become new creatures, before we are saved, before we are justified, or sanctified, or redeemed — before we receive the Spirit, or bear the fruits of the Spirit, as love, joy, peace, &c. and before we become members of one body of Christ, and one in him."[39] This argument came as a shock to many who had known him over the years. John Rogers was incredulous and wrote to Stone,

> I have just read, with astonishment, a piece from your pen. . . . I have read it over and over again, and still my astonishment increases. I have been ready to say, '*This* surely is a misprint, or *that* was a slip of the pen;' and yet I fear I am mistaken. What! I have said to myself, can these be the sentiments of Father Stone? Is it possible, that he who has looked upon a number of us as a little too straight, upon some points, — who has regarded bro. Campbell as rather ultra upon these points, is it possible, that *he* has gone beyond us all — has quite out Campbelled bro. Campbell himself?[40]

Stone assured Rogers that there had been no misprint and no slip of the pen.[41]

But Rogers's astonishment underscores the point I am making here: thousands of Stone's followers had understood him to teach for many years that the pious unimmersed should be fellowshiped as Christian brothers and sisters, full of the Holy Spirit and of hope for salvation. It was precisely here that the revival tradition of the Great Awakenings defined Stone's understanding of nondenominational Christianity. Stone rejected out of hand the view of many in the Campbell tradition that nondenominational Christianity involved only those in the Church of Christ movement who had been immersed and who therefore belonged to the "true church" rather than to a denomination. In Stone's view, nondenominational Christianity had far more to do with a lifestyle of simple holiness that cut across all denominational boundaries. Stone objected to confining the label *Christian* exclusively to the immersed on the grounds that "we see no more fruits of the Spirit in them — no more holiness in their lives — no more humility, and self denial" than in the unimmersed. "Do we not see as much conformity to the world manifested — as much pride — as much injustice — as much avarice?" he asked. ". . . Talk no more of being washed from your sins by immersion, when we see you living in sin; and many of you living on the gains of oppressing the poor African."[42]

More than this, Stone chastised those who made immersion the *sine qua non* of the Christian faith on the grounds that it "steeled the breasts of our brethren of all denominations against us." He complained especially of the younger Christians in his movement who wanted "to concentrate religion in immersion and weekly communion" to the neglect of what Stone called "Christian experience" — love for God and for the brethren. Without that experience, Stone wrote, "religion is not worth a straw."

For all these reasons, Stone insisted that he could "pray with unimmersed, holy people, and praise, and perform every act of divine worship with such," and that he "found nothing in scripture to forbid me to commune with them at the Lord's table." Indeed, Stone noted as late as 1841 that "it is common with us that Baptists, Methodists and Presbyterians commune with us, and we with them."[43]

Further, by the mid-1830s Stone had found reason to complain that many in the movement — especially, one presumes, such sectarians as Tolbert Fanning, John Howard, and Arthur Crihfield — were using the nondenominational ideal for denominational purposes.

> Some among ourselves were for some time zealously engaged to do away [with] party creeds, and are yet zealously preaching against them — but instead of a written creed of man's device, they have substituted a nondescript one, and exclude good brethren from their fellowship, because they dare believe differently from their opinions, and like other sectarians endeavor to destroy their influence in the world.[44]

Stone explicitly contrasted the sectarian spirit with the ecumenical spirit that had been generated by the revivals in the early years of the nineteenth century. Looking back nostalgically to the great Cane Ridge Revival of 1801, Stone asked in 1827, "What but this [sectarian spirit] terminated the revival of religion in Kentucky and the West, twenty five years ago?"

> Then were living christians happily united; their distinctions and notions were almost lost in the glory of religion. It was evidently seen that if this state of things continued all parties must sink into oblivion, human Creeds be

neglected, and all christians would flow together into one body. [But] party spirits . . . , fearing the downfall of their party, . . . began the horrid work of drawing disciples after them, and of dividing the flock of Christ, that they *might glory in their flesh.* . . . Thus terminated that glorious revival, which had caused the earth to quake for fear, and multitudes to turn to the Lord.[45]

Similarly, Stone roundly condemned debating in the interest of the Christian faith. We noted in Chapter 2 that Alexander Campbell inaugurated a tradition of debate in Churches of Christ that lasted for generations. Stone rejected this tradition, claiming that "debates tend to strife, deaden piety — destroy the spirit of prayer — puff up the vain mind, . . . and destroy the comforts of true, heavenly religion." He claimed that it was rare to find "in the same person, a warrior and an humble devoted christian." He admitted that debates might win many to a given cause, but he questioned the conviction of those converted in this way: "The children are like the parents, lean and pigmy things." In 1844, near the close of his life, Stone complained that many of his own people increasingly placed biblical knowledge, religious controversy, and debate above "godliness, piety and brotherly love." "Do we see genuine christianity promoted by such controversies and debates? Look around and enquire for these fruits. Do you know of any person spiritually renewed or refreshed with spiritual understanding? Do you find brotherly love and christian union advanced? On the contrary, do you not find their opposites promoted?"[46]

Finding this strong ecumenical emphasis in Stone, many historians, especially within the tradition of the Disciples of Christ, have interpreted Stone chiefly as an apostle of unity and a harbinger of the modern ecumenical movement.[47] This reading of Stone renders him little different from the older, more mature Alexander Campbell — a progressive ecumenist, uniting all Protestants in one grand "common Christianity." Such a view makes it easy to understand how the Stone and Campbell movements could have united as easily as they did at Lexington in 1832.

But such a reading misses altogether the genius of Barton W. Stone, because it ignores a final theme in Stone in which every other aspect of his thought was deeply rooted: his apocalyptic worldview. If we appropriately take into account Stone's apocalypticism, we can see that he could never have favored a vapid ecumenism, as though one denomination were just as good and as biblical as another. Quite the contrary. Stone always insisted that all denominational structures were equally fallen and therefore equally wrong; together, they constituted what Stone described as "Babylon" and "a wilderness of confusion." He allowed that there were authentic Christians within this denominational "Babylon," to be sure, but he routinely called on these Christians to abandon "Babylon" and unite on the New Testament alone.[48] He believed that once all Christians abandoned "Babylon," all denominational structures would collapse into the dust.

In Stone's view — and this is the critical point — the collapse of denominational structures and the final triumph of primitive Christianity would characterize the millennium, not the present fallen age. Stone's willingness to fellowship with people from a variety of denominations was a measure adapted only to a fallen world. He believed that in the millennium there would be only one true Church of Christ, governed by Jesus Christ himself.

Stone's vision of nondenominational Christianity, then, was both sectarian and apocalyptic, precisely because it despaired of the values and the structures of the present world and stood in judgment on both. That is to say, his vision had far more in common with the growing sectarian emphasis of the early Churches of Christ than with the ecumenical interests of the early and later Disciples. By the 1830s, however, the Stone tradition began to take an interesting turn. Many from the ranks of the Stone movement, nurtured on an apocalyptic, countercultural worldview, began to be more attracted by the sectarian exclusivism of those who had radicalized the teachings of the early Alexander Campbell. But to understand these developments more clearly, we need first to explore both the sectarian and the apocalyptic themes in the thought of Barton W. Stone.

Barton W. Stone: Apocalyptic Sectarian

In connection with our survey of Alexander Campbell's postmillennial optimism, we took note of his rather spirited exchange with Samuel M. McCorkle in 1833/34. McCorkle was critical of Campbell's cultural and religious optimism, and Campbell thought McCorkle badly out of touch with the progressive spirit of the age. By 1844, McCorkle found himself drawn more to Stone's *Christian Messenger* than to Campbell's *Millennial Harbinger*. Stone allowed McCorkle to contribute a lengthy series of articles to the *Messenger* in which he launched a massive counterattack on Campbell's views. "'*Restoration* of *ancient order*,' is a pleasing *dream* — a brilliant phantom," McCorkle began in July. He specifically called on Campbell to show how the "man of sin" might be destroyed by merely "moral means." By August, McCorkle took off the gloves and came out swinging.

> Great names in the Christian church have vetoed the doctrine of a personal reign of Messiah, and our credulous brethren following in the perilous *wake!* . . . Half inebriate with the *fumes* of Babylon, . . . [editors] are harping upon, "Christianity restored," when we are approaching a *time of trouble,* such as never was. . . . Will they counteract by the "Ancient Order" the strong delusion that God has promised to send . . . ?

It is significant that McCorkle chose to publish these criticisms in Stone's *Christian Messenger* and that Stone agreed to print them. Perhaps even more significant is McCorkle's confession to Stone that, "with the exception of yourself, I have the editorial corps [of the movement] against me."[49] While Stone did not approve of all that McCorkle wrote, he did share McCorkle's pessimistic outlook on human potential and progress. In spite of their rejection of Calvinist theories of conversion, Stone and his followers — most of whom came from Presbyterian or Baptist backgrounds — continued to nurture for many years a basically Calvinist assessment of human nature.[50] Stone expressed the views of many when he wrote, "That mankind are depraved, is a lamentable truth, abundantly attested by the word of God, and confirmed by universal experience and observation. . . . All are in want of what they were made to enjoy, which is God; and have a propensity to satisfy that want with meaner things."[51]

In addition, Stone's followers generally joined to their Calvinist appraisal of human nature an experience of poverty and deprivation. John Rogers, one of the early Stone preachers in Kentucky, later recalled that the pioneers "were mostly men of small means" who "knew nothing of the luxuries and refinements of modern society." And Isaac Jones recalled that all the preachers in Middle Tennessee and south central Kentucky early on were "poor men, (some having no homes of their own) having but little education."[52]

Poverty, however, was hardly unique to the Stone tradition. As we already have seen, some on the Campbell side of the movement — Benjamin Franklin, for example — shared the experience of cultural and economic deprivation. This was especially true in the South, where poverty haunted most in the movement, regardless of whether their principal allegiance was to Stone or to Campbell. B. F. Hall made this clear in his autobiography:

> We had in those days but few meeting houses. When the weather would allow, we worshipped in groves and under sheds. But, as such places were not suitable for preaching in the winter, we had to occupy private houses. No one now can have any idea of the sacrifices which were made by the vetrean [*sic*] pioneers of the present great religious movement. . . . [Their] adherents . . . were generally of the poorer class, and without great personal influence. The preachers too were poor, and received but little pecuniary aid. They had, consequently, to resort to some secular pursuit in order to make a living.[53]

None of this is surprising, since deprivation was quite in keeping not only with the outsider mentality of the Stone tradition but also with the outsider mentality of the *Christian Baptist*. At an economic level, then, the Stone tradition shared a great deal with the outsider perspective of the early Campbell and his followers.

But Campbell did not retain the perspective of an outsider for long. It is true that he praised simplicity, as, for example, when he described the ideal building for Christian worship as "humble, commodious, and free from all the splendor of this vain and sinful world,"[54] but he never idealized poverty as a

Christian virtue as many of the Stoneites did, and he finally "died the wealthiest man in West Virginia," according to his biographer, having plowed an inheritance from his father-in-law into farming, land speculation, book publishing, and educational enterprises.[55]

While Campbell often preached in urban meetinghouses, Stone's early preaching is described as largely itinerant, being "done under an Elm and Oak" and "under a Beech Tree, covered with a summer grapevine." And while Campbell increasingly moved among the cultured and the sophisticated, the work of Stone and his colleagues remained principally among rustic and unlettered frontier people whose religious practices were often both primitive and emotional.[56]

Clearly, the issue of wealth and poverty provided considerable common ground for the followers of Stone and the devotees of Campbell's *Christian Baptist* — but it became a point on which Stone and his people were increasingly separated from the maturing Alexander Campbell. While Campbell evolved toward a growing accommodation of American secular and Christian culture, the apocalyptic orientation of Stone and his followers was leading them in decidedly countercultural directions, moving them to reject both worldly values and political activity.

Separation from the World

The notion of separating from the world and its values lies at the heart of the apocalyptic dimension of Stone's thought and abounds on almost every page of fourteen volumes of his *Christian Messenger,* running from 1827 through 1844. Stone consistently urged on his followers a radical code of ethics that required abandonment of self and service to the neighbor. For example, Stone summoned his followers to avoid extravagant attire, to care for widows and orphans, to minister to the poor and the hungry, and to free their slaves.[57] Stone summed up his life's orientation when he affirmed in 1842, "No Christian lives for himself — not self but the Lord is the great end of his living. . . . Like an obedient servant, he says, Lord what wilt thou have me to do? And when that will is known, he flies to do [it], not regarding how great the sacrifice of wealth, ease, or reputation."[58]

His own life was a case in point. Stone abandoned early plans for a law career in order to take up preaching. Then, when he and the other dissidents left the Presbyterian church in the aftermath of the Cane Ridge Revival, Stone voluntarily relinquished all salary and committed himself to a life of poverty in the interest of the kingdom of God. "Having now no support from the congregations, and having emancipated my slaves," he later recalled, "I turned my attention . . . cheerfully, though awkwardly, to labor on my little farm. . . . I had no money to hire laborers, and often on my return home, I found the weeds were getting ahead of my corn. I had often to labor at night while others were asleep, to redeem my lost time." Forty years later, he still prized the ideal of the impoverished preacher. "Decency in plain, coarse apparel displeases none but fops and dandies," he wrote, observing by the way that "we read of no rich preacher in the New Testament, nor in the best days of the church, before they were made rich by Constantine, when Heaven's order was prostrated by that deed." If Stone had a creed, he surely expressed it in 1841 when he admonished his readers that "you must not mind earthly things, nor set your affections on them — not to be conformed to the world. . . . Here you have no abiding place, but are as strangers and pilgrims seeking a better country."[59] This sentiment bespeaks the essence of the apocalyptic worldview embraced by Barton W. Stone.

Abner Hill provides another example of the separationist theme in the Stoneite tradition. An early Stone preacher in Tennessee, Hill wrote that "I had a good farm, a good house, . . . and a good prospect for living independent." But after a serious reading of Scripture, "I determined to give up my worldly prospects and to do all I could to turn people to righteousness. . . . I followed traveling preaching through the prime of my life."[60]

All of this stands in remarkable contrast to the world that Martha Wilson, a mountain girl from North Carolina, found at Campbell's Bethany College in 1858. Having accompanied her husband to Bethany, Martha wrote home to her Aunt Julia in Yadkinville that she and Virgil, her husband, had "had invitations to tea at Mr. Campbell's and most of the *Professors*. They are all very sociable and friendly but there are rather more grades and circles in society than I think ought to be in a christian community." In another letter, she complained that "I do not like to visit here — the people visit too fashionably." But her husband was awed with the prospects of Bethany graduates. "Tell Uncle that a great many young men go out from college to teach," he wrote, "but owing to the reputation of Bethany for its instruction, they command enormous prices never less than $800. One young preacher has been offered $1500 in S. Virginia to preach for three churches."[61]

Without a doubt, differences in orientation toward the world clearly separated the basic worldviews of the Stone and later Campbell movements. As we shall see, this theme of separation from the world and its values continued as a powerful motif among many in Churches of Christ until well into the twentieth century.

In some cases, the Stoneites' sense of being separate from the world went hand in hand with an explicitly premillennial eschatology.[62] Millennial excitement was central to the Stone movement from its inception at the Cane Ridge revival of 1801. John Dunlavy recalled after the revival that many thought "the day of the Lord, or Millennium, was at hand, and that that revival would never cease until that day should commence." Levi Purviance recalled that during the revivals, "many were fully persuaded that the glorious Millennial Day had commenced, and that the world would soon become the Kingdom of our Lord Jesus Christ."[63]

Due to a paucity of sources, it is difficult to trace the progress of Stone's millennial thought between the time of the revivals and 1827, when he launched the *Christian Messenger*. But by the early 1830s, no one could doubt where he stood on the millennial question. One sample of his thinking — a reply to an Elder William Caldwell — will suffice: "The second coming of Christ is at the commencement of his millenial [sic] reign on earth — here on earth he will reign till the 1000 years be finished — nor will he cease to reign on earth till he has raised from death the wicked, and judged them according to their works."[64] While the widespread excitement prompted by the millennial predictions of William Miller in the early 1840s fueled Stone's interest in this theme, his convictions regarding the premillennial kingdom of Christ predated those events by many years.[65]

Rejection of Politics

It is precisely here, tucked away in the union of separatism and apocalypticism, that one finds the origin of another theme central both to Stone and to a major stream in Churches of Christ for over a century. This tradition held that civil government — including American democracy — was both demonic and illegitimate and that Christians should refuse all active participation in government and politics, including voting. One finds the presuppositions of this theme spelled out clearly by Stone and his fellow dissidents from Presbyterianism in their *Observations on Church Government:*

> It will be granted that he who *creates* has a right to *govern*. Upon this principle God is acknowledged to be the governor of the world. . . . [But] men have been generally fond of mending what they supposed God had left imperfect, filling up and supplying what they judged deficient, and making plain what divine wisdom had left in the dark. Thus have they wandered from the plain simple rule of God's word, and taken the reins of government into their own hands.[66]

While they primarily addressed the issue of church government in this document, they also addressed the issue of civil government. Indeed, the two were inescapably connected in the thinking of the Stoneite Christians: they held all government devised by the wits of humankind, whether in church or state, to be simply illegitimate.

In fact, the Stoneites generally interpreted the vision recorded in the second chapter of Daniel to mean that in the last days the kingdom of Christ would fill the entire earth, destroy every human government, and inaugurate the rule of Christ on earth for a thousand years. Stone himself taught that the lawful King, Jesus Christ, will shortly put them [human governments] all down, and reign with his Saints on earth a thousand years, without a rival. . . . Then shall all man made laws and governments be burnt up forever. These are the seat of the beast. . . . Christians have no right to make laws and governments for themselves . . . [and] all should submit to the government and laws of our King. . . . We must cease to support any other government on earth by our counsels, co-operation, and choice.[67]

Working from this fundamental presupposition, the Stoneites time and again admonished one another to total noninvolvement in civil government other than paying taxes and obeying civil laws — and then only those laws that did not conflict with the kingdom of God. For example, James M. Mathes of Indiana wrote to Stone in 1836 complaining that some preachers "forget themselves" and "become candidates for posts of honor and profit in the civil department." Mathes observed that the primitive Christians left no such example. "They were subject to every ordinance of Caesar's government, for conscience sake, but took no part in law-making. Let us profit by their example."[68] And in 1835, an ad hoc committee representing various Stone churches addressed the readers of the *Christian Messenger* as follows: "Cease, cease, dear Brethren to be numbered among the Political aspirants — partake not of the evil of their midnight corruption. . . . While we take sides in the Political contests of this evil day, . . . we virtually renounce the laws of our King."[69]

It goes without saying that Stone and his people embraced an ethic of pacifism and grounded that ethic squarely in their anticipation of the final triumph of the kingdom of God. "If genuine christianity were to overspread the earth," Stone observed, "wars would cease, and the world would be found together in the bonds of peace. This is Christ's kingdom — the kingdom of peace." On the other hand, he noted, "A nation professing christianity, yet teaching, learning and practicing the arts of war cannot be of the kingdom of Christ."[70] It is clear that Stone implicitly rooted his pacifism in the first Christian age, and yet the apocalyptic vision of the final triumph of the kingdom of God, informed by the ancient faith, was most decisive for his thinking on questions of war and peace.

Alexander Campbell and many who embraced the *Christian Baptist* tradition shared Stone's aversion to war and violence. But Campbell based his rationale for pacifism mainly on the biblical pattern and the first Christian age rather than a vision of the final triumph of the kingdom of God. "War *ought to be abolished*," he wrote in 1834, "BECAUSE CHRISTIANITY FORBIDS IT" and because the Christian faith enjoined pacifism "in its uncorrupted, unsophisticated youth."[71]

So, while Campbell and Stone agreed on the issue of pacifism, they came to their positions from different directions. Their followers, through several generations, walked the same paths, bearing witness to their conviction that

Christianity was a religion of peace, albeit for different reasons. Even in the twentieth century, some among Churches of Christ whose roots were primarily Campbellian continued to preach this position.[72] But it was undisputably the Stoneite tradition that emerged as the principal carrier of the pacifist sentiment within this fellowship (a matter we will consider at greater length in Chaps. 6 and 7).

We should also note that the Stoneites' rejection of ecclesiastical societies (missionary, Bible, temperance, etc.) grew out of the same apocalyptic vision that governed their refusal to participate in civil government. They insisted that God had not ordained any of these societies and that his coming kingdom would destroy them, along with all human governments and institutions. The notion of belonging to a king whose kingdom would fill the earth in the last days simply proved a far more powerful and lasting motivation for Stone and his colleagues than did mere biblical patternism.

Once again on this point we can find a significant distinction between Stone and Campbell. Campbell opposed ecclesiastical societies only during the early years of his career (he had certainly abandoned such opposition by 1849, when he became president of the American Christian Missionary Society), and even then his opposition was based on his understanding of the biblical pattern rather than on an apocalyptic vision, as in the case of Stone.

And finally, since Daniel 2 was so key to the apocalyptic vision of Stone and his people, it is interesting to note that Campbell tamed that passage and placed its meaning squarely in the context of human history and progress. Campbell associated the little stone that would fill the entire earth not with the coming kingdom of God but with the Protestant Reformation: he associated the image that the stone destroyed not with human government but with the Roman Catholic Church.[73]

It will help at this point to sharpen the contrast between Campbell and Stone with reference to the restoration vision. If Campbell's vision can be described as *rational progressive primitivism* as I suggested in Chapter 2, Stone's vision can be appropriately described as *apocalyptic primitivism*. This is to say that Stone lived his life between the times. He was not so much interested in the church as in the *kingdom*, the rule of God over all human affairs. That rule, he felt, was manifest in the ancient church when God had made Jesus "Lord of all [and] the only law-giver of the world. While he reigned and ruled alone in the first centuries of the world, religion in her loveliest forms dwelt on earth." Things changed in the fourth century, when "christians became dissatisfied with [God's] . . . government" and invented their own.[74]

Stone believed that the same divine rule that prevailed in the first four centuries of the common era would be consummated again in the premillennial second coming of Jesus Christ. In this way, his vision of the ancient church and his vision of the coming kingdom of God essentially coalesced in one grand vision of the rule of God over all the earth.

But between the times, as Stone saw things, the kingdom of God remained a countercultural reality that stood in judgment on all Christian denominations; on all rational, scientific, and technical progress; on all governments; and on all human creations whatsoever. More than anything else, this conviction formed the basis for his sectarian, antimodern bias.[75] Further, this apocalyptic-countercultural perspective provided the mainspring not only for Stone but also for a sizable segment of Churches of Christ until well into the twentieth century, even after that perspective had joined itself to the biblicism of the early Campbell.

Stone and Campbell Joined

The apocalyptic perspective of the Stone tradition did, in fact, begin to merge with the biblicism of the early Campbell in 1823. Prior to that year, few in the Stone movement — which by then numbered perhaps 15,000 to 20,000[76] — had ever heard of Alexander Campbell. But in that year, Campbell traveled to Kentucky to debate the Presbyterian W. L. McCalla. As it happened, he had just begun publishing the *Christian Baptist,* and he took copies of the new journal with him to Kentucky. Campbell's oratorical presence, his journal, and most of all his clear and lucid description both of the ancient gospel and the ancient order won over thousands of the followers of Barton W. Stone.

Stoneites, many of whom were Calvinists, found Campbell's presentation of the *ancient gospel* immensely appealing, chiefly because Campbell's theology of conversion eliminated the emotional burden that frontier Calvinism often imposed on believers. Calvinism dictated that a person is saved only if God has predestined that person for salvation. Many understood this to mean that it was futile to attempt to respond to the gospel call apart from a conviction that one had been predestined by God for redemption. This theology wrought emotional havoc within the Stoneite community. Many reported in their autobiographies that they had wept and wailed for weeks, months, and in some cases years at a time, seeking conversion but not knowing if salvation was for them. Seventeen-year-old B. F. Hall, for example, spoke of seeking God "back of the field, near a hollow, in a briar thicket. . . . I knealt for some moments in silence, for words came not to my lips. I could think of nothing to say. My pent-up grief was intence [*sic*]. . . . Tears gushed unbidden from my eyes. I sobbed aloud." Hall finally reached conversion, but when he did, his mother was astonished at "how Benjamin got through so soon. He was only about four weeks under conviction; and it was seven years before I obtained comfort, and I was all the while earnestly seeking the Lord."[77]

But in 1823 Campbell offered the Stoneites a theology that cut through the struggle and the pain, for in his debate with W. L. McCalla he developed his contention that immersion is for forgiveness of sins. This notion became the linchpin in what Campbell increasingly would call the *ancient gospel*. It meant that one no longer had to undergo weeks and months of uncertainty, seeking all the while for a sign that one was in fact among the redeemed. It meant, rather, that one simply submitted to immersion and, then and there, was saved. John Rogers, an early Stoneite preacher in Kentucky, marveled at how easy it was. The primitive Christians, he noted, were immersed and therefore were "pardoned, & knew it, & rejoiced in it . . . & never spoke in the language of doubt or fear upon the subject."[78]

If Campbell's baptismal theology provided the Stoneites with a certainty of salvation where before there had been only insecurity and bewilderment, his theology of the *ancient order* provided certainty in another way. For Campbell sketched out in detail the outline and shape of the primitive church — its organization, its worship, its patterns of benevolence, its celebration of the Lord's supper, and a host of other practices, as we saw in Chapter 2. In so doing, Campbell provided structure and therefore security for a people whose theology of freedom had brought ambiguity and insecurity. The Stoneites, who had failed to develop any meaningful theology of the church because of their overriding concern to preserve Christian freedom, now welcomed Campbell's portrayal of the ancient faith.

Samuel Rogers was a case in point. Both baptized and ordained by Stone, Rogers nevertheless worried about his call. He thought he should have "credentials" like those of the apostles. "I attempted to draw from dreams and visions and vague impressions, some super-human aid. . . . I thought I ought to perform miracles." Finally, he discovered "the 'Christian Baptist' and found relief." Rogers recalled that Campbell "preached no new gospel . . . , but taught us to worship intelligently the God whom we had ignorantly worshipped." If "Stone had given me the book, . . . Campbell taught me how to read it in its connection."[79]

Moreover, as we have seen, Campbell also urged on the Stoneites the notion that the Spirit works in conversion only through the written Word, and he completely rejected such "exercises" as jerking, barking, and dancing. As a consequence, Isaac Jones, born in east Tennessee in 1822, recalled that "by degrees . . . these [exercises] all passed away, and people began to do things 'decently and in order.'"[80]

Conclusion

These developments are of the greatest importance for an understanding of the earliest formation of Churches of Christ, because they were the means by which two sectarian traditions were fused into a single movement. The sectarian tradition of Barton Stone focused chiefly on an apocalyptic foundation for a distinctly Christian lifestyle, standing against the world. The sectarian tradition of the early Alexander Campbell focused on human potential and a rational reconstruction of the Christian faith, standing against the denominations. At the most fundamental level — that of foundational presuppositions — these two traditions were simply incompatible. Yet, they shared considerable common ground at less foundational levels, such as their emphasis on the restoration of primitive Christianity and the unity of all Christians. And since Campbell provided the basic structure for achieving these goals, many Stoneites received him as an ally.

Consequently, and especially at the urging of Barton Stone, the Campbell and Stone traditions formally united in Lexington, Kentucky, in 1832. Many Stoneites perceived the fundamental differences between their own perspective and that of Alexander Campbell and refused to enter the union. Most of these eventually united with the eastern Christian movement known as the Christian Connection, which was led in the late eighteenth and early nineteenth centuries by Elias Smith in New England and James O'Kelley in Virginia and North Carolina. Typical in this regard was the Ohio preacher Matthew Gardner, who complained that preachers in the Campbell tradition "seem to labor more especially to reform the churches of other denominations over to their views, than they do to reform the wicked from the error of their ways." Gardner recalled that the Stone movement "arose upon the liberal ground of each individual enjoying and exercising his own private opinion," and he lamented that "Mr. Campbell has obviated all these difficulties." He was also upset by the fact that Campbell had made immersion "the *sine qua non*" of his movement, "and any man who does not tacitly receive it, is loaded with the odious epithet of being an opposer of the glorious reformation."[81]

But many other Stoneites rejoiced in their union with the forces of Alexander Campbell. They did not see the fundamental theological differences that would in time produce the rupture between Churches of Christ and the Disciples. For the rupture that the United States Bureau of the Census recognized in 1906 was not, in the final analysis, a result of disagreements over the validity of missionary societies and instrumental music in worship. It was a result of a clash of radically conflicting worldviews. Those who had never known the theology of Barton W. Stone, who were disciples only of the mature Alexander Campbell, celebrated progress and human potential and simply could not fathom a pessimistic, apocalyptic perspective that viewed this world with profound skepticism. Most of these people lived in western Pennsylvania, Ohio, Virginia, and Kentucky, where Campbell's influence was the strongest.

On the other hand, many Christians of southern Kentucky, Middle Tennessee, and northern Alabama, whose earliest roots reached deeply into the apocalyptic soil of Barton Stone, had just as much trouble fathoming the progressivism and this-worldly optimism of the churches to the north. These southerners, who had fused the visions of Campbell and Stone, had also fused their understanding of primitive Christianity with an apocalyptic worldview.

Their rejection of missionary societies and instrumental music in worship symbolized their allegiance to the apocalyptic kingdom of God. Here, there was no room for progress, change, or allegiance to human potential.

As a result, when their brothers and sisters to the north began pushing for missionary societies and instrumental music in worship, these southerners imagined that their northern counterparts had abandoned "the original ground of primitive Christianity." But in many instances, northerners had simply modified their understanding of primitive Christianity with an infusion of the Campbellian allegiance to progress and human potential. They were genuinely shocked when the southerners began suggesting that they had abandoned the restoration vision. The truth is that many — perhaps most — of the northern Christians continued to call for a restoration of apostolic Christianity well into the twentieth century. It was just that apostolic Christianity meant something quite different to them than it did to those further south. The problem — which few then or since have understood — lay in the fact that the surface agreement between the Stoneite and Campbellite traditions, which prevailed for twenty to thirty years following their union, masked a fundamental difference in worldview.

This difference in worldview does not entirely explain the eventual division between Disciples and Churches of Christ. Many who went with Churches of Christ knew little or nothing of the worldview of Barton W. Stone; their opposition to the progressivism of the Disciples was rooted in their allegiance to the early Campbell and to the ideals of the *Christian Baptist* or Benjamin Franklin's *American Christian Review*. Significant numbers of such people migrated from Ohio and Indiana through Missouri to the plains of Texas and Oklahoma, where they joined people with roots in the old Stoneite worldview who had migrated there from Tennessee, Kentucky, and Alabama. Despite the fact that these two groups had different theological and geographical roots, they at least shared a common sectarian vision grounded in a vision of primitive Christianity, and in time they formed an alliance against those Campbellian progressivists who remained in the Middle West and followed Campbell in his transition from sect to denomination.

CHAPTER 6

The Apocalyptic Tradition
of Churches of Christ

If Churches of Christ in Middle Tennessee, northern Alabama, and southern Kentucky fused the Campbellian vision of the *Christian Baptist* era with the apocalyptic perspectives of Barton W. Stone, the person most responsible for the original fusion was Tolbert Fanning. And the person who stabilized that fusion and perpetuated the apocalyptic primitivism of the Stone/Campbell tradition among Churches of Christ well into the twentieth century was David Lipscomb.

Tolbert Fanning

As we have seen, Tolbert Fanning was the great second-generation leader of Churches of Christ who was deeply indebted to the ideals of Alexander Campbell, especially from the *Christian Baptist* period. But Fanning is a classic example of how Churches of Christ in the mid-nineteenth century built their theology not from Campbell alone but rather from the competing and sometimes contradictory perspectives of Alexander Campbell *and* Barton W. Stone. For while Fanning constructed his theological agenda squarely on Lockean epistemology, and while he fully embraced the sectarian notion that the Church of Christ to which he belonged was the one true church of God and that all other denominations were simply false churches, he also fully embraced the Stoneite vision of countercultural sectarianism, apocalypticism, and apoliticism. Fanning so completely merged the ideals of Stone and Campbell that in his view the kingdom of God that would finally triumph over all the earth was simply the Church of Christ he knew in Middle Tennessee.

A native of Tennessee, Fanning soon moved with his family to Alabama, where he received his earliest religious instruction from several Stoneite preachers in that region, including Ephraim D. Moore, James E. Matthews, and Ross Houston.[1] In 1860 Fanning wrote, "We are more indebted to . . . E. D. Moore, for our early religious instruction and impressions than to any other man dead or alive."[2] One can only surmise that Moore, Matthews (who baptized Fanning), and Houston must have shared with young Fanning the separatist, apocalyptic, and apolitical mentality that so pervaded the early Stone movement.

The fact is, one finds precisely those themes in Fanning's writings throughout his editorial career. It is true that the apocalyptic dimension was muted in Fanning's thought and that in 1846 he claimed to have no certain knowledge of the prophecies of the book of Revelation.[3] Nonetheless, the standard Stoneite interpretations of Daniel 2 appeared routinely in Fanning's *Christian Review*. In 1844, one contributor suggested that the church is indeed the kingdom of God, "but only in its *stone* form. . . . It is yet to be established in its mountain form — yet to break the image to pieces, and fill the whole earth. . . . When the day of the glory of the Son of Man shall come, the kingdoms of this earth will fall, and the kingdom, and the dominion, and the greatness of the kingdom under the whole heaven, shall be given to the saints. Thus I am taught by Daniel, and by present events, that this period draws nigh."[4]

Fanning himself, in a sermon entitled "The Mission of the Church of Christ," speculated that the time was "not far distant when the problem of self-government, civil and ecclesiastical, will have been worked out — when, from the utter failure of worldly-wise organizations," the Church of Christ would finally triumph. And in 1861, when the Civil War dominated the thoughts of most Americans, Fanning wrote that the "church of Christ" would "'break in pieces and consume' [the] kingdoms of the world." He asserted that human beings tragically deceived themselves when, "by their efforts in constructing governmental plans and systems," they imagined "they could essentially aid the Almighty. . . . They had just as well hold up their feeble tapers at noon to help the sun shine." And as late as 1872, Fanning sounded the same refrain: "That the cause of our Master, the Lord Jesus Christ will eventually triumph; and that the governments of the world, will finally yield to the higher authority of the Spirit there can be no question." The following year, he affirmed once again his conviction that the church would "break into pieces and consume all other kingdoms."[5]

There is no evidence that Fanning was explicitly premillennial, but there is abundant evidence that his outlook was profoundly apocalyptic. Further, it is likely that he learned this apocalyptic perspective from Ephraim D. Moore and the other Stoneite preachers who taught him the Christian faith when he was young. "From our earliest acquaintance with the Sacred Oracles," Fanning wrote, "we have entertained not a doubt that the Church of God is . . . destined, finally, . . . to triumph over all the powers of the earth."[6]

Fanning's apocalypticism bore its practical fruit in the characteristic position of the Stoneites regarding civil government. In August of 1844, Fanning strongly warned against voting and electioneering, and David Lipscomb reported in 1867 that Fanning himself had not voted in some twenty years, "holding it to be incompatible with the Christian profession."[7] Further, in May of 1846, the month in which the United States declared war on Mexico, Fanning placed democracy in the same category with monarchy and aristocracy, criticizing them all: "Monarchies, aristocracies, and democracies were all the same to them [primitive Christians]. . . . The church of Christ is an institution . . . in which there is no necessity of elections, or legislation. . . . Neither has God constituted them [Christians] law-makers for the wicked, or rulers, in any place but in the kingdom of his dear Son."[8] In light of all this, it is not surprising to find that Fanning was a consistent pacifist who opposed Christian participation both in the Mexican War and in the Civil War.[9]

Fanning's pacifism was not a product of a southern bias against the North or a reaction to the horrors of the Civil War; rather, it grew out of deeply held theological convictions — in part his adherence to the model and example of the primitive church and in part his apocalyptic anticipation of the day when that church would triumph over all the kingdoms of the earth. He viewed the period between those times as essentially irrelevant to the Christian's task. He simply took his stand on the kingdom of God that manifested itself in the first Christian age, that would manifest itself again in the final days, and that stood in judgment continuously on all the kingdoms of humankind. This is the principal reason Fanning consistently refused either to vote or to fight in his nation's wars.

Fanning's apocalyptic worldview differed from that of Barton W. Stone in the extent to which Fanning had absorbed the rational and technical perspectives of Campbell. Stone viewed the kingdom of God as a transcendent reality standing in judgment on human creations and institutions that would not be completely realized in this world until the end of time. Fanning's extreme rationalism led him to particularize the transcendent in ways that had been foreign to Stone. As a result, he virtually identified the kingdom of God with the Church of Christ he knew in Tennessee and the Mid-South.

David Lipscomb

The man who more than anyone else carried the Barton Stone tradition into the twentieth century was David Lipscomb, clearly the most influential person among Churches of Christ from the close of the Civil War until his death in 1917; for most of those years he served as editor of the immensely influential *Gospel Advocate,* based in Nashville. Lipscomb often acknowledged an immense debt to his mentor, Tolbert Fanning, from whom he picked up the rational and legal perspectives of the early Alexander Campbell as well as the apocalyptic outlook of Barton W. Stone.

In many ways the father of Churches of Christ in the American South, David Lipscomb (1831-1917) combined the rational and legal perspectives of Alexander Campbell with the apocalyptic outlook of Barton W. Stone.
(Photo courtesy David Lipscomb University)

Lipscomb and Alexander Campbell

There is no question that Lipscomb was in many ways a Campbellite, embracing a rational view of Scripture and even turning Campbell's biblicism toward legalism. Lipscomb routinely employed the Baconian common sense method of Bible interpretation, though not nearly as self-consciously as had Campbell and Fanning. That is to say, he spent little time discussing either the method as such or Francis Bacon, its alleged founder. But when he did discuss the method, he placed himself squarely in the Campbellian tradition of biblical interpretation. He flatly asserted that "the Bible is science, is knowledge, classified by God." On another occasion he argued that "the Christian religion . . . is addressed to the common sense in man," and he defined common sense as that "sound, practical judgement . . . in regard to first principles in which all men in general agree." This means, he continued, that "you must use common sense to do what he commands in the best way your common sense directs. That in no way interferes with our doing all that God commands — adding nothing thereto, taking nothing therefrom."[10] In 1868 he stated that the editors of and contributors to the *Gospel Advocate* were determined to make that publication "more perfectly the reflex of the Divine Will as revealed in the Bible than any human production now in existence."[11]

His Baconian common sense outlook not only contributed to his legalism but also nurtured within him an unwavering conviction that, in matters of the Christian faith, his interpretation of Scripture was virtually synonymous with Scripture itself. Though he was fully capable of dialogue with those with whom he disagreed (see Chap. 9), he felt strongly in such situations that he was simply right and that those who disagreed were simply wrong. So in 1907, when division finally came, Lipscomb viewed things in black-and-white terms. "Can you walk with him [God] while you insist on making laws and changing his order?" he asked the liberals in the movement. "Can two walk together when one insists on walking in God's ways and the other insists on going another way? . . . If division must come, let it come along the lines of love and loyalty to God."[12]

It is no wonder, then, that Lipscomb inevitably stood at the heart of the fights between the emerging Churches of Christ and the emerging Disciples of Christ over missionary societies, the propriety of instrumental music in the worship of God, the role of women in the church, and basic attitudes toward Scripture. Further, it was Lipscomb who responded to S. N. D. North, director of the Federal Census of 1906, who thought he detected a major rupture in the Stone-Campbell movement. North was right, Lipscomb responded, and he urged him to list Churches of Christ separately from Disciples of Christ.[13] Reflecting in 1916 on his long career of leadership in Churches of Christ, Lipscomb expressed his satisfaction with "knowing we have opposed all innovations and changes upon his [God's] order at every point along the line of duty drawn by him."[14] He clearly stood in the legalist tradition foreshadowed by Alexander Campbell in his *Christian Baptist* and perpetuated by such people as Arthur Crihfield, John R. Howard, Tolbert Fanning, and Benjamin Franklin.

Lipscomb and Barton W. Stone

But if Lipscomb was a Campbellite who turned Campbell's biblicism toward legalism, he also stood squarely in the Stone-Fanning tradition of separatism, apocalypticism, and apoliticism. His success in combining the Campbell and Stone perspectives in his own outlook was key to establishing the tremendous power and influence he exercised throughout the heterogeneous fellowship of Churches of Christ. Had Lipscomb focused exclusively on the rational and legal side of Alexander Campbell, he would have alienated those whose roots ran deeply into the separatist piety of Barton W. Stone. And had he focused only on the traditions of Stone, he would have alienated the legalists whose roots reached into the rationalism and biblicism of Alexander Campbell. Lipscomb's genius lay in the way he coherently combined those two perspectives into one. As it turned out, Lipscomb was the last major leader in the history of Churches of Christ to combine these two perspectives successfully. Following his death in 1917, the mainstream of Churches of Christ increasingly relegated the perspectives of the Stone movement to the status of heresy and built their house instead on the world-affirming foundation laid by Alexander Campbell, buttressed by the rational and legal themes that grew out of Campbell's biblicism. Lipscomb stands, therefore, at a pinnacle in the history of Churches of Christ, looking backward to both Stone and Campbell and forward to a monolithic Church of Christ that would expel Stone's apocalyptic outlook from its agenda.

During his lifetime, however, Lipscomb was an articulate proponent of the Stoneite worldview. In the years immediately following the Civil War, he published a series of articles on the Christian's relation to the world and especially to civil government, and in 1889 he gathered these articles into a small book that received wide circulation among Churches of Christ. He called the book simply *Civil Government*,[15] and a year after its publication he judged that "nothing we ever wrote affects so nearly the vital interests of the church of Christ and the salvation of the world as this little book."[16]

Separation from the World

The fundamental premise of Lipscomb's book — and of his life — was his conviction that the Christian belongs to a kingdom ruled by God, not to the kingdoms ruled by humankind.[17] This conviction led him to advocate an active separation from the world and from its concerns with fashion, wealth, and power. Benjamin Franklin, who, as we have seen, thought plainness a mark of the apostolic order, praised Lipscomb as "a plain and unassuming man, with the simplicity of a child. . . . He lives in utter disregard of the notions of the world, puts on no airs, wears just a coat, hat and pants as suit him. . . . It is refreshing to meet one content to be the *plain man of God*."[18] On this point, Lipscomb not only stood indebted to Barton Stone and Tolbert Fanning but readily acknowledged debts to Anabaptists, Waldensians, Lollards, Hussites, Paterines, and the followers of Arnold of Brescia.[19]

When Lipscomb described what separation from the world might mean in practical terms, he made it clear that he did not mean mere morality. "There is no doubt the devil is willing to turn moral reformer and make the world moral and respectable," he observed. Instead, he advocated "a full surrender of the soul, mind, and body up to God," leading to "the spirit of self-denial, of self-sacrifice, the forbearance [*sic*] and long suffering, [and] the doing good for evil." Most important, separation from the world meant for Lipscomb, as it had for Stone, reliance on the sovereign power of God. It was in this context that he found human institutions so objectionable. The spirit of those institutions, he claimed, "corrupts the church, drives out the spirit of God, destroys the sense of dependence upon God, causes the children of God to depend upon their own wisdom and devices, and the arm of violence, and the institutions of earth rather than upon God and his appointments."[20]

The very existence of human institutions and human governments represented for Lipscomb a departure from God's primordial design. In *Civil Government,* he argues that God from the beginning intended to be sovereign over all the earth. His sovereignty, in fact, formed the very essence of the Garden of Eden before the fall. But "the act [by Adam and Eve] of . . . disobedience culminated in the effort of man to organise a government of his own, so that he himself might permanently conduct the affairs of earth, free from the control of God, and independent of God's government." Similarly, the Jews rejected God's sovereignty when they called for a king. Lipscomb took very seriously God's words to Samuel on that occasion: "For they have not rejected thee, but they have rejected me, that I should not be king over them."[21] Lipscomb viewed the rejection of God's sovereignty, first by Adam and Eve and then by the Jews, as evidence that humanity had transferred its allegiance from God to Satan. This explained to him the meaning of Satan's statement to Jesus that all the kingdoms of earth "were delivered to me": human government was nothing less than "Satan's dominion in rebellion against God."[22]

Following humanity's rejection of divine government, Lipscomb claimed, it had been God's intent to restore his sovereignty over the earth. This was the point of the Jewish wars against the Caananite tribes. "The work to which they were called was a war of extermination against all people maintaining a human government." Lipscomb argued that the advent of Jesus Christ into the world constituted another of God's attempts at restoration. This attempt succeeded to the extent that Jesus conquered "death and hell and the grave," said Lipscomb, but it failed to the extent that it did not ultimately destroy sin and rebellion.[23]

Apocalyptic Eschatology

It was in this context that Lipscomb introduced the apocalyptic themes that characterized both Barton Stone and Tolbert Fanning before him. The day would come, Lipscomb maintained, when God would re-establish his sovereignty over all the earth and destroy all human governments, the best along with the worst. And, like Stone and Fanning, Lipscomb rooted this vision in Daniel 2:

> The end of all conflicts and strifes of earth, will be the complete and final destruction, the utter consuming of the last vestige of human governments and institutions, and the giving of the dominion, and power, and authority of the whole earth to the people of the saints of the Most High. . . . All these kingdoms are to be broken in pieces, and *consumed . . .* but the little stone

cut out of the mountain without hands is to become a great mountain, and fill the whole earth.

Lipscomb considered these themes to be the very "key notes . . . of the Old and New Testaments." Without them, the Bible was "without point or meaning."[24]

At this point Lipscomb differed significantly, however, from Fanning, who had particularized the transcendent and had virtually identified the eschatological kingdom of God with the temporal Church of Christ. Lipscomb agreed that when God established the church, he also re-established his kingdom, rule, and authority. But the kingdom of God in its church form was by no means the same as the eschatological kingdom that would break in pieces all the kingdoms of the earth. Lipscomb made this point abundantly clear in an article entitled "The Kingdom of God," which he wrote in 1903: "The kingdom in its present stage is not called 'the everlasting kingdom,' but it will grow into it. It is the same kingdom in a lower stage and development."[25] And in *Civil Government,* he spoke of the church as the present manifestation of the coming kingdom of God.[26] Like Stone before him, Lipscomb could not imagine human perfection between the times of primordium and millennium.

Clearly, Lipscomb's apocalypticism embodied an eschatological expectation that governed his worldview. But was Lipscomb also premillennial? This question is important, because premillennialism became a pivotal issue for Churches of Christ during the first half of the twentieth century, and Lipscomb's position on that issue was hotly disputed following his death. The answer to the question hangs on our understanding of what it means to be a premillennialist.

It seems safe to say that Lipscomb did not believe that Jesus would one day return to sit on the throne of David in Jerusalem for a literal thousand years. For one thing, he displayed little or no interest in the role of Israel or the throne of David in the millennial age. For another, Lipscomb always maintained that the kingdom of God would "fill the whole earth, and stand forever."[27] He envisioned the millennium not as a thousand-year interlude but as the eternal rule of God on this earth.

But Lipscomb did clearly contend that Jesus' return to earth will precede and inaugurate the final golden age of God's rule on earth. To this extent, Lipscomb's position was clearly premillennial. We can find glimpses of this position in an assortment of articles Lipscomb wrote for the *Gospel Advocate* over a period of years. For example, in 1878 he commented favorably on the First American Bible and Prophetic Conference, convened at the Holy Trinity Episcopal Church in New York City in October of that year.[28] He noted that speeches at the conference focused on "the idea of the re-appearance of the Savior before and preparatory to the advent of the millenium [*sic*]," and he commended those speeches as doing "honor to the word of God." While Lipscomb expressed some uncertainty about whether Christ's coming would precede or follow "the conversion of the world to God," he urged his readers to acquire copies of the speeches by writing to the *New York Tribune* — cautioning only that no one make this topic "a hobby to disturb the peace of churches." Years later, Lipscomb spoke explicitly of a "reign of Jesus on earth" and declared that "'the times of restoration of all things' must be when Jesus returns again to earth — the restoration of all things to their original relation to God."[29]

Further, there can be no doubt that the millennium Lipscomb envisioned was a literal kingdom on this earth. He spoke, for example, of "the glorious millennial morn" in connection with "the re-establishment [of] the kingdom of God on earth." He stated that "the one purpose of God was to re-establish his authority and rule on earth." He wrote that "this earth in the material, moral and spiritual world must become a garden of God's own planting." Further, to those who asked, regarding God's rule on earth, "How would the mails be carried? How could the affairs of Railroads, Manufactures, and the many large corporations . . . be managed?" Lipscomb simply replied, "We will cheerfully commit the adjustment and management" of these things to God.[30]

Many in Lipscomb's circle shared this basic position, though with differences in emphasis. James A. Harding, cofounder with Lipscomb of the Nashville Bible School, first president of that institution, and coworker with Lipscomb on the *Gospel Advocate,* candidly and explicitly advocated a view much more in keeping with classic premillennialism:

> When the saints are caught up to meet him, Christ comes with them to earth. . . . Satan is then caught, chained and cast into the abyss . . . [where] he is confined for one thousand years . . . [while] Christ and his saints reign; but the rest of the dead live not until the thousand years are expired. This, the resurrection of the righteous, is the first resurrection.[31]

Others in Lipscomb's circle revealed their premillennial assumptions time and again, often in an offhanded way. For example, when answering a question from a reader of the *Gospel Advocate,* E. G. Sewell simply assumed a millennium bounded by a "first resurrection" of the righteous and a "second resurrection" when "the thousand years of peace are finished."[32] And Philip S. Fall wrote in an open letter to Mrs. Alexander Campbell, "In regard to the pre-millennial advent, . . . the New Testament . . . impresses me with the hope that this earth . . . is to be the home of the righteous. . . . I can conceive of no higher ideal of heaven than that [we] . . . will dwell together with him . . . in this renovated spot."[33]

Generally speaking, Lipscomb and those in his circle strongly resisted elaborating on their premillennial perspectives or engaging in speculation about "what the millennium is or when it begins or ends."[34] They refused to speculate on the millennium because they did not wish to press beyond what they viewed as the bounds of Scripture. Further, they did not argue or debate the premillen-

The Nashville Bible School, established in 1891 by David Lipscomb and James A. Harding, trained a small army of preachers who embraced the apocalyptic worldview so characteristic of Barton Stone, Lipscomb, and Harding and who provided positive leadership for Churches of Christ well into the twentieth century. Pictured above are (1) the first building the school occupied in 1891 and (2) the faculty shortly after the turn of the century.
(Photos courtesy David Lipscomb University)

nial question simply because it was not an issue. It was rather a working assumption, and one that characterized many in Middle Tennessee, along with others in Churches of Christ in surrounding regions from the days of Stone throughout the nineteenth century. Indeed, Stanford Chambers, a leader among premillennial Churches of Christ throughout the first half of the twentieth century, recalled late in his life that while he had been raised in an overwhelmingly premillennial environment in southern Indiana, "I had never heard the term [*premillennial*] used by any brethren whom I knew [and] had never seen it in any of their writings [until 1911]."[35] Rather, the premillennial idea was simply a working assumption for many in this tradition. In spite of all this, few historians have taken note of the fact that Lipscomb or those in the Stone-Lipscomb heritage were premillennial at all.[36]

Rejection of Politics

The third component in Lipscomb's outlook was his rigorous pacifism and refusal to vote or otherwise participate in politics or the affairs of government. "The mission of the kingdom of God is to break into pieces and consume all these kingdoms, take their place, fill the whole earth, and stand forever," Lipscomb declared. "How [then] could the individual citizens of the kingdom of God found, enter into, and become part and parcel of — upbuild, support, and defend, that which God's kingdom was especially commissioned to destroy?" Further, Lipscomb flatly rejected the postmillennial suggestion that God would re-establish his sovereignty over the earth "by the conversion of all the people, and the civil governments will then be manned by Christians." To this, Lipscomb only reiterated his position: the kingdom of God "shall break in pieces and consume all these and it shall fill the whole earth and stand forever."[37]

In this context, Lipscomb argued that the common Protestant understanding of the biblical term "Babylon" was surely wrong. "It is usually interpreted as reference to the Romish Church, and the confusion of sects springing from Rome," he wrote. The truth was, however, that "Babylon" signified human government. "This human institution has never lost or changed its leading characteristics; it is still confusion and strife. All human government rests for authority upon the power of the sword; its mission has been strife and bloodshed." For this reason, Lipscomb contended, "Every act of alliance with or reliance for aid upon the human government on the part of the church or any of its members, is spiritual adultery." He insisted that "to come out of Babylon is to come out of the affiliation and association with human governments. The fall of Babylon is the down fall of all human governments and the destruction of human institutions and authority, and the reinstation of God's rule and authority on earth and through his own institutions."[38]

Fanning, Lipscomb, America, and the South

By now, it must be abundantly clear that when Lipscomb characterized human government as the dominion of Satan that God's kingdom would break in pieces and consume, he had in mind the government of the United States along with all the others.[39] Given his judgment upon the government of the United States, therefore, one might suspect that Lipscomb's antipolitical posture chiefly reflected his status as a southerner, his partiality toward the Confederacy, and his bitterness over the Civil War.

David Edwin Harrell has argued that Churches of Christ were, to a significant degree, the product of postwar southern sectionalism. Harrell concedes that a sectarian emphasis was present in the Stone-Campbell movement from the beginning. Yet, "the church in the South emerged from the Civil War more strongly than ever committed to the extreme sectarian emphasis in Disciples thought." He concludes, "sectarian theology was a natural reaction to the sociological forces which spawned the *Gospel Advocate* and the Church of Christ." For this reason, he argues — as we noted earlier — that "the twentieth-century Churches of Christ are the spirited offspring of the religious rednecks of the post bellum South."[40]

It would be absurd to deny the importance of sectionalism and social factors in shaping the thinking of many among the postwar Churches of Christ. Harrell, for example, points instructively to the American Christian Missionary Society, which in 1863 affirmed a resolution of loyalty to the Union, an action that alienated many among Churches of Christ in the South.[41] Further, Harrell accurately reports that Fanning and Lipscomb, in the aftermath of the war, routinely chastised their brethren in the North. "Those brethren," wrote Fanning and Lipscomb, "who believe that political resolutions are the Gospel can do so; and those who desire to contribute to such an object can do so; *we cannot do it.*"[42] And it is perfectly true that Lipscomb spoke of the resurrection of the *Gospel Advocate* in 1866, after a four-year hiatus during the war, in sectional terms: "The fact that we had not a single paper known to us that Southern people could read without having their feelings wounded by political insinuations and slurs, had more to do with calling the *Advocate* into existence than all other circumstances combined."[43] It is even true that Fanning, following the war, proposed a "consultation meeting" for southern Christians only, as we noted in Chapter 4.[44] Further, many southerners, for years following the war, clearly blended their theology with their sectional prejudices. Harrell cites as a case in point Thomas R. Burnett's assertion that "we know the doctrine advocated by them [writers in the largely northern *Christian Standard*] comes from the *North*. It is neither scriptural nor *Southern*, and is not suited to Southern people. But it is the determination of the *Standard* and its *Northern* allies . . . to force the new things upon the churches of this section."[45]

Harrell contends that when Fanning and Lipscomb opposed their northern brothers and sisters following the war, they "were making a thinly veiled appeal for backing to the supporters of the lost cause."[46] I would suggest that such a reading is shortsighted, however, because it obscures the significance of the sectarian tradition that Fanning and Lipscomb inherited from Barton Stone and his cadre of preachers in Middle Tennessee in the early years of the nineteenth century.

One of the central themes of this book — that there were two kinds of sectarianism present in the movement from the beginning — will help us gain perspective on this problem. Those who followed Alexander Campbell and built their sectarian house on the foundation of postmillennial optimism, Baconian rationalism, and the "biblical pattern" could hardly avoid confusing their religious faith with political and sectional prejudices. After all, there was nothing in their theology that explicitly stood in judgment on the world or their culture. To the contrary, Campbell's postmillennial outlook encouraged such confusion, because it suggested that the prevailing culture was at least compatible with the kingdom of God and was perhaps even the vessel on which God's kingdom would arrive.

But there was another sectarian tradition in this movement, a tradition that stood in judgment on this world and all its achievements — the tradition of Barton W. Stone, which profoundly influenced Fanning and Lipscomb and a host of other members of Churches of Christ in Middle Tennessee and throughout the South.

This is the point we must bear in mind when interpreting the rhetoric of both Fanning and Lipscomb during and after the war. For while one might conceivably construe their rhetoric as essentially southern and prejudicial, opposing northern Christians because they were Yankee sympathizers, one might also understand their rhetoric in light of their allegiance to the kingdom of God, which stood in judgment, they felt, on political activities of all kinds.

Lipscomb tells us that he arrived at his conclusion regarding the illegitimacy of all civil government "early in life," long before the Civil War.[47] He also made a point of stating his belief that the government of the Confederacy was as fully in rebellion against God as the government of the United States. "*Every man* who voted to bring on or perpetuate that war, was just as guilty before God as the men who actively participated in it. . . . The same is true of *every man* that supports and maintains human government."[48] In fact, when the southern civic faith celebrated the Confederate veteran in a variety of organizations and activities during the 1880s and 1890s, Lipscomb and others on the *Advocate* staff resolutely stood against such celebrations on the grounds that they promoted immorality, crime, and the "principles of war."[49] In 1861, Fanning ventured the opinion that, from a strictly political viewpoint, northerners and southerners simply could not "live together" and that if granted the right of revolution, "we doubt not the civil right of citizens South to resist to the last extremity." But Fanning, characteristically, had no interest in his "civil right" in that regard; he preferred instead to speak of his responsibilities as a citizen in the kingdom of God. "Christianity . . . is so transcendently superior to civil institutions," he wrote, "that members of the church can heartily cooperate, religiously, under antipodal civil governments, and they should not, indeed, be the least influenced by political struggles. . . . As religionists, they should know neither north nor south."[50]

Perhaps even more telling, Lipscomb reflected in 1881 on the brutal nature of civil governments in comparison with the peaceable kingdom of God:

> In the beginning of the late strife that so fearfully desolated our country, much was said about "our enemies." I protested constantly that I had not a single enemy, and was not an enemy to a single man North of the Ohio river. I had never been brought into collision with one — but very few knew such a person as myself existed. . . . Yet, these thousands and hundreds of thousands who knew not each other . . . were made enemies to each other and thrown into fierce and bloody strife, were embued with the spirit of destruction one toward the other, through the instrumentality of human governments.[51]

When Fanning and Lipscomb, therefore, criticized their northern counterparts "who believed that political resolutions are the Gospel," one may well violate their intentions if one argues only that they were "making a thinly veiled appeal . . . to the supporters of the lost cause." They may well have appealed to sectional prejudices, for they were human and surely they felt the pain of war. But they also criticized their northern counterparts because these northerners had participated in politics and had confused political considerations with the gospel.

When Lipscomb indicated that he and Fanning had resurrected the *Advocate* following the war because there was "not a single paper known to us that Southern people could read without having their feelings wounded by political insinuations and slurs," he may well have betrayed a sectional prejudice, but he also expressed his conviction that incendiary political rhetoric was altogether alien to the long-standing apolitical tradition of Churches of Christ in Middle Tennessee. Likewise, Fanning may have reflected sectional sentiments when he proposed a "consultation meeting" for southern Christians only, but he also recognized that Christians in the South, who stood in the separatist tradition of Barton W. Stone, shared a perspective that was largely foreign to Christians further north, schooled in the optimistic, postmillennial perspectives of Alexander Campbell. Nothing made these differences more apparent to Fanning and Lipscomb than the Civil War itself.

Does this mean that social factors played no role in shaping the Stone-Fanning-Lipscomb tradition? By no means. Harrell is absolutely correct in pointing out the importance of economic deprivation in shaping the tradition (a point we noted in our consideration of Benjamin Franklin). But poverty was a factor for decades prior to the Civil War.[52] In Chapter 5, we saw how poverty plagued both Stone and many of his corps of preachers in the early nineteenth century and how, in fact, they viewed poverty as a Christian virtue. This strong bias against wealth characterized the Stone tradition throughout the nineteenth century. Fanning, for example, asserted that "churches formed of the wealthy, speculative, and idle are little more than synagogues of Satan."[53] And Lipscomb recalled that Fanning established Franklin College specifically for the "common working people," not for the "children of wealth."[54] In 1847, Fanning specifically advised his students to avoid careers in law, medicine, the military, or merchandising but commended teaching, preaching, farming, and working with their hands. Ten years later, in 1857, Fanning flatly stated that "all classes not versed in the arts of industry are beyond the reach of the gospel of Christ." Celebrating the simple yeoman farmer, Fanning suggested that while it was sadly the case that "many of the poor . . . are too degraded to be reached by the gospel of Christ," it was also the case that "most of the rich are too much under the influence of the flesh to open their hearts for the entrance of the word."[55]

Much the same can be said of David Lipscomb, who directed his favor far more toward the poor than toward the working classes. And yet Lipscomb himself was not a poor man, having inherited substantial means from a moderately wealthy father.[56] This would seem to suggest that his bias in favor of the poor had more to do with the religious tradition in which he had been nurtured than with his own economic background.[57] In fact, Lipscomb reported that, from an early age, he took as a model for his own life one Madison Love, "a poor shingle-maker" who preached and baptized over five thousand people in the course of his life.[58]

At the same time, there can be little doubt that the poverty and suffering the Civil War brought to the South intensified Lipscomb's bias toward the poor. More than this, the tragedy of the war intensified the entire apocalyptic-separatist worldview in which his bias toward the poor ultimately was rooted. When Lipscomb was only twenty-four years old, for example, he defied the traditions of both Stone and Fanning in a speech he delivered to the Alumni Society of Franklin College on July 4, 1855. He praised the American government as "the first political fruit of Christianity," and went on to argue that "every patriot lover of liberty [should] accept, and jealously preserve inviolable, the franchises of freedom as the gifts of God. We would especially have every American freeman approach the ballot box of his country as the sacramental altar of his God — with bared feet and uncovered head, conscious that he treads upon holy ground."[59] And five years later, in 1860, Lipscomb did cast his vote for John Bell, the presidential candidate of the Constitutional Union Party.[60] Yet, by the close of the Civil War, Lipscomb had returned to the tradition of his forebears and advised his people not to vote.

His return to this tradition, clearly influenced by the ordeal of war, doubtless intensified his long-standing rejection of wealth and his concern for the poor. Shortly after the close of the war, when the American Christian Missionary Society issued a hymnbook that Lipscomb considered more fit for the wealthy than for the poor, he complained bitterly.

> Almost three times the bulk of the former book, it may answer well the needs of city congregations, stationed ministers and pastors, and the wealthy who ride to church in carriages and similar equipages. . . . [But] to the great masses who must go to the meeting house on foot, and at best on horseback, to the true, earnest evangelist, who . . . in apostolic style, goes to the poor of the earth, to the offcast neglected places of our backwoods, with his staff in hand, and often times without purse or change of garments, . . . it is ill-adapted.

In Lipscomb's view, all aspects of the church — its books, its houses, and its customs — should be adapted "to the necessities of God's elect — the poor of this world, rich in faith toward God."[61] Two months later, Lipscomb's rhetoric on behalf of the poor was even stronger. The church, he proclaimed, "is the especial legacy of God to the poor of the earth. . . . It is the rich that are out of their element in Christ's Church."[62] As late as 1906, Lipscomb's position remained unchanged: "Christ," he wrote, "intended his religion for the poor, [and] adapted it to their necessities."[63]

Members of Churches of Christ throughout Middle Tennessee and beyond doubtless appreciated Lipscomb's rhetoric, for they had been poor before the war, and they were poorer still afterward. E. W. Sewell recalled in 1907 that by war's end members of Churches of Christ "had seen the emptiness and uncertainty of earthly institutions and earthly wisdom, and were ready to look up to God and to trust him, his word and appointments, to an extent never before manifested in this country." As a result, wrote Sewell, "We have never witnessed such general, such almost universal, interest in the Christian religion as was almost everywhere manifested for some years after the war. There was scarcely a meeting held that there were not from half a dozen to thirty or forty additions, and that, too, in one week's time."[64]

Lipscomb continued to favor the poor and to advocate their causes for the rest of his life. During the gilded age, he registered strong criticism of such barons of industry as John D. Rockefeller and Cornelius Vanderbilt, and he spoke regularly on behalf of labor and of the causes of working people.[65] His overriding concern continued to be the interests of the kingdom of God, and by 1906 his convictions regarding the preeminent place of the poor in that kingdom remained firm. "Christ," he flatly declared, "intended his religion for the poor."[66]

Conclusion

Social forces clearly shaped and molded David Lipscomb in a variety of ways, but on the whole they seem to have done so in ways that reinforced the theological tradition of Stone and Fanning that had nurtured Lipscomb since the days of his youth. Further, it is safe to say that no one kept that tradition more fully alive in the late nineteenth century than did David Lipscomb. This is why, by the late nineteenth century, Lipscomb stood so completely at odds with the Disciples of Christ who perpetuated the Campbellian tradition of postmillennial optimism regarding this world and human progress. Lipscomb held to his conviction that the kingdom of God would "break into pieces" all the kingdoms of this earth, while the editor of the Disciples-oriented *Christian Oracle* argued for "a very intimate relation between the advancing influence of Christian nations and the advancement of the kingdom of God."[67] J. C. Tully typified the Campbellite/Disciples faith in progress when he asked, "Will the earnest desire in the hearts of men for freedom from the shackles of the past ever fade away and die?" and then rejoiced,

> Never, never, no never. The forces are going forward, not back. . . . So rapidly has the spirit of the age come upon us, that it may be affirmed of a truth: We are not in the same world, although on the same planet, with those who lived in the last century. We live in the age of progress in civilization and in all things which, in human judgment, minister to its perfection.[68]

These two opposing worldviews, more than anything else, stood at the heart of the debates over missionary societies and instrumental music in the late nineteenth century, at least so far as the Churches of Christ in Middle Tennessee were concerned. And the difference between those worldviews finally helped create, by 1906, two well-defined denominations: Churches of Christ and Disciples.

Lipscomb's commitment to the kingdom of God sheds light on the genius of his restoration vision and helps explain why he took the positions he did on missionary societies, the use of instrumental music in worship, and a host of other issues. To perceive Lipscomb as nothing more than a legalist committed to restoring the forms and structures of the primitive church is to miss the heart of the man. Lipscomb was a legalist, to be sure, but his legalism pointed beyond itself in two directions: first, to Eden before the fall, when God's sovereign rule prevailed in sublime perfection, and second, to God's inevitable, final, and future rule over all the earth, when the perfections of Eden would be restored.[69] He viewed the church between these times of perfection as the finite manifestation of God's kingdom on earth. And because he viewed the restoration of the primordial and Edenic rule of God as absolutely certain, he insisted that Christians should live their lives and order their churches according to God's law in its every detail. In this sense, Lipscomb's efforts to restore biblical forms of worship and biblical patterns of church organization all pointed beyond themselves to the restoration of the kingdom of God in "the glorious millennial morn."

In this light, we begin to see how Lipscomb managed to hold together in a single movement the modernizing heirs of Alexander Campbell and the antimodern heirs of Barton W. Stone. The heirs of Stone fully understood the apocalyptic context of Lipscomb's legalism and ethics. They recognized his rejection of instrumental music in worship and his refusal to vote as two sides of the same apocalyptic coin. On the other hand, those who rooted their legalism in the biblicism of Alexander Campbell were content to ignore Lipscomb's apocalyptic thrust as well as his position on civil government. It was enough for them that Lipscomb railed against departures from the "ancient order" among the emerging Disciples of Christ. His refusal to vote was an idiosyncrasy they could tolerate. The main thing was his fidelity to "the old paths."

During Lipscomb's lifetime, however, more and more of his people abandoned the antimodern, apocalyptic vision of Stone for the rational, progress-oriented outlook of Alexander Campbell. Lipscomb acknowledged this shift in 1880 when he lamented that a majority of the readers of the *Gospel Advocate* did not share his antipolitical position.[70] Those who made this shift were key players in the evolution of Churches of Christ in the twentieth century from sect to denomination. They continued to embrace the sectarian vision of the early Alexander Campbell, but they were no longer persuaded by the apocalyptic sectarianism of Barton W. Stone — and without the restraining influence of that tradition, their movement toward denominational status was inevitable. On the other hand, those who continued to embrace the apocalyptic, separatist, and apolitical perspectives of Stone, Fanning, and Lipscomb would soon be cast from the mainstream as heretics. That process began during World War I, as we shall see in Chapter 7.

PART II

CHURCHES OF CHRIST:
THE MAKING OF A
DENOMINATION

CHAPTER 7

A Shifting Worldview:
The Premillennial Controversy

By the end of the nineteenth century, the Church of Christ had solidified its status as a full-fledged sect, standing in judgment on denominations as well as on the values of the larger culture. By World War I, however, the Church of Christ had embarked on its journey from sect to denomination. Heated disputes over three issues — premillennialism, institutionalism, and liberalism — directed the course of that journey throughout the twentieth century. In this chapter we will explore the great controversy over premillennialism that virtually consumed Churches of Christ from 1915 to 1940 and placed them squarely on the path that led to denominational status.

James A. Harding

During the waning years of the nineteenth century and the early years of the twentieth, no one within Churches of Christ embraced premillennial eschatology with more fervor than did James A. Harding, cofounder and first president of the Nashville Bible School.[1] But in many ways, premillennialism was not Harding's principal concern. His formal eschatology reflected a deeper worldview that pervaded and sustained his theology at every significant point. Simply put, that worldview consisted of his conviction that he belonged to the kingdom of God rather than to any institution or kingdom reflecting human contrivance and ingenuity. This conviction created within Harding a level of trust in God that awed or baffled many of his contemporaries. R. C. Bell, one of his students at the Nashville Bible School, later wrote that "Brother Harding possessed more fully than any other Christian I have known Paul's absolute confidence and unqualified trust in God's promise to supply every need."[2] Harding refused to rely on salaries, contracts, or other measures that might have guaranteed financial security, and gave away much — perhaps most — of the material wealth that came his way. He was convinced, as he put it, that God would supply all his needs.

In many ways, Harding represented the epitome of the apocalyptic tradition that had flourished in the Mid-South for a hundred years. He refused to place faith in human institutions, human schemes, or human progress, trusting instead not only that God would triumph over all the earth in the last days but also that God would care for his children in the here and now, removing any need to rely on human accomplishments. Perhaps more than any other person in this tradition, Harding made it clear that premillennial eschatology was merely a facet — an expression — of a worldview defined chiefly by faith in the overarching providence and kingdom of God.

Harding's almost otherworldly allegiance to the kingdom of God and trust in God's providential care affected his views on a number of key issues in the tradition. For one thing, it undergirded his opposition to missionary societies. He maintained that loyalty to missionary societies reflected trust in human schemes and institutions rather than in the kingdom and providence of God. "Every

A noted turn-of-the-century educator among Churches of Christ, James A. Harding (1848-1922) cofounded the Nashville Bible School in 1891, served as the first president of that institution, and then established Potter Bible College in Bowling Green, Kentucky, in 1901. Harding was especially known for his trust in the grace and providence of God.
(Photo courtesy David Lipscomb University)

missionary society on earth," he stated flatly, "is built on unbelief."[3] And when the Nashville Bible School that he had served for many years finally moved in the late nineteenth century to incorporate under a board of trustees in order to ensure that the property would always be used for the purposes for which the institution was founded, Harding strongly objected. "I could not work as a teacher of the doctrine of Christ under such control," he wrote. "In doing the work of Christ, a Christian should not submit himself to be directed and controlled by any other authority than that of Christ, nor should he belong to any other institution for the advancement of the Lord's cause than the church of God."[4]

In addition, Harding — like Fanning, Franklin, and many others before him — strongly warned against located preachers who relied on regular salaries for their support. Harding maintained that such preachers rebuffed the promise and providence of God. He idealized both the itinerant preacher and the system of "mutual edification" whereby a variety of resident males in a given congregation took up the leadership of all aspects of the worship service, including preaching. This had been the practice of Churches of Christ for most of the nineteenth century and, we should recall, was the model for which Tolbert Fanning argued so strenuously in the aftermath of the Jesse Ferguson affair. When a Texas preacher asserted in 1883 that "the brethren in Texas know that the churches that pay their preachers best will always have the best preachers," Harding was stunned. He knew, he said, that more and more men were preaching for hire, "but I was not prepared to find that even one of them would boldly, in public prints, approve of such a course."[5]

It is precisely in this context that one finds an early, major shift among Churches of Christ toward institutional and denominational status. In 1910, a full-blown written debate on this issue erupted between Harding and L. S. White, who preached for the Pearl and Bryan congregation in Dallas. There can be little doubt that both the larger shift and the debate were, at least to some degree, regionally and economically inspired. After all, while the shift toward the "pastor system" occurred chiefly among people of greater means, it also occurred mostly west of Nashville and especially in Texas. The Nashville churches, rooted in the apocalyptic outlook of Harding and Lipscomb, remained firmly committed to the older system of itinerant preaching and mutual edification. Harding reported that the Nashville Bible School had sent perhaps 125 preachers into the field. Fewer than a dozen of these, he thought, favored the pastor system. Further, not a single teacher at the Nashville Bible School supported this innovation. His own congregation, which met in the school's chapel, was "led in its meetings by its elders, who encourage every brother who will to take part in speaking, in prayer, or in song." In fact, he reported that "Nashville has a greater number of congregations that conduct their meetings without 'the pastor' than any other city in America, so far as I can learn."[6]

L. S. White, however, found the Nashville practice a scandal and an offense. He charged that it retarded not only the development of a strong corps of preachers in the United States but also the development of missions abroad. He argued that Harding's views were "doing untold harm."[7] White's chief concern was the growth and institutionalization of Churches of Christ, objectives that he felt could hardly be realized if churches remained tied to Harding's apocalypticism.

At the heart of this debate, however, was a dispute not simply over the pastor system, or even over institutionalization, but over two radically differing world-views which, to a significant degree, reflected the circumstances in which Harding and White lived. In Harding, one finds a poor man, governed almost entirely by the sectarian and apocalyptic perspective that had long characterized Churches of Christ in his region. In White, one finds a man governed by hard-nosed prag-matism and a rigorous doctrine of self-reliance — the sort of attributes that characterized people living on the rough-and-tumble Texas frontier.

Harding professed that

> for thirty-six years I have endeavored to follow the directions of Jesus literally. I have avoided the accumulation of property. There have been few, if any, times in these thirty-six years that I have had money enough to bury me if I had died. I have owned two horses, at different times, and a buggy. I have owned two cows, at different times, and a calf. . . . I doubt if there has been a time in these thirty-six years when all of my possessions would have brought as much as five hundred dollars if they had been sold at public auction.[8]

This, in Harding's view, was virtue: a Christian should get by on as little as possible and give the surplus to the poor.[9]

But White considered Harding's arguments to be out of touch with reality — or at least out of touch with the reality of early twentieth-century Texas culture. When Harding suggested it was wrong to "lay up 'treasures on earth,'" where moth and rust doth corrupt, White retorted, "I insist that nothing will 'rust or corrupt' as long as it is used. . . . When we have money, or other property, as long as we use it to the glory of God, it will never 'rust or corrupt.'" Further, White totally rejected the notion that God might supernaturally pro-vide apart from human arrangements and foresight. "Creation began in miracle," he said, "but ended in natural order." And in that natural order, he insisted, there is only one way to secure the necessities of life: hard work. In addition, White conceded that while Jesus did indeed feed the poor through miracles, "after the Church was established the disciples were taught to relieve people by giving of their means." And while Jesus taught his disciples "to 'pray for their daily bread,' after the Church was established we are taught 'to do your own business, and to work with your hands. . . .'" When Harding suggested that the reason "David never saw the righteous forsaken, nor his seed begging bread" was that he had trusted in God, White disagreed. David's prosperity had nothing to do with trusting God, he insisted, but everything to do with the great, general prosperity that characterized his age. "Had David lived at a later period, he would have seen the righteous forsaken."[10]

In L. S. White, one finds the pragmatic, progressive primitivism of Alexander Campbell fully triumphant and complementing the circumstances in which he lived. Preoccupied as he was with the need to build churches in the growing city of Dallas, he rejected out of hand any possibility of divine providence in his own time and place and focused his gaze entirely on the pragmatic possibilities of the here and now. Harding's apocalyptic frame of reference made no sense to him at all.[11]

Though Harding fully embraced the apocalyptic, sectarian mentality of the Stone-Lipscomb tradition, he also stood squarely within the sectarian tradition of the radicalized *Christian Baptist*. We see the latter heritage in his confident assertion that "our business is to fight everything and everybody that impedes the success of our Master's cause."[12] He was especially eager to debate and fight those within his own fellowship who refused to take a stand on issues such as instrumental music. One such man was T. B. Larimore, a popular Church of Christ preacher widely known for his kind and gracious spirit. Because Larimore refused to involve himself in the controversy over instrumental music, however, Harding in 1900 refused to permit him to speak at the Nashville Bible School, of which Harding was president at the time. "He will never come here to lecture to the boys, as long as I am president of the school, till he takes a stand on the music question," Harding was reported to have said.[13]

As this incident suggests, Churches of Christ were still very much united in 1900 on the sectarian outlook bequeathed to them by the radicalized *Christian Baptist*. But the other source of the sectarian tradition — the apocalyptic outlook of Barton Stone — was slowly unraveling. In that regard, the Harding-White affair was but a prelude to a larger issue that would finally separate most Churches of Christ from their apocalyptic underpinnings and place them squarely on the road toward denominational standing. That issue was the great debate over premillennial eschatology.[14]

The R. H. Boll Affair

In 1915, and continuing for more than a third of a century, the emerging mainstream of Churches of Christ launched a sustained, and at times ferocious, attack against premillennial thinking of all kinds. The chief object of this attack for all those years was a mild-mannered German immigrant named Robert H. Boll, who enrolled in 1895 in the Nashville Bible School. There he studied under David Lipscomb and James A. Harding, from whom he learned the separatist and apocalyptic perspectives that had energized those in the Stone-Lipscomb tradition throughout the nineteenth century.

Stridently antimodern, Boll questioned whether "the boastful splendor of the twentieth century" and "the roar of its civilization" represented any serious progress at all. When the United States entered World War I in 1917, Boll

By virtue of his training at the Nashville Bible School, R. H. Boll (1875-1956) embraced an apocalpytic perspective that eventually turned in explicitly premillennial directions. For a full third of a century beginning in 1915, Boll was the acknowledged leader of the premillennial movement within Churches of Christ and the principal target of the campaign to destroy the premillennial sentiment.

counseled Christians to refuse to fight. He dismissed the notion that the war was "a struggle . . . to make the world safe for democracy" and grounded his pacifist counsel in the Stone-Lipscomb vision that the Christian does not belong to the kingdoms of this world.[15]

There is no question but that Boll had learned his apocalyptic lessons from his teachers at the old Nashville Bible School, but Harding appears to have been especially influential. Indeed, Harding viewed Boll in many respects as a model student and commented, "I wouldn't take a million dollars for him."[16]

Substantial evidence suggests that most — perhaps all — of the leaders of the premillennial movement in Churches of Christ came directly from the Stone-Lipscomb tradition. Such was the case with Stanford Chambers, who in 1908 cofounded and edited the *Christian Word and Work*, an important premillennial periodical issued first from New Orleans and later from Louisville, Kentucky, where Boll served as its editor.[17]

Chambers was born in 1877 and reared in Sullivan County, Indiana. Barton Stone had migrated to Illinois prior to the Civil War in order to emancipate his slaves, and many of his followers made similar moves north to Illinois and Indiana for the same reason.[18] It is not surprising therefore that Chambers, raised in one of the Stoneite communities that resulted from this migration, imagined well into his adulthood that practically everyone in Churches of Christ shared the premillennial position.[19]

Among the first indications he received that many in Churches of Christ opposed this view was the published debate between L. S. White of Dallas and Charles Taze Russell, founder of the Jehovah's Witnesses. Chambers "had no sympathy with Chas. T. Russell's theory," but he also reported that "I could not find in my Bible all that Brother White taught. But to my surprise his position met with general approval."[20]

Significantly, those in Churches of Christ who opposed the premillennial outlook routinely sought to discredit its proponents by labeling them "Russellites," implying that Russell's teachings had convinced them to adopt the position.[21] In the case of Boll and Chambers, this was pointedly not the case. Both men adopted the position after having "sat at the feet of Lipscomb, Harding, [J. N.] Armstrong, et al." at the Nashville Bible School.[22]

We should note, though, that Boll received only a basic apocalyptic frame of reference at the Nashville Bible School. He later expanded this apocalyptic outlook to include the dispensationalism of such protofundamentalists as Dwight L. Moody, Arno Gaebelein, Isaac M. Haldeman, Philip Mauro, James M. Gray, Reuben Torrey, W. E. Blackstone, and Cyrus I. Scofield — thereby developing a perspective that was altogether foreign to the nineteenth-century apocalyptic tradition of Churches of Christ.[23]

Perhaps in part because of the great faith that Harding and presumably even Lipscomb placed in Boll, the owners of the *Gospel Advocate* made Boll their front-page editor in 1909. For several years, Boll presented his apocalyptic and premillennial notions in the *Advocate,* until, in 1915, those ideas began to encounter stiff resistance from his fellow editors. The resistance grew so intense, in fact, that in December of that year Boll resigned from the *Advocate* staff and moved on to become editor of the previously mentioned *Word and Work,* which had recently moved from New Orleans to Louisville.

The ouster of Boll from the staff of the *Gospel Advocate* marked the beginning of a great war on premillennialism that preoccupied and sapped the energies of preachers and editors in the emerging mainstream of Churches of Christ until well into the 1940s. It seems clear that their rejection of apocalypticism reflects the final triumph of Alexander Campbell's rational, progressive primitivism over the Stone-Lipscomb tradition, precisely in the region where the Stone-Lipscomb tradition had exerted its greatest influence. But why? Why were Churches of Christ so concerned to destroy the premillennial sentiment when the mainspring of the Stone-Lipscomb side of that tradition had been anchored to a profoundly apocalyptic worldview throughout the nineteenth century? Why would they so completely cut themselves off from the wellsprings that had nourished them for over a hundred years?

Causes for the Decline of Apocalypticism

One is tempted to suggest that Churches of Christ made war on R. H. Boll because he had adopted a dispensational position with which they were largely unfamiliar. That explanation is inadequate, however, because dispensationalism was by no means the principal target of attack and because Churches of Christ rejected not just dispensationalism but the entire apocalyptic frame of reference. There are three more compelling reasons why Churches of Christ finally rejected the apocalyptic tradition.

Legalism versus Grace

First, Boll's premillennial eschatology was grounded in his understanding of the grace of God — a theme he cherished and often discussed. Indeed, the very notion of premillennialism suggests reliance on divine initiative. Increasingly, however, the mainstream of Churches of Christ had built its house on the foundation of human initiative and self-sufficiency inherited from Alexander Campbell. By the late nineteenth and early twentieth centuries, that mainstream had defined itself not only in terms of human initiative but also in terms of keeping God's law. To a tradition with so much invested in human initiative and an ability to keep the law, the grace-centered theology of R. H. Boll would represent an enormous threat. And so it did. Gregory Alan Tidwell has argued that the inability of the mainstream of Churches of Christ even to understand — much less appreciate — Boll's doctrine of grace was the principal reason for its complete rejection of the apocalyptic worldview.[24]

During the first half of the twentieth century, however, Boll was not the only person in Churches of Christ to maintain a serious understanding of God's grace. There were others as well, almost all descended from the Stone-Lipscomb tradition. The rift between the legal side and the grace-centered side of Churches of Christ grew increasingly wide during the 1930s and 1940s, a point we will consider at greater length in Chapter 8.

Primitivist Identity of Churches of Christ

Second, Boll's premillennial outlook completely undermined the prevailing identity of Churches of Christ in the early twentieth century — namely, the conviction that Churches of Christ were identical, in all essential respects, to the churches of the apostolic age.

As we have seen, many throughout the nineteenth century embraced this perspective. But developments in the early twentieth century rendered the outlook more important than ever before, to the point that it hardened into a rigid, all-pervading orthodoxy.

One of those developments occurred between roughly 1880 and 1906, when Churches of Christ underwent their bitter division from the Disciples. The Disciples retained most of the buildings and the majority of the wealthy and influential members, especially in urban settings. In effect, Churches of Christ were left to begin all over again. Angered and defensive, Churches of Christ increasingly embraced the conviction that they, and they alone, were the true church, descended from the days of the apostles.

Boll's emphasis on the grace of God clearly conflicted with such a view — as did the explicitly premillennial terms of Boll's eschatology. Boll argued that the church most assuredly was *not* the kingdom of God in its fullness of perfection, either in its Pentecost beginnings or in its modern manifestation. He insisted that the kingdom would come only in the last days, when Christ would rule the earth with his saints. In the meantime, the church was a manifestation of that kingdom but was in no sense perfect or complete.[25] By and large, this had been the position of James A. Harding and David Lipscomb in the previous generation, but few were prepared to accept that position now. J. C. McQuiddy, publisher of the *Gospel Advocate*, typified the mainstream response when he charged in 1919 that Boll's doctrine "belittles the church of Christ" and was "calculated to destroy every congregation of disciples."[26] Partisans of the exclusivist self-understanding of Churches of Christ were still railing against Boll's views in the late 1930s. For example, N. B. Hardeman, one of the church's most popular preachers during that era, told an audience in Nashville in 1938 that premillennial eschatology made "the church of Christ absolutely an accident."[27]

Moreover, Boll provided a concrete demonstration of his own rejection of the sectarian exclusivism of Churches of Christ when he routinely ran articles from such early fundamentalists as Gaebelein, Mauro, Torrey, and Blackstone in the pages of his journal *Word and Work*. While most in the emerging mainstream of Churches of Christ sympathized with the fundamentalists' fight against modernism, they nonetheless stood separate and apart from the formal fundamentalist movement for two reasons: they viewed the various denominations that fundamentalism represented as false churches, and they opposed the premillennial sentiments held by many in the fundamentalist camp as simply unbiblical. Many viewed Boll's fraternization with fundamentalists as nothing short of scandalous.

Social Respectability, World War I, and Pacifism

The third issue that helped erode the apocalyptic viewpoint in this period was related to two factors: the loss of cultural respectability Churches of Christ experienced in the aftermath of their separation from the Disciples in 1906 and the entry of the United States into World War I in 1917.

Simply put, Churches of Christ, in their separation from the Disciples, lost not only thousands of members and hundreds of church buildings but also their social standing in scores of communities from Tennessee to Texas. In city after city where they once had boasted strong and prosperous congregations, they now started essentially from scratch in tents and storefront churches with only a handful of members, who, according to the records, were mostly poor. In 1940, for example, J. N. Armstrong recalled, "Not only did the defection leave us without schools, but those who introduced the music carried with them, also, the best church property, most of the wealth, big businesses, banking, and so forth. All colleges, scholarships, church property, wealth, and big businesses became the inherited asset of the Christian Church."[28]

Then, in little more than a decade following the division, the United States entered World War I. Popular and government pressure on Americans to support the war was intense, and those who refused support became the objects of scorn, ridicule, and harassment. Their division from the Disciples, costing them both members and property, already had relegated Churches of Christ to a degree of social marginality. Retention of their historic commitment to pacifism would have marginalized them yet further. Facing that prospect, many members of Churches of Christ elected to support the American involvement in the war.

However — and here one finds the fundamental issue — they could not support the war and at the same time cling to the apocalyptic/pacifistic perspective of the Stone-Lipscomb tradition. To support the war, they needed a theology far more progressive, far more amenable to militarism, far more centered on the concerns of this world, and far less focused on the coming kingdom of God. Such a theology was readily at hand. The rational, progressive primitivism of Alexander Campbell was as much a part of their heritage as the apocalypticism of Barton W. Stone. All that remained was for the former to triumph over the latter.

This suggests that R. H. Boll, consumed as he was with sectarian, pre-millennial perspectives, was simply the wrong man in the wrong place at the wrong time. As pacifism grew increasingly objectionable to Churches of Christ throughout the war, apocalypticism — which provided the theological foundation for pacifism — came increasingly under attack.

Several other factors also facilitated the erosion of pacifism.[29] First, pacifism had always been a minority position among Churches of Christ, though pacifists were especially strong in Middle Tennessee. Not surprisingly, then, the record on pacifism among Churches of Christ in World War I was mixed. On the one hand, many members and congregations petitioned the government for conscientious objector status, and a number of young men from the church faced prison terms for refusing to support the war effort.[30] E. A. Elam wrote in 1918 that "thousands in the church of Christ . . . cannot conscientiously engage in carnal warfare."[31] On the other hand, J. H. Lawson, who was intimately involved with evangelistic work both at Camp Travis near San Antonio and Camp Bowie near Fort Worth, registered his observation that there were "thousands of members of the church" in the army.[32]

Second, among those families that held pacifism as an article of faith, a new generation of young people during World War I simply failed to share their elders' convictions. Many sons of strongly pacifist families participated in the war, including sons of J. M. McCaleb, J. C. McQuiddy, L. R. Sewell, and Jesse Kling-man.[33] The participation of their sons in the armed services no doubt prompted many of the older generation to rethink lifelong positions. Further, the death of David Lipscomb in 1917 deprived the younger generation of the most articulate defender of the pacifist position the church had known for half a century.

Third, the growth of Churches of Christ in Texas, far from the Middle Tennessee heartland of the pacifist and apolitical sentiments, also contributed to this change. David Lipscomb himself, reporting on a tour of Texas in 1872, wrote that political strife "is the one great cause of inactivity of the churches throughout Texas," and that Christians there "are more ready to turn politician — run for sheriff — the legislature — become post-master or prosecuting attorneys, clerks, etc., etc., than they are in the older settled countries."[34] By the early twentieth century, two of the most powerful figures in Texas Churches of Christ were G. H. P. Showalter, editor of the Austin-based *Firm Foundation,* and Jesse P. Sewell, president of Abilene Christian College. In June of 1918, Showalter argued that any Christian who was a patriot in peacetime was obligated to be a patriot in wartime as well, and therefore "should the more carefully discharge his duty as a citizen now."[35] And Sewell, urged in 1916 to run for the Texas legislature, declined but commented, "I have always felt a deep interest in the affairs of State, and as a citizen have taken considerable interest in public matters." We should not be surprised to learn, then, that in the fall of 1918 Abilene Christian College established a Student Army Training Corps in which students received military training along with academic studies and became eligible, upon graduation, for officers' training.[36] There were clear and profound cultural differences between the churches in Texas and the churches in Middle Tennessee.

Fourth, the sheer power of wartime propaganda and the tremendous pressure exerted by the United States government to rally support for the war, epitomized by the Espionage and Sedition Acts of 1917-1918, hastened the demise of the pacifist sentiment among Churches of Christ.[37] In fact, the United States Attorney General for Middle Tennessee, Lee Douglas, threatened J. C. McQuiddy, publisher of the *Gospel Advocate,* with arrest if he continued to publish "seditious" articles in the *Advocate* that discouraged "registration of young men under the Selective Service . . . Act."[38]

McQuiddy forthwith tempered his rhetoric, advised conscientious objec-tors to "be careful that they do not say anything against the government of the United States during the present crisis," and counseled each Christian to "manifest his love for his country and . . . [to] show his patriotism in every way possible without violating his conscientious convictions."[39] McQuiddy's new course apparently satisfied the attorney general, who later wrote McQuiddy that "I came to respect you as a man for your sincere religious convictions and your fine patriotism."[40] Not everyone, however, was so kind to McQuiddy. For ex-ample, J. N. Armstrong, perhaps the leading defender of the Stone-Lipscomb tradition in that period, criticized McQuiddy severely: "I believe he . . . has never accepted the antiwar position for Christians, but he knew the Advocate had so taught. . . . So he tried to keep in line with the life long policy of the paper, while all the time his own convictions were contrary."[41] Shortly after the incident with the attorney general, McQuiddy simply put a stop to all promotion of pacifism and all criticism of militarism on the pages of the *Advocate*.

The fifth factor that helped erode pacifism among Churches of Christ was the popular understanding of Germany as both demonic and barbaric and America as the last defense of Christian civilization. George Marsden has pointed out that this mythic perspective helped transform an assortment of conservative Christians, many of whom were explicitly pacifist, into proponents of a patriotic form of militant fundamentalism by the end of the war.[42] Much the same thing happened among Churches of Christ. C. A. Buchanan typified this outlook when he charged following the war that "Germany armed herself and set out to rob and plunder the whole world, . . . and the only way to punish her was by armed

Publisher of the *Gospel Advocate* J. C. McQuiddy (1858-1924) contributed in important ways to the collapse of the apocalyptic/pacifist heritage of Churches of Christ. When Lee Douglas, United States Attorney General for middle Tennessee during World War I, threatened McQuiddy with arrest for publishing articles on pacifism, McQuiddy backed down, then opened the *Advocate* to articles hostile to the apocalyptic orientation.

(Photo courtesy Disciples of Christ Historical Society)

force. . . . The United States acted as a legal and divinely authorized agent."[43] Likewise, M. C. Kurfees, one of the *Advocate*'s editors, proclaimed that the war had "been a contest between barbarism and civilization."[44]

This is not to say that the pacifist sentiment simply vanished from Churches of Christ at large during World War I, however. Its power had been so strong for so many for so long that it continued in many locales as a formal orthodoxy until World War II, when it suffered another major decline. From that time on, a gradual disintegration of the pacifist sentiment persisted until, by the time of the Vietnam War in the 1960s, pacifism had almost entirely vanished from the fellowship.

Demise of the Apocalyptic Perspective

But if pacifism did not vanish altogether, what did disappear, by and large, was the basic Stone-Lipscomb worldview that invigorated the pacifist sentiment. Humpty Dumpty–like, the themes of apocalypticism, separation from the world, and reliance on the power of God rather than on human wit and ingenuity — all these themes took a great fall, and all the preachers and all the editors were unable to piece them together again with any semblance of coherence. For the most part, no one even tried.

The demise of the Stone-Lipscomb worldview was most apparent in the attitude of the editorial staff of the *Gospel Advocate* toward Woodrow Wilson's League of Nations. For example, while Stone, Fanning, Lipscomb, and Harding had all held that human institutions were powerless to renovate the world and that God, at his initiative alone, would bring the millennial dawn, J. C. McQuiddy now suggested that the League might do God's bidding: "I ask those who are pessimistic, I ask those who are fighting the policy of our President [regarding the League], how do they know but that this is the time of which the prophet prophesied and that the day is soon to dawn when nation shall not lift up sword against nation?"[45] M. C. Kurfees was even more explicit. "Who knows," he asked, "but . . . [that the League's] adoption may be a long step toward the glad time when the nations 'shall beat their swords into plowshares, and their spears into pruning hooks;' and when 'nation shall not lift up sword against nation, neither shall they learn war any more.' "[46] Boll and his followers, on the other hand, viewed the League as the prophesied "last form of the Gentile power . . . that men are looking for as the Golden Age but which God . . . shows us will be the climax of all the world's great wickedness."[47]

It is clear that a major change overtook the Stone-Lipscomb tradition in general and the *Gospel Advocate* in particular during the World War I era. The heart and soul of that change involved a fundamental reappraisal of human potential. The issue of pacifism was simply the most important symbol of that reassessment. Throughout the nineteenth century, poverty and social marginality coupled with a lingering Calvinist perspective had informed the basic outlook of the Stone-Lipscomb tradition, prompting those in that tradition to exalt the sovereignty of

God and to downgrade the potential of human wit, human ingenuity, and human institutions to achieve any lasting good. In a word, the Stone-Lipscomb tradition was fundamentally *pessimistic* about human possibilities.

But by World War I, it was precisely that pessimism regarding human potential that the editors of the *Gospel Advocate* sought to undermine. "It is not Christlike, it is not manly, it is not noble," McQuiddy complained in 1919,

> to sit down and whine that it is impossible to bring about such a condition [as the end of all war]. . . . The same spirit would never have broken the Hindenburg line; the same spirit would never have conquered Germany and made her sue for peace. . . . The same spirit will never overcome the world, the flesh, and the devil, and bring the crown that is sure to come to the faithful.[48]

In fact, recognizing the problems that the old-time pessimism posed for those who sought acculturation, the editors of the *Gospel Advocate* featured in 1916 a lengthy symposium entitled "Is the World Growing Better?" With few exceptions, participants answered in the affirmative. F. W. Smith of Nashville, a frequent contributor to the *Advocate*, offered a typical assessment:

> The pessimist sees only the dark side of every picture. If he were to gaze through the mighty telescope upon the mighty sun, he would see only the *black spots*. . . . To deny that the world is growing better in some ways is to deny what our very eyes can see, our ears can hear, and our hearts can feel. In fact, it would be to say that Christianity is a failure.[49]

Precisely for this reason, several *Advocate* writers found serious fault with themes that stood at the very heart of apocalypticism and premillennialism. Smith, again, was typical. He argued that the traditional Calvinist understanding of the grace of God "comes as near making a nonentity [*sic*] of mankind as anything ever invented by the wild imagination of man . . . [and] leaves man a hopeless wretch."[50]

The confrontation between these two perspectives — the cultural pessimism of R. H. Boll and the cultural optimism of the *Gospel Advocate* — reached a climax of sorts in 1928 in a major debate between Boll and H. Leo Boles, president of David Lipscomb College. Boles contended that "good men are getting better and better . . . , Brother Boll and I . . . , if faithful to the Lord, are growing better and better; and as the Lord's people grow better, conditions in the world are better." To argue otherwise, Boles charged, "makes the church an absolute and monumental failure on the earth." Boll simply stuck to his premillennial guns: "The one and only goal of hope set before the Christian is the Lord's return."[51]

F. L. Rowe, publisher of the Cincinnati-based *Christian Leader*, may have embodied in his outlook the greatest irony of the anti-Boll crusade. Standing resolute in a movement that prided itself on its allegiance to the Bible, Rowe groused, "I sometimes wish that some Bible House would get up a Bible or a

H. Leo Boles (1874-1946) served as president of the Nashville Bible School from 1913 to 1917 and of David Lipscomb College from 1917 to 1920 and again from 1923 to 1932. In 1928, a published debate between Boles and R. H. Boll on prophecy and premillennialism gained widespread attention in Churches of Christ and contributed to the final collapse of the premillennial movement. (Photo courtesy Disciples of Christ Historical Society)

New Testament, and leave the Book of Revelation off. . . . The twenty-six books preceding Revelation have everything we need in the way of faith and practice."[52]

From Sect to Denomination: Transition at Harding College

By the 1930s, those in Churches of Christ intent on thrusting premillennialists from their fellowship focused their guns not only on R. H. Boll but also on tiny Harding College in Searcy, Arkansas. J. N. Armstrong, Harding's president from 1924 to 1936, was the son-in-law of James A. Harding and, other than R. H. Boll, was perhaps the most prominent early twentieth-century representative of the apocalyptic piety of the Stone-Lipscomb tradition. A former student at the Nashville Bible School, Armstrong professed in 1903 that Lipscomb and Harding had there "impart[ed] to me 'principles and spiritual truths that enter into and affect and control' your own lives, and thus I was made a new man — your child."[53] By 1928, one observer wrote that "no man among us . . . stays so much with the 'old Nashville Bible School spirit' fostered by D. Lipscomb and

James A. Harding as J. N. Armstrong."[54] It was because of Armstrong's reputation in this regard that, by 1934, those determined to drive premillennialism from Churches of Christ made him one of the principal objects of their attack.

Over and again, Armstrong denied that he upheld premillennial eschatology.[55] At the same time, however, he staunchly maintained the apocalyptic worldview that characterized his teachers. He repeatedly affirmed his conviction that two principles of government vied with one another for control of the world — human government and the rule of Jesus Christ — and he proclaimed his undivided allegiance to the kingdom of Christ, who he believed would ultimately triumph over all human kingdoms and all civic governments and extend his reign over all the earth.[56] This notion, for Armstrong, was not a mere theory or a matter of theological speculation; it formed the basis for a life of radical discipleship that included, among other things, his refusal to participate in human warfare. One should recall, for example, that it was Armstrong who so severely criticized J. C.

J. N. Armstrong (1870-1944), a graduate of the Nashville Bible School and the son-in-law of James A. Harding, embodied the apocalyptic perspective perhaps more completely than any other leader among mainstream Churches of Christ in the early twentieth century. Armstrong launched several fledgling institutions of higher learning that finally culminated in Harding College, where he served as president from 1924 to 1936.

(Photo courtesy Gospel Advocate Company)

McQuiddy for conforming *Gospel Advocate* policy to government pressure on the issue of pacifism during World War I. Further, because he understood that the apocalyptic worldview was, in the final analysis, the fundamental issue even for R. H. Boll, Armstrong refused to join the effort to destroy Boll and his movement. Instead, he maintained his friendship with Boll throughout the controversy.

Moreover, Armstrong gathered around him a core of faculty who shared his apocalyptic outlook and who also had sat "in the long ago at the feet of David Lipscomb and James A. Harding." Of that faculty, Armstrong affirmed in a radio address in 1941 that "there has never been one doctrine taught in the colleges over which I have presided that either one or both of those great men did not teach on the housetops."[57]

The controversy over premillennialism had become so heated by the mid-1930s, however, that many within Churches of Christ had difficulty distinguishing between varieties of premillennialism on the one hand and an apocalyptic worldview on the other. As a result, Harding College soon acquired the reputation throughout Churches of Christ as a veritable hotbed for the premillennial heresy. Though that reputation was largely unjustified, it nonetheless was the case that Harding was one of very few places among Churches of Christ at this time where people with premillennial sympathies found acceptance and shelter.

The prehistory of Harding College is complex. With strong ties to the Nashville Bible School, there is a sense in which Harding had its beginnings when James A. Harding left the Nashville Bible School in 1901 to establish a similar school, Potter Bible College, in Bowling Green, Kentucky. There he assembled a faculty that included four younger men who shared his worldview: J. N. Armstrong, B. F. Rhodes, R. C. Bell, and R. N. Gardner. In 1905, those four men, wanting to establish a comparable institution west of the Mississippi River, founded Western Bible and Literary College in Odessa, Missouri, with Armstrong serving as president. In 1908, Armstrong, Rhodes, and Bell left Odessa to help with a newly established school in Cordell, Oklahoma: Cordell Christian College. Once again, Armstrong served as president.

The apocalyptic worldview that dominated the thinking of Armstrong, his faculty, and almost all the members of his board, however, finally led to the closing of Cordell Christian College as World War I was coming to a close. In the midst of the patriotic fervor that surrounded American involvement in that war, Armstrong and his faculty made no attempt to hide their pacifist position. Not everyone at the college shared their viewpoint, however. Even though some thirty-eight persons from the college community entered the armed services, that was not enough for the local Selective Service board in Cordell. In July of 1918, the board demanded that the "institution be so reorganized as will unreservedly conform to all military policies and requirements of the government in order to successfully carry on the war and that no half-way compliance will be tolerated." The board further demanded the immediate resignation of Armstrong and all of the faculty and board of trustees who shared his pacifist

In 1908, J. N. Armstrong, B. F. Rhodes, and R. C. Bell founded Cordell Christian College (pictured above) in Cordell, Oklahoma, one of the predecessors to Harding College. With a distinctly pacifist faculty, administration, and board, the college came under fire during World War I from the local Selective Service board, which demanded support for United States military policies. Unwilling to conform, the college closed its doors in 1918.
(Photo courtesy Mike Casey)

position. Because that would have meant a total reorganization of the institution, Cordell had little choice but to close its doors.[58]

In the fall of 1919, Armstrong took his seemingly migrant faculty to Harper, Kansas, where Armstrong assumed the presidency of yet another fledgling school, Harper College. In 1924, Harper College merged with Arkansas Christian College at Morrilton, Arkansas. The school thus created became known as Harding College. In 1934, it moved to its present location, Searcy, Arkansas.[59]

As one might suspect, all the schools over which Armstrong presided had limited financial resources. Moreover, with his highly idealistic orientation, Armstrong apparently was not an especially strong financial manager.[60] Compounding that problem, Armstrong doubtless damaged his ability to raise funds for Harding among members of Churches of Christ when he refused, in 1934, to join the presidents of the other Church of Christ–related colleges in condemning the teachings of R. H. Boll.[61] Consequently, in 1936 Armstrong elected to resign from the presidency of Harding College and turn the reins over to a younger man who might place Harding College on a firm financial footing. That younger man was George S. Benson.[62]

Armstrong's decision to pick Benson as his successor was surely one of the events most symbolic of the transition of Churches of Christ from sect to denomination in this period. Trained at Harper College in the apocalyptic orientation of the Stone-Lipscomb tradition, Benson graduated in 1923 from Harper, where he studied both Greek and Bible under J. N. Armstrong.[63] He served as an instructor at Harding College in the 1924-25 academic year, and then worked almost continuously as a missionary in China from 1925 until 1936, when he returned home to assume the presidency of Harding.

His experience with Chinese Communism in Canton exerted a significant influence on Benson's outlook and largely severed whatever commitment he may have had to the apocalyptic perspectives of the Stone-Lipscomb tradition. Communist-inspired mobs harassed Benson shortly after his arrival in Canton, and by the end of his second year there (1926) the Communist-controlled government forced him, along with all other foreign missionaries, to leave the mainland. He returned to mainland China in 1929 and stayed until 1936, but his negative experiences with Communism profoundly shaped his outlook.

When Benson returned to the United States in the aftermath of the Depression, he thought he saw in President Franklin Roosevelt's program for

Handpicked by J. N. Armstrong to succeed him as president of Harding College, George S. Benson (1898-1991; pictured above) served in that position from 1936 to 1965. In the 1930s, Harding labored under a cloud of suspicion, since many in Churches of Christ erroneously thought Armstrong held premillennial sentiments. Benson therefore turned to business and civic leaders for funding, and promoted Harding as a bastion of Americanism and anti-Communism. In this way, Benson helped undermine the apocalyptic orientation that Armstrong had sought to preserve.
(Photo courtesy Gospel Advocate Company)

recovery a greatly expanded government that approached nationalization of American industry. He also sensed a significant erosion of respect for both American government and the American economic system.[64] Coupling those perceptions with his bitter experiences with Chinese Communism, Benson increasingly abandoned the apocalyptic worldview he had learned from J. N. Armstrong and others at Harper College and adopted instead a stridently patriotic, pro-capitalist, anti-Communist perspective. He institutionalized that perspective at Harding in his National Education Program, an organization through which Benson tied Christianity to Americanism and the principles of free-enterprise capitalism for a full quarter of a century.

We can safely conclude that when Armstrong invited Benson to succeed him as president of Harding College, he had no idea he was choosing a man who would devote his presidency to objectives so alien to the apocalyptic principles upon which Armstrong had built the school. In that regard, the significance of Benson's presidency can hardly be overestimated.

Benson's tenure, in fact, marks not only a radical tear in the apocalyptic fabric of the Stone-Lipscomb-Armstrong tradition but also a radical tear in the political fabric of this tradition. First, Benson helped move the tradition from rejection of politics toward political involvement. And second, within a tradition of essentially left-wing sympathies for labor, the poor, and the downtrodden, Benson helped bring respectability to such right-wing concerns as laissez-faire capitalism, anti-Communism, and Christian patriotism. In this regard, Benson stands as a major transitional figure in Churches of Christ, for in the decades that followed, Churches of Christ moved increasingly toward Benson's kind of right-wing political involvement — a story we will examine in some detail in Chapter 11. For now it will be enough to observe that Benson, with his strongly patriotic emphasis on a Christian America, contributed greatly toward moving Churches of Christ from sect to denomination.

But while Benson's strident pro-Americanism weakened the apocalyptic, world-rejecting milieu at Harding College over the years, his political posture did help stabilize the school financially. The institution's mortgage debt was retired by November of 1939, and by the time Benson retired from the presidency in 1965, Harding's assets approached $25,000,000.[65] Ironically, Benson might never have achieved such remarkable financial success had it not been for opponents who fought Harding College on the grounds that the school harbored premillennialists. Such complaints effectively dried up funding from within Churches of Christ and forced the college to look to alternate sources.

More than anyone else, the man who suggested and helped Benson reach those sources — a man without whom Benson might never have succeeded at Harding College — was Clinton Davidson, another person reared in the James A. Harding–J. N. Armstrong apocalyptic milieu. Davidson was a shadowy but pivotal figure for many developments within Churches of Christ during this period. Among those developments were the transition at Harding College

Clinton Davidson (1888-1967), a graduate of James A. Harding's Potter Bible College, later made a fortune in New York City by selling life insurance to major American industrialists. In 1936, Davidson taught George S. Benson, the new president of Harding College, how to raise funds from these industrialists by promoting Americanism, free enterprise, and limited government. Davidson also funded development of the new *Christian Leader,* a short-lived (1939-40) journalistic enterprise designed to counteract the negative brand of journalism promoted by Foy E. Wallace Jr.
(Photo courtesy Charles Carpenter)

from apocalypticism to Christian patriotism and, as we shall see, the larger transition of Churches of Christ from sectarian to denominational status.

Reared near Bowling Green, Kentucky, Davidson attended Potter Bible College, where he came under the influence both of James A. Harding and of J. N. Armstrong.[66] In time, he made his way to New York, where he became immensely successful in the life insurance industry, setting the pace worldwide for sales in life insurance for seven consecutive years. He also served as a financial consultant to significant corporate executives, establishing two corporations for this purpose. Fiduciary Counsel, Incorporated, served clients with a combined wealth exceeding half a billion dollars. Then, through his Estate Planning Corporation, Davidson planned the disposition of estates of clients with a combined wealth exceeding three billion dollars.[67]

In 1935, gratefully recalling J. N. Armstrong's impact on his early life,

Davidson offered financial assistance for Harding College. Armstrong informed Davidson of his imminent retirement, and the two men determined to defer the gift until Benson became president. The following year, Benson and Davidson developed what eventually became an immensely profitable relationship for Harding College. After Harding had liquidated its mortgage in 1939, Benson acknowledged that Davidson "has not only been a liberal contributor but he has put us in contact with men of means, a number of whom have contributed liberally. In fact, fully 55% of the total amount raised has been directly through his efforts and through men with whom he has put us in contact."[68] These men of means included Lammot du Pont, president of the E. I. du Pont Company; Alfred P. Sloan Jr., president of General Motors; Daniel Willard, president of the Baltimore and Ohio Railroad; and the presidents of major steel and oil companies, the Morton Salt Corporation, and International Harvester.[69]

Davidson not only put Benson in contact with major contributors to the college but also taught him fund-raising skills. He apparently encouraged Benson to use the message of free enterprise and limited government in order to appeal to corporate executives disillusioned with the big-government dimensions of Roosevelt's economic recovery program.[70] The strategy worked and, in the final analysis, seems to have been crucial to the survival of Harding College. Beyond this, the partnership of Benson and Davidson contributed enormously to shifting Churches of Christ toward mainstream participation in the world's affairs and away from the apocalyptic, apolitical, and separationist posture that had characterized the Stone-Lipscomb tradition for over a hundred years. In short, working together, Benson and Davidson helped move Churches of Christ from sect to denomination.

In this regard, Benson and Davidson represent an ironic trend among Churches of Christ. As we will see later in this chapter and again in Chapter 9, those who helped lead Churches of Christ in the 1930s and 1940s toward full participation in political and cultural affairs were almost always people whose roots ran deeply into the soil of the Stone-Lipscomb tradition or who had been shaped by the ideals of that tradition at some point along the way. But how could that be? After all, apocalyptic pessimism regarding human progress had stood at the heart of that tradition since the days of Barton W. Stone.

The answer lies in the fact that, when the explicitly apocalyptic dimensions of the Stone-Lipscomb tradition began to erode in the period after World War I, those with roots in this tradition typically went one of two ways. Many who opposed the premillennial position of R. H. Boll simply exchanged the sectarian posture of Stone for the sectarian posture of the radicalized Alexander Campbell. Where they had once arrayed themselves against the world and its values, they now arrayed themselves against the surrounding denominations. We have already seen this pattern in the *Gospel Advocate*'s opposition to R. H. Boll. Others took a different path. Refusing to fight premillennialism, but at the same time finding the apocalyptic perspective increasingly irrelevant to the world in which they lived, they shifted their focus to another aspect of the Stone-Lipscomb tradition: the emphasis on faith in a sovereign God. Severed from its apocalyptic underpinnings, however, this faith quickly became faith in self, faith in nation, faith in the economy, and faith in God to sustain the American system. In suppressing their emphasis on the coming kingdom of God, these people suppressed as well their sense of divine judgment on human progress and potential. Ironically, in this fashion they often replaced pessimism regarding this world with faith in faith or the power of positive thinking.

Clinton Davidson typified this trend. Ironically, in 1961 Davidson attributed his financial success to biblical principles he had learned from James A. Harding at the old Potter Bible College: "A large part of my business success I attribute to the influence of those [daily chapel] talks [at Potter Bible College] by President James Harding. . . . [He] drove home again and again the fundamental facts of faith in God, the need of serving Him and our fellow men, [and] the possibility of doing big things by His help."[71] Over the years, however, Davidson had radically transformed Harding's meaning. Harding viewed the Bible as an apocalyptic manual for countercultural living; Davidson viewed the Bible as a manual for financial success. "Anyone in this world with normal intelligence, and industry enough to apply himself to the task, can succeed by simply following the principles laid down in the Bible," Davidson proclaimed.[72]

Among the principles Davidson prized most was the biblical affirmation that "all things work together for good to them that love God." Harding took this passage to mean that God sometimes sends us hardships to make us better people. He by no means precluded the tragic dimensions of life. "If God cares for a man, . . . He gives him all the hunger, thirst, toil, discouragement, persecution, affliction, cold, nakedness, sickness that are good for him; he also gives him all the gladness, joy, peace, comfort, food, raiment, shelter, friends, houses, horses, buggies and everything else that he needs for his happiness and usefulness."[73] Davidson, on the other hand, interpreted the passage to mean that even misfortunes ultimately would contribute to the financial success of those who loved God.[74] Or again, Harding would have read Mark 10:43-44 ("Whoever wants to become great among you must be your servant, and whoever wants to be first must be slave of all") as counseling radical servanthood; Davidson read it as a key to amassing riches. He thought it "unfortunate . . . [that] many people still believe that the reward from service comes only in the afterlife."[75] He viewed the Bible as a sort of casebook of success stories. David, Joseph, Daniel, Moses, Jesus, and Paul — Davidson viewed them all as remarkable salespersons who knew how to persuade people to think and behave as they wished.[76]

Davidson imagined that he still stood in the tradition defined by James A. Harding, but in reality, he, Benson, and a host of others in this period turned the teachings of Harding and Armstrong into little more than moralistic advice along the lines of *Poor Richard's Almanac* or entrepreneurial principles along the lines of Bruce Barton's *The Man Nobody Knows* (1925) — a best-selling book of the period promoting an approach to life, business, and religion much like Davidson's. In many ways, Davidson and Benson reflected the cultural beliefs of the America in which they matured — the first quarter of the twentieth century, when many Americans reaped the harvest of the Gospel of Wealth and shared the conviction of Calvin Coolidge that "the business of America is business."

Clearly, Clinton Davidson and George Benson shared that conviction, and when one couples that conviction with Benson's strident affirmation of capitalism and opposition to Communism, one realizes how the friendly heirs of the Stone-Lipscomb tradition unwittingly launched an assault on their own religious heritage.

The Little General: Foy E. Wallace Jr.

To some degree, this battle launched by friendly troops against the Stone-Lipscomb-Armstrong tradition made unnecessary the battle waged by the foes of premillennial thought. Nonetheless, those intent on purging Churches of Christ of all premillennial sentiments remained blissfully unaware that people like Benson and Davidson were, at a very basic level, their allies rather than their enemies. And so, when Davidson and Benson refused to condemn R. H. Boll and J. N. Armstrong, the antimillennial zealots mistook them for mortal enemies, declared war on them both, and sought to destroy their bulwark, Harding College.

The man who more than anyone else marshaled the attack against Armstrong, Boll, Harding College, and the entire premillennial/apocalyptic orientation was Foy E. Wallace Jr., a Texan who edited the *Gospel Advocate* from 1930 to 1934. In 1935, Wallace established his own paper, the *Gospel Guardian*, for the express purpose of purging premillennialism from Churches of Christ, and in 1938 he established another paper, the *Bible Banner*, in which he published stinging attacks on premillennialism, pacifism, and the entire apocalyptic worldview.[77]

Wallace was another major transitional figure in the history of Churches of Christ, especially in that side of the heritage defined chiefly by those who had radicalized Alexander Campbell's *Christian Baptist* in the early nineteenth century (see Chaps. 3 and 4). Wallace gave the hard style a hardness it had never known before.

The son of well-known preacher Foy E. Wallace Sr., Wallace gained fame among Churches of Christ early in life as a boy-wonder pulpiteer. As a skilled and intimidating speaker and debater, and especially as a fighting editor, he soon marshaled an enormous following, especially west of the Mississippi River. In the 1930s and 1940s, he emerged as the single most influential preacher in

Churches of Christ, with the power to crush most who resisted his opinions and his leadership.

Wallace added little of substance to the ongoing attack on R. H. Boll and premillennial eschatology. But he did turn that attack into a withering barrage by combining rational analysis with biting ridicule and sarcasm, name-calling, and charges that premillennialists were willfully divisive. By 1949, when he discontinued the *Bible Banner*, premillennialism — and the entire apocalyptic worldview along with it — was a lost cause among Churches of Christ except for a group of congregations located in and around Louisville and New Orleans that remained loyal to the position. Wallace and his troops had convinced most members of mainstream Churches of Christ that premillennialists were at best badly deceived and at worst fundamentally evil.

The fact that Wallace was able to consolidate and direct such inordinate power tells us some important things about the polity of this tradition. Churches of Christ often claimed that because they possessed no organizational structure over and above the local congregation, they therefore had no power structure at all. The truth is that the absence of any *formalized* power structure allowed ambitious leaders to seize power they likely could not have claimed otherwise.

The Battle against Harding College

We have already noted J. N. Armstrong's refusal in 1934 to side with other presidents of Church of Christ colleges in condemnation of the premillennial sentiment. Pressed hard by his critics, Armstrong a year later declared his rejection of certain tenets of dispensational premillennialism, but he by no means disavowed his apocalyptic orientation.[78] He thereby left open the door for his enemies to pursue his destruction.

The man Wallace most trusted to clean up Harding College and secure the ouster of Armstrong was the preacher at the Fourth and State Street Church of Christ in Little Rock, Arkansas, E. R. Harper. Harper moved to Little Rock in 1933, and for his first five or six years there he supported Harding in a variety of ways, even while questioning its alleged premillennialism. He eventually became convinced, however, "that it was impossible to get the Administration to take a definite stand for 'the old paths' and definitely renounce 'Bollism.'"[79] From that time on, Harper was an implacable foe of Harding College. He maintained that Benson's great sin was his retention of J. N. Armstrong as chair of the Bible Department after he had stepped down from the presidency of the college. Harper insisted that Armstrong was a rank premillennialist and should be fired. If Benson would take that step, Harper would be satisfied.

The extent of Foy Wallace's immense power in the Churches of Christ, even in the fight against Harding College, became apparent when Harper struck an agreement with Benson in late 1939 to drop his fight against Harding if

Benson would hire an assistant to Armstrong who was *not* premillennial. When Wallace learned of Harper's agreement, "without any changes having been made, with the same regime in control, on such a far-reaching action involving the destiny of the cause of Christ in a whole section of the country," he was enraged. He concluded that "the school must have got the drop on Brother Harper and brought him out with his hands up," and he intimated that he might no longer use "someone who hits and runs" in a significant way in the *Bible Banner*.[80]

Apparently desperate to reclaim his standing with Wallace, Harper explained that he never raised his hands "because some one gets the drop on me." He took the action he did because "we had an opportunity to win the fight." He asked Wallace to view his proposed agreement with Benson as "but a 'shifting of battle grounds' to carry on the fight. We were hoping to get 'inside the camp' where the fighting could be 'at close range' and the 'bull's eye' more easily hit." Specifically, he had in mind working "our way into the Bible Department. . . . We thought we had a way into the 'temple' where we could render help in cleansing it of its money changers and Boll sympathizers."[81]

Throughout the 1930s and into the 1940s, Foy E. Wallace Jr. marshaled a massive campaign to destroy the premillennial sentiment in Churches of Christ. E. R. Harper (1897-1986; pictured above), preacher at the Fourth and State Street Church of Christ in Little Rock, served as Wallace's lieutenant in Arkansas. Harper directed his attack especially against Harding College, which he suspected harbored premillennial sympathizers.

(Photo courtesy Gospel Advocate Company)

Harding College responded with an official college *Bulletin* in which officials expressed outrage at Harper's confession that his proposed agreement had been "merely a trick to 'get inside the camp' " and condemned Harper's actions as the sort of "Nazi treachery" that "we thought . . . belonged only to the unscrupulous dictator who feels himself above all moral law." In addition, the *Bulletin* suggested that "Harper's article reflects almost an abject submission before Brother Wallace. He seems almost ready to kiss the hand that had lashed him so severely."[82] Such was the power of Foy E. Wallace Jr., and such was the nature of the struggle over premillennial thinking in Churches of Christ.

Foy E. Wallace Jr. versus David Lipscomb

Wallace's own objection to premillennialism rested on the standard complaint that it undermined the restoration of true apostolic Christianity and therefore the identity and integrity of Churches of Christ. "The [Boll] theory," he charged, "makes the church an accident, . . . the result of a prophetic default; a mere afterthought." For that reason, "there was never anything taught by [Charles Taze] Russell, [Judge] Rutherford, or impostor Joe Smith, or any other leader of a stray cult, which was more vitiating to the gospel of Jesus Christ, the character of the New Testament church and the entire scheme of human redemption."[83]

As early as 1938, Harper had egged Wallace on to declare Boll and his premillennial following no longer bona fide members of Churches of Christ, and two months later Wallace did just that.[84] By 1944, Harper could rejoice that "R. H. Boll has been fought by every paper, pulpit, preacher and most schools," and that he and his people had been rejected "as unsound and therefore have been 'marked and avoided' by the church in general." He added that "the papers no longer allow him space to write his views and the pulpits are closed to him, . . . and most schools will not allow him to enjoy their fellowship."[85] Boll died in 1956.

In the meantime, America entered the Second World War. The pacifist sentiment among Churches of Christ, though severely wounded during World War I, was nonetheless still alive, and even Foy Wallace emerged at the beginning of the war as a champion of nonresistance. But Wallace experienced a sudden conversion to militarism sometime prior to March of 1942, apparently in reaction to Japan's attack on Pearl Harbor in December of 1941.[86]

Wallace wasted no time turning his conversion into a crusade against pacifists and conscientious objectors in Churches of Christ, and by the close of World War II, pacifism among mainstream Churches of Christ was essentially dead.[87] The very month in which Wallace announced his renunciation of pacifism, he lambasted conscientious objectors as "impractical," "misguided," "men with a dwarfed conscience," and "freak specimen[s] of humanity."[88] If anything, his brother Cled was more vicious toward pacifists than Foy, calling pacifists "crackpots" and people with "dwarfed minds" and characterizing their doctrine of nonresistance as "a screwy philosophy" and "idiotic drivel and unpatriotic rot."[89]

There can be no doubt that Wallace desperately wanted Churches of Christ to be accepted by the surrounding culture, especially in wartime. Accordingly, he castigated those who sought to present the Church of Christ to the government as a peace church. "It is . . . a 'stigma,'" Wallace wrote, "to have such a doctrine pinned on the churches in the records of our government and in the eyes of the world."[90] In this way, Wallace contributed toward denominational status for Churches of Christ just as effectively as George S. Benson did at Harding College. Though separated geographically by hundreds of miles, and though at odds theologically in many ways, these two men unwittingly became partners in a common enterprise — namely, the movement of Churches of Christ toward acculturation in mainstream American society.

But Wallace had sufficient insight to see that pacifism and premillennialism in this movement were often connected.[91] He must have concluded that he could not destroy pacifism unless he first destroyed the apocalyptic worldview that sustained it. To this end, he wrote,

> The whole question of civil government appears to be in the background of the premillennial theory, if not in the foreground. It has a distinct connection with the premillennial scheme of things. Premillennialists generally hold that human governments belong to Satan, hence the time will come when Christ will abolish every government in the world and set up his own. . . . Therefore, those who advocate the theory that civil government belongs to the devil are the ones who are helping the premillennialists.[92]

For these reasons, in 1942 Wallace opened the pages of the *Bible Banner* to an attack on David Lipscomb himself. W. E. Brightwell fired the first shot, noting that the pacifists in the church were only "those who have attended certain schools or have read a certain book" — that being Lipscomb's *Civil Government*. Brightwell simply could not fathom how Lipscomb could claim that human government was the domain of Satan. "The purpose of civil government is good," he wrote. "The devil does not have anything to do with it. The Lord does. And the fallacy of this foolish theory ought to be patent to all."[93]

Brightwell's comments reflect the extent to which the two World Wars separated Churches of Christ from their nineteenth-century intellectual origins. He, along with many others in this period, displayed a complete inability to comprehend the Stone-Lipscomb position that human institutions were flawed to the core. To the contrary, they viewed government as good — especially the government of the United States. These moderns granted that minor defects may have existed, but they dismissed as myth the notion that government was fundamentally flawed because of human sin.

Perhaps no one reflected this new perspective more completely than did

O. C. Lambert, who maintained that government was bad only if it did bad deeds. "I have been living some time and the United States government has never persecuted me for my religion," Lambert observed. "If that is the way the devil resists the church it seems to me he is wonderful." Lambert was simply dumbfounded that Lipscomb would make "the devil . . . the head of the United States government." He rightly pointed out that "Lipscomb recognizes no difference in the kingdoms. The United States government is just as bad as the rest. The government that gives so much freedom to Christians is no better than one that persecutes them." Though he had earlier accepted Lipscomb's positions, Lambert now announced, "I lose faith in the Lipscomb Lion and Lamb story!" Further, he felt certain that "the Lipscomb book would be outlawed now if the FBI knew its contents," and he encouraged Churches of Christ to "call all of them [copies of *Civil Government*] in and burn them."[94]

By October 1943, Wallace himself joined the attack, focusing on the foundational apocalyptic perspectives of Lipscomb's *Civil Government.* "In looking back over the years in which this book and others like it were circulated among the brethren, it is not hard to see how the theories of Premillennialism found soil in which to grow among churches of Christ." He rightly observed that "premillennialism calls for the very things that are taught in 'Civil Government' by David Lipscomb. The two theories go together; they fit each other perfectly." For these reasons, he concluded that Lipscomb's book was "about as rank with false doctrine as one book of its size could be," and he expressed his shame "that any recognized leader in churches of Christ, past or present, should espouse and promote such a doctrine" as that of David Lipscomb.[95]

While Wallace and his soldiers in the *Bible Banner* attacked Lipscomb head-on, the *Gospel Advocate* undermined Lipscomb and his position by misrepresenting him. By the mid-1940s, mainstream Churches of Christ so completely rejected premillennialism that the *Advocate* simply refused to acknowledge that David Lipscomb had ever taught such a notion. The denial came when a young preacher named Hulen Jackson called attention to an apparently premillennial passage in a commentary Lipscomb had written. Regarding Lipscomb's comments on Ephesians 4:9, Jackson wrote, "I hereby charge that the comments by David Lipscomb on this passage teach premillennialism." *Advocate* editor B. C. Goodpasture and writer John T. Lewis flatly denied that this was true. If anything, Lewis wrote, Lipscomb was describing a time when this earth will have passed away.[96] When the *Advocate* had done its work, the real Lipscomb of history, like Alice's Cheshire cat, had disappeared, leaving only an optimistic, disembodied smile.

Wallace wrote the epitaph to the premillennial controversy in 1945, when a majority of Churches of Christ in Houston, Texas, invited him to deliver a series of sermons in their city's Music Hall "exposing modern millennial theories." The churches intended these lectures to rebut premillennial teachings in the city of Houston, but Wallace and his colleagues had already defeated the premillennial vision among mainstream Churches of Christ, and the book that resulted from Wallace's lectures — *God's Prophetic Word* [97] — served more than anything else to celebrate the triumph.

The premillennial Churches of Christ emerged from that period severely damaged, and they continued to decline in numbers afterward. By 1990, they could claim only seventy-six congregations — forty-six in Kentucky and twenty in Louisiana.[98]

Conclusions

How are we to assess the significance of the anti-Boll crusade among Churches of Christ? First, it represented a rite of passage from the culturally pessimistic, separatist mentality that had characterized the Stone-Lipscomb tradition in the nineteenth century to the culture-affirming, patriotic mentality that would increasingly characterize the mainstream Churches of Christ in the twentieth century. Politically, this passage entailed a loosening of the ties to the apolitical and pacifist stance that had characterized Barton Stone, Tolbert Fanning, David Lipscomb, James A. Harding, J. N. Armstrong, and thousands of their followers for over one hundred years. Religiously, it meant — at long last — the near-complete triumph of the *rational progressive primitivism* of Alexander Campbell that had both coexisted and competed for a century and more with the pessimistic *apocalyptic primitivism* of Barton W. Stone. And sociologically, it meant the beginnings of the shift from sect to denomination.

More specifically, what might we say of Foy E. Wallace? Clearly, Wallace successfully pulled apart the two sectarian traditions that had coalesced over the years to form Churches of Christ, and he marshaled the one against the other. In so doing, he enhanced the sectarian side of Churches of Christ that had descended from Campbell's *Christian Baptist,* but he effectively destroyed the sectarian side of Churches of Christ that had descended from Barton W. Stone. This led Churches of Christ, paradoxically, to become increasingly sectarian vis-à-vis the surrounding denominations but increasingly denominational vis-à-vis the larger world of politics, militarism, and the values of the surrounding culture. In this sense, for all their differences, Foy Wallace and George S. Benson both proved to be effective agents of modernization, and Wallace, Benson, and Davidson were all responsible for moving Churches of Christ toward denominational status.

This helps explain the paradox that historian of southern religion Samuel S. Hill described when he wrote some years ago of the place of Churches of Christ in the American South: "It is the astonishing blend of being very much at home and quite alien in the South that helps make this religious tradition so difficult to comprehend and yet so captivating." A whole host of leaders in this tradition — from J. C. McQuiddy during World War I to Foy E. Wallace during World War II — took pains to move Churches of Christ into community with the larger southern culture, while at the same time they sought to intensify the alienation of Churches of Christ from the larger Christian community that surrounded them.

But there is more. Hill observed that Churches of Christ, with their emphasis on the "Truth," rationally presented and understood, had been out of step for years with mainstream Protestantism in the South, which historically had focused on revivalism and spirituality.[99] By accentuating the legacy of the *Christian Baptist* and by driving from Churches of Christ the heritage of Barton Stone, Wallace and his followers not only turned Churches of Christ in a radically sectarian direction by accentuating exclusivist truth claims, but they also very nearly severed the only tie Churches of Christ might have had to the larger religious landscape in the American South: the deep sense of piety and spirituality that grew from the revivalist roots once so carefully nurtured by Barton W. Stone.

Finally, with their nineteenth-century apocalyptic roots, one might think that Churches of Christ would have stood shoulder to shoulder with fundamentalists in the early twentieth century, hurling judgment on proponents of modernity. Indeed, Churches of Christ, with their biblical primitivism, were deeply sympathetic with the biblicism of the fundamentalist movement, but their exclusivism prevented them from formally joining the fundamentalists. Further, in the extent to which they defended human progress and adopted a strident stand against apocalypticism during the World War I era, Churches of Christ actually shared significant ground with modernists. In opposing the apocalypticism of R. H. Boll, Churches of Christ in principle joined hands with such mainline Protestant liberals as George Eckman, Shailer Mathews, Shirley Jackson Case, James Snowden, and George Preston Mains, who engaged in a similar effort to drive premillennialism from America's churches.[100] Of all those in the fellowship of the Churches of Christ, Boll was most in tune with the fundamentalist outlook and most at odds with the modernist worldview. When Churches of Christ turned their back on Boll and the apocalyptic spirit, they put themselves on the path of accommodation to modern American culture.

Before we proceed, we might do well to review briefly some of the alignments that had emerged among Churches of Christ by the 1930s. First, the mainline was represented by the *Gospel Advocate* and its editors, who defended the religious exclusivism of Churches of Christ but who also sought to expel from their heritage all traces of apocalypticism and pacifism. Second, Foy Wallace and his followers sought to control the mainline but actually represented a radical version of the mainline. Wallace edited the *Gospel Advocate* from 1930 to 1934, differing from most of his *Advocate* colleagues in style but not in substance. Third, the premillennial wing of Churches of Christ was slowly bowing to defeat. And fourth, there was within the mainline tradition a coalition of leaders who appreciated the spirituality of Boll and the premillennial tradition, who resisted the belligerent style of Wallace and his followers, and who sought to define for Churches of Christ a more gracious orientation. It is to this "grace tradition" of Churches of Christ that we turn in Chapter 8.

CHAPTER 8

Grace, Law, and the Fighting Style

In 1968, Stanford Chambers was ninety-one years old. He had been among the leaders of the premillennial movement from its beginning, and now, reflecting in the twilight of his life on decades of struggle with the mainstream of Churches of Christ, he concluded, quite simply, that "the real issue [was] . . . not prophecy but grace." In a fundamental sense, Chambers was right, for no one in the history of Churches of Christ possessed a keener sense of divine grace than did R. H. Boll. Divine grace, in fact, was the central feature of Boll's theology, and his premillennial outlook was but a pale reflection of it. Put another way, the idea of the premillennial second coming of Jesus underscored for Boll the helplessness of humankind: we would all be doomed apart from divine intervention.

On the other hand, many in Churches of Christ — especially those in the radicalized tradition of the *Christian Baptist* — had nurtured for years a confidence in human potential and a legalistic understanding of the Christian faith that rendered them inevitably hostile toward Boll's message. Clearly, this was the case with most in the mainstream Churches of Christ represented by the *Gospel Advocate* on the one hand and by Foy E. Wallace Jr. on the other.

In addition to the traditions defined by Boll, the *Advocate*, and Wallace, there also existed within the mainstream of Churches of Christ in this period a minority voice defined by an emphasis on grace. Like Wallace, these people rejected premillennialism and even the apocalyptic outlook that sustained it. Unlike Wallace, however, they held tenaciously to God's grace in a variety of other expressions. Not surprisingly, most of these people descended in one way or another from the Stone-Lipscomb tradition. Because they tended to be gracious themselves, and because they understood that grace was the starting point for all of Boll's thought, they resolutely refused to condemn him. On the contrary, they sought to put an end to the premillennial squabble and to bring peace to a fellowship deeply disturbed and divided by the harshness of the crusade against premillennialism. Their refusal to condemn Boll, however, only inflamed Wallace and his people all the more, and elicited additional invective.

The tradition of grace contributed enormously to the movement of Churches of Christ from sectarian to denominational status, but we must wait until Chapter 9 to explore the dynamics of that contribution. In this chapter, we will distinguish between two competing theological traditions in Churches of Christ — the legal tradition and the heritage of grace — and we will explore the relation of the legal tradition to the hard and fighting style, especially as that style took root in Texas.

R. H. Boll's Theology of Grace

Stanford Chambers traced the tradition of grace especially to James A. Harding at the old Nashville Bible School, where he had studied. "To Harding," he recalled, "... the Holy Spirit was a personality and His help in our infirmities real. Salvation 'by grace . . . through faith' rather than by 'works' or deeds of merit was a cherished truth." But even at the Nashville Bible School, Harding's teachings provoked a split in the student body on this issue. "The one class had their spirituality deepened, and others in a measure became crystallized in a legalistic attitude." Significantly, he recalled, "Robert Boll was one who drank it in."[1]

In Churches of Christ, those who spoke of unmerited grace were so rare and provoked such opposition that it is important to explain precisely what Boll meant when he used this language. Practically everyone in Churches of Christ professed to teach God's grace, but a world of difference separated the orthodox understanding held by the vast majority from the understanding of grace held by R. H. Boll.

In many respects, Boll's understanding of the gospel closely resembled that of Martin Luther — and, since Boll grew up in Germany, one can only wonder if the Lutheran theological tradition had shaped his insights. In the first place, Boll made it clear time and again that his interest in the millennium had everything to do with the sinfulness of humankind and the unmerited favor of God. "I am not debating about the millennium as such, though I believe in it," he pointedly told H. Leo Boles in the famous Boles-Boll debate of 1928.

> [I] am merely seeking to show that before there is or could be such a period, Christ must come. . . . Call it "millennium" or whatever you please, let it be on earth or in heaven, let it be a thousand years or longer, the one and only point is that *that future time of the final triumph of the saints and universal glory and bliss cannot be before the coming of Christ.*[2]

Boll's opponents often claimed that when he used the phrase "imminent second coming," he was speaking of an immediate return of Christ, perhaps in their own lifetimes. Boll himself insisted that "by '*imminent*' I mean impending in the sense of being *always liable to occur.*"[3] This, of course, was hardly the essence of premillennialism, but it was the very essence of the apocalyptic worldview. Further, Boll's version of the apocalyptic outlook pointed directly to God's initiative and grace. It was only natural, he said, that those who trusted in their own good works to save them would not be comfortable with the idea of an imminent second coming. "Can we ever have a minute's real peace with God or feel anything more than anxiety and fear toward Him so long as we stand upon this miserable plan of salvation by works?" Happily, he rejoiced, there was "a way in which we may have present peace and assurance . . . *right now. . . . 'Being therefore justified by faith we have peace with God through our Lord Jesus Christ. . . .'* (Rom. 5:1, 2)." With this peace, Boll maintained, one might confidently affirm, " 'Even so, Come Lord Jesus!' "[4]

Like Luther, Boll often spoke of the great gulf that separates the unrighteousness of human beings from the absolute righteousness of God but also of the righteousness with which God, through his grace, makes his children clean and spotless in his sight. For example, in 1917, he wrote,

> Our own righteousness is indeed as filthy rags, and no apron of leaves can clothe our nakedness in the presence of God's searching holiness. . . . The question . . . [then] arises, how then can any man be saved? . . . The answer lies *in the gospel.* The gospel is the power of God unto salvation: "for *therein is revealed a righteousness of God* from faith unto faith" (Rom. 1:17). This "righteousness" is not the fruit of our own works, but a free gift from God (Rom. 5:17).[5]

What place did Boll see for works, then? Again, he sounded remarkably like Luther: "Our good work is the *fruit* of the life and of the good blessings before-hand received, and not the means with which we purchase those favors of God." Or again, "in proportion as they have known and appreciated His grace they *will* work. For the faith by which we are justified is also the faith that afterward worketh by love."[6]

By 1943, Boll had suffered for almost thirty years the kind of rejection and abuse that might have disabused many others of their notions of divine love and grace. But Boll, more tenaciously than ever, now grounded his life in the themes so central to his career, and he spoke of the freedom enjoyed by the one who serves in response to grace and not from constraint.

> If you are burdened and distressed, and the price of righteousness seems too much, and you find yourself estimating that you have done as much as was expected of you, and thinking God ought to be satisfied with you, then you are a bondman, and yours is inferior work. [But] if you do God's will, not to make Him love you, but because He loves you; not to obtain His grace, but because that grace works in you mightily; if you don't work by the piece or

by the day, but bring your whole self a willing sacrifice, willing to spend and be spent, and rejoicing in the privilege, you are a free man and happy, a son of God.

Then Boll turned to those in Churches of Christ who had not understood this theme. He asserted that many had been "slow to believe and seize the blessing." He exclaimed, "See what frantic efforts have been made to reduce the beautiful, living Gospel of Christ to a bony skeleton of precepts. . . . There are Christians who would be happy to see the New Testament turned into a code of laws and regulations, emphasized with compelling threats." But Boll admonished his people to resist such threats, to "be free and grant others their freedom." He wrote, "Let no man lord it over your conscience, and do not tyrannize over the consciences of others. The dingdonging and scolding so common in pulpit and papers, is worse than nothing."[7]

The Legal Tradition in Churches of Christ

Boll may have thought the "dingdonging and scolding" worse than nothing, but in spite of his objections, it was a fixture among Churches of Christ in those days and refused to go away. To a significant degree, it grew out of the legal tradition that had characterized the Campbell side of the movement since the days of the *Christian Baptist*. We noted in Chapter 2 some of the legal connotations that characterized Campbell's early thinking, but we also saw some indications that Campbell understood the notion of grace in its classic form.

Campbell clearly affirmed in his famous "Sermon on the Law," preached before the Redstone Baptist Association of Pennsylvania in 1816, that salvation was "not by legal works or observances, in whole or in part, but through the abundance of grace."[8] And he argued in the *Christian Baptist* that "the Gospel . . . is emphatically called *the grace of God* . . . [which] signifies the *favor* of God towards sinners . . . no where so fully exhibited as in the gift of his Son."[9]

The legal overtones of Campbell's doctrine of grace came from the distinction he made between the divine origination of the gospel and human enjoyment of the gospel. Campbell viewed the *origination* of the gospel as a pure gift of sovereign grace, but he maintained that human beings must fulfill certain conditions in order to *enjoy the benefits* of the gospel. At the same time, he insisted that such a distinction did not imply conditional grace or a contract between humanity and God.[10]

Understandably, many of Campbell's successors found such subtle distinctions difficult to comprehend. Members of the emerging Churches of Christ had already been shaped by Campbell's emphasis on human initiative and ability, and so they were prepared in a sense to understand God's grace as conditional, predicated on obeying his commands.

An essay appearing in the 1835 edition of Campbell's *Christian System* typified the outlook that, more than anything else, helped define the traditional understanding of grace among Churches of Christ. There, Campbell praised Luther's conception of justification but held that Luther restored the ancient gospel only partially: "Emerging from the smoke of the great city of mystical Babylon, he saw as clearly and as far into these matters as any person could in such a hazy atmosphere." At the same time, he asserted that if Luther's views were "carried out to their legitimate issue, . . . we should have the ancient gospel as a result." Presumably Campbell believed that he was carrying Luther's views "to their legitimate issue" when he suggested that God manifests his grace when he grants human beings the opportunity to obey his commands. "To present the gospel in the form of a command is an act of favor," he wrote, "because it engages the will and affections of men, and puts it in their power to have an assurance of their salvation from which they would be necessarily excluded if no such act of obedience were enjoyed."[11] In part, Campbell's effort to "present the gospel in the form of a command" that "engages the will" was part of his reaction against a Calvinist system of predestination that minimized human will and effort.

Campbell held that the one command through which God uniquely conveyed his grace was the command to be immersed.[12] In good scientific fashion, he observed that "no relation in which we stand to the material world . . . can be changed by believing, apart from the acts to which that belief or faith induces us." In the Christian religion, he wrote, faith is merely "the principle of action, and . . . the cause of those acts by which such blessings are enjoyed." Further, he argued that faith "without those acts is nothing." On this basis he reasoned that if Scripture says we are "justified by faith," it actually means that by faith *"we have access"* to justification — and that "access" is achieved only through a material action — namely, immersion.[13] In other words, Campbell maintained that while God's grace is unmerited and free insofar as its origination is concerned, only a human response can appropriate its enjoyment.

Such was Campbell's understanding of grace, and such was the foundation for the legal tradition among Churches of Christ. Even among the followers of Barton W. Stone, many found Campbell's baptismal theology immensely attractive, as we noted in Chapter 5. The notion of conditional grace, however, posed a knotty theological problem for people who came from the Stone tradition: how might they reconcile what seemed to be a doctrine of conditional grace that emphasized human initiative with an apocalyptic worldview that emphasized divine initiative?

Both Tolbert Fanning and David Lipscomb implicitly addressed this problem. They taught that obedience to all of God's commands, obviously requiring human initiative, was the only proper response to a sovereign God who would eventually triumph over all the earth. In this way, they reconciled human initiative with the apocalyptic outlook that might well have pointed them toward a theology of grace. Certainly the apocalyptic outlook pointed R. H. Boll in that direction. As it turned out, however, the extraordinary influence of Alexander Campbell over Fanning and Lipscomb led them to derive a more legal understanding of the Christian faith from their apocalypticism, an understanding focused chiefly on human initiative and obedience rather than unmerited favor.

Lipscomb is a case in point. In his commentary on Romans 1:16-17 — the passage that had sparked Luther's insight into unmerited grace and that stood at the fountainhead of the Protestant Reformation — Lipscomb focused on the theme of obedience: "He who would be saved by the gospel must not trust to faith only, for the divine order is, 'obedience of faith.' (1:5; 16:26.) Faith is the principle from which obedience springs. God's arrangement is: first faith, then obedience. From this there must be no departure. . . . Hence, 'faith apart from works is barren.' (James 2:20)."[14]

In 1874, T. W. Brents, a medical doctor in Tennessee who pursued preaching, debating, and religious writing as avocations, published a massive volume entitled *The Gospel Plan of Salvation*. This book soon came to serve as a kind of systematic theology for Churches of Christ, both reflecting the historic orthodoxy of the tradition and defining its orthodoxy for generations to come. The title was immensely significant, for the contents did indeed outline Brents's conception of the "plan of salvation." The essence of this plan, according to Brents, was centered less in what God had done for humankind than in what human beings must do in order to be saved. The very structure of the book reflects this emphasis. There is not a single chapter devoted to the atonement, to the cross, or to God's grace. Brents spends the first 139 pages seeking to undermine the premises of Calvinism as he understood it, the next 43 pages defining the "one church," and most of the remainder of the book on the "plan of salvation," which squares remarkably well with Walter Scott's "five-finger exercise" and the "original marks" of the true church that John R. Howard had described in 1848. In short, Brents taught that the plan of salvation consists of faith, repentance, confession, and baptism. Of the 382 pages he devoted to the "plan of salvation," 327 focus on baptism.

Brents defined faith not as reliance on God's promise or grace but rather as intellectual assent to the proposition that Jesus is the Son of God.[15] Further, he insisted that faith should express itself in immersion.[16] This was the "plan of salvation" through which one was saved. Working from this premise, Brents concluded that when Paul wrote that justification was by faith in Christ and "'not of works, lest any man should boast,' he referred, first, to the origin of the plan of salvation, that it was by *grace* or *unmerited favor*."[17] That is to say, he restricted the domain of divine grace to God's action in devising the plan that he meant men and women to follow as they pursued their own salvation.

Four years later, F. D. Srygley succinctly expressed what by then had become Church of Christ orthodoxy on the question of grace — namely, that

God revealed his grace in his commands. "By obedience to his [God's] require-ments man may walk 'the way that leadeth unto life.' . . . Everything God has done in preparing the *city*, and revealing the *way* is of grace. . . . Hence salvation is of grace and not of works."[18]

By 1909, in the aftermath of the division with the Disciples of Christ, even David Lipscomb dealt with the issue of grace in starkly legal terms as he emphasized the "safety" one could find when one obeyed all of God's commands. In this context, he made no distinctions among immersion, the Lord's supper, instrumental music in worship, or missionary societies: all were matters of obeying God's commands in the interest of standing on "safe ground."

> A man in spiritual and eternal matters ought to stand on safe and solid ground. . . . If faith will save a man, a faith that works through love and leads one to show his faith in Christ by being baptized into Christ will not destroy his salvation. . . . One believes he can worship God acceptably without par-taking of the Lord's Supper on the first day of the week[, . . . but] all may safely partake of the Supper every Lord's day. Some people believe Christians may worship with an organ[, . . . but] all may worship without the organ. This is safe ground. Many think human societies may be formed to collect the money and direct the preaching. . . . [But] no one doubts we may all work through the church. This is safe ground on which all may stand.[19]

In 1920, C. R. Nichol and R. L. Whiteside published four volumes in-tended for "Sunday School classes, prayer meetings, private study, college classes, etc." that also served Churches of Christ as a kind of systematic theology. The authors affirmed that "the greatest exhibition of God's grace is seen in the gift of his Son, Jesus Christ" — but they quickly added that "next to that, his greatest favor to man is seen in the very command he has given for man's guidance." On the day of Pentecost, they wrote, those who heard Peter preach "could save themselves only by performing the conditions upon which salvation was so graciously offered."[20]

By the 1930s, there were few preachers among Churches of Christ who proclaimed a message of "unmerited grace." One of the few who did was K. C. Moser, a native Texan and a preacher in Oklahoma and Texas from the 1920s through the 1970s.[21] Moser became convinced early in his career that God's grace was to be found not in his commands but in the cross. He published his views in 1932 in a book he entitled *The Way of Salvation*. But it was not until 1934, when he published an article on this issue in the *Firm Foundation*, that Churches of Christ paid any serious regard to his perspective. The response, when it came, was almost entirely negative.

Quite simply, Moser argued that while baptism and good works were important, the proper response to the gospel was not so much a matter of

In the 1930s and 1940s, when Foy E. Wallace Jr. dominated Churches of Christ with a legalistic theology and a hard, fighting style, a scattered few promoted a strong theology of grace. K. C. Moser (1893-1976; pictured here) was especially notable in this regard. He published his views in a small book, *The Way of Salvation,* in 1932, but gained widespread attention for his perspective among Churches of Christ only when he described the grace of God in an article published in the *Firm Foundation* in 1934. (Photo courtesy Fran Winkler)

believing facts and obeying commands as it was of trusting in "Christ crucified, buried and raised for our justification."[22] The editor of the *Firm Foundation,* G. H. P. Showalter, rejected Moser's claim and pressed him to "speedily abandon such fantastic speculation and urge the lost not only to believe, but to obey."[23]

Soon, a storm of controversy erupted over Moser's emphasis on unmerited grace. He became *persona non grata* in many quarters of Churches of Christ for the next forty years. At Harding College, however, where several strategic people continued to embrace the apocalyptic perspective, Moser was welcomed.[24]

Even more significantly, Moser complained in 1937 that the message he regarded as "gospel" had, by and large, been lost from pulpits of Churches of Christ. He had confirmed his sense that this was the case, he said, by reading numerous sermons and sermon outlines and listening to many sermons from a variety of preachers. Time and again, he "noticed that the gospel was not being preached." Symptomatic of the problem, he suggested, was a sermon he had read on John 3:16.

Naturally one would expect the gospel to be preached with such a subject. But alas, it was not preached. According to the sermon, the death of Christ was merely for the purpose of displaying God's love for man and giving him a law to obey that would bring life. Christ is said to save by furnishing man an EXAMPLE. He simply showed man how to save himself![25]

In spite of his efforts to point Churches of Christ toward a more grace-centered theology, however, Moser never carried the day. He had friends and supporters at Harding College and in Tennessee, but for the most part, back at home, his was a voice crying in a Texas and Oklahoma wilderness.

By the 1930s, Churches of Christ had identified God's grace with his commands for almost one hundred years. Predictably, the growing strength of the legalistic perspective in Churches of Christ did much to weaken the apocalyptic tradition, even in the heartland of Middle Tennessee. Those steeped in the legalistic outlook of Churches of Christ, whether in Texas or in Tennessee, quite naturally viewed R. H. Boll's theology of grace as a gross aberration from biblical principles. Moreover, the legalistic outlook created an environment in which the "dingdonging and scolding" that Boll complained about could thrive.

Texas, the Fighting Style, and Foy E. Wallace Jr.

We cannot really understand Wallace unless we understand the climate that prevailed among Churches of Christ in Texas, where Wallace grew up in the early twentieth century. There, in the context of a church that stood on the economic margins of a rough-and-tumble frontier society, Wallace learned not only the legal tradition of Churches of Christ but also the combative style that he would hone to perfection. While Wallace's this-worldly theology opened wide the door to modernization, as we saw in Chapter 7, his hard and graceless style increasingly alienated Churches of Christ from other Christian denominations. Clearly, then, one of Foy E. Wallace's great contributions was to reinforce and perpetuate the sectarian mentality that Churches of Christ had inherited from the radicalized *Christian Baptist* tradition.

Nowhere among Churches of Christ did the legalistic tradition more thoroughly join itself to the scolding style than in Texas. This is not to say that the legalistic dimension was not pervasive in other regions of the Church of Christ heartland, for it was — notably in Arkansas and Tennessee. Nor is it to say that Texas was altogether lacking in grace-oriented leaders. My point here is simply that the Texas experience contributed to the hard, legalistic side of Churches of Christ in significant ways.

Many factors helped account for this, chief among them being the wild and wide open qualities of the nineteenth-century Texas frontier. Legitimate settlers and outlaws competed with one another for a toehold in this raw, developing society, and Native Americans and Mexicans reacted to the Anglo-Saxon invasion in ways that made life for whites uncertain.

In such a climate, softer, gentler souls had difficulty even surviving. One preacher, a Mr. Bush, who had emigrated to Texas following the Civil War, learned that the church in Lagarto in Live Oak County badly needed a preacher.[26] When Bush arrived on Sunday morning at the home of a "Brother Stillwell," a leading member of the congregation, he found

> several men gathered around the home, all heavily armed, with knives and guns. Bush inquired for Stillwell, found him, introduced himself, and then inquired what was happening. Stillwell replied, "We are glad to see you; don't be alarmed at appearances; you go over to town, and the brethren will care for you. We have three or four Mexicans to hang, and then we will be ready for a meeting."[27]

Offering welcomes like that, it is little wonder that Texas proved most attractive to those among Churches of Christ who were already given to a hard and legal style — or that those who nurtured such themes as unmerited grace or who embraced an apocalyptic worldview and refused either to vote or fight should have found Texas less hospitable. Little wonder that Benjamin Franklin's *American Christian Review*, with its strongly legal and dogmatic spirit, proved popular with members of Churches of Christ in Texas, or that David Lipscomb found Texas resistant to his apocalyptic worldview.[28] All these factors helped ensure that the radicalized tradition of Alexander Campbell's *Christian Baptist* would reign supreme in the Lone Star state.

Further, while Texas attracted a sizable population from Tennessee, it also attracted many from such midwestern states as Illinois, Indiana, and Ohio. Thus Texas became home not only to conservatives with loyalties to the emerging Churches of Christ but also to progressives with loyalties to the emerging Disciples of Christ. As a result, Texas became the preeminent battleground for wars over instrumental music and missionary societies. That fact, coupled with the division between Churches of Christ and the Disciples that was very much in progress during the waning years of the nineteenth century, further nurtured the hard and legal style already so much a part of the intellectual landscape of Texas Churches of Christ.

For all these reasons, the cultural experience of turn-of-the-century Churches of Christ in Texas sustained and reinforced the sectarian model of the *Christian Baptist* tradition. Churches of Christ in Texas would eventually move toward denominational status, but that movement would be a long time coming.

Austin McGary and the Firm Foundation

Fully a product of this hard, embattled culture, Austin McGary launched in 1884 the *Firm Foundation,* the paper that in time would mean for Texas what the *Gospel Advocate* meant for Tennessee. The *Firm Foundation* differed dramatically from the *Gospel Advocate,* however, just as Austin McGary differed dramatically from David Lipscomb. McGary's father, Isaac, served under Sam Houston in the Texas army and guarded the defeated General Santa Anna the night following his capture in 1836. Ten years later, in 1846, Austin McGary was born in Huntsville. When the Civil War broke out, McGary enlisted in the Huntsville Grays.

In 1872, during the height of Reconstruction, McGary entered politics, running for sheriff as a Democrat in Republican-controlled Madison County. Knowing that Republicans would depend on the black vote to defeat him, McGary determined to do what he could to keep blacks from the polls. When he learned that a white organizer from nearby Hempstead was heading to Madison County, McGary intercepted the man en route, forced him at gunpoint

Austin McGary (1846-1928) founded the noted Texas journal the *Firm Foundation* in 1884, expressly to fight David Lipscomb on the issue of rebaptism. A legalist who stood in the lineage of Benjamin Franklin and Alexander Campbell's *Christian Baptist,* McGary required rebaptism for Baptists who wanted to convert to the Church of Christ, since Baptist baptism was not intended "for the remission of sins." Plain and rustic, McGary typified the hard style of preaching and teaching that characterized the Texas frontier. (Photo courtesy R. L. Roberts)

to drink castor oil, and turned him back home. Blacks did not vote in that election, and McGary won by a slim margin.

After serving as sheriff, McGary worked as a conveying agent for the state penitentiary. The job involved transporting convicted criminals to prison from the far corners of the state and coping not only with the criminals under his care but also with outlaws and hostile Native Americans as he made his way back home. By the early 1880s, McGary was a hard-bitten and much-feared lawman with values a world away from those of David Lipscomb. Such was the early life of the man who launched the *Firm Foundation* in 1884.

Significantly, when McGary finally became interested in religion, he undertook a study of the Alexander Campbell–Robert Owen Debate. He was converted near the close of 1881 in response to the preaching of a British emigrant, and he became a member of the Church of Christ. Three years later he began publishing the *Firm Foundation.*[29]

McGary brought to his religion the same tough, fighting style he employed as a lawman. Indeed, he established the *Firm Foundation* for the express purpose of fighting David Lipscomb on the issue of rebaptism. One finds played out in his campaign against Lipscomb some of the issues that separated the apocalyptic perspective of the Stone-Lipscomb tradition from the more legalistic outlook that descended from Alexander Campbell. True to his allegiance to a sovereign God, Lipscomb insisted that one should be baptized for one reason only: to obey God. To make the validity of immersion "turn upon any other point than this," Lipscomb argued, "is transferring the healing virtue from God to ourselves."[30] In keeping with this principle, Lipscomb and his colleagues in Middle Tennessee gladly received Baptists who wanted to become members of the Church of Christ.

McGary, on the other hand, stood squarely in the Campbell tradition, insisting that remission of sins was contingent on immersion and hence that one must be baptized for the express purpose of forgiveness of sins. Since Baptists typically submitted to immersion because they believed that their sins had *already* been forgiven, McGary argued that any Baptist who wanted to become a member of the Church of Christ had to be rebaptized. Inherent in McGary's position was a strongly sectarian attitude toward the thousands of Baptists in Texas — an outlook Lipscomb simply did not share. For over fifteen years, McGary fought Lipscomb and the *Advocate* over this issue, and, as a result, Churches of Christ in Texas, largely sympathetic to McGary's position, increasingly embraced the legal and sectarian tradition that had descended from Alexander Campbell and the *Christian Baptist.*

On the other hand, in 1884 McGary voiced strong support for Lipscomb's assertion that Christians should not be involved in politics. "We fully and heartily agree with Bro. Lipscomb on this question," he wrote, "believing that he has clearly sustained it by Scripture." Obviously, this man who had served both as sheriff and as conveying agent for the state penitentiary had undergone a significant conversion on this issue, and he confessed as much: "We have heretofore gone heart and soul into politics; but in the election that has just passed we took 'neither part nor lot,' although the voting place was in sight of us. The 'old man' yearned to vote for Cleveland and Hendricks, but was kept 'under subjection' by a law that is higher in our estimation, than those of earthly governments and potentates."[31] By 1900, however, he had changed his mind again, and now criticized Lipscomb severely for his "crude and unreasonable teaching."

> We confess that for several years we were swept off of our feet and stood upon our head, as it were, by the teachings of others upon what was called "The Christian's Relation to Civil Government." Many of our friends are yet in that same confused state of mind on this question that we were. . . . Those who deny that the Christian sustains any proper relation to civil government that entitles him to the right of suffrage . . . are trying to make Gods out of ordinary mortals.[32]

In the rough-and-tumble Texas culture of the late nineteenth century, the legal tradition, not the apocalyptic tradition, was destined to prevail.

The True Church and the Hard Style: Texas Version

In this context, Churches of Christ in Texas gave a whole new meaning to the combative tradition that Campbell himself had fathered during the *Christian Baptist* era. In the inaugural issue of the *Firm Foundation*, Austin McGary specified that the publication was being launched "to battle for the truth, ignoring the conventionalists of so-called 'polite society.' "[33] And, indeed, when David Lipscomb complained that McGary had attacked him unfairly, McGary responded like a Texas sheriff dealing with a common criminal: "He richly deserves the castigation that is in store for him, and he should stand up bravely and take it. He plaited the whip with his own hands, and if he aimed it for a plaything, he should not have made it so *heavy!*"[34]

When McGary's critics complained that he was too heavy-handed, McGary admitted that "we have said some cutting things some times, that we are now sorry for." But he also insisted that "the man who proclaims 'the truth as it is in Jesus' . . . must wound a large per cent of the people."[35]

To understand Austin McGary and his hard and caustic style, one must take into account the fact that he identified completely with common people and had little use for fashionable society. Like Benjamin Franklin and David Lipscomb, McGary felt that a faithful preacher "is apt to be a poor man in this world's goods[, for] wealth and Bible Christianity . . . are not often found walking hand in hand."[36] He believed that the fashionable classes had inundated the church in Austin, excluding and ignoring the common people — himself included. He had nothing but praise for Elijah Hansbrough, a Texas preacher and agent for the *Firm Foundation* who, he said, "wields the old Jerusalem blade with telling effect." But he complained that "a majority of the brethren in the vicinity of Austin are too slacktwisted to appreciate Bro. H.'s preaching."[37]

McGary's deep-seated lower-class biases played an enormous role in shaping the *Firm Foundation,* both in content and in style. As far as McGary was concerned, the greatest source of corruption in the church in the 1880s was the growing class of salaried preachers, men McGary regarded as "raving wolves" who cared only for money, fashion, and reputation. If primitive Christianity was to be restored, McGary argued, "the system of the 'modern pastor' must be relegated to the bats and owls with all its worldly trumpery." It was time, he wrote, to "call in the old pioneer preachers, who have been pushed aside to give place to gay college striplings who have been taught preaching as a trade, and let these old soldiers reorganize the Churches after God's plan."[38]

When McGary sought to justify his combative style, he pointed first of all to the growing class of wealthy and fashionable Christians "who are for peace, peace, peace!" Such people, he charged, would readily make "peace with the organ, the grab-bag, the church sociable, jug-breaking, parlor-dancing, modern pastor (who lords it over God's heritage), immodest apparel (such as jewelry, bangs, frizzes, silks, satins, etc., etc., jockey caps and fine hats with tropical birds roosting on them), and . . . the 'missionary society,' and sectarian immersion."[39] Faced with these sorts of serious threats to his conception of primitive Christianity, McGary regarded the hard style as altogether necessary and appropriate.

Among the economically deprived members of Churches of Christ throughout Texas and the surrounding regions — a people living on the margins of a rough, frontier society — the hard style became standard fare near the turn of the century. When a Church of Christ congregation in neighboring New Mexico appealed for a preacher in 1890, it warned, "One of those soft-going, milk-and-cider, one-by-three preachers need not apply. Soft teachers will not likely accomplish much in this territory."[40] Thirty years later, J. D. Tant, a crusty Texas preacher, felt compelled to defend his plain, Texas language to his Tennessee critics:

> It is . . . true that my language is blunt and plain; but having been reared in the West, where we all use plain speech, and being an Irishman also . . . , we all use language out there that can be understood; and when I heard many of my brethren, especially among the pure-hearted preachers, claiming that my language was offensive because I said "bull" in the pulpit, I hardly knew what to do.[41]

Some Texas preachers cast the plain-spoken tradition in terms of the proverbial Texas shoot-out and admonished one another to fire "mighty salvos of shot and shell . . . into the ranks of the enemy" and "put the foe to rout."[42]

When Texas preachers of the early twentieth century fired their "shot and shell," more often than not they took aim at one of two targets: the "fashionable" Disciples of Christ, with their organs and missionary societies, or the competing denominations. One Texas preacher who routinely took aim at both was T. R. Burnett, who wrote three volumes of satirical poetry published by the *Firm Foundation*. A sample of Burnett's lyrical talent can be found in his rendition of "Alas and Did My Saviour Bleed," which he rewrote to satirize the Baptists:

If you will in the straw-pen roll,
    And wrestle hard, my boy,
You'll get salvation in your soul,
    And shout and jump for joy!

At the bench, at the bench, there I first saw the light,
And excitement took my senses all away,
It was there in the straw that I wrestled all the night,
And now I'm deluded all the day.[43]

Such was the climate, by and large, among Churches of Christ in Texas during the late nineteenth and early twentieth centuries. It was a climate that supported the hard-scrabble lifestyle of underprivileged settlers — settlers who generally lived on the underside of society and knew little of the refinements of a more settled social order. It was a climate that sustained the sectarian model of the church that members of Churches of Christ had inherited from Alexander Campbell, Tolbert Fanning, Benjamin Franklin, and other nineteenth-century luminaries. And it was the climate into which Foy E. Wallace Jr. was born — in Montague County, Texas, in 1896.

The Fighting Style and Foy E. Wallace Jr.

Perhaps more than any other person of his period, Foy Wallace embodied all the qualities we have discussed, from a hard style to a theology that focused squarely on human initiative. His theology is perhaps most clearly revealed in his sermons. In 1937, he published a small volume of his sermons under the title *The Certified Gospel*. In the sermon bearing the title of the volume, Wallace explained his conception of the gospel. Though the sermon occupies five pages in print, Wallace devoted only five lines to the themes of the cross and the atonement. "The cross," he said, "declares God's infinite hatred of sin, and God's infinite love for the sinner." Beyond that, he did not elaborate.

The bulk of the sermon was given over to two issues: (1) a list of evils that Wallace especially wanted to combat — evolution, modernism, denomi- nationalism, and faith-only revivalism — and (2) a discussion of the true

Foy E. Wallace Jr. (1896-1979) was perhaps the most pivotal and influential figure in Churches of Christ throughout the 1930s and 1940s. Through his papers the *Gospel Guardian* and the *Bible Banner*, Wallace launched a crushing attack against the entire nineteenth-century apocalyptic heritage, focusing his attack especially on pacifism and premillennialism. Wielding enormous power, Wallace also popularized among Churches of Christ a hard, fighting style and attacked those who refused to support either his tactics or his objectives as sympathizers with his enemies.
(Photo courtesy Gospel Advocate Company)

church. Wallace claimed that "the certified gospel is that of Christ and the Church" — not just any church, but the *one* church. "Considering the fact that Christ built one, died for one, purchased one, and is the head of but one — deep down in your heart, what church do you, yourself, think you should belong to, friend?" He then amplified his definition of the "certified gospel" to include "the gospel of Christ and the church versus men and their movements." And how does one enter the church? Here Wallace focused on "the divine plan," which entails "faith to change the heart, . . . repentance to change the will, . . . and baptism to change the state (or location). . . . Friends," he declared, "this is the certified gospel."[44]

Neither Wallace nor those who looked to him for leadership had much conception at all of "unmerited grace." Little wonder, then, that when one of Wallace's writers preached in Cincinnati, F. L. Rowe complained that the man's four sermons were "forceful" but "largely pugnacious." Rowe "asked him at the supper table to preach a sermon on the Prodigal Son. He hesitated a minute and then said, 'Brother Rowe, I cannot do it. I never have studied that subject.'"[45]

In addition, in his campaign to save the Churches of Christ as he had known them as a boy, to discredit those whose style he considered too soft, and to destroy R. H. Boll, Wallace transformed the hard style he had inherited from his turn-of-the-century Texas upbringing into a swashbuckling, fighting style that he urged upon all his followers. In the very first issue of the *Bible Banner*, he complained that "a general softness is pervading the church. Firm faith and plain preaching, once universal and unanimous among those devoted to the ancient gospel, are now yielding to the persuasions of the plush-mouthed and velvet-tongued moderns." He blamed this decline, not unexpectedly, on "the Bollistic blight [that] has been a malignant growth in the body of Christ" and on "the spirit of pacifism . . . [which] is taking the fight out of the church."[46] He called instead for "militant preaching . . . and teaching and writing that defends the truth against all errors, teachers of error and institutions of error by name, make, model and number."[47] To give biblical sanction to this campaign, Wallace appealed to Paul, arguing that he "was as personal in preaching and in writing as any man ever was; and when he denounced heresy and heretics, our strongest language is mild beside his."[48]

Wallace's followers were not slow to get his message. They soon virtually filled the *Bible Banner* with calls for militant preaching. Many of these calls perpetuated the familiar lower-class bias that favored sectarian religion and reflected an implicit awareness that the Church of Christ, here and there even in the late 1930s, was moving toward denominational status. R. A. Turner was a case in point. He condemned the "window-dressed-with piety, lily-fingered, please-let-us-pray type of . . . preacher-pastor[s], with pensively sweet manners, who serve as social secretaries to the congregation and make hop-calls on the women while the men are at work." He put such preachers in a class with "the near-nude bathers, the wibble-wabble, dancing church members, cigarette-smoking, beer-drinking, card-playing men and women of the church (including preachers), adultery, [and] the movies (hatched from the incubator of whoredom in Hollywood)."[49]

Others expressed alarm that "soft" preachers had apparently joined ministerial alliances. A. B. Keenan complained that such alliances existed only for "the stifling of religious investigation by the fostering of union meetings and pulpit exchanges; by the extolling of a 'common heritage'; [and] by the willingness to let each seeker for salvation 'join the church of his choice.'" He went on to say that "the unsullied restoration platform agrees as well with membership in a pastors' union as God with the devil."[50]

No one, however, echoed with more precision Wallace's call for militant preaching and writing — and for calling the names of sinners and compromisers — than did Hugo McCord. "There are those among us who believe in being soft, noncontroversial, nonfighting," McCord complained. "But the old Book still tells us to fight the good fight and to put on the whole armor of God."[51]

McCord practiced what he preached. He explained that when he attended a Church of Christ in Greenfield, Tennessee, he was "shocked to hear them call on a Presbyterian preacher" to lead in prayer. McCord "debated what to do" and then decided to "condemn it publicly, right now. So I pointed out the heinousness of what had been done." Within three minutes, half a dozen people left the church. Though McCord assumed they were all Presbyterians, he later learned "that all of them were members of the church [of Christ]" embarrassed by his actions. Then McCord made his point: "The church is softening! We want to get along with sect neighbors regardless of the cost."[52]

McCord especially condemned in this regard Boll's *Word and Work,* which he said "does not mention names of those it attacks," and the *Truth-Seeker,* published at Harding College, "which is determined to be sweet-spirited, never pugnacious." On the other hand, he praised the *Firm Foundation,* the *Gospel Advocate,* the *Christian Leader,* and the *Christian Worker,* which, he said, "are not hesitant in calling the names of denominations and in uprooting their doctrines." Similarly, he compared Harding College and David Lipscomb College (successor to the Nashville Bible School), on the one hand, with Freed-Hardeman College (Henderson, Tenn.), which was "positively outspoken." And he contrasted such preachers as E. H. Ijams (on whom more in Chap. 9), who "will call a Methodist preacher at New Hope, 'Brother,'" on the one hand, with N. B. Hardeman and E. R. Harper, whose preaching "draws the line between truth and error [and] . . . calls the names of errorists," on the other.[53]

Simply put, one finds in the *Bible Banner* of the late 1930s evidence of a serious cleavage within Churches of Christ. Wallace and his followers rose in opposition to those who sought to move the Church of Christ more into the mainstream of American life and culture. Further, as Wallace and his followers grew increasingly shrill regarding those they viewed as "modernizers," these more gentle spirits sought to undermine Wallace's work, to temper Churches of Christ with a measure of grace, and to render Churches of Christ less odious in the eyes of its neighbors. It is to this phase of the story that we now turn.

G. C. Brewer and the Heritage of Grace

Throughout the history of Churches of Christ, there were few, indeed, who conceived of "unmerited grace" in the radical, uncompromising fashion of R. H. Boll or K. C. Moser. There were some, however, especially in Tennessee and Arkansas, who carried the banner of grace more successfully than Moser and who, through the force of their personalities and/or their adherence to orthodoxy on other critical points, nonetheless managed to enjoy widespread acceptance among mainstream Churches of Christ.

Standing in the mainstream but dissenting from the legalisms that the mainstream often fostered, these people typically refused either to support or to condemn R. H. Boll and his premillennial movement. On the other hand, they did take a stand in forthright opposition to the tactics of Foy E. Wallace. We might say that they celebrated a doctrine of grace that downplayed premillennial eschatology.

Significantly, these people not only rejected premillennialism but typically abandoned the apocalyptic outlook that had driven the premillennial sentiment within Churches of Christ for over a hundred years. They were thus prepared to make their peace with the surrounding culture in ways that might have shocked Barton Stone or David Lipscomb.

Typical of this grace-oriented tradition was G. C. (Grover Cleveland) Brewer. Brewer spent most of his life in Tennessee and northern Alabama, and there as a boy came under the influence of T. B. Larimore, one of the truly generous and kind-spirited preachers of the late nineteenth and early twentieth centuries. Brewer also attended the Nashville Bible School and absorbed much of its spirit — to the extent, in fact, that shortly before his death in 1956 he recalled, "I have never even voted in my life."[54] It is also true that Brewer largely jettisoned the apocalyptic framework of his forebears in his efforts, beginning in the 1930s, to engineer a strongly patriotic, anti-Communist movement among Churches of Christ (a development we will survey in Chap. 11). But that does not alter the fact that Brewer spoke regularly of unmerited favor and challenged what he saw as a strongly legalistic outlook among his people.

Thus, for example, when K. C. Moser's book *The Way of Salvation* appeared in 1932, Brewer strongly endorsed it and criticized those among Churches of Christ who had turned the gospel into a legal system:

> In showing that man can and must obey God in order to be saved, *some of us have run to the extreme of making salvation depend on works.* Some have been wont to show that there is a *human side* and a *divine side* to salvation, and in doing so they have made the *human side coordinate with the divine.* Worse, in the minds of some the *divine* has been completely ruled out and salvation made a matter of human achievement — except that the *"plan"* was divinely given.

Brewer maintained that such teaching flatly "perverts 'the gospel of the grace of God.'" Further, in the context of efforts to exclude R. H. Boll and his people from the fellowship of Churches of Christ, Brewer suggested that if anyone among Churches of Christ should be "'*marked*' and *avoided*," it should be the legalist who undermines the gospel. Concerning Moser's book, Brewer ended by saying that "if there is a conclusion in it from which I differ, I do not now recall it."[55]

This emphasis on "unmerited favor" continued to characterize Brewer's thinking and preaching. In 1945, he scolded those among Churches of Christ who have "faith in faith, faith in repentance, faith in confession, faith in baptism!" Such emphasis on "a plan," he argued, "is to build according to a blueprint; and if you meet the specifications your building will be approved by the great Inspector!" Such a notion "is all wrong," he insisted. "We are saved by a *person,* not by a ceremony" or "a plan."[56]

Brewer refused for many years to condemn R. H. Boll, even though he rejected Boll's premillennial outlook. Brewer knew full well that Boll's premillennial eschatology was but a reflection of a deeper theological commitment to unmerited favor, a position that Brewer himself shared. Further, Brewer felt that if he had received God's grace, he should in turn extend that grace to others, in spite of disagreements.

Consequently, as early as 1925, Brewer suggested that the premillennial issue was not worth discussing.[57] He objected in 1932, when Foy Wallace, then editor of the *Gospel Advocate,* sought to charge Boll and his people with heresy.[58] And again in 1933, he objected when Wallace prepared to debate Charles Neal on the issue of premillennialism.[59]

Then, in 1934, Brewer laid all his cards on the table. Wallace had been scheduled to speak at the Abilene Christian College lectureship that year but canceled his engagement at the last minute. The college secured Brewer as a replacement, and he used the occasion to criticize Wallace for his attack on Boll and the premillennial wing of the church and to urge a greater spirit of tolerance among Churches of Christ. His criticisms of Wallace were sufficiently strong that the editors of the annual lectureship book for 1934 replaced them with more generic — though still quite pointed — remarks. But G. H. P. Showalter, editor of the *Firm Foundation,* provided readers with his own summary of Brewer's speech, which he had heard.

According to Showalter, Brewer dismissed the "Boll issue" as lacking "sufficient significance to justify the division it had occasioned." Brewer claimed that Boll and his people were "pure-minded men, with strong faith and deep reverence for the word of God," and added that Boll "had entered his own life at a crucial period and he believed had been the actual means of his salvation." Brewer noted that he and Wallace "differed widely on . . . 'Bollism,'" and suggested that preachers who push debates on inconsequential issues often do so "to distinguish themselves."[60]

Though Wallace's name does not appear in the text of Brewer's lecture that appeared in the official volume, Brewer's meaning is nonetheless unmistakable even there:

> The divisions that exist in local congregations or in any particular sections of the country, whatever may be the ostensible cause, are caused by carnality. . . . Those who are involved in a division always claim that some vital point is in question. They strive to justify the condition that exists by citing

some doctrinal disloyalty, or some unfaithfulness to the word of God. Frequently, however, it is only our opinion or our judgment that has been disregarded and not the word of God.

But Brewer was not through. He added,

> Our efforts sometimes are similar to the solicitous servant who jealously guarded his master's slumbers. The master had given orders to the servants not to allow him to be disturbed, but he was awakened by a bright flash and a sudden roar in the room which almost deafened him. In great excitement he inquired of the servant what this meant; the servant standing with a smoking revolver in his hand said that there was a mouse gnawing paper in the corner of the room and he feared that it would disturb the master and therefore shot it. Brethren, let us quit shooting mice and therefore stop exciting people to the extent of heart failure and death.[61]

When Wallace read the report in the *Firm Foundation,* he could hardly believe his eyes. He complained that "the injury to the cause of truth could not have been greater had R. H. Boll appeared on the program in person." He took Brewer's speech as "an attack on all the faithful preachers who are opposing this new party in the church" and as "an effort to break the influence of the Gospel Advocate's opposition to this new party."[62] Though Brewer would later become more openly critical of Boll's premillennial position, the relation between Brewer and Wallace was never the same.

Conclusions

In seeking to trace the evolution of Churches of Christ from sect to denomination, one cannot afford to ignore the importance of those who opposed premillennialism but embraced the heritage of grace. As we shall see in Chapter 9, those who sought in the 1930s to blunt the sectarian spirit and to move Churches of Christ in the direction of progress, modernization, and denominational status typically stood squarely in that tradition.

Further, one has to appreciate the essential irony associated with this "grace tradition." Who could have imagined that people with theological roots reaching so deeply into the soil of the sectarian, apocalyptic, and countercultural tradition of Barton W. Stone would have provided the principal impetus for moving Churches of Christ from a sectarian to a denominational posture? And yet they did so. As the pounding waves of modernization slowly ate away the apocalyptic perspective of the Stone-Lipscomb tradition and the principles of pacifism and refusal to participate in politics slowly washed out to sea, the theological moorings of the "grace tradition" also underwent radical transformation. Even among the proponents of the grace tradition, the apocalyptic perspective inevitably declined. There remained among them a strong doctrine of grace, but it was a doctrine of grace largely estranged from a sense of divine judgment on the common culture.

Thus the early twentieth-century heirs of the Stone-Lipscomb tradition, already anxious to accommodate Churches of Christ to the best of mainstream American culture, came into possession of the theological tool that would facilitate that accommodation: a doctrine of grace cut loose from its apocalyptic moorings. Scattered representatives of the "grace tradition" increasingly focused their energies on "positive, constructive" teaching that in many cases differed little from the moral values of the surrounding culture and transformed grace into a kind and gentle spirit. In this way, they nudged Churches of Christ further down the road of cultural adaptation and respectability. It is to this story that we now turn.

CHAPTER 9

Resisting the Fighting Style: From Primitivism to Modernization

Apocalypticism often translated itself into a rich understanding of justification by grace through faith, as we saw in Chapter 8. Yet, few prominent leaders of Churches of Christ articulated the theme of grace as forthrightly as did R. H. Boll, K. C. Moser, or G. C. Brewer.

But there were other leaders, also rooted in the apocalyptic heritage, who conceptualized grace more in terms of tolerance for competing perspectives and a reverential search for truth. Their apocalypticism led them to affirm that God was God and stood in judgment on all human pretensions, and that only God — and no human being — had a corner on the market of truth. Within the Stone-Lipscomb tradition, this belief in a sovereign God who defines truth and who himself is truth often inspired a passionate search for truth and a tolerance for perspectives that differed from their own. They viewed such tolerance as a form of divine grace embodied in the common life.

At the same time, the notion of a sovereign God also inspired among these people a sense of judgment. Truth was truth and right was right, after all, especially since God himself had made those determinations. The sense of divine sovereignty that inspired a search for truth thus also inspired a categorical rejection of compromise and error. For this reason, the themes of judgment and grace often went together and stood in dialectical tension within the Stone-Lipscomb heritage well into the twentieth century.

But the dialectical relation between judgment and grace tended to dissolve in the acid bath of the premillennial controversy. As those in the Wallace camp increasingly focused on judgment to the neglect of grace, many in the Stone-Lipscomb tradition who opposed Wallace gravitated toward affirmations of grace rather than affirmations of judgment.

This almost singular preoccupation with grace — whether in its classic, biblical form or in its more democratic, social manifestation — brought striking changes to the Stone-Lipscomb tradition and to the entire fellowship of Churches of Christ. In the first place, those who opposed Wallace by focusing on various aspects of grace subtly transformed the long-standing tradition of tolerance for differing viewpoints into a tradition of consensus. Given the highly polarized intellectual climate that prevailed among Churches of Christ in the 1930s, it was difficult at best to engender tolerance for differing perspectives or to air those differences civilly in the public arena. Under the circumstances, many settled on consensus as the next best option. Over the years, the church's most progressive leadership proved more inclined to search for consensus than to undertake free and open discussions of differing points of view. At the same time, the progressives increasingly came to identify the old debating tradition fostered by Alexander Campbell and his heirs in the nineteenth century with intolerance and with the most sectarian segments of Churches of Christ.

Second, in seeking to shape consensus, those who opposed Wallace increasingly endeavored to build that consensus around positive and constructive themes and to eliminate negative themes altogether. If Wallace called for hard, negative preaching and writing, his opponents increasingly called for positive thinking, positive preaching, and positive writing, and they often confused criticism with cynicism. Throughout the remainder of the century, this emphasis on positive thinking increasingly became a hallmark of the progressive leadership of Churches of Christ.

And third, in the context of their preoccupation with consensus built on positive thinking, those who opposed Wallace determined that theological issues germane to the Christian heritage often generated considerable controversy, whereas biblically rooted cultural values often generated the consensus they sought. In the interest of harmony and consensus, therefore, they increasingly ignored the theological issues that had proved so divisive in the past and focused instead on biblically rooted cultural values that might serve as the basis for unity and peace — the practical value of providence and prayer, for example, and the values of family life, Christian unity, Christian business ethics, Christian education, kindness, goodness, basic morality, and the role of Christianity in promoting mental health.

This concern to build consensus around cultural values is strikingly reminiscent of the eighteenth-century Enlightenment model through which leading thinkers of that age sought to bring peace and harmony to a warring Europe — the model that shaped the thinking of Alexander Campbell as he sought to bring unity to American Christendom. But Campbell had infused that model with explicitly Christian content, whereas his most progressive heirs among Churches of Christ in the 1930s often found Christian doctrine too divisive and turned instead to more broadly palatable, biblically inspired cultural values.

This affirmation of cultural values was not produced solely in reaction to the doctrinal divisiveness of Wallace and his people, however; it was also associated with the heightened level of education and the growing sense of middle-class propriety that was rapidly gaining ground within Churches of Christ. Indeed, virtually all who led in the effort to circumvent Wallace's program had been exposed to substantial higher education. Several were college presidents, and others either had graduate degrees or were enrolled in graduate studies programs. Further, this group of leaders self-consciously appealed to a relatively educated, urban audience, whereas Wallace generally appealed to a less sophisticated audience that was on the whole suspicious of cities, wealth, and education. Wallace found supporters in urban areas as well, but these often were people estranged from the city and its ways. We will pick up on this theme at greater length in Chapter 10.

The key point here is that many in Churches of Christ during the 1930s and 1940s took a decisive turn toward an acculturated faith that was grounded in grace, tolerance, and middle-class American values — a faith largely divorced from the radical sense of judgment that characterized their nineteenth-century forebears. We have already noted this shift of emphasis on the part of George S. Benson and Clinton Davidson in the mid 1930s. In the late 1930s, the shift appeared again in two new journals: the *Christian Leader* and the *20th Century Christian.*

Before exploring these developments and the cultural shifts they represented, however, we should first consider the tradition of tolerance and free and open discussion in the interest of truth that prevailed within the Stone-Lipscomb tradition. It was this tradition on which the progressives among Churches of Christ in the 1930s self-consciously based their opposition to Foy E. Wallace.

The Search for Truth in the Stone-Lipscomb Tradition

One need not look far to find within the Stone-Lipscomb heritage the concern with an ongoing search for truth. In fact, this theme was central as well to Alexander Campbell — though, as we have seen, many of those who radicalized the *Christian Baptist* perspective lost sight of its meaning and significance. In the early years of the nineteenth century, however, most Campbellites and Stoneites stood shoulder to shoulder in their agreement on this point.

For example, under the leadership of the influential Stoneite-turned-Campbellite minister John Rogers, the entire Church of Christ at Concord, Kentucky, affirmed in 1830 that

> the *fatal error* of all reformers has been that they have too hastily concluded *that they knew the whole truth, and have settled back upon the same principles of proscription, intolerance and persecution, against which they so strongly remonstrated.* . . . Having, then, full in our view, this fatal rock, on which so many reformers have split, may we studiously avoid it. We have no reason to con-

clude, we know all the truth. . . . We have nothing to lose in this inquiry after truth. We have no system to bind us to human opinions.[1]

Rogers represented both the Campbell and the Stone sides of this movement in its early years. As time went on, however, those who embraced the search for truth most strongly were those who had at least one foot planted squarely in the apocalyptic tradition inspired by Barton W. Stone.

David Lipscomb is perhaps the most notable case in point. When asked in 1875 about the question of excommunication, Lipscomb responded,

> So long as a man really desires to do right, to serve the Lord, to obey his commands, we cannot withdraw from him. We are willing to accept him as a brother, no matter how ignorant he may be, or how far short of the perfect standard his life may fall from this ignorance. . . . What is needed is patient instruction and discipline in the church, instead of withdrawal from the weak.[2]

In 1907, he criticized preachers within the Church of Christ who "spend their time to combat the sects, to expose their errors, and show the mistakes they make." He charged that among such people "this party zeal becomes a substitute for love of truth and practice of godliness."[3]

In addition, at the old Nashville Bible School, Lipscomb routinely promoted debate and discussion on all sides of controverted issues. Jesse P. Sewell recalled in 1940,

> When I was a student in Nashville Bible School, each year they brought Brother G. G. Taylor there. He and Brother Lipscomb would debate the Civil Government question. They brought Brother [T. W.] Brents. He and my uncle E. G. Sewell would debate the Laying On of Hands question. . . . The people were allowed to hear the strongest that could be presented on both sides of these controverted questions.[4]

Further, in his role as editor of the *Gospel Advocate,* Lipscomb assiduously practiced the policy of open journalism and routinely printed articles and opinions that differed from his own. He reserved the right to challenge those opinions — not in order to vanquish his writers but to encourage dialogue and conversation in the ongoing search for truth.[5] A case in point involved F. D. Srygley, who wearied in 1885 of what he called the "Southern journalism and theology" that appeared regularly in the *Gospel Advocate.* In fact, Srygley disagreed with practically every position Lipscomb took, including those on participation in politics, on instrumental music, and on missionary societies. He went so far as to propose that a group of progressives buy stock in the *Advocate,* neutralize Lipscomb, and suppress "the six-for-a-nickel jackasses that are now braying in it." Four years later, in 1889, Lipscomb added this same F. D. Srygley to the *Advocate* staff. By 1892, with Srygley still on his staff, Lipscomb observed that "Brother Srygley feels under no obligation yet to agree with Brother Lipscomb."6

No wonder that when B. C. Goodpasture, editor of the *Advocate* in the 1940s, sought to rebuke Foy Wallace for his hard and arrogant style, he simply reprinted an editorial from David Lipscomb: "A true lover of truth seeks out and appropriates as his own every truth he finds, no matter who holds or teaches it. . . . The love of truth is a spirit of kindness and love toward all, even to the holder of error."7 Indeed, the ideal of the grace of God often expressed itself precisely in this way among nineteenth-century Churches of Christ, especially among those with strong roots in the Stone-Lipscomb tradition. And this was also the case with the two new papers born among Churches of Christ in the decade of the 1930s: the new *Christian Leader* and the *Twentieth Century Christian*.

A Kinder Journalistic Style

We have already noted the major movement toward progress, modernization, and denominational standing that was made when many key leaders among Churches of Christ turned their backs on the apocalyptic worldview of the Stone-Lipscomb tradition during the World War I era. A second major push toward progress and modernization occurred when heirs of that tradition sought to undermine the sectarian spirit fostered especially by Foy E. Wallace. Since Churches of Christ had no formal power structure, and since, as we noted in Chapter 1, powerful editors effectively functioned as bishops, this struggle inevitably occurred in the field of religious journalism. When the would-be reformers of the 1930s sought to make a serious difference among Churches of Christ, they had only one real way of doing so: they had to create a new and different brand of journalism.

The New Christian Leader

Of the new papers that appeared in the late 1930s, by far the most controversial was the "new" *Christian Leader* — an updated version of an older paper that first appeared in 1886 in Cincinnati and that now emerged — all polished, scrubbed, and refurbished — from Nashville. Employing two-color graphics on its cover, a handsome typeface, a content that focused on biblically rooted cultural values, and a kind and gentle spirit, the new *Christian Leader* stood in marked contrast to traditional journalism among Churches of Christ.

Though the new *Christian Leader* survived for only two years — 1939 and

1940 — its story is pivotally important for understanding Churches of Christ in the twentieth century. For this story involves far more than the mere launching of a new paper. It is the story of a titanic struggle between those committed to preserving the Churches of Christ as a sect and those committed to moving Churches of Christ toward more mainstream denominational status.

Those involved with the new *Christian Leader* clearly thought of themselves as a distinct, reforming movement, committed to breaking the sectarian spirit and fighting style that increasingly characterized their heritage. And while they ultimately failed so far as the *Christian Leader* was concerned, in the long run they succeeded and contributed to the pattern that would increasingly characterize the more progressive wing of Churches of Christ for the remainder of the twentieth century.

The struggle between the sectarian and denominational ideals implicit in the "war of the papers" that ensued had its roots in both theological and social factors. On the one hand, it was a struggle, to a significant degree, between the tradition of grace and the more legalistic tradition among Churches of Christ. To some degree, therefore, it perpetuated the long-standing split between the iconoclastic Alexander Campbell of the *Christian Baptist* era and the irenic Barton W. Stone. On the other hand, the struggle also reflected social divisions within Churches of Christ — divisions between the educated and the unschooled and between urbanites and rural folk, as we already have noted. And finally, the struggle was to some degree a contest between Tennessee and Texas. Leaders who represented the genteel Tennessee tradition of Stone and Lipscomb more often than not provided the core of the leadership on behalf of more positive, constructive journalism. Many of the key defenders of the old sectarian spirit had their roots in the rough-and-tumble environment of the Texas frontier.

By the late 1930s, Wallace had to a great extent stamped journalism among Churches of Christ with his hard, fighting style, and many in this tradition saw only two alternatives: they could either line up behind Wallace or risk a schism within the church. E. H. Ijams, president of David Lipscomb College, confided to Jesse P. Sewell in 1938 his conviction that "this movement will be lost unless there is a great improvement in the journalistic situation that has existed within recent years."[8] Sewell agreed. In his view, journalism among Churches of Christ had been governed too long by "a leadership of suspicion, distrust, criticism and distruction [sic]."[9] Feeling the same need for change, a small group of church leaders determined to provide Churches of Christ with a meaningful alternative in Christian journalism — an alternative that would stress the positive rather than the negative and that would emphasize the values on which all within Churches of Christ might agree.

The core of that group — Clinton Davidson, Jesse P. Sewell, and E. W. McMillan — represented the wealthier and better-educated segment of Churches of Christ. Davidson, we should recall, was the millionaire salesman and businessman who had helped stabilize Harding College when George Benson went there as president in 1934. Sewell and McMillan had both acquired advanced academic degrees, and Sewell had served as president of Abilene Christian College. The three reached out to include other like-minded individuals, including E. H. Ijams (president of David Lipscomb College), George Benson (president of Harding College), J. F. Cox (president of Abilene Christian College), S. H. Hall, and G. C. Brewer. Almost all these men had connections with the old Nashville Bible School and had been influenced in significant ways by David Lipscomb, James A. Harding, or both.

McMillan was a native Texan who learned the message of grace only indirectly from the Nashville Bible School. He grew up in the anti–Sunday school wing of Churches of Christ that had little connection with the Nashville tradition (a faction we will look at more closely in Chapter 10). But at Gunter Bible College (Gunter, Texas), he met and married Elizabeth Baxter, a cousin of Batsell Baxter, who became a significant force among Churches of Christ in his own right. McMillan later said that Elizabeth gave him his education. He also received rich stores of spiritual and devotional wisdom from the president of Austin College, a Presbyterian school in Sherman, Texas, where he completed his bachelor's degree, and from the Baptists at Baylor University, where he earned his master's degree.

As McMillan was nearing completion of his program at Baylor, Elizabeth died. The kindness that the Baylor community extended to McMillan in that hour of crisis deepened his conviction that the Christian faith had far more to do with a life of devotion and spirituality than with sectarian orthodoxy.[10] Appropriately enough, McMillan's crowning publication was a book published in 1959 entitled *The Minister's Spiritual Life*. McMillan served as chairperson of the Bible Department at Abilene Christian College from 1928 to 1934. During the period in the late 1930s when he played such a significant role in launching the new *Christian Leader*, he was pulpit minister for the Central Church of Christ in Nashville.

In many ways, Jesse P. Sewell was the most important leader in the effort to provide a more positive thrust in Christian journalism among Churches of Christ. Sewell was a well-known and highly respected figure throughout the fellowship of Churches of Christ. This was especially true in Texas, where he had served as president of Abilene Christian College from 1912 through 1924 and served in the late 1930s as preacher for the Grove Avenue Church of Christ in San Antonio. Sewell's correspondence for the 1930s and 1940s reflects the extent to which he provided leadership in the movement to derail Foy Wallace and to offset the fighting style Wallace had brought to Churches of Christ.

Though he now was a Texan, Sewell — like so many others in this movement for a kinder, more constructive brand of journalism — had roots in Tennessee. He had been a student at the Nashville Bible School from 1894 through 1898, and he readily acknowledged his debt to that institution. "It was there," he recalled, "from David Lipscomb, J. A. Harding, Dr. J. S. Ward, J. W.

Grant and others that we received the inspiration for whatever work we have done, and whatever good we have accomplished."[11]

It is true that he eventually rejected the apoliticism and pacifism that he undoubtedly learned there, and by World War I he took a great interest in Texas politics and even permitted the formation of a Student Army Training Corps at Abilene Christian College, as we noted in Chapter 7. But he did retain from his Nashville training a deep commitment to an unbiased search for truth conducted in a fair and impartial manner, and he sought to apply it in the midst of the bitter and divisive premillennial crusade. In 1940 he wrote to Thornton Crews that he had tried to foster at Abilene Christian College the same kind of open investigation that he had experienced at the Nashville Bible School:

> I believe that . . . [open investigation] is the only scriptural and safe course and I am unreservedly commited [*sic*] to it. It might interest you to know

Along with Clinton Davidson and E. W. McMillan, Jesse P. Sewell (1876-1969; pictured here) provided the pivotal leadership in the fight for more positive, constructive journalism among Churches of Christ in the late 1930s and early 1940s. The president of Abilene Christian College from 1912 to 1924, Sewell attended the Nashville Bible School in the late 1890s and readily acknowledged the extent to which that institution had shaped his thinking.

(Photo courtesy Abilene Christian University)

that I made not a half-hearted but a very persistent effort to get this very thing done during the lecture week which has just closed at Abilene. I suggested that R. H. Boll be invited to present his views and that Foy Wallace be invited to present the other side. . . . My suggestions were considered and much correspondence was carried on with reference to it, but the management finally decided against it.[12]

In the field of journalism, however, Sewell chiefly supported positive and "constructive teaching so thoroughly in harmony with the word of God that, every time they [the Wallace people] strike, the blow will react against them."[13]

Many in this group of reformers hoped that the *Gospel Advocate* might emerge as the much-needed voice of positive and constructive teaching, but there was reason to doubt that this would be the case. In the first place, Foy Wallace had edited the *Advocate* from 1930 through the spring of 1934, and he had left a strong stamp on the paper. When Wallace's successor John T. Hinds died on New Year's day 1938, the future of the *Advocate* — and, many believed, the future of Churches of Christ as well — was very much up for grabs.

The selection of the next editor and hence the editorial direction of the *Advocate* rested with the paper's owner and publisher, Leon McQuiddy. Jesse Sewell represented many who were convinced of the gravity of McQuiddy's decision, and so he wrote a series of stern letters to the publisher in 1938, urging him to choose as editor someone who transcended factional interests.

Already, Sewell noted, Churches of Christ suffered from an implicit division. He pointed on the one hand to "a conservative group, (which some would call a radical group) headed by N. B. Hardeman," a leading preacher and debater among Churches of Christ who had cofounded and at that time was serving as president of Freed-Hardeman College in Henderson, Tennessee. Given the political climate in Tennessee at the time, Sewell was doubtless right in identifying Hardeman as the leader of the "conservative group," but he recognized that Hardeman was allied with "such men as Foy E. Wallace, [E. R.] Harper, Charlie Nichol, W. L. Oliphant, [and] Dee Bills."

On the other side of the existing division, said Sewell, was "a liberal group (which would by some be designated the soft group) headed by E. W. McMillan and backed by such men as [E. H.] Ijams, Sam Hall, G. C. Brewer, Geo. Benson, J. F. Cox [president of Abilene Christian College], and etc." Then Sewell made his point: "Now, Brother McQuiddy, the division is here already in sentiment, spirit and attitude. The question is, shall it be defined, and become distinct and permanent or shall it be destroyed . . . ?"[14] So far as Sewell was concerned, McQuiddy held the answer to that question in his own hands.

McQuiddy's actions, however, suggested to many that his real sympathies lay with the Wallace faction. Early in 1938, he offered to bankroll Wallace's *Bible Banner*[15] and, so far as most could see, took no discernibly positive steps to

A noted educator, evangelist, and debater, N. B. Hardeman (1874-1965) cofounded Freed-Hardeman College with A. G. Freed in 1908 (Freed-Hardeman grew from earlier institutions dating to 1869) and in 1923 became president of that institution. Five times between 1922 and 1942, Hardeman delivered his famous Tabernacle Lectures in Nashville's Ryman Auditorium. At least two generations of Church of Christ preachers cut their theological teeth on those lectures, which received wide distribution in published form. In 1938, Jesse P. Sewell identified Hardeman as the leader of "a conservative group" that promoted east of the Mississippi River the tactics and ideas popularized by Foy E. Wallace Jr.
(Photo courtesy Gospel Advocate Company)

reform the *Advocate*. On that score, E. W. McMillan complained to Sewell in August of 1938,

> Brother McQuiddy has dalleyed [*sic*] so much that I do not believe he is going to do anything toward allowing the *Gospel Advocate* to be a part of the [reform] movement. . . . It is my conviction that he is marking time in the hope that the movement may lose its momentum and allow the Advocate to plod on in the old rut. . . . Moreover, it is my conviction that he ultimately will lend the Advocate to the extreme, radical element.[16]

For some time, however, Sewell nurtured the hope that McQuiddy would be part of the solution, not part of the problem. He wrote to him about the hate factor then dominating Churches of Christ. "There is no question that some men in these groups make it a test of fellowship that every one else hate the men they hate."[17] And he warned McQuiddy of the "combination of from six to ten . . . fellows in high places, pulling every wire possible to control every center of influence in the brotherhood." McQuiddy should know, Sewell wrote, that "there is a wide spread and growing resentment against it."[18] And he wrote to Davidson, spelling out his concerns precisely:

> If he [McQuiddy] selects a Hardeman-Wallace man, then there will have to be a new paper or the restoration movement will be destroyed. . . . If he doesn't select a Hardeman-Wallace man and should select an extreme factionalist on the other side, the Hardeman-Wallace group will rally to the Wallace new paper [*Bible Banner*] and there will be war.[19]

Finally, even Sewell grew despondent over McQuiddy's course and abandoned all hope that the publisher would work for a more constructive style of journalism among Churches of Christ. When Sewell's name surfaced as a possible editor of the *Advocate*, he told McQuiddy in no uncertain terms that, under the circumstances, he had no interest.

> Now, let's get it straight. There are *no conditions* under which I would accept the editorship of the Advocate. If it is to continue with the present spirit, attitude and lack of constructive program I certainly would not be interested — and your letters indicate to me that . . . you have not at any time intended to make any constructive changes and that you do not now intend to.[20]

It was at this point that Sewell, Davidson, McMillan, and others seriously began considering a new paper that would challenge the fighting style. Following a conference in Nashville to explore the status of religious journalism among Churches of Christ,[21] Davidson distributed a questionnaire early in 1938, seeking to learn the feelings, especially among preachers, regarding publications within Churches of Christ. When the results were in, Davidson announced triumphantly that "97% of those who answered the questionnaire were opposed to articles in which one writer criticizes another writer by name."[22] Then, in August of that year, Davidson reported to Sewell that he had "purchased an option on the Christian Leader. . . . I have the promise of sufficient capital to publish . . . twice monthly a magazine with better paper stock, better typography, and better cover than any paper in the brotherhood. . . . The policy will be 100% constructive."[23] The first issue of the new *Christian Leader* appeared on January 1, 1939, and combined the old *Christian Leader*, the *Truth Seeker* (formerly published in Searcy, Arkansas, the home of Harding College), and the *West Coast Christian* (published by James L. Lovell of Los Angeles). E. W. McMillan served as the editor of the new publication.

Needless to say, Foy Wallace was less than happy when he learned of the plans for the new journal. He viewed it as a weapon in "a campaign against plain writing and preaching."[24] Further, since Davidson copyrighted the results of the questionnaire and refused to release them in full, Wallace suspected that it had been sent to a very small group of preachers and hence was not representative of grassroots sentiment in the church. He cited as warrant for that suspicion communications he had received from large numbers of preachers who either had not received the questionnaire or who had refused to complete it.[25] And, indeed, when the new *Leader* finally appeared in January 1939, many rejected it precisely on the grounds that it was "soft." Eugene Smith, for example, complained that "men may desire journalistic excellence but as for me and mine give me Bible [*sic*]. . . . God never authorized any course but an open and condemning one."[26]

For many reasons, Davidson quickly earned Wallace's undying contempt. Most of all, Wallace suspected that Davidson intended to promote in a variety of ways the premillennial theories of R. H. Boll.[27] That offense alone would have been sufficient to ignite all of Wallace's wrath. But Wallace registered other complaints as well. Not only did Davidson copyright the results from his questionnaire; he also copyrighted materials in the new *Christian Leader* — in order, Wallace thought, to hide behind legal protection.[28] And then Davidson issued a veiled threat to sue the *Bible Banner* over an article he viewed as libelous.[29] Wallace later claimed that Leon McQuiddy withdrew his financial support from the *Bible Banner* precisely because of that threat, leaving him "with a publication on my hands, to sink or swim, live or die."[30]

Further, many in the Wallace camp resented Davidson because of his wealth. One writer gave voice to a sentiment common among *Bible Banner* readers when he characterized Davidson as a "man who for twenty years bowed himself in supplication and adoration at the altar of material success and there to the neglect of his soul and his God amassed a fortune."[31] Others charged that for many of his years in New York, Davidson had worshiped with a "fashionable" and "digressive" Disciples congregation rather than with a Church of Christ.[32] "While he was hibernating twenty years in this fashionable Christian Church," Wallace wrote, "he was making big money in the insurance business." He dismissed Davidson on the grounds that he was "a *business* man" rather than a serious Christian.[33] More than that, he charged that Davidson was "the leading menace of the church today." "The church has its Fifth Columnists," he said, and "Clinton Davidson is [their] leader."[34]

North/South and rural/urban class distinctions played a significant role in separating the new *Christian Leader* from the readership not only of the *Bible Banner* but of virtually all the traditional journals that served Churches of Christ. Almost one full year into publication of the new *Leader*, Davidson assessed the problems that differences in social class had posed for the paper: "The old circulation of the Leader was almost entirely among farming people

and country churches. I believe that a large percentage of them do not like the
Leader. They express dislike for the cover. . . . The new subscribers have come
largely from the city churches."[35] In addition, the old *Leader* had built its base
in the Middle West — in Ohio and Indiana where the legacy of the *Christian
Baptist* and Benjamin Franklin predominated. Everyone connected with producing the *Leader* quickly sensed the significant differences between the leadership that emanated from Nashville and the mentality that had characterized the
Leader's former midwestern constituency. Davidson noted that the old, midwestern readers "criticize the writers on the grounds that many of them are
Southern writers and also on the grounds that these writers are too well educated."[36] McMillan candidly acknowledged that

> the problem of sectionalism is not to be lightly considered. True it is that
> such should not be, but "we" have a "North" and "South" as definitely as does
> Methodism. . . . With this sectional spirit, augmented by the suspicion so
> rapidly spread over the field where most of the old subscribers and writers
> live, it has been quite difficult to get material from old writers.[37]

At least part of the North/South sectionalism that plagued the *Leader* can be
attributed to animosities left over from the Civil War, but an even more
important factor was the long-standing breach within Churches of Christ
between the legacy of the *Christian Baptist* on the one hand and the legacy of
Barton W. Stone and David Lipscomb on the other. The midwestern readers
of the old *Christian Leader* simply could not relate to the kinder, more grace-
centered perspective appearing in the new journal. Further, the citadels of
higher education among Churches of Christ were all in the South; all of the
movement's educational institutions in the North now served the Disciples.
And the growing split between city dwellers and farmers simply exacerbated
the situation.

Faced with this daunting barrier to consensus, the directors of the
Leader decided that, to the extent they had to, they would ignore the objections coming from down "on the farm" and from those "accustomed to . . .
the old fighting material" and "concentrate our subscription efforts [instead]
among city churches."[38] Having thus determined their direction, they committed the *Leader* to a vigorous program of positive and constructive journalism. It featured articles on such topics as the Christian in business, persistence, love and unity, prayer and providence, the virtues of American
democracy, the value of a Christian home, spirituality, and the power of
positive thinking.[39]

Time and again the new *Leader* denied any sympathies with premillennial
eschatology.[40] At the same time, its frequent emphases on pacifism and conscientious objection in the face of World War II gave evidence of the apocalyptic
soil in which most of its writers had their roots.[41] Clinton Davidson even went

beyond advocacy of pacifism to argue for a spirit of Christian "internationalism" in which "there were no favored races or favored nations."[42]

The arrival of of the *Leader*, with its constructive policy, had an immediate impact on the course of the *Gospel Advocate*. On March 2, 1939, it was announced that B. C. Goodpasture would assume the editorship of the *Advocate*,[43] and in his opening editorial Goodpasture rejected the fighting style and appealed to the memory of Tolbert Fanning and David Lipscomb to justify the change in policy: "These venerable men exalted principles above persons, and sought to be free from personal bitterness and recriminations. Their example is worthy of our consideration and emulation."[44]

Quite simply — and quite accurately — Wallace accused Leon McQuiddy and the *Advocate* of selling out to pressures from Clinton Davidson.

> Our fight is with this New Deal of Liberalism — commonly known as soft-pedalism, compromise and neutrality. It is born of the Clinton Davidson movement — "conceived in sin and brought forth in iniquity." . . . As for the Gospel Advocate, it has apparently succumbed to the New Deal mania and is doing Davidson's bidding. Their revamped policy is exactly what Clinton Davidson commanded.[45]

Others in the Wallace camp shared that opinion. Price Billingsley characterized Goodpasture as "a panty-waist editor," not unlike "that hand-picked softie E. W. McMillan," editor of the *Leader*. He urged McQuiddy not to betray further the great "mass of common folk" that constituted the heart and soul of Churches of Christ. These people, Billingsley urged, "were bred to fight, born in a storm," and would abandon the *Advocate* as soon as they sensed weakness on McQuiddy's part.[46]

Sewell, on the other hand, was convinced that Davidson had saved the church from ruin. "The entire situation in the field of Christian journalism is changed wonderfully for good," he wrote Davidson. "Had you gone back from the meeting which we held in Nashville and withheld your money from the Christian Leader there would be an open, bitter division running throughout the churches all over the land today."[47]

Sewell's optimism proved unfounded, however, for the "open, bitter division" was far from ended. While Wallace continued his attacks on Davidson, he also sought to discredit both E. W. McMillan, the new editor of the *Christian Leader*, and the Central Church of Christ in Nashville where McMillan preached.

While serving as chair of the Bible department at Abilene Christian College in the mid-1930s, McMillan had strongly supported a member of his faculty whom some accused of harboring premillennial sentiments. That man was R. C. Bell, who had served with James A. Harding at Potter Bible College and with J. N. Armstrong at both Western Bible and Literary College in Missouri and Cordell Christian College in Oklahoma earlier in the century (see Chap. 7). McMillan knew full well that Bell embraced not premillennial speculation but rather the traditional apocalyptic worldview that had characterized the Stone-Lipscomb tradition. Further, Bell developed an extensive reputation for his grace-centered teaching at Abilene Christian College. In this, he occupied common ground with such individuals as G. C. Brewer, K. C. Moser, and R. H. Boll. In defending Bell, McMillan made himself suspect in the eyes of Wallace and his people.[48]

Moreover, many viewed the Central Church, which now housed the offices of the *Leader,* as rife with premillennial sentiment. While some of Central's members no doubt held premillennial beliefs, the congregation was not predominantly premillennialist. Like R. C. Bell, most of Central's members identified with the apocalyptic worldview of the Stone-Lipscomb tradition. The congregation's founding literature gives evidence of scant concern to promote itself in terms of Church of Christ orthodoxy. Rather, in a statement published in 1925, the year of

E. W. McMillan (1889-1991) preached for the Central Church of Christ in Nashville from 1938 to 1941. During that period, this congregation resisted the hard style of teaching and preaching and accelerated its tradition of outreach to the poor and the dispossessed. McMillan chaired the Bible department at Abilene Christian College from 1928 to 1935, and in 1948 founded Ibaraki Christian College in Japan and served as that school's first president until 1952. In 1950, McMillan helped establish the predominantly black Southwestern Christian College in Terrell, Texas. He served as Southwestern's president from 1950 to 1953, simultaneously leading both Ibaraki and Southwestern for a period of two years. (Photo courtesy Central Church of Christ, Nashville)

E. H. Ijams (1886-1982; pictured here), a professor at David Lipscomb College, worked alongside A. M. Burton to establish the Central Church of Christ in Nashville in 1925. This remarkable congregation provided free medical and dental care along with food and clothing for the poor, living quarters for homeless young people, daily worship, and family counseling. Ijams preached for this congregation for its first three years. He also served as president of David Lipscomb College from 1934 to 1944 and president of Georgia Christian Institute in Valdosta from 1951 to 1953.
(Photo courtesy David Lipscomb University)

its founding, the congregation described its principal commitment as "seeking first the Kingdom of God, thus worshipping God, and serving man — REALLY SERVING 'in spirit and in truth.'" Further, they shaped their commitment around a self-conscious awareness of apocalyptic judgment, basing

> all of its objectives as a church on the Biblical quotation, "Then shall the King say unto them on his right hand, Come ye blessed of my Father, inherit the Kingdom prepared for you from the foundation of the world, for I was hungry and ye gave me to eat; I was thirsty, and ye gave me to drink; I was a stranger and ye took me in; naked, and ye clothed me; I was sick and ye visited me; I was in prison and ye came unto me."[49]

This congregation grew from a concern shared by two men — E. H. Ijams, then a faculty member at David Lipscomb College (heir to the old Nashville

Bible School), and A. M. Burton, founder and president of Nashville's Life and Casualty Insurance Company and chairman of the Board of Trustees of David Lipscomb College. Forty years later, Ijams explained that concern: "Churches of Christ, as I had observed them during the first quarter of the twentieth century, were commendably strong in doctrine, but were often very, very weak in good works."[50] Ijams and Burton therefore determined to put their Christian faith into action among the poor and dispossessed in Nashville's inner-city district. Within a year, the congregation's good works had caught the attention of the *Nashville Banner,* which ran a full-page pictorial story on its social outreach programs, including its free dental and medical services and its efforts to dispense food and clothing to those in need.[51]

By 1941, the congregation had grown from 45 to 1,200 members and once again attracted attention from the *Nashville Banner,* which reported on the

A. M. Burton (1879-1966), founder and president of Life and Casualty Insurance Company, Nashville, and chairman of the board of trustees of David Lipscomb College, worked with E. H. Ijams to launch the Central Church of Christ in that city in 1925. Burton articulated his vision for that congregation in a booklet entitled *Real Religion — Practical Christianity* and purchased in downtown Nashville two buildings that served as a home for this congregation. Burton also provided substantial financial support for African American evangelist Marshall Keeble and for the school Keeble served as president, the Nashville Christian Institute (see Chap. 12).

(Photo courtesy David Lipscomb University)

Nashville's Central Church of Christ provided live-in facilities for homeless and destitute young people. The boys' home housed 60, while the girls' home (shown here) housed 100. According to a story in the *Nashville Banner* in 1926, for less than forty cents a day a child could rent a room with heat, lights, water, and linens, and had access to other privileges the church provided.
(Photo courtesy Central Church of Christ)

hundreds of meals and thousands of articles of clothing that the church had given away during the previous six months; on its facilities for homeless youth, which housed at that time "60 boys" and "100 girls"; and on its extensive mission and teaching programs. Further, the *Banner* noted, "Central Church facilities remain open practically the entire day and night, and emergency welfare calls are given close attention, regardless of the hour."[52] This was the church for which E. W. McMillan began preaching in 1938 — the very year in which he, Sewell, and Davidson began serious discussions about launching the new *Christian Leader*.

That same year, however, the Central church helped to confirm suspicions regarding its alleged premillennial sympathies. In that year, N. B. Hardeman held the fourth of his massive evangelistic events — the fabled "Hardeman Tabernacle Meetings" — in Nashville's Ryman Auditorium. The first of these meetings was held in 1922, the second in 1923, and a third in 1928. Now, ten years later, he returned for another series. This time, however, he focused not so much on evangelism as on issues disturbing Churches of Christ — most notably, the premillennial controversy. Significantly, he appealed extensively in his opening lecture to the memory and theology of Thomas and Alexander Campbell, making no mention at all of Barton W. Stone.[53] The *Gospel Advocate* reported that from 4,000 to 6,000 people attended the meetings each night for two full weeks; "we are a fighting bunch," the report stated, "and we should fight together against error."[54]

The Central church neither supported nor opposed the meeting. It simply ignored it, declining even to announce it publicly.[55] Not surprisingly, this omission brought down upon both E. W. McMillan and the Central church the full fury of Foy Wallace's *Bible Banner*.[56]

The suspicion Central engendered was so strong that by November of 1939, Fred L. Rowe, former editor of the *Christian Leader,* wrote to Clinton Davidson urging him to get the new *Leader* out of Nashville and "back to the old paper with the old writers." The "Central Church," he declared, "is regarded throughout the Southland as . . . the line of separation between our faithful brethren and those that the unfair critics denominate 'Bollites.'" The issue for him was urgent indeed: "You cannot imagine the bitterness that exists in Nashville and throughout the south and southwest."[57] Even Sewell became alarmed

Nashville's Central Church of Christ provided day-care facilities for children of lower-income mothers. Shown here are some of those children in 1927, two years after the congregation was established. (Photo courtesy Central Church of Christ)

and wrote McMillan, "Under the present circumstances and conditions I would not continue with the Central Church."[58]

Aware that he was losing his influence with a large segment of Churches of Christ, McMillan left Central in 1941 and took the pulpit of the Union Avenue congregation in Memphis. But his reputation as a man "soft" on the premillennial issue followed him there. By September of 1942, a group of disgruntled Union Avenue members drafted an open letter criticizing McMillan's preaching.

> Shall we have the TRUTH the WHOLE TRUTH and NOTHING but the TRUTH . . . or shall we have only "soft" "everybody can accept it" preaching such as: "Uncle Ben" and the "Gassers," "somewhere in Arizona," or "Way down on the farm."

Their open letter included affidavits from other preachers who had little appreciation for McMillan's emphasis. Gus Nichols of Jasper, Alabama, was a case in point:

> Frankly I think he is too soft to preach the gospel, and I . . . was surprised that the Union Ave. Church in Memphis would use a man whose record was questionable. They have gone over to the drifters and softies. . . . If one wants human wisdom in abundance, and pretty words, and lectures, etc., then he is all right, but for a gospel preacher I frankly say I consider him a failure.

With no sense of history whatsoever, the sponsors of the open letter called instead for "that ancient Jerusalem gospel preached by, the Campbells, Stone, [John T.] Johnson, Raccoon Smith, Harding, [E. G.] Sewell, [and] Lipscomb."[59]

The *Leader's* experiment in positive, constructive journalism came crashing down in 1940. In the spring of that year, Davidson delivered two speeches at Abilene Christian College. Sewell considered these speeches favorable to premillennialism, and he felt betrayed. He wrote to Davidson, "Since hearing your two speeches in Abilene I cannot go further with the Christian Leader."[60] And to McMillan he wrote, "I heard those speeches and I am through."[61] Sewell expressed the hope that the Pepperdine Foundation of Los Angeles might take over the *Leader*.[62]

By 1937, George Pepperdine, founder of Western Auto stores, had already established Pepperdine College, an institution related to Churches of Christ (it later became Pepperdine University). But George Pepperdine's fortunes had declined since 1937, and McMillan reported in July of 1940 that "income for the Pepperdine Foundation has been decreased by the war" and hence "'the Christian Leader' will not go to the west coast, at least for the present."[63] In fact, it never did. Instead, G. H. P. Showalter, editor of the *Firm Foundation* in Austin, Texas, announced in December of 1940 that he had acquired ownership of the *Leader* and would assume sole responsibility for its contents.[64]

Following Showalter's announcement, Wallace crowed, "The Davidson-

Leader movement is dead."[65] And he was right, at least for the moment. But the new *Christian Leader* had pioneered a kind of journalism — and a kind of theology — that would increasingly characterize the progressive wing of Churches of Christ for the remainder of the twentieth century. The new journalism and associated theology would move Churches of Christ further and further away from the sectarian mentality of the nineteenth century and would increasingly celebrate the values of conservative Protestant culture in the United States.

In this way, the *Christian Leader* initiated a transition fundamentally similar to the one Alexander Campbell had made in 1837 (see Chap. 2), when he elected to defend American Protestantism. The difference was that while Campbell acknowledged that transition, those directing the *Leader* apparently possessed little or no awareness of this dimension of their work. Their naivete in this regard was closely connected to their continued commitment to the primitive Christian faith.

The truth was that since the days of Campbell and Stone, the notion of primitive Christianity had become so central to the thinking of Churches of Christ — and so foundational to orthodoxy in every aspect of this tradition — that no one who cared about his or her standing in the church could afford to waffle on the theme, much less abandon it outright. Put another way, primitive Christianity had become the defining, foundational myth for this tradition. In this context, few progressives sensed any disjunction between the celebration of modern values and commitment to the primitive Christian faith. On the other side of the fence, however, Foy Wallace and his people were fully convinced that the progressives had abandoned their historic, sectarian posture.

The 20th Century Christian

Of all the literature of Churches of Christ through this period, the *20th Century Christian* perhaps most graphically depicts the fusion of conservative twentieth-century Protestant values with a commitment to primitive Christianity. And once again, the individuals who led this project had all enjoyed opportunities in higher education.

Four graduate students at Nashville's Peabody College — M. Norvel Young, James D. Bales, George DeHoff, and Woodrow Whitten — conceived the idea for this journal in 1938. Disillusioned with the fighting style that increasingly characterized journalism in Churches of Christ and concerned that Churches of Christ had failed to communicate effectively with the younger generation, these students determined to bring the message of Churches of Christ more into line with contemporary concerns — a goal strikingly similar to that of the new *Christian Leader*. Further, like those who pioneered the new *Christian Leader*, these young men also were committed to positive, constructive journalism.

But when Young took this idea to E. H. Ijams, at that time president of David

Lipscomb College in Nashville, he received little or no encouragement. Ijams informed Young that a group of older men was about to launch a significant journal, backed by substantial funding, that would accomplish precisely what these younger men had in mind. Ijams therefore advised Young and his colleagues to stand aside and entrust their common vision to the older generation.

Despite this advice, the graduate students determined to press ahead. With their own funds and their own resources, they issued the first number of the *20th Century Christian* from the basement of Nashville's Hillsboro Church of Christ in October 1938 — only three months before the new *Christian Leader* appeared. Knowing that none of them carried sufficient weight among Churches of Christ to serve as editor, they secured for that position J. P. Sanders, at that time the preacher of the Hillsboro Church of Christ. They also signed on Hugh Tiner (dean of Pepperdine College in Los Angeles) and Athens Clay Pullias (vice president of David Lipscomb College) to serve along with Sanders and themselves on an editorial council.

Far from being disillusioned with the core message of Churches of Christ, these students were deeply committed to the traditions of their heritage and to the ideal of primitive, nondenominational Christianity. They sought, however, to make that traditional message relevant to their own time. The cover of this periodical, for example, bore the motto, "New Testament Christianity in the Present Age." Further, Young and his cohorts found inspiration for the title of their journal — *20th Century Christian* — in two sources. First, it played on the theme of first-century Christianity and implicitly pointed backward, in good primitivist fashion, to the first Christian age. Second, it celebrated the present and the modern. The Hollywood film studio Twentieth Century Fox, for example, helped to inspire the title *20th Century Christian*.[66] When the magazine changed its name to *21st Century Christian* in January 1990, it dropped from its cover the motto "New Testament Christianity in the Present Age."

In spite of their preoccupation with the modern world, though, these students maintained significant links to the Stone-Lipscomb tradition. James D. Bales, George DeHoff, and Woodrow Whitten, on the one hand, all graduated from Harding College, where they had been influenced by J. N. Armstrong. Norvel Young had been immersed in this tradition from his earliest years, growing up in Middle Tennessee. His mother's father and uncle both owned farms adjoining David Lipscomb's, and his mother, Ruby Morrow Young, studied not only under Lipscomb but also under James A. Harding and T. B. Larimore. Young himself graduated from David Lipscomb College, the successor to the old Nashville Bible School. In later years, Young claimed no memory of either a legalistic or exclusivist outlook in the churches of his youth in Middle Tennessee. Rather, he recalled a pietistic perspective, centered on prayer, love, and one's relation to God through Christ.[67] Further, in the 1930s all four of these students had embraced the pacifist tradition that for years had been central to the apocalyptic worldview.

The *20th Century Christian* was fundamentally shaped by the extent to which these students were rooted in the Stone-Lipscomb tradition on the one hand and their preoccupation with the modern world on the other. These influences helped make the journal a bridge between the apocalyptic outlook of the nineteenth century and the pragmatic perspectives of the twentieth. On balance, however, the fascination of the founders with technological, scientific, and cultural progress eventually weakened and transformed the apocalyptic perspective to the extent that it finally bore little resemblance to the outlook of their forebears.

To understand the nature of this change, we must recall that the apocalyptic perspective in the nineteenth-century Stone-Lipscomb tradition pointed in two directions — backward to the perfections of primitive Christianity and forward to the last age when those perfections would triumph over all the earth. The eschatological dimension injected into the tradition the note of judgment on human culture. Thousands in the tradition, from Stone to Lipscomb and beyond, argued that God's eschatological kingdom stood in judgment on all human creations. As we have seen, R. H. Boll questioned whether *all* human progress was not perhaps illusory when viewed from the standpoint of the infinite, which would relativize all human creations and institutions in the last age (see Chap. 7).

The students who launched the *20th Century Christian*, however, had come of age not in the old, blighted South of their parents, but in the New South, which flourished especially in such urban centers as Nashville and in such centers of higher learning as Vanderbilt University and Peabody College. Further, these students lived in the interval between the two world wars, a period that witnessed a veritable explosion of scientific and technological advancements, and they were deeply impressed not only with the wonders of the modern world but also with its general faith in progress. It is not surprising, then, that they sought to reconcile Churches of Christ to the spirit of the modern age. But the old apocalyptic perspective of the nineteenth century constituted an obstacle to such a reconciliation.

In order to realize their vision, the students made two fundamental alterations to the tradition. First, they scuttled almost entirely the eschatological side of their inheritance and adopted instead a primitivist vision divorced from any serious expectation of a divine apocalyptic triumph over the powers and principalities of this earth. Second, they reinterpreted the traditional primitivist vision to a significant extent, redefining primitive, nondenominational Christianity in spiritual and practical terms, largely divorced from the legal and rational understandings that informed the doctrinal controversies of their age. Further, they positioned their new journal as inspirational rather than polemical, thereby withdrawing from the battlefield that Foy Wallace claimed as leader and watchdog. Hugh Tiner, for example, argued that "undenominational" Christianity "is not a system of theology, but is a practical life to be lived," centered in the person of Jesus Christ.[68] And since contributors to the *20th Century Christian* defined that "practical life" almost entirely in individualistic and privatistic terms, the sort of primitive Christianity that appeared on the pages of the journal seldom stood in judgment on the larger world of science, technology, human progress, and economic growth.

In a word, these students embraced *modernization* for Churches of Christ by scuttling eschatological considerations and recasting primitive Christianity in terms of spiritual ideals. Perhaps nowhere in the early years of the *20th Century Christian* does one find this new emphasis more fully expressed than in an article by Woodrow Whitten entitled "Progress in Christianity." Whitten asserted that "if we focus our attention on the last century, the advances made truly startle us. . . . The materialist's utopian dream of a mechanically perfect world is much nearer realization than ever before. In terms of technological advances and material developments, man has truly progressed." But he also affirmed the traditionally restorationist position that "the grandest spiritual ideas and achievements occurred once for all in the early morning of civilization." In the spiritual realm, there could be no progress beyond the truths of primitive Christianity.[69] It was this distinction that allowed these sons of the Stone-Lipscomb tradition to celebrate the modern world in a way that was foreign to their fathers and at the same time to affirm time and again the virtues of "primitive, nondenominational Christianity." For all practical purposes, those who began the *20th Century Christian* managed to stand in the Stone-Lipscomb tradition despite having abandoned the apocalyptic worldview.

If we understand this dimension of the *20th Century Christian,* we understand the rationale behind its two principal foci: the devotional and spiritual life on the one hand and human progress and potential on the other. Its focus on human potential appeared time and again. Wade Ruby, for example, granted that the modern world was plagued by war, greed, crime, and persecution, but he asked, "why brood . . . over these things? Their vast ugliness suggests the supreme beauty of their contrasting opposites." Indeed, Ruby insisted, one "enamored with his potentialities . . . must be always a *becoming* creature, always achieving, always attaining, always climbing toward the ideal in human personality."[70] In the same vein, Paul Southern praised the virtue of success. "Successful living does not depend upon work alone," he wrote. "Work without vision is drudgery. Vision without work is visionary. But vision plus work is Christianity."[71]

In that context, the *20th Century Christian* also sought to lead Churches of Christ to a sense of mission to the larger world. Norvel Young had returned in 1937 from a seven-month trip around the world on which he came into contact with cultures and civilizations of which many in Churches of Christ were not aware. He was inspired to call on Churches of Christ to "catch a larger vision" and " 'lift up your eyes, and look on the fields, that they are white already unto harvest.' "[72]

Through all of this, though, one note of the apocalyptic outlook lingered on the pages of the *20th Century Christian* — namely, a continued emphasis on pacifism.[73] In many ways anticipating the theme of civil religion that would be widely discussed in the years after World War II, James D. Bales even went so far as to quarrel with the religious dimensions of nationalism that always, he claimed, lay at the root of war.[74] Bales later abandoned this position, however, along with his pacifist convictions, in the interest of preserving American civilization.

The progressives' efforts to counteract the scolding legalism within Churches of Christ and to create a kinder tradition no doubt helped to prevent many young people from abandoning their heritage. Harry Robert Fox Jr., a missionary to Japan from 1947 to 1958, was an adolescent in the 1930s, living in Nashville. Years later, he spoke of the "hate factor" that characterized that period. "Well do I remember it and how terribly I was troubled by it!" But he credited "E. H. Ijams, George Klingman, E. W. McMillan, J. P. Sanders, J. N. Armstrong, R. C. Bell, G. C. Brewer, Norvel Young, Robert G. Neil, Norman Parks, E. V. Pullias, Ralph Wilburn" and others for helping him "to get the bigger picture." Without them, he remarked, "I doubt that I could have survived spiritually or remained with Churches of Christ."[75]

Conclusion

Over the long term, the *20th Century Christian* and the new *Christian Leader* helped move Churches of Christ out of the nineteenth century and into the twentieth. But there is more to the story than that, for these two journals helped shift a sizable segment of Churches of Christ from preoccupation with primitive Christianity to preoccupation with the modern world.

This is not to suggest that those involved with the new *Christian Leader* and the *20th Century Christian* self-consciously rejected the traditional vision of primitive Christianity. Leaders of both these journals continued to speak of primitive Christianity as a noble ideal, and they routinely sought to justify both their theology and their practice by appealing to the first Christian age. At the same time, however, for many in Churches of Christ the notion of primitive Christianity increasingly became a shibboleth, a badge of orthodoxy, albeit divested of its nineteenth-century power.

This is not surprising, for primitivism in America — at least as Churches of Christ embraced that theme — was essentially a nineteenth-century ideal. As I suggested in the Introduction, it flourished in the radically utopian climate of the early nineteenth century, borne on the wings of a variety of millennial and apocalyptic expectations and sustained by the philosophical underpinnings of Scottish Common Sense Realism. It also proved attractive to many in Churches of Christ who experienced poverty and social alienation. All these factors ensured the vitality of Christian primitivism in Churches of Christ throughout most of the nineteenth century.

But the nineteenth century passed. Educated leaders of Churches of Christ no longer experienced poverty and deprivation firsthand. Among mainstream Churches of Christ, both millennialism and apocalypticism died off, and in the larger culture Baconianism lost much of its power. It was simply inevitable that primitivism would lose its power as well, especially among those concerned to relate Churches of Christ to the values of twentieth-century American culture. The new *Christian Leader* and the *20th Century Christian* played significant roles in helping Churches of Christ to abandon, however slowly, the restoration vision as it had been defined in the nineteenth century. Indeed, these two papers helped Churches of Christ turn their attention from the golden age of the first century (as viewed through a nineteenth-century lens) to the golden age of the twentieth century, in which, in the ensuing decades, the first Christian age came to be viewed as increasingly irrelevant. Inevitably, this transition also entailed a turn from the sectarian outlook of the nineteenth century to an increasingly denominational orientation both toward the world and toward other Christian traditions.

In all these ways, the *20th Century Christian* represented at least as much of a threat to the legal and sectarian side of Churches of Christ as did the new *Christian Leader*. Yet it altogether escaped attack from Foy Wallace and those who shared his concerns. The new *Christian Leader*, launched by older men who were well established in Churches of Christ, died after only two years. But the *20th Century Christian*, begun by a group of graduate students in a church basement, survived and prospered throughout the twentieth century. By 1955, it boasted more than fifty thousand subscribers.[76] How can this be? The answer lies in the nature of the politics of Churches of Christ during the period in question: these churches lacked organizational structure beyond the local congregation and hence depended on informal relations in their political activity.

The four graduate students who launched the *20th Century Christian* took advantage of this situation in several ways. First, they never called attention to themselves or their enterprise. They never sent out a questionnaire or announced in any way their plans to challenge the fighting style of so many of the periodicals that served Churches of Christ at that time. They just did it.

Second, they steered clear of all discussion of premillennialism, focusing instead on positive, constructive values that many, if not most, among Churches of Christ could accept.

Third, they sought not to refurbish an existing journal but rather to begin a new one. In this they differed crucially from the group that purchased the *Christian Leader*. This latter group essentially sought to impose aspects of the Stone-Lipscomb tradition on a journal that stood squarely in the lineage of the *Christian Baptist*. The man who had established the *Christian Leader* in 1886 — John F. Rowe — attended Bethany College, held Alexander Campbell as a hero, and worked alongside Benjamin Franklin for eleven years as associate editor of the *American Christian Review.*[77] It is little wonder that the loyal readers of the old *Christian Leader* found the new sound emanating from Nashville under Clinton Davidson and E. W. McMillan unacceptable. But the four graduate students who established the *20th Century Christian* ran no such risks. They started from scratch and created a publication that would reflect all the major currents flowing through Churches of Christ at that time — with the exception of the fighting style. They rooted the *20th Century Christian* in the pietistic primitivism of Barton Stone on the one hand and in the progressive primitivism of Alexander Campbell on the other. They avoided the extreme apocalyptic worldview that had dominated the Stone side of the movement throughout the nineteenth century, but they also avoided the extreme rationalist perspective that had dominated the Campbell tradition within Churches of Christ. In a word, the *20th Century Christian* found a middle road, a *via media,* that borrowed from all the elements of the movement's history while avoiding all its extremes. And it survived.

For all these reasons, Foy Wallace and others of his stripe never sensed the threat to sectarian values implicit in the *20th Century Christian.* But that threat became increasingly easy to detect in the period during and following World War II. Many of the people who, in the 1930s, prized a kind and gentle spirit, who refused to attack R. H. Boll, and who sought to undermine the fighting style of Foy Wallace worked to develop the institutional machinery of Churches of Christ in the 1940s. Their efforts set the stage for the next major battle in this communion and the next major transitional move from sectarian status among Churches of Christ toward full-fledged denominational standing. We turn to that story in Chapter 10.

CHAPTER 10

The Fight over Modernization

John F. Rowe complained in 1880 that the line dividing Churches of Christ from Disciples was "becoming more distinct every day." He observed that "there are two classes among us — those who represent 'The Ancient Order of Things' and those who represent 'The New Order of Things,'" and that "the men of the New Order of Things are determined to crush down, if possible, the Ancient Order of Things."[1]

By 1895, J. A. Clark of Thorp Spring, Texas, had decided that those who stood for the "New Order of Things" had pretty well appropriated the spirit of the Gilded Age. He believed that these compromisers made up the Disciples of Christ who had abandoned the "Ancient Order of Things," so highly prized by Churches of Christ, and he satirized them unmercifully.

> *What do men say this fifty-dollar gold coin is?* Some say it is filthy lucre; some say it is the price of the gospel; and others say it is the measure of a man's piety, or one of his passports into heaven.
>
> "But what do you say that it is?" resumed the pastor.
>
> The Disciple evangelist answered and said: "It is the chief corner stone of the Disciple church."
>
> Blessed art thou, sensational evangelist, for the gullible dupes who give us these coins have not revealed this to you, but sanctified common sense that rules our actions. And thou shalt be called coin-gatherer; and upon this metal I will build my church.[2]

Had Rowe and Clark lived into the late twentieth century, they might have been shocked to read descriptions that now portrayed their own Churches of Christ much as they, themselves, had portrayed the Disciples some hundred years before. For example, one noted historian of the American South, Thomas L. Connelly, observed in 1982 that in spite of the fact that "some of its

beliefs . . . smack of the primitivism associated with rough-hewn frontier religion," the Church of Christ had become, since World War II, "a middle-class
establishment" and "one of the larger Protestant denominations" in the South.
Connelly reported that even in Nashville, Tennessee, once dominated by an
otherworldly, apocalyptic perspective, Churches of Christ now embraced the
pragmatic methods and strategies of the surrounding world. There, he noted,
"acres of asphalt church parking lots, 110 separate congregations, scores of
buses, multimillion-dollar church buildings, television and radio, and local
political power — all rest in this body."[3]

The principal story of Churches of Christ in the 1940s and 1950s is their
transition, as Connelly put it, to the status of a modern "middle-class establishment." Whatever else that might have entailed, it surely entailed adoption
of the norms and principles of modernization. In the case of Churches of Christ,
modernization involved the development of an expanding network of
bureaucratized institutions that, through a variety of "technological innovations" and "capitalist initiatives," developed momentum and, over the years,
took on lives of their own.[4]

The process of modernization involved two important theological revi-
sions in Churches of Christ. First, it involved a shift in emphasis from reliance
on divine providence and the power of God to reliance on technique and
institutionalization — a radical change from the the apocalyptic perspective of
the nineteenth-century Stone-Lipscomb tradition. Second, the focus on institutions meant serious modification of the radically individualistic and democratized polity that members of Churches of Christ had long identified with the
New Testament pattern (see especially Chap. 4).

In another sense, however, modernization demanded no change in
Churches of Christ at all. Alexander Campbell himself, we should recall, had
sown the seeds of modernization with his postmillennial emphasis on progress
through human ingenuity, reason, and initiative. In the years following World
War I, the Campbellian faith in human progress slowly eroded the apocalyptic
outlook within the Stone-Lipscomb tradition; by World War II, the only theological resistance to modernization remaining among Churches of Christ was
their allegiance to a radically democratized polity.

One should not underestimate the power of that allegiance, however, for
it was more than just an allegiance to polity. Those who held most tenaciously
to the democratic vision did so in the name of the primitive church. They
believed that to shift from democratization to institutionalization would be to
abandon the entire primitivist vision upon which Churches of Christ based
their very reason for existence.

The Non-Class and One-Cup Churches of Christ

One rupture over institutions began in the early twentieth century when a small faction, centered especially in Texas, protested the emergence of Sunday schools.[5] In 1925 this faction drew up its own directory of churches, thereby excluding itself from the larger, mainstream fellowship, which had fully embraced the Sunday school phenomenon. By 1990, this faction counted between 500 and 600 congregations with a total membership of roughly 25,000, mainly in Texas, Oklahoma, and Arkansas.[6]

There was far more to this movement, however, than its protest against the institution of the Sunday school. First, these churches rejected Sunday schools because Sunday schools generally employed women to teach the Bible in the church. Taking literally such passages as 1 Corinthians 14:34 — "As in all the congregations of the saints, women should remain silent in the churches" (NIV) — these people felt that women should not teach even children. Accordingly, their 1974-75 directory of faithful non-class churches invited those "congregations to list, whose work and worship is patterned after the teaching of the New Testament . . . such congregations that believe in an undivided assembly for teaching the word of God . . . and let their women keep silence in the Church."[7] In fact, the gender issue has emerged over the years as the predominant point of distinction between non-class and mainline Churches of Christ. According to Larry Branum, a minister in the non-class wing, "Many have come to see the question about women teachers as the only real issue, and no longer view the question about dividing into classes as of great significance."[8] Mainline Churches of Christ have allowed women to teach children and other women but have generally prohibited them from teaching classes that included both men and women — although, as we shall note in Chapter 14, discussion of the role of women in the work and worship of the mainline congregations increased significantly during the 1990s.

The legalism that had informed the Campbellian/*Christian Baptist* dimension of Churches of Christ for so many years also contributed to the rise of the non-class movement. By 1930 the non-class churches embroiled themselves in another schism, this time over whether one cup or multiple cups should be used in the communion service.[9] The one-cup adherents based their argument on such passages as Matthew 26:27, in which the Gospel writer narrates the Last Supper. Jesus never instituted multiple cups, they claimed; rather, the biblical record clearly says, "Then he took the cup, gave thanks and offered it to them, saying, 'Drink from it, all of you' " (NIV). By 1990, one-cup congregations numbered 530, with concentrations in Texas, Oklahoma, California, and Missouri.[10]

Alongside its legalism, the non-class tradition has also embraced a commitment to pacifism. Though that commitment declined in these churches by World War II, it did not disappear. The one-cup churches continued to identify themselves as peace churches in the 1990s.[11]

The Larger Battle over Institutions

The non-class schism, however, was only a minor skirmish compared to the far larger battle over institutions that would rend Churches of Christ in major ways by mid-century. As early as 1934, W. E. Brightwell saw this second fight looming menacingly on the horizon and predicted with deadly accuracy, "The next religious war will be fought around the issue of institutionalism."[12] Two years later, Brightwell described the problem in more specific terms. Churches of Christ were growing large and prosperous, he said, and many had begun to concern themselves with "gaining prestige for the church." They were building colleges that exalted "human wisdom." They had abandoned the countryside for the city, heedless of the fact that their strength throughout their history had been "rural — and rugged." They had built some fine buildings and hired stationed pastors who often sought not so much to preach the truth as to please their employers. And in their zeal for growth, they had experimented with radio preaching, which, by its very nature, undermined plain, hard preaching. Because there was "no 'amen corner' in a radio audience," Brightwell complained, the temptation was therefore strong "to play safe and build up a clientele of regular listeners." For all these reasons, Brightwell lamented, Churches of Christ were in crisis,[13] and he therefore joined the fight against the building of institutions within this tradition.

Brightwell was but one of a cadre of anti-institutional leaders among Churches of Christ from the late 1930s through the 1950s, but the principal leader, at least through the 1940s, was — once again — Foy E. Wallace Jr. As a principal heir to the radically democratic sentiments of nineteenth-century Churches of Christ, Wallace was just as concerned to combat the institutionalizing tendencies of Churches of Christ as he was to combat premillennialism. Ironically, by fighting premillennialism, he undermined the apocalyptic perspective that might have lent substance to his crusade against modernization. Moreover, by promoting self-reliance, militarism, and values that ran counter to the apocalyptic orientation, Wallace helped lay the intellectual foundations for those aspects of modernization he later would strenuously oppose.

But Wallace never saw that point. From his perspective — and that of many of his colleagues — premillennialism and institutionalization were the two greatest threats to the integrity of the Churches of Christ. Premillennialism threatened the church's ultimacy and finality, while institutionalization threatened its New Testament polity, which Wallace believed to be essentially democratic. The fact that Wallace and his colleagues could fight on both these fronts with equal vigor suggests the extent to which they had absolutized the democratic experience as itself a principal manifestation of the kingdom of God.

Be that as it may, the institutional controversy, having conducted dress rehearsals throughout the 1930s, moved toward center stage in the 1940s, just as the premillennial controversy was slipping into the wings. Wallace launched several journals to facilitate both these fights. He resigned from editing the *Gospel Advocate* in 1934, and in 1935 he founded the *Gospel Guardian,* which ran through 1936. Then, beginning in 1938, as we have seen, he edited the *Bible Banner* and used it to vanquish the last remnants of the premillennial heresy within the mainstream of Churches of Christ. By 1949, having slain the dragon of apocalypticism, Wallace ceased publication of the *Bible Banner.*

But the dragon of modernization still roamed the landscape of Churches of Christ, destroying the simple, democratic values of this tradition and seducing the faithful with the allurements of big city churches, centralized control, bureaucracies, and modern institutions. If Wallace was too old or too tired to slay this second dragon, younger men were determined to take up his sword. In 1949, they revived Wallace's first paper, the *Gospel Guardian.* Roy Cogdill of Lufkin, Texas, published the paper and appointed Fanning Yater Tant as editor. The battle against institutions raged throughout the 1950s, but it proved ultimately to be a lost cause, at least in the context of the mainstream of Churches of Christ.

Events in the 1960s revealed all too clearly that mainstream Churches of Christ had accommodated themselves to the values and mores of modernization in a variety of ways — a development we shall explore in Chapter 11. Modernization, however, often hid behind primitivist rhetoric and, for that reason, went largely undetected by the progressive leaders of the mainstream church. In point of fact, primitivism — the historic center and core of this tradition — was rapidly becoming an empty myth with little connection to the modern world in which mainstream Churches of Christ now lived.

Understanding the Dynamics of Change

At this critical stage of a long, complex story, it will be helpful to take a closer look at some of the factors that led to this transition, exploring along the way the critical impact of World War II.

Of first importance — as we have noted throughout this study — was the progressive loss of the apocalyptic perspective during and following World War I. In the context of this chapter, however, it is equally important to observe how the loss of apocalypticism also undermined in significant ways the primitivist dimensions of Churches of Christ. The orthodox presumption was that the millennium would be nothing more and nothing less than that time when the perfections of the first age would be restored. Apocalypticism infused primitivism, therefore, with hope and expectation. For this reason, some form of apocalypticism — whether postmillennialism, premillennialism, or simply an apocalyptic worldview — served to power the primitivist perspective among Churches of Christ throughout the nineteenth century.

Apart from that source of power, primitivism sputtered and either collapsed into a system of legal constraints or simply became irrelevant. This was clearly the fate of the primitivist vision among the nineteenth-century followers of Alexander Campbell. Conservatives like Benjamin Franklin, alienated from the postmillennial progressivism of the Campbell tradition, came to view primitivism as little more than a legal code grounded in the pattern of the ancient church. Progressive followers of Campbell simply rejected primitivism as outdated and irrelevant to the world in which they lived.

In the aftermath of World War I, a similar split occurred among those with primary roots in the Stone-Lipscomb tradition. Cut loose from their apocalyptic moorings, many in this tradition — especially the rural, the poor, and the less educated — found ever more compelling the barren legal tradition established by those who had radicalized Alexander Campbell's *Christian Baptist* in the early nineteenth century (see Chaps. 2-4). As we have observed time and again throughout this book, that outlook had long been part of their heritage. So long as it was joined to an apocalyptic perspective, it remained alive, expectant, and dynamic. But when the apocalyptic engine lost power, primitivism also lost its dynamic quality. For all of this, however, many of those hardy, rural souls who clung to the primitivist perspective mounted a furious attack on the modernizers who, they claimed (with considerable justification), had abandoned the ways of the fathers.

But others in the Stone-Lipscomb tradition — especially the more well-to-do and educated urbanites — increasingly came to view the primitivist perspective as irrelevant except as a measure of traditional Church of Christ orthodoxy. The appeal to primitive Christianity continued to hold Churches of Christ together, to be sure, but for the children of the modern world in the 1930s and 1940s, primitivism increasingly became a banner without a cause, a body without a soul, an orthodoxy divorced from a truly meaningful worldview. Already we have seen early stirrings of those changes in the late 1930s, reflected in such journals as the new *Christian Leader* and the *20th Century Christian*.

Second, if the spirit of the Gilded Age had facilitated acculturation and modernization among Disciples in the late nineteenth century, the emergence of the New South between 1913 and 1945 facilitated similar changes among Churches of Christ, especially during the 1930s. As George Tindall, another noted historian of the American South, has written, precisely during those years "Southern people moved into a far more diversified, pluralistic society." And then, as if describing the dynamics that characterized Churches of Christ during that period, Tindall wrote, "For many Southerners the stresses of change set off defensive reactions against the new and unfamiliar, but for many others change offered at last an escape from poverty, both economic and cultural."[14]

Many traditionalists among Churches of Christ were among those Southerners reacting defensively to the stresses of change. It was the progressives among Churches of Christ who found an escape from economic and cultural poverty in the New South. They sought to chart new directions for Churches of Christ, focusing especially on constructive journalism and a theology that would take modernity seriously. Even more important, these progressives created a theological climate that would sustain the institutionalizing phase of modernization yet to come.

Third, while a more moderate, progressive theology created a climate in which institutionalization could thrive, World War II proved to be the single most decisive factor prompting Churches of Christ toward greater moderniza-tion and efficiency and toward the expansive program of institution building that took place in the 1940s and 1950s. During the postwar period, Churches of Christ identified ever more closely with the values of the dominant culture; by 1960 they had practically completed their long, tortured journey toward full-fledged denominational status.

World War II prompted Churches of Christ toward institutionalization in three distinct areas: education, world missions, and general acculturation.

First, the postwar period focused attention on colleges and universities as thousands of G.I.'s returned home from Europe to begin or complete their college education. By the close of World War II, Churches of Christ already had five major colleges in place: David Lipscomb College in Nashville, the successor to the Nashville Bible School, founded in 1891; Abilene Christian College, founded in Abilene, Texas, in 1906; Harding College (the history of which we surveyed in Chap. 7); Freed-Hardeman College in Henderson, Tennessee, founded in 1869; and George Pepperdine College in Los Angeles, founded in 1937. The massive influx of students after the war, coupled with the postwar religious revival, implicitly raised the question of the extent to which the colleges could promote the growth and maintenance of Churches of Christ, both in the United States and abroad. That question, in turn, raised the critical question of support for these colleges. Should they be funded solely by individual contributions, or should they be supported by congregations? The former option would inevitably hobble their growth; the latter option would, in effect, render the colleges institutional agencies of the congregations that provided support — a situation that would clearly run counter to the radically democratic and individualistic traditions that had defined Churches of Christ since the early nineteenth century.

Second, the war sparked among Churches of Christ an unprecedented awareness of other parts of the world that led to a growing interest in missions. During the war itself, some congregations of Churches of Christ began making plans to evangelize Germany and Japan after the cessation of hostilities. But it was clear that a single congregation, faced with such a momentous task, could do relatively little. To solve the problem, some congregations proposed that groups of churches channel funds to a single receiving congregation, which would then provide support for missionaries in the field. Partisans of a radically democratic polity, however, thought they smelled the stench of centralized control in such schemes.

When Churches of Christ embarked in the early 1950s on a massive program of domestic evangelism through a radio and television program called the "Herald of Truth," they used the "sponsoring church" arrangement to facilitate the project, much to the chagrin of the anti-institutional partisans. The "Herald of Truth" exerted an even greater impact on Churches of Christ, however, by subtly redefining both the theology and the power structure of the tradition.

Third, by the early 1950s, Churches of Christ were not only establishing institutions to serve a variety of causes but were establishing the church itself as a formidable institution on the religious landscape of its geographic heartland. For most of their history, Churches of Christ had been poor and socially marginal, standing over against other Christian denominations as well as the larger culture and typically viewing themselves as sojourners in a strange and foreign land, but by the 1950s all that had changed — or was rapidly changing. The theme of "sojourner" rapidly gave way to the theme of "settler," as Churches of Christ settled into their cultural environment and felt increasingly at home in the world in which they lived.

Nothing symbolized this development more graphically than the construction boom among Churches of Christ during that decade. In part, this boom constituted a response to the post–World War II religious revival that fed thousands of people into conservative and/or evangelical Christian denominations — Churches of Christ included.[15] But the boom also served as symbolic celebration of the modernization that had occurred among Churches of Christ since the 1930s and as symbolic proclamation of the extent to which Churches of Christ now sought to take their place among the respectable religious establishments of their time and place. Accordingly, the colleges rapidly expanded with new buildings that were both permanent and substantial, and a host of new junior colleges sprang up all over the country, some even before the war concluded. The list of these junior colleges included Alabama Christian College, Montgomery (1942); Florida Christian College, Temple Terrace (1944); Oklahoma Christian College, Oklahoma City (1950); Southwestern Christian College, Terrell, Texas (1950); Michigan Christian College, Rochester (1959); Columbia Christian College, Portland, Oregon (1956); Northeastern Christian College, Villanova, Pennsylvania (1959); York College, York, Nebraska (1956); Lubbock Christian College, Lubbock, Texas (1957); and Ohio Valley College, Parkersburg, West Virginia (1960).

At the same time, many congregations launched major building campaigns. Many of these congregations had met in small clapboard dwellings in poorer neighborhoods or on the edge of town. Now, many constructed new and elaborate houses of worship in more fashionable districts, strategically situated to serve not the poor but the middle class and perhaps even some of the more wealthy and influential members of the community.

The battle over institutionalization was thus in many ways a struggle involving class distinctions. Proponents of institutionalization typically lived in larger towns or cities, had gained at least some higher education, and were commensurately wealthier. On the other hand, while several key churches in the anti-institutional movement were city congregations, opponents of institutionalization typically lived in smaller towns and rural areas and generally came from the lower end of the socioeconomic scale. Though some of the anti-institutional preachers had attended college, few had earned graduate degrees. To some extent, their protest against institutionalization was an expression of their opposition to the growing power of those with more wealth and education. But it was also a lamentation over the demise of a way of life they long had identified with the primitive Christian faith.

Beyond issues of social class, there were also theological factors involved in this struggle. Those who led Churches of Christ in this pivotal phase of institutionalization were heirs to the tradition of grace that we surveyed in Chapters 8 and 9; their oldest and deepest roots were in the apocalyptic heritage that reached back to Stone and Lipscomb. It is ironic that the champions of institutionalization should have descended from people who maintained that the kingdom of God would triumph over all human institutions, but it is also quite understandable that people in the Stone-Lipscomb tradition would foster the building of institutions, given that most of the institution builders had roots in the first permanent institution among Churches of Christ in the South — the Nashville Bible School. The real irony, then, involves the Nashville Bible School itself and suggests the extent to which David Lipscomb compromised his apocalypticism when he also embraced the self-reliant progressivism of the *Christian Baptist* tradition (see Chaps. 2-4).

At any rate, the twentieth-century generation of institution builders, though descended from the Stone-Lipscomb tradition, was far removed from the apocalyptic orientation of its forebears. Proponents of institutionalization tended to speak not of the kingdom of God but rather of the primitive church, which they identified, largely out of habit and tradition, with the increasingly modern Churches of Christ of their own time and place. Orthodoxy among Churches of Christ increasingly demanded that the faithful omit from the Lord's Prayer the phrase "thy kingdom come," since it was presumed that the kingdom had come long ago on Pentecost, had been restored in the modern age, and was therefore nothing more or less than the primitive church now clothed in thoroughly modern garb.

Moreover, by identifying primitive Christianity, at least in formal ways, with their own time and place, the proponents of institutionalization allowed themselves to believe that whatever they did by way of modernization might be justified entirely by the primitive model. Those who sought to move Churches of Christ toward greater institutionalization consistently did so in the name of primitive Christianity and with regular appeals to the New Testament pattern. Typically, they manifested no awareness at all of the ever-widening gap that separated progressive, mainstream Churches of Christ in the mid-twentieth century from their nineteenth-century primitivist foundations.

The opponents of modernization and institution building came from the Stone tradition as well as from the Campbell tradition, and they often collapsed those perspectives into one. On the one hand, they drew on the radically democratic bias of such people as Benjamin Franklin, Tolbert Fanning, and David Lipscomb. On the other hand, they routinely appealed to the anti-institutional posture that was so central to the apocalypticism of the Stone-Lipscomb tradition. For example, some of their early leaders, such as the fiery Texas preacher J. D. Tant — father of Fanning Yater Tant, editor of the *Gospel Guardian* — also identified in many ways with Lipscomb and the old Nashville Bible School.

This means, first, that the anti-institutional movement among Churches of Christ was not a product solely of the Campbell tradition nor solely of the Stone-Lipscomb tradition but was rather a product of both mixed together, blended, and amalgamated. Second, it means that those who opposed the development of institutions stood squarely in the democratic, anti-institutional mainstream of their nineteenth-century heritage, contrary to the assertions of mainstream Churches of Christ that they were deviants, radicals, and schismatics.

Not only did these people stand squarely in the historic mainstream of Churches of Christ by virtue of their democratic biases and their opposition to anything smacking of institutions and centralized control but they also stood squarely in the legal tradition of Churches of Christ. In this regard, they simply carried to a higher key the outlook popularized by Arthur Crihfield, John R. Howard, Moses Lard, Benjamin Franklin, and others who had radicalized Alexander Campbell's *Christian Baptist* (see Chaps. 3-4).

Among the anti-institutional people, the legal dimension revealed itself especially in their Baconian hermeneutic, which rendered the Scripture undiscriminatingly flat and binding at every point. Thus, Roy Cogdill, publisher of the *Gospel Guardian* beginning in 1949 and a key leader in the anti-institutional crusade, attacked centralized oversight of missions on the grounds that "one unscriptural practice is as serious as another unscriptural practice." *How* one does missions, he argued, was just as critical "as whether one sprinkles or immerses, . . . [or] whether Moses spoke to the rock as God commanded or struck it taking glory to himself."[16] The anti-institutional tradition fully embraced the ideal that Moses Lard had laid out for Churches of Christ one hundred years before — namely, "the *minute* conformity of our practice to the revealed will of Christ."[17]

Moreover, the anti-institutional movement also stood squarely within the historic mainstream of Churches of Christ in its intolerance and its exclusivist, sectarian response toward other Christians. Fanning Yater Tant argued in 1935, for example, that "the spirit of religious tolerance is the very antithesis of the spirit of Christianity. The attitude of Christ and the apostles was always one of *im-*

Fanning Yater Tant (1908-) edited the *Gospel Guardian,* the principal voice of the anti-institutional movement of the 1950s, from 1949 to 1971. Through the *Guardian,* he and his corps of writers assailed all forms of bureaucratization that they felt supplanted in any way the autonomy of the local church. (Photo courtesy R. L. Roberts)

placable intolerance toward all forms of error in religion." And as late as 1969, Tant baldly announced in the headline of one of his editorials, "I Have a Closed Mind." He proceeded to explain, "I'm not ashamed of it; I'm proud of it. It has been closed for a long time, and I expect to die with it closed as tightly as it now is. I like to think it is not closed on every subject, and in every area. But there are some areas in which I am definitely NOT 'searching for truth.' I have the truth."[18]

The anti-institutional tradition as a whole typically rejected other Christian churches as fundamentally un-Christian. Tant typified his tradition in this regard when he wrote in 1953,

> There is not a Christian on this earth who is not a member of the church of Christ. There has never been one. There will never be one. . . . De [*sic*] we mean that denominational people are not true Christians? We mean exactly that. . . . Do we contend that among all the millions of Baptists, Lutherans, Catholics, Methodists, Presbyterians, and other denominational people on the earth there is not even one single, solitary faithful Christian? That is our contention.[19]

While the mainstream of Churches of Christ was moving headlong toward denominational standing, the anti-institutional movement renewed its resolve to perpetuate the old sectarian posture of the nineteenth century.

In truth, the two major heresies of the twentieth century — premillennialism and anti-institutionalism — were not heresies at all when measured by the standards of the nineteenth century. The premillennial movement kept alive the apocalyptic orientation of the Stone-Lipscomb tradition, while the anti-institutional movement kept alive the democratic and legal biases that can be traced especially to those who radicalized Campbell's *Christian Baptist*. Their allegiance to the ideals of the nineteenth century became heretical only in the context of the modernizing tendencies of twentieth-century Churches of Christ.

Finally, one cannot fully understand the battle over institutions unless one appreciates the lust for power and control that often drives contestants in struggles such as this.

The Issues

We turn now to explore, in more detail than we have to this point, the specific issues and developments that aroused the opposition of the anti-institutional movement. The efforts to build institutions among Churches of Christ, raising the spectre of centralized control, triggered a prolonged debate even more rancorous, if that was possible, than the debate over premillennialism earlier in the century.

Colleges

Opposition to higher education among nineteenth-century Churches of Christ revolved especially around Benjamin Franklin, who, as we noted in Chapter 4, unhesitatingly condemned higher education for preachers, especially following the Civil War. "We have no patience," he complained, "with this mere butterfly twaddle, toploftical, aircastle, highfalutin and empty thing."[20]

Franklin died in 1878, and his *American Christian Review* passed into the hands of one of his disciples, John F. Rowe. By 1886 the *Review* had fallen on hard times, and Indianan Daniel Sommer, another protégé of Franklin, purchased the *Review* with the intention of expanding the legacy of his mentor.[21] That he did, and more, for Sommer soon led a sizable group of radicals, centered especially in the Middle West, and determined to preserve the lower-class, democratic values to which Benjamin Franklin had devoted his life and work.

Like Franklin, Sommer was a plain and rustic man, dogged by poverty all his life and devoted to plainness as a principal Christian virtue. In a book he entitled *Plain Sermons*, he claimed to set forth "plain truth . . . in plain sentences."[22] According to Sommer, "Christ was a plain man, the apostles and other Christians were all plain people, the gospel is a plain document, and the Church is a plain institution." Not surprisingly, Sommer connected the virtue of plainness with simple, rural living, in contrast to the ostentation he associated with "larger towns and cities."[23]

Like Franklin, Sommer was a misfit in the postbellum North. He found himself estranged from developments associated with the rapid urbanization and industrialization of that region. His alienation led him to play a principal role at a "mass meeting" held at Sand Creek, Illinois, in 1889, where conservatives within the Campbell tradition virtually excommunicated progressives for the sins of endorsing church festivals, choirs, missionary societies, and stationed pastors.[24] To understand both Franklin and Sommer, one must view them in the context of the Holiness crusade mounted by simple, rural people of the postbellum North against similar vices in their own denominations.

In this context, Sommer became a ruthless foe of higher education among Churches of Christ. He attended Campbell's Bethany College for two years, beginning in 1869, but found the experience to be counterproductive. Indeed, he wrote, "I should have gone to a common school," since no one ever went to college "more ignorant than I."[25] Further, he saw at Bethany "disciples . . . of the primitive or apostolic type" and "others . . . of a modern or plastic type."[26] In the first article he ever wrote for Franklin's *American Christian Review* (in 1848), Sommer asserted that colleges help produce "a sort of preachers, for which a restoration of primitive Christianity has no use whatever."[27] Several months later, he targeted Bethany directly:

> Bethany's pile of buildings, presenting a four-hundred-and-twenty-feet front, has produced an amount of pride and poverty among our churches which can not be estimated. With her capacity for six hundred students, and her occupancy by one hundred, and her bankruptcy published by both friend and foe, Bethany is a grand failure.[28]

When David Lipscomb and James A. Harding established the Nashville Bible School in 1891, Sommer renewed his attack on church-related colleges. He grew even more vocal when Harding established Potter Bible College in 1901 (see Chap. 7).

Sommer routinely objected to church-related colleges on the same grounds that he objected to missionary societies: both institutions usurped the power of the local church. Ultimately, however, his argument was grounded more in social than theological concern; it was centered principally in the struggle shaping up between nineteenth-century rustics like himself and younger, more educated preachers. Quite simply, Sommer feared that the younger generation of preachers would render people like himself obsolete. "It is interesting," he thought, "to watch the moves of self-importance among young men and women when they come home from college. . . . They look down upon the ones who are not educated as they are." And in such a climate, he feared, "the poor preacher who has had few school advantages, and so knows nothing but the Bible, is a back number and is ostracized." Sommer also feared that the colleges would, in time, come to control the churches by producing a class of educated clerics who would "PUSH ASIDE THE GOD-GIVEN ELDERS."[29] Sommer's struggle against colleges clearly involved far deeper issues of power and control.

By the 1940s and 1950s, the anti-institutional movement among Churches of Christ sounded remarkably like Daniel Sommer. Indeed, representatives of mainstream Churches of Christ routinely sought to discredit the movement with the label "Sommerite."[30] But did the proponents of that movement really stand in that tradition? Were they latter-day Sommerites? The anti-institutional people themselves typically denied any organic connection with or descent from the Sommer tradition.[31] And on the whole they were right.

In the first place, the anti-institutional people of the 1940s and 1950s hailed, by and large, not from the Midwest but from Texas, Tennessee, and points in between, and they had little connection with the older Sommerite churches. And in the second place, they framed the issue in terms that differed significantly from Daniel Sommer's chief concern. Sommer questioned the very legitimacy of church-related colleges throughout most of his career; people in the anti-institutional movement of the 1940s and 1950s seldom pressed that issue. It is true that they often were suspicious of colleges and college-bred preachers, but their chief concern in this regard involved the question of how church-related colleges should be supported. As Roy Cogdill put it in 1947, the real issue was a matter of "whether or not it is right for a congregation of the Lord's church to contribute to a college or school in which the Bible is taught when that school is organized as a human institution doing a secular work under a board of trustees."[32] Churches of Christ had supported colleges for many years, but often that support derived — in good democratic fashion — from interested individuals rather than from congregations. Many believed that placing colleges in congregational budgets would involve those congregations in supporting institutional structures comparable to the missionary societies of the nineteenth century. Further, such schemes would take initiative away from the individual and would enable congregations with greater wealth to exert greater influence by virtue of their ability to support the colleges more substantially.

In spite of their differences, however, the Sommer movement in the Midwest in the late nineteenth/early twentieth centuries and the anti-institutional movement of the 1940s and 1950s were fundamentally similar in several respects. First, the anti-institutional movement, like Daniel Sommer, ultimately descended from the radically democratic impulse of the *Christian Baptist*. Second, the anti-institutional movement was often characterized by the same socioeconomic class prejudices that had characterized both the Sommer movement and the Franklin movement of the Midwest. Indeed, regarding old-time, unschooled preachers, Roy Cogdill asked, "How many of those men, even if they were in their prime, would be acceptable to the churches today? In many of the congregations would they appear too uncouth, uneducated, unpolished to fill the need now? How many of them could fill a place teaching the Bible in one of 'our' schools?"[33] C. R. Nichol concurred. "Call the roll in Texas," he demanded, "and view the men who were to the fore as the 'best prepared preachers.' Were they 'college graduates', products of 'Christian Colleges'?"[34]

Not surprisingly, the "Sommerites" and the "anti's," as they often were called, shared a common rejection of modernization. Sommer and his people resisted modernization among the midwestern *Disciples of Christ* in the late nineteenth century, as had Sommer's mentor Benjamin Franklin, and the anti-institutional tradition resisted modernization among *Churches of Christ* half a century later and further south. This explains why J. D. Tant, by 1937, saw in Daniel Sommer a spiritual comrade. "It was thought that you were 'extreme' on the college work," Tant wrote to Sommer, "but of late years I have said the time will come that we will go so far from Bible Christianity that we can well say, 'We had a prophet among us but did not know it.' "[35]

In truth, if mainstream Churches of Christ wanted to saddle the anti-institutional movement with the stigma of "Sommerism," they should in fairness have recognized their own similarities to the proponents of modernization among Disciples of Christ a half-century before. That, however, was a step they would never take, because it would have undermined their understanding of themselves as Christians of the "ancient order." This point is important, because it illumines the critical difference between modernization among nineteenth-century Disciples and modernization among twentieth-century Churches of Christ. The Disciples of Christ were able to accommodate themselves to modernization easily and forthrightly because they did so, from the beginning, under the banner of human progress. When Churches of Christ undertook modernization, they did so in the name of primitive Christianity, which means that they essentially backed into the modern age, often with great reluctance. The process of modernization for Churches of Christ was at best ambiguous and at worst an exercise in self-deception.

G. C. Brewer typified the ambiguity. Consistently pleading the cause of primitive, undenominational Christianity, Brewer was perhaps the first influential leader among Churches of Christ to encourage congregations to support colleges from the congregational treasury. He did so, first, in an important address at the Abilene Christian College lectureship in 1931 and again in a series of articles in the *Gospel Advocate* in 1933.[36] Significantly, none of these appeals raised much opposition. It is true that throughout the 1930s Foy Wallace and others questioned the growing power of the colleges,[37] but it was not until the late 1930s and the early 1940s that the college-in-the-budget question became a burning issue in its own right.

Significantly, this issue first became a matter of contention only insofar as it related to politics connected with the earlier premillennial controversy. When G. C. Brewer, at the Abilene Christian College lectureship in 1934, criticized Wallace's stand on the premillennial movement (see Chap. 8), he drove a wedge between Wallace and himself and made it unlikely that Wallace would view any of his proposals with much favor. Even more important were the efforts of several college presidents and former college presidents — most notably Jesse P. Sewell and James F. Cox of Abilene Christian College, George Benson of Harding College, and E. H. Ijams of David Lipscomb College — to undermine Wallace and his work by lending support to the new *Christian Leader* (see Chap. 9). As early as September 1938, Wallace thought he saw a "combination" emerging that would "set out at once to control schools, churches, and preachers."[38] Not surprisingly, therefore, he and his people increasingly opposed the college-in-the-budget scheme.

Even more important than premillennial politics, however, was the sudden influx of students into America's colleges at the close of World War II. Colleges everywhere sought to raise funds for new facilities to accommodate the growing student demand, and colleges among Churches of Christ increasingly appealed for congregational support. Two instances illustrate the point. In 1947, Robert Alexander of Abilene Christian College sought to raise $3,000,000 for expansion of the college, in part by appealing to congregations. Roy Cogdill of Lufkin, Texas, then publisher of Foy Wallace's *Bible Banner,* was incensed. He informed Alexander that "we are old fashioned . . . down here in East Texas" and that "we are not in sympathy in any way with your efforts to enlist the churches to support your school."[39]

Of far more importance than Alexander's efforts on behalf of Abilene Christian College, however, were N. B. Hardeman's efforts on behalf of Freed-Hardeman College in Henderson, Tennessee. Hardeman's position in this regard surprised almost everyone, since he had allied himself so closely with Foy Wallace in the premillennial controversy. But as a college president, Hardeman had a school to run, and early in 1947 he launched a strong appeal for congregational support for his college. He also vigorously criticized those who fought congregational support for colleges, including Foy Wallace. These people, he claimed, would erect "a beautiful meeting house, . . . put carpets on the floor, fans in the ceiling, install a baptistry, provide for the water to be heated, buy baptismal robes, hire a janitor, buy fuel, provide nurseries, and hire baby sitters" — would do practically anything, in fact, "except to make a donation to a school in which the Bible is taught. If we are not careful, we will be straining out gnats and swallowing camels."[40]

Hardeman and Wallace quickly came to a parting of the ways over this issue, dramatizing the serious tensions that attended the institutionalizing efforts of Churches of Christ. Recalling that Wallace had earlier changed his position on the issue of pacifism, Hardeman now sought to discredit Wallace as unfit to lead the church. "Being unstable," Hardeman concluded, "he cannot be a safe teacher." Indeed, "He is 'double-minded' and 'a double-minded man is unstable in all his ways.'"[41] Wallace responded by saying that "N. B. Hardeman has never been a friend to any man beyond the use that he can make of that man" and that "when he learned that I do not have a price tag on the lapel of my coat, he turns on me."[42] Though Hardeman later apologized, Wallace was hurt — so much so that he abandoned his leadership position within the anti-institutional movement. When Wallace's *Gospel Guardian* re-emerged in 1949, Wallace was not involved; Roy Cogdill, Wallace's heir apparent, provided leadership for that venture.[43]

This was by no means the end of the story, however, for Hardeman sought to force the issue by comparing congregational support of colleges to congregational support of orphans' homes.[44] The strategy backfired: he simply succeeded in making orphans' homes the object of the same sort of dispute that already focused on the colleges.[45]

By 1951, in a Harding College lecture dealing with the support of orphans, G. C. Brewer flatly accused the anti-institutional movement of Pharisaism. "The Pharisees who gave a tenth even of their garden herbs but showed no *mercy* to the suffering," he argued, "cared nothing for *justice* . . . and had no real *faith* in God."[46] Indeed, most among mainstream Churches of Christ by now viewed the anti-institutional movement as cranky and hopelessly legalistic. The anti-institutional people, in turn, regarded the mainstream of Churches of Christ as irretrievably devoted to modernizing schemes, institutional structures, and denominational standing.

Missions

Missions began in earnest among Churches of Christ following World War II. Already during the war, various members stationed in the European theater submitted articles for the *Gospel Advocate* and the *Firm Foundation* urging a massive program of evangelism in that part of the world. But how could hundreds of congregations, all radically autonomous and independent, undertake such a massive task without some form of cooperation?

Once again, people with primary roots in the Stone-Lipscomb tradition took the lead in addressing this problem. Early in 1943, G. C. Brewer revealed, both in the *Firm Foundation* and in the *Gospel Advocate,* that the Broadway Church of Christ in Lubbock, Texas, where he now served as pulpit minister, would "sponsor the plan" for cooperative evangelism of postwar Europe.[47] According to his "plan," the Broadway congregation would receive funds from numerous other smaller congregations and then supervise distribution of those funds in support of European missions.

Though arrangements of this sort were not altogether new, it was obvious that those who seized the initiative in postwar missions would inevitably build a significant power base among Churches of Christ. For that reason, the "plan" drew immediate criticism from the *Bible Banner*. "Just what authority does . . . [the Broadway congregation] have to 'sponsor' a 'Plan' for somebody else?" asked Cled Wallace.[48] But the criticism did not grow to serious proportions for several more years.

In the meantime, M. Norvel Young succeeded Brewer as pulpit minister at Broadway in 1944, and for the next several years, three men from that congregation stirred enormous interest among Churches of Christ in German missions in particular. Those three included Young, Paul Sherrod (an elder for the Broadway congregation), and Otis Gatewood, who soon became the best-known missionary to postwar Germany among Churches of Christ. Time and again, these three promoted the Broadway congregation as sponsor of the German work, receiving and distributing funds from an extensive network of smaller congregations.[49] Soon the Union Avenue Church of Christ of Memphis,

During and following World War II, leaders of the Broadway Church of Christ in Lubbock, Texas, stirred among Churches of Christ a great interest in European missions, especially in Germany. From 1947 to 1957, the Broadway congregation sponsored Otis Gatewood (1911- ; pictured here) as a missionary in Frankfurt, Germany, and he became during those years one of the best-known missionaries within this fellowship. In more recent years, he has spearheaded missions in Austria and the former Soviet Union. (Photo courtesy Gospel Advocate Company)

Tennessee, where G. C. Brewer preached after having left Broadway, undertook a similar coordination of missions in Japan. And the Crescent Hill Church of Christ in Brownfield, Texas, undertook coordination of Italian missions.

In the twenty years following the war, foreign mission activity among Churches of Christ increased significantly. Indeed, in 1946-47 Churches of Christ sponsored only 46 missionaries, whereas by 1967 that number had grown sixteen-fold to 724. Those figures reflect not only a growing interest in missions but also a significantly enlarged domestic base: Churches of Christ grew from 682,000 members in 1946-47 to perhaps 2,350,000 members by 1967.[50]

In the meantime, however, people within the anti-institutional movement grew more and more wary of the mission methods employed by mainstream Churches of Christ. Their concern was not with missions per se but with what they viewed as the mushrooming institutional machinery through which mission work now was accomplished. They objected as well to what they saw as a corresponding interest among many for standing, status, and prestige, both at home and abroad, for a "denomination" come of age.

These feelings smoldered among the anti-institutional people for several years following World War II and broke into the open in a major way in 1950. In that year, word came from Italy that Italian Catholics had attacked Church of Christ missionaries in a rock-throwing incident. Churches at home responded with mass meetings in Houston and Dallas and registered strong protests both with Congress and the State Department.[51]

Protests to the government seemed natural enough to mainstream Churches of Christ by 1950. To the anti-institutional people, however, they reflected a high degree of acculturation and a loss of the old sectarian perspective. Cled Wallace ridiculed the protests and mass meetings on the grounds that they reflected nothing more or less than a denominational orientation to the world.

> Maybe if we keep our shirts on and our hats on straight, "our" denomination may be able to appoint enough committees and draft enough resolutions to influence the pope to call off his rock throwing. . . . I am not very optimistic over the prospect of persuading the President and the State Department to bomb the Vatican. It is doubtful that "our" denomination is that popular in Washington at the present time.[52]

Wallace's article stirred up a veritable hornet's nest within the mainstream Churches of Christ. Many interpreted Wallace's criticism as support for the Italian Catholics against the missionaries. Those who registered protests against his article along these lines, however, revealed that they had virtually no comprehension of the point he was trying to make. For example, Mr. and Mrs. Oscar Paden, parents of two of the Italian missionaries, complained about Wallace's "reference to the church of our Lord as our denomination. We're not a denomination, even in fun."[53] And J. R. Chisholm couldn't understand why Wallace was so upset. "Is it wrong for Christians to become concerned and indignant over injustice?"[54] Fanning Yater Tant, editor of the *Gospel Guardian*, felt he had to explain the point to a variety of innocents within the mainstream tradition who had no awareness of the shift among Churches of Christ from its historic sectarian posture to a latter-day denominational standing. Cled, he wrote, had

> shocked many brethren into taking a "breather" in their wild rush toward a typical denominational pressure campaign on our State Department. For the turn the campaign was taking — mass protest meetings, drawing of resolutions, forming of committees, appointment of representatives, etc., etc. — was so typically denominational procedure that it might have been lifted right out of the "Methodist Handbook for Political Action."[55]

In the context of the rock-fight incident, the anti-institutional people stepped up their campaign against the "Broadway plan" for missions, which in their view stood at the center of the problem. Cogdill claimed, "Many have . . . overlooked the question that is of real importance in the matter . . . [which] is, 'Does our work in foreign countries rest upon a scriptural basis?'" Cogdill and his colleagues were convinced that it did not. "We would propose the question," wrote Cogdill, "if the Broadway elders at Lubbock can supervise the 'mission' work in Germany for two congregations could they not supervise it for two hundred? Or for all the churches throughout the world? Why don't we just elect them our 'missionary society' . . . and let Lubbock be our denominational headquarters?"[56]

In response, Cecil N. Wright of Denver sought to provide intellectual and biblical justification for the "sponsoring church" arrangement in a lengthy series of articles that appeared in the *Gospel Advocate* and the *Firm Foundation* as well as in the *Gospel Guardian*, where Fanning Yater Tant routinely reviewed them.[57] Wright maintained that the anti-institutional people had raised a phony issue, "calculated to leave a sinister impression . . . that maybe congregational autonomy is being violated by the 'sponsoring' church method of cooperation, and [this method] is therefore unscriptural."[58] Though many among the mainstream churches heaped praise on Wright's work, Cogdill charged that the material was "as full of sophistry as it is lacking in scriptural proof."[59]

Though Wright sought to maintain a scholarly approach to the discussion, relations between the anti-institutional movement and the mainstream Churches of Christ continued to deteriorate. The "anti's" held fast to the old nineteenth-century vision, viewed the mainstream as hopelessly modern and denominational, and grew increasingly strident in their condemnation of mainstream compromise. For their part, the mainstream took the new modern arrangement for granted but continued to use the language of nineteenth-century sectarianism and biblical primitivism to justify it, and they tended to dismiss the anti-institutional people as merely obtuse. It was only a matter of time before the mainstream would effectively expel the anti-institutional people from their ranks, just as they had expelled the premillennial people some years before.

The event that triggered the expulsion occurred in 1951, when a dispute between two representatives of the anti-institutional movement — Cled Wallace and Roy Cogdill — divided the Church of Christ in Lufkin, Texas, home of the *Gospel Guardian*. Wallace retained the loyalty of the core of the established congregation and continued to serve it as preacher. Cogdill led the breakaway congregation, preaching at meetings in the city's courthouse.

This local split became a church-wide issue when B. C. Goodpasture, editor of the *Gospel Advocate,* published a "Statement of Fact" provided by the older congregation, adding his own sarcastic commentary:

> From the foregoing, the reader might be able to determine where the "overflow" editor would attend church if he were in Lufkin on Sunday; but still it might remain for him to show the exact technique for starting a new congregation according to the "Lufkin plan": and also he might tell how it was done "without circumventing the elders."[60]

In this statement, Goodpasture sought to depict the leaders of the anti-institutional movement as inherently divisive, even to the point of promoting division among themselves.

Not surprisingly, Cogdill thought the *Advocate* had meddled in a local situation for no reason other than to discredit the anti-institutional leadership. The dispute between the *Advocate* and the *Gospel Guardian* now became personal. "The editor of the *Gospel Advocate,*" Cogdill complained, "seems to have a disposition that makes it difficult for him to refrain from casting slurs, and trying to discredit those who differ from him."[61] For his part, Goodpasture scorned Cogdill's response as "a vial of journalistic wrath" that was "bombastic, blusterous, and bitter" and served to expose the Lufkin troubles even further.[62] Cogdill responded to this criticism by attacking the *Advocate* itself.

> *Never in her long history has the Advocate stood for so little, and never has she given her influence to so many false and hurtful doctrines as during the present administration.* . . . The fact that she is "enjoying the largest circulation in her history" only means that her influence for evil and compromise is more widely extended.[63]

By 1954, Goodpasture had had enough. Judiciously, and with his own commendation, he published a letter calling for a " 'quarantine' " against the anti-institutional people.[64] In effect, he had drawn the line in the sand. As William Wallace (son of Foy Wallace Jr.) later wrote,

The spirit of quarantine swept the country and the Guardian movement was subjected to the same kind of pressures which had been exerted on the premillennial movement in previous years. Churches were divided, preachers had their meetings cancelled, some left the movement making confessions of their "error" in the journals, and the Guardian movement hardened into a strong minority entity.[65]

Along with the mainstream Churches of Christ and the premillennial Churches of Christ, there was now a third major wing in this tradition: the anti-institutional Churches of Christ. By 1990 they numbered some two thousand congregations, centered mainly in Texas and Alabama.[66] Significantly, the anti-institutional tradition never developed much of a following in the old Stone-Lipscomb heartland of Middle Tennessee.

Two postscripts conclude this phase of the story. First, as we noted in Chapter 9, B. C. Goodpasture was the man Leon McQuiddy appointed to edit the *Gospel Advocate* in 1939, and he assumed those duties with a commitment to resist the fighting style of Foy Wallace. As David Edwin Harrell has pointed out, Goodpasture came on the scene when Churches of Christ were becoming increasingly concerned with institutional management and maintenance of well-established dogma, and, as Harrell has further noted, Goodpasture served essentially as a manager. More than this, he managed by technique. "Foy Wallace scorched heretics," observed Harrell; "Goodpasture warned them that they would lose their position in the brotherhood." It was his commitment to manage well — to cut his losses and to consolidate his assets — that finally led him to break with the anti-institutional people altogether. In Harrell's judgment, he managed so well that he quickly became "the most influential single man on the course taken by churches of Christ between 1940 and 1970."[67]

On the other hand, Foy Wallace — Goodpasture's nemesis — finally disassociated himself from both the *Gospel Guardian* and the anti-institutional movement that he had helped establish. These decisions were largely the result of a series of personal disagreements with the editor of the *Gospel Guardian*, Fanning Yater Tant, and the involvement of his brother Cled in the Lufkin church split. In 1955, Foy wrote that "in several years I have not received or read an issue" of the *Gospel Guardian* and that "no copy of it has come to my hand."[68] By the mid-1960s, Wallace had returned to the right wing of the mainline Churches of Christ, which honored him numerous times before his death in 1979.

After a decade characterized by negative journalism, publisher Leon McQuiddy appointed B. C. Good-pasture (1895-1977; pictured here) as editor of the *Gospel Advocate* in 1939. Goodpasture used the *Advocate* to create a more constructive journalistic style. Serving in that post until his death in 1977, he arguably became the most influential man among Churches of Christ and the epitome of the "editor-bishop." He demonstrated that fact in 1954, when he successfully "quarantined" the anti-intitutional movement.
(Photo courtesy Gospel Advocate Company)

The "Herald of Truth" and the New "Electronic Bishops"

Any discussion of institutionalization and modernization among late twentieth-century Churches of Christ is incomplete without a consideration of the "Herald of Truth," a national radio broadcast that Churches of Christ inaugurated in 1952 and expanded to television in 1954.[69] While various congregations of Churches of Christ had engaged in regional radio preaching as early as 1922, the idea that Churches of Christ should undertake programming on a nation-wide scale awaited the visionary leadership of two young preachers, James Walter Nichols and James D. Willeford.

The originators of the idea believed that a project of that magnitude would clearly require a "sponsoring congregation" arrangement. The Highland Church of Christ in Abilene, Texas, assumed oversight of the project from its inception.

Predictably, the anti-institutional wing of the movement registered strong opposition to the prospect of a single congregation controlling both the finances and the content of a project that represented Churches of Christ worldwide. Such an arrangement, they thought, presented the same problems as a nineteenth-century missionary society, deceptively cloaked in the garb of congregational autonomy. The battles over the "Herald of Truth" raged furiously for the remainder of that decade and helped solidify the division between mainstream Churches of Christ and their anti-institutional antagonists.

Yet, the greater significance of the "Herald of Truth" lies in the changes that occurred in the content of its preaching between 1952 and the 1970s. In its early years — indeed, throughout the 1950s — speakers for the program focused on the traditionally sectarian themes that had long been central to Churches of Christ. For example, they routinely portrayed the Church of Christ as the one true church described in the New Testament, attacked the "false doctrine" of both Protestants and Catholics, presented the Bible as a legal

Two midwestern preachers — James Walter Nichols (1927-1973) in Cedar Rapids, Iowa, and James D. Willeford (1916-1992) in Madison, Wisconsin — merged their radio ministries in 1950 and created in 1952 the first national radio ministry of Churches of Christ, the "Herald of Truth," sponsored by the Highland Church of Christ in Abilene, Texas. This ministry expanded to television in 1954. Shortly, activists in the anti-institutional movement made the "Herald of Truth" one of their primary targets. In this photograph, taken in the early years of the ministry, James D. Willeford preaches over ABC radio. (Photo courtesy Gospel Advocate Company)

pattern, and urged listeners and viewers alike to comply with the "plan of salvation" — a theme discussed in Chapter 3. The elders of the Highland Church of Christ who supervised production of these programs required, in fact, that the "plan of salvation" be presented on every program, regardless of the announced topic.

The late 1950s, however, brought subtle changes in sermon content. To understand those shifts, one must recall the kind of piety that dominated American religion throughout the 1950s. During that decade, practically all major denominations promoted the role religion could play in fostering peace of mind. That emphasis found nationally recognized proponents in Judaism with Joshua Liebman's *Peace of Mind* (1946), in Catholicism with Fulton Sheen's *Peace of Soul* (1949), and in Protestantism with Norman Vincent Peale's *Power of Positive Thinking* (1952). In such a climate, messages that extolled the "true church" and that condemned "the denominations" for their "false doctrine" were not likely to develop a significant following beyond the ranks of the faithful. This ministry was at a crossroad: it could continue to preach to the converted or it could seek to extend its reach. But if Churches of Christ wanted to reach out, conventional wisdom suggested that they could not expect to compete effectively in the denominational free market of souls unless they embraced the sort of "peace-of-mind" piety that had dominated the national religious landscape for more than a decade.

That is precisely what happened, beginning in 1960. In that year, Batsell Barrett Baxter, professor of Bible at David Lipscomb College and a nationally known preacher among Churches of Christ, began his career as a "Herald of Truth" television evangelist, later adding radio programming to his duties. He continued to serve "Herald of Truth," both on radio and television, through 1981, producing his last programs only months before his death in 1982. Through all these years, however, Baxter never had full responsibility for these programs; he always shared preaching duties with other evangelists.

During the early 1960s, Baxter continued to preach on the traditional themes pertaining to Church of Christ identity, to be sure, but he also introduced subtle shifts in emphasis that would be far-reaching in their impact on Churches of Christ. With increasing frequency, he explained to national radio or television audiences how to achieve spiritual growth and peace of mind, how to develop healthy family relationships, and how to cope with anxiety and fear or with the various stages along life's way.[70]

By the 1970s, these sorts of themes increasingly dominated "Herald of Truth" programming, and the sectarian themes so much a part of the identity of Churches of Christ for a century and a half receded far, far into the background. If "Herald of Truth" strategists during the 1950s had simply sought to communicate the traditional message of Churches of Christ, "Herald of Truth" strategists by the 1970s engaged in market analyses to determine the kinds of messages that would be most likely to capture the attention of a secular listening audience. Aside from its consistent presentation of "the plan of salvation," the

Batsell Barrett Baxter (1916-1982) preached on the "Herald of Truth" radio and television ministry from 1960 until 1981. Noted for his kind and generous spirit, Baxter helped transform the content of "Herald of Truth" programming from an almost exclusive preoccupation with doctrinal issues that defined Churches of Christ to a broader agenda. Without neglecting Church of Christ doctrine, Baxter regularly explained to national radio and television audiences how to achieve spiritual growth and peace of mind, how to develop healthy family relationships, and how to cope with anxiety and fear. In this way, he helped move Churches of Christ more into the mainstream of conservative American Protestantism. (Photo courtesy Gospel Advocate Company)

"Herald of Truth" routinely conformed its preaching to the therapeutic gospel that prevailed among conservative religionists in the United States. This shift held significance not just for the "Herald of Truth," however, but for Churches of Christ at large.

We noted in Chapter 1 that editors had served throughout the history of Churches of Christ as the functional equivalent of bishops. People in the pew voted for these "bishops" with their subscriptions and turned them out by dropping their publications. But in an age dominated by electronic media, traditional print media among Churches of Christ became less and less important. Speakers on the "Herald of Truth" increasingly displaced the editors of gospel papers as "bishops" within the tradition. These newer "bishops" still drew their support from the people — not from individual subscriptions but collectively from congregations, which could choose to support or refuse to support the "Herald of Truth."

And yet, these newer "bishops" were a breed apart from their predecessors. The "print media bishops" historically had defined orthodoxy on a variety of issues, but only on those issues that the church at large had deemed worth discussing. Further, the "print media bishops" were intramural bishops: they spoke only within the confines of the Churches of Christ. The "electronic bishops," however, spoke to a national audience well beyond the boundaries of Churches of Christ. That alone gave them symbolic power that far transcended the power wielded by any "print media bishop." As a consequence, the "electronic bishops" did not so much speak to issues already established as they symbolically defined, by virtue of the issues they chose to address and those they chose to ignore, which issues were worth discussing and which were essentially irrelevant.

And so, as the "electronic bishops" increasingly focused on issues pertaining to self-esteem, anxiety, marriage and the family, and the like, pulpit preachers throughout the fellowship of Churches of Christ quickly followed suit. By the late 1970s, especially in large congregations in urban centers, one could listen to preachers in Churches of Christ for weeks and months on end and never hear anything remotely approaching the traditional sectarian message that had defined the tradition for a century and a half.

This is the proper context in which to assess the lasting impact that Batsell Barrett Baxter, especially, had on Churches of Christ, for Baxter was the first — and by far the most powerful — of all the "electronic bishops." Significantly, Baxter's principal roots — like those of G. C. Brewer, Norvel Young, E. W. McMillan, Jesse P. Sewell, and a host of other "modernizers" of that generation — were in the Stone-Lipscomb tradition. His father, Batsell Baxter, graduated from the old Nashville Bible School in 1911 and later served as dean of Cordell Christian College under president J. N. Armstrong (see Chap. 7) and as a member of the faculty of Harding College. He went on to serve as president of three colleges related to Churches of Christ: Abilene Christian College from 1924 to 1932, George Pepperdine College from 1937 to 1939, and David Lipscomb College from 1932 to 1934 and from 1943 to 1946. While the son, Batsell Barrett Baxter, had no sense of the nineteenth-century apocalyptic perspective, he did inherit from that tradition a gracious outlook and demeanor. His generous spirit enabled him to redefine in subtle ways, through his radio and television preaching on "Herald of Truth," the theological task of Churches of Christ.

The symbolic power of the "electronic bishops" went largely unrecognized by all involved — by the "bishops" themselves, by the elders of the Highland Church of Christ, by the multitude of congregations that supported the "Herald of Truth," and even by the anti-institutional wing of Churches of Christ. Since Churches of Christ had historically denied the existence of any power that transcended the local congregation, no one was really prepared to appreciate the enormous power associated with national television programming.

Nonetheless, the "electronic bishops" effectively — and very quickly —

defined themselves out of existence. For the more they focused on issues that concerned the larger secular public rather than on issues that concerned the historic appeal of Churches of Christ, the more they eliminated the need for any in-house "bishop" at all. By the mid-1970s, in fact, the message of "Herald of Truth" had become almost indistinguishable from messages being presented by a variety of other conservative and/or evangelical radio and television ministries. And by then, many among Churches of Christ — ministers and laity alike — looked more to these evangelical ministries than to the "Herald of Truth" for intellectual and spiritual direction. Thus it can be said that the "electronic bishops" sowed the seeds of their own destruction. By the 1980s, they were gone. Few looked to "Herald of Truth" to provide theological leadership, and the "print media bishops" had long since passed from power. Little wonder, then, that Churches of Christ found themselves in considerable theological disarray.

For all of this, the anti-institutional people gave little evidence of having recognized that the issue of modernization and institutionalization had taken a critical new turn with the emergence of "Herald of Truth." They typically combated the "Herald of Truth" by focusing on the shop-worn issue of the "sponsoring congregation." To all appearances, they remained oblivious of the symbolic power wielded by this national television program and its "electronic bishops." The "Herald of Truth" triumphed by rejecting the arguments of the anti-institutional people, amassing power in spite of their objections, and proceeding to define new issues that rendered the perspective of the "anti's" completely irrelevant to the life of the mainstream church. The de facto exclusion of the "anti" movement accomplished in this way by the "Herald of Truth" proved far more effective than the "quarantine" imposed by B. C. Goodpasture in 1952, simply because the symbolic power of the "electronic bishops" far transcended the power of the traditional editor.

Symbols of Modernization: The Institutional Church Building

In the early 1920s, Churches of Christ were just beginning their long, turbulent transition from sect to denomination. Behind them were the first hundred years when they stood against the values of the world, celebrated poverty and social marginality, and — in the case of those who descended from the Stone-Lipscomb tradition — anticipated the coming kingdom of God. Before them, however, lay a glorious future marked by striking numerical growth, upward social and economic mobility, and increased participation in the mainstream of American life.

Nothing symbolized this transition more effectively than the houses of worship that Churches of Christ erected in the twentieth century. As we have seen, many Churches of Christ lost their property in the division with the

Disciples. For several decades after the turn of the century, many congregations worshiped in store fronts, tents, and small, dilapidated structures in poor, out-of-the-way neighborhoods. By the early 1920s, however, Churches of Christ had begun rebuilding, and construction accelerated to a stunning pace by the 1950s — the decade when the fight over institutions reached its peak.

These new houses of worship were significant in several respects. Often elaborate and sometimes even ostentatious, they frequently served a highly symbolic function, proclaiming to the surrounding community that it should no longer view the Church of Christ as a tiny, offbeat sect on the wrong side of town. The structures also served a pragmatic function, providing facilities for an increasingly institutionalized religious organization. In a word, the houses of worship that Churches of Christ constructed, especially in the 1950s, symbolized everything the anti-institutional tradition rejected.

Even as early as the 1920s, a few progressive preachers committed their congregations to taking their place on the upscale side of southern life. A case in point was John Allen Hudson, who moved from Oklahoma City to Memphis in 1922 to work with the Harbert Avenue church of that city. In December of 1925 Hudson submitted an article to the *Gospel Advocate* describing his role in the construction of a new and elaborate building for the congregation on Union Avenue. From then on, it would be known as the Union Avenue Church of Christ. Its location was significant, for Union Avenue even then symbolized status and financial respectability.

When Hudson first arrived in Memphis, he found a small group of Christians meeting in a ramshackle old building "poorly located on a fifty-foot lot in the middle of a block" and "rotting down over our heads." Hudson determined to replace that building with "a commodious house of worship adequate to every need." To that end he regularly visited all the members of the congregation and "systematically and indefatigably agitated the building of a new church home in every home that I entered." Once completed, the building and grounds were "worth one hundred and twenty-five thousand dollars," though, he claimed, "the finances of the congregation are in good condition." Hudson hoped this successful venture in growth and construction might "serve as an example to inspire others."[71]

James A. Allen, a descendant of the old school in Churches of Christ and editor of the *Advocate* at the time, was not impressed. Placing Hudson's work in the category of the "fads and fancies suggested by professional promoters," Allen resolutely declared that "a meetinghouse that has one hundred and twenty-five thousand dollars tied up in it is a satire on the spirit and genius of Christianity." After all, "Jesus was born in a stable. He selected to be his apostles men who were penniless. In the age when the church grew most rapidly most of its members were common laboring people; and while some few of its members were men of wealth, they were taught to preserve their wealth by giving it away." Christian meetinghouses, Allen argued, should be "free from all

When John Allen Hudson moved to Memphis, Tennessee, to preach for the Harbert Avenue Church of Christ in that city, its members met in a ramshackle, old building, "rotting down over our heads" *(top)*. Hudson spearheaded a campaign to build on fashionable Union Avenue an up-to-date building, which opened in 1925. Symbolizing the slow transition of Churches of Christ from sect to denomination, the Union Avenue building drew the wrath of James A. Allen, editor of the *Gospel Advocate*, who judged the Union Avenue building "a satire on the spirit and genius of Christianity."
(Photos courtesy Woodland Hills Church of Christ, Memphis)

the luxury of this vain and sinful world." He disputed Hudson's claim that the finances of his congregation were in good condition, stating that "the ghost of a frightful sixty-five-thousand-dollar debt is hanging like a pall over these Memphis brethren." He concluded that "God has put his stamp of disapproval upon the centralization of wealth and power, upon monopolies of every kind, upon big businesses and big churches."[72]

Allen's was a voice, however, crying in a rapidly receding wilderness. By the late 1940s, the once apocalyptic Stone-Lipscomb tradition had produced a generation that clamored for the upscale, institutional structures that Allen had found so objectionable. A notable case in point was M. Norvel Young, who, as we already have noted, helped redefine, in subtle but significant ways, the theological task of Churches of Christ with the *20th Century Christian* and who helped popularize G. C. Brewer's "Broadway plan" of missions coordinated by a "sponsoring church."

In the late 1940s, Young contributed again to the process of modernization among Churches of Christ when he embarked on a systematic effort to encourage construction of modern and strategically located houses of worship. Young was convinced that Churches of Christ would benefit significantly from the postwar religious revival, and he was right. By 1954, Reuel Lemmons, soon to be editor of the *Firm Foundation*, claimed that "churches of Christ are growing faster than any other religious order" in the United States.[73] While it is difficult to sustain Lemmons's claim statistically, it is nonetheless true that Churches of Christ grew at a phenomenal rate for fifteen to twenty years following World War II.

Given this rate of growth, it was inevitable that Churches of Christ would have to build new, expanded facilities. Since they would have to build anyway, Young encouraged congregations to construct facilities that would be not only serviceable but also substantial, attractive, and prominently located. No one among Churches of Christ played a more significant role in this regard than he.

Young pressed this issue at the Abilene Christian College lectureship in 1947, and he followed up with related articles in both the *Firm Foundation* and the *Gospel Advocate*, urging congregations to plan buildings that would accommodate babies with "cry rooms," professional preachers with a centrally located "minister's study," support staff with a secretary's office, congregational fellowship with "a large fellowship room" and "cooking facilities near this room," benevolent activities with a storeroom that would house "food and clothing for . . . the poor," educational needs with significant classroom space and a church library, and media needs with a "mimeograph room" and "electric outlets in each classroom so that visual aids may be used."

Further, Young urged, "the building should be designed so that it 'looks like a church.' . . . The exterior should be attractive, though simple, without unnecessary ornamentation, but with good lines of architecture." More than that, "it would be wise to have enough ground to permit attractive landscaping." It would be especially important, he argued, to "locate the new building on a prominent site — one that will advertise the meetings of the church. . . . Do not tuck it away in a secluded spot." Further, Young implicitly suggested that Churches of Christ take seriously the religious architecture of various denominations.[74]

Then, in 1956, Young and James Marvin Powell published a significant book entitled *The Church Is Building*. They surveyed a variety of architectural styles for church buildings and explored every aspect of construction from the engagement of the architect to the final design of the building. In addition, the book featured photographs of a variety of buildings constructed by Churches of Christ — among them, the Union Avenue Church of Christ in Memphis, built under the leadership of John Allen Hudson in the 1920s.

The real significance of this book lay in the way it symbolized the transition of Churches of Christ from a lower-class sect to a respectable, middle-class denomination. This was so despite the fact that Young and Powell remained committed to important elements of the old sectarian, primitivist, and nondenominational understanding of the church and that both men would surely have rejected the denominational nomenclature. It was simply the case that their emphasis on financial assets, attractive architectural design, and upscale location reflected a preoccupation with conformity to the denominational mainstream of American Protestantism. "Early church buildings among our people," the authors lamented, "were a one room affair with no thought for class rooms. We finally got a few basement rooms, but thank God we are out of the musty basement." They went on to report that since 1940 Churches of Christ had built over 1,000 buildings "representing assets of more than $147,000,000.00."[75]

In the introduction to the book, Burton Coffman, then the prominent minister of the Central Church of Christ in Houston, noted that modern facilities among Churches of Christ involved far more than auditoriums for worship. They also included

> parking lots, public address systems, germicidal lights for nurseries, rugs, draperies, venetian blinds, art windows, spires, crosses, buttresses, heating, plumbing, air-conditioning, elevators, kitchens, dining rooms, Bible school rooms, visual aid equipment, baptisteries, flannel graphs, movie projectors, cinema screens . . . , etc.

While praising the fruit of modernization, however, Coffman also celebrated the continuing commitment of Churches of Christ to primitive Christianity, free of modern innovations. In the buildings that Churches of Christ had erected, he noted, "there are no choir lofts, no high altars, no instruments of music. . . . In short there is nothing for use as an innovation in the pure worship of Jesus Christ according to the New Testament."

Coffman also argued that church buildings provided effective advertising

M. Norvel Young (1915-) was arguably the quintessential builder among Churches of Christ in the twentieth century. In an effort to improve the quality of journalism among Churches of Christ, he and several fellow graduate students established in 1938 the *20th Century Christian,* a journal that sustained a substantial circulation throughout the twentieth century. When Churches of Christ experienced record growth following World War II, Young encouraged congregations throughout the United States to move across the tracks and build new facilities that would be substantial, attractive, and prominently located. Young took his own advice and, while preaching for the Broadway congregation in Lubbock, Texas, led in the construction of the largest sanctuary anywhere among Churches of Christ in 1950 (shown above). In Lubbock, he also played a critical role in founding Lubbock Christian College, the Children's Home of Lubbock, and the Smithlawn Maternity Home. In 1957, Young became president of George Pepperdine College in Los Angeles, and in the early 1970s he and chancellor William S. Banowsky led in the construction of a glittering new campus in Malibu, California. Young is pictured here in the president's office at Pepperdine in 1957.

(Photos courtesy Helen Young)

for the gospel. Indeed, he wrote, "There is no better advertisement of one's faith than that provided by a modern, beautifully constructed church edifice in a prominent location."[76] Young and Powell argued for attractive landscaping on the same grounds.

> Church lawns that are well kept will bring many people to the church services who would not otherwise come. On the other hand an ill-kept, slovenly appearing lawn will drive many people away who might otherwise come. . . . Many people have the erroneous impression that in order to be orthodox we must be downright "tacky."[77]

All in all, *The Church Is Building* revealed that by the 1950s many mainstream Churches of Christ had abandoned their sectarian social standing, were seeking to appeal to a more affluent clientele, and had accommodated themselves both to the spirit and to the technical strategies of the modern world. But it also revealed that Churches of Christ continued to maintain important aspects of their traditional primitivist theology, inherited from the nineteenth century.

In 1950, Norvel Young took seriously his own advice and led the Broadway Church of Christ in Lubbock, Texas, in the construction of a beautiful, modern facility situated on an important thoroughfare and boasting an auditorium capable of seating 2,100 worshipers — the largest at that time among Churches of Christ. G. C. Brewer, a former minister of that congregation, preached on the evening of the building's inaugural Sunday on the topic "The Undenominational Nature of the Lord's Church." He recalled and celebrated what he believed Churches of Christ were still about — namely, the attempt "to restore New Testament simplicity, [and] to bring back to earth the ancient order of things."[78]

Conclusion

Though the 1950s was a decade of transition for Churches of Christ, it was only a springboard for greater changes still to come. One can gauge those changes, to some degree, by tracking the career of the quintessential builder among Churches of Christ in the twentieth century, M. Norvel Young. After serving as a successful minister in Texas, Young went to California in 1957 to save George Pepperdine College for the Churches of Christ after the board of trustees expressed concern that the school had drifted from its original religious moorings. In the early 1970s, Young capped his building career when, as president (later chancellor) of Pepperdine, then located in south-central Los Angeles, he and Chancellor William S. Banowsky developed a glittering new campus in the exclusive beach community of Malibu.

While preaching for the Broadway Church of Christ in Lubbock, Texas, William S. Banowsky (1936- ; shown above) achieved fame among Churches of Christ as something of a giant slayer when, in 1967, he debated Anson Mount, religion editor of *Playboy* magazine (see Chap. 13). He subsequently debated theologian Joseph Fletcher and Episcopal bishop James A. Pike on questions of morality and situation ethics. As chancellor in the early 1970s for Pepperdine University in Malibu, Banowsky and president M. Norvel Young built that campus into one of the most magnificent in the United States. Banowsky subsequently served as president of Pepperdine from 1971 to 1978.

(Photo of Banowsky courtesy Gospel Advocate Company; photo of Pepperdine University courtesy Pepperdine University)

The very idea that Churches of Christ might be connected in a significant way to such an enterprise would have boggled the minds of most in nineteenth-century Churches of Christ, and it no doubt startled many even in the 1970s. But the new Malibu campus, which would become famous as one of the most beautiful university campuses in the world, simply symbolized the extent to which many in Churches of Christ now felt at home in the world their forebears had rejected.

In truth, Pepperdine's Malibu campus symbolized trends and transitions that had come to dominate the cultural landscape of Churches of Christ. In 1966, Norman Parks, a professor at Middle Tennessee State University and a former dean at David Lipscomb College, reported the changes in his own region — the historic heartland of the Stone-Lipscomb tradition. There, he noted, the Church of Christ now included "the congressman, the university president, the county judge, the city mayor, the sheriff, bank executives, bar leaders, medicos and dentists, and sundry business executives."[79] And all this was true in a region where members of Churches of Christ had once refused even to vote.

By now we begin to see what Thomas L. Connelly had in mind when he wrote in 1982 that Churches of Christ in Nashville constituted a "middle-class establishment." Through the process of modernization and the development of various parachurch institutions, the Church of Christ developed almost everywhere in the United States into a well-established *institution* in its own right. Put another way, the Church of Christ was no longer a sect, much less an informal movement; it had become instead a full-blown denomination, at least in terms of its social standing in the context of American culture. This was the issue to which leaders in the anti-institutional movement had pointed all along.

In spite of all this, however, most leaders of mainstream Churches of Christ never fully comprehended the issues that the anti-institutional people sought to raise. They remained convinced, in spite of all their concessions to modernization, that Churches of Christ persisted unscathed as the twentieth-century embodiment of primitive, nondenominational Christianity.

Even more ironic, the anti-institutional Churches of Christ themselves could not escape, in the final analysis, the corrosive effects of change and modernization. By 1979, David Edwin Harrell, a respected leader in the anti-institutional movement, wrote that it was "hard to get used to preachers who are well-educated, well-fed and well-paid" even though he knew "that they ought to be all of those things." He confessed that the anti-institutional churches were "filled with bright young people who say all the right things but leave me wondering."[80]

During the turbulent and transitional decade of the 1960s, however, the faithful among mainstream Churches of Christ got a rude awakening from a most unlikely source: their own children. Mainstream Churches of Christ had by that point largely adopted the social values of conservative Protestantism in the United States. They were Protestant and they opposed Catholics; they were overwhelmingly white and usually resisted integration; they were male-dominated and often resisted equal opportunity for women; and, having long since abandoned notions of pacifism, they typically stood shoulder to shoulder in support of America's military venture in Vietnam.

It was precisely these values that many of their children rejected. More than this, having been reared on the rhetoric of Christian primitivism, the children quickly discerned the discrepancy between the primitivist rhetoric of Churches of Christ and the reality of their social accommodation. The children typically reacted in one of two ways. Either they dismissed the primitivist vision as an empty shell, rejected it, and left Churches of Christ entirely, or they turned the sectarian vision in prophetic judgment on the cultural accommodation of their parents. This latter reaction placed Churches of Christ, which had successfully rejected the sectarian challenges of premillennialism and anti-institutionalism over the course of the twentieth century, in the ironic position of having to deal with a similar sectarian challenge from their own children. This is the story to which we turn in Chapters 11, 12, and 13.

CHAPTER 11

Understanding the 1960s:
The Fundamentalist Connection and the
Defense of Christian (Protestant) America

At the outset of this book, I suggested that the central story of Churches of Christ over the course of almost two centuries was its slow evolution from sect to denomination. A sect is by definition estranged from the culture in which it lives and from the religious bodies that reflect the culture's values, and it typically stands in judgment on both. A denomination, on the other hand, has made its peace both with the dominant culture and with the larger Christian community.

By definition, then, Churches of Christ were for the most part clearly a sect throughout their nineteenth-century experience. By the 1960s, Churches of Christ still for the most part resisted recognition of other denominations as Christian bodies, and in this sense they maintained their sectarian status. But by this time they also overwhelmingly supported the conservative cultural values that ruled the American South. By and large, they identified with the values of white cultures as opposed to the values of people of color, with patriarchalism as opposed to gender equality, with middle-aged adults as opposed to the youth counterculture, with Protestantism as opposed to Catholicism, with the American military venture in Vietnam as opposed to the peace movement, and with the policies and politics of conservatism and law and order. In this way they betrayed their evolution toward denominational standing.

In some respects, this transition is astounding, especially in light of the distinctly countercultural dimensions of the Stone-Lipscomb tradition in the nineteenth century. While it is difficult to identify all the factors that facilitated this transition, it is possible to point out certain benchmarks along the way.

Fundamentalism and Anti-Communism

Of all those benchmarks, none was more crucial than the ideological alliance that Churches of Christ made with the fundamentalist movement following World War I. *Ideological* is a key word in this context, for while Churches of Christ supported much of the fundamentalist agenda, they refused to ally themselves in any formal sense with the fundamentalist movement itself.

This ambiguous relationship is, in some respects, surprising. One might expect that Churches of Christ would have supported the fundamentalist movement at every step along the way. After all, Churches of Christ, like fundamentalists, had built their theological house squarely on the Bible, read the Bible from a decidedly Baconian perspective, and categorically rejected Darwinian evolution, biblical criticism, and all other aspects of modernity that seemed to undermine the authority of an inerrant biblical text.[1]

Yet, Churches of Christ stood aloof from the fundamentalist movement, especially during the movement's earliest years (1910-1918), and they did so for two principal reasons. First, fundamentalism in that period often connected itself to dispensational premillennialism — a perspective that mainstream Churches of Christ found abhorrent, as we have seen. R. H. Boll was among the few leaders among Churches of Christ during that period that could be characterized as thoroughly fundamentalist, and in the end the mainstream churches expelled him from their fellowship (see Chap. 7). Second, most in Churches of Christ, steeped in a highly exclusivist perspective, remained convinced that fundamentalists, connected as they were with a variety of sects and denominations, were pseudo-Christians at best. James Allen spoke for many among Churches of Christ when he praised William Jennings Bryan's attacks on evolution but questioned whether Bryan was an authentic Christian. "As to Mr. Bryan's being a Christian," he wrote, "we are not able to say. He is a great and good man, but many great and good men are not Christians. He is also an elder in the Presbyterian Church, but to be a Presbyterian and to be a Christian are two separate and distinct things."[2]

Fundamentalists and Churches of Christ: A Common Worldview

In spite of all this, however, Churches of Christ and fundamentalists increasingly had a common worldview and common cultural concerns, especially following World War I. It was not simply that Churches of Christ suddenly moved closer to the historic tenets of fundamentalism; rather, fundamentalism and Churches of Christ both underwent a massive cultural reorientation in the aftermath of World War I. For all their dissimilarities, that reorientation brought Churches of Christ and fundamentalists into a common orbit of cultural concern.

George Marsden has described the postwar reorientation of fundamentalism in substantial detail in his landmark study *Fundamentalism and American Culture*. Like Barton Stone, most fundamentalists descended from a distinctly Calvinist heritage and concerned themselves preeminently with the question of God's sovereignty over human culture. In the late nineteenth century, faced with the rise of Darwinian evolution, biblical criticism, and the new psychology that explained God chiefly in terms of human need, many of these Calvinists saw little evidence of God's rule over American culture. They saw instead a yawning chasm separating the kingdom of God from the world in which they lived. Marsden explains that, prior to World War I, many Calvinists embraced distinctly premillennial perspectives, stood separate and apart from politics and culture, found their identity exclusively in their allegiance to the kingdom of God (which they viewed as transcending all the kingdoms of this world, the United States included), and maintained a profoundly pessimistic outlook regarding human progress in science, technology, and politics. In a word, the fundamentalist worldview prior to World War I often resembled rather remarkably the worldview I have described in this book as the Stone-Lipscomb heritage within Churches of Christ.

World War I thoroughly transformed this fundamentalist tradition. Many fundamentalists came to view Germany not merely as the wartime enemy of the United States but as the source of virtually all the ideas that threatened to undermine the Christian dimensions of American culture. They came to believe that if they could only discredit and destroy such characteristically German notions as evolution (associated with Nietzsche's concept of the *Übermensch*) and biblical criticism, they could bring America once again under the sovereign rule of God. And so it was that they launched a coordinated attack on all those German ideals they thought atheistic and anti-Christian — ideals that they believed were preventing America from becoming an outpost of the kingdom of God.

In the very process of attacking these German ideals, however, fundamentalists subtly and prematurely collapsed America and the kingdom of God into a single, unified vision. If the heresies that separated America from the rule of God were foreign rather than domestic, then was it not reasonable to infer that America, in its essence, was a clear manifestation of the kingdom of God — a pure kingdom that had regrettably been infected with foreign impurities? Almost overnight, the political and cultural separatism that had characterized much of fundamentalism before the war largely collapsed. In its place appeared a strident anti-German, pro-American patriotism that increasingly identified America with God's kingdom and charged that the Germans were seeking to subvert it.[3]

By 1919, with World War I now behind them, Americans experienced the short-lived postwar "Red Scare," and many fundamentalists saw in Bolshevism the next great threat to the kingdom of God in America. By the early 1920s, many fundamentalists were linking Communism with evolution as twin faces of atheism, and by the mid-1930s a strident anti-Communist defense of "Christian civilization" had become a pivotal part of their worldview.[4]

As fundamentalists after World War I shifted their focus to a defense of the "Christian civilization" of the United States, they betrayed the extent to which they had assumed all along that biblical ideals informed and shaped American culture at its deepest, most critical levels. Their defense of the Bible was aimed not just at preserving the Bible in its own right but also at preserving an imagined biblical civilization — a veritable kingdom of God — that they identified with the United States of America.

Much the same kind of transition occurred within Churches of Christ. In order to understand the dynamics of this transition, however, we must first understand the strategic role of Calvinism in shaping the Stone-Lipscomb worldview. At first glance, the suggestion that Calvinism shaped this tradition in any sense whatsoever may seem wildly off base. After all, did not Stone strongly oppose the notion of predestination? And was it not true that Campbell rejected out of hand the Calvinist understanding of conversion, presupposing as it did the direct operation of the Holy Spirit on the heart of the believer?

Still, one simply cannot understand Barton Stone apart from his Calvinist yearning for the kingdom of God. For Stone, "the kingdoms of this world" *had not* "become the kingdoms of our Lord, and of His Christ." Far from it. In truth, it was precisely the enormous gap between the kingdoms of this world and the kingdom of God — a gap that seemed so apparent to Stone for a number of reasons — that fueled his apocalypticism. The same can be said for David Lipscomb and a host of others among Churches of Christ who shared this perspective.

But, as we noted in Chapter 7, this vision began to die away among mainstream Churches of Christ during and following World War I. Many heirs to the Stone-Lipscomb tradition no longer viewed the kingdoms of this world as fundamentally antagonistic to the kingdom of God. Instead, they came to believe that the chasm separating the kingdoms of this world from the kingdom of God had, for all practical purposes, been bridged. In an effort to gain respect and standing in the larger wartime culture, many rejected their historic apocalyptic heritage and turned instead to the cultural optimism of their other principal founder, Alexander Campbell. We noted that M. C. Kurfees and J. C. McQuiddy praised the League of Nations as God's instrument for bringing about the millennial dawn, for example, and we noted the growing cultural optimism of other leading preachers, such as F. W. Smith.

Like their fundamentalist counterparts, many leaders among Churches of Christ viewed World War I as a cosmic struggle between the American kingdom of God and the German kingdom of Satan. Most leaders among mainstream Churches of Christ believed that German culture and civilization threatened to undermine the Christian foundations of the United States. Kurfees attacked

German theology and philosophy as a "corrupt fountain" that threatened the pulpits and colleges of America. McQuiddy charged that "German criticism" of Scripture "has corrupted many of our universities" and that its theories "nullify the revelation that God gave us." Smith complained about the "German rationalism that has spread its slime across the face of the earth."[5]

Having been similarly transformed during World War I, Churches of Christ quite naturally began to make common cause with fundamentalists in a number of areas. Two recent studies — one by Michael Casey and the other by Stephen Wolfgang — have demonstrated the complicity of Churches of Christ in a whole variety of fundamentalist cultural concerns, especially during the 1920s.[6] Many leaders among Churches of Christ in this period routinely attacked biblical criticism, upheld theories of biblical inerrancy, scorned the theory of Darwinian evolution, defended and praised William Jennings Bryan, fraternized with fundamentalists in informal ways, and generally cast their lot with fundamentalism on almost every critical issue with the single exception of dispensational premillennialism. But it is critical to note that those in Churches of Christ who embraced these concerns not only defended the Bible but, like mainstream fundamentalists, implicitly defended as well a civilization they believed to have been built on solidly biblical foundations. This was the legacy that World War I bequeathed to Churches of Christ.

The Political Career of G. C. Brewer

While this legacy was not immediately apparent for a number of years following the war, it grew abundantly evident in the mid-1930s, the very period when fundamentalists were growing increasingly shrill regarding the menace of international Communism. In that same period, key leaders among Churches of Christ launched their own campaign against the Communist peril.

As we noted in Chapter 7, George S. Benson, the new president of Harding College in 1936, adopted a strong anti-Communist position, impressing leaders of American industry who helped place Harding on a firm financial footing. Benson's anti-Communist campaign affected Churches of Christ only minimally, however, at least in those early years, when Harding College still labored under the stigma of premillennialism.

For this reason, Benson was not the person chiefly responsible for promoting pro-American, anti-Communist sentiment within the church itself. That distinction falls to G. C. Brewer, the popular and highly influential preacher whose stand against Foy Wallace we noted in Chapter 7, whose doctrine of grace we surveyed at some length in Chapter 8, and whose leadership in the institutionalization of Churches of Christ we explored in Chapter 10. Coupling all of that with Brewer's efforts to promote what he called "Americanism," we can see why Norman Parks identified him as "one of the two leading 'architects'

By any measure, G. C. Brewer (1884-1956) was one of the most strategic figures among Churches of Christ in the twentieth century. A noted preacher in Texas and Tennessee, Brewer resisted Foy Wallace's attacks on R. H. Boll and the premillennialists, promoted a strong doctrine of grace when few among Churches of Christ thought or spoke in those terms, and provided strategic leadership in the 1940s and 1950s for intercongregational cooperation, especially on behalf of missions. Though Brewer's roots ran deep into the apocalyptic soil of Barton Stone and David Lipscomb, he used his immense influence to promote Americanism, anti-Communism, and anti-Catholicism and, in this way, helped align Churches of Christ with some of the most conservative forces in American politics.
(Photo courtesy Elizabeth Mason)

of the contemporary 'mainline' Church of Christ as it moved . . . along the historic track from sect to denomination."[7]

Like so many others who helped move Churches of Christ toward denominational standing, Brewer came directly from the apocalyptic Stone-Lipscomb tradition, having spent six years as a student at the old Nashville Bible School, graduating in 1911. During World War I, Brewer strongly resisted military service. He later recalled,

> I had been reared under the teaching of Brother David Lipscomb and I believed it was wrong for Christians to participate in civil government in any sense. I didn't want to buy bonds or savings stamps or contribute one penny toward the shedding of blood. This was the teaching under which all of us had been reared and no member of our family had ever voted.[8]

Although in those early years Brewer identified himself with the kingdom of God and refused to support the kingdoms of this world, all that began to change in the early 1920s. By 1922, in the aftermath of the postwar "Red Scare," Brewer had telescoped the kingdom of God and American culture into a single vision that formed the basis for his lifelong patriotic crusade against Communism.[9] In muddling the kingdom of God with American nationalism, Brewer simply reflected the cultural transformation overtaking both fundamentalism and Churches of Christ in that period.

In 1936 Brewer made headlines both in the Nashville press and in church periodicals when he delivered a celebrated lecture on Communism before the Nashville American Legion. In that speech, as reported by F. B. Srygley, Brewer called "upon all 'red-blooded' American citizens to fight communism — if need be — to the last ditch; [and] to spill every last ounce of blood — if need be — in defense of our government." He proclaimed that, "if and when this nation must fight to prevent the overthrow of Americanism, I, for one, am ready to give the last drop of blood in my veins in the cause my forefathers fought and died for."

Brewer's speech drew criticism in the *Gospel Advocate* from Srygley, who still embraced, at least in certain respects, the perspectives of David Lipscomb. "The attitude of the entire speech," Srygley complained, "was to glorify America rather than the teaching of Christ and the apostles."[10] But Srygley's criticism had little effect on Brewer, who remained convinced that Communism not only threatened the liberties of all Americans but also threatened to destroy the Christian faith.

Brewer took his case directly to the church in a series of eight articles published in the *Gospel Advocate* in 1936. That same year, the *Advocate* issued those articles as a book entitled *Communism and Its Four Horsemen*.[11] Brewer sought to persuade others among Churches of Christ "that the communists already have an alarming hold on the United States; that they are in our schools and universities and even in the churches; that communism is in many text-books and that millions of high-school students are enrolled in the party."[12] Citing a Congressional investigation as his authority, Brewer specifically singled out as notorious advocates of Communism in the United States such scholars as Charles Beard, Carl Becker, and John Dewey; he also criticized such well-known publications as the *Scholastic Magazine*.[13] He went so far as to assert that "we have more communists in Los Angeles alone than they had in all of Russia when that country was seized by gangsters, the government overthrown, and the people made slaves."[14]

Three factors prompted Brewer's concern. One was the Communist commitment to eradicate traditional religion, a point of particular concern to him because he viewed Christianity as one of the fundamental supports for traditional American culture.[15] A second source of Brewer's concern was the fact that the Roosevelt administration had extended diplomatic recognition to

Soviet Russia — something that "Wilson, Harding, Coolidge, and Hoover steadfastly refused" to do.[16] Surprisingly, the third source of Brewer's concern was the growing commitment to pacifism and disarmament in the United States following revelations of the horrors of World War I. One 1934 poll reported that over 60 percent of American ministers had urged their churches to refuse "to sanction or support any future war."[17] Brewer maintained that it was Communism, not idealism, that was prompting church leaders, students, and American citizens throughout the nation to rally behind such peace advocates as Kirby Page.[18] He insisted that it was the Communist commitment to pacification of the United States that "accounts for the great hue and cry against war in our country — not among Christians, but among atheists. This accounts for the oath that so many college professors and students are taking not to fight, even if our country is invaded. The colleges are full of communism."[19]

Even so, Brewer himself claimed to be an advocate of peace. "All Christians are peace lovers, peace promoters, and peacemakers," he wrote. But he also insisted that Christians "do not make a political platform out of pacifism and agitate and campaign against preparedness on the part of our nation while other nations are arming and fighting and menacing the very existence of all nations."[20] Clearly, Brewer had abandoned the radical pacifist posture of his youth, just as he had abandoned the apocalyptic orientation he had learned from his teachers at the old Nashville Bible School.

With such influential leaders as George Benson and G. C. Brewer doing what they could to promote American nationalism within the church, it is not surprising that the pacifist tradition of Churches of Christ was essentially dead by World War II. A few isolated voices sought to keep the tradition alive, but for the most part they were voices crying in the wilderness. In 1943, Bennie Lee Fudge published a book entitled *Can a Christian Kill for His Government?* Fudge said "No," but his answer provoked displeasure from many within the fellowship of Churches of Christ.[21]

Throughout the 1940s, G. C. Brewer continued to write and lecture on the perils of Communism. By the late 1940s, however, he also targeted Catholicism[22] — a concern neither new nor novel in the history of this tradition. Alexander Campbell's decision to "defend Protestantism," for example, grew directly from his fear of papal designs on the United States, as we noted in Chapter 2. Moreover, anti-Catholicism had always stood at the heart of the primitivist perspective that had powered Churches of Christ from their beginning. This was because Churches of Christ, since the early nineteenth century, had identified the historic apostasy of the church with the rise of the Catholic tradition and the power of the Roman pope.[23]

Brewer's determination to expose Catholicism, then, was nothing new. His innovation lay in his determination to link Catholicism and Communism as twin threats to the American way of life. In 1953, Brewer joined five other highly influential leaders among Churches of Christ in Middle Tennessee and adjoining states in launching a journal dedicated to exposing both Catholicism and Communism. They called the new journal the *Voice of Freedom,* and Brewer explained its rationale. Catholics, he argued, sought "to make people believe . . . that Catholicism is the only antidote for Communism — that it is the only alternative. We do not believe this, but we believe that Catholicism is another form of totalitarianism and that our freedom would be lost if the Catholics gained power."[24] The harassment of Church of Christ missionaries by Italian Catholics in 1950 (see Chap. 10) convinced Brewer that "the Catholic Church does not allow religious freedom in countries where that Church is in control," and it thus helped provoke the creation of this new journal.[25]

Given the considerable standing and influence that G. C. Brewer enjoyed among Churches of Christ for many years, dating back to the 1930s, it is easy to understand why his vigorous campaigns against both Communism and Catholicism, stretching over several decades, had an enormous impact on this tradition. Further, as Harding College slowly but successfully erased its image as a hotbed of premillennialism, its influence within Churches of Christ grew as well. Significantly, Harding, under the strong leadership of George Benson, replaced its old, premillennial image with an image of patriotism and strident anti-Communism, thereby making these ideas increasingly acceptable to the rank and file among Churches of Christ.

The five men who, along with Brewer, provided leadership for the *Voice of Freedom* included B. C. Goodpasture, editor of the *Gospel Advocate,* and Batsell Barrett Baxter, professor of Bible at David Lipscomb College and, by 1960, speaker on the national "Herald of Truth" television program.[26] Put another way, the *Voice of Freedom* was no off-the-wall venture, representing a mere fringe within Churches of Christ; it enjoyed the full support of the Nashville establishment — a point that speaks loudly of the theological transition that had occurred among Churches of Christ since World War I.

Further, none of the leaders who promoted either anti-Communist or anti-Catholic sentiment among Churches of Christ seemed to sense that these campaigns represented any significant departure from the historic nondenominational and primitivist identity of Churches of Christ. To the contrary, they believed that these cultural and political campaigns grew quite naturally out of their vision of primitive Christianity, thereby illustrating Henry Bowden's contention that primitivists peering into the well of history and seeking to discern there the outlines of the ancient faith often wind up seeing only a reflection of their own concerns.[27]

This was particularly true of Brewer and the *Voice of Freedom.* If the Bible provided a principal support for American civilization, then a defense of America seemed necessary to defend the Bible itself — or at least to defend its principles. Likewise, to expose Catholicism was to expose the corruptions that had befallen the primitive church.[28] Brewer and his colleagues thus sacralized the *Voice of Freedom* — and at the same time sacralized the America they sought to defend — with the mythology of primitive and biblical Christianity. On the masthead of the very first issue appeared the slogan "An undenominational, nonsectarian publication devoted to telling the truth, the whole truth, and nothing but the truth, about the threat to our freedom from Catholicism and Communism."

Mainstream Churches of Christ thus approached the decade of the 1960s as religious defenders of American civilization, and especially of the white, Anglo-Saxon, Protestant civilization they had known in the American South. This was a cause, they imagined, altogether compatible with their historic commitment to primitive Christianity. Accordingly, these churches no longer stood separate and apart from their culture, hurling apocalyptic judgment on the kingdoms of this world. Instead, they viewed America as the kingdom of God, and they sought to defend that kingdom.

Having adopted such a posture, Churches of Christ were singularly unprepared for the ethical challenges that the events of the 1960s presented to all of America. During that decade, most among Churches of Christ sided time and again with the cultural status quo against progressive causes of all sorts, a pattern we shall see as we turn now to those issues.

The Election of John F. Kennedy

With a tradition of anti-Catholicism extending a full century and a half into their past and a legacy of anti-Communism reaching back over a quarter-century, most in Churches of Christ staunchly opposed the election of John F. Kennedy to the presidency of the United States. Later, most members of mainstream churches strongly supported the Vietnam War, which they viewed as a war against Communist aggression.

Most members and leaders of Churches of Christ, in virtually every quarter of the tradition — from Foy Wallace to the *Christian Chronicle,* from the *Gospel Guardian* to the *Gospel Advocate,* from the *Firm Foundation* to the *Twentieth-Century Christian* — opposed the election of John F. Kennedy.[29] They feared the prospect of America being governed by a Catholic president because they imagined that such a president would be subservient to Rome — that in effect the United States would end up being governed by the pope. And so they mobilized a massive crusade, in a myriad of their publications, to warn their own members and Americans at large of the grave dangers to the United States that would be posed by a Kennedy presidency.

Of course Churches of Christ were not alone in publicizing such concerns. The National Association of Evangelicals resolved in April 1960 to oppose Kennedy's election because of his Catholicism, and Southern Baptists throughout the South announced much the same stand.[30] While normally shunning relations with other Protestant bodies, Churches of Christ worked hand in glove with a variety of Protestant churches and anti-Catholic groups to work out strategies for defeating Kennedy. Their newfound denominational status had never been more apparent than it was in this particular crusade.

This is how Churches of Christ greeted the decade of the 1960s. Little did they know that before the decade was through, they would have to come to terms with a genuinely multicultural America. In this context, a Catholic president would be the least of their concerns.

But in 1960, the prospect of a Catholic president still troubled them greatly. Carroll Ellis, writing in the *Gospel Advocate,* offered in classic form the argument that characterized most in Churches of Christ. The Roman Catholic Church, he suggested, is not just a religion but a temporal power that claims a divine sanction. "The ideal relationship," therefore, "is one in which the civil government will foster the teaching and claims of Catholicism." Kennedy would be morally bound as a Roman Catholic president, warned Ellis, to enforce the will of the Catholic Church in America.[31]

Editor B. C. Goodpasture intimated that Catholics might even kill those who resisted their control. "Those who think no danger to our religious freedom is involved are evidently not acquainted with history," Goodpasture warned. "They do not know about the fires of Smithfield, the horrors of the Spanish Inquisition, the bloody Massacre of St. Bartholomew's Day, and the frightful slaughter of the Waldenses and Albigenses."[32] In one of his editorials, Goodpasture promoted a book entitled *Mr. Kennedy, We Challenge You,* which invited the candidate

> to prove that your Church does not claim the right to put Protestants, Jews, and liberals and other heretics to death, and that your becoming President would not hasten this happy day. . . . Do you intend to help the church put to death any and all heretics and evangelicals when "Der Tag" arrives?[33]

Reuel Lemmons, editor of the Texas-based *Firm Foundation,* suggested that Catholicism and democracy were simply inimical to one another. "One cannot be loyal to both, regardless of how he may try." On the other hand, Lemmons asserted that Communism and Catholicism were two peas in a pod. "Structurally the two are identical. Philosophically they are identical. Militantly they are identical. Their aim at world domination is identical." For all these reasons, Lemmons strongly resisted the presidential aspirations of John F. Kennedy.[34]

Writing for the *Firm Foundation,* W. A. Holley described in some detail his vision of what a Catholic America might be like. Should the Catholic Church ever gain control of the United States, he explained,

> she would force upon the citizens of our country, union of church and state . . . ; she would raid our public treasury for funds to promote her

sectarian doctrines; she would place her stooges in key positions and thus dominate our domestic and foreign policy; she would censor our media of communications; she would bind upon our children all the backwardness and superstition of her outmoded educational system; she would saddle our doctors, nurses, and hospitals with her medieval and unscientific medical practices; her priests would become masters of marriage, home, and children; [and] she, through the Index of Forbidden Books, would enslave our minds, telling us what to read and what to think!![35]

No publication among Churches of Christ spoke more loudly against a Kennedy presidency than the *Voice of Freedom* under the editorship of L. R. Wilson of Cleburne, Texas.[36] Even more explicitly than had G. C. Brewer, Wilson fused the primitivist biblicism of his Church of Christ heritage with historic American ideals. "The Constitution was based upon the principles laid down in God's Word," he argued, and he rejoiced in "a President [Eisenhower] who believes in the Supreme God, who believes in the Bible as God's revelation, and who prays to Almighty God." In Wilson's view, the *Voice of Freedom* was "committed only to New Testament Christianity, our American ideals and to the Constitution of the United States."[37]

Wilson charged that the Roman Church had acted as accomplice to many of the evils that had befallen the Western world in the nineteenth and twentieth centuries, from the assassination of Abraham Lincoln to Hitler's rise to power.[38] Even now, Wilson argued, the Catholic Church in America sought "to control the education of our youth, to curtail the freedom of the press, . . . to restrict our individual freedom . . . and . . . to control the minds of the people."[39]

Some among Churches of Christ even found subtle Catholic propaganda in the popular music of the period. One man complained to his local radio station that such songs as "The Lady of Fatima," "Village of St. Bernadette," and "Shrine on Top of the Hill" were "subtle means of indoctrination" designed to promote the Kennedy candidacy. "I for one," he wrote, "cannot let my child be taught through songs of this kind, doctrines that are not found in my New Testament."[40]

Churches of Christ gained national publicity for their near-uniform views on this issue in two particular instances. First, in October of 1960, just weeks before the election, NBC camera crews arrived at the upscale and prestigious Hillsboro Church of Christ in Nashville to film, for broadcast on "Chet Huntley's Views," a sermon by Batsell Barrett Baxter on the threat of Catholicism to American liberties. Baxter concluded his sermon with the warning, "If the Roman Catholic Church should ever become large enough and strong enough to dominate the United States of America, the rest of us would lose our religious freedom," and he urged Christians to "oppose the growth and spread of the Roman Catholic Church in every legitimate and honorable way." As Baxter brought his sermon to a close, Representative Joe Evins, a member of the United

States Congress and also a member of that congregation, stepped up from the audience and asked Baxter if he might speak for a few minutes. "I came here to worship," Evins objected, "but I have heard a political speech." He went on to call for tolerance for other religious persuasions.[41]

The *Christian Chronicle* reported, however, that "the reaction of the 1,152-member congregation . . . was an overwhelming endorsement of the sermon that had been preached." And B. C. Goodpasture, an elder of that congregation, defended Baxter's "exposure of Romish error" and described Evins's remarks as "most ill-advised and unfortunate."[42]

In the second incident that gained national publicity for Churches of Christ, V. E. Howard, a radio evangelist, confronted Kennedy directly when the candidate appeared in a televised meeting with the Houston Ministerial Association in September of 1960. After publicly reading selections from the *Catholic Encyclopedia* on "the doctrine of Mental Reservation," Howard asked Kennedy if he accepted or rejected "these authoritative Catholic declarations."

"I have not read the *Catholic Encyclopedia*," Kennedy responded, "and I don't know all the quotations you are giving me. I don't agree with the statements. I find no difficulty in saying so, but I do think probably I could make a better comment if I had the entire quotation before me." Howard reported in the *Gospel Advocate* that Kennedy had sought "to evade the issue," and the *Christian Chronicle* proclaimed, "The Catholic doctrine of mental reservation was placed squarely in John F. Kennedy's path here Sept. 12 and he dodged it."[43]

When all was said and done, the campaign launched by Churches of Christ against the election of John F. Kennedy revealed two new dimensions that had recently come to characterize the tradition. First, it revealed the considerable extent to which Churches of Christ had abandoned the separatist, apolitical, and apocalyptic outlook that had governed the thinking of so many in the nineteenth century. And second, it revealed the extent to which Churches of Christ now identified with and even defended the conservative Protestant culture of the American South. In a word, the anti-Kennedy campaign revealed the fact that Churches of Christ had now become a denomination — a luxuriant plant thriving on the conservative slope of America's cultural landscape, in spite of all their protests to the contrary.

Anti-Communism and the Vietnam War

If most among Churches of Christ drew on their long-standing anti-Catholic sentiments to oppose the election of John F. Kennedy, they drew on their more recent opposition to Communism to support the Vietnam War, which they typically viewed as a war to stop Communist aggression in Southeast Asia. While most journals serving mainline Churches of Christ produced little direct discussion of the merits of the war itself, they did engage in sustained and vigorous criticism of war protesters. Reuel Lemmons offered a typical argument when he asserted that "the rebellion now in progress on university campuses is not a protest against the war in Viet Nam" but an exercise in lawlessness and immorality. "We deny," he stated categorically in the *Firm Foundation*, "that pot smoking freaks, soaked in alcohol and high on drugs have a right to protest anything."[44]

Neither Lemmons nor any of his editorial colleagues serving the mainline churches acknowledged that any dimension of the antiwar protest might have stemmed from a moral or patriotic base. Rather, they consistently described the antiwar movement as Communist inspired. "Karl Marx laid down the strategy for communist revolution," wrote Lemmons, and the "strategy seems to be working in America." His editorial counterpart on the *Gospel Advocate*, B. C. Goodpasture, concurred and often published, from the writings of F.B.I. Director J. Edgar Hoover, stern warnings of a Communist conspiracy at work on America's college campuses such as the following: "The students for a Democratic Society (SDS), largest of the New Left groups, is rapidly gaining a definite Marxist-Leninist coloration. . . . Never before in this country has there been such a strong revolutionary Marxist movement of young people which is so eager to destroy established authority."[46]

The themes of "established authority" and "law and order" were important to mainline Churches of Christ, and they often obscured the questions of justice, economic imperialism, environmental destruction, and the legitimacy of the war that many in the antiwar movement sought to raise. For example, after protesters disrupted the Democratic convention of 1968 in an effort to call attention to what they regarded as the atrocities of an unjust war, commentators from Churches of Christ routinely condemned the disruption as Communist inspired and praised the Chicago police and others who sought to maintain order. Typical was a sermon preached by Dan Harless at Nashville's Hillsboro Church of Christ — the same congregation that heard Batsell Baxter's warning in 1960 about the dangers of electing a Catholic president of the United States. The Democratic convention in Chicago, Harless claimed, was

> a convention unique in the annals of American history — a convention in which the forces of disorder and disunity and anarchy openly challenged the police department of a great city and the National Guard of a great state by attempting to carry out their oft-repeated threat to bring the authorities to their knees. During this past week millions of Americans witnessed the degrading spectacle of a presidential aspirant defending the Communist inspired and the Communist led hippies and yippies and other purveyors of violent dissent.[47]

During the period from World War I to the war in Vietnam, Churches of Christ had come a very long way indeed. In the earliest years of the twentieth century, many members and leaders identified their interests with the kingdom of God as distinct from the kingdoms of this world and often rejected the militarist values of their own culture, but by the 1960s all of that had changed. If on the whole at the outset of World War I Churches of Christ presented themselves as a countercultural community of faith in which pacifism rooted in religious conviction was still a serious option, by the 1960s mainstream Churches of Christ presented themselves as an almost united front of support for the American military venture in Vietnam. For the most part, the ethical and moral criticism of the war raised in the larger culture carried little weight with most among mainstream Churches of Christ, who remained far more interested in issues of authority, law and order, and opposition to Communism.

Conclusion

When all was said and done, Churches of Christ underwent a far-reaching cultural transformation during and after World War I, a transformation that by the 1960s had aligned them with the most conservative forces in American politics. Further, it was a transformation that moved them, over some forty years, from the status of a backwater southern sect resisting the values of the culture in which they lived to the status of a Protestant denomination defending the values of Protestant America. This transformation was most apparent in their strident anti-Catholicism, resulting in their almost unanimous rejection of the presidential bid of John F. Kennedy, in their concern to save America from the inroads of international Communism, and in their strong support for American involvement in the Vietnam War.

Nor was this political conservatism a mere passing phase. In the mid-1980s, political scientist Mel Hailey, a faculty member at Abilene Christian University, conducted a major survey of Church of Christ ministers, assessing their political attitudes. He found that 76 percent of those ministers described themselves as political conservatives, while only 5 percent described themselves as political liberals; that 74 percent identified with the Republican party, while not a single one claimed to be a "strong Democrat"; that 95 percent supported Ronald Reagan over Walter Mondale in the 1980 presidential election; and that when asked to respond to the statement "It would be hard to be both a true Christian and a political liberal," 82 percent either agreed or strongly agreed. Little wonder, then, that a vast majority stood in almost complete agreement with the agenda of the New Religious Right. Hailey concluded that Churches of Christ preachers were, "almost to a man, a self-described bastion of political conservatism."

At the same time, Hailey found that these ministers, by and large, held themselves aloof in the 1980s from the various religio-political organizations that promoted these ideals, just as they had held themselves aloof from the fundamentalists whose values they shared a half-century before. Only one of the 195 preachers surveyed, for example, belonged to the Moral Majority, and most were completely unaware of such right-wing organizations as Christian Voice and the Religious Roundtable.[48]

This is to say that as late as the 1980s Churches of Christ managed to adapt themselves to the conservative contours of the cultural and political landscape of the United States without abandoning their sectarian status vis-à-vis other Christian organizations. Put another way, Churches of Christ managed to preserve their historic vision of the primitive apostolic faith with reference to the threats they perceived in Catholicism and Protestantism. But they had lost the substance of that vision insofar as they had given up their earlier allegiance to the radical values of the kingdom of God and accommodated themselves to the conservative values of the larger culture.

We have surveyed the path that Churches of Christ took during the twentieth century toward affirmation of a Christian America and adoption of conservative politics. We have not yet considered another interesting dimension of the changes that were evident in the tradition by the 1960s, however — the ways in which Churches of Christ responded to issues of social justice, particularly in the context of the civil rights movement of this period. To that issue, then, we will turn in Chapter 12.

CHAPTER 12

Blacks and Whites:
The Struggle for Social Justice
in the 1960s

This chapter does not present a history of African American Churches of Christ. For all practical purposes, black and white Churches of Christ have gone their separate ways. Though, for the most part, this has been the case for two centuries, it has been true especially since the 1960s. Hubert Locke, a minister in the black Churches of Christ until 1971, has pointed out that

> many of us who were dissenters in the 1960s were being shaped by (and trying to shape) events quite unrelated to the stance of the white church. Our congregations were struggling with the most important social upheaval in a lifetime. . . . For all practical purposes, we had given up on the white churches; their "agonies" were simply no longer our concerns.[1]

Any serious history of the African American heritage in the Stone-Campbell tradition, therefore, would require a separate book — a book still waiting to be written.

My intent in this chapter is to assess the dominant response of white Churches of Christ to issues of social justice and racial equality raised in the 1960s. This issue is worth raising in this book because it casts light on many of the changes that overtook Churches of Christ in the course of their transition from sect to denomination. It provides striking evidence that white Churches of Christ had long since abandoned their apocalyptic and countercultural emphasis on the kingdom of God and turned to embrace instead the values common to the Protestant establishment of the white South.

To assess the response of white Churches of Christ to issues of social justice, we will first have to consider the roots of that response, which ran deep into the soil of the nineteenth century. There we find two very distinct perspectives regarding social justice, one belonging to the heritage of Barton W. Stone and the other belonging to the heritage of Alexander Campbell. Those two perspectives come clearly into focus when we examine the attitudes of the Stone and Campbell traditions toward the questions of racial equality and slavery.

Race and Justice: Perspectives of the Stone-Lipscomb Tradition

An early and telling clue regarding the attitude toward slavery on the part of Barton Stone and the "Christian" movement emerges in the autobiography of Joseph Thomas, published in 1812. Thomas informs us that in 1810/1811, he traveled from his home in North Carolina to Kentucky to learn more about Stone and the "Christian" movement he led. Thomas was especially impressed with their strong opposition to slavery; he reported that

> the christian companies in this settlement and about Cane Ridge have been large; but within a few years, many of them, who held black people as slaves, emancipated them, and have moved to the state of Ohio. I will observe that the christians of these parts *abhor* the idea of *slavery,* and some of them have almost tho't that they who hold to slavery cannot be a christian.[2]

What should we make of this report? David Edwin Harrell has suggested that the powerful abolitionist sentiment so central to the early Christian movement grew from the humanitarian dimensions of the Second Great Awakening.[3] No doubt this is true. But the Stoneites' abhorrence of slavery also grew from their overarching apocalyptic worldview, which focused on the sovereignty of God and the future triumph of his kingdom. Generated in part by the revivals, in part by the Calvinism so prominent on the southern frontier, and in part by the fact that life was hard and often haunted by poverty, disease, and malnutrition, this perspective characterized many in Stone's movement, as we have seen.

Moreover, one cannot assess or even understand the convictions the Stoneites held regarding social justice apart from this apocalyptic perspective. The Stoneites believed that those who shared the values of the world might well hold slaves, pursue wealth and power, seek their own self-interests at the expense of others, participate in the politics of this world, and fight in this world's wars. But those who took seriously the values of Jesus would refuse either to vote or to fight, would free their slaves, and would turn their backs on wealth, power, and selfish advantage over other human beings. That, they were convinced, was the way of the kingdom that would triumph over this world in due time.

This means, quite simply, that the early Stoneites wove a commitment to social justice into the very fabric of their faith. They believed that social justice belonged to the very essence of the Christian gospel. If we grasp this point, we can begin to understand the significance of Joseph Thomas's observation that "some of them have almost tho't that they who hold to slavery cannot be a christian." One's attitude toward race, therefore, became for many early Stoneites a test of Christian fellowship.

A commitment to social justice in the context of the church endured in the old Stoneite heartland of Middle Tennessee for many years, though by the late nineteenth century this conviction had been compromised in many ways. By the end of the century congregations had come to be segregated by color, and some had been for decades. This situation troubled many, and none more greatly than David Lipscomb and his close associates in Nashville.[4]

As we have seen, Lipscomb inherited the apocalyptic perspective of Barton Stone and made that perspective the mainspring of his life and his ministry. This explains why Lipscomb so strongly resisted racial discrimination in the context of the church, in spite of the fact that, in so doing, he flew directly in the face of the dominant values of his region and his time. In 1878, Lipscomb learned about a church in McKinney, Texas, in which some members had resisted a black Christian who had presented himself for membership in the congregation. Incensed, Lipscomb penned in the *Gospel Advocate* strong words of protest that, as much as any statement he ever made, reflected his convictions regarding racial prejudice within the church:

> We believe it sinful to have two congregations in the same community for persons of separate and distinct races now. . . .
>
> God saves the negro equally with the white man when he believes in Christ and puts him on by being buried with him in baptism. . . . I had as soon think of the worst blasphemer in the land, steeped in the vilest of crimes being saved as a man or woman who would stand between that individual and his obedience to God. He sets at defiance God's law, assumes to be greater than God, and is guilty of a presumptuous sin in the sight of God, for which we can hardly believe pardon can be found.
>
> God saves the believing negro or white through his obedience, and can one claiming to be a child of God say no? . . . How dare any man assume such power and authority? How dare a church tolerate the persistent exhibition of such a spirit? Such a church certainly forfeits its claims to be a church of God. . . .
>
> We mean simply this, a church which cannot bring an individual to see his rebellion against God in such a course, ought to withdraw from that individual as one who with a heart full of pride, bitterness and treason fights against God. For our part we would much prefer membership with an humble and despised band of ignorant negroes, than with a congregation of the

[most] aristocratic and refined whites in the land, cherishing such a spirit of defiance of God and his law, and all the principles of his holy religion.[5]

In addition to giving us a general sense of Lipscomb's perspective, this passage offers us important insights into three specific aspects of his position. First, Lipscomb expresses serious doubts about whether a racist can be saved. Second, he calls for congregations to excommunicate those who seek to refuse membership to Christians of other races. And third, he unambiguously argues that a church which failed to take this step was simply not a Church of Christ. Clearly, in Lipscomb's view, issues of justice and equality in the context of the church belonged to the very essence of the gospel, just as they had for the Stoneites seventy years before. No wonder, then, that attitudes toward race in the church were for Lipscomb, as they had been for the Stoneites, a test of Christian fellowship. He believed that racism in the church reflected the values of the world, not the values of the kingdom of God.

Lipscomb had occasion to address this issue again in 1907, when S. E. Harris and other members of the Bellwood Church of Christ in the Nashville area sought to exclude from their membership a young black girl who, for all intents and purposes, had been adopted by Mr. and Mrs. E. A. Elam, also members in that church. Elam was a close friend of Lipscomb and a coworker on the *Gospel Advocate*.

When Harris told Elam that many in the congregation were "sore" over this girl's attendance in an otherwise all-white congregation and asked that Elam make her attend "the colored church," Elam and Lipscomb both rejected Harris's request on the grounds that it was fundamentally anti-Christian. "I have no patience whatever," Elam wrote, "with that corrupt and abominable heresy that negroes have no souls. . . . This heresy is responsible for all this disturbance at Bellwood. Those who hold to it, and who have disturbed the church over it, are the heretics, the sinners, and should have been dealt with by the church years ago."[6] Lipscomb concurred:

> No one as a Christian . . . has the right to say to another "Thou shalt not," because he is of a different family, race, social or political station. . . . Jesus Christ personates himself in the least and in the most despised of his disciples; and as we treat them, we treat him. . . . To object to any child of God participating in the services on account of his race, social or civil state, his color or race, is to object to Jesus Christ and to cast him from our association. It is a fearful thing to do.[7]

The passion for social justice and for racial equality that manifested itself here and there in the Stone-Lipscomb tradition did not endure long, however. It slowly evaporated, leaving Churches of Christ largely unprepared for many of the issues involving social justice that would confront them throughout the twentieth century. Most of all, it left them unprepared for the demands for social justice that confronted all of America during the decade of the 1960s, as we shall see. The question we must ask at this point, however, is Why? Why did the passion for social justice largely disappear from the ranks of Churches of Christ?

Race and Justice: Perspectives of Alexander Campbell

Answers to this question are both several and complex, and they have much to do with Alexander Campbell's understanding of the Christian faith. Indeed, when we turn to Campbell, we find an approach to social ethics very different from that of the early followers of Barton W. Stone. To understand Campbell at this point, we must assess his theological agenda in three respects.

1. *The Reading of Scripture.* Campbell's preeminent goal was the unity of all Christians, and he sought to achieve that goal through a scientific reading of the biblical text, based on the presuppositions of Scottish Common Sense Realism. As we observed in Chapter 2, Campbell believed that if all Christians read the Bible as a kind of scientific manual for church and Christian life, they would attain a uniformity of faith and practice, at least with regard to "the essentials" or "matters of faith." In keeping with this, Campbell viewed as essentials only those issues for which the Bible provided precise and unmistakably clear directions. He relegated to the category of opinion all issues of social justice on which positions might be inferred from broad biblical principles but for which there were no precise instructions. Important though such issues may have been, he maintained that they simply did not stand at the core of the Christian gospel and hence were not suitable issues for debate in the larger Christian community. This reasoning determined Campbell's approach to the question of slavery as well.

Campbell rejected slavery for a variety of reasons and emancipated his own slaves, to be sure. But he rooted his opposition to slavery in his judgment that *"in this age and in this country it* [slavery] *is not expedient."*[8] He viewed slavery as "not in harmony with the spirit of the age nor the moral advancement of society," and he judged it "not favorable to individual and national prosperity."[9] But he refused to argue that slavery was sinful for the simple reason that the Bible never pronounced it either right or wrong. As he put it in 1845, "there is not one verse in the Bible inhibiting it, but many regulating it. It is not, then, we conclude, *immoral."*[10] In fact, he suggested, "in certain cases and conditions," slavery might be "morally right."[11]

For this reason, Campbell refused to "unchristianize or non-fellowship any Christian master," and he argued that *"no Christian community can religiously make the simple relation of master and slave a subject of discipline or a term of communion."*[12] Campbell stood in fundamental agreement, therefore, with his colleague Walter Scott, who offered the following conclusion to the whole matter: "Slavery is radically a political, not a religious evil."[13] These men simply maintained that the issue of slavery had little or nothing to do with the Christian gospel.

2. *Individual Conversion versus Social Ethics.* Campbell privatized the Christian faith by making the issue of individual conversion paramount and focusing especially on individual obedience to "first principles" — faith, repentance, confession, and immersion. It would be unfair to suggest that Campbell had no interest in ethics as part of the Christian life beyond mere conversion, but it is nonetheless true that his battles on two fronts led him to place a disproportionate emphasis on the conversion process: (1) Campbell did battle with Calvinists of all stripes over the nature of conversion — insisting that it occurred not through a supernatural operation by the Holy Spirit but through a rational decision of the human will — and (2) his emphasis on immersion for the forgiveness of sins led him into endless discussions of the point at which one becomes a Christian in the fullest sense — whether at baptism or before. His inordinate focus on individual conversion allowed little serious attention to the ethical content of the Christian life. Thus, Campbell's focus on personal conversion reinforced his scientific reading of the biblical text and helped push questions of social justice even further to the peripheral realm of private opinion.

3. *The Canon within the Canon.* As we saw in Chapter 2, Campbell insisted that the essentials of the Christian faith are found in the New Testament, not in the Old, and that the New Testament alone contained the laws and regulations that should govern the church. Further, he argued that only that portion of the New Testament which actually reflects the Christian age is finally pertinent in this regard. Since Campbell identified the day of Pentecost as the birth of the Christian age, he restricted his canon to that section of the New Testament bounded by Acts 2 on the one end and Revelation 22 on the other.[14]

This is not to say that Campbell did not value the remainder of the biblical text. He did. But by placing such heavy emphasis on that portion of the New Testament beginning with the second chapter of Acts, he effectively downplayed those biblical materials that spoke most directly to questions of social justice — the Old Testament prophets, for example, and the Gospels, which contain the pointed teachings of Jesus regarding compassion and social concern.

Campbell's positions and those of his close associates on all these points are critical since, as we have seen, Campbell began to exert a considerable influence on the Stoneite churches in Kentucky beginning in 1823. He brought to those churches the scientific reading of the biblical text, the privatistic understanding of the Christian faith, and the emphasis on the restricted canon that we have just surveyed. It did not take many years for Stoneite congregations to begin treating slavery precisely as Campbell and Scott did — as a serious social problem that was nevertheless unrelated in any fundamental way to the Christian gospel and therefore as an issue that ought not to be subject to dispute in the Christian churches.

When John Secrest, an avowed abolitionist, traveled to Carlisle, Kentucky, in 1828 to raise the issue of slavery, the congregation there warned him "not to broach that subject among us. We are living in peace & harmony, & do not wish our peace interrupted." They went on to say, "We would rejoice to hear you preach that simple gospel, which you have been preaching in Ohio. But we do trust, that if you have intended to introduce the question of slavery, you will . . . abandon that idea." Moreover, John Rogers reported that the Christians at Cane Ridge who in 1810-1811 had viewed slavery as incompatible with the Christian faith had by 1828 sustained sufficient "connection with slavery" that Secrest "greatly abused the brethren, on [that] account."[15]

As the years went by, no one epitomized the Campbellian response to slavery any more than did Benjamin Franklin, who wrote in 1859,

1. If those who labor on the subject will show where the Lord ever gave a decision or opinion, we will publish and maintain it.
2. The same goes for the Apostles.
3. If they will show where the Lord or the Apostles ever discussed the subject, we will discuss it.
4. If they didn't discuss it, we won't.
5. Those who condemn us for ignoring it condemn Jesus and the Apostles. We follow them.[16]

Like Campbell, Franklin maintained his focus on the "first principles" of individual conversion for which he felt the Bible gave clear and precise instructions, especially in the book of Acts and in the epistles.

Collapse of the Ethical Vision in the Stone-Lipscomb Tradition

But there is more, for the Stone-Lipscomb tradition itself finally provided its own incentive for Churches of Christ to view questions of social justice as essentially penultimate considerations. In this regard, the apocalyptic perspective was a two-edged sword. On the one hand, it encouraged believers to conform their lives to the will of a sovereign God whose values differed radically from the values of the world. On the other hand, by drawing such a clear and distinct line of demarcation between the world and the kingdom of God and by radically disassociating the two, the apocalyptic perspective encouraged believers to conclude that matters of social justice might well be germane in the context of the church but had little pertinence in the context of the larger world.

Thus, while David Lipscomb could condemn racism in the church in no uncertain terms and could even argue that churches which tolerated racial discrimination were no churches at all, he refused to condemn slavery in the larger culture. This was so because Lipscomb had merged his apocalyptic outlook with the more legal, technical perspective of Alexander Campbell. Lipscomb fully subscribed to Campbell's premise that slavery was a political, not a religious question. As he put it,

> Slavery is a political relation, established by political governments. . . . Christ did not propose to break up such relations by violence. He recognized the relationship, regulated it, and put in operation principles that in their workings would so mold public sentiment as to break down all evil relations and sinful institutions.[17]

Because Lipscomb's apocalyptic worldview assured him that all human government and political activity belonged to the realm of Satan, Lipscomb could essentially regard the public debate over slavery as fundamentally irrelevant to the gospel, to Christians, and to the church. Put another way, proponents of the apocalyptic dimension of the Stone-Lipscomb heritage finally turned it in distinctly otherworldly directions and came to view the political affairs of this world as irrelevant to the kingdom of God.

In addition, at this stage in its evolution, the apocalyptic worldview assured believers that they could belong to the kingdom of God alone and stand altogether separate and apart from the values of the world. In fact, however, the values of the world intruded themselves on these believers far more than they knew. They fell captive to their culture precisely when they imagined they had escaped its constraints.

Nowhere is this more apparent than in the attitudes these Christians held toward blacks. For example, John Rogers, the preacher for the Church of Christ in Carlisle, Kentucky, for most of the first half of the nineteenth century, regarded blacks as "the most immoral, the most indolent, shiftless, & therefore the most worthless & unfortunate class in our Country." At the same time, he imagined that God had "permitted the horrible slave-trade, & thus brought the savage heathen black man to this country, to be benefitted by his contact with the white race."[18] Even David Lipscomb admitted that he had "always felt the race instincts strong," and when he defended the rights of the Elam girl in the Bellwood church, he spoke unabashedly of "the sins common to her race."[19]

If such attitudes could prevail at a time when many in Churches of Christ self-consciously sought to live their lives in the kingdom of God as a realm apart from the world, it was inevitable that racism would intensify in later years when such aspirations grew weaker and less urgent. When leaders among Churches of Christ abandoned the apocalyptic vision following World War I and embarked on a program of systematic acculturation, most Churches of Christ not only failed to resist racism in the larger culture but increasingly failed to resist racism within the church itself. Once the apocalyptic vision died, there were few serious theological resources either to sustain a vision of social justice or to prevent the racism in the larger culture from making serious inroads into the church.

Churches of Christ and the Social Gospel

Finally, to understand the response of Churches of Christ to issues of social justice in the 1960s, one must also realize that Churches of Christ in the early years of the twentieth century, like their fundamentalist counterparts in the same period, reacted strongly against the "social gospel" promoted by those they perceived as theological liberals.[20]

In the first place, many in Churches of Christ, especially those standing in the more legal tradition of the radicalized Alexander Campbell, defined the gospel in terms of law and pattern for the organization and worship of the church. They naturally tended to view the social gospel as simply irrelevant to the fundamental issues of the Christian faith. We can see something of this view in their reaction to Charles Sheldon's *In His Steps* — a popular presentation of the social gospel in the early twentieth century.[21]

Sheldon told the story of a fashionable urban church whose pastor and members determined that before they made any critical decisions they would ask, "What would Jesus do?" This question led them into a variety of social ministries, directed especially toward the poor and the dispossessed. After reading the book, Austin McGary, the crusty editor of the *Firm Foundation,* wrote a series of articles in which he asked "what Jesus would *not* do if He were on earth." With little interest in the social gospel, McGary not only turned Sheldon's question upside down but also gave it an entirely different focus. He charged that social gospelers were "teaching for doctrines the commandments of men," and he insisted that "Christ would not, if He were here, approve of their teaching, nor recognize them as the people of God."[22] Nor, McGary argued, would Jesus condone instrumental music in the worship of the church. To underscore this point, he ironically appealed to one of the favorite passages of the social gospel movement, Amos 5:23-24 and 6:4-7 — completely missing the central meaning of the text:

> Let us hear what God said upon the matter through His prophet Amos: ". . . Take away from me the voice of thy songs; for I will not hear the melody of your viols." Again, through the same prophet, and in the same connection, He, after pronouncing woes against other things pronounces a solemn one against those who "chant to the sound of the viol, and invent to themselves instruments of music like David."

From this McGary concluded that "Christ could not, if He were here now, tolerate instrumental music in the worship without putting himself in antagonism with the will of His Father."[23]

If McGary's resistance to the social gospel grew out of his Campbellian conception of the Christian faith, others grounded their resistance in a perspective that grew more directly from the Stone-Lipscomb tradition: they contended that the church was not in the business of saving this world but rather of saving souls. These two positions were not mutually exclusive, however, and few who embraced one would have quarreled with the other.

N. B. Hardeman provided an especially notable example of this latter perspective when he delivered his second series of Tabernacle Sermons in Nashville in 1923. Hardeman criticized those who called themselves Christians and who emphasized social relief. He argued that in biblical times people subsisted "in dirt and filth and thickly settled districts, living in unsanitary surroundings; and yet neither Paul nor any of the apostles were ever engaged primarily in work of that sort." He concluded that "the function and the work of the church of God is not primarily for the furnishing of temporal help or assistance, but the paramount work of the church . . . is to spread the gospel."[24]

Speakers at the Abilene Christian College Bible lectureship in the early years of the twentieth century similarly resisted exploring the social implications of the gospel, and for reasons much like those advocated by Hardeman. As William S. Banowsky explained in his book on the lectureships,

> The very weight of the Lectureship lodged the standard conservative objection [to the social gospel]: that the socially-conscious liberals had forsaken the one great purpose of the church, namely, the salvation of individual souls. The speakers made virtually no reference to such questions as labor-management relations, capitalistic control, mass unemployment, bread lines, slum clearance, political reform, racial discrimination, or education for the handicapped and under-privileged.[25]

Banowsky explained that when lectureship speakers did express interest in support for orphans, widows, or the destitute, they almost invariably viewed these activities as a means to individual conversion and justified them on those grounds.

To be sure, there were exceptions to this pattern throughout the twentieth century. For example, the Central Church of Christ in Nashville organized a massive program of outreach to the destitute and homeless, as we noted in Chapter 9. The Church of Christ in Madison, Tennessee (metropolitan Nashville), carried out an active social ministry to orphans, the elderly, the homeless, and the destitute throughout the middle and later years of the twentieth century. But exceptions like these were relatively few and far between.[26]

By the 1960s, little in this regard had changed. In 1963, for example, the Brookline Church of Christ in Brookline, Massachusetts, established an interracial urban ministry called the House of the Carpenter. Led by graduate students from Harvard, Boston University, and M.I.T. who were members of that congregation, the House of the Carpenter sponsored an after-school tutoring program — including Bible classes — for neighborhood youth, a summer day camp, and special classes for neighborhood residents offering training in a variety of fields from sports to cooking. This was one of the earliest forays into inner-city ministry among Churches of Christ, and it thrived. In 1967 the Boston Renewal Authority razed the old storefront church that had been home to the House of the Carpenter from its inception in order to make room for new high-rise buildings. Undaunted, the Brookline Church of Christ purchased a new property that contained "six classrooms, library, recreation facilities and offices for staff and teachers."[27] The entire enterprise came crashing down, however, in the aftermath of the Grove Hall riot, June 3, 1967.[28]

When Reuel Lemmons, editor of the *Firm Foundation,* learned that the House of the Carpenter had collapsed, he caustically wrote,

> We can hardly stifle a yawn when some of our young radicals . . . begin to push for the social gospel through such projects as House of the Carpenter, etc. Incidentally, we understand that House of the Carpenter has been given up as an experiment that failed and has been closed down. We have no desire to say, "we told you so" but when we pick up things the denominations, the Salvation Army and others have tried for years without results we can expect them to fail.[29]

Like most others in Churches of Christ in those years, Lemmons smelled "liberalism in the church" among those less concerned with "soul saving" than "with helping downtrodden people." He hammered on this theme time and again. "Entirely too much of today's radicalism is aimed in one direction only, i.e., toward the social gospel," he complained in 1969. "The things many young Christians are pulling for make good social fodder, but are poor Bible."[30]

Six years later, in the aftermath of the turbulent 1960s, H. A. (Buster) Dobbs provided a classic statement, reflecting the dominant perspective of both mainstream and conservative Churches of Christ on issues of social justice:

> The gospel of Jesus places the emphasis on the individual. The social gospel puts the emphasis on the community. The gospel of Jesus teaches soul salvation. The social gospel proclaims a community salvation. The gospel of Jesus encourages an emphasis on heaven and not on earth. The social gospel employs all of its energy in worldly, not heavenly interests.[31]

A variety of theological factors thus contributed to the decision of most among Churches of Christ essentially to ignore the question of racial justice for most of the twentieth century. These factors included Campbell's scientific and individualistic gospel, his canon within the canon, the collapse of the apocalyptic vision of Stone and Lipscomb, and the failure of most in Churches of Christ to acknowledge that the Christian faith had any social implications.

The Growth of Institutionalized Racism

We must add to this theological context the social setting in which Churches of Christ, for the most part, lived and moved and had their being: the American South. Following the collapse of any serious theological resistance to racism, we should not be surprised to discover that by the 1920s and 1930s, racism had institutionalized itself within the church just as surely as it had within the larger culture.

One sign of this increasingly institutionalized racism is that some — perhaps many — among Churches of Christ belonged to the Ku Klux Klan in the 1920s. James Allen, editor of the *Gospel Advocate* at that time, claimed that "many of the preachers" were members, and one student of race relations among Churches of Christ reported that many members of Churches of Christ belonged to the Klan in that period.[32]

The clearest evidence of institutionalized racism within the church, however, was the pattern of segregation that increasingly dominated the lives of both individuals and congregations of Churches of Christ in the early twentieth century. This was not a matter of mere separation of the races by mutual consent; it was a matter of whites excluding blacks from their fellowship because they did not view them as their equals.

G. C. Brewer, for example, candidly recalled the years of his youth in Tennessee in the early twentieth century. "None of us thought of inviting Negroes into our homes as guests or of sitting down to eat with them at the same table; we felt, as a matter of course, that they should have the same food that we ate, but that they should eat in the kitchen or in the servants' quarters." Brewer acknowledged that "this was the condition that prevailed and this we accepted as right and satisfactory." At the same time, he could resolutely affirm that "we were not prejudiced against the Negroes."[33]

The standard pattern of institutional segregation is exemplified in the poignant story of Marshall Keeble. Because of his ability to move crowds and win converts, Keeble distinguished himself as the most successful of all the black preachers among Churches of Christ during the twentieth century. He routinely made hundreds of converts in weeklong gospel meetings and revivals in black communities throughout the South from the earliest years of the twentieth century until the 1960s. Throughout his career, Keeble remained almost entirely dependent for financial support on the white power structure in Churches of Christ. One of his biographers contends that "no other religious group in the South has singled out a lone Negro and heaped upon him more personal honors than [has the Church of Christ] on Marshall Keeble."[34] Keeble made the most of the situation, using the white support for purposes he deemed important.

In the early 1940s, Keeble had an exchange with Foy Wallace Jr. that reflects the pattern of segregation that had become routine by that point. Wallace initiated the exchange when he complained that certain black preachers were

African American evangelist Marshall Keeble (1878-1968), in a preaching career that ran from 1897 to 1968, distinguished himself as the most successful preacher, black or white, among twentieth-century Churches of Christ. The president of Nashville Christian Institute, Keeble baptized over 25,000 people, established over 200 congregations, and individually trained scores of African American preachers. Keeble led one of two major streams in African American Churches of Christ: Keeble relied on extensive white support for his work, even to the point of tolerating indignities; others rejected white support if that support carried with it racist requirements.
(Photo courtesy Gospel Advocate Company)

attracting large numbers of whites to their meetings. Wallace doubtless had Keeble in mind when he complained that "if any of the white preachers should say everything they [the black preachers] say to a word, it would sound so common that the brethren would stop it. But when a negro says it, in negro manner, the brethren paw up the ground over it." He went on to say that "reliable reports have come to me of white women, members of the church, becoming so animated over a certain colored preacher as to go up to him after a sermon and shake hands with him *holding his hand in both of theirs.*" In Wallace's view, "that kind of thing will . . . make fools out of the negroes." Further, "for any woman in the church to so far forget her dignity, and lower herself so, just because a negro has learned enough about the gospel to preach it to his race, is pitiable indeed." Wallace commended another model instead:

When N. B. Hardeman held the valley-wide meeting at Harlingen, Texas, some misguided brethren brought a group of negroes up to the front to be introduced to and shake hands with him. Brother Hardeman told them publicly that he could see all of the colored brethren he cared to see on the outside after services, and that he could say everything to them he wanted to say without the formality of shaking hands.[35]

No one protested Wallace's harangue, in print at any rate. But relations between the races were such among Churches of Christ in the 1940s that Keeble felt constrained to abase himself before Wallace in the next issue of the *Bible Banner*. "For over thirty years," Keeble wrote,

I have tried to conduct my work just as your article in the *"Bible Banner"* of March suggested. Taking advice from such friends as you have been for years has been a blessing to my work. So I take the privilege to thank you for that instructive and encouraging article. I hope I can conduct myself in my last days so that you and none of my friends will have to take back nothing they have said complimentary about my work or regret it.[36]

Wallace was quick to commend Keeble's compliant spirit. "This letter," he wrote, "is characteristic of the humility of M. Keeble. It is the reason why he is the greatest colored preacher that has ever lived." Black preachers like Keeble, Wallace affirmed, "know their place and stay in it, even when some white brethren try to take them out of it."[37]

Yet, according to blacks who knew Keeble well, Wallace's portrayal of Keeble was way off base. Dewayne Winrow, a Keeble understudy for several years, claims that

although Keeble advocated for blacks an *adaptive life* philosophy similar to that of Booker T. Washington, he should not be mistaken to have been an "Uncle Tom" for whites. Some of us who knew him and traveled with him often characterized him as "a preacher ahead of his time." We saw him as a black preacher who was able to communicate effectively across racial lines. The "Keeble Style" of wit and logic coupled with straightforwardness and skill of expression enabled him . . . to say things to white audiences that would have required a great deal of courage for other black preachers of his day.[38]

One finds in Marshall Keeble, therefore, a man who exploited the prevailing patterns of institutionalized racism in order to preach the gospel to as wide an audience as possible.

The pattern of institutionalized racism was evident throughout Churches of Christ at a fairly early date. Many had already abandoned David Lipscomb's example by around 1890 and had begun to establish segregated congregations.

By the early twentieth century, white congregations were funding and constructing separate buildings for blacks in a deliberate effort to foster segregation. As
S. E. Harris noted in 1907, "as soon as there were enough negroes in the white
church to start a colored church, we would build them a house to worship in,
like the old brethren did here fifteen or twenty years ago."[39]

A. B. Lipscomb, David Lipscomb's nephew, submitted to the *Gospel Advocate* a classic description of this pattern in 1931:

> The second meeting among the Negroes of Valdosta, Georiga [*sic*], conducted
> by the colored evangelist, Marshall Keeble, of Nashville, Tenn., came to a close
> on August 9. All told, one hundred and sixty-six persons were baptized, chiefly
> adults. . . . Through the effort of the white disciples a large commodious
> house has been secured and regular worship prevails.

The younger Lipscomb proudly announced his conviction that "we [the whites]
have never made a better investment for the Lord nor any which brought such
quick and happy results." He added that the "new religious and moral status
for the Negro element . . . means that we now have better farm hands, better
porters, better cooks, [and] better housemaids than ever before."[40]

Without meaning to do so, Foy Wallace Jr. offered perhaps the most telling
reason for the growth of institutionalized racism among Churches of Christ in
the twentieth century when he wrote that an acceptable black preacher is one
who "knows what his relationships are in the church in the light of his relationships with society."[41] In the 1930s, 1940s, and 1950s, the values of white southern culture increasingly defined the racial posture of white Churches of Christ.

The Black Heritage among Churches of Christ

The most convulsive aspects of the civil rights movement in America took place
between 1955, when police officers in Montgomery, Alabama, arrested Rosa
Parks for refusing to give up her seat on a city bus to a white man, and 1968,
when Dr. Martin Luther King Jr. fell victim to an assassin's bullet. Though the
events of those years were surely the most revolutionary to transpire in America
since the Civil War, one scarcely would have known of them at all if one's only
source of information during the period had been the *Firm Foundation,* the
Gospel Advocate, or almost any other media outlet related to mainstream
Churches of Christ. It is true that James Willeford spoke boldly against racism
in national "Herald of Truth" radio broadcasts in 1955.[42] With few exceptions,
Willeford's was a voice crying in the wilderness. Andrew Hairston, black minister of the Simpson Street Church of Christ in Atlanta, Georgia, lamented in
1963 that on the issue of racial justice, the white press had been "for the most
part . . . as silent as the grave."[43]

To a very significant degree, that silence reflected the extent to which black and white Churches of Christ had become, by those years, two very different churches, with almost no meaningful interaction. As Hairston wrote in 1964, "There is with rare exception in every town a 'White' Church of Christ and a 'Colored' Church of Christ."[44] Blacks had their own bishop in the editor of their leading paper, the *Christian Echo.* They had their own lectureships and crusades. And they had their own college, Southwestern Christian College, which opened its doors in Terrell, Texas, in 1950. W. E. Brightwell, the "News and Notes" editor of the *Gospel Advocate,* estimated in 1948 that there were more than a thousand African American congregations in the United States. By 1990, the most authoritative record available pegged that number at 1,218.[45] The extent to which blacks felt the sting of segregation is reflected in the fact that they sometimes counted their membership only in terms of blacks, not whites. For example, V. L. Cathey wrote in 1965 that "with a church membership of more than 40,000, we can put Southwestern Christian College in the class with all other accredited colleges in America any day we decide to."[46]

Most white members of Churches of Christ knew next to nothing about the African American churches and institutions, as the *Christian Chronicle* noted in 1968:

> The average white member of a local church knows less about his Negro fellow-Christians than he does about local politics or the latest TV heroes. There have been, indeed, two separate brotherhoods with their own leaders, schools, missionaries, lectureships, and geographical areas of strength. Even the white churches who have supported Negro mission work and building projects are largely unaware of life on the other side of the "middle wall of partition."[47]

If we wish to understand black Churches of Christ in America, we must realize that two traditions coexisted in that heritage from the earliest years of the twentieth century. On the one hand, Marshall Keeble perhaps best reflected the tradition of dependence on white paternalism. But throughout the century black Churches of Christ also developed a separate, independent tradition fully capable of launching vigorous critiques against white racism. G. P. (George Phillip) Bowser provided early and undisputed leadership for this tradition.[48]

Born in Alabama but raised in Nashville, Bowser was both a preacher and an educator who founded and directed several schools for black preachers. Reared a Methodist and educated in a Methodist college, this "one-eyed, one-armed preaching wonder" had a good working knowledge both of the biblical text and of the original biblical languages.[49] In 1907, he established a school in Nashville; two years later, it moved to Silver Point, Tennessee, and was renamed the Silver Point Christian Institute. In 1938 Bowser began another school, the

Bowser Christian Institute, and operated it out of his home in Fort Smith, Arkansas. There he trained a corps of men who would provide leadership for black Churches of Christ in the critical years to come. Notable in that group were J. S. Winston, R. N. Hogan, Levi Kennedy, and G. E. Steward.

Bowser was also a capable editor, and in 1902 he launched the *Christian Echo,* a publication that served to unify and mobilize black Churches of Christ for the remainder of the century. Throughout the civil rights struggle of the 1960s and beyond, R. N. Hogan, one of Bowser's students at the Silver Point

G. P. (George Phillip) Bowser (1874-1950; pictured here) was one of the two most influential leaders of African American Churches of Christ in the twentieth century, the other being Marshall Keeble. While white financial support helped to sustain Keeble's preaching ministry for seventy years, Boswer fostered a tradition that spurned white support when whites insisted on racist behavior and practice. For example, A. M. Burton funded in 1920 the Southern Practical Institute, a school for blacks in Nashville, and invited Boswer to serve as principal under a white superintendent, C. E. W. Dorris. When Dorris insisted that the black students conform to southern custom and enter the school through the back door, Bowser objected. Though Keeble urged Bowser to overlook this indignity, Bowser refused, packed up, and returned to Louisville. Bowser was especially noted for a lifetime devoted to the training of African American preachers. He established two schools for this purpose: the Silver Point Christian Institute in East Tennessee (1907-1920) and the Bowser Christian Institute in Fort Smith, Arkansas (1938-1946). Bowser also launched in 1902, and edited until 1949, the *Christian Echo,* the principal publication that has served African American Churches of Christ throughout the twentieth century.
(Photo courtesy Vernon Boyd)

Christian Institute, edited the *Christian Echo* and made it the principal voice of black protest within Churches of Christ.

Despite the obvious differences between the Bowser and Keeble traditions, both contributed to a cohesive pattern of development in the black Churches of Christ in the United States. Almost uniformly, these churches have nurtured a theological orientation as conservative as any within white Churches of Christ. S. R. Cassius, a leader among black Churches of Christ in the early years of the twentieth century, complained in 1915 that black congregations seldom moved beyond what he called "first principles." "We are teaching too much faith, repentance, confession, and baptism," he wrote, "and not grace, love, truth, and mercy."[50] Steeped in Campbellian rationalism, they have long tended to be literalistic in their reading of the biblical text and exclusivistic in their attitudes toward other Christian traditions. Likewise, their worship style is far more subdued and controlled than that of most other black Christian traditions. Marshall Keeble underscored this dimension of black Churches of Christ when he wrote that "the gospel can take the dance out of the man, stop him from dancing, pull him out from under a mourner's bench, and set him up on a seat."[51]

Yet, to a great extent, the conservatism of the black Churches of Christ was cut from a different piece of cloth than that of their white counterparts. Campbellian rationalism, for example, does not entirely explain the literalism with which black Churches of Christ tend to approach Scripture. Another important factor has been the degree to which African Americans have understood a literal reading of Scripture to speak directly and powerfully to their experience. As Dewayne Winrow has pointed out, "The white Church of Christ, for the most part, values the nineteenth-century historical-critical technique," which

> suggests that in order to read and understand the Bible or any literary work 'properly,' one must abandon oneself completely to the world of that literary work. In particular, one must renounce one's experience of reality, suspend one's understanding of life, and waive one's right to one's own values, so that one may without encumbrances surrender oneself to the experiences, world view, values, and assumptions embedded in the work. This method of reading has had little influence in black Churches of Christ.[52]

Instead, blacks in Churches of Christ take the Bible both literally and authoritatively, because they understand it to speak directly to the issues of the slavery, racism, oppression, and economic deprivation that they have experienced in the United States.

The Struggle for Equal Rights: Segregated Colleges

One compelling gauge of the seriousness of the struggle that black members of Churches of Christ waged for equal treatment within the church and its institutions between 1955 and 1968 can be found in the issue of racial segregation within Church of Christ–related colleges. For many years, Church of Christ–related colleges in the South simply reflected the racial attitudes of the region. In 1928, for example, the editors of the Abilene Christian College yearbook, the *Prickly Pear,* chose black minstrel caricatures for the volume's theme. Alongside degrading cartoons there appeared verses containing derogatory racial terms and demeaning stereotypes such as the following:

> Ain't no use o' my workin' so hard
> For I got a gal in de white folks' yard;
> She brings me meat an' she brings me lard,
> Dere ain't no use in my workin' so hard.

It goes without saying that Abilene Christian College in those years, along with every other Church of Christ–related college, refused admission to blacks as a matter of stated policy.

The U.S. Supreme Court handed down its landmark ruling in the *Brown v. Board of Education* case in 1954, declaring segregation in America's public schools to be unconstitutional. But as late as 1960, all Church of Christ–related colleges located in the South still refused admission to blacks.[53] The same held true for practically every other institution related to Churches of Christ. Hubert Locke, assistant to the police commissioner in Detroit and minister to the largely black Conant Gardens Church of Christ, complained in 1965 that "Churches of Christ have, for the most part, remained a religious symbol of all that is distasteful about the 'southern way of life.'" He indicted "our leading southern educational institutions" on the grounds that all but one refused to admit African Americans. He went on to note that "there are no Negro children admitted to our church-related orphanages or Negro residents to our homes for the aged." He concluded by saying that "we are the only major religious body in America whose voice has not been raised in the present conflict on the side of racial equality."[54]

Many blacks simply refused to accept this state of affairs as compatible with the Christian faith. Reflecting the traditional restorationist perspective of Churches of Christ, Andrew Hairston complained that segregation had "practically devoured the true church and nearly convenced [*sic*] the world that the existence of the true Church of Christ must yet be prayed for and hoped for, but has not yet appeared."[55]

Of all the black critics of segregation among Churches of Christ, however, none was more unrelenting than the editor of the *Christian Echo,* R. N. Hogan. Hogan grieved especially because blacks were "admitted to Denominational

Richard Nathaniel Hogan (1902-), trained by G. P. Bowser from age fourteen, has been a leading African American preacher for the duration of the twentieth century. For many of those years, Hogan preached in a gospel tent that he took to various communities throughout the United States. He is pictured here (left) in the late 1930s, standing in front of his tent with Fred Lee, minister of the 9512 Compton Avenue Church of Christ in Los Angeles. In 1949, Hogan took over the editorship of G. P. Bowser's *Christian Echo* and continued to produce that publication into the 1990s. He used the *Echo* in the 1960s to attack racism among white Churches of Christ and especially in Church of Christ–related colleges. (Photo courtesy Jerry Rushford)

schools as well as State schools, but cannot enter a christian (?) school operated by members of the church of Christ." Hogan therefore argued time and again that those who ran these schools should "stop calling themselves Christians, stop calling their schools christian schools, and stop calling their churches, churches of Christ."[56]

By 1960, Hogan found an ally at Abilene Christian College in Bible professor Carl Spain. At the college's annual Bible lectureship for that year, Spain rebuked his own institution and, by implication, the southern white fellowship of Churches of Christ and all the colleges they supported. Pointing to the slowness of Churches of Christ to respond to the issue of racial justice, Spain proclaimed, "God forbid that churches of Christ, and schools operated by Christians, shall be the last stronghold of refuge for socially sick people who have Nazi illusions about the Master Race." Then he announced,

I feel certain that Jesus would say: "Ye hypocrites! You say you are the only true Christians, and make up the only true church, and have the only Christian schools. Yet, you drive one of your own preachers to denominational schools where he can get credit for his work and refuse to let him take Bible for credit in your own school because the color of his skin is dark!"[57]

There were critics of Spain's speech, to be sure. But the speech evoked such strong, broad-based support from the board, the administration, the faculty, the students, and the school's constituency that Abilene Christian College began admitting blacks to its graduate school in 1961 and to its undergraduate programs in 1962. According to John C. Stevens, assistant president of the college during those years, the additional year of delay at the undergraduate level was not a result of reluctance to alter policy but rather reflected an effort

Carl Spain (1917-1990), Bible professor at Abilene Christian College (University), delivered a stinging rebuke to Churches of Christ for their racial prejudice when he spoke on the Abilene Christian College Bible lectureship in 1960. In his history of those lectures, William S. Banowsky called Spain's speech "the most spectacular . . . ever delivered" in the Abilene lecture series. After Spain's controversial speech, the college responded and admitted blacks to its graduate school in 1961 and to its undergraduate programs in 1962.

(Photo courtesy Gospel Advocate Company)

Southwestern Christian College in Terrell, Texas, near Dallas, has served the black community in Churches of Christ continuously since it opened its doors in 1950. Pictured here is the Hogan-Steward Learning Center on that campus.
(Photo courtesy Southwestern Christian College)

to avoid damaging the largely black Southwestern Christian College in Terrell, Texas, which at that time was only twelve years old and still struggling to attract students.[58]

Hogan praised Abilene Christian College for its actions but continued to scold the other schools. "It is almost an insult," he wrote,

> for a Negro to ask to be admitted into the David Lipscomb College in Nashville, Tenn. Yet it is supposed to be operated by Christians; what reason can David Lipscomb, Harding, Freed Hardeman, Florida Christian (?) and other such schools who are refusing to allow Negroes to be trained in their schools, give for such practice, but sheer prejudice and hate?[59]

Hogan found it especially ironic that the school that bore Lipscomb's name was among the last bastions of segregation in Churches of Christ.[60] By 1963, however, Harding College had integrated, and David Lipscomb College followed suit in 1964.

Still, as late as 1969, some black leaders strongly suspected that integration, in at least some of the colleges, had been prompted chiefly by government threats to cut off federal funds. G. P. Holt, for example, stated in the *Christian Echo* that he was not impressed when some college president or Dean or representative of a (quote) "Christian College" tells black brethren, "Look at us, we are not segregated; we have ten Black students at our College. See we love you." We know and you know and God knows that our Colleges have not had a *Change of Heart* — but that the Government of our land is responsible for these ten Black students in the College.[61]

The Struggle for Equal Rights:
The Nashville Christian Institute

Another important gauge of the black struggle for equal treatment within Churches of Christ can be found in the story of the Nashville Christian Institute, an educational institution that served blacks in Churches of Christ from 1941 to 1967. The Institute's story actually began as early as 1919, however, when A. M. Burton, founder and president of the Life and Casualty Insurance Company of Nashville and a chief benefactor of Marshall Keeble, established a school for blacks called the Southern Practical Institute. Burton persuaded G. P. Bowser to leave temporarily his ministry in Louisville, Kentucky, and to help with the new school in Nashville. Unfortunately, the white man whom Burton had installed as president of the Institute, C. E. W. Dorris, insisted that the all-black student body enter the school through the rear door. According to R. N. Hogan, the students "packed up and went home."[62]

Angered and disappointed, the Institute's intended constituency decided to build a school of their own that would offer elementary and secondary education, principally for black youth. They raised the money chiefly from within the black community of Churches of Christ, secured the property, and opened the Nashville Christian Institute (N.C.I.) in 1941 with an all-black board of directors.[63] Sometime before 1943, several whites were added to the board, and in 1943 several other whites with strategic positions at David Lipscomb College joined the board as well, including the college president, Athens Clay Pullias, and two college board members, chairman A. M. Burton and J. E. Acuff.

Over the years, Burton contributed approximately half a million dollars to N.C.I.[64] When he died in 1966, N.C.I. lost its chief benefactor. Athens Clay Pullias, still president of David Lipscomb College, succeeded Burton as president of N.C.I.'s board of directors.

By 1967, the physical plant of N.C.I. was in poor repair, and its teachers were receiving salaries roughly half those of teachers in the city's public schools. Enrollments dropped as many black parents elected to send their children to Nashville's public schools, which were by that time integrated. Overall, N.C.I.'s enrollment "declined from a high of 683 in 1947-48 to the low of 138 in 1967."[65] With insufficient funds to correct all these deficiencies, the N.C.I. board decided

In 1941, African Americans within Churches of Christ opened in Nashville, Tennessee, a new school for black youth, the Nashville Christian Institute (pictured here). Launched with funds raised almost exclusively from within the black community, and governed at its inception by an all-black board of directors, the school opened the board to several whites within two years of its founding. In 1967, with the school in poor repair and enrollment down, the board closed the school and transferred its assets to a scholarship fund for black youth at David Lipscomb College.
(Photo courtesy Maxine Cato)

to close the school in 1967 and transfer its assets of roughly $500,000 to the Burton-Keeble Scholarship Fund for black youth at David Lipscomb College.

The N.C.I. board and officials at David Lipscomb College considered these actions proper under the circumstances. Some blacks agreed. Marshall Keeble, for example, wrote that "while Sister Keeble and I regret to see Nashville Christian Institute close her doors, we wholly support what we thought had to be done."[66]

But R. N. Hogan and a host of other blacks felt betrayed. Several alumni of N.C.I soon filed suit in federal court, seeking an injunction against the board of N.C.I. The attorney for the plaintiffs was Fred Gray, a black Church of Christ minister who also represented at various times both Rosa Parks and Martin Luther King Jr. The suit claimed that David Lipscomb College, which historically had refused to accept graduates of N.C.I. because of their race, now sought to close N.C.I. "for the purpose of enriching the David Lipscomb College Foundation and . . . David Lipscomb College."[67]

To Hogan, especially, the issues were clear. He maintained that N.C.I. had been built with money given by "poor Negroes, some of . . . [whom] were on pensions, [and] others of very meager income gave to this school in order that young Negro Boys and Girls could receive an education in a wholesome Christian environment." In time, charged Hogan, "under the guise of wanting to help the Negro, some white brethren, who claimed to be Christians, became members of the Board of Directors of this Negro School." Finally, he wrote, these men "decided to grab the assets of N.C.I. and close it's [sic] doors." He asserted that "these men who claim to be Christians are guilty of robbing poor Negroes who struggled and gave of their meager income in order to build a Christian School for their children who were denied the privilege of attending the white so-called christian school." He called on blacks to rally and support the litigation effort with contributions.[68]

In the end, however, the court denied the effort to secure an injunction against the N.C.I. board, and the effort only served to drive yet another wedge between black and white Churches of Christ. G. P. Holt no doubt spoke for many when he confessed that he wept when he learned of the closure of N.C.I. *"We wept,"* he wrote, *"because* a great brotherhood had been stabbed in the

Many African Americans felt betrayed when the board of the Nashville Christian Institute closed the school and transferred its assets to David Lipscomb College. Several N.C.I. alumni unsuccessfully filed suit in federal court, seeking an injunction against the N.C.I. board. Fred Gray (1930- ; shown here), a prominent civil rights attorney and Church of Christ minister from Tuskegee, Alabama, represented the plaintiffs in this case. Gray previously had represented both Rosa Parks and Martin Luther King Jr. (Photo courtesy Fred Gray)

back. . . . (We have felt the power structure of the Nashville hierarchy.)"[69] As late as 1990, Jack Evans, president of Southwestern Christian College, observed that "because the Institute was closed against the will of the black churches of Christ . . . , a feeling of an injustice and unfairness still exists among some black people."[70]

The Legacies of Marshall Keeble and Martin Luther King Jr.

By 1968 the nation had experienced the murder of Emmett Till, the Montgomery bus boycott, the presence of federal troops in Little Rock enforcing racial integration in the public schools, race riots at the University of Mississippi, white attacks on freedom riders who integrated interstate buses in the South, the march on Selma, the Birmingham riots, the murders of four black children attending Sunday School at a Birmingham church, the murders of four young civil rights workers in Mississippi, the assassination of Medgar Evers, the 1963 March on Washington, the assassination of Malcolm X, and, finally, the assassination of Martin Luther King Jr.

During that same period, white leaders of Churches of Christ heard blacks including Andrew Hairston, Zebedee Bishop, Roosevelt Wells, Floyd Rose, Franklin Florence, G. P. Holt, Eugene Lawton, Humphrey Foutz, R. N. Hogan, and Hubert Locke severely criticize the system of segregated churches and church-related institutions. And blacks and whites both endured the struggle over the Nashville Christian Institute.

But during all those years, with few exceptions, the white press serving Churches of Christ responded to these issues with deafening silence.[71] For the most part, the *Gospel Advocate* maintained its silence until well into 1968. The *Advocate* ignored not only the murder of Martin Luther King but also a race relations workshop sponsored by a local black congregation in its own city of Nashville.

It took the death of Marshall Keeble on April 20, 1968, to shake the *Advocate* from its silence. An entire issue was dedicated to the memory of the evangelist — though the *Advocate*'s praise for Keeble was intermingled with criticism of the civil rights movement. "He never led a march or demonstration," wrote Karl Pettus, "peaceful or otherwise. He was never connected with a riot. . . . He didn't march for school integration, but he worked and spent himself for most of his life for Christian education."[72]

In September and October, the *Advocate* followed the Keeble issue with two articles dealing with prejudice written by Batsell Barrett Baxter, the influential Nashville preacher and popular speaker on the national "Herald of Truth" television program. These articles essentially trivialized the issue of racial justice in America, however, by treating the problem of racism as just one aspect of the generic problem of prejudice — rich against poor, educated against uneducated, young against old — that had existed throughout "the history of the world."[73]

Like the *Gospel Advocate,* the *Firm Foundation* remained essentially silent on the issue of racial discrimination until 1968, when it joined the *Advocate* in taking note of Keeble's death.[74] Editor Reuel Lemmons penned an infamous editorial that praised and eulogized Keeble, denounced the course of the civil rights movement and the work of Martin Luther King, and argued that Keeble had never suffered from discrimination and that Churches of Christ were essentially free from racial prejudice. Lemmons's editorial created such a storm of controversy and protest that it deserves to be quoted at some length. Keeble, he wrote,

> never led a riot; he never burned out a block of buildings; he never marched on Washington. But he marched toward heaven from the day he obeyed the gospel. . . . He traveled — without discrimination — for seventy years among blacks and whites alike. . . . If he ever knew there were segregation lines he never indicated it. Indeed, because of his life and work there has been an infinitesimally small amount of racial prejudice in the Church of Christ.[75]

Among the first to take issue with Lemmons was a black preacher, Norman Adamson. "I have searched myself deeply," Adamson wrote, "trying to decide if the editorial is based upon unbelievable racism on your part, gross ignorance of the conditions that have existed and still are very much in evidence in the Church, or maybe you were so emotionally upset by the death of Marshall Keeble that you lost sight on reality."[76]

Howard A. White, dean of undergraduate studies at Pepperdine College, pointed out to Lemmons that "Keeble was the victim of discrimination *most* of the time. During the five years I taught at David Lipscomb College," White wrote, Keeble

> came every year to speak at the lectures. Not once was he invited to join a luncheon or a dinner or to do anything else beyond speaking. His students and associates from the Nashville Christian Institute were segregated in one corner of the balcony. Because of his great and generous spirit, Brother Keeble suffered all these indignities in silence and without any observable resentment.[77]

Jennings Davis, a Pepperdine professor, questioned not only Lemmons's assessment of racial prejudice among Churches of Christ but also his assessment of Martin Luther King Jr. On this issue, Lemmons dug in his heels even more firmly than he had regarding the question of racial prejudice in the church. "With reference to your paragraph on my thinly veiled criticism of Martin Luther King," Lemmons wrote, "my only regret is that the criticism was veiled at all."[78]

Vastly different perspectives on King and the civil rights movement in

America produced a great chasm among Churches of Christ, revealing how polarized the tradition had become in two respects. First, it revealed the extent to which Churches of Christ separated social action from a spiritualized gospel of individual conversion, in some cases to the point of viewing them as antithetical. When Rex Turner, the president of Alabama Christian College during the time of the marches in Selma in 1965, learned that some members of Churches of Christ supported King and his nonviolent protests, he condemned them in no uncertain terms. He charged that such people were seeking "to displace the gospel of Christ with a social gospel . . . that has little or no concern for the fundamental doctrines of Christianity." He condemned King as "a rank modernist" and placed most of "those white 'ministers' who crusade with him" in the same category.[79]

Second, the civil rights movement revealed the extent to which most mainstream Churches of Christ championed the law-and-order values of conservative politics in the face of the civil unrest associated with racial tensions and growing opposition to the country's involvement in Vietnam. Reuel Lemmons refused to admit that the riots of the summer of 1967 had anything to do with "a downtrodden element of society struggling for its fair share of effluency [sic]." He insisted that the riots were simply "the signs of a decaying and dying society. . . . When a nation turns away from God and rejects eternal verities of moral conduct, the Sodomitish atmosphere soon manifests itself."[80]

Robert Taylor, writing in the *Firm Foundation*, also emphasized the close relation between religion, authority, law, and order. "Citizens governed by God, led by the Christ, and guided by the Inspired Volume," he claimed, "are *not* going to burn entire city blocks, loot whole communities, cause rivers of precious blood to flow in the streets of our major cities and defy every vestige of constituted authority which seeks to restore law and order to a bewildered populace."[81]

Many among Churches of Christ believed that the entire civil rights movement was being surreptitiously directed by Communist conspirators whose true goal was to weaken or destroy America. Reuel Lemmons stated baldly that "Communism is behind most of these riots."[82] And in a letter to Jennings Davis, Lemmons wrote,

> A lot of people wanted to compare Martin Luther King to Jesus Christ. In reality, King was a modernist, and denied faith in Jesus Christ as taught in the Bible. . . . If he was not an outright Communist, he certainly advocated Communist causes. His absolute disregard for law and order except those laws and orders which he wanted to obey leaves me cold. . . . J. Edgar Hoover branded King as a notorious liar and Harry Truman said he was a troublemaker. This kind of man, black or white, I cannot conscientiously praise.[83]

James Bales, a professor at Harding College, produced a considerably more extended argument that King was connected to international Communism. "His contribution to anarchy within the United States, his cooperation with Communists within the United States, and his efforts to render us defenseless in the face of external Communist aggression," Bales wrote, "all add up to defeat for freedom and victory for communism if he and others like him prevail."[84]

Predictably, many blacks believed judgments like those of Lemmons and Bales to be the product more of blind racial prejudice than reason. They wearied of the persistent refusal of such authors to view the civil rights movement and the work of King as authentic expressions of protest against a racist society. The Communist conspiracy theories and the inflamed rhetoric in which they were typically couched did much to increase the level of alienation between blacks and whites within Churches of Christ. Jesse Johnson, a black preacher in Detroit, denounced Bales's book in uncompromising terms:

> The book's accusations are preposterous, its conclusions are not based upon facts, it is against every rule of journalistic ethics, should be publicly exposed as being hate literature and should be condemned as "racist" in its intent. . . . Black people, both inside and outside the church, will not stand idly by and see their heroes scandalized in such a manner.[85]

Noble Patterson, editor of the Fort Worth–based *Christian Journal*, made another attempt to link the civil rights movement to a Communist conspiracy just a few days after King's assassination. John Allen Chalk, a young progressive preacher among Churches of Christ who at the time was the featured speaker on the "Herald of Truth" radio broadcast, eulogized King at a student gathering on the campus of Oklahoma Christian College in Oklahoma City, Oklahoma. Following his address, Chalk led the students in singing the black protest anthem "We Shall Overcome." Taking note of this meeting in the *Journal*, Patterson objected that "the current version of 'We Shall Overcome' is a modern adaptation of the Negro church song, 'I'll Overcome Someday' and was written by Pete Seeger," who "has been identified under oath by an FBI undercover agent as having been a member of the Communist Party." He also claimed that "when Fidel Castro was still considered by many as 'The Robin Hood of the Caribbean' and was leading his so-called 'agrarian reformers' in their overthrow of the Cuban government, the official slogan was 'Venceremos,' i.e., 'We shall overcome.'" This was sufficient evidence for Patterson that "some in the church today are being 'overcome' rather than 'overcoming.'"[86] On reading this, Humphrey Foutz, a black preacher in Baltimore, wrote in despair to John Allen Chalk, "I have been hoping against hope for the changes that must come, to come peacefully. Then this kind of lunacy reminds you, shakes you back to the harsh reality of our times."[87]

Most blacks in Churches of Christ at the time of the assassination of Martin Luther King were convinced that most whites in mainstream Churches of Christ had little understanding of the issues that drove the civil rights movement. Blacks saw mainstream whites as far more concerned with issues of law and order than with issues of social justice. Overall, the response of Churches of Christ to the civil rights movement and Martin Luther King simply compounded the problems that had troubled relations between blacks and whites in Churches of Christ for many years.

Tentative Signs of Change: 1968

Still, there were some within white Churches of Christ who felt deep concern over the issue of racism and racial injustice. John T. Willis, a Bible professor at David Lipscomb College and a speaker on the David Lipscomb College lectureship in June of 1967, publicly challenged the notion that "white people should have their separate building for worship and negroes should have theirs." One might think that this sort of message, delivered as late as 1967, would have received resounding support. It did draw "some affirmations," but it also drew considerable criticism.[88] White Churches of Christ in Nashville remained reluctant to abandon deep-seated patterns of segregation.

Aside from challenges from various individuals like Willis, the greatest impetus for change came in a series of integrated race relations workshops initially prompted by a group of white activists. In January of 1966, the first of these workshops took place in Nashville. It was a private, by-invitation-only, "underground" event organized under the leadership of Walter Burch (a public relations consultant then living in Abilene, Texas), George Gurganus (a professor at the Harding Graduate School of Religion, Memphis), Ira North (minister of the Madison Church of Christ, Madison, Tennessee), Dwain Evans (minister for the Church of Christ in West Islip, New York), and John Allen Chalk.[89]

Walter Burch, in particular, provided leadership for a variety of efforts to promote racial justice within Churches of Christ. He later recalled that from 1965 through 1972, "I was a one-dimensional character. I equated the responsible Christian life almost exclusively with the issue of racial equality."[90]

While Burch was not an organizer of a second workshop held in March of 1968, he played a pivotal role in the gathering in a variety of ways; that event was hosted by the mostly black Schrader Lane Church of Christ in Nashville, under the leadership of its minister, David Jones. Since support from white Churches of Christ in Nashville was relatively meager, Burch proposed that the *Christian Chronicle* publish the workshop proceedings in a tabloid supplement for which he served as guest editor, and in that way gave the workshop substantial exposure within Churches of Christ.[91]

Then, in February of 1968, Burch and Dwain Evans, along with two black ministers, Roosevelt Wells of Harlem and Eugene Lawton of Newark, New Jersey, met in Harlem to plan for a major race relations workshop in Atlanta. Because the activism of Burch and Evans had tarnished their reputations within

Walter Burch (1927-), a public relations consultant in Abilene, Texas, in the late 1960s, provided key
leadership for the improvement of race relations in Churches of Christ during that period. Burch helped
plan and publicize several race relations workshops and, in his speaking and writing, encouraged white
Churches of Christ to take race relations with greater seriousness. He also served on the founding editorial
board of *Mission* magazine, guiding that journal's organizational development for over a year.
(Photo courtesy Walter Burch)

Churches of Christ, Wells and Lawton secured Jimmy Allen, a Bible professor
at Harding College, to help organize the conference. This meeting finally took
place in June in a suburb of Atlanta, hosted by Andrew Hairston, the African
American minister of the Simpson Street Church of Christ in Atlanta.[92]

When all was said and done, the conference succeeded in attracting some fifty
influential leaders among Churches of Christ, both black and white, representing
a broad ideological spectrum. When the conference concluded, the majority of the
delegates signed a statement confessing "the sin of racial prejudice which has existed
in Churches of Christ and church-related institutions and businesses." The statement went on to recommend a variety of measures to promote racial healing
throughout Churches of Christ and its various institutions.[93]

Burch later concluded that while this conference raised the level of awareness on the part of a number of individuals, "as far as visibly affecting institutional change, it was a 'toothless tiger.'"[94] Several presidents of Church of

Christ–related colleges along with an elder in the Highland Church of Christ (Abilene, Texas), sponsoring congregation for the "Herald of Truth" radio and television ministries, refused to sign the confessing statement for fear of detractors, although John Allen Chalk did sign the statement. And there *were* detractors. Glenn Wallace, for example, writing in the *First Century Christian* (see Chap. 13), claimed to know "the ultimate goals and aims" of the group: "They are set to RESTRUCTURE the church. They want our pulpits to ring with the social gospel theme. They want the 'urban ministry' to become the cry of our day. They are tired of the story of the 'old rugged cross.' "[95]

The same month the Atlanta workshop occurred — June 1968 — the *Firm Foundation* published a hard-hitting article by Burch accusing Churches of Christ of majoring in minors. This article provided such a telling assessment of the situation and stirred such controversy that it is worth considering it in some detail.

Burch wrote that he could hardly believe that "the most flaming moral issue perhaps in the history of Christianity is evaded, ignored, or shunned with maddening indifference by the Church of Christ." He charged that many in Churches of Christ appeared to believe that there was no clear-cut scriptural principle at stake in the matter of race relations in the United States. In taking this position, Churches of Christ stood squarely on the Campbellian side of their heritage. On the issue of racial justice, they occupied precisely the same ground that Alexander Campbell had occupied on the issue of slavery over a hundred years before.

But Churches of Christ had not uniformly turned their backs on social issues, noted Burch. They may have felt no particular urgency regarding the issue of racial justice in the 1960s, but they embraced a variety of other social causes in the same period. For example, Reuel Lemmons penned strong editorials in the 1960s urging Churches of Christ to oppose legislation that would permit legalized gambling at the race tracks, the sale of liquor by the drink, and textbooks that advocated the theory of evolution.[96] In each of these instances, Lemmons — and others in Churches of Christ who supported these causes — offered further evidence of the dramatic shift of Churches of Christ from sect to denomination. Their stated rationale for endorsing their various causes all boiled down to their belief that they needed to support the moral foundations of the larger conservative culture with which they now identified; they seldom mentioned, in their explanations, the vision of the kingdom of God that drove their nineteenth-century forebears. We find an example of their reasoning in Lemmons's rationale for attacking gambling and pari-mutuel betting:

> The undermining of the moral fiber of a nation is tragic. . . . Nations do not fall because of a single stroke of apoplexy. They, rather, crumble, as one by one virtues are surrendered and moral fiber slowly disintegrates. If good men give ground, inch by inch, it is not long before the good have their backs to the wall. It will be too late for the unconcerned to join the ranks of the concerned after the foundations of moral society have been eaten away.[97]

But Burch found little evidence that Churches of Christ were disturbed by the slow disintegration of moral fiber with regard to racial justice. In the end, he wrote dejectedly, "The camel has been swallowed."[98]

Lemmons published Burch's article, but in a later issue of the *Firm Foundation* he also published a sampling of the overwhelmingly negative response to Burch's conclusions. Most critics accused Burch of preaching a gospel different from that proclaimed in the primitive church. One man admonished *Firm Foundation* readers, "Let's not use [the] language of philosophers, Ashdod, liberalists, sectarians, humorists, evolutionists, atheists, and worldlings — but use true spiritual words for spiritual ideas, and contend for such until we die." Another suggested that the proper response to the racial crisis was simply to "*preach* the gospel! Convert sinners! Teach the principles that change lives! If we should do otherwise . . . , why didn't the apostles, other ministers, and all early Christians do it?" And Lemmons himself affirmed again his conviction that "racial prejudice is gross in an infinitesimally small part of the body of Christ. Blaming the whole church for individual cases of discrimination is like blaming a whole nation for the deeds of a single assassin."[99]

Nonetheless, John Allen Chalk was so encouraged by the workshops that he addressed these issues in a series of sermons entitled "Three American Revolutions" that he preached on the nationally broadcast "Herald of Truth" radio program.[100] In the sermons, Chalk explored the rapid changes in American life, especially regarding crime, sex, and race, and he argued that racial prejudice was simply incompatible with the Christian faith.[101]

Chalk's sermons on race evoked a record response to a "Herald of Truth" program, and the response was largely positive.[102] But critics made their voices heard as well. One preacher objected that Chalk's sermons sounded "too much like the Social Gospel themes of the liberals!"[103] Another wrote from Georgia, "For years I listened to brother [E. R.] Harper and to brother [James] Willeford [two of Chalk's predecessors on 'Herald of Truth'] preach the fundamentals of the gospel — the Church, The New Birth, Baptism, The Authority of the Bible, etc. — but now you have a new philosophy; Brethren, it is the wrong philosophy."[104]

There were other developments as well. In July of 1968, for example, the *20th Century Christian* published a special issue entitled *Christ and Race Relations* featuring articles by black leaders Clyde Muse, Roosevelt Wells, Zebedee Bishop, Humphrey Foutz, and Eugene Lawton along with articles by several whites including Jennings Davis, Dwain Evans, Walter Burch, John Allen Chalk, Steven Lemley, and Carl Spain. Almost immediately after publication of this issue, circulation of the *20th Century Christian* dropped from 40,000 to roughly half that number.[105]

It is little wonder that black leaders in Churches of Christ remained thoroughly disheartened and discouraged. G. P. Holt lamented in 1969 that "so many brethren both black and white . . . do not know that tension, mistrust, and misunderstanding exists among us," and he expressed his belief that the black church and the white church were "growing farther apart each day."[106]

John Allen Chalk (1937-) served as speaker for the national "Herald of Truth" radio ministry from 1966 to 1969. In that capacity, he played a significant role in helping promote improved race relations among Churches of Christ. Addressing over national radio the social issues convulsing the United States at that time, Chalk argued that racial prejudice and Christian faith were incompatible. He helped organize race relations workshops and worked in Campus Evangelism, a national college campus ministry. (Photo courtesy John Allen Chalk)

Some frustrated black leaders sought to bring their concerns and frustrations directly to the white church. In 1969, for example, Harding College invited Roosevelt Wells, the Harlem minister who had helped shape the Atlanta race relations workshop the year before, to appear on its annual Bible lectureship. In preparing the text of his speech, Wells minced no words:

> The white church has joined the pitiful parade of psychological propagandizing, and loving traditional ties more than timeless truth, and being more wedded to cultural priorities than Christian principles. They scraped [*sic*] their Bibles except for the first principles of conversion, and piece-mealed, southernized, culturized, and Americanized the rest, endorsing racism, segregation, exploitation, discrimination and white supremacy.

Wells made it clear that he was "for revolution. As a Harlemite, I must be committed to this course: there are no alternatives." He went on to explain, however, that he did not seek "the blood of the oppressor" or "the death of segregationists." He sought instead "the death of segregation and scriptural sanctification for the segregating sinner." Wells submitted the text of his speech to Harding College in advance of the lectureship, but found his invitation canceled. The school objected that the speech did "not relate itself to the subject which has been assigned."[107]

Franklin Florence, another important black leader among Churches of Christ and a close friend of Malcolm X, raised the level of confrontation with white Churches of Christ to an even higher level. A product of the Nashville Christian Institute, Florence later served as preacher for the Reynolds Street Church of Christ in Rochester, New York. There, blacks targeted the Eastman Kodak Company for alleged hiring discrimination and organized FIGHT (Freedom, Integration, God, Honor, Today), the organization through which they

Roosevelt Wells (1933-), preacher for the Church of Christ in Harlem, New York, helped lead resistance to white racism in Churches of Christ in the 1960s. Wells helped plan the Atlanta Race Relations Workshop of 1968, which attracted some fifty influential leaders among Churches of Christ, both black and white. The following year, Harding College invited Wells to speak on its annual Bible lectureship, though Harding officials canceled Wells's appearance when they read his prepared text. That speech was later published in *Mission* magazine.
(Photo courtesy Harding University)

While preaching for the Reynolds Street Church of Christ, Rochester, New York, in the 1960s, Franklin Florence *(left)* was elected president of FIGHT (Freedom, Integration, God, Honor, Today), an organization through which blacks successfully targeted the Eastman Kodak Company for alleged hiring discrimination. A graduate of the Nashville Christian Institute, Florence had broad contacts within the black community. Here he is pictured with Malcolm X, who had come to Rochester to speak at a rally protesting a police raid on a Black Muslim mosque. The photo was taken on Wednesday, February 17, 1965, only four days before Malcolm's assassination.
(Photo courtesy Franklin Florence and Constance M. Mitchell)

confronted Kodak. As president of FIGHT, Florence brought Stokely Carmichael, leader of the Student Non-Violent Coordinating Committee (SNCC), to Rochester, and, under their leadership, FIGHT won significant concessions from Kodak, including six hundred new jobs for Rochester blacks.[108]

Early in 1969, Florence told a black church in Oklahoma City that "brethren in the Church of Christ" were "doing absolutely nothing about the problems of our day." He complained that the "white Church of Christ" was "reactionary and racist." He suggested that white Churches of Christ were interested in aiding only those dispossessed people who had the proper religious affiliation. And he lamented the "dilapidated churches" and "worn out song books" that whites often gave to their "black brothers."

Hugo McCord, a leader among white Churches of Christ in Oklahoma City, wrote a stinging response, accusing Franklin of manifesting "a sorry viewpoint." Regarding Florence's complaint that white Churches of Christ did nothing about the issues of the day, McCord said that "the chief problem of our day, as it was in Jesus' day, is sin." McCord argued that Churches of Christ were actually doing a great deal to alleviate the racial tensions, "but they are not preaching that love requires artificial integration." And as for Florence's remarks about "dilapidated churches" and "worn out song books," McCord admonished Florence, "Thanks be to God, there are many black brothers who have appreciated getting something rather than nothing."[109]

Conclusion

Over the next several years, attitudes toward blacks did begin to change among mainstream Churches of Christ — although the change tended to be more individual than institutional, largely because the chasm between the black and white churches had been so wide for so long. By the early 1990s, only a few congregations of Churches of Christ were seriously integrated, with blacks and whites sharing equally in the leadership of those congregations. Many largely white, urban congregations had a few black members, but few black congregations had any white members. Most white members of Churches of Christ still remained ignorant of black publications such as the *Christian Echo,* of black lectureships, and of other dimensions of the black church.

No wonder, then, that by 1990 many black leaders among Churches of Christ saw little reason for optimism. Eugene Lawton, for example, lamented that "we still have two churches in the brotherhood: the black church and the white church."[110] Jack Evans, president of Southwestern Christian College, concurred: "It is glaringly apparent that there are two racially divided fellowships in churches of Christ — one black and one white."[111] And David Jones, black minister of the Schrader Lane Church of Christ in Nashville, wrote more pointedly still that

> the divided relationship of the "black church of Christ" and the "white church of Christ" is as pervasive as the practice of "Jim Crow" in the southern United States prior to the late 1960s, with one exception: The church did not keep pace with the changes that took place in the legal arena of the "New South."[112]

This state of affairs is not really surprising because, as we have seen, the historic theology of Churches of Christ left them unprepared, by and large, to deal with issues of social justice and racial equality. By the 1960s, most mainstream Churches of Christ were far more concerned to win acceptance into the dominant "Christian" culture of white America than to battle for social justice, racial or otherwise. There are doubtless those who would like to believe that Roosevelt Wells exaggerated when he claimed in the 1960s that white Churches of Christ had "scraped [*sic*] their Bibles except for the first principles of conversion, and piece-mealed, southernized, culturized, and Americanized the rest." In many crucial respects, however, the evidence suggests that he was not far off the mark.

CHAPTER 13

Fragmentation: Left and Right

Having already fought two major battles in the twentieth century (one over premillennialism and one over institutionalization), in the 1960s Churches of Christ took up a third battle that proved to be the most crucial of all — a battle that involved nothing less than the legitimacy of their traditional mission and identity. In many respects, this third battle pitched old against young, parent against child, and, as we have seen, white against black.

Many in the younger generation, well educated and driven by the social agenda of that period, found the traditional concerns of twentieth-century Churches of Christ inadequate and irrelevant to the world in which they lived. As a result, they seriously questioned almost every aspect of their tradition, from the Baconian hermeneutic to the way church leaders had formulated the restoration vision.

At the same time, these youthful critics often revealed themselves to be authentic children of the restorationist heritage. Nowhere was this more apparent than in their strong allegiance to the Bible. But they differed significantly from their parents in the way they read the Bible. They declined to take it as a blueprint that lined out in detail the forms and structures of the primitive church, for example. They believed that it spoke more about compassion than about true doctrine, that it taught more about the Holy Spirit than about forms of worship, and that it addressed the ethical issues of the 1960s head-on.

The third great battle of the twentieth century was directly related to the two previous battles. Churches of Christ had progressively made their peace with the values of the larger culture first by systematically destroying their apocalyptic heritage in the 1920s and 1930s and then by institutionalizing themselves as a middle-class southern denomination in the 1950s; their behavior in the 1960s revealed how completely they had accommodated themselves to the culture in which they lived. Confronted with the pressing social issues of the 1960s, Churches of Christ came down, in almost every instance,

on the side of the cultural status quo. To a significant extent, the third great
battle was a matter of youthful protesters among Churches of Christ rejecting
precisely that accommodation.

Putting this in terms of the argument I have developed thus far in this book,
mainstream Churches of Christ had evolved, by the 1960s, into a full-fledged
denomination. In reacting against that development, the younger generation
essentially worked to recover the sectarian vision that had prevailed before the
move to denominational status. Therein lies the final irony of the tradition: the
older generation characterized the younger generation as deviant, liberal, and
subversive when in fact that younger generation upheld many of the sectarian
ideals of the nineteenth century, especially the ideals that had descended from the
Stone-Lipscomb tradition that their parents had rejected. Judged by standards of
the nineteenth-century Churches of Christ, the mainstream leadership had become liberal, and their children were the true conservatives.

From another perspective, the protests of the younger generation among
Churches of Christ significantly paralleled the protests of America's larger youth
counterculture. Few among the countercultural generation claimed that American ideals were fundamentally flawed. Rather, they claimed that their parents
had betrayed those ideals — by fostering racially segregationist policies at home,
for example, and by engaging in an immoral war in southeast Asia. In much
the same way, young people among Churches of Christ charged their elders
with having betrayed the ideals of their religious heritage.

The third great battle split Churches of Christ into three informal but
identifiable traditions: a mainstream that embraced some diversity but that
sought, by and large, to preserve the dominant vision of the 1950s; a group of
progressives who challenged that vision; and a group of conservatives who, in
reaction to both the progressives and the relativizing tendencies of the 1960s,
absolutized the historic vision of Churches of Christ, claimed to understand
absolute truth absolutely, and maintained that Churches of Christ were not
"Christians only" but the "only Christians." So it was that in 1969, *Firm Foundation*
editor Reuel Lemmons, a voice from the mainstream known for his moderate
stance on church disputes, criticized both conservatives and progressives.

Lemmons maintained that the ranks of the progressives contained many
outright "modernists" and "liberals."[1] He claimed that modernists dismissed
the restorationist agenda as little more than "reluctance to part with outmoded
patterns and an outmoded book." Liberals were "concerned most with education
and social change" and felt the "the church's task is to foster race relations and
better housing." Moreover, liberals and modernists had so completely absorbed
the revolutionary spirit of the age that their presence in Churches of Christ had
created "an hour of unprecedented crisis."[2]

The number of radicals who think the church is nothing more than another
denomination is increasing rapidly. The number of intellectuals who believe

the Genesis account of creation is a myth is increasing. That coalition of social revolutionaries and quoters of left-wing theologians that has set itself to revolutionizing the church is gaining boldness with every brazen insult to Biblical loyalty that goes unrebuked. More and more are the platforms and publications open to them. They are scattered through the church like cancer cells.[3]

At the same time, Lemmons worried about conservatives who, in reacting against liberals and modernists, confused their traditions with biblical truth. "There will be a dangerous tendency," he wrote, "on the part of those who contend for 'The Old Paths' . . . to fail to see that some of these paths were made by human feet." Moreover, he defended the right of young people to think

Reuel Lemmons (1912-1989) edited from 1955 to 1983 one of the two most influential papers circulated among Churches of Christ, the *Firm Foundation,* based in Austin, Texas. The great power he exercised in that capacity made him one of the "editor-bishops" among Churches of Christ during those years. Especially during the highly polarized 1960s, Lemmons opposed reactionaries on both the left and the right and sought to steer mainline Churches of Christ in a moderate direction. He created considerable controversy when he claimed in 1968 that "there has been an infinitesimally small amount of racial prejudice in the Church of Christ."
(Photo courtesy Gospel Advocate Company)

for themselves and severely chastised the traditionalists who sought to purge the church of intellectuals and nonconformists. "We deplore the seemingly systematic campaign to kill them off with criticism," he wrote. "They are not going to buy the traditional ways that are such a part of our heritage. They don't have to."[4]

Lemmons charged conservatives with having abandoned their historic position of "liberty in the realm of opinion." Of all people, he charged, "we are often the most restrictive." He called them back to a spirit of tolerance and mutual respect. "Differences in viewpoint are not only tolerable; they are desirable." He conceded that differences would produce tensions, but he argued that such tensions should be dealt with "in an atmosphere of mutual respect, tolerance, fairness, trust, patience and love."[5]

Lemmons's criticism of both liberals and traditionalists confused many of his readers. In his own mind, however, his position was clear. He simply advocated a middle ground that conceded nothing to social activists or biblical critics on the one hand or to hyper-traditionalists on the other.

The question we now must raise is this: Who were those people who increasingly stood on the right and left wings of Churches of Christ, and what were the issues that divided them?

The Progressives

The progressive movement in Churches of Christ could never have arisen apart from the institutions of higher learning that Churches of Christ established earlier in the century (see Chap. 10). It is ironic, but scarcely unprecedented, that these colleges should have helped to produce a movement that in many significant ways undermined their original aims and intentions. As a rule, these colleges were founded to promote and even institutionalize the orthodox agenda of Churches of Christ. Once established, however, they effectively promoted genuine education rather than simple indoctrination. Further, the colleges inevitably moved Churches of Christ beyond insular concerns and into a larger world of ideas as they graduated students who served in urban centers as teachers, bankers, attorneys, and corporate executives. Having engaged the larger world in this fashion, it was inevitable that some in Churches of Christ would grapple with the ethical and intellectual concerns of the 1960s and seek to promote a larger ethical and theological vision within their fellowship.

The progressive movement in Churches of Christ was also shaped significantly by the graduate theological education that began in earnest among Churches of Christ in the 1950s. W. B. West established the first graduate program in Bible and religion among Churches of Christ at George Pepperdine College in 1944. Then, in 1952, West led in founding a similar program at Harding College. By 1958, that program occupied its own separate campus in

W. B. West (1907-1994) launched at George Pepperdine College in 1944 the first graduate program in Bible and religion among Churches of Christ. In 1952, he established a similar program at Harding College, Searcy, Arkansas, and then served from 1958 to 1972 as dean of the Harding Graduate School of Religion, Memphis, Tennessee.
(Photo courtesy Gospel Advocate Company)

Memphis, Tennessee, where it came to be known as the Harding Graduate School of Bible and Religion.[6] In 1953, Abilene Christian College launched a comparable program, offering a master's degree in biblical studies.[7]

In order to offer graduate programs in religion, these colleges had to secure significant numbers of professors with doctoral degrees in biblical and related studies. Of pivotal importance in this regard was LeMoine G. Lewis, who, after earning his doctorate from Harvard, returned to his alma mater, Abilene Christian College, as professor of church history in 1949; he continued to serve in that capacity until 1986. Lewis successfully encouraged scores of his students over the years to pursue doctoral studies in religion at Harvard and similar institutions. "By the mid-1950's," Don Haymes observed, "the first generation of 'LeMoine's boys' had arrived at Harvard — Everett Ferguson, Pat Harrell, and Abraham Malherbe." Others soon followed, including Roy Bowen Ward and Harold Forshey from ACC and Thomas H. Olbricht and Don McGaughey, who had done undergraduate studies at Harding.[8] Ferguson, Malherbe, and Olbricht eventually accepted teaching posts at ACC, where they, in turn, continued to

LeMoine G. Lewis (1916-1987), professor of church history at Abilene Christian University from 1949
to 1986, perhaps did more than any other person to initiate a tradition of biblical and theological
scholarship within Churches of Christ. After earning his doctorate from Harvard Divinity School in
1949, Lewis sent a steady stream of his students to Harvard and other comparable institutions, where
they pursued doctoral work in various fields of religious studies. Many of his students were at the core
of a progressive movement that emerged among Churches of Christ in the 1960s.
(Photo courtesy Abilene Christian University)

promote high-level scholarship among enterprising young students from
Churches of Christ.[9] This was the beginning of a virtual host of aspiring scholars
from Churches of Christ who would soon take up doctoral-level studies at
prestigious institutions of higher education throughout the United States and
abroad, including Harvard, Yale, Princeton, Union Theological Seminary in New
York, Hebrew Union College, the University of Iowa, the University of Southern
California, Boston University, Vanderbilt University, Claremont School of Theology, the University of Chicago, Cambridge University, the University of Tü-
bingen, the Pontifical Institute in Toronto, the Ecumenical Institute in Jerusalem, and the School of Oriental Research in Jerusalem.

New Journals and Publications

There is a sense in which the progressive tradition among Churches of Christ in the context of the 1960s was founded by Carl Ketcherside and Leroy Garrett, two men who, on the eve of that decade, called Churches of Christ to abandon both legalism and exclusivism, to cultivate a greater appreciation for the grace of God, and to manifest a greater tolerance for Christians of other traditions. Garrett grew up among mainline Churches of Christ, but as an adult he embraced the anti-institutional position. Ketcherside, on the other hand, came from the Sommerite tradition of Churches of Christ, a tradition hardly known for its sense of grace or its ecumenical spirit (see Chap. 10). Even in the middle years of the twentieth century, this small wing of Churches of Christ maintained a radically democratic tradition of opposition to Bible colleges, located preach-

W. Carl Ketcherside (1908-1989), a product of the Sommerite wing of Churches of Christ, published the *Mission Messenger* in St. Louis, Missouri, from 1939 to 1975. Intensely sectarian in his early years, Ketcherside underwent conversion to a more ecumenical, grace-oriented perspective in 1951. For the remainder of his career, he called on Churches of Christ to abandon legalism and exclusivism, to cultivate appreciation for the grace of God, and to extend fellowship to Christians of other traditions. Together with Leroy Garrett, Ketcherside helped pioneer the progressive tradition among Churches of Christ that flowered in the 1960s.

(Photo courtesy Mr. and Mrs. G. B. Ketcherside)

Through his graduate studies at Southern Methodist University, Princeton, and Harvard, Leroy Garrett (1918-) concluded that Churches of Christ in the twentieth century had perverted the original ecumenical vision of Alexander Campbell. His journals, *Bible Talk* (1952-1958) and *Restoration Review* (1959-1992), challenged Churches of Christ to a greater sense of grace and a larger ecumenical spirit. (Photo courtesy Disciples of Christ Historical Society)

ers, missionary societies, and any other "innovation" that might challenge the independence of the local congregation. It also sustained a highly exclusivist sensibility: members tended to identify their own wing of Churches of Christ with the fullness of the kingdom of God. By the early 1950s, however, the thinking of Ketcherside and Garrett began to change.

As in so many other cases, higher education led Garrett to an appreciation of Christians in other traditions and prompted him to question many of the fundamental presuppositions of Churches of Christ. From 1938 through 1942, Garrett attended colleges related to Churches of Christ: Freed-Hardeman College first, and then Abilene Christian College. In 1943, he earned a master's degree from Southern Methodist University, and in 1948, a bachelor of divinity degree from Princeton Theological Seminary. Hungry for further learning, he enrolled at Harvard in 1949 and graduated with a doctorate in philosophy of religion in 1957.

In 1952, three years after enrolling at Harvard, Garrett launched *Bible Talk*, a publication that regularly accused Churches of Christ of having perverted the nineteenth-century ecumenical vision articulated especially by Alexander Campbell. In fact, Garrett claimed, Churches of Christ in the twentieth century stood for the very kind of sectarianism and exclusivism that Campbell had sought to destroy. For that reason he renounced his allegiance to a denomination called the "Church of Christ" and identified himself instead with the universal kingdom of God. "I now make no choice among the denominations, including the Church of Christ," he insisted. "I consider myself a Christian and a brother of all saints of God wherever they may be — in the Church of Christ, the Christian Church, and other churches as well."[10] Garrett discontinued *Bible Talk* in 1958, but in 1959 he launched *Restoration Review,* in which he continued to challenge Churches of Christ to a greater sense of grace and a larger ecumenical spirit.[11]

Carl Ketcherside came to many of the same conclusions, though by an entirely different route. A child of a poor midwestern miner, Ketcherside never had the luxury of attending college. But he did read voraciously as a child and as a young man. He later recalled that when the Carnegie Library was built in his hometown of Marshalltown, Iowa, he read "a book per day and sometimes more."[12]

Ketcherside left his Lutheran roots to join the Sommerite wing of Churches of Christ in 1920, when he was only twelve years old, and as he grew older, he became a formidable debater and well-known defender of that position. In 1951, however, he experienced a shattering change of perspective. He had occasion to preach that year "in the little Presbyterian meetinghouse at Ahorey, near Rich Hill [Northern Ireland], where Thomas Campbell was once the minister." As Ketcherside himself recalled the story,

> The recognition of what we had done to the noble Restoration Movement this humble man helped to launch caused me to completely re-examine my own life, and the whole movement as it now exists. From 1951-57, I re-read virtually everything of importance written in conjunction with the restoration movement and when I became convinced we had abandoned both that movement and the word of God, I started in to help us regain some sense of sanity, in the midst of our divided state.[13]

Already in 1939, Ketcherside had begun a journal called the *Mission Messenger* that had a significant circulation among Sommerite Churches of Christ. In 1957, he turned the *Messenger* in more ecumenical directions, urging Churches of Christ at large to abandon "the myth that there is no difference between the church for which Christ died, and the particular 'Church of Christ' in which we have always lived."[14] In time, the *Mission Messenger* attained a worldwide circulation of some eight thousand readers.[15]

When Ketcherside and Garrett first began circulating their views, most leaders among mainstream Churches of Christ found it easy to dismiss them as representatives of small, schismatic traditions fixated on opposition to the modernizing tendencies of the larger denomination. As their perspectives changed, however, they began to attack the bedrock presuppositions not only of the Sommerite and anti-institutional traditions but also of Churches of Christ at large. Leaders among Churches of Christ then began to characterize them as fundamentally unstable men who had ridden the swinging pendulum from one extreme to the other. The truth, however, was quite the reverse. Despite the fact that Ketcherside and Garrett adopted more tolerant perspectives, both men maintained their allegiance to radically democratic, anti-institutional perspectives for the rest of their lives.[16]

No incident more dramatically illustrates this point than Garrett's visit in 1955 to Freed-Hardeman College in the small southern town of Henderson, Tennessee. En route from Cincinnati Bible College to his home in Dallas, Garrett stopped over in Henderson, where he found the annual Freed-Hardeman College lectureship in full swing. His mere presence there fired up a storm of interest and controversy.

For three years, as editor of *Bible Talk*, Garrett had challenged the exclusivist identity of Churches of Christ on the one hand and their efforts to modernize and institutionalize on the other. Now at Freed-Hardeman, in private conversation with small groups of people, he questioned the very right of the school to exist, comparing it to a missionary society usurping the work of the church. Learning of these conversations, the school's administration warned Garrett "not to stir up any confusion" and forthwith threatened him with legal action. When the students invited him to discuss his perspectives with them in their dormitory rooms, the administration repeatedly advised Garrett that they would not permit him to visit the dormitory and would have him arrested if he tried to do so. Garrett informed the administration that he fully intended to visit the dormitory on the grounds that he was a Freed-Hardeman alumnus and, in fact, had done nothing wrong. True to their word, the administration summoned the police, who arrested Garrett, charged him with "creating a public nuisance," and locked him up in the city jail for the night.[17]

While the work of Ketcherside and Garrett reflected the rising educational level among Churches of Christ and appealed to a more educated clientele, neither of these men belonged to the growing network of biblical and theological scholars who emerged within mainstream Churches of Christ especially in the 1960s. Further, as heirs to the anti-institutional and Sommerite traditions, Ketcherside and Garrett focused their work almost exclusively on questions of sectarianism and exclusivism, calling Churches of Christ to fellowship with the larger Christian world. The new generation of scholars that emerged in the 1960s concerned themselves chiefly with critical questions raised by contemporary biblical and theological scholarship — questions that neither Garrett's *Restoration Review* nor Ketcherside's *Mission Messenger* addressed with any regularity.

To fill that vacuum, a new publishing venture emerged among Churches of Christ in 1957: the *Restoration Quarterly,* a scholarly journal conceived and produced by two of "LeMoine's boys" — Abraham Malherbe and Pat Harrell.[18] These founders set two goals for the *Quarterly:* to "create a community of scholarly discourse" among religion scholars in Churches of Christ and to enrich the theological agenda of Churches of Christ with ideas from the larger world of biblical and theological scholarship.[19]

As it turned out, however, the *Restoration Quarterly* had an impact that extended well beyond the confines outlined by these goals. The scholars contributing to the journal had been taught to look at the Bible and the world in ways that ranged well beyond the confines of the comparatively insular vision of the Churches of Christ at that time. Indeed, these scholars began to grapple with theological questions that far transcended the premillennial and anti-institutional controversies. Moreover, the methods and conclusions of biblical criticism that they employed more often than not seemed to render inadequate and obsolete the old Baconian approach to the biblical text.

Still, the *Restoration Quarterly*'s new vision remained largely restricted to the scholarly community within Churches of Christ. It was not until the late 1960s that scholars began disseminating the results of biblical and theological scholarship to a broader, largely lay audience. Two journals undertook that task. One was *Integrity,* a journal that began in 1969 as a regional publication in Michigan but quickly achieved a national circulation among the progressive wing of the church. Perhaps an even better barometer of the progressive wing of Churches of Christ by the late 1960s, however, was a lively publication called *Mission,* which began publication in July 1967.

Dwain Evans, the young minister for the West Islip Church of Christ on Long Island, New York, provided in 1965 the leadership that ultimately led to the creation of *Mission.* In the fall of that year, Evans invited five other men — his brother Ralph Evans, John Allen Chalk, William Banowsky, Wesley Reagan, and Walter Burch — to meet with him in Midland, Texas, to discuss the need for a journal that would "speak to contemporary man in vital, energetic language" with "a message of renewal."[20] Other strategic meetings followed in Queens, Nashville, Abilene, Memphis, and Searcy, Arkansas. Those involved in these meetings pursued Evans's vision even further. When the Memphis meeting convened in June 1966, participants agreed that Churches of Christ desperately needed a journal that would address, from a biblical point of view, the social and intellectual issues convulsing modern America. One participant in the Memphis meeting stated the case for *Mission* in unequivocal terms:

> No extant publication is speaking to our brotherhood in bold, fresh, and
> relevant terms. No periodical exists which deals with the most pertinent issues
> of modern life. . . . Many are hungry for such a publication. . . . They are
> more concerned in searching than in perpetuating the illusion that we have
> utterly restored pure Christianity.[21]

For sixteen months, Walter Burch guided the efforts to organize the journal, traveling from coast to coast to raise funds and secure support. He received little encouragement from mainstream Churches of Christ.[22]

Significantly, many of the scholars involved with the *Restoration Quarterly* also involved themselves in *Mission*'s inception and early years of publication. Among others, these included Thomas H. Olbricht, Roy Bowen Ward, Abraham Malherbe, Everett Ferguson, Carl Spain, Frank Pack, and J. W. Roberts.

From the beginning, the contributors to *Mission* aimed its message directly at the pulpit and the pew and sought to redirect the theological interests of Churches of Christ away from what they viewed as the provincial battles of the past toward what they viewed as more pressing ethical and biblical concerns, largely inspired by the ferment of the 1960s. More than this, they sought to make *Mission* an open forum in which voices from a variety of perspectives could be heard — a genuine alternative to the lockstep orthodoxy that had characterized the *Gospel Advocate* and, to a lesser extent, the *Firm Foundation* for many years. For these reasons, *Mission* provides a unique window on the variety of concerns that divided Churches of Christ in that period.

Social Justice, Racial Equality, and the Vietnam War

Time and again, *Mission* chided Churches of Christ for their failure to deal forthrightly with issues of racial justice. John McRay, for example, suggested that "no element of our nation or of our world . . . stands in greater need of self-evaluation on this point than Churches of Christ." Jennings Davis criticized the "thoughtless gaze of Christians" who had condoned the systematic "terrorism and violence perpetrated against blacks" in American culture. And Thomas Langford suggested that, in the absence of serious leadership by the church, God had raised up Robert Kennedy and Martin Luther King to provide examples in the realm of racial justice.[23]

Mission was among the few periodicals serving Churches of Christ that reported on such events as the Atlanta Conference on Race Relations or the struggle for equal employment opportunities that black Church of Christ minister Franklin Florence led against Eastman Kodak in Rochester, New York (see Chap. 12).[24]

Many *Mission* writers, especially among the younger generation, complained that Churches of Christ showed vast concern for doctrinal orthodoxy but relatively little concern for social ethics. These people concluded simply that Churches of Christ had majored in minors for so long that its message had become irrelevant to the pressing concerns of the 1960s. For example, Dan Danner, a Church of Christ scholar who taught theology at the Roman Catholic University of Portland, lamented the many debates over such issues as "how we can scripturally help an orphan or widow" or "whether we can help the needy

If the youthful counterculture among Churches of Christ in the 1960s reflected in many ways the sectarian, apocalyptic outlook of Barton Stone and David Lipscomb, no one exemplified that perspective more completely than Don Haymes (1937-). Committed to justice for the poor and the dispossessed — with whom he cast his own personal lot — Haymes routinely voiced his concerns in *Mission* and *Integrity,* journals that served the countercultural community within Churches of Christ. He called on scholars in that tradition, for example, to speak out on issues of social justice and rebuked them for their silence. Regarding the legalism that had become so prevalent among Churches of Christ, he charged that many in this tradition had "managed to sidetrack the real issues in a desperate search for gnats to strain." And he lamented the fact that Churches of Christ had evolved from sectarian status to the denominational mainstream in the American South. In his view, the real issues had little to do with instrumental music or even with baptism by immersion, but everything to do with "whether we can do the Gospel on Jesus' terms; whether we will serve God or mammon."
(Photo courtesy Betty Haymes)

who are not in our fellowship from the church treasury, while children go uncared for [and] unfed."[25]

Don Haymes, a young activist and scholar, concluded that Churches of Christ had "managed to sidetrack the real issues in a desperate search for gnats to strain." By consistently looking to the pattern of the primitive church reflected in the book of Acts instead of to the example of Jesus revealed in the Gospels, Churches of Christ had missed the central point, charged Haymes. "The basic issue is whether we can do the Gospel on Jesus' terms; whether we will serve God or mammon, and not, unfortunately, whether we will sing without an instrument, or say 'thee' or 'you' in prayer or even baptize by immersion." Then Haymes specifically addressed the problems of the 1960s.

So long as we harbor the illusion that God cares more about what transpires within the hallowed walls of church buildings than about the sickening bloodshed of Vietnam, or the struggle for freedom of men and women in the chains of poverty, or the willful treachery of governmental bureaucracy, or even the routine of our offices, classrooms, farms or factories, then we are still kidding ourselves.[26]

Gary Freeman also took Churches of Christ to task for their preoccupation with fine points of doctrine to the neglect of social justice. In 1969, Harper and Row published Freeman's book *A Funny Thing Happened on the Way to Heaven*, which satirized Churches of Christ on this and a variety of other issues. The book never mentions Churches of Christ by name, but it was based almost entirely on well-known figures in Churches of Christ and on incidents that actually occurred when he was a student at Abilene Christian College. The

Gary Freeman (1932-) helped focus the issues of the 1960s through his biting satire of Churches of Christ, which earned him plaudits from progressives and condemnation from conservatives. Sweet Publishing Company, a Church of Christ–related press, published his 1967 book, *Are You Going to Church More but Enjoying It Less?* Two years later, Harper and Row published his second book, which received extensive circulation both inside and outside Churches of Christ: *A Funny Thing Happened on the Way to Heaven*. Freeman continued his satirical review of Churches of Christ in a series of columns that appeared in *Mission* magazine for four years, beginning in December 1969.
(Photo courtesy Gary Freeman)

foibles it lampoons were universal enough to attract a significant readership across a wide spectrum of American denominations.

The book features Cletus Kinchelow, an enterprising Bible major and boy preacher who attends Sinai Christian College on the dusty plains of West Texas and goes on to become a preacher in the True Church. After Cletus slowly becomes disillusioned with the True Church — its backroom politics and its teachings not only regarding religion but also regarding race, Communism, Catholicism, and a host of other issues — the power structure of the True Church has Cletus committed to a mental institution. Needless to say, the book inflamed both the conservative wing and the mainstream of Churches of Christ.

What made this book even more significant was the fact that, soon after it appeared, Freeman began a regular column in *Mission* entitled "Balaam's Friend." There he continued the exploits of Cletus and held up to scathing ridicule what he, and many readers of *Mission,* viewed as the reluctance of the leadership of Churches of Christ to come to terms with the pressing issues of the 1960s.

In one of those columns, Freeman juxtaposed the Churches of Christ's concern for doctrinal purity with their general failure to address the issue of racial justice, and in that connection he satirized Reuel Lemmons's claim that racial prejudice among Churches of Christ was almost non-existent (see Chap. 12).

> I guess everybody in the brotherhood knows and appreciates S. T. All-bright, editor of *The Militant Contender.* . . . Last week, . . . S. T. wrote in an editorial that there wasn't a trace of race prejudice in the True Church. . . . S. T. was all lathered up about some of the young turks in the church who had been accusing us of racism. Personally, I'm pretty turned off by all that bleeding heart stuff. But on the other hand I couldn't help feeling that we might be guilty of a *little* bit of racism. . . . So I called on him to ask him about it. He was very cordial.
>
> "Whatta ya mean racism in the True Church, you effete snob," S. T. screamed, pleasantly. He hit the desk so hard that the complete works of Harry Rimmer went sliding off, like a domino theory come to life.
>
> "Well," I said, apologetically, already sorry I had brought it up, "how many blacks or Mexican-Americans have ever been editor of one of our prestige journals, like *The Militant Contender?* And take our big colleges, like Sinai Christian. How many blacks, or Mexican-Americans, or Indians, or Japanese-Americans, or, gee whiz, Italians, for that matter, have ever been president or bursar or vice-president or dean of men or chairman of the board, or head coach, or student body president, or homecoming queen? How many of our really prestige pulpits, like 6th and Izzard in Dallas, have local ministers who are black or Puerto Rican?"
>
> "Cletus, let me explain something to you, boy. No, don't flinch. I ain't mad at you. You're a good boy. But there are some things you don't understand

yet. Take my job, for instance. Editor of *The Militant Contender*. When we select an editor, we're color blind, boy. I mean it. Absolutely color blind. We don't look for a race or a nationality. The only things we look for are soundness, godliness, ability, background, soundness, intelligence, literary ability and soundness. True, we've never picked anyone from your so-called minority races, as your pseudo-intellectuals and pussyfootin' professors are always reminding us."

"But *why*, S. T.? Why haven't we?"

"It's very simple, Cletus. Got nothing to do with racism. Look, take your average Nigra. Or your average Taco. Or Redskin. What does he know about the intricacies of the *psallo* argument? Tell me that, Cletus. What does he know about the nuances of the premillennial theory? What does he know about the orphan home controversy, and all the other fundamental issues that threaten the very existence of our planet? I'll tell you what he knows about those things. Next to nothing, that's what."

"You mean . . . ," I said, beginning to see the light.

"Yes, Cletus. Your minority groups aren't ready for real integration in the True Church."

"You may be right," I said, satisfied.[27]

Further, *Mission* writers typically had little patience with suburban congregations that had built elaborate and comfortable facilities in the postwar period to serve an essentially middle-class and suburban membership and that often turned a deaf ear to the problems of the inner city. One writer, styling himself "Pseudo-Amos," proclaimed,

Thus says the Lord:

> For three transgressions of the Churches of Christ
>   and for four, I will not revoke the punishment;
> because they sell the inner city for suburban sanctuaries
>   and the ghetto for heated baptistries and soft lights;
> they that trample the head of the indigents and immigrants
>   and turn aside the way of the addicts and alcoholics.

Hear the word that the Lord has spoken against you, O Churches of Christ: You only have I known of all the churches of the earth; therefore, I will punish you for your iniquities.

*   *   *

> Woe to us who sit on padden pews
>   and relax ourselves on theatre seats;
> Who sing spiritual ditties without the sound of the harp
>   and unlike David, do not invent for ourselves instruments of music;

Who drink Welch's grape juice in individual cups
　　and anoint ourselves with the finest cosmetics;
But are not grieved over the ruin of our people!
Therefore, we shall now be the first to go into exile,
　　and the revelry of those who are relaxed shall pass away.[28]

On the strength of such contributions, *Mission* emerged as a radically
sectarian publication critiquing a church that had traded its sectarian birthright
for a bowl of denominational porridge. To be sure, few if any *Mission* writers
embraced an apocalyptic worldview; nonetheless, with its strong ethical witness,
Mission offered something that resembled in many ways the ethical emphasis
of the old Stone-Lipscomb tradition. Likewise, few if any *Mission* writers shared
all the biases of the anti-institutional movement of the 1950s, and yet many of
them called on Churches of Christ to abandon their preoccupation with institutional maintenance, especially when that maintenance drowned out the cries
of the offcast and the poor and obscured the need for racial and economic
justice.

Though contributors to *Mission* often addressed such issues as racial
justice and the problems of the inner city, they seldom spoke of either the
morality of the Vietnam War or the morality of the protests against that conflict.
In its inaugural year, *Mission* did devote one entire issue to the general question
of Christianity and warfare, but that issue contained the only article critical of
American involvement in Vietnam that would appear in the journal for the next
four years.[29] This is not to suggest that *Mission* readers and writers typically
supported the war, for in all likelihood most did not. It does suggest, however,
that *Mission* readers were principally concerned with domestic matters, especially civil rights and urban issues. In this regard at least, *Mission* followed the
pattern of the rest of Churches of Christ: few journals that served the tradition,
whether progressive, mainstream, or conservative, made any aspect of the war
in Vietnam an issue in any sense at all.[30]

Redirecting Traditional Theology

In addition to social issues, *Mission* published a variety of articles over the years
that specifically sought to redirect the theology of Churches of Christ. Others
had done the same in the *Restoration Quarterly*, but more gently. Roy Bowen
Ward, for example, had suggested in 1965 that the traditional restoration hermeneutic, involving commands, examples, and necessary inferences, could not
be found within the text of the New Testament but rather was "derived from a
certain logical system imposed from outside the text."[31]

Contributors to *Mission* attacked the restoration ideal and the Baconian
hermeneutic head-on. Lanny Hunter, for example, argued that the restoration

Roy Bowen Ward (1934-) served on the original editorial board and as founding editor of *Mission* magazine. One of LeMoine G. Lewis's students at Abilene Christian College, Ward completed doctoral studies at Harvard in 1967 and, in many ways, typified the young scholars who called for rethinking the theology of Churches of Christ during that period. In an essay published in the *Restoration Quarterly* in 1965, " 'The Restoration Principle': A Critical Analysis," he argued that the way Churches of Christ read the Bible had little to do with the Bible itself but "derived from a certain logical system imposed from outside the text." That essay became a classic for many of Ward's generation.
(Photo courtesy Miami University, Oxford, Ohio)

vision "first requires that everyone accept our [Baconian] philosophical view of scripture, after which they must accept our private interpretation of scripture based upon that philosophy." For this reason, he suggested, restoration theology, as Churches of Christ had understood it, dethroned Christ and turned the Christian faith into a barren system of legal constraints. "Our sense of justification," he wrote, "does not derive from anything so flagrantly obvious as being morally good, but from the virtue of being doctrinally correct."32

Likewise, William Davis questioned the very notion of a New Testament pattern that must be reproduced in the present age. "We must have the courage to ask if possibly we are not on a wrong track altogether with regard to the whole business of a pattern," he wondered. "When one considers the matter, it almost seems that the New Testament is *intentionally* vague on all the 'mechanical' points which have been so long debated in restoration circles."33

The Attack on Mission

It is hardly surprising that many among mainstream Churches of Christ were deeply suspicious of *Mission* and its revisionist agenda. Accordingly, Norvel Young, Batsell Barrett Baxter, and Ira North (the pulpit preacher for the largest Church of Christ in the world at that time, the Madison Church of Christ, Madison, Tennessee) declined to lend active support to *Mission,* apparently viewing any such connection as "a serious liability."[34] Their suspicions proved correct. Within six months of the launch of *Mission,* Reuel Lemmons, powerful editor of the *Firm Foundation,* issued an attack against the progressives, if not against *Mission* in particular.

> We have an increasing number among us who think of the church as just another denomination. . . . They publish scandal sheets that blaspheme the body of Christ, and defame the character of the Bride, the Lamb's wife. Their writings make us cry in anguish, "How long, Oh Lord, how long?"[35]

Soon the *Firm Foundation* published statements describing *Mission* as "the mouthpiece for a far-out liberal movement in the church."[36] The criticism quickly intensified. Maxie Boren typified many when he wrote in 1968, "I believe *Mission* is serving as a 'sounding-board' for intellectual-liberals in the church who delight in promulgating revolutionary concepts and ideas."[37] By 1972, Guy N. Woods charged that *Mission* was leading the church into "digression and apostasy. Men who forsake the truth, as many of your writers have done, under the guise of scholarship, disgrace both truth and scholarship."[38] The critics of *Mission* soon pressured the board of trustees at Abilene Christian College to force four of its faculty members — Olbricht, Ferguson, Spain, and Roberts — to resign from *Mission*'s board, though not all did.[39] Such was the resistance that the revisionist policies of *Mission* engendered among Churches of Christ in the late 1960s and early 1970s. Yet *Mission* continued to serve a progressive constituency among Churches of Christ for a full twenty years. It finally dissolved in 1987, when its editorial board decided that much of the leadership of mainstream Churches of Christ had internalized a great deal of what *Mission* had attempted to communicate over the years.

The Conservatives

If many of the progressives of the 1960s stood in the apocalyptic and ethical heritage of Barton W. Stone, there can be little doubt that the conservative wing that emerged among Churches of Christ in the 1960s belonged to the tradition of the radicalized *Christian Baptist.* These conservatives stood squarely in that long train of believers going back to the youthful Alexander Campbell, Arthur Crihfield, Tolbert Fanning, Benjamin Franklin, Austin McGary, and Foy Wallace Jr. — men who were deeply concerned with biblical authority, law, rationality, and order. Thus we cannot properly say that this wing of Churches of Christ *emerged* in the 1960s, for it had been there all along; rather, the conservatives rose to prominence in the sixties.

Various factors motivated them to intensify their message and become especially vocal and extraordinarily visible. The relativistic side of the 1960s challenged their concern for law and authority; the existential dimension of the 1960s challenged their passion for Lockean and Baconian rationality; and the fact that American culture in that period stood in such disarray challenged their concern for neatness and for order.

More of these conservatives lived in small towns and rural areas than lived in large cities, and on the whole they had little acquaintance with the results of graduate-level theological scholarship. They gave little evidence of interest in the dominant ethical issues of the period, but they did express a great deal of concern over what they called "liberalism" in the church, and they sought to preserve the restoration vision as they had received it from such individuals as Foy E. Wallace Jr.

These conservatives tended to view the 1960s as a period of degeneracy and decay rooted in moral relativism and a collapse of law, order, and social structure. Johnny Ramsey, for example, attributed "American degeneracy" to the breakdown of "respect for authority." In the face of this onslaught, he looked to Churches of Christ, with their "back to the Bible" plea, for real solutions to the nation's problems. "The absolute nature of truth," he maintained, "will take care of the new morality with its 'everything is relative' approach."[40]

Another conservative, William Reeves, ascribed "our modern peace cults, love cults, nonviolence cults, etc." directly to "modernism and liberalism." "Liberals," he complained, "want a god who is only 'good,'" and "protestantism is one large grace cult, rejecting the truth about works of obedience, such as baptism." The God of the Bible, however, was rigorous and demanding, and certainly not "a candidate for membership in some peace cult." Reeves went on to argue that the problems facing America called for rigorous and demanding responses: "Civil rulers are to . . . use the sword whenever necessary (Rom. 13:4). Please note that a sword is an instrument of death. . . . The Christian is to support all of this (Rom. 13:6). God wants evil suppressed on every level — local, national, international."[41]

Rubel Shelly — a man who began his career in the conservative fold but who underwent a conversion to a more grace-oriented perspective between 1975 and 1980[42] (see Chap. 14) — argued in 1972 that America's problems grew chiefly from existentialism. "This anti-authoritarian philosophy . . . denies all absolutes," he asserted, and under its influence "men defy the authority of Christ and the Bible in religious matters" and "citizens defy the civil authority which

God has delegated to policemen, mayors, governors and other officials by obeying only those laws which they like and disobeying the rest."[43]

Mainstream Churches of Christ shared these convictions to a significant degree. It is hardly surprising, therefore, that *Star* magazine, a mainstream publication in Forth Worth, Texas, devoted a special issue in 1968 to law and order, featuring on its cover a uniformed police officer standing beside his patrol car. The entire issue was dedicated to a consideration of "the obligations we all have to civil authorities."[44] Churches of Christ had moved far, indeed, from the nineteenth-century apocalyptic vision that viewed human governments as agents of Satan.

Yet there was a decisive difference between mainstream Churches of Christ and the new conservative wing. First, mainstream Churches of Christ were increasingly urbanized, were flirting with evangelical understandings of the gospel, had undergone significant acculturation, and many had become open to the implications of higher education. With a few significant exceptions, the new conservatives had resisted all of these changes in their efforts to maintain the nineteenth-century, rational and authoritarian vision in as pure a form as possible. Further, most among mainstream Churches of Christ had made a decisive turn away from the hard and strident style best represented by Foy Wallace Jr. in the 1930s and 1940s. Many in the new conservative wing, however, still regarded Wallace as a hero and viewed his tactics as worthy of emulation.

At the time, however, the lines between the conservatives and the mainstream were not so clearly drawn as would be the case in later years. By remaining focused and very vocal in defense of their views, therefore, the conservatives managed to exert an influence in this period far out of proportion to their numbers. We have already seen, for example, the effectiveness of their demands that members of the Abilene Christian College faculty terminate their involvement with the board of *Mission*. Several other professors of Bible and religion at Harding College, the Harding Graduate School of Religion in Memphis, and Abilene Christian College were removed from their positions during this period because of complaints and agitation on the part of conservatives. At David Lipscomb College, none were terminated, but three faculty members — John McRay, George Howard, and John T. Willis — resigned in order to escape the scrutiny that severely diminished the delight of college teaching.[45]

New Journals

Because they were convinced that the journals and editors within mainstream Churches of Christ were not waging the battle against modernism as effectively as they might, many conservatives felt constrained to establish new periodicals of their own. Three in particular deserve mention, all of which, in one way or another, sought to defend the restoration of primitive Christianity, as their editors understood that theme, from the inroads of modernism, liberalism, and relativism.

In 1967 Roy Hearn of Memphis and Franklin Camp of Birmingham launched the *First Century Christian,* a title that stood in clear juxtaposition to that of the mainstream, progressive journal founded in the 1930s, the *20th Century Christian.* Significantly, the *First Century Christian* featured as the lead article of its inaugural issue an essay by Foy Wallace Jr. extolling the King James Version of the Bible and lamenting the modernism implicit in the new translations of Scripture.[46]

In 1969 Thomas B. Warren, professor of Bible at Freed-Hardeman College in Henderson, Tennessee, and Rubel Shelly, one of his former students, launched the *Spiritual Sword.* Warren held an earned doctorate from Vanderbilt in philosophy, and Shelly earned the same degree at Vanderbilt in 1981. As already noted, Shelly adopted more progressive positions within a very few years, but at this

In the aftermath of a troubled decade, Thomas B. Warren (1920- ; pictured here) and one of his students, Rubel Shelly, began publication in 1969 of the *Spiritual Sword,* a journal that served conservatives in Churches of Christ. Rooted squarely in the rational side of that tradition, Warren especially sought to combat relativism in Churches of Christ. With a doctorate in philosophy from Vanderbilt, he sought to prove through logical demonstration what he felt was a bedrock principle of the restoration heritage, that human beings can know absolute truth absolutely.
(Photo courtesy Gospel Advocate Company)

point both men stood squarely in the traditions of Lockean empiricism and Common Sense Realism, and both were concerned to resist relativistic philosophies that undermined what they viewed as a cardinal principle of the restoration heritage: the notion that human beings can know absolute truth absolutely. In his opening editorial, Warren explained, "This journal is launched both in determined opposition to skepticism, liberalism and relativism and in strong affirmation that the Bible is the infallibly inspired word of God and that men *can* learn and obey the truth."[47]

Finally, in 1970, Ira Y. Rice Jr., a former missionary to Singapore who had returned to Nashville, launched perhaps the most flamboyant and sensational of all the new journals, *Contending for the Faith.* Rice announced his intention to join "the mortal . . . struggle now raging . . . between those who really *believe* in the Restoration Movement — based strictly on what the New Testament teaches — and those who really *do not believe* in it — but would *liberalize it*

Following an extended mission tour in southeast Asia, Ira Y. Rice Jr. (1917-) undertook the study of Mandarin Chinese at Yale University in 1964. In the Church of Christ that served that campus, Rice encountered notions he considered liberal. Over the next six years, he issued three volumes of *Axe on the Root,* in which he sought to expose the people and institutions he thought responsible for liberalizing trends in all quarters of Churches of Christ, but especially in Church of Christ–related colleges. He followed those three books with an extended exposé, a regularly published newsletter that he called *Contending for the Faith.*
(Photo courtesy Gospel Advocate Company)

beyond all recognition."[48] Rice embraced wholesale the tactical strategies of Foy Wallace, routinely identifying "heretics" in print "by name, rank, and number," as Wallace once put it.

The fact that all three of these journals originated in Tennessee and/or Alabama suggests that the older, more traditional regions east of the Mississippi River now constituted a major heartland for Church of Christ conservatism. And since most of the leadership for *Mission* and the *Restoration Quarterly* had their roots, in one way or another, at Abilene Christian College, the suggestion of a regional dimension to the liberal/conservative split in Churches of Christ may have some merit.

Yet, there were major exceptions to this pattern, such as the progressive journal *Integrity*, published in Michigan, and one could find progressive thinkers at David Lipscomb College and the Harding Graduate School of Religion in Memphis. On the other hand, Texas, the original breeding ground for the hard, fighting style, still served as a stronghold for the extreme right wing of Churches of Christ. Houston, for example, was the birthplace of yet another conservative periodical in 1969 — the *Anchor*, which was designed "to add another voice to those already being heard calling for a return to the old paths, and for a jealous maintenance of ancient truths already recovered."[49]

All of these conservative journals launched strong attacks against those they perceived as "liberals," seeking to restructure the Churches of Christ. Ira Rice, for example, specifically singled out *Mission* as the "VOICE OF APOSTASY AMONG THE CHURCHES OF CHRIST!"[50] Rice's chief purpose in his second volume of *Axe on the Root*, in fact, was to expose *Mission* before it began publication.[51]

New Schools

The new conservatives did not just establish new papers; they also established new schools — specifically, preacher-training schools. In part, these schools were established in response to the widespread feeling that Church of Christ–related colleges were not producing enough preachers to keep up with the rapid increase in membership following World War II. But there was more to the preacher-school phenomenon than that. Conservatives had largely lost faith in the ability of colleges related to Churches of Christ — especially Abilene Christian — to produce *acceptable* pulpit preachers. The conservatives were convinced that such institutions had become hotbeds of the sort of biblical and theological scholarship that characterized the progressive movement and that as a result they were now producing scholars rather than preachers.

Historically, Churches of Christ have never required academic degrees for preachers. Indeed, there have never been any requirements beyond those established by the local congregation. On the nineteenth-century American frontier, many preachers were self-educated. In the twentieth century, more and more preachers — but by no means all — prepared for their task by taking a four-year liberal arts curriculum, *possibly* majoring in Bible and religion. A few who taught in these programs in Church of Christ–related colleges had earned doctorates in religion from recognized universities, but many did not. By the 1960s, however, more and more professors in these programs were beneficiaries of high-level critical training, especially in biblical studies. Some congregations found these changes threatening and unacceptable.

We can detect evidence of this sort of distrust in a speech presented by John Adams at Freed-Hardeman College as part of the 1970 lectureship devoted to the theme "The Church Faces Liberalism." "We have seen what Bultmann, Barth, and Brunner think about the Bible," said Adams. "For all practical purposes they are infidels." Then, by way of contrast, he pointed his audience to conservative leaders among Churches of Christ. "The choice is yours," he concluded. "You may take your stand with Barth, Brunner and their cohorts who ridicule the Bible and reject it as the authority of God. Or, you may stand with those men whom we have quoted, along with a host of others, who believe that the Bible is the only authority in religion."[52]

In no case was the hostility toward theological scholarship more apparent than in Ira Rice's journal *Contending for the Faith*. Rice returned from a mission tour in Singapore in 1965 in order to study Mandarin Chinese at Yale. In New Haven, he encountered two Yale divinity students, Robert M. Randolph and Derwood Smith, and a local preacher, Bob Howard, whose perspectives troubled him greatly. "I kept hearing reference," Rice later wrote, "to 'the best divinity schools'; and kept asking myself how a *denominational* or *secular* so-called 'divinity' school could be even *good,* much less *better* or *best!*" In one instance, one of the students "used the word 'Christendom' in such a way that the true church was lumped with those in error." Another "made it appear that *Martin Luther was a Christian*" and that "churches of Christ are *just another denomination.*"[53]

Rice was so distressed that in 1966 he issued a volume entitled *Axe on the Root,* in which he attacked not only Randolph, Smith, and Howard but graduate education generally, especially in religion and theology. He suggested, for example, that it was probably impossible for young Christian students to attend "secular or sectarian 'divinity' school[s], and to come out untainted."[54] Over the next four years, he issued two more volumes of *Axe on the Root,* and all three sold well.

His distrust of higher education also became a central theme in the pages of *Contending for the Faith*. He claimed that the concern among Church of Christ–related colleges for "academic accreditation" was "the primary source of infiltration by liberalism/modernism," for example. "It would appear that ACC's seduction by accreditation is practically complete," he wrote. "And what is true at ACC . . . largely either has already become true at several of our other campuses or rapidly is heading in that direction!"[55]

Rice and the other new conservatives were hardly alone in their distrust of theological scholarship. Dismissive assessments of such scholarship routinely appeared in such mainstream publications as the *Firm Foundation* and the *Gospel Advocate,* despite the fact that growing numbers of preachers in mainstream Churches of Christ were employing the results of modern theological scholarship in the pulpit. Articles in the *Gospel Advocate* criticized "sermons filled with quotations from Niebuhr, Barth, Cox, [and] Bonhoeffer," attributed the spread of "liberalism" to "graduate education," and specifically attacked Bultmann's call for demythologizing the New Testament as subversive of the entire restoration vision of Churches of Christ.[56]

Convinced that many liberal arts colleges related to Churches of Christ were no longer training preachers sufficiently orthodox in the faith, a variety of congregations determined to establish their own "schools of preaching" to train new preachers. Schools that grew from this sort of motivation included the Memphis School of Preaching, the Brown Trail School of Preaching in Fort Worth, and, to a lesser degree, the Bear Valley School of Preaching in Denver. Other schools of preaching grew from a somewhat different motivation. The Sunset School of Preaching in Lubbock, Texas, and the White's Ferry Road School of Preaching in West Monroe, Louisiana, for example, tended by the mid-1970s toward a warm evangelical pietism, and Sunset in particular emphasized a strong theology of grace.

Batsell Barrett Baxter identified ten schools of preaching operating within the United States in 1970.[57] According to Baxter's statistics, these schools trained over 25 percent of all the students studying to preach among Churches of Christ. And of course many of these schools were established by people who stood squarely in the conservative wing of the tradition.

These schools typically focused entirely on the Bible and did not require the completion of any additional courses in the liberal arts or sciences. Roy Hearn, co-editor of the *First Century Christian,* described the curriculum of the Getwell Road School of Preaching in Memphis, which later came to be known as the Memphis School of Preaching: "During two years of intensive study the Bible is the main text and is covered thoroughly by textual study, largely verse by verse. At least three other courses give a survey of the Bible making four times it is covered. Forty-eight courses are offered in Bible and related subjects, as Bible Geography, Church History, Homiletics, Introduction, [and] Christian Evidences." He went on to explain that schools of preaching had been established in order to serve aspiring ministers who, for one reason or another, were unable to attend four-year liberal arts colleges.[58] That was true as far as it went, but Ira Rice suggested some deeper motivations when he contemplated establishing his own preacher training school in San Francisco:

What most of our *supposed*-to-be *Christian* colleges cannot seem to comprehend is that if they had been faithfully performing their function — training both the *number* and the *kind* of men required as ministers to the churches — in all likelihood this present "school-of-preaching" phenomenon . . . never would have arisen at all![59]

Glenn Wallace, writing in the *Firm Foundation,* concurred. The "growing number of preacher training schools [reflects a] *deficiency* among us," he wrote. "Our Bible departments — in some colleges — are being overloaded with Harvard specialists. . . . Many are tainted with sectarian philosophy and are totally ignorant of the sickness in our land. They speak — not in a relevant message — but in intellectual nothingness or just plain denominational terms."[60]

Controversy over the Holy Spirit

Progressives and conservatives battled seriously over the identity of Churches of Christ, biblical hermeneutics, and issues relating to social justice, but arguably no issue raised in the 1960s generated more heat among all segments of the movement than that of the Holy Spirit. As we have seen, many who stood in the *Christian Baptist* heritage of Alexander Campbell virtually identified the Spirit with the biblical text or viewed the Bible as the "sword of the Spirit" and maintained that the Spirit works solely through the written word. In the 1960s, those assumptions came under attack.

To some extent at least, this change in perspective on the Holy Spirit can be attributed to the subjectivism of the counterculture movement in the 1960s. Throughout America, youthful protesters rejected what Theodore Roszak called the "myth of objective consciousness."[61] That myth — a legacy of the post–World War II era — enshrined as virtual gods rationality and its offspring, science and technology. After all, had not science and technology introduced a host of labor-saving devices, raised the standard of living for post-Depression Americans to levels previously unimagined, and made America a world power? Had science not provided the technology that secured victory in World War II? Most of that generation assumed that science and technology would solve all the significant problems of modern life.

In this light, it is little wonder that Churches of Christ experienced such phenomenal growth during the postwar period. To some extent it was a matter of a rising tide raising all ships, but Churches of Christ were set to benefit more than most communions from the postwar revival because their rationalist, empirically oriented theology so neatly matched the temper of the times.

This objectivist approach to life that reigned over the American psyche in the 1950s, however, left unanswered one fundamental question: the question of life's meaning. Protesters of the 1960s, therefore, routinely charged that American universities were teaching them how to make a living but not how to live. Further, countercultural activists typically imagined that American business preoccupied itself with profit at the expense of truth, integrity, and basic human values. Finally, the technological air war over Vietnam exploded for many the "myth of objective consciousness." In that war, airmen flying many miles above the earth simply pressed a button and released deadly accurate bombs and missiles that wreaked enormous destruction on men, women, and children below. Then the airmen returned to base, never compelled to come face to face with the human suffering and death their technical instruments of destruction had inflicted. In other words, this highly technological war had excised the human dimension with surgical skill.

For many in the counterculture, the war symbolized the absurdities of a worldview that extolled science and technology as gods and yet downgraded fundamental questions of human meaning and value. Many youthful protesters rejected objective consciousness and exalted the subjective instead. This partially accounts for the rise of interest in Eastern religions that opened believers to subjective realms largely suppressed by Western faiths as well as the growing fascination with mind-expanding drugs.

This is the context in which the controversy over the Holy Spirit occurred among Churches of Christ. If the counterculture at large found absurd the focus on rational objectivity enshrined in science and technology, many young people among Churches of Christ found absurd the focus on rational objectivity enshrined in the biblical text. They moved toward the belief that lashing the Holy Spirit of God to an objective book of paper and ink — or, indeed, circumscribing the Spirit with any kind of rational constraints — ultimately impoverished the soul and drained life of its meaning.

The Dwain Evans Affair

While the controversy over the Holy Spirit swirled on many fronts, three are particularly notable. The first involved Dwain Evans, whom we have already encountered as one of the principal agents involved in establishing *Mission*.

In the early 1960s, Evans conceived a bold new vision of evangelism among Churches of Christ: the exodus movement. The strategy was for large numbers of families to sell their homes, quit their jobs, and move en masse to a region of the United States where Churches of Christ were weak.[62] Evans led the first such movement in 1963, to Bay Shore, New York, situated on Long Island.[63] Commonly known as "Exodus Bay Shore," this experiment attracted significant media attention, both inside and outside the Churches of Christ. *Time* magazine ran Evans's picture and proclaimed, "The Campbellites are coming."[64] The congregation that resulted from this experiment became the West Islip Church of Christ.

By virtue of this bold step, Evans quickly became the fair-haired boy among mainstream Churches of Christ. His calendar rapidly filled with speaking

Dwain Evans (1933-) pioneered the "exodus movement" concept of domestic missions, leading "Exodus Bay Shore" to Bay Shore, Long Island, New York, in 1963. Because of this bold step, he became almost overnight a sensation within Churches of Christ. Just as quickly as his star had risen, however, it came crashing down, when he spoke about the power of the Holy Spirit to a lectureship audience at Abilene Christian College in 1966. ACC officials explained that Churches of Christ were not ready for Evans's message. Evans helped organize several race relations workshops in the 1960s, provided initial motivation for the creation of *Mission* magazine, and worked in Campus Evangelism.
(Photo courtesy Dwain Evans)

engagements. Colleges related to Churches of Christ scheduled him for their lectureships. Local congregations scheduled him for guest sermons. He was in great demand.

Then, in 1966, Evans delivered an address at the Abilene Christian College lectureship that pulled his star from the sky and sent it crashing to the ground. In those days, because the college's facilities were limited, each lecturer presented the same address for two nights running. In his lecture for the first evening Evans proclaimed,

> If I were asked to cite the greatest blessing that the Exodus to Long Island was [*sic*] brought it would have to be this: a greater understanding of the power of the Holy Spirit. Time and time again there was confrontation with the challenge of the impossible. In each case the power of the Holy Spirit at work within enabled us to overcome. Although Jesus speaks of special Holy

Spirit power which the apostles were to receive which we have not received, we must not conclude that His power is not available to us today. He works in different ways but He is fully as powerful today to accomplish His purpose as He was in the first century. . . . We must come face to face with the "impossibility" of our challenge. . . . Only then will we see the miracle-working power of the Holy Spirit.[65]

Those words set off alarms in the collective imagination of the college's administration. The president, the dean, and the bursar summoned Evans to an emergency meeting in the president's office. Their message: he must not repeat that speech the second evening. The Churches of Christ, they said, were simply not ready for such teachings regarding the Holy Spirit. But Evans refused to be pressured. The second evening, he delivered the same speech, perhaps with even more vigor than the night before.[66]

Repercussions for Evans came swiftly and decisively. Within weeks of his speech, Reuel Lemmons penned an editorial that, at the very least, would inevitably destroy Evans's preaching career if he refused to repent. Lemmons conceded that those who were "placing undue emphasis upon the direct guidance of the Holy Spirit" were "sincere men" whose "dedication and devotion surpasses that of most," but he warned they had not "weighed the consequences of the new, strange doctrine" they were preaching. "One recently made this statement," Lemmons went on: " 'Too long we have taught the people that the Spirit operates only through the word. I stand here tonight to deny it!' Well, I stand here to affirm it."

For Lemmons, and for most among mainstream and conservative Churches of Christ in the 1960s, the notion of an indwelling Holy Spirit undermined the Bible as the empirically objective word of God and relativized Churches of Christ in relation to other Christian traditions. Accordingly, Lemmons wrote,

> If the Holy Spirit can furnish us unto a single good work that the Word of God does not lead us into, then the New Testament is not a perfect law of liberty. If these claims are true, then the Roman Catholic doctrine of continuing revelation is true, and all the battles we have fought with both R.C.'s and Protestants have been for naught.[67]

Within a matter of weeks following Lemmons's editorial, colleges and churches throughout the fellowship of Churches of Christ canceled every speaking engagement on Evans's heavily booked calendar. That fact alone attested to the efficiency of the informal political structure that governed the denomination and underscored Lemmons's role as a *de facto* editor-bishop.

In the meantime, the controversy Evans had uncorked continued to rage. By late summer, Lemmons noted that "we have received enough articles on the indwelling of the Holy Spirit to fill the entire paper for several months."[68] Most of those articles reaffirmed the traditional position of Churches of Christ and expressed fears of Pentecostal exercises.[69] One man wondered, for example, "how long it will be before some will be speaking in tongues, and practicing miraculous healing."[70] A similar concern was registered in the *Gospel Advocate* by Guy N. Woods, who expressed amazement that any among Churches of Christ would presume to question the position "so ably argued and successfully defended" throughout their collective history. Woods asserted that Evans's position was perilously close to that of "a fullfledged Mary Baker Eddy or a Joseph Smith who also claimed special direction." And Woods restated in unequivocal terms the position he held as true: *"All influences, wrought upon the human mind by the Holy Spirit of God, are accomplished by means of the inspired Word of God."* That, for Woods, was unvarnished empirical truth.[71]

Finally, Evans felt compelled to clarify his position, and so he published "A Statement of My Convictions" in the *Firm Foundation.* "I believe," he wrote,

> that the Bible reveals that the Holy Spirit is to indwell every Christian baptized for the forgiveness of sins. This indwelling is never contrary to the written word. There is no new revelation. The indwelling of the Spirit does not manifest himself today as he did in the lives of the apostles by enabling them to "cast out demons, speak with new tongues, take up serpents, and drink deadly poison." The Holy Spirit does not operate separate and apart from the word in conversion.[72]

But there was no undoing the initial response to his speech. In the end, the controversy effectively put an end to his preaching career. Within a few years, he left the congregation he had established in New York and moved to Houston, where he became a real estate developer. He continued his ministry, however, as an active member and elder in the Bering Drive Church of Christ in that city.

The Pat Boone Affair

Three years after Evans delivered his fateful lecture, the popular entertainer Pat Boone created another storm of controversy within Churches of Christ when he revealed that he had received the Holy Spirit and now spoke in tongues.[73] A native of Donelson, Tennessee (a suburb of Nashville), a graduate of David Lipscomb High School, and a former student at David Lipscomb College, Boone grew up in the very bosom of Churches of Christ and, at twelve years of age, was baptized by M. Norvel Young. In 1954, his musical abilities attracted national attention when he won competitions on Ted Mack's *Amateur Hour* and Arthur Godfrey's *Talent Scouts*. In 1955, he rocketed to stardom and fame with two gold records.[74]

Through it all, however, Boone maintained close ties with Churches of Christ. More than that, his moral and religious scruples quickly earned him a national reputation as a fundamentally wholesome and clean-cut kid — something unique in the world of Hollywood. Needless to say, Churches of Christ prized Boone as an important symbol of their own rapid ascent to middle-class social respectability.

Then, in the mid-1950s, Boone's career took him to New York. There, he encountered Clinton Davidson, the man who had helped save Harding College from fiscal collapse in the 1930s (see Chap. 7) and who had led in the effort to subvert Foy E. Wallace's hard style of journalism (see Chap. 9). In the intervening years, Davidson's spirituality had developed from a simple trust in the providence of God to include an interest in signs, wonders, and latter-day miracles. He shared this interest with Boone, explaining, for example, that if he found himself running late for an important financial meeting, he would simply pray, and, as Boone put it, "a cab would come out of nowhere [and] he would jump in and arrive just in the nick of time. He would thank God, tip the driver and stroll in, chuckling." Davidson also told Boone that his wife, Flora, had suffered for years with an injured hip, until he finally took her to a healing revival led by Oral Roberts, the well-known Pentecostal evangelist, and within days the hip was healed. Boone was impressed. "As I listened to Clint in our den, I'll admit it was hard to believe. Here was a millionaire business man, a business consultant to men whose combined worth was over 300 million, a Washington consultant and financial brain telling me he had *seen* miracles of healing. But this was only the beginning for me."[75]

In the following months, Boone experienced other powerful spiritual encounters. He read David Wilkerson's book *The Cross and the Switchblade,* which relates tales of miraculous healings and speaking in tongues. "If he's telling the truth," Boone thought, "then there's another whole dimension of Christian living that I . . . didn't let myself experience, didn't expect."[76] Only months later, Boone met George Otis, a financial consultant and former president of the Lier Corporation. Like Davidson and Wilkerson, Otis told of stunning signs and wonders performed in the power of the Holy Ghost. Boone found his testimonies all the more convincing because, like Davidson, Otis was "a highly respected, analytical kind of guy, a man who can't afford to be fooled. And in broad daylight and in a business suit — not in a late night ghost-storytelling session — Otis is saying that *God performs miracles today!*" Further, Boone noted, when Otis surrendered himself to God, "his business career flourished. Now God was his partner."[77]

Some months later, shortly after the death of her father, country-western singing star Red Foley, Shirley Boone reported that she had received the Holy Spirit and had spoken in tongues. It was a time when Pat, himself, was facing possible financial ruin. Having witnessed spiritual deliverance in the lives of Davidson, Wilkerson, Otis, and now his wife Shirley, Boone determined "that the gift of the Holy Spirit *could* be for me — if I was willing to claim it." In January of 1969, he went to the home of George Otis and, after a time of Bible study, Boone exclaimed, "Oh, precious Jesus — be my baptizer. *Baptize me right now* in Your Spirit, the Spirit of the living God." Within minutes, he later recalled, "I sang a lovely, quiet song . . . in an infinitely expressive prayer language." He determined now to relinquish his career if God so willed, but instead found his career rejuvenated and his financial difficulties resolved. He characterized the whole experience as "a fantastic miracle of God."[78]

News of Boone's charismatic reliance on the Holy Spirit spread quickly within Churches of Christ. For those who doubted, partial proof appeared on their television screens late in the summer of 1969, when Boone appeared on the nationally broadcast programs of Pentecostal preachers Rex Humbard and Oral Roberts. Foy Smith reported in the *First Century Christian* that when he encountered these broadcasts, "I almost dropped my bridge work!" Smith charged Boone with helping to "foster false doctrines," and he called on him to publicly repent.[79]

Firm Foundation editor Reuel Lemmons, however, saw things somewhat differently. Representing the middle-class mainstream of Churches of Christ, Lemmons rejoiced that "Pat Boone is perhaps the only member of the Lord's church with a worldwide image. He can, and does, reach millions. . . . Power to him."[80] But many thought otherwise. James Bales, Bible professor at Harding College, believed that Lemmons had been deceived and really had no clear idea of Boone's beliefs, and he wrote an entire book in which he sought to expose Boone's errors.[81]

In the meantime, *Testimony* magazine, an evangelical journal originating in Rosemead, California, ran on its front cover a picture of former mainstream Church of Christ minister Ben F. Franklin and his wife, Geneva, both of whom now ministered to Christ's Center Church of Christ in San Diego. In an article inside, the Franklins proclaimed, "We once offered a thousand dollars for a miracle; but since receiving the Holy Spirit, with tongues, we have miracles in our own Church of Christ!" In another article in the same issue, Boone told how he had "received the Holy Spirit and Tongues." In a third article, Dean Dennis, a former minister of the Northside Church of Christ, Santa Ana, California, told how he had approached the Boones in an effort to dissuade them from their error only to be convinced that it was he, not they, who was mistaken. Elsewhere, Dennis reported that before he left the Boones' home, he had received the baptism of the Holy Spirit and the gift of tongues.[82] Now, in the *Testimony* article, he boldly declared that he had witnessed healing miracles involving a "man stricken with cancer" and an arthritic woman.[83]

That issue of *Testimony* magazine circulated widely among Churches of Christ and provided all the evidence required to convict Boone and his family of heresy. Conservatives quickly mounted a crusade to bar Boone from access to any channels of communication within Churches of Christ. Perry B. Cotham, for example, writing in both the *Gospel Advocate* and the *First Century Christian*, called on colleges, papers, and individual congregations to lock Boone out. "I do not intend to keep silent," he declared, "and let the Lord's church be turned into some kind of 'Pentecostal Holiness' denomination."[84] Wayne Jackson in the *Christian Courier* went further: "It is our firm conviction that both individuals and congregations who continue to condone or use Pat Boone should be publicly marked."[85]

Ira Y. Rice criticized the *Testimony* articles in the June 1970 issue of *Contending for the Faith*,[86] and five months later he complained bitterly that the elders in the Inglewood, California, Church of Christ that the Boones attended had taken no substantial action to resolve the problem: "It is not just *Inglewood* that is being made to suffer by all this heretical, false teaching being done — worldwide — by Pat and Shirley Boone. Individual after individual, congregation after congregation — here, there and everywhere — not only is being *disturbed* by their doctrines but *corrupted* as well." In Rice's view, "the time is far past when they [the Inglewood congregation] should have withdrawn from Pat and Shirley Boone on grounds of heresy."[87] Finally, after many months of discussion with the Boones, the Inglewood congregation expelled them from their fellowship in April of 1971.[88]

That same year, halfway across the country in Nashville, events were set in motion that soon would involve Boone's parents, Archie and Margaret Boone, in similar ways. In 1971, Nashville's Belmont Church of Christ, long a staid congregation, invited Don Finto to serve as its preacher. Finto had a doctorate in German literature from Vanderbilt and had taught at Lipscomb from 1963 until 1971, when he resigned to accept Belmont's invitation. Deeply moved by the spiritual and ethical concerns of the countercultural generation, Finto led the Belmont church in outreach to the poor, the disenfranchised, and the alienated. Soon, the character of the congregation dramatically changed. Worshipers embraced the power of the Holy Spirit and spoke in tongues. By 1979, the congregation's elders voted to allow musical instruments in the worship. That action effectively ended Belmont's standing as an orthodox Church of Christ.

Prior to Finto's arrival at Belmont, Archie and Margaret Boone had been members of the Granny White Church of Christ. Inspired by their son and daughter-in-law, Pat and Shirley, the elder Boones professed in 1970 that they had received the baptism of the Holy Spirit. The Granny White Church of Christ quickly expelled them from their fellowship, but the Boones soon discovered Finto and became active members of the Belmont congregation — in many ways, the most visible stronghold of progressivism among Churches of Christ in Tennessee during that period.[89]

What ought we to conclude about the episodes involving Dwain Evans and Pat Boone? Certainly there are differences between the two cases — Boone moved considerably further from traditional Church of Christ beliefs than did

Evans — but they nonetheless point to a variety of common themes. First, the swiftness with which Churches of Christ moved to minimize the influence of both Evans and Boone within the tradition provides yet more evidence of the efficiency of their informal political structures — despite their frequent denials that such structures even existed. Indeed, the success with which they essentially barred Evans and Boone from all channels of communication and influence within the denomination reminds one of the success with which their forebears destroyed the influence of the premillennial leader R. H. Boll earlier in the century. Second, there is a sense in which both Evans and Boone stood at least partially in the Stone-Lipscomb tradition, with its emphasis on the mysteries of God's sovereign rule. At the same time, however, both Evans and Boone were distinctly the children of their own time and place. Their ministries reflected the subjective emphases so common to the countercultural generation of the 1960s, including a general rejection of the scientific, the technical, and the merely rational. And third, the response of Churches of Christ to both men suggests the extent to which the tradition still drew nourishment from Enlightenment ideology and, for that reason, stood fundamentally estranged from the intellectual currents that informed the younger generation. In this regard, the Evans and Boone episodes paint a picture of a modern church with roots sunk deep into the Age of Reason, coming into conflict with an increasingly postmodern culture that was in the process of rejecting Enlightenment presuppositions. To a great extent, this conflict would be the dominant motif among Churches of Christ for the next quarter-century.

Campus Evangelism

The struggle in Churches of Christ with encroaching postmodernism was especially evident in the battle they fought over an organized effort to evangelize America's colleges — an effort called Campus Evangelism. This program placed more emphasis on a personal relation with Jesus than on the institutional church, and it sought to present the gospel in language that would speak to America's youth. To understand the battle over this program, we must understand the dynamics of yet another periodical, the *Christian Chronicle,* which worked hard to keep the story of Campus Evangelism in the forefront of the consciousness of Churches of Christ.

Olan Hicks founded the *Chronicle* in June of 1943, intending that it serve Churches of Christ as a newspaper focusing chiefly on overseas and domestic missions. In June of 1967, the executive editor of the *Chronicle* at that time, James Walter Nichols, announced that the *Chronicle* had been sold to Ralph Sweet, owner of the Sweet Publishing Company, which specialized in books and Bible school materials designed especially for Churches of Christ.[90] Sweet immediately installed as the journal's new editor Harold Straughn, a man very much a part of the growing world of biblical and theological scholarship among Churches of Christ. With a B.A. and an M.A. in biblical studies from Abilene Christian College and an S.T.B. from Harvard, Straughn was sensitive to the cultural and religious ferment that increasingly convulsed Churches of Christ.

Within a matter of weeks, it became clear that Straughn would not confine his reporting to the bland and the traditional. He was determined to use the *Chronicle* to inform Churches of Christ of the struggle for the church's soul, and to that end he ran features and news articles that focused time and again on the developing story of Campus Evangelism. He reported the events as they unfolded — the activities of Campus Evangelism as well as the criticisms lodged against it by conservatives. Disturbed by these open reports of the political struggles within Churches of Christ, many conservatives began to link the *Chronicle* with *Mission, Integrity,* and the writings of Gary Freeman as part of a liberal conspiracy.

The idea for Campus Evangelism began at an Abilene Christian College lectureship in 1965, when Wesley Reagan, a preacher in Pasadena, Texas, challenged Churches of Christ to link their autonomous campus ministries in a national program of campus evangelism.[91] Jim Bevis, a minister at the Broadway Church of Christ in Lubbock, took the challenge to heart and began prodding his congregation to accept the job of coordinating Church of Christ missions to college campuses nationwide in much the same way that it had accepted the task of coordinating overseas missions following World War II. He got approval to organize a Campus Evangelism Steering Committee.

Bevis began by looking closely at a program that seemed to him an effective model for campus evangelism on a national scale — Bill Bright's Campus Crusade for Christ. In June of 1966 Bevis attended a ten-day Campus Crusade Leadership Training Institute at Bright's headquarters in San Bernardino, California. Bevis was impressed with Campus Crusade, and Bright, in turn, was impressed with Bevis and the plans he and the Campus Evangelism Steering Committee were formulating; he invited Bevis to attend his Staff Training Institute later that year.[92]

Bevis shared his enthusiasm about this invitation with John Allen Chalk: "If our elders allow us to attend this crucial meeting, I'm confident that it will place this work ahead fifteen years immediately. This organization, Campus Crusade, is literally turning the college campus upside down. We must get on the inside and find out how they are going [*sic*]."[93] The elders did grant permission, and Bevis returned to San Bernardino in August. This time, he "heard men and women like Dr. Roy Moon of Moody Institute, Betty Eliot [*sic*], wife of the slain missionary, and Roy and Dale Rogers."[94]

By December of that year, the Steering Committee held a "Campus Leaders' Seminar" in Dallas that was attended by over 350 college students, campus ministers, elders, and local preachers. One of the principal speakers for the seminar was Bill Bright, president of Campus Crusade for Christ International.[95]

There were no objections to this obvious effort to build yet another centralized institution to help coordinate campus ministries nationwide — that battle had been fought and decided in the 1950s. But the Steering Committee did take some bold and innovative steps that made the Dallas meeting both significant and controversial in several respects. For one thing, they invited as a principal speaker for a seminar in Church of Christ evangelism a man who came not from Churches of Christ but from the "denominational world." That step alone made this fledgling movement vulnerable to considerable criticism.

Jim Bevis (1937-), a minister for the Broadway Church of Christ in Lubbock, Texas, in the 1960s, responded in 1965 to a challenge to link the various campus ministries of Churches of Christ in a national program of campus evangelism. He turned to Bill Bright's Campus Crusade for Christ as a model for his work. One can measure the impact of Campus Evangelism, the organization that resulted from Bevis's work, in several ways. (1) Campus Evangelism trained over four thousand young people in methods borrowed from Campus Crusade, thereby linking Churches of Christ to the world of evangelical Protestantism. Many of those students became leaders in Churches of Christ in later years. (2) Campus Evangelism transcended the cultural norms of Churches of Christ and shared its message with drug addicts, hippies, conservatives, radicals, and students of all races and economic classes. In the end, however, the ministry proved too revolutionary for Churches of Christ and died in 1970 for lack of funding. Bevis is pictured here, participating in a Campus Evangelism worship service. Behind him is John Allen Chalk.

(Photo courtesy John Allen Chalk)

Perhaps even more important, Bevis and his Steering Committee opened Churches of Christ to the influence of evangelical Christianity. Throughout their history and at many levels, with precious few exceptions, Churches of Christ had stood poles apart from the world of evangelicalism.[96] Evangelicals emphasized salvation through faith by grace; Churches of Christ emphasized the importance of immersion. Evangelicals stressed the power of the Holy Spirit; Churches of Christ had largely confined the Spirit to the Bible. Evangelicals preached an experiential religion; Churches of Christ insisted on a rational faith, structured along the lines of Baconian logic. But now, here in Dallas, Churches of Christ were giving birth to a movement that was in many respects evangelical in its approach and in its theology.

This development would be critical for the future of Churches of Christ, since Campus Evangelism would eventually train in its seminars over four thousand students, many of whom would rise to positions of influence in local congregations throughout the United States. Further, the sort of theology these students were picking up in Campus Evangelism was in some ways reinforced by younger professors at various Church of Christ–related colleges who counseled them to develop a biblical theology centered on "the crucified Christ." For those with eyes to see, it was clear that Churches of Christ were inching their way toward an increasingly evangelical identity.

In July of 1967, Campus Evangelism became a reality, and Jim Bevis and Rex Vermillion, associate ministers of the Broadway Church of Christ, were named codirectors of the program.[97] As the movement spread to some 350 college and university campuses,[98] it became increasingly clear that it would encourage students to submit themselves first of all to the claims and demands of Jesus Christ and that it would downplay the claims of the traditional institutional church. The official publication of Campus Evangelism, *GO*, editorialized, "There is little evidence in our time of the kind of church Jesus foresaw."[99] Speakers at the 1968 seminar in Dallas resonated to this theme. Dwain Evans told the students, "Christ didn't strive to be editor of the Jerusalem Advocate or chief minister of the Temple Church of Christ. He said, 'I am among you as one who serves.'" And John Allen Chalk observed, "There is little awe in our religion because we don't have a relationship with Jesus. It's institutional and our awe comes from great preachers and leaders."[100] Indeed, "repeated throughout the whole seminar came the same piercing questions: 'Do you really know Jesus Christ in your life? Are you really redeemed? Do you personally know the Lord Jesus Christ?'"[101] Campus Evangelism clearly appealed to the anti-institutional biases that were central to the youth culture in the 1960s.

The genius of Campus Evangelism, however, went far beyond its anti-institutional appeal. The program also sought to transcend the traditional cultural norms of Churches of Christ: it shared its message with students of all races and all economic classes, with drug addicts and hippies, with conservatives and radicals. And it sought to address issues of concern to students in a language they understood. At Daytona Beach in 1969, Campus Evangelism workers manned a beachside coffee shop and passed out 10,000 copies of "The Inside Story," J. B. Phillips's translation of Luke, John, Acts, and Romans. Meanwhile, both Pat Boone and Ray Walker performed in the 5,000-seat Daytona Beach bandshell, attracting students to hear speakers talk about Jesus.[102] In 1967, on the campus of Texas Tech University in Lubbock, Campus Evangelism sponsored a debate on the "Playboy Philosophy" between William S. Banowsky, the pulpit minister of Lubbock's Broadway Church of Christ, and Anson Mount, public affairs editor of *Playboy* magazine.[103] Campus Evangelism also sponsored campus forums on war and peace and on race relations, the latter featuring such leading black preachers among Churches of Christ as Humphrey Foutz of Baltimore, Zebedee Bishop of Detroit, David Jones Jr. of Nashville, Andrew Hairston of Atlanta, and Ron Wright of Los Angeles.[104] The point, quite simply, is that Campus Evangelism sought to build bridges to students by emphasizing student concerns in an idiom students understood.

Yet, by April of 1970, Campus Evangelism was dead. As Reuel Lemmons wrote in the *Firm Foundation,* "It is hard to determine whether it committed suicide or was murdered. There seemed to be ungovernable suicidal tendencies present, as well as plenty of evidence that its critics stoned it to death."[105] In any event, its critics effectively managed to dry up funding for the organization.

The critics of Campus Evangelism were the same people who assailed *Mission, Integrity,* and the scholars who brought the fruits of higher learning to Church of Christ–related colleges. Some of these critics stood squarely in the mainstream of Churches of Christ, but by and large the most vocal critics belonged to the newly emerged conservative wing. They pressed three fundamental objections: Campus Evangelism was accommodating denominational influences and concerns, abandoning the traditional forms and structures of Churches of Christ, and inappropriately emphasizing the power of the Holy Spirit in the lives of believers.

Franklin Camp voiced the first objection when he flatly complained in *First Century Christian* that "Campus Evangelism has decided to join forces with [the] denominations."[106]

Glenn Wallace voiced the second objection, warning his conservative colleagues that Campus Evangelism was indulging in the same sort of revolutionary spirit that was convulsing American society at large:

> Listen to these Campus crusades that feature such rebellion against the "old way of life." Make a note of the speakers in youth forums who are talking about "the establishment" and "traditionalism" as they deride the "old church of Christism." Listen well to those who speak of the "elders who will not permit us to do our thing." This modern cry is not for any needed reform.

It is a rebel yell for the destruction of Bible authority and Scriptural practice and speech.[107]

Sharing similar fears, conservatives criticized a broad variety of new and innovative strategies. Anthony E. Emmons, for example, could hardly believe that Campus Evangelism would accept "hippies" as Christians.

> Christian hippies, INDEED! This is enough to turn the stomach of every God-fearing, Bible-loving Christian on earth. If there ever were two terms more diametrically opposed to each other than Christian and hippy, we have never cast our eyes upon them. Hippies are called the lost generation, and also drop-outs from society. We hear that their habits are unclean. They are inevitably connected with LSD and pot. . . . What is Christian about the hippy movement?[108]

Oklahoman W. R. Craig objected to a confessional service on the ground that it consisted mainly of "crass emotionalism with little or no understanding of Christ and His gospel." Quoting extensively from *Advance,* a publication of Campus Evangelism, Craig wrote,

> It was called a "FAGGOT SERVICE." First they erected a cross and at its base was built a blazing camp fire. Each student was given a stick of wood on which he was to mentally write the name of some sin which he was "going to give to Jesus." And as he "committed a part of himself to Christ, he flung the faggot into the fire to watch it consumed entirely as Christ himself takes away sins." Jesus said, "If we confess our sins He is faithful to forgive our sins. . . ." [But] is it to be done with "flung faggots?" God forbid!![109]

When Campus Evangelism announced its Daytona Beach crusade of 1969, Jerry Brewer wrote in the *First Century Christian,* "It should be interesting to see how one would go about preaching to a nearly-nude sun bather who is there for 'sand, suds and sex.'" And in the aftermath of the crusade, Glenn Wallace wondered if it was "in keeping with the spirit of the Master to walk about on a beach, exposing a hairy chest, carrying a Bible in one hand, offering free donuts and coffee in the other and seeking to communicate with bikini clad girls?"[110]

Evidence of the third fundamental conservative objection, concerning the emphasis that Campus Evangelism placed on the power of the Holy Spirit in the lives of believers, surfaced in a significant way at the Freed-Hardeman College lectureship of February 1969. Each year the lectureship featured an "Open Forum," conducted by legendary preacher and debater Guy N. Woods, focusing on some particular issue of concern to the church. That year, the "Open Forum"

Guy N. Woods (1908-1993), legendary author, preacher, and debater in Churches of Christ, presided over the annual "Open Forum" at the Freed-Hardeman College lectureship for thirty years, beginning in 1954. In 1969, Woods turned the Forum's searchlight on the Campus Evangelism Seminar held in Dallas the previous year and thereby joined the growing list of critics concerned about the orthodoxy of that campus ministry. Of particular concern to Woods were reports that Campus Evangelism seminar instructors had taught that "the Holy Spirit operates apart from and independent of the Word." (Photo courtesy Gospel Advocate Company)

focused on the 1968 Campus Evangelism seminar in Dallas, and several representatives of the organization attended to defend themselves from implicit accusations of heresy. At one point in the interchange, Woods turned to the issue of the Holy Spirit. According to the transcript of the conversation later published in the *Christian Chronicle*, the interchange that followed went like this:

> W [Woods] — All right. There, uh, they also taught that the Holy Spirit operates apart from and independent of the Word. Do you accept that view?
> S [Charles Shelton] — No, sir, we believe that the Holy Spirit indwells the Christian according to Romans 8, Ephesians 3 and other passages of scripture . . . but it does not work apart from the Word, but in harmony with the Word. Now I don't believe that statement was made.
> W — But you can't say that you know it wasn't then.

S — No, sir, because there were a hundred different classes and individual groups.

W — That's our very point. . . . Now, here's the thing about it, Brother Shelton, if you are not responsible for the statements and they are made, then the next time you ought to see to it that you have speakers that don't make statements like that.

S — Well, Brother Woods, we can't be any more responsible for that than the administration of Freed-Hardeman College can be responsible for everything that's said in a lectureship.

W — If you can't you ought to disband then. You ought not to go around (Brother Woods is interrupted by amens from the audience), you ought not, you ought not to go (Woods is interrupted by applause), you ought not to go around the country carrying speakers under your banner who are teaching false doctrine.[111]

Concerns about the Holy Spirit surfaced in other ways as well. When Alabama preacher Franklin Camp read that someone had described a Campus Evangelism seminar as "Spirit filled," he charged that the seminar "was not a thing in the world but a high classed 'Holiness Camp Meeting' moved from a tent and sawdust to the carpets of a hotel." In Camp's view, the emphasis that Campus Evangelism placed on the Holy Spirit was not "one whit different from that which is claimed in any denominational meeting from Billy Graham down to Oral Roberts."[112]

Likewise, Glenn Wallace bemoaned the shift from the rationally restrained, highly structured worship services characteristic of traditional Churches of Christ to the emotional worship experiences that increasingly characterized the student generation. "At these 'spiritual love ins,'" Wallace objected, "the atmosphere is charged with excitement and the youth are led to give their personal testimony and tell of the moving of God in their lives. They are urged to let go and permit God to take full control of their whole self; and this includes their voices. They are led to believe that God can and does speak through them."[113] For all these reasons, the conservative wing of Churches of Christ, and many in the mainstream as well, launched such a sustained attack on Campus Evangelism that it eventually became a serious political liability for its supporters. Finally, without sufficient financial backing, it simply collapsed and disappeared.

Departure of a Generation

During the course of the 1960s, youthful reformers and protesters within Churches of Christ found that the mainstream and the conservative wings of Churches of Christ either resisted or rejected practically every new idea, every new institution, and every new periodical that reflected the concerns of their generation. No wonder they found themselves increasingly estranged from the perspectives in which they were reared. As time went on, increasing numbers of these young people abandoned Churches of Christ for other more socially concerned, more ecumenical, or more spirit-filled Christian traditions. Many left organized Christianity altogether.

By the early 1970s, this exodus became a significant concern. In 1973 Thomas H. Olbricht lamented in the pages of *Mission*, "It is no secret that a whole generation born between 1930 and 1950 has become Church of Christ drop-outs. Visit churches in St. Louis, in Houston, in Nashville and you won't see them. Oh, there are some, but they aren't the bright [and] the creative."[114] Then Olbricht noted that different groups in the church offered different explanations for the "mass exodus." On the one hand, he wrote,

> Those who like the church as it is, or better yet, as it was in 1938, have a ready answer. All these people who leave the church are liberals and modernists and have been educated in atheistic northern universities. The church is better off if all those fast talking, theologian quoting, long hairs leave. . . . If they would accept the church as it is they could stay. But they want to change it.

On the other hand, he noted, "the under-forty crowd claims that the lost generation is because of the church itself. The leadership of the church is not interested in Jesus Christ, but in church politics . . . [and] in the 1930s Church of Christ understanding [of Scripture]."

Olbricht himself believed that neither of these explanations was correct; the chief reason for the exodus, he insisted, was the failure of Churches of Christ to come to terms with "the crucified Christ" and the implications of the Christ-event for biblical theology. "I find it no longer useful to confess the weaknesses of young liberals or of stodgy churches," he wrote. "There are plenty. . . . So I have one message to churches and [to] those who would leave. Keep the crucified Christ before you."[115]

Olbricht was an influential figure who, by the mid-1980s, had helped to shape a whole generation of preachers through his nineteen years of teaching at Abilene Christian University.[116] Several other biblical scholars at Abilene Christian, Harding Graduate School of Religion, and elsewhere shared his viewpoint and, together, they had a significant impact on a new generation of preachers who sat in their classrooms. Olbricht's message, therefore, is worth assessing. What did he mean?

Over the years he made clear in numerous articles, lectures, and classroom presentations his belief that the central task of Churches of Christ was to recover a biblical theology. For all their talk of restoration, he said, this was something they had as yet failed to do. "In spite of announcements from the pulpit for the need to declare the whole council of God," he wrote in the *Firm Foundation* in 1969, "it was seldom declared. . . . If leaders among Churches of Christ had conceived Biblical doctrine as broad as the Bible itself, the distaste for doctrinal preaching [current in the 1960s] might not now be with us to the extent it is."[117]

Then, in a *Mission* article in 1979, Olbricht summarized his emphasis over the years and tied it directly to the historic restoration vision of Churches of Christ. "The predispositions against the overarching message of the Scripture," he wrote, "fostered by many of our forefathers including Campbell, has [*sic*] impoverished the effort to restore New Testament faith." Olbricht called for Churches of Christ to focus instead on the "core message" of Scripture, centered in "the mighty acts of God and his final and crucial act in the death, burial, and resurrection of Jesus Christ."[118] These were themes that, by the 1980s, became increasingly important to preaching and teaching among Churches of Christ, as we shall see in Chapter 14.

Conclusion

What can we say at this point about the polarization between conservatives and progressives within Churches of Christ during the 1960s and the early 1970s?

First, the polarization was profoundly theological in character, with roots on both sides of the rupture reaching far back into the nineteenth century. But it was not simply theological; it also grew out of long-standing cultural, educational, and demographic rifts in the tradition that were widened by the dramatic changes taking place in American culture during the 1960s.

Further, Thomas Olbricht was undoubtedly correct when he suggested that the hostility of both conservative and mainstream Churches of Christ toward the progressives grew, to a significant degree, from the dismantling of an old, entrenched power structure that had resided for years in the "editor-bishops" (see Chap. 1).[119] Glenn Wallace said much the same thing in 1967, when he compared *Mission* to the new *Christian Leader* of the 1930s, funded by Clinton Davidson (see Chap. 9):

> Those who are acquainted with religious history among us will remember a man by the name of Clinton Davidson, now deceased, who about 30 years ago came out of New York with the announced intention of taking over the bad journalism among us and giving the brotherhood a real up-to-date magazine. . . . This watered down gospel that was advocated 30 years ago was a failure and we would earnestly pray that any repetition of the same ideas today will meet the same failure.[120]

Third, the progressive/conservative rupture was no mere skirmish in the backwater of Churches of Christ; it was a major war fought in the heartland of the heritage in which both sides sought to claim the soul of the tradition. This created enormous problems for the leadership of Churches of Christ at large, for, when all was said and done, few of those leaders could escape having to take a stand. In the short term, as we have seen, many among mainstream Churches of Christ feared the progressives, their message, and their tactics, and so they identified — though often reluctantly — with the aims and perspectives of the conservatives.

By the close of the 1980s, most progressives had either made their way back into the mainstream of Churches of Christ or had left the tradition altogether. But it was also the case that many mainstream congregations now reflected bits and pieces of the agenda that the progressives had laid out in the 1960s. The conservative wing, on the other hand, continued as a vocal but increasingly isolated minority in urban areas and a dominant force in many small towns and rural regions.

By the close of the 1960s, it had become apparent to those who had eyes to see how thoroughly the "nondenominational" Churches of Christ had become a denomination, standing in near-lockstep formation with the conservative interests of the larger culture. This meant that one key support of the tradition's identity stood in jeopardy: the myth of nondenominational Christianity. Further, the attempt by conservatives and some mainstream members of Churches of Christ to link the historic restoration vision with reactionary politics and exclusivist claims regarding the one true church convinced many moderates and progressives that the restoration vision, itself, was seriously flawed. In this way, yet another key support of the tradition's identity began to deteriorate. And finally, increased acculturation coupled with doubts regarding the tradition's validity led many to abandon evangelistic activity.

Churches of Christ thus entered the 1970s experiencing minimal growth and anxiety over their institutional identity. In Chapter 14 we shall consider how Churches of Christ sought to address this crisis.

CHAPTER 14

Conclusion:
Renewal and Reform

By the 1960s, the theological house that Churches of Christ had built for themselves in the nineteenth century had all but collapsed. As we have seen, that house rested on twin pillars that stood, like majestic sentinels, at opposite ends of history — or at least at opposite ends of the only history that really mattered for people in this tradition. The first pillar, the primitive church of the apostolic age, stood at the beginning of that history. The second, the apocalyptic kingdom of God, stood at its end. Because these two pillars not only bracketed meaningful time but were also secured to one another, they virtually defined reality for believers and sustained for them the only meaningful life there could possibly be.

The house that rested on these supports, therefore, stood for over a hundred years in the realm of sacred time and space. Those who lived within its precincts hurled implicit judgment on ordinary human culture and proclaimed the final triumph of the restored kingdom of God.

By World War I, however, strong cultural pressures began to weaken the apocalyptic pillar, and the house had to depend more and more on the single pillar of primitive Christianity. But that pillar had also suffered fracture. For years, Churches of Christ had altered and adapted the restoration vision to fit the worldly considerations they originally sought to escape: the particularities of time and place. In this way, the realities of history swallowed the ideals of the ancient faith, and the strength of the restoration vision slowly ebbed away.

By the close of the 1960s, the restoration vision had fallen on especially hard times for a variety of reasons. Perhaps most important, Churches of Christ increasingly behaved like a denomination that had made its peace with the larger culture even though they continued to employ the sectarian, countercultural language of primitive Christianity to define their basic identity. Members who felt at home with the church's public behavior increasingly found the restorationist rhetoric irrelevant if not offensive, and many who prized the restoration vision above cultural accommodation felt betrayed. Put another way, Churches of Christ could not decide if they constituted a sect or a denomination — though they resisted both labels. In the midst of their indecision and confusion, the restoration vision grew blurred.

Beyond this, other factors undermined faith in the restoration ideal. The general failure of Churches of Christ to speak meaningfully to the pressing ethical issues of the 1960s convinced many, especially the young, that the restoration vision — at least as it was understood and defined by Churches of Christ — was ethically impotent. The historic exclusivism of Churches of Christ, illumined especially by forty years of personal attacks from such leaders as Foy Wallace and Ira Rice on those with whom they disagreed, led many to think of the restoration vision as inherently legalistic and productive of mean-spirited divisiveness. And finally, the postmodern climate that emerged after the 1960s proved especially corrosive to the Enlightenment foundations of Churches of Christ. Fewer and fewer people found meaningful or spiritually enriching a restoration vision built on the presuppositions of Lockean empiricism and Scottish Common Sense Realism. Put another way, the historic concerns of Churches of Christ seemed increasingly irrelevant to the spiritual needs of the new, post-1960s generation.

Highlighting these disjunctions was the widespread perception that Churches of Christ, which had experienced such rapid growth in the post–World War II era, were now merely holding their own numerically, or perhaps even declining. The malaise was only compounded by suggestions that the total membership of Churches of Christ might be less than half of previous estimates — down from earlier estimates of some 2,500,000 to perhaps between 1,000,000 and 1,250,000.[1]

Given the general religious climate in the United States during the 1970s, when liberal denominations were rapidly losing members and conservative denominations were growing by leaps and bounds, leaders of Churches of Christ found the stagnation of their congregations all the more disturbing. This was a time when Churches of Christ, by any measure, should have been making their greatest gains. It was a time marked, for example, by Dean M. Kelley's much-heralded book *Why Conservative Churches Are Growing*, by *Newsweek*'s proclamation that 1976 was "The Year of the Evangelical,"[2] and by the sudden proliferation of "nondenominational Bible churches" that attracted hundreds and thousands of members in suburban neighborhoods throughout the United States. This time, however, the playing field belonged to fundamentalists, Pentecostals, and evangelicals of various stripes, and Churches of Christ, for the most part, were left looking on from the sidelines.

Churches of Christ formulated three major responses to these disappointments, each geared toward renewal and revitalization — responses that had not fully played themselves out even by the 1990s.

The Promotional Response:
Perpetuating the Sect/Denomination Confusion

Many mainline Churches of Christ — and institutions related to those churches — located the problem precisely in the separatist dimension of their heritage that for many years had alienated Churches of Christ from the broader culture. Accordingly, while still affirming the historic restoration heritage of Churches of Christ, they sought to present that heritage in ways that might be relevant to broad cultural concerns shared by many conservative Americans — saving the American family, for example, or saving the American nation by returning America to God. In effect, this approach involved using a blatantly denominational hook to interest people in a fundamentally sectarian message.

A case in point was the "Herald of Truth" radio and television ministry that we considered in Chapter 10. In 1979, "Herald of Truth" launched a new publication it called *UpReach* magazine. Emerging in the aftermath of the national descent into cynicism triggered by the Vietnam War and exacerbated by the Watergate scandal, *UpReach* billed itself as "a magazine for better living."

Its inaugural issue featured the words "Happy Families" emblazoned in large type across its multicolored cover and focused on "the problems families face."[3] Two months later, its cover featured a photograph of the U.S. Capitol building over the heading "The Timeless Standards That Made America Great." One of the principal articles that month, "When We Cease to Be Good," featured an extract in bold type: "America is great because America is good, and if America ever ceases to be good, America will cease to be great."[4] In June of that same year, the cover featured a pastoral scene with a heading denoting the issue's theme: "America's Search for a Better Way." If *UpReach* conveyed any fundamental message in these early issues, it was this: America was born a Christian nation and could be saved from slipping into national decline only by returning to its Christian roots and traditional family values.

There can be little doubt that *UpReach*, along with its parent, the "Herald of Truth," stood in the tradition of the new *Christian Leader* (see Chap. 9) and sought to present the Christian faith in positive and attractive terms. *UpReach* even offered a theological breath of fresh air with a strong emphasis on the love and grace of God. Yet, *UpReach* and the "Herald of Truth" found it difficult to abandon the sectarian message that had characterized Churches of Christ for a century and a half.

In its first several issues, *UpReach* provided its readers with hardly a hint of either the historic restoration commitment of Churches of Christ or their sectarian orientation. It made only passing references to Christian theology, and in those references it emphasized only basic biblical themes held in common by most Christian denominations. Its opening editorial, for example, described its Christian orientation in the following terms:

UPREACH is a magazine for better living. To us, better living is righteous living. We believe that God is the almighty creator, that Jesus Christ is his only begotten son, the gift of God's love, sent to lead man back to God. We believe that the Bible is God's inspired revelation, the instruction manual supplied by the Creator. We believe that man is made in the image of God, that man has been corrupted by sin, and that man's greatest need is to fulfill the expectations of his Maker. We believe that the church is Christ's body on earth, and that participation in it is essential to the right relationship with God.[5]

The casual reader who chanced to see *UpReach* magazine during its first few months of existence might well have considered it a publication much like *Guideposts* or even *Readers' Digest*, devoted principally to the promotion of conservative American values, sustained by broad Christian sentiment. If *UpReach* represented Churches of Christ, then those first several issues surely portrayed Churches of Christ as a conservative Protestant denomination, fully in sync with traditional American values.

Then, eight months later, *UpReach* published an unflinchingly sectarian and restorationist issue, centered on the theme "What to Do When Your Church Leaves You." An article with that title suggested that many denominations had left their original moorings and now floundered in a maze of liberalism. It counseled disillusioned church members to seek out

fellowships of people who seek to be Christians only. Churches of Christ around the world, though independent and autonomous, are seeking to restore the faith and order of the church which Christ died to establish. . . . If your church has left you, perhaps you are ready to take a fresh look at the church Jesus built.[6]

Another article identified "the church Jesus built" as the Church of Christ, describing that tradition in terms almost identical to those employed by John R. Howard in his classic 1848 sermon "The Beginning Corner; or, The Church of Christ Identified" (see Chap. 3). The article concluded,

With the Bible as our only guide, we seek to find what that original church was like and restore it exactly. . . . We do not conceive ourselves as being a denomination, nor as Catholic, Protestant or Jewish, but simply as members of the church which Jesus established and for which He died.[7]

So no one could miss the point, *UpReach* included in that issue a two-page chart with the heading "A Quick Look at Church History." The chart listed a number of well-known denominations along with the circumstances surrounding their origins and the dates of their foundings. The Church of Christ headed the list with the founding date of A.D. 33; no mention at all was made of the nineteenth-century origins of Churches of Christ. On the other hand, there were listings for such nineteenth-century "man-made" denominations as the Latter-day Saints, Seventh-Day Adventists, Christian Scientists, the Salvation Army, the Christian and Missionary Alliance, and Jehovah's Witnesses.[8]

Thirteen years later, when the presidential campaign of 1992 pitted Republican incumbent George Bush against Democratic challenger Bill Clinton, Republicans routinely pressed the theme of family values as a campaign issue. This political climate seemed almost tailor-made for the historic emphasis of the "Herald of Truth," and, indeed, the ministry sought once again to connect its primitivist sectarian vision with current political and cultural concerns.

With considerable fanfare, "Herald of Truth" produced a video entitled "In God We Trust," which aired on national television February 14, 1993.[9] Reflecting a strong commitment to America's civil-religion tradition, this film called for leaders at all levels of government to return America to "the religious roots that have nurtured the growth and development of our nation, and therefore our families." Copies of the video were sent to every member of Congress, every Supreme Court Justice, and the President of the United States as "an open letter to America's leaders from members of churches of Christ."

The film affirmed that America's "connections to Christian principles . . . have made this a great nation" and that "only a Christian commitment can conceive a nation of freedom and peace, a nation tolerant of diversity." It concluded, "It's time for us to turn back to God." The overall message of the video differed hardly at all from the sort of thing Americans had heard time and again from fundamentalist and evangelical leaders of various stripes since the mid-1970s. The only really unique content appeared at the conclusion, when the video suddenly shifted to a restorationist, sectarian orientation. With footage portraying baptisms and various acts of worship in a Church of Christ congregation, it portrayed their vision of "New Testament Christianity" as the last, best hope for America's future. Then, to tie that vision unmistakably with the American-born Churches of Christ, it described those churches in terms that could have been lifted directly from John R. Howard's description of 1848:

> The church that Jesus established is made up of people in the process of being changed by God. . . . If you visit a worship service of the church of Christ, you'll see us partaking of the Lord's supper each week, singing together to honor and glorify God, praying to God to praise him and thank him, studying the Bible as God's written word, and contributing financially as we have been prospered to help others. . . . I hope you'll make an opportunity soon to visit a church of Christ in your neighborhood.[10]

Why would the "Herald of Truth" and *UpReach* magazine seek to blend the uniquely restorationist and exclusivist identity of Churches of Christ with an explicitly denominational appeal in this way? There are several possible explanations.

Perhaps it was because some fundamentalists and evangelicals had employed right-wing political and cultural themes to great advantage, and "Herald of Truth" sought to emulate their success.

Perhaps the video reflected the fact that the restoration vision, while still embraced as orthodoxy among Churches of Christ, was now subservient to an increasingly dominant conservative political theology.

A third possible explanation is that, ever since World War I, Churches of Christ had slowly been accommodating themselves to conservative Protestant values while simultaneously insisting that they were not a denomination but "the church that Jesus built." Among these conservative Protestant values was a belief that America was fundamentally a Christian nation — a proposition that David Lipscomb and his peers had rejected out of hand in the late nineteenth century. If America was fundamentally Christian, and if Churches of Christ represented the only completely authentic Christian impulse in the nation, then it stood to reason that Churches of Christ represented the nation's last, best hope. From such a perspective, the various "Herald of Truth" productions would have been sincere and genuine efforts to implement what seemed a logical conclusion: the growth of Churches of Christ and revitalization of the nation went hand in hand.

Or perhaps the producers of "Herald of Truth" — and many supporters within Churches of Christ — had never seriously considered the fact that a sectarian message, seriously embraced, squares poorly with a broad denominational appeal.

These developments would not be so significant were it not for the fact that the "Herald of Truth" broadcasts reflected the sentiments of many mainline Churches of Christ. As the new "electronic bishops" (see Chap. 10), spokespersons on the "Herald of Truth" radio and television ministries helped define Church of Christ orthodoxy, which in turn helped shape the content of "Herald of Truth" programming. When the "Herald of Truth" ministry described the "In God We Trust" video as "an open letter to America's leaders from members of Churches of Christ" and thus presumed to speak for the entire tradition, it did in fact speak for a very sizable segment of mainline congregations.

The Sectarian Response:
The Crossroads Church of Christ and the Boston Movement

Some among Churches of Christ, however, found the political and cultural theology sometimes preached by the "Herald of Truth" and by many mainstream congregations fundamentally confused and confusing. For them, the proclamation of a sectarian message under the guise of denominational concerns offered no solution to the malaise of Churches of Christ; to the contrary, they insisted, such preaching stood at the heart of the problem.

The most visible expression of protest and the most significant effort to revitalize Churches of Christ along specifically sectarian lines occurred in a University of Florida campus ministry led by Charles H. (Chuck) Lucas under the oversight of the Crossroads Church of Christ in Gainesville.[11] A product of the Campus Evangelism movement (see Chap. 13), Lucas began work with the Crossroads congregation in October 1967, only two months after the birth of Campus Evangelism itself.

But Lucas brought to his campus ministry a dimension lacking in the larger Campus Evangelism movement. He combined the sectarian, exclusivist heritage of Churches of Christ with discipling methods he claimed he found in the ministry of Jesus. Lucas maintained that the method of evangelism em-

Charles H. (Chuck) Lucas (1938-), a product of the Campus Evangelism movement, became director of a campus ministry to the University of Florida, sponsored by the Crossroads Church of Christ in Gainesville, in 1967. Lucas emphasized a discipling strategy that called on each disciple to make disciples of others on a one-to-one basis. It also called on disciples to monitor the lives of one another in an effort to produce "total commitment." When Lucas's work produced a staggering number of conversions, it attracted the attention of Churches of Christ nationwide. Soon, however, many accused Lucas of cultic procedures. Lucas, shown here at right, shares his message with a student at a Campus Evangelism outreach at Daytona Beach, Florida, in 1969.
(Photo courtesy *Christian Chronicle*)

ployed by Jesus himself called on each disciple to make disciples of others on a one-to-one basis. He argued that modern churches were in decline because they were not following that simple strategy; instead, they had set up programs and devised institutional strategies that allowed individual Christians to avoid the task of confronting others directly with the gospel.[12]

But Lucas added another key dimension to his discipling strategies. He insisted that discipling another person entailed a good deal more than simply winning that person as a convert: it entailed entering into a relationship with the convert, monitoring his or her behavior, and calling each convert to nothing less than "total commitment." This total commitment required, first of all, that each convert dedicate his or her life to converting others, who in turn would convert others, and so on. Anything short of this kind of commitment, said Lucas, should be grounds for discipline.

Using these strategies, Lucas achieved results on the campus of the University of Florida that were truly startling. The Crossroads congregation grew from a total membership of 275 in 1970 to over 1,000 by 1977, with most of that growth coming from student converts.

By 1979, however, many mainstream Churches of Christ were accusing Lucas of leading a cult. T. Pierce Brown, for example, argued in the *Gospel Advocate* that

> to challenge young and old with "total commitment" and sacrificial living for Christ, and have them respond is thrilling. But when I see an insidious and creeping cultism, mind control, and perverted Christianity masquerading under the guise of positive mental attitude, progress and enthusiastic devotion to the Lord, I weep.[13]

Kip McKean, one of Lucas's student converts at the University of Florida, inaugurated a whole new chapter in this movement in 1979, when a small, struggling Church of Christ in Lexington, Massachusetts, invited him to become their minister. McKean agreed to come, but only if each member would "vow to become . . . 'totally committed.'"[14] The congregation agreed, and over the next ten years it grew from a straggling band of fifty to a thriving community of 3,200 members that routinely met in the Boston Garden.

This congregation soon became known as the Boston Church of Christ, the mother church of equally prosperous congregations both in the United States and abroad. By 1990, daughter churches in Atlanta, Denver, Miami, and Orlando were attracting more than a thousand people each Sunday; churches in Chicago, Los Angeles, San Francisco, and San Diego were attracting more than two thousand; and in Boston, the mother church occasionally attracted as many as 6,500. The Boston Church also spawned highly successful congregations in London, Kingston, Manila, and Toronto and undertook active missions in Johannesburg, Paris, Stockholm, Bombay, Mexico City, Buenos Aires, Hong Kong, Munich, Tokyo, Cairo, Honolulu, Bangkok, and elsewhere.[15]

One of Chuck Lucas's students, Kip McKean (1954-), introduced discipling strategies in 1979 to the Church of Christ in Lexington, Massachusetts. McKean's work in New England launched the "Boston Movement" that *Time* magazine described in 1992 as "a global empire of 103 congregations from California to Cairo with total Sunday attendance of 50,000." Little fellowship remains between mainline Churches of Christ and the Boston Movement, which now describes itself as the International Churches of Christ.
(Photo courtesy Kingdom News Network)

So stunning were its gains that *Time* magazine ran a full-page story on the Boston movement in 1992, calling it "one of the world's fastest-growing and most innovative bands of Bible thumpers," having grown into "a global empire of 103 congregations from California to Cairo with total Sunday attendance of 50,000."[16] But charges of cultism persisted. *Time* went on to report that

> a loose network of "exit counselors" seeks to pressure church members into quitting. Universities that welcome all manner of oddball groups on campus actively seek to curb these evangelists. Critics mail out booklets and tapes denouncing them. Some defectors — who number half the converts since 1979 — charge that the church has done them psychological or spiritual harm. Many are crying "cult."[17]

Student dropouts from the Champaign-Urbana Church of Christ, near the campus of the University of Illinois, testified that "the church employs mind-control and manipulation tactics in its teachings." Students at the University of Southern

California claimed "the church harassed ex-members, threatened opponents and isolated recruits from their friends and families." And at Santa Monica College in southern California, students "expressed concerns about being 'harassed' in the cafeteria by LACC [Los Angeles Church of Christ] proselytizers." Representatives of the Boston movement categorically denied all these charges.[18]

Given such conflicting assessments, what are we make of the Boston movement? We might begin by noting that the movement radicalized much that was central to historic Churches of Christ. In addition, it is characterized by a radical moral fervor connected with the values of the youth counterculture of the 1960s. McKean confessed that, "like many young men of the '60s, I was inspired by those who refused to compromise and were willing to sacrifice for 'the worthy cause.' " He added that his "heroes became John F. Kennedy and Dr. Martin Luther King, Jr. who paid the ultimate price for their dreams."[19]

It was precisely this radical moral fervor that led adherents of the Crossroads/Boston movement to weigh traditional Churches of Christ and find them wanting. After graduating from the University of Florida in 1975, for example, McKean took a job as campus minister for Northeastern Christian College, a Church of Christ–related institution in Villanova, Pennsylvania. He later wrote that he saw on that campus "how uncommitted the so-called Christian students were: drugs, drunkenness, prejudice, immorality, and lukewarmness were in many of the students' lives. I came to a deep conviction that being religious is not the same as being righteous."[20] Then, between 1976 and 1979, his firsthand acquaintance with a number of Churches of Christ led McKean to believe that "the spiritual condition of most of the Churches of Christ ranged from lukewarm to disgusting."[21]

When leaders of mainstream Churches of Christ publicly lamented their own numerical decline, Boston leaders thought they saw hard, empirical evidence of spiritual stagnation. On the basis of his own survey work, for example, mainstream leader Flavil Yeakley somberly declared, "In 1980 the church of Christ in the United States did stop increasing and started decreasing in total membership. It is clear that if the 1965-1980 trend were to continue unchanged, the church of Christ would cease to exist in this nation in just a few years." Likewise, *Firm Foundation* editor Reuel Lemmons conjectured in 1982 that some eight thousand congregations of Churches of Christ had died out in the previous quarter century.[22] Leaders of the Boston movement took these reports to indicate that traditional mainline Churches of Christ were "heading toward extinction."[23]

In many ways, then, the Boston movement constituted an effort to revitalize traditional Churches of Christ. It drew much of its inspiration from the historic Church of Christ tradition, but at every step along the way it developed perspectives and practices that served to distance it from the parent tradition. One can trace the ambiguous relationship between the established fellowship and the upstart movement in several ways.

In the first place, congregations in the Boston orbit committed themselves to the restoration of primitive Christianity. "True restorations occurred," McKean explained of his movement, "as first-century Bible doctrines were once more rediscovered."[24] But McKean had not grown up in Churches of Christ, and in fact he largely rejected the understanding of restoration that prevailed in the mainstream tradition. For instance, mainstream Churches of Christ viewed the silence of Scripture as prohibitive, whereas McKean and the movement he led viewed biblical silence as permissive.[25] This fundamental difference in biblical interpretation led to increasing differences in practice. By the 1990s the Boston movement had embraced instrumental music in worship — something mainstream Churches of Christ had rejected since their beginnings in the nineteenth century.

In the second place, the Boston movement affirmed the sectarian conviction that their particular movement was the kingdom of God, and yet McKean also affirmed the existence of Christians in other traditions.[26] McKean based his definition of true and authentic Christianity on a notion central to mainline Churches of Christ since the days of Alexander Campbell — namely, that the chief task of a Christian is evangelism (see Chap. 12). But mainstream Churches of Christ had grown lukewarm regarding this notion by the late twentieth century and seldom engaged in serious evangelistic outreach. McKean, on the other hand, was passionate about it. He argued that one cannot "be saved and . . . a true Christian without being a disciple also" — by which he meant that one could not be saved unless one was actively involved in converting others. It followed from this that "a true church is composed only of disciples," and on the basis of this reasoning, McKean insisted that people coming into the Boston Church of Christ from the mainline tradition submit to rebaptism, since "they had not been baptized as disciples themselves."[27]

Third, like traditional Churches of Christ, the Boston movement placed great emphasis on good works — understood as discipleship — with little sense of mercy or grace. Further, in its efforts to sustain the "total commitment" of its members, it kept in place the system of "discipleship partners" that had been implemented by the earlier Crossroads movement.[28] It was this system, more than anything else, that occasioned the charge of "cultism" from both the general public and the mainstream tradition. Flavil Yeakley, a leader among traditional Churches of Christ and one of the Boston movement's chief critics, complained that

> the word "discipling" is used in this movement to mean much more than making converts. It is used primarily to describe a system of intense training and close personal supervision of the Christians being discipled. . . . The person being discipled is taught to submit to . . . [and] imitate the discipler. Christians being discipled are required to confess their sins to their discipler. Such confession is followed by rebuke, correction, admonition, and prayer. If the person being discipled seems reluctant to confess sins, the discipler asks probing personal questions to elicit the confession.[29]

Fourth, McKean led the Boston movement to embrace an organizational structure radically different from that of traditional Churches of Christ. As we have seen throughout this book, from the outset in the nineteenth century traditional Churches of Christ had practiced a radically democratic polity and had prized their congregational autonomy. Churches of Christ always argued that the only legitimate spiritual shepherds in a given congregation were its elders, to whom even the minister was accountable. But the Boston movement devised an altogether different organizational strategy. Its phenomenal and often unwieldy growth in urban centers, coupled with a concern to provide effective care and governance for an increasingly far-flung membership, led McKean to devise a hierarchical system of church administration in which evangelist/administrators worked in various parts of the United States and abroad but ultimately all evangelistic work remained directly under his own supervision. He also specified that, in every congregation, "the lead evangelist worked with and, for the most part, led and discipled the elders to direct the affairs of a local church."[30]

Though originally designed to revitalize Churches of Christ, these various strategies of the Boston movement increasingly led to a break with the denomination that it had sought to reform.[31] By 1990, there was hardly any fellowship between these two traditions at all. And no wonder. By any measure, the Boston movement was a sect, standing against the larger culture and its various religious expressions. The more traditional Churches of Christ, on the other hand, though still tied to the language of sectarian orthodoxy, had become a denomination, fully in sync with the conservative values of the larger culture. By the 1990s, few in the mainstream tradition had much interest in "total commitment," at least as the Boston Church of Christ defined and implemented that notion.

The Theological Response: Rethinking the Restoration Vision

In 1963, Jimmy Allen, Bible professor at Harding College, lectured to over one hundred undergraduates in a course on the book of Romans. These students had come to Harding from congregations of Churches of Christ scattered all over the United States and abroad. Few if any were prepared for what they would hear when Allen came to Romans 8:1: "Therefore, there is now no condemnation for those who are in Christ Jesus."

When Allen read those words, he waxed warm and eloquent. The students sat in rapt attention. Their teacher explained that Christians are forgiven and redeemed solely through the grace of God in spite of their sins and failures, not because of their goodness or merit, and that no one can possibly be good enough, smart enough, or right enough to earn or deserve salvation. This was the first time most of these students had heard the doctrine of grace explained

With their rational approach to the Christian faith, Churches of Christ have typically shunned revivalism and revivals in favor of sponsoring "gospel meetings" that focus on rational explanations of the biblical text. Yet, a few preachers among Churches of Christ have developed a message and a style that could only be described as revivalistic. One such preacher was Jimmy R. Allen (1930-), Bible professor at Harding University, who baptized over 7,000 people in evangelistic campaigns from 1964 to 1982. Allen's exposition of the grace of God in a class on Romans sparked a virtual revival on the Harding College campus in 1963.
(Photo courtesy Harding University)

in this way, though they had all grown up in Churches of Christ. Most of them had heard grace defined in terms of God's response to human effort, not as unmerited favor. That night a virtual student revival erupted in the dormitories at Harding College.[32] In the years to come, many of the students involved in this event would help lead a sizable segment of Churches of Christ in new directions.

Rediscovering the Theme of Grace

The fact is, Allen's class at Harding College was only a small slice of a significant revival that swept through a large number of Churches of Christ in the 1960s, reorienting many in the tradition away from a preoccupation with law and pattern toward a preoccupation with the grace of God and the power of the Holy Spirit.

It is hardly surprising that a grace-oriented revival would occur at Harding College: the institution had been the stronghold of a grace-oriented theology in Churches of Christ since the days of J. N. Armstrong (see Chap. 7). But why did this revival occur on a national scale, and why did it happen when it did?

In the first place, Churches of Christ found the themes that dominated this revival in their core scriptural text — the New Testament. Second, there was considerable precedent for this emphasis, since many Churches of Christ, especially on the Stone-Lipscomb side of the tradition, had held strongly to notions of divine grace and power throughout the nineteenth century. Though weakened, these themes persisted into the twentieth century in the thinking of such people as R. H. Boll, K. C. Moser, and G. C. Brewer (see Chap. 8) and the legacy they left behind. Indeed, the text Jimmy Allen used in his 1963 course on Romans at Harding College was K. C. Moser's *The Gist of Romans*.

But why a revival of this sort in the 1960s? There are several possible answers to this question, but two seem especially compelling. Within the church, the legalism that had dominated the tradition since World War I did much to discredit the restoration vision, especially for the younger generation of the 1960s. Many within Churches of Christ began to question or reject outright the rational and legal ideals associated with their heritage. Many began to long for a more subjective, relational understanding of the Christian faith.

A similar shift occurred in the larger culture. As we noted in Chapter 13, many of the troubling issues of the 1960s — the persistence of racism, the spread of environmental pollution, and unending war in Vietnam — helped discredit the Enlightenment-based notion that the application of reason would somehow solve all the problems of the world and usher in a golden age. Americans generally turned away from unconditional faith in scientific objectivity and sought out instead the subjective dimensions of human life, the supernatural, and the power of human relationships.

Caught up in these general trends, many Churches of Christ began to define themselves less in terms of legal codes and more in terms of relationships, both with God and with other human beings. Many found the basis for this new orientation in the biblical documents that had been their focus for so many years. There they inevitably discovered the love and grace of God and the power of an indwelling Holy Spirit, and these themes revitalized a substantial portion of Churches of Christ throughout the 1970s and 1980s.

The Hermeneutic Crisis

But that was only half the story. If the generation of the 1960s and 1970s rediscovered a theology of grace, the generation of the 1980s inherited a far more difficult task. It fell to them to ask whether the older restoration vision that had defined Churches of Christ since the early nineteenth century was compatible with the new theology of grace and, if so, how. It also fell to them to ask how the fundamentally modern, Enlightenment foundations of Churches of Christ might comport with the new postmodern culture of the United States, which resisted Enlightenment empiricism.

These challenges demanded nothing less than a reevaluation of the traditional hermeneutic of Churches of Christ — that is, how they understood the Bible. For many years, most in this tradition had understood the Bible as a blueprint or scientific manual offering rational guidelines for reconstructing the primitive church. Now, in a culture skeptical of unadorned rationalism, many in Churches of Christ turned to subjective and relational ways of understanding both the Bible and the Christian faith. Almost every nook and cranny of Churches of Christ felt the impact of these transformations in one way or another. Only those congregations most entrenched in nineteenth-century patterns of rationality and empiricism escaped them.

Events surrounding the sale of the *Firm Foundation* in its hundredth year of publication provide one measure of the wrenching hermeneutical changes that engulfed Churches of Christ in those years. Reuel Lemmons had edited this paper since 1955 and, with reference to the doctrinal issues that divided Churches of Christ, had pursued a course of moderation. Many viewed him as an enlightened spokesperson who opposed liberalism on the one hand but who also resisted legalism and radical conservativism. But in 1983, the *Firm Foundation*'s owner sold the paper to H. A. (Buster) Dobbs and Bill Cline, representatives of the conservative wing of Churches of Christ. These "new owners have made it clear," Lemmons lamented, "that they intend to select an entire new staff and direct the paper in a direction entirely different from the middle-of-the-road course in which we have kept it." Lemmons made no attempt to disguise his disappointment.

> We find this new direction incompatible with our thinking. For 28 years and 8 months we have plead [*sic*] for unity and not division. We have been willing to allow a brother to express an opposing viewpoint, and have been willing to give a brother the benefit of the doubt until all the facts were in. We have . . . refused to fan the flames of controversy.[33]

When the new *Firm Foundation* appeared in August of 1983, it was an altogether different venture from the journal Lemmons had edited for almost thirty years.

Almost immediately, people loyal to the old *Firm Foundation* began to dream of a new journal that might provide Churches of Christ with another voice of moderation. Under the leadership of Denny Boultinghouse, a young journalist from West Monroe, Louisiana, the new journal appeared in June of 1985 with the title *Image* and with Reuel Lemmons as its editor.[34] Lemmons's opening editorial clearly reflected the hermeneutic shifts that were overtaking Churches of Christ. In the course of stating the purpose of the new journal and explaining the significance of its name, Lemmons said nothing about the biblical pattern for proper worship or church organization. In fact, he said nothing about the *Bible* as pattern at all. Instead, he spoke of *Jesus* as the pattern for authentic human life. "This magazine," Lemmons wrote, "shall have one goal and one purpose — to mould men more perfectly into the image of Jesus Christ."[35] This is not to suggest that either Lemmons or his new journal had abandoned the New Testament as a pattern for the church, for they had not. But the hermeneutic lens had changed focus dramatically since Lemmons became editor of the *Firm Foundation* in 1955.

If preachers and editors had to grapple with the hermeneutic shifts overtaking Churches of Christ, so did the scholars. Several young teachers in Church of Christ–related colleges and universities formally addressed these issues in the summers of 1992 and 1993 when they called together colloquia of scholars and church leaders to consider the topic "The Churches of Christ in a Post-Modern World."[36]

In the course of their deliberations, they were unavoidably confronted with the issue of the nature of the Bible. Was it primarily an ancient constitution or blueprint that must govern every aspect of church life, from its terms of admission to worship and church organization? That had been the position of Alexander Campbell, who had shaped the way Churches of Christ had understood the Bible for almost two centuries. Or was the Bible principally a theological treatise, describing a God who seeks relationship with his children and whose relationship with them sustains their relations with one another? Put another way, would the traditional understanding of the Bible as blueprint or pattern for the church sustain the new theology of grace? Would it sustain the Churches of Christ in a postmodern world? Or was another paradigm in order? These questions constituted what many described as the "hermeneutic crisis" among Churches of Christ.

Stated in this way, the problem inherited by this generation was difficult enough. But a long-standing assumption regarding biblical interpretation compounded the problem immeasurably. Churches of Christ leaders had long maintained that New Testament law is manifested in three categories: direct commands, examples, and necessary inferences. Implicit in the thought of Alexander Campbell and explicit in the writings of Moses Lard (see Chap. 3), this assumption prevailed among Churches of Christ throughout the twentieth century. In 1958, J. D. Thomas, the influential head of the Bible Department at Abilene Christian College, virtually canonized this theme in his book *We Be Brethren*, an attempt to legitimate efforts by mainstream Churches of Christ in the 1950s to create institutions that transcended the local church (see Chap. 10). To substantiate his own hermeneutical base, Thomas argued that the command–example–necessary inference hermeneutic had "in general been accepted by all of us since the beginning of the Restoration period of church history."[37] But while the hermeneutic issue of the 1980s was indeed shaped by the full two-century history of Churches of Christ, the institutional controversy of the 1950s was especially important in establishing the terms of the debate.

Granted, there were many in the churches in the 1980s who never bothered with questions regarding hermeneutics. For many traditionalists, the questions never arose at all, and many progressives chose to ignore them as they happily pressed ahead with visions of grace and a spirit-filled life. Yet, the progressives implicitly raised these questions by structuring their churches around concerns fundamentally different from those that guided their forebears throughout most of the history of Churches of Christ.

Thus Thomas H. Olbricht was correct when he argued that the "herme-neutic crisis" actually reflected a "paradigm shift" at the grassroots level. He characterized the new paradigm as one in which church members concerned themselves not so much with biblical patterns for the church as with "a more meaningful relationship with God and the members of his body."[38]

While few at the grassroots level of the churches addressed the sorts of questions that the paradigm shift inspired, many younger intellectuals — espe-cially those who had been trained in graduate programs in religion — found they

As a professor of Bible and biblical theology for nineteen years at Abilene Christian University (1967-86) and for ten years at Pepperdine University (1986-96), Thomas H. Olbricht (1929-) exerted a significant impact on the content of preaching in Churches of Christ in the closing years of the twentieth century. Olbricht argued that Churches of Christ should focus their restorationist lens on a recovery of biblical theology centered in the "core message" of Scripture and in "the mighty acts of God." He claimed that the starting point for a proper understanding of the Bible "is God, Christ, and the Holy Spirit, rather than commands, examples, and necessary inferences." Olbricht articulated his emphasis in several books, including *The Message of the New Testament, He Loves Forever,* and *The Power to Be.*
(Photo courtesy Thomas H. Olbricht)

could not escape them. Several older scholars had, in fact, addressed these questions some twenty years before, when the paradigm shift was only beginning. Olbricht, for example, confronted the issues as early as 1965. "In my opinion," he wrote,

> Campbell got us headed in the wrong direction. . . . I think he was wrong in seeing it [the Bible] as a collection of facts, the unity of which emerges from the individual facts themselves. What he should have done is to raise the question of what are the great themes of the scriptures of God's love shown in his deeds of sin and salvation and then interpreted the individual facts in that light.[39]

But in 1965 it was still far too early for a widespread assessment of this problem.

By the mid-1980s, however, the dilemma was apparent to far more people than had recognized it in the mid-1960s. Theological confusion now abounded in both pulpit and pew, and a variety of younger scholars attempted to diagnose the problem. Russ Dudrey, for example, suggested that Churches of Christ had arrived "at an impasse." Why? "Because our model is ill-suited to the nature of biblical literature." Dudrey then lamented,

> As a Christian and as a restorationist, I know that in the final analysis what is at stake in our hermeneutic is not merely the success of Restorationism; at stake is our knowledge of the Father. Hardline patternism approaches Scripture as a revelation of propositional truths rather than of the heart of the Father. Surely we subvert our model of the character of God if we require our hermeneutic to address such scholasticizing issues as . . . how we should read the blueprint of New Testament case law.

Dudrey went on to suggest that while "Protestant Scholasticism hypostatized Justification by Faith, making it a sort of theological talisman, we have hypostatized Justification by Necessary Inference."

What should be done? "We must make a shift in our model of biblical literature," Dudrey argued, "a shift perhaps as radical as the change of paradigms that Thomas S. Kuhn argues takes place in scientific revolutions." He urged Churches of Christ to abandon the notion that the Bible is a collection of empirical facts and embrace the New Testament instead as a collection of documents, "far less systematic and far more historical, particular, and occasional — far more 'missionary' — than we have recognized."[40]

Along similar lines, Gary Collier bemoaned the fact that Churches of Christ, with their traditional emphasis on the "objective" facts of Scripture, finally left little room for the "subjective" dimensions of biblical faith.[41] In Collier's view, traditional Churches of Christ had created a Bible

> that does not relate to people where they live (mired in sin), but only requires of them a rigid attention to commands, examples, and necessary inferences

to decipher God's pattern requirements — in spite of theoretical statements to the contrary; and we have churches that are dying because they have forgotten the meaning of Jesus' statement, "I desire mercy and not sacrifice," or at least they have not figured out how such a statement can fit into the rationalist/inductive approach as it exists.[42]

Thomas Olbricht, who had been working with these issues for some thirty years, offered perhaps his most cogent assessment of the problem in 1991, when he addressed a group of graduate students at Princeton Theological Seminary. There, Olbricht lamented that Churches of Christ

> have probed in depth neither a Biblical doctrine of atonement nor Christ's word and work as the forerunner for our life style. We have focused rather on a plan of salvation which culminates in baptism. . . . While we suppose God to be very important as creator and sustainer and the father of our Lord Jesus Christ, we have reflected little upon his steadfast involvement with humankind. . . . We have viewed man as sinner and in need of salvation, but chiefly as a violator of rules rather than as one who fails to love God with all his heart, soul and strength.

Olbricht argued that in fact "the focal point in scripture is the mighty loving action of God on behalf of man made in his image and the universe he has created" and hence that the starting point for hermeneutics should be "God, Christ, and the Holy Spirit, rather than commands, examples, and necessary inferences, regardless of how helpful these may be in regard to specific matters of church order."[43]

These kinds of critiques both reflected and fed the storm of controversy that now engulfed the Churches of Christ. In September of 1989, under a banner headline reading "Bible Interpretation Controversy Smoulders," the *Christian Chronicle* reported that "one subject keeps cropping up in sermons, articles, retreats and lectureships these days — how to interpret the Bible." Indeed, the question of biblical hermeneutics went straight to the heart of the traditional identity of Churches of Christ.

In many ways, Rubel Shelly's career reflects in microcosm the hermeneutic changes that were occurring in the tradition during this period. In the late 1960s, Shelly was a protégé of Thomas B. Warren, one of the principal leaders of the conservative wing of the church and a cofounder (with Warren) of the *Spiritual Sword* (see Chap. 13). By the late 1970s, however, Shelly was seriously rethinking that orientation, and in the early 1980s he emerged as a leader of a new generation of reformers within Churches of Christ.[44]

In 1984, Shelly made what amounted to his personal declaration of independence from sectarian orthodoxies in a book entitled *I Just Want to Be a Christian*. He wrote the book in an effort to reclaim for twentieth-century Churches of Christ the nondenominational vision that had driven the tradition

Rubel Shelly (1945-), a young and celebrated spokesperson for the conservative wing of Churches of Christ in the late 1960s, underwent a conversion in the late 1970s and, by the early 1980s, emerged as a leader of a new generation of reformers within Churches of Christ. In his new role, Shelly pointed Christians not so much to the pattern of the ancient church as to the pattern provided in the life and death of Jesus Christ. In 1992, along with Phillip Morrison and Mike Cope, Shelly launched a new publication called *Wineskins* intended, as Shelly put it, "to be a catalyst for reform within a heritage of reformers."

(Photo courtesy Jerry Rushford)

in its earliest years. Though he had abandoned his earlier exclusivist orientation, this book still reflected the traditional nondenominational agenda — and the traditional hermeneutic — of Churches of Christ.

Then, in 1992, along with Randall Harris, a young philosophy professor at David Lipscomb University, Shelly wrote *The Second Incarnation: A Theology for the Twenty-first Century Church*. In this book, Shelly and Harris returned in some degree to the apocalyptic orientation that had characterized the Stone-Lipscomb tradition in the nineteenth century. "We resist," they wrote, "the arrogant claim that we [the Churches of Christ] embody the fullness of the kingdom of God. Yet we long for a 'rich welcome into the eternal kingdom of our Lord and Savior Jesus Christ' . . . [and] commit ourselves to pursuing the kingdom lifestyle."[45] At the same time, they categorically rejected the notion that Churches of Christ had reproduced the "golden age" of the church. Such a claim, they suggested, was "both historically inaccurate and theologically dangerous," since it "claims ultimacy and perfection for human efforts at some particular point in history."[46]

Instead of prescribing a new pattern for Churches of Christ, Shelly and Harris sought to underscore relationship — the same theme that according to Olbricht stood at the heart of the paradigm shift. Specifically, they argued, relationship with Christ himself was the central dimension of authentic Christian faith: "Why are we the church? Is it just because we have duplicated a pattern? No, but because we have been made alive in Christ. To be the church is the meaning of our new life, to live as his spiritual body in the world."[47]

In 1992, Shelly, Phillip Morrison, and Mike Cope (another young reformer and preacher for the Highland Church of Christ in Abilene, Texas) launched a new journal called *Wineskins* devoted to communicating the gospel in the language of contemporary culture. "The church must be light on its feet," declared the new journal's statement of purpose. "It must address the spirit of time and place without absorbing it. The body of Christ must be an elastic wineskin for the gospel wine rather than a brittle liability to it."[48]

Further, as Shelly noted, *Wineskins* was "intended to be a catalyst for reform (i.e., bold and responsible change) within a heritage of reformers."[49] But the sort of reform that *Wineskins* sought was inconsistent with the traditional notion of Scripture as constitution or blueprint for the church. Specifically, the founders of the journal sought to foster "Christocentric study of scripture that can challenge the church to act out the meaning of Christ for this age."[50]

Thus Shelly, Morrison, and Cope championed many of the ideals held by Barton Stone, David Lipscomb, and R. H. Boll, but they pointedly backed away from the highly rational orthodoxy that had descended from the Campbell side of the movement and that had dominated Churches of Christ since World War I. No one saw this more clearly than the conservatives from whom Shelly had declared his independence. As Shelly later recalled, the reaction he experienced from those quarters was "quick and severe," though not unexpected. After all,

> I have sat in their council meetings; I know the strategy of attacking and defaming. I, too, have refused to hear, hurled my theological missiles, and thought myself "contending for the faith" all the while. I deserve the fate I have suffered at their hands, for it is right for one to reap as he has sowed.[51]

In a fundamental sense, *Wineskins* served the same function for the generation of the 1990s that *Mission* had served for the generation of the 1960s and 1970s. Both publications sought to communicate the gospel to a contemporary culture in language that the culture could understand, and both assumed the mantle of reformer. The difference lay chiefly in the fact that in the 1960s Churches of Christ largely resisted the kind of renewal that *Mission* sought to achieve, thereby relegating *Mission* to the status of gadfly to the mainstream tradition.

By the 1990s, however, *Wineskins* found widespread receptivity to its message — testimony to the extent to which many Churches of Christ had changed since the 1960s. But the change taking place among Churches of Christ was no mere reform, no mere evolutionary development within the bounds of traditional nineteenth-century assumptions. Rather, it was fundamentally a paradigm shift — a shift from a patternistic version of Christian primitivism filtered through the grid of Lockean empiricism and Scottish Common Sense rationalism to an emphasis on the subjective dimensions of the Christian religion — faith, hope, and love realized in the lives of believers through the power and grace of God. Put another way, the new understanding of Scripture emphasized the power of God to create relationships with and among human beings and to inaugurate thereby a new community of believers.

To a great extent, Churches of Christ were moving squarely into the orbit of American evangelical Christianity. A telling indication of that fact was the immense popularity in evangelical circles of the various books written by Max Lucado, a Church of Christ preacher in San Antonio.[52] But, even more significantly, Lucado's popularity in evangelical circles seemed to render him even more acceptable among Churches of Christ. He regularly spoke on Church of Christ–sponsored forums and lectureships throughout the United States.

Disagreement and Resistance

Having said all this, two caveats are in order. First, while dissatisfaction with the old rational paradigm was widespread among Churches of Christ in the waning years of the twentieth century, and while many Churches of Christ were groping for a more relational model that might inform their theology and identity, there was little agreement on precisely what that model might be or how it might be developed. Put another way, Churches of Christ still were caught in an identity crisis of significant proportions.

Second, while reassessment of tradition swept through Churches of Christ and touched thousands of individual believers, it nonetheless failed to touch a sizable segment of this communion. Most of the churches that remained unaffected by the renewal were in small towns and rural areas, but some urban congregations also resisted the winds of change. The renewal also failed to touch in any meaningful way the predominantly African American congregations, whether urban or rural; they remained deeply committed to the Enlightenment paradigms of the past and typically believed without qualification that the Church of Christ was the one true church, outside of which there was no salvation.

One significant gauge of the depth and power of resistance to both renewal and change in the early 1990s was the immense popularity of a book entitled *The Cultural Church,* by F. LaGard Smith, a professor in Pepperdine University's School of Law. A product of the anti-institutional movement of the 1950s who had subsequently moved into the mainstream of Churches of Christ, Smith did not think well of the various efforts to rethink the traditional hermeneutic of his heritage. The immediate catalyst for his book was a presentation by Michael Casey, another Pepperdine professor, who argued for a narrative approach to Scripture.[53] Smith held to the traditional belief that the Bible is essentially a book of rules and guidelines and that the "command–example–necessary inference" hermeneutic provides the only way to be faithful to the biblical text. He was convinced that proposals like Casey's could deprive Churches of Christ of the authority of Scripture altogether.[54]

Smith went on to argue that efforts to rethink the traditional Church of Christ hermeneutic were nothing more than responses to popular culture. Proponents of the "new hermeneutic," he suggested, were more interested in being politically correct than in being faithful to Scripture. And he claimed that a single cultural/political issue was at the bottom of all the ferment — what he

In their almost two hundred–year history, Churches of Christ have seldom interacted in meaningful ways with the world of American evangelical Christianity. Yet, by the 1990s, that was changing. No one demonstrated this fact better than Max Lucado (1955-), pulpit preacher for the Oak Hills Church of Christ in San Antonio, Texas, since 1987, whose books were national best-sellers in the evangelical book market. Among those titles were *No Wonder They Call Him the Savior, God Came Near, Six Hours One Friday, The Applause of Heaven, In the Eye of the Storm, And the Angels Were Silent, He Still Moves Stones, When God Whispers Your Name,* and *A Gentle Thunder.*
(Photo courtesy Jerry Rushford)

called "the women's issue." This issue was a "perfect catalyst" for radical change, he said, because

> it combines utilitarian practicality, current notions of political correctness, and an obvious case for tolerance — all in one neat package. . . . And here is the connection with hermeneutics: Those who support a wider role for women have little choice but to get rid of the "old hermeneutic." Taking "command, example, and necessary inference" seriously would mean having to accept the well-documented biblical principle of male spiritual leadership at face value.[55]

The Role of Women

Smith was correct when he identified the role of women as a pivotal issue troubling many congregations of Churches of Christ throughout the United States in the early 1990s. But there is reason to believe he was wrong in arguing that this issue had spawned the hermeneutic crisis. In fact, the evidence suggests that it worked the other way around. During the 1970s and 1980s, literally hundreds of congregations experienced theological reorientation while failing to address in any meaningful way the role of women in either their worship assemblies or their organizational structure. The women's issue rose to prominence later.

Moreover, it seems unlikely that the women's issue could have arisen in Churches of Christ in a significant way had the ground not been prepared by the widespread shift in biblical understanding that occurred in the 1970s and the 1980s. Certainly the issue had shown no significant signs of life within the tradition during the previous hundred years. But the hermeneutical shift both allowed and demanded consideration of the role of women in the worship and organization of the church. It *allowed* consideration of the topic by calling into question the basis on which meaningful female participation had to that point been denied — namely, a patternistic reading of Scripture. It *demanded* consideration of the topic, since the new understanding of Scripture focused on relationship within a community of believers — the relationship God had established with human beings and the relationship they now shared with one another through divine redemption. Many reached the conclusion that excluding women from meaningful roles in the church would violate the basic principles of a relationship- and community-centered theology.

Of course, changes occurring in the larger culture also influenced the debate over this issue within Churches of Christ. Between the 1960s and the 1990s, the campaign for women's rights effected significant changes in American society. Increasing numbers of women worked outside the home, in an increasing diversity of professions. These sorts of changes had taken place among the

Charlotte Fall Fanning (1809-1896), educator, philanthropist, and writer, worked with her husband, Tolbert Fanning, to open a short-lived school at Franklin, Tennessee, in 1837. After she and Tolbert in 1840 successfully established Franklin College, a school for young men located five miles east of Nashville, Charlotte launched a school for young women which met in her home. The Franklin College building burned in 1865, and Charlotte and Tolbert opened in 1866 a school for girls which they called Hope Institute and which operated until Tolbert's death in 1874. Ten years later, in 1884, Charlotte launched the Fanning Orphan School, which continued to operate until 1943 when the city of Nashville purchased the property for construction of the municipal airport. As a young woman, Charlotte learned Hebrew, Greek, Latin, German, and French, and taught French at the Female Academy of Nashville before she met Tolbert. She wrote for the *Gospel Advocate*, which Tolbert began in 1865, signing her articles simply, "C. F."
(Photo courtesy David Lipscomb University)

membership of Churches of Christ as well. But the women who had attained new prominence and power in the business world and the professions found the opportunities available to them in the churches to be greatly restricted by comparison. They began to view Churches of Christ as seriously out of sync with the other spheres of their lives. Many younger professional women began leaving Churches of Christ for other fellowships that afforded them greater opportunities for participation.

Thus, for a variety of reasons, the women's issue rose to prominence throughout the fellowship of Churches of Christ in the late 1980s and early 1990s. While a few women called for opportunities to preach, many more sought to participate in such roles as chairing committees, serving as deaconesses, making announcements in the context of Sunday morning worship, officiating at the communion service, passing the communion to the congregation, leading singing, leading in public prayer, reading Scripture before the entire congregation, or teaching a Bible class composed of adults of both genders. With few exceptions, Churches of Christ had restricted all these roles to males for over a hundred years. It was symbolic of the tradition's male orientation that the term used most frequently by its members — both male and female — to designate their own fellowship was "the brotherhood."

This had not always been the case, however. In the earliest years of the tradition, it was not uncommon for women to preach, exhort, or testify among those Churches of Christ associated with Barton Stone. Isaac Jones told of Nancy Mulkey, who preached powerful sermons in the first decade of the nineteenth century. She was a daughter of John Mulkey, the former Separate Baptist preacher who led many Separate Baptists into the Stone movement shortly after the turn of the century. Jones reported that she

> was a shouter, as then called. While the popular style was to shout "Glory Hallelujah," or simply to scream one scream after another, accompanied by violent jerks, jumping up and down, or clapping of hands till exhausted, she would arise with zeal on her countenance and fire in her eyes, and with a pathos that showed the depth of her soul, and would pour forth an exhortation lasting from five to fifteen minutes, which neither father nor brother could *equal*, and which brought tears from every feeling eye.[56]

Joseph Thomas also told of hearing her preach — "surely by the power of the Holy Ghost" — in 1810. He recalled that "many felt the weight of her exhortation, and some were mourning under conviction the greater part of the night."[57]

Many of the Stoneite congregations that utilized women in these ways, however, rebelled against Stone's union with Alexander Campbell in 1832 and joined the Christian Connection that descended from Elias Smith and Abner Jones in New England and James O'Kelley in Virginia (see Chap. 5). For this reason, few if any of these congregations ever flowed directly into the lineage of Churches of Christ.

Still, the evidence suggests that at least some Churches of Christ influenced by both Stone and Campbell utilized both deacons and deaconesses throughout the first half of the nineteenth century. The early "creed" that John R. Howard drew up in 1848, for example, which was designed to explain the "original marks" of the true church, acknowledged both "deacons and deaconesses."[58] Further, an ad hoc committee from various Stoneite congregations in Tennessee

Selena M. Holman (1850-1915) wrote often in the *Gospel Advocate* regarding the role of women in the home and in the church, and provided pivotal leadership for the temperance crusade in her home state of Tennessee. In published articles, she took issue with David Lipscomb and other *Gospel Advocate* editors and writers who sought to restrict women to a traditional and subservient role in the church. Holman believed that if a woman could speak on religious topics to a small group of men and women within a home, she could speak to hundreds in the context of the church. Claiming that "a good wife earns her own living," she ridiculed the notion that husbands "support" their wives. A life-long advocate of temperance, Holman became president of the Tennessee Women's Christian Temperance Union in 1896, and, under her leadership, membership in the state organization increased from 200 to 4,000. David Lipscomb, editor of the *Advocate,* described Holman as a "strong minded woman," resisted her activities in a temperance society, and claimed her articles gave him "the blues." The state of Tennessee honored Holman in 1917 when her portrait was placed in the capitol building in Nashville.

issued a report in 1835 with recommendations for proper organizational structures in the churches. Among other things, that report suggested, "Let us choose
Bishops, Deacons, and deaconesses. Let them rule and minister according to
the law of God. Let the churches submit to their rulers, as those who watch
over them for good."[59] While it is difficult to know how to appraise these reports,

Sarah S. Andrews (1893-1961) served from 1916 to 1961 as a missionary to Japan, where her work proved the most enduring of any mission activity undertaken in that country by members of Churches of Christ. From 1916 to 1919, she studied Japanese language and customs in Tokyo, then moved to Okitsu-machi in Shizuoka Prefecture, where she opened a public nursery, established women's societies, and shared the Christian gospel with those with whom she came into contact. She built two churches in Shizuoka Prefecture, one in Okitsu and one in Shizuoka City. By the time of her death in 1961, her work had produced a total of eight congregations. During World War II, the Japanese government placed her in a prison camp until September, 1942, then confined her to house arrest for the remainder of the war. She later recalled that "after months of meatless days I relished grasshoppers for meat." Her weight dropped during those years to seventy-five pounds. In 1946, a Japanese official wrote in a letter of commendation, "Throughout the 30 years that she has been here, her career has been wholly devoted to social work, such as the preaching of the Gospel, managing of [her] Kindergarten, and relief of the sick and the helpless. She has often suffered insufficient funds for her work and went home to America three times to raise the necessary funds, while she herself has been living in contented poverty, which fact is making a deep impression upon people about her." In 1952 Andrews began mission activity in Namazu City, and erected a church building there in 1954. When she died in Japan in 1961, the Japanese people, both Christian and non-Christian, built a memorial at her burial site.
(Photo courtesy Harry Robert Fox Jr.)

Annie C. Tuggle (1890-1976) served African American Churches of Christ as a missionary, an educator, and a historian. While attending G. P. Bowser's Silver Point Christian Institute in 1913, she became a field agent for that school, raising funds throughout Tennessee, Arkansas, and Mississippi. In the 1940s, Bowser commissioned her to serve in a similar capacity on behalf of his Bowser Christian Institute in Fort Smith, Arkansas. Before moving to Detroit in 1944, she taught in the Nashville Christian Institute, presided over by Marshall Keeble. Following several years of mission activity in Jamaica, the Bahamas, and Haiti, Tuggle compiled and published the first directory of African American Churches of Christ, which she entitled *Our Ministers and Song Leaders of the Church of Christ*. Drawing on a rich store of personal experience within that tradition, she published in 1973 her autobiography, *Another World Wonder*, which effectively served as a history of black Churches of Christ for most of the twentieth century.
(Photo from Annie C. Tuggle, *Another World Wonder*)

meaningful involvement of women in both the worship and governance of the churches had largely disappeared by the century's end. Several reasons for this decline might be suggested.

First, in a society in which the power structure had traditionally been both white and patriarchal, the realities of Reconstruction likely prompted a backlash not only against blacks but also against women. The eclipse of female involvement in southern Churches of Christ, therefore, might have been part of a general reassertion of white, male power in the aftermath of the Civil War. That, at least, is a thesis worth exploring.[60]

Second, as we have already noted, Churches of Christ, following Alexander Campbell, had long prized objective rationality and deemphasized the emotional component of faith and worship. Perhaps stereotypical beliefs that women were more emotional (and hence less rational) than men motivated the male leadership of the tradition to exclude them from positions of power. There is evidence of this sort of thinking in David Lipscomb's objections to congregations that allowed women too much latitude. Such congregations, he wrote, permitted "perversions of the service of God," since a woman's "strong emotional nature demands whatever strikes her fancy, whether authorized by the Lord or not."[61] Put another way, Churches of Christ excluded women for the same reason they excluded the Holy Spirit: both appeared unmanageable and therefore threatening to a "brotherhood" that put a high priority on preserving order and control based on strictly rational considerations.

Third, in the context of the struggle for women's suffrage, women in the liberal wing of the Stone-Campbell movement organized the Christian Woman's Board of Missions in 1874. This organization offended southern conservatives, including David Lipscomb, on a number of grounds. For one thing, it was formed in the context of the larger struggle to gain for women the right to vote — a right Lipscomb judged as questionable at best and demonic at worst, since he believed that Christians should not vote at all. Furthermore, southern conservatives viewed the organization as just one more human society seeking to undermine the God-given prerogatives of the church. Finally, Lipscomb and his colleagues considered the people involved in the formation of the board fundamentally disrespectful of the Bible because they ran with the crowd that accepted missionary societies, instrumental music in the worship, and the new critical understandings of Scripture. It was a classic case of guilt by association. For all these reasons, contributors to the *Gospel Advocate* in the 1880s voiced strong objections to women voting on the one hand and preaching on the other.

This general opposition to an expanded role for women in the churches escalated in 1892, when David Lipscomb launched a consistent and sustained attack on the Christian Woman's Board of Missions.[62] In that year, the CWBM met jointly with the General Christian Missionary Society in David Lipscomb's own backyard — Nashville, Tennessee. This was more than Lipscomb could tolerate, and he vociferously complained, "Every man who encourages [the women's board] works against God, the church, womanhood, the interest of the family, motherhood, and against true manhood itself."[63] Five years later, in 1897, Lipscomb essentially disfellowshiped the Disciples of Christ.[64]

Fred Bailey, the authoritative historian of these nineteenth-century dynamics, has suggested that the struggle over the role of women may well have been the single issue that finally pushed Lipscomb to break fellowship with the Disciples.[65]

Through her speaking and her writing, Bobbie Lee Holley (1927-) actively promoted a more meaningful role for women among Churches of Christ several years before mainline Churches of Christ undertook consideration of this issue in the 1980s and 1990s. For example, she served as the keynote speaker for a "Women in Christ" seminar at the University Church of Christ, Austin, Texas, in 1975, and as one of several keynote speakers for a seminar involving black and white Christian women in Detroit in 1969. From that seminar grew at least one integrated congregation, the Strathmoor Church of Christ in Detroit. She also was the first woman to serve on the board of trustees of *Mission* magazine, later served as book review editor for that publication, and finally served as editor of *Mission* from 1982 to 1988. (Photo courtesy Bobbie Lee Holley)

If so, that action virtually canonized as formal orthodoxy for Churches of Christ the subjection of women in church affairs. In any event, the acrimonious debate over this issue in the 1880s and 1890s contributed greatly to defining the identity of Churches of Christ in terms of a male-dominated fellowship.

Finally, in seeking to understand the decline of meaningful involvement on the part of women among Churches of Christ, we ought not to ignore the "pattern" hermeneutic that Alexander Campbell introduced into the tradition. A scientific, literal reading of such key passages of Scripture as 1 Corinthians 14 and 1 Timothy 2 provided conclusive evidence to many that women were obligated to "remain silent in the churches" — even though a handful of notable preachers in the history of Churches of Christ (e.g., C. R. Nichol and J. D. Tant) dismissed that consensus as a fundamental misinterpretation of Scripture.[66]

Helen M. Young (1918-), perhaps the most visible and influential woman among Churches of Christ in the second half of the twentieth century, has spoken regularly since the late 1940s for women's classes in local congregations and on lectureships sponsored by Church of Christ–related colleges. With deep roots in the Stone-Lipscomb tradition of Churches of Christ, she has emphasized practical Christian living, the spiritual life, and the role of the Christian woman in the modern world. In 1950, she and her husband, M. Norvel Young — at that time the pulpit minister for the Broadway Church of Christ, Lubbock, Texas — began production of a daily devotional guide called *Power for Today,* which quickly achieved a remarkable circulation among Churches of Christ. From 1950 to 1975, Helen served as managing editor, assigning and editing virtually all the articles that appeared in *Power for Today* during those years. Arguably, this publication helped enhance the spiritual dimensions of a tradition dominated by rational analysis of the biblical text and haunted since the 1930s by internal quarrels over a variety of doctrinal issues. In 1958, Helen founded Associated Women for Pepperdine, a women's auxiliary dedicated to the support of George Pepperdine College where her husband served as president from 1958 through 1971. She has also served on the board of directors of a number of civic organizations including Freedom's Foundation in Valley Forge, Pennsylvania; and the Los Angeles Area Chamber of Commerce.
(Photo courtesy Helen Young)

By the late 1960s, however, the "pattern" hermeneutic came under close and severe scrutiny, especially in *Mission* and *Integrity.* Not surprisingly, several writers in those two journals pressed for greater and more meaningful involvement of women in the worship and leadership of Churches of Christ.[67] For the most part, however, those who addressed this issue in *Mission* and *Integrity* wrote and spoke only to themselves. Few among the larger fellowship of Churches of Christ were listening.

At the same time, however, the various campus ministries of the 1960s and 1970s implicitly — and perhaps unwittingly — prompted reconsideration of this question. The significant growth of those ministries created the need for ministers to serve both the male and female populations on college campuses. Without much theological discussion, some churches began to employ women to minister to female students. Although these ministers were usually called "women's counselors" rather than ministers, their employment was nonetheless a significant step, because it marked the first time, at least in the twentieth century, that a woman was actually paid by a local congregation to teach the Bible, to provide leadership in campus ministry activities, and to evangelize in the campus community. The fact that these ministries were oriented toward women and restricted to college student communities does not diminish the indirect acknowledgment on the part of some congregations that women were capable of thinking, teaching, evangelizing, and leading in the same ways as men.

By the 1980s and 1990s, as a major paradigm shift rapidly worked its way through Churches of Christ, the question of the role of women in the tradition increased in importance, and a few congregations took steps to offer women more meaningful opportunities to minister.[68] In the 1990s, a host of congregations throughout the United States were discussing this issue. Many people apparently concluded that such a reexamination was in order once they began to read the Bible more as a theological treatise and less as a legal blueprint, more in terms of relationship, community, and the subjective dimensions of faith, hope, and love, and less in terms of scientific objectivity.

Underscoring the extent to which this question was increasingly coming to the fore among Churches of Christ were the various public forums on the issue that were held at colleges and universities connected with the tradition. For example, Freed-Hardeman University, long regarded as a bastion of conservatism among Churches of Christ, sponsored such a forum in 1990, as did the Harding Graduate School of Religion in 1993. While these forums examined both the pros and cons of the issue, each featured men who had pioneered efforts to expand the opportunity for greater female participation in their own congregations. Robert M. Randolph of the Brookline, Massachusetts, Church of Christ and Lynn Mitchell, an elder of Houston's Bering Drive congregation, both spoke in favor of more meaningful involvement for women at the Freed-Hardeman forum, while Mitchell — this time alone — did so at Harding.[69]

Finally, it must be said that while many congregations were considering the issue of gender equality, there remained a good deal of resistance to greater involvement of women, especially in public worship, in a great many congregations throughout the United States. The resolution of this issue will eventually tell much about the depth of the renewal that came to Churches of Christ in the late twentieth century, but as of the early 1990s the issue was far from resolved.

Conclusions

As the final decade of the twentieth century dawned, the monolithic nonde-nominational temple that Churches of Christ had undertaken to build almost two hundred years before was in serious disrepair. Several factors had inflicted the damage.

First, at various points in its history, the residents of this temple had made subtle changes and additions to the original structure, claiming all the while that they had made no change at all. Some of these alterations provoked virulent family fights that badly damaged the temple's interior. More often than not, the losers in those fights, under considerable duress, simply packed their bags, moved out, and built a smaller temple somewhere else, following their inter-pretation of the original blueprints.

Second, in an effort to drive the premillennial side of the family out of the temple in the early years of the twentieth century, the majority of the family removed the apocalyptic pillar, one of the temple's two most important sup-ports. This alteration weakened the structure far more than anyone suspected at the time.

Third, only one support was still in place — a brittle restorationist pillar poured from a rationalist mold over two hundred years before. In the late twentieth century, a younger generation examined that support and found it riddled with cracks from having supported all of the temple's enormous weight. They reported the damage to their elders, but many of those elders accused them of fraud and misrepresentation. Others ignored both the report and the danger and proceeded with efforts to modernize and beautify the temple's interior as though nothing were amiss.

Over time, however, increasing numbers of people accepted the report. Convinced that the temple was in danger of collapsing, they and their children together undertook the urgent task of making repairs. In an effort to secure the temple firmly to a Christocentric foundation, they strengthened the restora-tionist support with faith, hope, and love and restored as well bits and pieces of the apocalyptic pillar that had been removed some fifty years before.

But as the work proceeded, serious questions remained. After all these years, who really were the inhabitants of this temple? Who and what had they become? Did they have a usable past? And more important, did they have a future as a cohesive Christian tradition?

Those are questions that must be answered by the people who make up this tradition. After all, they are the ones who have told, and will continue to tell, "the story of Churches of Christ in America."

Notes

Abbreviations Used in the Notes

ACR	*American Christian Review*
BB	*Bible Banner*
CB	*Christian Baptist*
CC	*Christian Chronicle*
CE	*Christian Echo*
CF	*Contending for the Faith*
CG	David Lipscomb, *Civil Government: Its Origin, Mission and Destiny, and the Christian's Relation to It* (Nashville: n.p., 1889)
CL	*Christian Leader*
CM	*Christian Messenger*
FCC	*First Century Christian*
FF	*Firm Foundation*
GA	*Gospel Advocate*
GG	*Gospel Guardian*
MH	*Millennial Harbinger*
RQ	*Restoration Quarterly*
SS	*Spiritual Sword*
20th CC	*20th Century Christian*
WW	*Word and Work*
Sewell Papers	Sewell Papers, Center for Restoration Studies, Abilene Christian University

Notes to Chapter 1

1. *The Encyclopedia of American Religions,* ed. J. Gordon Melton, vol. 2 (Tarrytown, N.Y.: Triumph Books, 1991), pp. 98-101.

2. *Churches of Christ in the United States,* comp. Mac Lynn (Nashville: Gospel Advocate, 1991), p. xiii.

3. See Richard T. Hughes, "Two Restoration Traditions: Mormons and Churches of Christ in the Nineteenth Century," *Journal of Mormon History* 19 (Spring 1993): 34-51.

4. On this theme, see Don Haymes, "The Road More Traveled: How the Churches of Christ Became a Denomination," *Mission Journal* 20 (March 1987): 4-8.

5. See Richard T. Hughes and C. Leonard Allen, *Illusions of Innocence: Protestant Primitivism in America, 1630-1875* (Chicago: University of Chicago Press, 1988).

6. Batsell Barrett Baxter and Carroll Ellis, "Neither Catholic, Protestant Nor Jew" (Nashville: Hillsboro Church of Christ, n.d.), p. 12. This pamphlet was first published by the Church of Christ that Meets on Granny White Pike (Nashville, 1959). See also Batsell Barrett Baxter, "What Is the Church of Christ?" — a pamphlet based on a sermon Baxter preached at the Hillsboro Church of Christ in Nashville, 23 January 1955, and also published by the Church of Christ that Meets on Granny White Pike in 1959. For these publication dates, see the congregational bulletin of the Church of Christ that Meets on Granny White Pike, *AIM*, 20 March 1959.

7. Srygley, "Are Christians in All Denominations?" in *The New Testament Church* (Nashville: Gospel Advocate, 1910), pp. 65ff.

8. Srygley, "The Current Reformation Not the Church," in *The New Testament Church*, pp. 25-26.

9. Campbell, *The Christian System* (1839; reprint, Cincinnati: Standard Publishing Co., 1901), p. 55.

10. Campbell first took this position in a debate with W. L. McCalla; see *A Public Debate on Christian Baptism* (1842; reprint, Kansas City: Old Paths Book Club, 1948), p. 100.

11. Concerning Campbell's vacillation during the *Christian Baptist* period, see Richard T. Hughes, "A Critical Comparison of the Campbells (1823-1830) and the Anabaptists (1524-1560)" (master's thesis, Abilene Christian University, 1967), pp. 97-113.

12. While the *Christian Standard* published this poem in its 21 October 1871 issue (p. 333), John Rogers recalled that a Kentucky Methodist preacher named William Phillips had produced it around 1833. Rogers also noted that this verse "was circulated by thousands, if not tens of thousands" ("The Life and Times of John Rogers," in John Rogers Books, 1800-1859, Book I, pp. 252-53, in Southern Historical Collection, Manuscripts Department, University of North Carolina at Chapel Hill). The poem has four additional verses.

13. The best study of the sectarian perspective among Churches of Christ is Myer Phillips's "Historical Study of the Attitudes of the Churches of Christ toward Other Denominations" (Ph.D. diss., Baylor University, 1983).

14. Rogers, *A Discourse Delivered in Carlisle, Kentucky, . . . 1860* (Cincinnati, 1861), p. 22.

15. Logan J. Fox, "Destiny or Disease?" in *Voices of Concern: Critical Studies in Church of Christism*, ed. Robert Meyers (St. Louis: Mission Messenger, 1966), pp. 14-15.

16. Readers seeking a more detailed history of Churches of Christ are advised to consult Earl Irvin West's four-volume *Search for the Ancient Order* (vol. 1: *1849-1865* [Nashville: Gospel Advocate Co., 1964]; vol. 2: *1866-1906* [Indianapolis: Religious Book Service, 1950]; vol. 3: *1900-1918* [Indianapolis: Religious Book Service, 1979]; and vol. 4: *1919-1950* [Germantown, Tenn.: Religious Book Service, 1987]).

17. Moore, *Comprehensive History of the Disciples of Christ* (New York: Fleming H. Revell, 1909), p. 12.

18. For the text of "The Last Will and Testament of the Springfield Presbytery," see Charles A. Young, *Historical Documents Advocating Christian Union* (Chicago: Christian Century Company, 1904), pp. 19-26.

19. For the text of the "Declaration and Address," see Young, *Historical Documents Advocating Christian Union*, pp. 27-209.

20. On that era's postmillennialism, see chap. 8 ("From Primitive Church to Protestant Nation: The Millennial Odyssey of Alexander Campbell") in Hughes and Allen, *Illusions of Innocence*.

21. For years, Earl Irvin West's four-volume *Search for the Ancient Order* was the only serious effort to trace the history of Churches of Christ as a tradition in its own right. More recently, Robert Hooper has written a history of Churches of Christ focusing especially on the twentieth century: *A Distinct People: A History of the Churches of Christ in the Twentieth Century* (West Monroe, La.: Howard Publishing, 1993). Readers should also consult Leroy Garrett's *The Stone-Campbell Movement: An Anecdotal History of Three Churches*, rev. ed. (Joplin, Mo.: College Press, 1994).

22. See, e.g., W. E. Garrison and A. T. DeGroot, *The Disciples of Christ: A History* (St. Louis: Bethany Press, 1948), pp. 404-6; and William E. Tucker and Lester G. McAllister, *Journey in Faith: A History of the Christian Church (Disciples of Christ)* (St. Louis: Bethany Press, 1975), pp. 251-54.

23. Ahlstrom, *A Religious History of the American People* (New Haven: Yale University Press, 1972), pp. 822-23; Gaustad, *A Religious History of America*, rev. ed. (New York: Harper & Row, 1990), p. 258; Hudson, *Religion in America*, 4th ed. (New York: Macmillan, 1987), p. 260n.25; and Wentz, *Religion in the New World: The Shaping of Religious Traditions in the United States* (Minneapolis: Fortress Press, 1990), p. 217.

24. West, *The Search for the Ancient Order*, 2:448.

25. Harrell, *The Social Sources of Division in the Disciples of Christ, 1865-1900* (Atlanta: Publishing Systems, 1973), pp. 7-8.

26. Harrell, "The Sectional Origins of the Churches of Christ," *Journal of Southern History* 30 (August 1964): 264, 277.

27. Harrell did speak of the "divided mind" of the movement, noting that "two distinct emphases emerged. One group conceived of Christianity in the denominational framework of practical religion, social and political activism, and, often, a nationalistic postmillennialism. A second group emphasized the sectarian tradition of Biblical legalism, a fanatical disposition, and uncompromising separation from the world" (*Quest for a Christian America: The Disciples of Christ and American Society to 1866* [Nashville: Disciples of Christ Historical Society, 1966], p. 60). Harrell did not recognize, however, the apocalyptic dimensions that often accompanied the sectarian phase of the movement, especially in the South.

28. Note, e.g., the titles of his two major books on this history: *The Social Sources of Division in the Disciples of Christ, 1865-1900*, and *Quest for a Christian America: The Disciples of Christ and American Society to 1866*.

29. Roberts, " 'Church of Christ': 1830 or 1889?" *Firm Foundation* 92 (30 September 1957): 614.

30. See "The Autobiography of B. F. Hall," p. 20. Typescript in Center for Restoration Studies, Abilene Christian University.

31. "The Autobiography of B. F. Hall," pp. 75, 87, 91.

Notes to Chapter 2

1. No contemporary biography of Alexander Campbell is available for readers interested in learning more about him. Such individuals should consult the memoirs prepared by Campbell's personal physician and colleague at Bethany College, Dr. Robert Richardson, *Memoirs of Alexander Campbell*, 2 vols. (1897; reprint, Nashville: Gospel Advocate Company, 1956); and Benjamin Lyon Smith, *Alexander Campbell* (St. Louis: Bethany Press, 1930).

2. The seven volumes of the *Christian Baptist* went through many editions and are still in print. The most recent edition was published in 1955 by the Gospel Advocate Company, publisher as well of the *Gospel Advocate*, a journal that has served Churches of Christ since 1855.

3. Rudolph, *Hoosier Faiths*, unpublished manuscript, pp. 30-31 (scheduled for publication by the University of Indiana Press).

4. Campbell, "Introductory Remarks," *MH* 3 (2 January 1832): 6; and "A Restoration of the Ancient Order of Things, No. 1," *CB* 2 (7 February 1825): 134-36.

5. Campbell, *The Christian System*, 5th ed. (1835; reprint, Cincinnati: Standard Publishing, 1901), p. ix; "Christendom in Its Dotage: A Hint to Reformers," *MH* 5 (August 1834): 374; "A Restoration of the Ancient Order of Things, No. 1," *CB* 2 (7 February 1825): 134-36; and "Prefatory Remarks," *MH* 1 (4 January 1830): 8.

6. See Campbell, "Events of 1823 and 1827," *MH*, n.s., 2 (October 1838): 466ff.

7. Campbell, *The Christian System*, pp. 154, xi-xii.

8. See Campbell, "Events of 1823 and 1827," *MH*, n.s., 2 (October 1838): 466ff.

9. Jeter, *Campbellism Examined* (New York: Sheldon, Lamport, & Blakeman, 1855), pp. 83-84.

10. Campbell developed these themes in a series of articles he entitled "The Restoration of the Ancient Order of Things," which ran in the *Christian Baptist* in thirty separate installments from February 1825 to September 1829.

11. Rogers, "The Life and Times of John Rogers, 1800-1867," *Lexington Theological Quarterly* 19 (January-April 1984): 76.

12. Jeter, *Campbellism Examined*, p. 23.

13. Campbell, "Prefatory Remarks," *MH* 1 (4 January 1830): 8; "Religious Controversy," *MH* 1 (4 January 1830): 41, 44; and "Notices of the War and the Campaign of 1834," *MH* 5 (December 1834): 619-20.

14. Campbell, quoted by Robert Richardson in *Memoirs of Alexander Campbell*, vol. 2 (1897; reprint, Nashville: Gospel Advocate, 1956), p. 90. On Campbell's debates, see Bill J. Humble, *Campbell and Controversy* (Rosemead, Calif.: Old Paths Book Club, 1952).

15. See Hatch, *The Democratization of American Christianity* (New Haven: Yale University Press, 1989), pp. 68-81.

16. See, e.g., Jefferson's letter to James Smith of 8 December 1822, in Norman Cousins, *"In God We Trust": The Religious Beliefs and Ideas of the American Founding Fathers* (New York: Harper, 1958), p. 159.

17. Campbell, "Remarks," *MH*, n.s., 4 (November 1840): 492-93; and Christianos, "Baptism," *MH*, n.s., 4 (May 1840): 198.

18. Campbell, "A Restoration of the Ancient Order of Things, No. 4," *CB* 2 (6 June 1825): 221.

19. Campbell, *The Christian System*, p. xii.

20. On Campbell's millennial understandings, see Tim Crowley, "A Chronological Delineation of Alexander Campbell's Eschatological Theory from 1823 to 1851," *Discipliana* 54 (Winter 1994): 99-107.

21. Campbell, "A Restoration of the Ancient Order of Things, No. 1," *CB* 2 (7 February 1825): 136; and Campbell and Robert Owen, *The Evidences of Christianity: A Debate* (St. Louis: Christian Board of Publication, n.d.), p. 385.

22. McCorkle, "Signs of the Times," *MH* 4 (October 1833): 483.

23. A Reformed Clergyman [Campbell], "The Millennium — No. 3," *MH* 5 (October 1834): 549-50; "The Millennium — No. 7," *MH* 6 (March 1835): 105; and "The Millennium — No. 8," *MH* 6 (April 1835): 148.

24. Campbell, "The Millennium," *MH*, 5th ser., 1 (June 1858): 335-36.

25. On the Puritans, see T. Dwight Bozeman, *To Live Ancient Lives: The Primitivist Dimension of Puritanism* (Chapel Hill, N.C.: University of North Carolina Press, 1988); on the Anabaptists, see Franklin H. Littell, *The Origins of Sectarian Protestantism* (New York: Macmillan, 1964).

26. See Campbell, "Education — New Series. No. 1," *MH* 3 (6 August 1832): 408-11. Campbell did, however, place a priority on the ancient languages. See Thomas H. Olbricht's discussion of the Bethany College curriculum in "Alexander Campbell as an Educator," in *Lectures in Honor of the Alexander Campbell Bicentennial, 1788-1988* (Nashville: Disciples of Christ Historical Society, 1988), pp. 89-90. On the value of classical civilization for understanding the biblical text, see Olbricht, "Alexander Campbell as an Educator," p. 95.

27. See Campbell, *Familiar Lectures on the Pentateuch,* ed. W. T. Moore (St. Louis: Christian Publishing, 1867), pp. 266-304. On Campbell's "canon within a canon," see M. Eugene Boring, "The Formation of a Tradition: Alexander Campbell and the New Testament," *Disciples Theological Digest* 2 (1987): 5-62.

28. Campbell, "Schools and Colleges — No. 2," *MH,* 3d ser., 7 (March 1850): 172. On "Baconianism," see T. Dwight Bozeman, *Protestants in an Age of Science: The Baconian Ideal and Antebellum American Religious Thought* (Chapel Hill, N.C.: University of North Carolina Press, 1977).

29. Richardson, "The Gospel — No. II," *MH,* n.s., 3 (April 1839): 149.

30. Campbell, *The Christian System,* pp. 6, 103-4.

31. On Campbell's anti-Catholicism, see Edward L. Hicks, "Republican Religion and Republican Institutions: Alexander Campbell and the Anti-Catholic Movement," *Fides et Historia* 22 (Fall 1990): 42-52; and David Edwin Harrell Jr., *Quest for a Christian America* (Nashville: Disciples of Christ Historical Society, 1966): 214-17.

32. Campbell, "The Christian Religion," *CB* 1 (4 July 1823): 14.

33. See Byron Cecil Lambert, *The Rise of the Anti-Mission Baptists: Sources and Leaders, 1800-1840* (New York: Arno Press, 1980), p. 207.

34. See Lambert, *The Rise of the Anti-Mission Baptists,* pp. 197, 210-12.

35. Campbell, "Catholic Controversy. No. 1," *MH,* 4 (November 1833): 538-39.

36. See Haymes, "A Battle of Giants: Alexander Campbell and Bishop John Baptist Purcell in Cincinnati, 1837," unpublished manuscript in possession of the author.

37. See Olbricht, "Alexander Campbell as an Educator," p. 82.

38. Campbell, "Essay on the Importance of Uniting the Moral with the Intellectual Culture of the Mind," *MH* 7 (Extra, December 1836): 579, 597.

39. Campbell quotes the text of the petition in "Roman Catholic Discussion," *MH* 7 (December 1836): 551-52.

40. Haymes, "A Battle of Giants."

41. See Robert Baird, *Religion in the United States of America* (1844; reprint, New York: Arno Press, 1969), p. 573.

42. See Daniel Aaron, "Cincinnati, 1818-1838: A Study of Attitudes in the Urban West" (Ph.D. diss., Harvard University, 1942), p. 264.

43. Campbell, "On Common Schools" (1841), in *Popular Lectures and Addresses* (St. Louis: John Burns, 1861), p. 259.

44. Campbell, "Address on the Anglo-Saxon Language: Its Origin, Character, and Destiny" (1849), in *Popular Lectures and Addresses,* p. 44.

45. Campbell, "To an Independent Baptist," *CB* 3 (1 May 1826): 204.

46. Campbell, "Extra, No. 1," *MH* 1 (December 1837): 578, 587-88, 581.

47. Jeter, *Campbellism Examined,* pp. 340-41. For further elaborations on Campbell's change, see pp. 338-53, 357-58.

48. Campbell, "Any Christians among the Sects?" *MH,* n.s., 1 (December 1837): 564-65.

49. See Campbell, "Preface," *MH,* n.s., 3 (January 1839): 3.

50. Campbell, "Any Christians among Protestant Parties," *MH,* n.s., 1 (September 1837): 411-14; and "Extra, No. 1," *MH,* n.s., 1 (December 1837): 588.

51. See Olbricht, "Alexander Campbell as an Educator," pp. 94-95. See also Lester G. McAlister, *Bethany: The First 150 Years* (Bethany: Bethany College Press, 1991), p. 31.

52. McAlister, *Bethany: The First 150 Years*, pp. 92-93.

53. M. Norvel Young, *A History of Colleges Established and Controlled by Members of the Churches of Christ* (Kansas City: Old Paths Book Club, 1949), p. 28.

54. Campbell, "Any Christians among the Sects?" *MH*, n.s., 1 (December 1837): 561.

55. Letter from T. M. Allen to John Allen Gano, Boon Co., Mo., dated 25 May 1840, in Gano papers, Center for Restoration Studies, Abilene Christian University.

56. Fanning, "The Origin of the Church of Christ Is Not Modern," *Christian Review* 2 (January 1845): 6; and "The Crisis," *Christian Review* 2 (October 1845): 10.

57. Lipscomb, "Tolbert Fanning's Teaching and Influence," in James Scobey, *Franklin College and Its Influences* (1906; reprint, Nashville: Gospel Advocate, 1954), p. 10.

58. Creath, "Old and New Things Contrasted," *GA* 19 (6 December 1877): 756; and "Arguments against Clerical Organization, No. 4," *Proclamation and Reformer* 1 (April 1850): 224-25.

59. Letter from George E. Taylor, Franklin County, Mo., to Jacob Creath, dated 16 April 1850, in Jacob Creath papers, Disciples of Christ Historical Society, Nashville.

60. Creath, "Conventions — No. V," *MH*, 3d ser., 7 (November 1850): 637; and "Arguments vs. Clerical Organization, No. 3," *Proclamation and Reformer* 1 (March 1850): 173.

61. Thornberry, "Conventions, Organizations, &c.," *GA* 20 (28 March 1878): 200.

62. Creath, "The Bible Alone Rejected by the Conventionists," *GA* 19 (22 November 1877): 724; and "Old and New Things Contrasted," *GA* 19 (6 December 1877): 756.

63. Lipscomb, "A Campbell and the Societies," *GA* 26 (4 June 1884): 358.

64. Lipscomb based this judgment on an assessment offered by Charles V. Segar in an introduction he wrote to Campbell's *Familiar Lectures on the Pentateuch* (Cincinnati: Bosworth, Chase & Hall, 1871), pp. 37-38. Segar claimed Campbell's family as authority for the information.

65. During his 1847 tour of Scotland, Campbell's opponents accused him of "man-stealing" because he had refused to condemn slavery, arguing that the Bible does not call slavery a sin (see Chap. 12). The incident escalated into a sideshow as Campbell was additionally accused of libel, arrested, and then jailed in Glasgow. The Scottish high court released him after a week. See "The Rev. James Robertson vs. the Rev. Alexander Campbell" and allied files in possession of Charles Marler, Abilene Christian University; and Thomas Chalmers, *Alexander Campbell's Tour in Scotland* (Louisville: Guide Printing and Publishing, 1892).

66. Lipscomb, "A Campbell and the Society," *Gospel Advocate* 26 (14 May 1884): 315; and "Solid Thoughts by Ernest Men," *GA* 26 (23 April 1884): 262.

67. Rowe, "Reminiscences of the Restoration," *ACR* 29 (6 May 1886): 148.

68. Robert Richardson in a letter to P. S. Fall dated 24 August 1857, in Philip S. Fall Collection, microfilm in Center for Restoration Studies, Abilene Christian University.

69. Franklin, "Anniversaries of Our Societies in Cincinnati," *ACR*, November 1856, p. 346.

70. Richard M. Tristano provides a judicious discussion of the issue in *The Origins of the Restoration Movement: An Intellectual History* (Atlanta: Glenmary Research Center, 1988), pp. 127-31.

71. Lard, "Can We Divide?" *Lard's Quarterly* 3 (April 1866): 336.

72. Campbell, "Any Christians among the Sects?" *MH*, n.s., 1 (December 1837): 561.

73. This was the wording of this sentence in the first edition of *The Christian System*, which bore the title *Christianity Restored*, printed in 1835. At least, this is the way Campbell interpreted the intent of that sentence, as he explained in "Any Christians among the Sects?" *MH*, n.s., 1 (December 1837): 562. However, in the revised edition of this work, first published

in 1839, under the title *The Christian System,* this meaning is not so obvious. There Campbell wrote, "We are so sanguine — perhaps many will say, so visionary — as to imagine that a *nucleus* has been formed, or may be formed, around which may one day congregate all the children of God" (*The Christian System* [Cincinnati: Standard Publishing, 1901], p. 86).

74. Campbell, *Christian Baptism* (1851; reprint, Nashville: McQuiddy Printing, 1913), p. x.

75. "Christian Church of Sand Creek et al. v. Church of Christ of Sand Creek et al., 219 Ill. 503 (1906)," appendix C in James Stephen Wolfgang, "A Life of Humble Fear: The Biography of Daniel Sommer, 1850-1940" (master's thesis, Butler University, 1975).

Notes to Chapter 3

1. Jeter, *Campbellism Examined* (New York: Sheldon, Lamport, & Blakeman, 1855), pp. 86-87.

2. Harrell, "The Sectional Origins of Churches of Christ," *Journal of Southern History* 30 (August 1964): 262.

3. Eva Jean Wrather has explored the radical dimensions of Scott's thought in " 'My Most Cordial and Indefatigable Fellow Laborer': Alexander Campbell Looks at Walter Scott," *The Christian-Evangelist* 84 (23 October 1946): 1044-48. It was Wrather who first suggested to me that Scott stands, in many ways, at the fountainhead of Churches of Christ.

Thomas H. Olbricht has argued that Churches of Christ are indebted to Walter Scott especially for their "plan of salvation," their emphasis on evangelism, and their "propensity to schematization." He correctly notes, however, that their preoccupation with ecclesiastical form and structure owes more to Campbell than to Scott ("Walter Scott's Vision of Restoration," paper presented at Restoration Center Lectures, Abilene Christian University, 1991, pp. 16-17).

4. On Sandeman and the Haldanes and their influence on Churches of Christ, see Lynn A. McMillon, *Restoration Roots* (Dallas: Gospel Teachers Publications, 1983).

5. See Dwight Stevenson, *The Bacon College Story, 1836-1865* (Lexington: College of the Bible, 1962), p. 10. The published version of Scott's inaugural address — no doubt much lengthier than what he actually said that day — appeared as "The State-System," *The Christian,* February-March 1837, pp. 25-72. See also "United States' System: An Address" (1837), *College of the Bible Quarterly* 23 (April 1946): 4-44.

6. See Dwight Stevenson, *Walter Scott: Voice of the Golden Oracle* (St. Louis: Christian Board of Publication, 1946), pp. 34-35.

7. Scott [pseud., Philip], "On Teaching Christianity — No. 1," *CB* 1 (1 September 1823): 30-32. The remainder of the series appeared in issues for 3 November 1823, pp. 66-71; 5 January 1824, pp. 110-14; and 2 February 1824, pp. 133-37 (Gospel Advocate edition, 1955).

8. Campbell, "Elder Walter Scott's Demise," *MH,* 5th ser., 4 (May 1861): 296-97.

9. On Scott's emphasis on "the ancient gospel" rather than "the ancient order," see Olbricht, "Walter Scott's Vision of Restoration," pp. 11-12.

10. Scott [pseud., Philip], "On Teaching Christianity — No. 1," *CB* 1 (1 September 1823): 31.

11. Scott [pseud., Philip], "On Teaching Christianity — No. 11," *CB* 1 (3 November 1823): 67.

12. For a discussion of the covenant theme in Scott's thought, see William Austin Gerrard, "Walter Scott: Frontier Disciples Evangelist" (Ph.D. diss., Emory University, 1982), pp. 126-30.

13. Scott, "Answer to the Above," *The Evangelist* 2 (2 September 1833): 209-11.

14. Scott, *To Themelion: The Union of Christians, on Christian Principles* (Cincinnati: n.p., 1852), pp. 78-79; "Address Given before the American Christian Missionary Society" (Cincinnati, 1854), p. 26; and *A Discourse on the Holy Spirit* (Bethany, Va.: n.p., 1831), pp. 20-21.

15. The subtitle further read, ". . . *and the Gospel in Its Various Parts Shewn to Be Adapted to the Nature and Necessities of Man in His Present Condition*" (Cincinnati: n.p., 1836).

16. Thomas Campbell quoted by William Baxter in *Life of Elder Walter Scott* (Cincinnati: Bosworth, Chase & Hall, 1874), pp. 158-59.

17. Scott, "From the Minutes of the Mahoning Association Report," *Christian Examiner* 1 (November 1829): 5-8.

18. See, e.g., Scott, "Circular Letter," *Christian Evangelist* 1 (2 January 1832): 17-18.

19. Scott, *The Gospel Restored*, pp. v-vi.

20. Campbell, "To Epaphras — No. 1," *MH* 3 (2 July 1832): 298.

21. Campbell, "Events of 1823 and 1827," *MH*, n.s., 2 (October 1838): 466ff.

22. Scott, "Sacred Colloquy, No. 7," *The Evangelist* 1 (6 August 1832): 182.

23. Letter from Scott to Philip Fall, dated 4 August 1840, in Philip S. Fall letters in the library of the Kentucky Historical Society, cited by Stevenson in *Walter Scott*, p. 179.

24. Richardson, "History of the Disciples of Christ," in *History of All the Religious Denominations in the United States*, ed. John Winebrenner (Harrisburg, Pa.: n.p., 1849), p. 228.

25. Lard, "The Reformation for Which We Are Pleading — What Is It?" *Lard's Quarterly* 1 (September 1863): 18.

26. "Items of Ecclesiastical Intelligence," *Heretic Detector* 3 (February 1839): 35.

27. J. W. Grant, "A Sketch of the Reformation in Tennessee," c. 1897, typescript in Center for Restoration Studies, Abilene Christian University, p. 83.

28. The earliest version of this sermon was entitled "Identification of the Church of Christ" (*Christian Magazine* 1 [September 1848]: 267ff.). It was then expanded and republished under the title "The Beginning Corner; or, The Church of Christ Identified" (*ACR* 1 [August 1856]: 225-36) and finally republished again under its second title in *Biographical Sketch and Writings of Elder Benjamin Franklin*, ed. John F. Rowe and G. W. Rice (Cincinnati: G. W. Rice, 1880), pp. 206-28. I am using here the 1856 version, published in *ACR*.

29. Howard, "The Beginning Corner; or, The Church of Christ Identified," pp. 226-29.

30. Howard, "The Beginning Corner; or, The Church of Christ Identified," pp. 226-35.

31. Howard, "The Beginning Corner; or, The Church of Christ Identified," p. 235.

32. Howard, "A Warning to the Religious Sects and Parties in Christendom," *Bible Advocate* 1 (January 1843): 82.

33. Crihfield, "Preface," *Heretic Detector* 2 (January 1838): 5; and "To T. M. Henley," *Heretic Detector* 1 (15 May 1837): 132.

34. Crihfield, *Heretic Detector* 3 (January 1839): 15f; Thomas Henley, "Sectarianism, Catholicism, Asa Shinn, &c.," *Heretic Detector* 1 (July 1837): 173-74; and G. A. Patterson, "Heaven," *Heretic Detector* 2 (April 1838): 108.

35. See Campbell, "Various Notices," *MH*, n.s., 5 (August 1841): 384.

36. Crihfield, in *The Cane Ridge Reader*, ed. Hoke S. Dickinson (N.p.: n.p., 1972), pp. 306-7.

37. Campbell, "The Heretic Detector," *MH*, n.s., 1 (September 1837): 432.

38. Campbell, "Essay on Heresy," *Heretic Detector* 3 (October 1839): 241f.

39. Crihfield, "Coming of the Lord — No. III," *Orthodox Preacher* 1 (February 1843): 25-31.

40. Campbell, "The Orthodox Preacher," *MH*, n.s., 7 (February 1843): 83.

41. Campbell, "The Orthodox Preacher," *MH*, 3d ser., 3 (January 1846): 56-58. The Crihfield quotation appears in this article.

42. See Walter Scott, "Editorial Correspondence," *The Protestant Unionist* 3 (31 March 1847): 66.

43. On Lard, see Kenneth L. Van Deusen, *Moses Lard: That Prince of Preachers* (Joplin, Mo.: College Press Publishing, 1987).

44. Jeter, *Campbellism Examined*, pp. 34-39.

45. Lard, *A Review of Rev. J. B. Jeter's Book Entitled "Campbellism Examined"* (Philadelphia: n.p., 1857), pp. 31-32.

46. Lard, "The Reformation for Which We Are Pleading — What Is It?" *Lard's Quarterly* 1 (September 1863): 14, 22.

47. Lard, "Have We Not Become a Sect?" *Lard's Quarterly* 1 (March 1864): 253, 248-49, 255, 258.

48. Lard, "Have We Not Become a Sect?" pp. 246, 259.

49. Lard, "Do the Holy Scriptures Authorize the Baptism of Infants?" 1 (December 1863): 158.

50. On the development of this threefold hermeneutic, see Michael Casey, "The Development of Necessary Inference in the Hermeneutics of the Disciples of Christ/Churches of Christ" (Ph.D. diss., University of Pittsburgh, 1986); "The Origins of the Hermeneutics of the Churches of Christ, Part One: The Reformed Tradition," *Restoration Quarterly* 31 (1989): 75-91; and "The Origins of the Hermeneutics of the Churches of Christ, Part Two: The Philosophical Background," *Restoration Quarterly* 31 (1989): 193-206. See also Russ Dudrey, "Restorationist Hermeneutics among the Churches of Christ: Why Are We at an Impasse?" *Restoration Quarterly* 30 (1988): 34.

51. See Campbell, "To 'Paulinus,' Letter II," *CB* 4 (2 April 1827): 188-89. For an extended discussion of Campbell's vacillation and his final inclination to require immersion following Scott's success in 1827, see Richard T. Hughes, "A Critical Comparison of the Restitution Motifs of the Campbells (1809-1830) and the Anabaptists (1524-1560)" (master's thesis, Abilene Christian University, 1967), pp. 97-113.

52. Lard, "Do the Unimmersed Commune?" *Lard's Quarterly* 1 (September 1863): 44, 49.

53. Lard, *Commentary on Paul's Letter to Romans* (Lexington: Transylvania Printing & Publishing, 1876).

Notes to Chapter 4

1. Howard, " 'Christian Review' and the Bible Advocate," *Bible Advocate* 2 (November 1843): 61. Alexander Campbell also noted the announcement of the *Christian Review* in "Proposals," *MH*, n.s., 7 (December 1843): 574.

2. See "The Autobiography of B. F. Hall," typescript in Center for Restoration Studies, Abilene Christian University, pp. 71-72.

3. See James R. Wilburn, *The Hazard of the Die: Tolbert Fanning and the Restoration Movement* (1969; reprint, Malibu: Pepperdine University Press, 1980), pp. 26-30.

4. Fanning, "Discourse, Delivered in Boston, July 17, 1836" (Boston, 1836), pp. 18-19. This lecture was printed at the request of the Boston Unitarians.

5. Fanning, "Discourse, Delivered in Boston, July 17, 1836," pp. 24-25.

6. Fanning, "The Christian Review," *The Christian Review* 1 (January 1844): 1.

7. Letter from William Ramsey to James E. Scobey, dated 8 June 1905, quoted in *Franklin College and Its Influences*, ed. James E. Scobey (1906; reprint, Nashville: Gospel Advocate, 1954), p. 238.

8. Fanning, "The Mission of the Church of Christ," in *The Living Pulpit of the Christian Church*, ed. W. T. Moore (Cincinnati: n.p., 1868), pp. 533-34.

9. Fanning, "Metaphysical Discussions — No. 4," *GA* 3 (January 1857): 3-4.

10. See Fanning, "Metaphysical Discussions — No. 1," *GA* 2 (October 1856): 315.

11. Samuel Robbins, "Modern Spiritualism," *MH*, 4th ser., 7 (October 1857): 580.

12. Fanning, "Spiritual Light," *Religious Historian* 1 (January 1872): 4.

13. Ferguson, quoted in "Spiritual Conference," *Nashville Union and American*, 12 November 1854, cited by Johnny Tucker in *Like a Meteor across the Horizon* (Fayetteville, Tenn.: Tucker Publications, 1978), p. 24. This book provides an excellent description of the Ferguson episode.

14. Fanning et al., *History and True Position of the Church of Christ in Nashville: With an Examination of the Speculative Theology Recently Introduced from Neologists, Universalists, Etc.* (Nashville: n.p., 1854), pp. 22-23.

15. This entire story, and its aftermath, is told in more detail than can be given here by Cloyd Goodnight and Dwight E. Stevenson in *Home to Bethphage: A Biography of Robert Richardson* (St. Louis: Christian Board of Publication, 1949), pp. 168-87.

16. See Richardson, "Misinterpretations of Scripture — No. 1," *MH*, 4th ser., 6 (September 1856): 505-7.

17. The student was W. S. Russell. On this, see Fanning, "Metaphysical Discussions — No. 2," *GA* 2 (November 1856): 326-29; Fanning, "To Editors of Periodicals and Papers Devoted to the Cause of the Christian Religion," *GA* 3 (July 1857): 221-22; Campbell, "The Real and the Ideal," *MH*, 4th ser., 6 (August 1856): 421; and Richardson, "Faith versus Philosophy — No. 4," *MH*, 4th ser., 7 (May 1857): 269-70.

18. Fanning, "Professor Richardson's Notice of the Senior Editor of the Gospel Advocate," *GA* 3 (June 1857): 190-91. See also Fanning, "The Church in Nashville," *GA* 3 (March 1857): 72ff.

19. Fanning, "Metaphysical Discussion — No. 2," *GA* 2 (November 1856): 326-27; "Metaphysical Discussions — No. 4," *GA* 3 (January 1857): 4-5; and "Professor R. Richardson's Second Notice of the Gospel Advocate," *GA* 3 (July 1857): 203, 209-10.

20. Fanning, "Metaphysical Discussion — No. 2," *GA* 2 (November 1856): 326-27.

21. Fanning, "Metaphysical Discussions — No. 1," *GA* 2 (October 1856): 314; and "Metaphysical Discussions — No. 4," *GA* 3 (January 1857): 3-4.

22. Richardson, "Faith versus Philosophy — No. 4," *MH*, 4th ser., 7 (May 1857): 273-75.

23. Richardson, "President Fanning's 'Reply,'" *MH*, 4th ser., 7 (August 1857): 447-48; see also "Faith versus Philosophy — No. 5," *MH*, 4th ser., 7 (June 1857): 330-31.

24. Richardson, "Faith versus Philosophy — No. 5," *MH*, 4th ser., 7 (June 1857): 331-34; and "Religious Herald — Again," *MH*, 4th ser., 7 (November 1857): 637-45.

25. Richardson, "Faith versus Philosophy — No. 5," pp. 335-36; and "Faith versus Philosophy — No. 4," p. 274.

26. Fanning, "Professor R. Richardson's Second Notice of the Gospel Advocate," *GA* 3 (July 1857): 204-5; and "Professor Richardson's Notice of the Senior Editor of the Gospel Advocate," *GA* 3 (June 1857): 189.

27. Campbell, "Christianity the True Philosophy," *MH*, 4th ser., 7 (September 1857): 481; and "The Religious Herald and Prof. Richardson," *MH*, 4th ser., 7 (October 1857): 576-77.

28. Richardson, in a letter to Philip S. Fall dated 15 December 1858, in Philip S. Fall letters, copy in Center for Restoration Studies, Abilene Christian University.

29. Richardson, "Faith versus Philosophy — No. 9," *MH*, 4th ser., 7 (December 1857): 703.

30. Richardson to Fall, 15 December 1858.

31. Richardson to Fall, 15 December 1858.

32. Campbell, "President Fanning," *MH*, 5th ser., 1 (June 1858): 353.

33. Campbell, in a letter to Philip S. Fall dated 4 January 1860, in Philip S. Fall letters, copy in Center for Restoration Studies, Abilene Christian University.

34. Richardson, "Faith versus Philosophy — No. 5," p. 328.

35. Lipscomb, "Tolbert Fanning's Teaching and Influence," in *Franklin College and Its Influences*, pp. 13-14.

36. Moore, "Tolbert Fanning," in *Franklin College and Its Influences*, p. 143.

37. Richardson, in a letter to Isaac Errett dated 16 July 1857, quoted by Cloyd Goodnight in "The Life of Dr. Robert Richardson," an unfinished manuscript containing a transcript of Richardson's private papers from the Fannie R. Thompson collection, Bethany College Library.

38. Richardson, in a letter to Philip S. Fall dated 19 December 1859.

39. Richardson to Fall, 19 December 1859.

40. Fanning, "Professor R. Richardson's Second Notice of the Gospel Advocate," p. 204; and "Professor Richardson's Notice of the Senior Editor of the Gospel Advocate," p. 191.

41. Fanning, "Metaphysical Discussions — No. 5," *GA* 3 (February 1857): 34-35, 37-38.

42. See Wilburn, *Hazard of the Die*, pp. 175-80; and Fanning, "Co-operation — Suggestions," *GA* 1 (October 1855): 109ff.

43. Lipscomb, "Tolbert Fanning's Teaching and Influence," p. 19.

44. Fanning et al., *History and True Position of the Church of Christ in Nashville*, p. 13.

45. See Wilburn, *Hazard of the Die*, pp. 149-55.

46. Fanning, "Temperance and Temperance Societies," *Christian Review* 2 (March 1845): 49-50.

47. Lipscomb, "The Death of Benjamin Franklin," *GA* 20 (31 October 1878): 677. On Franklin in general, see *Biographical Sketch and Writings of Elder Benjamin Franklin*, ed. J. F. Rowe and G. W. Rice (Cincinnati: G. W. Rice, 1880); Joseph Franklin and J. A. Headington, *The Life and Times of Benjamin Franklin* (St. Louis: Christian Publishing, 1879); Ottis L. Castleberry, *They Heard Him Gladly: A Critical Study of Benjamin Franklin's Preaching* (Rosemead, Calif.: Old Paths Publishing, 1963); and Earl I. West, *Elder Ben Franklin: Eye of the Storm* (Indianapolis: Religious Book Service, 1983).

48. Lipscomb, "Benjamin Franklin," *GA* 20 (5 December 1878): 758-59.

49. Lipscomb, "Benjamin Franklin," p. 758.

50. For a list of his published debates, see *An Author Catalog of Disciples of Christ and Related Religious Groups*, comp. Claude E. Spencer (Canton, Mo.: Disciples of Christ Historical Society, 1946), pp. 113-14. His two sermon books were *The Gospel Preacher: A Book of Twenty Sermons* (Cincinnati: Franklin & Rice, 1869) and *The Gospel Preacher: A Book of Twenty-One Sermons* (Cincinnati: Franklin & Rice, 1877). The journals with which he was associated included the *Reformer* and the *Western Reformer* (1843-1849), the *Proclamation and Reformer* (1850-1851), and the *American Christian Review* (1856-1878).

51. See, e.g., Franklin, "The Defection Again," *ACR* 2 (19 April 1859): 62; " 'American Christian Review' upon the Letter to James Challen," *British Millennial Harbinger*, 4th ser., 18 (1 April 1865): 134-35; and William E. Wallace, "Searching for a Method," *Vanguard* (May 1982): 10.

52. Franklin, "Alexander Campbell," *Proclamation and Reformer* 1 (November 1850): 713-16; "Anniversaries of Our Societies in Cincinnati," *ACR,* November 1856, p. 346; and "The A. C. Review," *ACR* 15 (16 April 1872): 124.

53. Franklin and Headington, *The Life and Times of Benjamin Franklin,* pp. 63, 267.

54. Franklin, "Still Going Ahead," *Proclamation and Reformer* 1 (February 1850): 105-6. Franklin's first published article was "A Discourse to the Unconverted," *Heretic Detector* (April-June 1837): 132-35.

55. Franklin, "Introductory Address," *ACR* 1 (January 1856): 3-4.

56. John F. Rowe, "Coquetting with the Sects," *ACR* 14 (27 June 1871): 204; and Franklin, "Open Communion," *ACR* 13 (16 August 1870): 261. Sentiments of this sort are legion in Franklin's *American Christian Review.*

57. Rowe, "Apologizing for Sectarianism," *ACR* 16 (14 January 1873): 13; and Franklin, "Sermon No. XX, Theme — Identity of the Church," in *The Gospel Preacher,* vol. 2 (Cincinnati: G. W. Rice, 1877): 475.

58. Franklin, "Reply," *Proclamation and Reformer* 1 (May 1850): 278-79; and "The New Defection," *ACR* 2 (5 April 1859): 54. For more on this episode, see West, *Elder Ben Franklin,* pp. 162-65.

59. On this theme in Franklin, see Wendell Willis, "A Sociological Study of the Restoration Movement in the North: 1866-1878" (master's thesis, Abilene Christian University, 1966), pp. 67-96.

60. Fanning, "A General Consultation Meeting Suggested," *GA* 8 (16 April 1866): 241-42; Franklin, "Comment of the American Christian Review, in Reference to the Contemplated Meeting of the Disciples in the Southern States," *GA* 8 (16 April 1866): 241-42; and Fanning, "Response to the American Christian Review," *GA* 8 (16 April 1866): 243.

61. West, *Elder Ben Franklin,* p. 195.

62. See Lipscomb, "Benjamin Franklin," *GA* 20 (5 December 1878): 758.

63. See Walter Scott, *Protestant Unionist* 17 (March 1847): 58.

64. Joseph Franklin (and J. A. Headington), *The Life and Times of Benjamin Franklin,* pp. 193-94.

65. Franklin, "Introduction," *ACR* 21 (1 January 1878): 4; and "Our Position Defined," *ACR* 10 (12 March 1867): 84.

66. See "Opening of the Central Christian Church," *ACR* 15 (20 February 1872): 61; and W. T. Moore, "Dedication of the Central Christian Church," *ACR* 15 (20 February 1872): 57.

67. Franklin, "Central Christian Church," *ACR* 15 (20 February 1872): 60.

68. Franklin, "Central Christian Church," *ACR* 15 (5 March 1872): 76; and "Central Christian Church," *ACR* 15 (20 February 1872): 60.

69. "To Benjamin Franklin," *ACR* 15 (16 April 1872): 125.

70. Richardson, "Correction," *ACR* 15 (16 April 1872): 124.

71. Moore, "The Central Church Once More," *ACR* 15 (16 April 1872): 122; and "Central Christian Church," *ACR* 15 (26 March 1872): 101.

72. See West, *Elder Ben Franklin,* p. 222; and *Biographical Sketch and Writings of Elder Benjamin Franklin,* p. 43.

73. Crabb, "Franklinian Stupidity," ACR 15 (2 April 1872): 105.

74. Franklin, "Introduction," *ACR* 21 (1 January 1878): 4.

75. Franklin, "Sermon No. XXI, Theme — The Simplicity of the Divine Economy," in *The Gospel Preacher,* 2:488ff., 500-502.

76. Franklin, "Sermon No. XII, Theme — Why Was the Primitive Church Persecuted? Why Were the First Christians Persecuted? Why Is the True Church Now Persecuted? Why Are the Christians Now Persecuted?" in *The Gospel Preacher,* 2:272, 275-76.

77. Franklin, "What Is Sectarianism?" *MH* 41 (January 1870): 356.

78. Lipscomb, "Benjamin Franklin," *GA* 20 (5 December 1878): 758.

79. See, e.g., Franklin, "Missionary Society," *ACR* 2 (March 1857): 90; and "Upward Tendency — Reformation Not a Failure — Missionary Work," *ACR* 2 (May 1857): 136.

80. Franklin, "Our Position Defined," *ACR* 10 (12 March 1867): 84.

81. Franklin, "Sermon No. XXI, Theme — The Simplicity of the Divine Economy," *The Gospel Preacher,* 2:495.

82. Franklin, "Instrumental Music in Churches," *ACR* 3 (31 January 1860): 18.

83. Pinkerton, " 'Instrumental Music in Churches,' " *ACR* 3 (28 February 1860): 34.

84. Lard, "Instrumental Music in Churches," *Lard's Quarterly* 1 (March 1864): 330-31.

85. Franklin, "Explanatory to Brother Franklin," *ACR* 13 (24 May 1870): 164.

86. See Lipscomb, "Christian Quarterly," *GA* 11 (29 April 1869): 394-95. For an excellent brief survey of the development of this issue, see William Woodson, *Standing for Their Faith: A History of Churches of Christ in Tennessee, 1900-1950* (Henderson, Tenn.: J & W Publications, 1979), pp. 26-31. On the number of adopting churches in Tennessee, see p. 29.

87. *Register of Christian Church of Springfield, Mo., at and from January 1, 1885,* housed at South Street Christian Church, Springfield.

88. Excerpt from the *St. Louis Globe Democrat,* 31 January 1887, reprinted in "Pen and Scissors," *Christian-Evangelist,* 24 (10 February 1887): 83.

89. Already during the late nineteenth century, the movement was also being divided along the lines of the incipient fundamentalist/modernist controversy. The liberal wing of the movement, represented during that period by J. H. Garrison's *Christian Evangelist,* squared off against the "moderates," represented by Isaac Errett's *Christian Standard.* On the role of the fundamentalist/modernist controversy in the schism that separated the conservative Christian Churches/Churches of Christ from the more liberal Christian Church (Disciples of Christ), see James B. North, "The Fundamentalist Controversy among the Disciples of Christ, 1890-1930" (Ph.D. diss., University of Illinois, 1973).

90. Franklin, "Labors in the Gospel," *ACR,* ser. 1, 1 (January 1856): 7; and "Evangelizing," *ACR,* ser. 1, 1 (February 1856): 55-56.

91. Franklin, "Ohio State Missionary Meeting," *ACR* 6 (23 June 1863): 98.

92. Franklin, "Do We Need a Theological School?" *MH* 36 (August 1865): 367.

93. Franklin, "The Situation," *ACR* 18 (4 May 1875): 140.

94. Rowe, "Are Colleges a Blessing or a Curse?" *ACR* 15 (5 March 1872): 76.

95. Franklin, "The Situation," *ACR* 18 (4 May 1875): 140.

96. Franklin, "Our Distinctive Plea," *ACR* 14 (5 December 1871): 388.

97. Franklin, "Introduction," *ACR* 21 (1 January 1878): 4.

98. Richardson in a letter to Fall dated 19 January 1859.

Notes to Chapter 5

1. On Stone, see Charles Crossfield Ware, *Barton Warren Stone: Pathfinder of Christian Union* (St. Louis: Bethany Press, 1932); and William Garrett West, *Barton Warren Stone: Early American Advocate of Christian Unity* (Nashville: Disciples of Christ Historical Society, 1954).

2. The phrase is that of Timothy P. Weber (*Living in the Shadow of the Second Coming: American Premillennialism, 1875-1925* [New York: Oxford University Press, 1979]).

3. See William D. Howden, "The Kingdom of God in Alexander Campbell's Hermeneutics," *Restoration Quarterly* 32 (1990): 90-91.

4. Campbell, *The Christian System,* 2d ed. (1839; reprint, Nashville: Gospel Advocate, 1970), p. 55.

5. On the differences between Stone and Campbell regarding the atonement, see John Mark Hicks, "What Did Christ's Sacrifice Accomplish? Atonement in Early Restorationist Thought," paper presented at Restoration Theology Fellowship, Chicago, November 1994.

6. Stone, *CM* 1 (25 November 1826): 4.

7. For valuable background on Caldwell, Hodge, and McGready, see Paul R. Conkin, *Cane Ridge: America's Pentecost* (Madison: University of Wisconsin Press, 1990), pp. 43-63.

8. Davies, *Sermons on Important Subjects*, vol. 1 (New York: n.p., 1842), pp. 217-18.

9. Whitefield, quoted by Winthrop S. Hudson in *Religion in America*, 4th ed. (New York: Macmillan, 1987), p. 79.

10. See Conkin's discussion of the Cane Ridge revival in the light of the traditional Scottish sacramental communion service (*Cane Ridge*, pp. 16-25).

11. Richard McNemar, Barton Stone, et al., *The Last Will and Testament of the Springfield Presbytery*, in *Historical Documents Advocating Christian Union*, ed. Charles A. Young (Chicago: Christian Century, 1904), pp. 19-23.

12. Thomas, *The Travels and Gospel Labors of Joseph Thomas* (Winchester, Va.: J. Foster, 1812), p. 90.

13. Haggard, quoted by W. E. MacClenny in *The Life of Rev. James O'Kelly* (Raleigh, N.C.: Edwards & Broughton Printing, 1910), p. 116.

14. This pamphlet has been reprinted with a preface by John W. Neth Jr. as *An Address to the Different Religious Societies, on the Sacred Import of the Christian Name: Footnotes to Disciple History, No. 4* (Nashville: Disciples of Christ Historical Society, 1954). See also Colby D. Hall, *Rice Haggard: The American Frontier Evangelist Who Revived the Name Christian* (Fort Worth: Stafford-Lowdon, 1957).

William E. Tucker and Lester G. McAllister argue that Davies, Haggard, and others connected with the two Awakenings ultimately learned the significance of the name *Christian* from a common source: a collection of sermons by Benjamin Grosvenor entitled *An Essay on the Name Christian*, published in London in 1728. See Tucker and McAllister, *Journey in Faith: A History of the Christian Church (Disciples of Christ)* (St. Louis: Bethany Press, 1975), p. 56n.15.

15. Robert Marshall and John Thompson, *A Brief Historical Account of Sundry Things in the Doctrines and State of the Christian, or as it is Commonly Called, the Newlight Church* (Cincinnati, 1811), p. 17.

16. Archippus, "Calvinism and Arminianism: Review of Elder D's Letter — No. III," *Christian Examiner* 1 (31 May 1830): 159.

17. T. S., "To the Editor of the Christian Messenger," *CM* 1 (25 September 1827): 249.

18. J. and J. Gregg, "An Apology for Withdrawing from the Methodist Episcopal Church," *CM* 1 (25 December 1826): 39-40.

19. See *The Biography of Eld. Barton Warren Stone* (1847), in *The Cane Ridge Reader*, ed. Hoke S. Dickinson (N.p.: n.p., 1972), pp. 39-42.

20. Joseph Thomas, *The Life of the Pilgrim Joseph Thomas* (Winchester, Va.: J. Foster, 1817), p. 186; see also pp. 151, 175.

21. Campbell, "Address to the Readers of the Christian Baptist, No. IV," *CB* 1 (1 March 1824): 148; *The Christian System*, 4th ed. (Bethany, Va.: n.p., 1857), p. 48; and *Christianity Restored* (Bethany, Va.: n.p., 1835), p. 350. See also Thomas Olbricht, "Alexander Campbell's View of the Holy Spirit," *Restoration Quarterly* 6 (1962): 1-11. Robert Richardson contended that Campbell downplayed the role of the Holy Spirit *only* in the context of his disputes with Baptists over the nature of conversion ("Religious Herald — Again," *MH*, 4th ser., 7 [November 1857]: 637-45).

22. Hall, "The Operation of the Spirit," *Heretic Detector* 1 (July 1837): 179.

23. Hall, "The Autobiography of B. F. Hall," typescript in Center for Restoration Studies, Abilene Christian University, pp. 49, 53.

24. Campbell, "To Paulinus," *CB* 4 (7 September 1826): 35 (reprinted from the *Gospel Advocate*).

25. See Stone's letter to Walter Scott published in *CM* 10 (January 1836): 13-14.

26. Crihfield, "Incidents of a Tour to Indianapolis, Chapter III," *Heretic Detector* 3 (October 1839): 267.

27. Stone, "Missionaries to Pagans," *CM* 14 (April 1845): 363 (Stone finished this article before his death in 1844); and Stone to Walter Scott, *CM* 10 (January 1836): 13-14.

28. Thomas, *The Travels and Gospel Labors of Joseph Thomas* (Winchester, Va.: J. Foster, 1812), p. 88.

29. Hall, "The Autobiography of B. F. Hall," p. 57.

30. Hall, quoted by John I. Rogers in *Autobiography of Elder Samuel Rogers* (Cincinnati, 1880), pp. 58-59.

31. Hall, "The Autobiography of B. F. Hall," pp. 60-61.

32. See Hall, "The Autobiography of B. F. Hall," p. 72. There were three articles in Matthews's series: "The Gospel Plan of Saving Sinners, No. I," *CM* 3 (April 1829): 125-29; "The Gospel Plan of Saving Sinners, No. II," *CM* 3 (May 1829): 150-54; and "The Gospel Plan of Saving Sinners, No. III," *CM* 3 (July 1829): 211-13.

33. See Stone, "The Christian Expositor," *CM* 1 (January 1827): 59-60. See also Stone, "Reply," *CM* 2 (May 1828): 152-55.

34. See Hall, "The Autobiography of B. F. Hall," p. 72. For some representative arguments made in debating the issue, see John O'Kane, "A Reply to James E. Matthews," *CM* 3 (July 1829): 213-16; and Stone, "Remarks on the Foregoing Reply," *CM* 3 (July 1829): 216-19.

35. See Roberts, "B. F. Hall: Pioneer Evangelist and Herald of Hope," *Restoration Quarterly* 8 (1965): 251-54. See also Thomas H. Olbricht, "The Invitation: A Historical Survey," *Restoration Quarterly* 5 (1961): 13-15. On Scott, Bentley, Rigdon, Smith, and Vardeman, see "Extracts of Letters," *CB* 5 (2 June 1828): 271.

36. Stone, *CM* (August 1830): 201.

37. Stone, "Reply," *CM* 4 (September 1830): 236; and "Reply to the Above," *CM* 5 (March 1831): 58.

38. Stone, *The Biography of Eld. Barton Warren Stone*, p. 78.

39. Stone, "The Way of Salvation," *CM* 12 (January 1842): 77.

40. Rogers, in a letter to Stone dated 17 February 1842, published in *CM* 12 (April 1842): 178.

41. Stone, "Reply to Eld. J. Rogers," *CM* 12 (April 1842): 180-87.

42. Stone, "Reply to Brother Gooch," *CM* 9 (October 1835): 221-23.

43. Stone, "Reply," *CM* 4 (September 1830): 236; and "Reply to the Above," *CM* 11 (June 1841): 340. For further discussion of Stone's reluctance to require immersion, see Myer Phillips, "Historical Study of the Attitudes of the Churches of Christ toward Other Denominations" (Ph.D. diss., Baylor University, 1983), pp. 34-37.

44. Stone, "Desultory Remarks," *CM* 10 (December 1836): 182.

45. Stone, "Partyism," *CM* 1 (August 1827): 239-40.

46. Stone, "To Young Preachers," *CM* 12 (August 1842): 316-17; and Stone and D. P. Henderson, "Introduction," *CM* 14 (May 1844): 4-5.

47. Anthony L. Dunnavant has thoroughly documented this tendency in his article "From Precursor of the Movement to Icon of Christian Unity: Barton W. Stone in the Memory of the Christian Church (Disciples of Christ)," in *Cane Ridge in Context: Perspectives on Barton W. Stone and the Revival,* ed. Anthony L. Dunnavant (Nashville: Disciples of Christ Historical Society, 1992), pp. 13-14. On Stone as a precursor of the modern ecumenical movement, see, e.g., Charles C. Ware, *Barton Warren Stone: Pathfinder of Christian Union* (St. Louis: Bethany Press, 1932), p. 10; and West, *Barton Warren Stone*, pp. 110-31, 137-202.

48. Stone, "Queries Answered," *CM* 1 (25 October 1827): 271-73. See also Stone, "Objections to Christian Union Considered," *CM* 1 (24 March 1827): 114; and "Reply: To Elder Spencer Clack, Editor of the Baptist Recorder," *CM* 2 (December 1827): 35.

49. McCorkle, "Conversion of the World, No. 4," *CM* 14 (July 1844): 70-71; "Conversion of the World — No. 4 [*sic* — it was actually no. 5 in the series]," *CM* 14 (August 1844): 97-98; and "The Laymen [*sic*]," *CM* 13 (March 1844): 349.

50. See D. Newell Williams, "Barton W. Stone's Calvinist Piety," *Encounter* 42 (Autumn 1981): 409-17; and Richard T. Hughes and C. Leonard Allen, *Illusions of Innocence: Protestant Primitivism in America, 1630-1875* (Chicago: University of Chicago Press, 1988), pp. 112-16.

51. Stone, "A Compendious View of the Gospel," in *The Cane Ridge Reader,* pp. 191-92.

52. Rogers, "Funeral Discourse on Elder H. Dinsmore [Part 2]," *ACR* 6 (17 November 1863): 181; Jones, "The Reformation in Tennessee," included in J. W. Grant's "Sketch of the Reformation in Tennessee" (c. 1897), typescript in Center for Restoration Studies, Abilene Christian University, p. 35.

53. Hall, "The Autobiography of B. F. Hall," pp. 67-68.

54. Campbell, "Meeting-Houses," *MH* 5 (January 1834): 8.

55. Benjamin Lyon Smith, *Alexander Campbell* (St. Louis: Bethany Press, 1930), p. 147.

56. Grant, "A Sketch of the Reformation in Tennessee," pp. 9-10. See also Jones, "The Reformation in Tennessee," pp. 31-32; and Thomas, *The Life of the Pilgrim Joseph Thomas,* pp. 124, 160, 162-63, and elsewhere.

57. See Stone et al., "The Brethren Appointed for That Purpose Report the Following Address," *CM* 9 (July 1835): 148; "Number 1," *CM* 10 (January 1836): 11-13; *The Biography of Eld. Barton Warren Stone,* pp. 49-50; and Joseph Thomas, *The Travels and Gospel Labors of Joseph Thomas* (Winchester, Va.: n.p., 1812), p. 56.

58. Stone, "Christian Expositor," *CM* 12 (July 1842): 272.

59. Stone, *The Biography of Eld. Barton Warren Stone,* pp. 49-50; "1,000 Spiritual Preachers Wanted," *CM* 13 (March 1844): 367-69; and "Christian Union, Lecture III," *CM* 11 (May 1841): 316-17.

60. Hill, "An Autobiography of Abner Hill, Pioneer Preacher of Tennessee, Alabama, and Texas" (c. 1861), typescript housed in Center for Restoration Studies, Abilene Christian University, pp. 19-20.

61. Letters from Martha Wilson to her Aunt Julia, Bethany, Virginia, dated 21 July 1858 and 11 September 1858, Jones Family Papers, Southern Historical Collection, Wilson Library, University of North Carolina, Chapel Hill. Virgil's remarks appeared in a postscript to the July 21 letter.

62. See Dan G. Danner, "A History of Interpretation of Revelation 20:1-10 in the Restoration Movement" (master's thesis, Abilene Christian University, 1963).

63. Dunlavy, *The Manifesto; or, A Declaration of the Doctrine and Practice of the Church of Christ* (New York: n.p., 1847), p. 437; Purviance, *The Biography of Elder David Purviance* (Dayton: n.p., 1848), pp. 248-49. See also B. W. Stone et al., *Observations on Church Government, by the Presbytery of Springfield* (1808), in *The Cane Ridge Reader,* p. 12.

64. Stone, "To Elder William Caldwell," *CM* 8 (May 1834): 148. See also Stone, "The Millennium," *CM* 7 (October 1833): 314; and "Reply," *CM* 7 (December 1833): 365-66.

65. See Stone, "The Signs of the Last Days," *CM* 12 (August 1842): 301-6; "Signs of the Last Days — Continued," *CM* 12 (October 1842): 363-67; and "The Coming of the Son of God," *CM* 12 (April 1842): 166-70.

66. Stone et al., *Observations on Church Government, by the Presbytery of Springfield,* pp. 3, 8-9.

67. Stone, "Reflections of Old Age," *CM* 13 (August 1843): 123-26. See also "Civil and Military Offices Sought and Held by Christians," *CM* 12 (May 1842): 201-5; letters to and

from T. P. Ware, *CM* 14 (October 1844): 163-71; and "An Interview between an Old and Young Preacher," *CM* 14 (December 1844): 225-30.

68. James M. Mathes, "Number III," *CM* 10 (May 1836): 65-66.

69. Jn. T. Jones, Jno. Rigdon, M. Elder, and D. P. Henderson, "Report," *CM* 9 (November 1835): 250-51.

70. Stone, "Lecture on Matt. V. VI. and VII. Chapters," *CM* 14 (July 1844): 65.

71. Campbell, "Duties of Laboring Assiduously and Praying Unceasingly for the Abolition of War," *MH* 5 (July 1834): 306, 309. See also "War and Christianity Antipodal," *MH*, 3d ser., 7 (September 1850): 523-24.

72. Homer Hailey, an anti-institutional Church of Christ preacher in the middle years of the twentieth century, is an excellent case in point. Hailey held resolutely to pacifist convictions despite the fact that he was in no sense a descendant of the Stone tradition. David Edwin Harrell Jr. makes this point in an as-yet-unpublished biography of Hailey, typescript in possession of author. Similarly, the Non Class, One-Cup Churches of Christ, which could hardly be classified as Stoneite, clung tenaciously to the pacifist sentiment throughout the twentieth century (see Chap. 10).

73. Campbell, "American Christian Missionary Society, President's Address," *MH*, 4th ser., 2 (March 1852): 124.

74. Stone, "Reflections of Old Age," *CM* 13 (August 1843): 124.

75. Most contemporary historians have not come to grips with the difference between Stone and Campbell regarding the restoration ideal. This is not surprising, for they also have failed to take seriously the apocalyptic worldview of Stone. David Edwin Harrell's work is a case in point. Harrell argues that both Stone and Campbell were committed to a "spirit of moderation" and to postmillennial visions of social progress (*Quest for a Christian America: The Disciples of Christ and American Society to 1866* [Nashville: Disciples of Christ Historical Society, 1966], pp. 36, 41, and 45). Indeed, he asserts that "prior to 1830, both [men] . . . linked their religious reform efforts with the eventual spiritual and social regeneration of the world." Interestingly, in the one passage from Stone that Harrell cites to support this claim, Stone is actually arguing just the reverse, vehemently criticizing the postmillennial vision and contending that "God would *overturn, and overturn, and overturn*, till Messiah shall reign alone, and all submit to his government" (Stone, "Remarks on Liberty of Conscience," *CM* 3 [February 1829]: 91, cited by Harrell in *Quest for a Christian America*, p. 41). Harrell does recognize that "the sectarian emphasis of nonparticipation in civil government centered around the influence of Barton Stone in the early years of the church," but he never connects that emphasis with the apocalyptic, countercultural worldview of either Stone or, later, Tolbert Fanning and David Lipscomb (*Quest for a Christian America*, pp. 54-55). Indeed, Harrell argues that all evidences of premillennialism in Stone and others were essentially aberrations in a fundamentally postmillennial movement (*Quest for a Christian America*, pp. 42-44; and *The Social Sources of Division in the Disciples of Christ, 1865-1900* [Atlanta: Publishing Systems, 1973], p. 25).

76. I base this estimate on the figures given by Joseph Thomas suggesting that as early as 1810/11, the Stone movement in Tennessee and Kentucky embraced roughly 13,000 adherents. See above, p. 108.

77. Hall, "The Autobiography of B. F. Hall," pp. 8, 22.

78. Rogers, "The Life and Times of John Rogers," in John Rogers Books, 1800-1859, Southern Historical Collection, Manuscripts Department, University of North Carolina at Chapel Hill, Book I, p. 8.

79. Rogers, quoted by Robert Richardson in *Memoirs of Alexander Campbell*, vol. 2 (1897; reprint, Nashville: Gospel Advocate, 1956), pp. 332-33.

80. Jones, "The Reformation in Tennessee," pp. 31-34.

81. Matthew Gardner in a tract published in 1836, cited by S. H. Ford in "Rise of the Current Reformation — Appendix," *The Christian Repository* 72 (March 1858): 205, 203.

Notes to Chapter 6

1. See James Wilburn, *The Hazard of the Die: Tolbert Fanning and the Restoration Movement* (Malibu: Pepperdine University Press, 1980), pp. 13-16.

2. Fanning, "Obituary," *GA* 3 (January 1860): 31.

3. Fanning, "Reply," *Christian Review* 3 (July 1846): 156.

4. Looker-On, "Interpretation of Prophecy — Desultory Thoughts," *Christian Review*, 1 (July 1844): 161-62. See also J. B. Ferguson, "Reflections on the Destiny of Human Society," *Christian Review* 1 (July 1844): 158-59.

5. Fanning, "The Mission of the Church of Christ," in *The Living Pulpit of the Christian Church*, ed. W. T. Moore (Cincinnati: R. W. Carroll, 1868), p. 536; "Reply to Brethren Lillard, Harding, and Ransome," *GA* 7 (September 1861): 265-76; "Salutatory," *Religious Historian* 1 (January 1872): 2; and "The Church of Christ in Prophecy, No. 2," *Religious Historian* 2 (February 1873): 40-44.

6. Fanning, "Ministers of Peace in the World's Conflicts," *GA* 7 (November 1861): 347-48.

7. Fanning, "Political Strife amongst Christians," *Christian Review* 1 (August 1844): 184-85; and Lipscomb, "The Gospel Advocate," *GA* 9 (7 March 1867): 65.

8. Fanning, " 'The Kingdom of Heaven': A Spiritual Empire," *Christian Review* 3 (May 1846): 101.

9. See Fanning, "Peace," *Christian Review* 3 (March 1846): 65.

10. Lipscomb, "The Bible and Evolution," *GA* 31 (26 January 1889): 56; and "Common Sense in Religion," *GA* 46 (25 February 1904): 120.

11. Lipscomb, "Our Subscribers," *GA* 10 (23 January 1868): 73.

12. Lipscomb, "Divisions Must Come," *GA* 49 (3 October 1907): 633.

13. Lipscomb, "The 'Church of Christ' and the 'Disciples of Christ,' " *GA* 49 (18 July 1907): 457.

14. Lipscomb, "After Fifty Years," *GA* 58 (6 January 1916): 1.

15. The original series of articles containing the material in *CG* appeared in the *Christian Quarterly Review* under the following titles: "Civil Government: The Origin, Mission, and Destiny of, and the Christian's Relation to, Civil Government, from the Old Testament" (7 [October 1888]: 545-73); "Civil Government — Its Origin, Mission, and Destiny, and the Christian's Relation to It, as Presented in the New Testament" (8 [January 1889]: 3-37); and "Civil Government, Its Relation to the Church" (8 [July 1889]: 413-34).

16. Lipscomb, "Religion and Politics," *GA* 32 (26 March 1890): 199.

17. See Lipscomb, *CG*, pp. 13-14, 16-17, 88-89, 91-92, 128, 145.

18. Franklin, "Visit to Tennessee," *ACR*, 13 July 1875, p. 220.

19. See Lipscomb, *CG*, pp. 121ff.

20. Lipscomb, *CG*, pp. 144-45 (cf. p. 134), 133, 91-92 (cf. pp. 143-44).

21. Lipscomb, *CG*, pp. 8-9, 19-20.

22. Lipscomb, *CG*, pp. 48, 9-10.

23. Lipscomb, *CG*, pp. 14, 46-47 (cf. "The Kingdom of God," *GA* 45 [21 May 1903]: 328; and *CG*, pp. 51ff.).

24. Lipscomb, *CG*, pp. 25, 27-28 (cf. pp. 83-84), 96.

25. Lipscomb, "The Kingdom of God," *GA* 45 (21 May 1903): 328.

26. Lipscomb, *CG,* p. 60.

27. Lipscomb, *CG,* p. 28.

28. For information on this conference, see Timothy P. Weber, *Living in the Shadow of the Second Coming: American Premillennialism, 1875-1925* (New York: Oxford University Press, 1979), p. 28.

29. Lipscomb, "The Prophetic Conference," *GA* 20 (21 November 1878): 725; "Queries," *GA* 37 (23 June 1898): 397 (cf. Lipscomb, *Queries and Answers,* ed. J. W. Shepherd [Cincinnati: F. L. Rowe, 1918], p. 360).

30. Lipscomb, *A Commentary on the New Testament Epistles: Ephesians, Philippians, and Colossians,* ed. J. W. Shepherd, vol. 4 (Nashville: Gospel Advocate, 1939), p. 76; *CG,* pp. iii, 28 (cf. pp. 12-13), 136.

31. Harding, "The Kingdom of Christ versus the Kingdoms of Satan," *The Way* 5 (15 October 1903): 929-31.

32. Sewell, "Queries," *GA* 37 (11 July 1895): 437.

33. Fall, "Interesting Reminiscences," *GA* 21 (15 May 1879): 310.

34. See Lipscomb, "Queries," *GA* 40 (23 June 1898): 397; and E. G. Sewell, "Queries," *GA* 37 (11 July 1895): 437.

35. Chambers, "It Is to Reminisce," *Exhorter,* April 1966, p. 9. See also Chambers, "It Is to Reminisce," *Exhorter,* October 1967, p. 6.

36. Three factors help account for this oversight. (1) The tendency of Disciples historians to understand their movement principally in terms of Alexander Campbell's faith in progress has obscured the premillennial sentiments of both Stone and Lipscomb. (2) The fervent refusal especially of Lipscomb and his circle to speculate on the second coming has led some to assume that he had little or no interest in millennial themes. Thus, David Edwin Harrell has argued that Lipscomb was "persistently unwilling to discuss the subject," something he attributes to the general decline of interest in premillennial themes dating from before the Civil War (*Quest for a Christian America: The Disciples of Christ and American Society to 1866* [Nashville: Disciples of Christ Historical Society, 1966], p. 44n.68). And (3) beginning in World War I, Churches of Christ launched a frontal attack on premillennialism that lasted a full third of a century. When that attack had run its course by the mid 1940s, most mainstream Churches of Christ had come to view premillennialism as a heresy. Historians working within the context of the church might for that reason have had some difficulty discerning the significance of such views among such revered leaders as Stone and Lipscomb. Both of Lipscomb's biographers — Earl West and Robert Hooper — simply ignore the premillennial theme in Lipscomb. West identifies the "kingdom" with the "church," and simply fails to see the apocalyptic dimension in Lipscomb's thought (*The Life and Times of David Lipscomb* [Henderson, Tenn.: Religious Book Service, 1954], pp. 97-99). Hooper spiritualizes Lipscomb's notion of the kingdom, suggesting that "a perfect kingdom," in Lipscomb's view, "could not be attained in this world" but only "in the world to come" (*Crying in the Wilderness: A Biography of David Lipscomb* [Nashville: David Lipscomb College, 1979], pp. 110-22, esp. 121).

37. Lipscomb, *CG,* pp. 28 (cf. pp. 83-84, iv), 97.

38. Lipscomb, "Babylon," *GA* 23 (2 June 1881): 340.

39. The evidence that Lipscomb counseled against participation in American democracy is overwhelming; for some representative references to the American situation, see *CG,* pp. 23, 127.

40. Harrell, *Quest for a Christian America,* pp. 173-74; and "The Sectional Origins of the Churches of Christ," *Journal of Southern History* 30 (August 1964): 277. Harrell goes on to argue that "social force, class prejudice, sectional bitterness, and theologies shot through with economic presuppositions were the base upon which doctrinal debates were built," and

that "the institutional history of the church is largely a mirror of class conflict within the movement" (*The Social Sources of Division in the Disciples of Christ, 1865-1900* [Atlanta: Publishing Systems, 1973], pp. ix, 3).

41. See Harrell, "The Sectional Origins of the Churches of Christ," p. 268.

42. Fanning and Lipscomb, "A Reply to the Call of W. C. Rogers, Corresponding Secretary of the A.C.M. Society for All to Disseminate the Gospel," *GA* 8 (27 March 1866): 109 (cited by Harrell in "The Sectional Origins of the Churches of Christ," pp. 269-70).

43. Lipscomb, "The Advocate and Sectionalism," *GA* 8 (1 May 1866): 273.

44. See Fanning, "A General Consultation Meeting Suggested," *GA* 8 (16 April 1866): 241-42

45. Burnett, "Our Budget," *Christian Evangelist* 29 (21 July 1892): 456 (cited by Harrell in "The Sectional Origins of the Churches of Christ," p. 271).

46. Harrell, "The Sectional Origins of the Churches of Christ," p. 270.

47. Lipscomb, *CG*, p. iii. Further, Lipscomb implied that he had learned his lessons in this regard in part from Tolbert Fanning: "A number of our most studious and devoted brethren of the older class adopted and maintained this position. Among the older ones were T. Fanning, P. S. Fall, and B. U. Watkins" (*CG*, p. 153).

48. Lipscomb, *CG*, pp. 139-40; italics mine.

49. Lipscomb, "Passing Events," *GA* 25 (30 May 1882): 338; "From the Papers," *GA* 37 (22 August 1895): 529; and "From the Papers," *GA* 17 (29 August 1875): 545-46. On the celebration of the Confederate soldier following the war, see Charles Reagan Wilson, *Baptized in Blood: The Religion of the Lost Cause, 1865-1920* (Athens: University of Georgia Press, 1980), pp. 30-32.

50. Fanning, "Religious Aspects of the American Revolution of 1861," *GA* 8 (July 1861): 206.

51. Lipscomb, "Babylon," *GA* 23 (2 June 1881): 340.

52. For Harrell's discussion of the importance of economic factors in the development of Churches of Christ in the period after the Civil War, see "The Sectional Origins of the Churches of Christ," pp. 272-77. Since he deals with evidence drawn only from the postwar period in this article, readers may infer — incorrectly — that poverty among southern churches was essentially a postwar phenomenon. In *Quest for a Christian America,* however, Harrell clearly demonstrates the lower-class prejudices of Christians from both the Stone and Campbell movements (see pp. 66ff.).

53. Fanning, cited by Lipscomb in "Tolbert Fanning's Teaching and Influence," in *Franklin College and Its Influences,* ed. James E. Scobey (Nashville: McQuiddy Printing, 1906), p. 24.

54. Lipscomb, "Tolbert Fanning's Teaching and Influence," p. 19.

55. Fanning, "Baccalaureate Address Delivered by T. Fanning to the Class of 1847," in *Franklin College and Its Influences,* pp. 282-83; and "Sermon Delivered by T. Fanning at Ebenezer Church" (October 1857), in *Franklin College and Its Influences,* pp. 295-97.

56. See Earl I. West, *Search for the Ancient Order,* vol. 2 (Indianapolis: Religious Book Service, 1950), pp. 9, 11.

57. See Anthony L. Dunnavant, "David Lipscomb on the Church and the Poor," *RQ* 33 (1991): 75-85; and "David Lipscomb and the 'Preferential Option for the Poor' among Post-Bellum Churches of Christ," in *Poverty and Ecclesiology: Nineteenth-Century Evangelicals in the Light of Liberation Theology,* ed. Anthony L. Dunnavant (Collegeville, Minn.: Liturgical Press, 1992), pp. 27-50.

58. See Earl I. West, *The Life and Times of David Lipscomb* (Henderson, Tenn.: Religious Book Service, 1954), p. 37.

59. Lipscomb, *The Religious Sentiment: Its Social and Political Influence* (Nashville:

Cameron & Fall, 1855), pp. 26, 34. A copy of this pamphlet is housed in the Tennessee State Library and Archives, Nashville.

60. See Lipscomb, "Our Positions," *GA* 54 (22 August 1912): 954.

61. Lipscomb, "New Publications," *GA* 8 (1 January 1866): 11-12.

62. Lipscomb, *GA* 8 (27 February 1866): 141.

63. Lipscomb, "Tolbert Fanning's Teaching and Influence," in *Franklin College and Its Influences*, pp. 59-60.

64. Sewell, "Reminiscences of Civil War Times, No. 4," *GA* (1 August 1907): 488.

65. See Robert E. Hooper, *Crying in the Wilderness: A Biography of David Lipscomb* (Nashville: David Lipscomb College, 1979): 231-333.

66. Lipscomb, "Tolbert Fanning's Teaching and Influence," p. 59.

67. "The Divine Law of Expansion," *Christian Oracle* 16 (18 January 1899): 2.

68. Tully, "Responsibility of the Disciples of Christ to the Present Age," *Christian Quarterly Review* 4 (1885): 581-82. For a brief discussion of the doctrine of Anglo-American progress among Disciples at century's end, see Harrell, *The Social Sources of Division in the Disciples of Christ, 1865-1900*, pp. 23-25.

69. See Lipscomb, *CG*, pp. 136-37, 53-56.

70. See Lipscomb, "Withdrawal," *GA* 22 (16 September 1880): 597.

Notes to Chapter 7

1. See Harding, "The Kingdom of Christ vs. the Kingdoms of Satan," *The Way* 5 (15 October 1903): 929-31.

2. Bell, "Studies in Philemon (3)," *FF* 77 (26 January 1960): 55.

3. Harding, "Can the Preacher Go in Faith without a Contract?" *GA* 27 (7 June 1885): 344.

4. Harding, "The Enemies of the Bible School," *The Way* 1 (November 1899): 163. Nashville Bible School incorporated despite Harding's objections, and he moved shortly thereafter to become the president of a new institution, the Potter Bible College in Bowling Green, Kentucky. His biographer argues, however, that the move was not directly related to his strong feelings over incorporation. See Lloyd Cline Sears, *The Eyes of Jehovah: The Life and Times of James Alexander Harding* (Nashville: Gospel Advocate, 1970), pp. 160-61.

5. Harding, "A Comfortable Doctrine," *GA* 25 (22 August 1883): 538.

6. Harding, "The Pastor — A Letter from Brother Je. E. Dunn and a Reply by the Editor," *The Way* 2 (June 1900): 83-84.

7. White, in *The Harding-White Discussion* (Cincinnati: F. L. Rowe, 1910), p. 19.

8. Harding, in *Harding-White Discussion*, pp. 14-15.

9. See *Harding-White Discussion*, pp. 16, 25.

10. White, in *Harding-White Discussion*, pp. 30, 11-12, 16, 21.

11. Before going to Dallas, White had utilized some of these pragmatic principles in a thriving ministry in Gallatin, Tennessee, clearly an exception to the prevailing pattern in that region. It is also worth noting that the preacher who preceded White at the Pearl and Bryan congregation in Dallas was Jesse P. Sewell (see Chap. 9).

12. Harding, "Scraps," *The Way* 1 (5 July 1899): 97.

13. See John T. Lewis, " 'His Heart Trembled for the Ark of God,' " *Bible Banner* 1 (October 1938): 7.

14. On the premillennial movement among Churches of Christ, see David M. Owen,

"The Premillennialist Movement in the Church of Christ" (master's thesis, Murray State University, Murray, Kentucky, 1989).

15. See Boll, "What Shall the End Be?" *The Way* 2 (April 1900): 60-61; and "The Christian's Duty as to War," *WW* 11 (December 1917): 493-94.

16. Harding, quoted by Sears in *The Eyes of Jehovah*, p. 155. Stanford Chambers notes that Boll had a special allegiance to Harding in "It Is to Reminisce," *Exhorter* (1 January 1968): 4.

17. See Chambers, "It Is to Reminisce," *Exhorter* (15 June 1964): 4; and "It Is to Reminisce," *Exhorter* (July 1964): 5.

18. R. L. Roberts has prepared biographical sketches of many early leaders in the Stone movement whose lives conformed to this pattern. These sketches will be published in Richard T. Hughes and R. L. Roberts, *The Churches of Christ* (Westport, Conn.: Greenwood Press, forthcoming).

19. See Chambers, "It Is to Reminisce," *Exhorter* (April 1966): 9.

20. Chambers, "It Is to Reminisce," *Exhorter* (October 1967): 7; and "It Is to Reminisce," *Exhorter* (April 1966): 9.

21. See Chambers, "It Is to Reminisce," *Exhorter* (April 1966): 9.

22. See Chambers, "It Is to Reminisce," *Exhorter* (December 1965): 3.

23. Evidence abounds concerning the influence of dispensational premillennialists on Boll. See, e.g., R. H. B., "About Books," *WW* 10 (February 1916): 88; "Bible Study Course," *WW* 10 (January 1916): 28; and "Jesus Is Coming," *WW* 10 (December 1916): 551. On Boll's dispensationalism, see Boll, *The Kingdom of God* (Louisville: Word & Work, n.d.).

24. Tidwell, "Autosoterism within Churches of Christ" (master's thesis, Vanderbilt University, 1986), p. 55.

25. See Boll, "Words in Season," *WW* 10 (July 1916): 338-39; and "The Olivet Sermon," *WW* 10 (November 1916): 487-92.

26. McQuiddy, "Do the Kingdom and the Church Mean the Same Thing?" *GA* 61 (17 April 1919): 367; and "Is the Church the Vestibule of the Kingdom?" *GA* 61 (20 March 1919): 271-72.

27. Hardeman, *Hardeman's Tabernacle Sermons*, vol. 4 (Nashville: Gospel Advocate, 1938), p. 157.

28. Armstrong, "A Piece of History," *Christian Leader* 54 (1 August 1940): 15.

29. On the erosion of pacifism among Churches of Christ in this period, see Michael Casey, "From Patriotism to Pacifism: The Emergence of Civil Religion in the Churches of Christ in World War One," *Mennonite Quarterly Review* 66 (July 1992): 376-90.

30. On petitions for conscientious objection, see, e.g., "Military Exemption," *Christian Leader* 31 (10 July 1917): 7; A. B. Lipscomb, "An Appeal for Exemption," *GA* 59 (28 June 1917): 145; A. J. Jernigan's open letter to President Woodrow Wilson in *FF*, 8 May 1917, p. 2; and Earl Irvin West, *Search for the Ancient Order*, vol. 3: *1900-1918* (Indianapolis: Religious Book Service, 1979), pp. 374-75.

Regarding imprisonment of conscientious objectors, J. N. Armstrong reported that in 1917, "twelve or more . . . brethren were sentenced for twenty years' imprisonment because their consciences could do no military service, [and] . . . other boys were meeting boards, pleading with military giants, and suffering all kinds of prosecution in all parts of this country, fighting for their consciences (" 'J. C. McQuiddy's Course and F. W. Smith's Complaint,' " *GA* 62 [9 December 1920]: 1191).

Regarding conscientious objectors, see Michael Casey, "New Information on Conscientious Objectors of World War I and the Churches of Christ," *RQ* 34 (1992): 83-96.

31. Elam, "Defining the Conscientious Objector," *GA* 60 (25 April 1918): 390-91.

32. Lawson, quoted by Earl West in "World War I and the Decline of David Lipscomb's Civil Government," an unpublished paper housed in Graves Memorial Library, Harding Graduate School of Religion, Memphis, p. 10.

33. See West, *Search for the Ancient Order*, 3:384.

34. Lipscomb, "Notes of Travel, No. 8," *GA* 14 (26 September 1872): 899-902.

35. Showalter, "The Relation of Christians to War," *FF* 35 (11 June 1918): 2.

36. Showalter made his comments in *GA* 58 (13 April 1916): 369; on the SATC training, see "Special from Abilene Christian College," *GA* 60 (13 October 1918): 953.

37. For an account of the telling impact of government propaganda and pressure on the Mennonites, a peace church by definition, see James C. Juhnke, *Vision, Doctrine, War: Mennonite Identity and Organization in America, 1890-1930* (Scottdale, Pa.: Herald Press, 1989), pp. 218-42, esp. p. 232.

38. F. W. Smith, "As a Matter of Simple Justice," *GA* 62 (23 September 1920), 931.

39. McQuiddy, "Conscientious Objectors," *GA* 59 (26 July 1917): 720-21.

40. Douglas, quoted by Smith in "As a Matter of Simple Justice," *GA* 62 (23 September 1920): 931.

41. Armstrong, " 'J. C. McQuiddy's Course and F. W. Smith's Complaint,' " *GA* 62 (9 December 1920): 1191.

42. See Marsden, *Fundamentalism and American Culture: The Shaping of Twentieth-Century Evangelicalism, 1870-1925* (Oxford: Oxford University Press, 1980), p. 149.

43. C. A. Buchanan, "Why the Change?" *GA* 61 (23 January 1919): 85.

44. Kurfees, "The Return of Peace with the Religious Outlook at the Dawn of 1919," *GA* 61 (2 January 1919): 10. The myth of demonic Germany and Christian America was particularly pronounced in the *Christian Leader*. See, e.g., J. Y. E., "Why Does God Permit the Kaiser?" *Christian Leader* 32 (10 September 1918): 6; and W. W. Freeman, "Christians and the War, No. 2," *Christian Leader* 32 (1 January 1918): 1.

45. McQuiddy, "The Peace League," *GA* 61 (27 March 1919): 297.

46. Kurfees, "The League of Nations and the Peace of the World," *GA* 61 (4 September 1919): 866-67.

47. See Charles Neal, "The United States of the Nations," *WW* 11 (September 1917): 378-80.

48. McQuiddy, "The Peace League," *GA* 61 (27 March 1919): 297-98.

49. Smith, in "Is the World Growing Better?" *GA* 58 (6 January 1916): 6-11.

50. Smith, "He Annihilated a Hobbyhorse," *GA* 58 (27 January 1916): 84.

51. Boles and Boll, *Unfulfilled Prophecy: A Discussion on Prophetic Themes* (Nashville: Gospel Advocate, 1928), pp. 335-36, 317; see also pp. 98-99.

52. Rowe, "How 'Revelation' Impresses Me," *CL* 47 (16 May 1933): 3.

53. J. N. Armstrong, "Words of Commendation," *GA* 45 (16 July 1903): 461.

54. S. H. Hall, "Harding College," *GA* 70 (22 November 1928): 1109.

55. See, e.g., Armstrong, "For Good Understanding," *FF* 52 (30 April 1935): 1; "The Living Message," *CL* 38 (18 November 1924): 3; and *Bulletin Harding College: Harding College on Premillennialism* 14 (May 1939): 2. Armstrong also affirmed this point in a letter to George Benson dated 10 April 1935, in possession of Richard Hughes.

56. See, e.g., Armstrong, *The Church* (Cordell, Okla.: Gospel Herald Printers, n.d.), p. 55; "The Beginning of the Kingdom of Heaven on Earth," *GA* 77 (24 January 1935): 84; "The Beginning of the Divine Rule on Earth," *FF* 61 (25 January 1944): 4-5; and "Allegiance Due to God First," *GA* 78 (7 May 1936): 444-45. This last article is perhaps Armstrong's clearest statement of his apocalyptic point of view.

57. Armstrong, in a radio address delivered 16 March 1941; ms. in possession of Clifton Ganus, former president of Harding College, Searcy, Arkansas.

58. See Lloyd Cline Sears, *For Freedom: The Biography of John Nelson Armstrong* (Austin: Sweet Publishing, 1969), pp. 155-57.

59. This brief history is based on James L. Atteberry's *Story of Harding College* (Searcy, Ark.: n.p., 1966), pp. 1-16. See also Adlai S. Croom, *The Early History of Harding College* (Searcy, Ark.: n.p., 1954); F. W. Mattox, "A History of the Development of Harding College, 1905-1939" (master's thesis, University of Oklahoma, 1940); Sears, *For Freedom*, pp. 65-263; and M. Norvel Young, *A History of Colleges Established and Controlled by Members of the Church of Christ* (Kansas City: Old Paths Book Club, 1949), pp. 129-47.

60. Frank Rhodes suggested as much in an interview with the author conducted 11 June 1990 in Searcy, Arkansas. Armstrong's biographer L. C. Sears concurs: "[Armstrong] would have denied being a financier at all; he was a teacher. He made no attempt to build endowments; he was building men" (*For Freedom*, p. 141).

61. See "College Presidents," *GA*, 11 October 1934, pp. 980-81; *GA*, 17 January 1935, p. 61; and J. N. Armstrong, "College Professor Goes on Record Again," *FF* 52 (8 January 1935): 1, 8. There is additional information supporting this in a letter from J. N. Armstrong to George S. Benson dated 10 April 1935, in possession of Richard Hughes.

62. On Benson, see John C. Stevens, *Before Any Were Willing: The Story of George S. Benson* (N.p.: n.p., 1991); and L. Edward Hicks, *"Sometimes in the Wrong, but Never in Doubt": George S. Benson and the Education of the New Religious Right* (Knoxville: University of Tennessee Press, 1995).

63. Benson recalled this in an interview with the author on 11 June 1990 at Searcy, Arkansas.

64. See chap. 1 of Hicks, *"Sometimes in the Wrong, but Never in Doubt."*

65. Atteberry, *The Story of Harding College*, p. 48.

66. According to John A. Scott in an interview with the author on 14 May 1991 in Memphis; and see Stevens, *Before Any Were Willing*, p. 128.

67. See Davidson, *How I Discovered the Secret of Success in the Bible* (Westwood, N.J.: Fleming H. Revell, 1961), p. 13.

68. *The Bison*, Harding College student newspaper (December 12, 1939), cited in Stevens, *Before Any Were Willing*, pp. 132-33.

69. See chap. 2 of Hicks, *"Sometimes in the Wrong, but Never in Doubt"*; see also Davidson, "Lessons from History," *CL* 53 (15 May 1939): 172.

70. Interview by the author with John A. Scott, 14 May 1991.

71. Davidson, *How I Discovered the Secret of Success in the Bible*, p. 82.

72. Davidson, *How I Discovered the Secret of Success in the Bible*, p. 128.

73. Harding, in *Harding-White Discussion*, p. 4.

74. See Davidson, *How I Discovered the Secret of Success in the Bible*, pp. 68-78.

75. See Davidson, *How I Discovered the Secret of Success in the Bible*, p. 99.

76. See Davidson, *How I Discovered the Secret of Success in the Bible*, pp. 19-20, 22, and 61.

77. Wallace's book *Modern Millennial Theories Exposed* (Houston: Roy E. Cogdill, 1945) contains most of his writings refuting premillennial theories.

78. See Armstrong, "For Good Understanding," *FF* 52 (30 April 1935): 1.

79. Harper, "The Objections to Harding College," *BB* 4 (August 1942): 15.

80. Wallace, "The Harding College Jubilee," *BB* 2 (January 1940): 4.

81. Harper, "An Explanation," *BB* 3 (September 1940): 18-19.

82. *Bulletin Harding College: Harper's Fight against Harding College* 17 (July 1941): 9-11.

83. Wallace, "What Is It All About — and What Difference Does It Make?" *BB* 1 (November 1938): 7; and "The 'New Spiritual Contingent Called "The Church"'; or, The Prophecies and Promises of God," *BB* 1 (August 1938): 3.

84. See Harper, "Defending the Truth: It Is the Duty of Every Christian to Oppose All Forms of Error That the Blood Stream of the Church May Be Kept Pure," *BB* 1 (August 1938): 12-13; and Wallace, "The Sin of Sectarianism," *BB* 1 (October 1938): 3.

85. Harper, "Is It the Truth — or the Person?" *BB* 6 (March 1944): 7.

86. See Wallace, "The Government — Civil and Military," *BB* 4 (July 1942): 2; and Cled Wallace, "What Pearl Harbor Did to Us," *BB* 6 (November 1943): 1. In a letter printed in the July 1942 issue of the *Bible Banner*, Glen E. Green wrote, "Just read your article in the March *Banner*. . . . I thought you were on the other side" ("The Christian and the Government," *BB* 4 [July 1942]: 7).

87. Regarding the collapse of pacifism among Churches of Christ in World War II, see Michael Casey, "Warriors against War: The Pacifists of the Churches of Christ in World War Two," *Restoration Quarterly* 35 (1993): 159-74; and "Churches of Christ and World War II Civilian Public Service: A Pacifist Remnant," in *Proclaim Peace: Christian Pacifism in America outside the Historic Peace Churches*, ed. Theron F. Schlabach and Richard T. Hughes (Champaign, Ill.: University of Illinois Press, 1996).

88. Wallace, "The Christian and the Government," *BB* 4 (March 1942): 8. This highly inflammatory article was unsigned. In July, however, W. E. Brightwell revealed that Foy Wallace had written the article, using Brightwell's notes (Brightwell, "For the Vindication of the Cause," *BB* 4 [July 1942]: 6).

89. Cled Wallace, "The Christian and the Government," *BB* 4 (June 1942): 4; and "The Big President of a Little College," *BB* 6 (June 1944): 3.

90. Wallace, "The Lipscomb Theory of Civil Government," *BB* 6 (October 1943): 5. See also Wallace, "We Are Also Conscientious," *BB* 6 (October 1943): 7.

91. While pacifism and premillennialism often went hand in hand, there were significant leaders in the movement who held to the one without holding to the other. For example, Daniel Sommer, a conservative preacher and editor in southern Indiana, was premillennial but also militaristic. On the other hand, H. Leo Boles, president of David Lipscomb College and an editor of the *Gospel Advocate*, fought premillennialism tooth and nail but was at the same time one of the last serious defenders of the pacifist doctrine among Churches of Christ.

92. Wallace, "The Government — Civil and Military," *BB* 4 (July 1942): 3-4.

93. Brightwell, "For the Vindication of the Cause," *BB* 4 (July 1942): 5, 7.

94. Lambert, "The David Lipscomb Book," *BB* 7 (September 1944): 9-10, 15; "Canonizing Campbell and Lipscomb," *BB* 6 (May 1944): 10; and a letter to Foy Wallace printed in Wallace, "The Lipscomb Theory of Civil Government," *BB* 6 (October 1943): 3.

95. Wallace, "The Lipscomb Theory of Civil Government," *BB* 6 (October 1943): 5-6; and " 'The Glorious Millennial Morn,' " *BB* 6 (May 1944): 5.

96. Helen Jackson, "David Lipscomb on Eph. 4:9," *BB* 6 (December 1943): 3; and John T. Lewis, "David Lipscomb on Eph. 4:9," *GA* 86 (May 1944): 330-31.

97. Wallace, *God's Prophetic Word* (Houston: Roy Cogdill, 1946).

98. See *Churches of Christ in the United States*, comp. Mac Lynn (Nashville: Gospel Advocate, 1991), p. x.

99. See Hill, "The Churches of Christ and Religion in the South," *Mission Journal* 14 (August 1980): 11, 15.

100. For examples of the liberal point of view, see George Eckman, *When Christ Comes Again* (New York: Abingdon, 1917); Shailer Mathews, *Will Christ Come Again?* (Chicago: American Institute of Sacred Literature, 1917), and *The Faith of Modernism* (New York: Macmillan, 1924); Shirley Jackson Case, *The Millennial Hope* (Chicago: University of Chicago Press, 1918), and *The Revelation of St. John* (Chicago: University of Chicago Press, 1919); James H. Snowden, *The Coming of the Lord: Will It Be Pre-millennial?* (New York: Macmillan, 1919), and *Is the World Growing Better?* (New York: Macmillan, 1919); and George P. Mains,

Premillennialism: Non-Scriptural, Non-Historic, Non-Scientific, Non-Philosophical (New York: Abingdon, 1920). For a discussion of the modernist attack on premillennialism, see Timothy P. Weber, *Living in the Shadow of the Second Coming: American Premillennialism, 1875-1925* (New York: Oxford University Press, 1979), pp. 117-21.

Notes to Chapter 8

1. Chambers, "It Is to Reminisce," *Exhorter* (1 January 1968): 4.

2. Boll, in H. Leo Boles and R. H. Boll, *Unfulfilled Prophecy: A Discussion on Prophetic Themes* (Nashville: Gospel Advocate, 1928), p. 380.

3. Boll, in Boles and Boll, *Unfulfilled Prophecy,* p. 321.

4. Boll, "Afraid of God and of Christ's Coming," *WW* 10 (August 1916): 34-35.

5. Boll, "The Righteousness of God," *WW* 11 (November 1917): 459-60.

6. Boll, "Words in Season," *WW* 11 (September 1917): 403; and "Afraid of God and of Christ's Coming," *WW* 10 (August 1916): 343.

7. Boll, "Words in Season," *WW* 37 (October 1943): 245-47.

8. Campbell, "Sermon on the Law," in *Historical Documents Advocating Christian Union,* ed. Charles A. Young (Chicago: Christian Century, 1904), p. 241.

9. Campbell, "Essays on the Work of the Holy Spirit in the Salvation of Men," *CB,* Burnet's edition, 2 (4 April 1825): 137.

10. See William J. Richardson, *The Role of Grace in the Thought of Alexander Campbell* (Los Angeles: Westwood Christian Foundation, 1991), pp. 35-43.

11. Campbell, *The Christian System,* 5th ed. (1835; reprint, Cincinnati: Standard Publishing, 1901), pp. 153, 166.

12. See Campbell, *The Christian System,* p. 189.

13. Campbell, *The Christian System,* pp. 166-67.

14. Lipscomb, *A Commentary on the New Testament Epistles: Romans* (Nashville: Gospel Advocate, 1943), p. 30.

15. Brents, *The Gospel Plan of Salvation,* 12th ed. (Nashville: Gospel Advocate, 1928), p. 211.

16. Brents, *Gospel Plan of Salvation,* pp. 479-570.

17. Brents, *Gospel Plan of Salvation,* pp. 548-49.

18. Srygley, "Salvation by Grace," *GA* 20 (28 November 1878): 743.

19. Lipscomb, "Stand on Safe Ground," *GA* 51 (28 October 1909): 1356.

20. Nichol and Whiteside, *Sound Doctrine,* vol. 1 (Clifton, Tex.: Nichol Publishing, 1920), pp. 146, 153.

21. On Moser, see John Mark Hicks, "The Man or the Plan? K. C. Moser and the Theology of Grace among Mid-Twentieth Century Churches of Christ," paper presented at the Eighteenth Annual W. B. West, Jr., Lectures for the Advancement of Christian Scholarship, 5 October 1993, Harding Graduate School of Religion, Memphis, Tennessee. The full text is available through the Harding University Graduate School library.

22. Moser, "Can the Gospel Be Obeyed?" *FF* 51 (6 February 1934): 2.

23. Showalter, "Obedience and Salvation," *FF* 51 (13 February 1934): 4.

24. For a somewhat more detailed version of this story, see Richard Hughes, "Are Restorationists Evangelicals?" in *The Variety of American Evangelicalism,* ed. Donald W. Dayton and Robert K. Johnston (Knoxville: University of Tennessee Press, 1991), pp. 124-25.

25. Moser, in a tract entitled "Are We Preaching the Gospel?" cited by Bill Love in *The Core Gospel: On Restoring the Crux of the Matter* (Abilene: Abilene Christian University Press,

1992), p. 245. Love argues that the patterns Moser described persisted well into the mid-twentieth century (pp. 243-58, 305-7).

26. Earl I. West assumes that the Mr. Bush in question was A. J. Bush (*Search for the Ancient Order,* vol. 2: *1866-1906* [Indianapolis: Religious Book Service, 1950], p. 411). R. L. Roberts thinks it more likely that the man was either W. T. Bush or Thomas Bush, both of whom are listed in the 1860 U.S. Census as "Christian clergymen" in Washington County, Texas. Of these two, Roberts names W. T. Bush, also known as Tandy Bush, buried at Salado, Texas, as the best candidate (in a letter to Richard Hughes dated 10 January 1995).

27. West, *Search for the Ancient Order,* 2:411.

28. Lipscomb, "Notes of Travel, No. 8," *GA* 14 (26 September 1872): 899-902.

29. This entire story is related by West in *Search for the Ancient Order,* 2:401-5.

30. Lipscomb, "Items Personal, Etc.," *GA* 26 (17 September 1884): 603. See also "Editorial Notice," *FF* 1 (October 1884): 37.

31. McGary, *FF* 1 (December 1884): 102.

32. McGary, "What Would Christ Not Do?" *FF* 16 (1 May 1890): 278.

33. McGary, *FF* 1 (September 1884): 1.

34. McGary, "Trying to Elude Detection by Pointing to Side Issues and Dodging behind Technicalities," *FF* 1 (November 1884): 72.

35. McGary, " 'Personalities,' " *FF* 1 (February 1885): 126.

36. McGary, " 'Personalities,' " *FF* 1 (February 1885): 128.

37. McGary, "A Good Meeting," *FF* 1 (September 1884): 20.

38. McGary, "A Good Meeting," *FF* 1 (September 1884): 22.

39. McGary, " 'Personalities,' " *FF* 1 (February 1885): 126.

40. S. L. Barker, "From New Mexico," *FF* 6 (13 March 1890): 5.

41. Tant, "That Apology," *GA* 62 (25 November 1920): 1140. Cf. "Pussyfoot's Religion," *GA* 62 (7 October 1920): 981.

42. Price Billingsley, "Betrayal Plus Bad Business," an open letter to Leon McQuiddy dated 17 May 1939, housed in the Center for Restoration Studies, Abilene Christian University.

43. Burnett, *Doctrinal Poetry,* vol. 1 (Austin: Firm Foundation, n.d.), pp. 58-59.

44. Wallace, "The Certified Gospel," in *The Certified Gospel* (Port Arthur, Tex.: O. C. Lambert & Son, 1937), pp. 1-5.

45. Letter from Rowe to J. Edward Meixner dated 23 June 1939, in Center for Restoration Studies, Abilene Christian University.

46. Wallace, "Imprimatur — Let It Be Printed," *BB* 1 (May 1939): 2; and "What the Church Must Do to Be Saved," *BB* 1 (July 1939): 3.

47. Wallace, " 'Jehovah-Nissi — The Lord My Banner,' " *BB* 1 (July 1938): 2-3.

48. Wallace, "Abraham and Lot — An Ill-Timed Editorial on a Misapplied Example," *BB* 2 (September 1939): 3.

49. Turner, "Long Live the Bible Banner!" *BB* 1 (December 1938): 11.

50. Keenan, "Shall We Join in a Conspiracy of Silence?" *BB* 1 (December 1938): 10.

51. McCord, "Casting Down Imaginations," *BB* 1 (October 1938): 10.

52. McCord, "We Are Softening," *BB* 1 (September 1938): 15.

53. McCord, "A Weak Attitude toward Error Is Inimical to the New Testament Church," *BB* 1 (August 1938): 13.

54. Brewer, *Autobiography of G. C. Brewer* (Murfreesboro, Tenn.: DeHoff Publications, 1957), p. 64.

55. Brewer, "Read This Book," *GA* 65 (11 May 1933): 434.

56. Brewer, "Confession and the Plan of Salvation," *GA* 87 (26 April 1945): 233. See also Love, *The Core Gospel,* pp. 211-17.

57. See Brewer, "Random Remarks," *FF* 42 (7 July 1925): 3.

58. See Wallace, "The Jorgenson Protest," *BB* 4 (June 1942): 2.

59. See Brewer, "A Letter with a Message to All," *FF* 51 (20 March 1934): 4.

60. Showalter, "Abilene Christian College and the Lectureship," *FF* 51 (6 March 1934): 4.

61. Brewer, "A Plea for Unity," *Abilene Christian College Bible Lectures, 1934* (Austin: Firm Foundation Publishing House, 1934), pp. 179-80, 182-83.

62. Wallace, "Brother G. C. Brewer's Abilene Lecture," *GA* 76 (22 March 1934): 284-85.

Notes to Chapter 9

1. Rogers, "The Church of Christ at Concord, to the Elders and Brethren Assembled in Conference at Caneridge, Sendeth Christian Salutation," *CM* 4 (October 1830): 258. See also Rogers, "The Life and Times of John Rogers," in John Rogers Books, 1800-1859, Book I, pp. 121-22, in Southern Historical Collection, Manuscripts Department, University of North Carolina at Chapel Hill.

2. Lipscomb, "Queries on Civil Government," *GA* 17 (17 April 1875): 399-400.

3. Lipscomb, "A Mistake," *GA* 49 (28 November 1907): 761.

4. Letter from Sewell to Thornton Crews dated 27 February 1940, from Sewell Papers.

5. See Richard Hughes, "The Editor-Bishop: David Lipscomb and the *Gospel Advocate*," in *The Power of the Press: The Forrest F. Reed Lectures for 1986*, comp. James M. Seale (Nashville: Disciples of Christ Historical Society, 1986), pp. 20-21.

6. Lipscomb, "Errett et al. vs. 'Southern Journalism and Theology,'" *GA* 34 (20 October 1892): 658.

7. Lipscomb, "A True Lover of Truth," *GA* 83 (7 August 1941): 745.

8. Ijams in a letter to Sewell dated 1 September 1938, in Sewell Papers.

9. Sewell in an undated letter to Leon McQuiddy, in Sewell Papers.

10. The information regarding McMillan related here is based on a telephone interview with McMillan's grandson Robert M. Randolph conducted by the author 9 September 1991 and on a letter from McMillan's daughter Elizabeth Randolph to the author dated December 1993. For a sketch of McMillan's life, see Jim Mankin, "E. W. McMillan Still Made an Impact at 100 Years of Age," *Christian Chronicle*, August 1993, p. 11.

11. Sewell, in a letter to Lacy Ellrod dated 27 March 1941, in Sewell Papers.

12. Sewell, in a letter to Thornton Crews dated 27 February 1940, in Sewell Papers.

13. Sewell, in a letter to Clinton Davidson dated 27 April 1939, in Sewell Papers. See also in the same collection, Sewell's letter to E. W. McMillan dated 11 November 1940.

14. Sewell, in a letter to McQuiddy dated 5 May 1938, in Sewell Papers.

15. See Wallace, "'Just the Facts,'" *BB* 1 (May 1939): 8-9.

16. McMillan, in a letter to Sewell dated 28 August 1938, in Sewell Papers.

17. Sewell, in a letter to McQuiddy dated 1 September 1938, in Sewell Papers.

18. Sewell, in an undated letter to McQuiddy, in Sewell Papers.

19. Sewell, in a letter to Davidson dated 26 August 1938, in Sewell Papers.

20. Sewell, in an undated letter to McQuiddy, in Sewell Papers.

21. See "Editorial," *CL* 53 (February 1939): 48.

22. Davidson, in a letter to all preachers who had responded to his questionnaire, dated 30 June 1938, in Sewell Papers. See also E. W. McMillan, "Our Aim and Why," *CL* 53 (1 January 1939): 6.

23. Davidson, in a letter to Sewell dated 24 August 1938, in Sewell Papers.

24. Wallace, "In-Cullings-Comments and Correspondence," *BB* 1 (September 1938): 10-11.

25. "Who Killed Cock Robin? — That Brotherhood Survey," *BB* 1 (May 1939): 14-19.

26. Smith, "Deliverance Has Come," *BB* 1 (March 1939): 16.

27. See, e.g., Wallace, "The Emergence of a New Movement," *BB* 1 (January-February 1939): 3; and "What Is It All About — And What Difference Does It Make?" *BB* 1 (November 1939): 5.

28. See Wallace, "Some Spoiled Fruit," *BB* 2 (October 1939): 2.

29. See Wallace, "The Spirit That Stoned Stephen," *BB* 1 (January-February 1939): 4.

30. Wallace, "The Bible Banner — Past, Present and Future," *BB* 8 (June 1945): 6-7.

31. Eugene S. Smith, "Deliverance Has Come," *BB* 1 (March 1939): 16.

32. E. W. McMillan explained these circumstances in " 'By Their Fruits,' " *CL* 53 (1 September 1939): 7-8.

33. Wallace, "The Man with a Program," *BB* 1 (July 1939): 9. See also Hugo McCord, "Viewing Some News," *BB* 2 (September 1939): 30.

34. Wallace, "Will There Be an Armistice?" *BB* 2 (January 1940), 3; and "The Accent on Love," *BB* 2 (May 1940): 2.

35. Davidson, in a letter to Sewell dated 11 December 1939, in Sewell Papers.

36. Davidson, in a letter to Sewell dated 11 December 1939, in Sewell Papers.

37. McMillan, in a letter to the directors of the *Christian Leader* dated 6 October 1939, in Sewell Papers.

38. Davidson, in a letter to Sewell dated 11 December 1939, in Sewell Papers.

39. On the Christian in business, see, e.g., George Pepperdine, "The Christian Business Man," *CL* 53 (15 February 1939): 4, 15. On persistence, see Clinton Davidson, "Through the Business Man's Eye," *CL* 53 (15 March 1939): 6, 17. On love and unity, see Jimmie Lovell, "Talking Things Over," *CL* 53 (15 May 1939): 3, 15; and E. W. McMillan, "In the Hope of Unity," *CL* 53 (1 June 1939): 7-9. On prayer and providence, see Clinton Davidson, "Examples of Answered Prayer," *CL* 53 (1 September 1939): 9. On the virtues of American democracy, see Batsell Baxter, "The Power of College Influence," *CL* 53 (1 April 1939): 6, 13-14. On the value of a Christian home, see E. J. Ijams, "Christians and Homes," *CL* 54 (1 May 1940): 3, 20. On spirituality, see E. W. McMillan, "The Spiritual Interpretation," *CL* 54 (1 October 1940): 6-7. On the power of positive thinking, see A. M. Burton, "Principles for Successful Living," *CL* 53 (1 January 1939), 5.

40. See, e.g., E. W. McMillan, "The Millennial Reign of Christ," *CL* 54 (15 May 1940): 8-9; "Editorial," *CL* 54 (15 December 1940): 7-8; and "Christ, Not Creeds," *CL* 53 (1 August 1939): 7-9.

41. See Norvel Young, " 'And Their Voice Prevailed,' " *CL* 54 (1 August 1940): 4; Max Leach, "The Christian and War," *CL* 54 (1 August 1940): 15; George Benson, "Advice from President Roosevelt," *CL* 54 (1 October 1940): 12; and A. B. Lipscomb, "A Young Man Speaks Out," *CL* 53 (15 September 1939): 3, 12.

42. Davidson, "Through the Business Man's Eye," *CL* 53 (15 April 1939): 10, 12.

43. H. Leo Boles, "The New Editor, B. C. Goodpasture," *GA* 81 (2 March 1939): 197, 205.

44. Goodpasture, "The Future Policy of the Gospel Advocate," *GA* 81 (2 March 1939): 196.

45. Wallace, "Abraham and Lot — An Ill-Timed Editorial on a Misapplied Example," *BB* 2 (September 1939): 4.

46. Billingsley, "Betrayal Plus Bad Business," an open letter to Leon McQuiddy dated 17 May 1939, housed in Center for Restoration Studies, Abilene Christian University.

47. Sewell, in a letter to Davidson dated 17 January 1940, in Sewell Papers. See also

Sewell's letter to S. H. Hall dated 29 December 1939, and Hall's letter to Jas. F. Cox dated 13 December 1939, in the same collection.

48. This opinion was expressed by Robert M. Randolph, grandson of E. W. McMillan, in an interview with the author on 9 September 1991.

49. "Welfare Program Including Social Service Emphasized by Central Church of Christ," *Nashville Banner,* 24 December 1941.

50. Ijams, "Acknowledging a Debt of Gratitude," a tribute to Andrew Mizell Burton on the occasion of his eighty-seventh birthday, February 5, 1966, typescript in possession of the author.

51. "Unique Work of Church Attracts Wide Attention," *Nashville Banner,* 30 May 1926.

52. "Welfare Program Including Social Service Emphasized by Central Church of Christ," *Nashville Banner,* 24 December 1941.

53. See Hardeman, "The Purpose of This Meeting," in *Hardeman's Tabernacle Sermons,* vol. 4 (Nashville: Gospel Advocate, 1938), pp. 11-13.

54. F. B. Srygley, "The Hardeman Meeting," *GA* 80 (3 November 1938): 1028.

55. McMillan noted this in a letter to Sewell dated 7 October 1938, in Sewell Papers.

56. See J. L. Hines, "Questions Asked E. W. McMillan," *BB* 1 (May 1939): 21.

57. Rowe in a letter to Davidson dated 21 November 1939, in Sewell Papers.

58. Sewell in a letter to McMillan dated 5 December 1939, in Sewell Papers.

59. J. W. Howell, J. B. Whitehorn, and W. L. Young in an open letter entitled "My Dear Fellow Christian," dated 25 September 1942, in Sewell Papers.

60. Sewell in a letter to Davidson dated 3 May 1940, in Sewell Papers.

61. Sewell in a letter to McMillan dated 3 May 1940, in Sewell Papers.

62. Sewell in a letter to Pepperdine dated 26 March 1940, in Sewell Papers.

63. McMillan in a letter to Sewell dated 24 July 1940, in Sewell Papers.

64. Showalter, "Future of the Christian Leader," *CL* 54 (15 December 1940): 6, 14.

65. Wallace, "Developments on All Fronts," *BB* 3 (January 1941): 2.

66. Young recalled this in an interview with the author in Malibu, California, 3 March 1992.

67. Young asserted this in an interview with the author, 24 January 1991.

68. Tiner, "The Challenge of Undenominational Christianity," *20th CC* 1 (November 1938): 11.

69. Whitten, "Progress in Christianity," *20th CC* 1 (December 1938): 19.

70. Ruby, "The Potentialities of Man," *20th CC* 1 (March 1939): 22-23.

71. Southern, "The Value of a Great Ideal," *20th CC* 1 (January 1939): 11.

72. Young, "Spiritual Vision," *20th CC* 1 (December 1938): 3.

73. See, e.g., Batsell Barrett Baxter, "When War Comes," *20th CC* 1 (November 1938): 1-3; and the series by P. D. Wilmeth, "A Square Look at War," *20th CC* 1 (May 1939): 20-23; (June 1939): 3-6; and (July 1939): 10-22.

74. James D. Bales, "Nationalism as a Religion," *20th CC* 1 (April 1939): 3-7.

75. Fox in a letter to Richard Hughes dated 21 June 1992.

76. "140,000 Readers This Month," *20th Century Christian,* April 1955, p. 2.

77. See Earl Irvin West, *Search for the Ancient Order,* vol. 2: *1866-1906* (Indianapolis: Religious Book Service, 1950), pp. 157-59.

Notes to Chapter 10

1. Rowe, "The Old and the New Order," *ACR* 23 (30 March 1880): 100.

2. Clark, "Views and Reviews," *GA* 37 (7 November 1895): 711.

3. Connelly, *Will Campbell and the Soul of the South* (New York: Continuum, 1982), p. 38.

4. I have adapted this understanding of modernization from Bruce B. Lawrence, *Defenders of God: The Fundamentalist Revolt against the Modern Age* (San Francisco: Harper & Row, 1989), p. 2.

5. On these "non-class" Churches of Christ, see Larry Hart, "Brief History of a Minor Restorationist Group," *RQ* 22 (1979): 212-32.

6. See Hart, "Brief History of a Minor Restorationist Group," p. 231; see also *Churches of Christ in the United States,* comp. Mac Lynn (Nashville: Gospel Advocate, 1991), p. ix.

7. Cited by Hart in "Brief History of a Minor Restorationist Group," p. 223.

8. Branum, "Those Anti-Non-Sunday School Churches," *Mission* 10 (July 1976): 8.

9. See Hart, "Brief History of a Minor Restorationist Group," p. 224; and James W. Russell, "The 'One Cup' Segment in American Church History," *Mission* 9 (March 1976): 180-82. See also Ronny F. Wade, *The Sun Will Shine Again, Someday: A History of the Non-Class, One Cup Churches of Christ* (Springfield, Mo.: Yesterday's Treasures, 1986).

10. *Churches of Christ in the United States,* p. x.

11. Michael Casey, "Churches of Christ and World War II Civilian Public Service: A Pacifist Remnant," in *Proclaim Peace: Christian Pacifism outside the Historic Peace Churches* (Chicago: University of Illinois Press, 1996); and Wade, *The Sun Will Shine Again, Someday,* pp. 153-57.

12. Brightwell, "A Religious Depression," *GA* 76 (29 November 1934): 1151.

13. Brightwell, "The Crisis We Are Facing," *GA* 78 (18 June 1936): 587; "The Crisis We Are Facing (No. 2)," *GA* 78 (25 June 1936): 611; and "The Crisis We Are Facing (No. 3)," *GA* 78 (2 July 1936): 635.

14. Tindall, *The Emergence of the New South, 1913-1945* (Baton Rouge: Louisiana State University Press, 1967), p. ix.

15. On the postwar religious revival, see, e.g., Joel Carpenter, "Youth for Christ and the New Evangelicals' Place in the Life of the Nation," in *Religion and the Life of the Nation: American Recoveries,* ed. Rowland A. Sherrill (Chicago: University of Illinois Press, 1990), pp. 128-51.

16. Cogdill, "What Does 'Sponsor' Mean?" *GG* 2 (22 June 1950): 15; and "Centralized Control and Oversight," *GG* 1 (20 April 1950): 1.

17. Lard, "The Reformation for Which We Are Pleading — What Is It?" *Lard's Quarterly* 1 (September 1863): 14; italics mine.

18. Tant, "The Evil Spirit of Tolerance," *GG* 1 (October 1935): 23; and "I Have a Closed Mind," *GG* 21 (9 October 1969): 356. On Tant, see Russell S. Fountain, "Captive of 'God's Blueprint' — Fanning Yater Tant and the Development of the Non-Institutional Churches of Christ" (master's thesis, Abilene Christian University, 1990).

19. Tant, "The Only Christians," *GG* 5 (8 October 1953): 340.

20. Franklin, "Ohio State Missionary Meeting," *ACR* 6 (23 June 1863): 98.

21. On Sommer, see Steve Wolfgang, "A Life of Humble Fear: The Biography of Daniel Sommer, 1850-1940" (master's thesis, Butler University, 1975); Mathew C. Morrison, *Like a Lion: Daniel Sommer's Seventy Years of Preaching* (Murfreesboro, Tenn.: Dehoff Publications, 1975); and *Daniel Sommer, 1850-1940: A Biography,* comp. William Wallace (N.p.: n.p., 1969). This last volume is a compilation of articles Sommer published in the *American Christian Review* under the title "A Record of My Life" during the early 1940s.

22. Sommer, "Preface," *Plain Sermons* (Indianapolis: Daniel Sommer, 1913), n.p.

23. Sommer, "The Simple Life," in *The Church of Christ* (Indianapolis: Octographic Review, 1913), pp. 354-55, 348-49.

24. For the significance of this event in the history of Churches of Christ, see Richard Hughes, "Twenty-five Years of Restoration Scholarship: The Churches of Christ — Part I," *RQ* 25 (1982): 250-56.

25. Sommer, in *Daniel Sommer, 1850-1940*, p. 76.

26. Sommer, in *Daniel Sommer, 1850-1940*, p. 91.

27. Evangelist [Sommer], "Educating Preachers," *ACR* 21 (29 October 1878): 349.

28. Evangelist [Sommer], "Educating Preachers, No. IV," *ACR* 22 (14 January 1879): 17.

29. Sommer, "The Perpetuation of the Clergy through Theological Seminaries, Bible Schools, and Colleges," in *The Church of Christ*, pp. 285, 290, 305.

30. See, e.g., N. B. Hardeman, "The Banner Boys Become Enraged," *GA* 89 (23 October 1947): 844.

31. See William Wallace, "Unwarranted Editorial Liberty," *Vanguard* (August 1983): 12; and "Onward Processes of the Movement (1)," *Vanguard* (June 1984): 20.

32. Cogdill, "The Persons and Personalities in the College Controversy," *BB* 9 (December 1947): 4.

33. Cogdill, "The Simplicity of the Gospel," *BB* 10 (June 1948): 4.

34. Nichol, " 'Christian Colleges,' " *BB* 9 (July 1947): 6.

35. Tant, *Apostolic Review* 81 (7 December 1937), p. 5, cited by Wolfgang in "A Life of Humble Fear," pp. 115-16.

36. Brewer's *Gospel Advocate* articles are reprinted in his book *Contending for the Faith* (Nashville: Gospel Advocate, 1941), pp. 199-238. In 1947, he reprinted three of the articles in a thirty-two-page pamphlet entitled "Congregations and Colleges."

37. See Wallace, " 'Jehovah-Nissi' — the Lord My Banner," *BB* 1 (July 1938): 3; and "Concerning Colleges," *BB* 1 (September 1938): 2.

38. Wallace, "In-Cullings-Comments and Correspondence," *BB* 1 (September 1938): 11. Cf. Wallace, "The Emergence of a New Movement," *BB* 1 (January-February 1939): 2-3.

39. Cogdill, "An Answer to the Announcement of Abilene Christian College for District Rallies for the Churches," *BB* 9 (May 1947): 6.

40. Hardeman, "Spending the Lord's Money," *GA* 89 (29 May 1947): 371.

41. Hardeman, "The Banner Boys Become Enraged," *GA* 89 (23 October 1947): 845; reprinted in *FF* 64 (28 October 1947): 1-3.

42. Wallace, "Reply to the N. B. Hardeman 'Hit and Run' Attacks," *BB* 8 (September 1947): 24.

43. See William E. Wallace, "The College Question," *Vanguard* (April 1983): 10.

44. Hardeman, "The Banner Boys Become Enraged," *GA* 89 (23 October 1947): 844; and "Foy Versus Roy, Cled, and Himself," *GA* 89 (28 August 1947): 656-57, 661. See also "Foy Versus Roy, Cled, and Himself," *FF* 64 (9 September 1947): 4-7.

45. Even in the 1930s, long before Hardeman raised this issue, some had questioned church support of orphanages. See William E. Wallace, "Orphan Homes," *Vanguard*, May 1983, p. 12; and William S. Banowsky, *Mirror of a Movement* (Dallas: Christian Publishing, 1965), p. 336.

46. Brewer, "Christ and the Problem of Orphans and Other Dependents in the Present Day World," *Harding College Lectures, 1951* (Searcy, Ark.: Harding College Press, 1952), p. 99.

47. Cf. Brewer, "Evangelizing the World in the Post War Period," *FF* 60 (16 February 1943): 1-2.

48. Wallace, "Sighting-in on 'Post-War Plans,' " *BB* 6 (August 1943): 7.

49. Sherrod and Young produced a pamphlet promoting the mission entitled "Germany for Christ: A Report on the German Mission Work." It was published by Broadway Church of Christ in October 1949 and widely distributed. On the development of the mission, see Banowsky, *Mirror of a Movement*, pp. 316-17.

50. Phillip Wayne Elkins, *Church Sponsored Missions: An Evaluation of Churches of Christ* (Austin: Firm Foundation, 1974), p. 6.

51. For a Catholic view of these events and a reply to Churches of Christ, see the Rev. Dr. L. Rumble, M.S.C., *"Churches of Christ" and "The Disciples"* (St. Paul: Radio Replies Press Society, n.d.).

52. Wallace, "That Rock Fight in Italy," *GG* 1 (19 January 1950): 1.

53. "A Letter from the Padens," *GG* 1 (23 February 1950): 5.

54. Chisholm, "An Answer To: 'That Rock Fight in Italy,'" *GG* 1 (23 February 1950): 1.

55. Tant, "Surveying the Scene," *GG* 1 (23 February 1950): 2.

56. Cogdill, "Centralized Control and Oversight," *GG* 1 (20 April 1950): 1; and "Now It Is All Settled," *GG* 2 (11 May 1950): 9.

57. The series began in the *Gospel Advocate*, 11 May 1950, in the *Firm Foundation*, 25 July 1950, and in the *Gospel Guardian*, 18 October 1951. The *Firm Foundation* gave nine of Wright's articles a wider circulation in pamphlet form. See Cecil N. Wright, *The Sponsorship-Cooperation Controversy* (Austin: Firm Foundation Publishing House, 1951).

58. Wright, "The Cooperation Controversy (3)," *GA* 93 (21 June 1951): 391.

59. Cogdill, "Brother Wright's Self Justification," *GG* 2 (17 August 1950): 9. There is evidence of the generally positive reception of the articles in a letter from M. Norvel Young to Cecil N. Wright dated 15 June 1950, in possession of author.

60. Goodpasture's commentary appeared under the heading "The Voice of the Turtle," *GA* 93 (12 July 1951): 434.

61. Cogdill, "'What Is That to Thee?'" *GG* 3 (2 August 1951): 1.

62. Goodpasture, "'What Is That to Thee,'" *GA* 93 (23 August 1951): 530.

63. Cogdill, "You Can See What I Meant," *GG* 3 (20 September 1951): 10.

64. "They Commend the Elder Who Wrote," *GA* 96 (9 December 1954): 962.

65. Wallace, "Onward Processes of the Movement (1)," *Vanguard*, June 1984, p. 20.

66. *Churches of Christ in the United States*, p. ix. Texas boasted 301 congregations, Alabama 214, Florida 147, and Kentucky 147.

67. Harrell, "B. C. Goodpasture: Leader of Institutional Thought," in *They Being Dead Yet Speak: Florida College Annual Lectures, 1981*, ed. Melvin D. Curry (Temple Terrace, Fla.: Florida College Bookstore, 1981), pp. 246-47, 249-50, 243.

68. Wallace, "For General Information," *GA* 97 (24 November 1955): 1056.

69. On the "Herald of Truth," see John Marion Barton, "The Preaching on Herald of Truth Radio, 1952-1969" (Ph.D. diss., Pennsylvania State University, 1975); and Robert Wayne Dockery, "'Three American Revolutions': A Study of Social Change in the Churches of Christ As Evidenced in the 'Herald of Truth' Radio Series" (master's thesis, Louisiana State University, 1973).

70. See Barton, "The Preaching on Herald of Truth Radio, 1952-1969," pp. 131-69.

71. Hudson, "My Work With the Union Avenue Church," *GA* 67 (5 December 1925): 1158.

72. Allen made his remarks under the heading of Hudson's article, "My Work with the Union Avenue Church," *GA* 67 (5 December 1925): 1158-59. Don Haymes also tells this story in "How the Church of Christ Became a Denomination," *Mission Journal* 20 (March 1987): 4-8.

73. Lemmons, "Some Facts about the World's Fastest Growing Church," *FF* 71 (8 June 1954): 1.

74. Young, "'So You Are Going to Build,'" *GA* 90 (29 January 1948): 104-5.

75. Powell and Young, *The Church Is Building* (Nashville: Gospel Advocate, 1956), pp. ix, 2-3.

76. Coffman, introduction to *The Church Is Building*, pp. ix-x.

77. Powell and Young, *The Church Is Building,* pp. 144-45.

78. Brewer, "The Undenominational Nature of the Lord's Church," sermon preached at dedication of the new building of the Broadway Church of Christ, Lubbock, Texas, 1950, transcript in possession of the author.

79. Parks, "Thy Ecclesia Come!" in *Voices of Concern: Critical Studies in Church of Christism,* ed. Robert Meyers (St. Louis: Mission Messenger, 1966), p. 78.

80. Harrell, "Emergence of the Church of Christ Denomination Update," *Vanguard* 5 (25 January 1979): 14-15.

Notes to Chapter 11

1. On fundamentalism in relation to these issues, see George M. Marsden, *Fundamentalism and American Culture: The Shaping of Twentieth-Century Evangelicalism, 1870-1925* (Oxford: Oxford University Press, 1980), pp. 55-62, 102-23.

2. Allen, "Current Comment," *GA* 67 (9 July 1925): 650.

3. Marsden, *Fundamentalism and American Culture,* p. 152.

4. Marsden, *Fundamentalism and American Culture,* pp. 208-10.

5. Kurfees, "Transylvania University and Destructive Criticism — The Situation at Lexington, Kentucky," *GA* 59 (7 June 1917): 554; McQuiddy, "Are the Germans a Chosen People?" *GA* 59 (12 July 1917): 672; and F. W. Smith, "The Cole Lectures at Vanderbilt," *GA* 64 (11 May 1922): 448.

6. See Casey, "The Interpretation of Genesis One in the Churches of Christ: The Origins of Fundamentalist Reactions to Evolution and Biblical Criticism in the 1920s" (master's thesis, Abilene Christian University, 1989); and James Stephen Wolfgang, "Fundamentalism and the Churches of Christ, 1910-1930" (master's thesis, Vanderbilt University, 1990). See also Casey, "Fundamentalism and the Churches of Christ," in *Encyclopedia of the Fundamentalist/Modernist Controversy,* ed. James Lewis (New York: Simon & Schuster, forthcoming).

7. Parks, "G. C. Brewer, Controversialist," *Discipliana* 44 (Winter 1984): 55. The other chief architect of Churches of Christ that Parks identifies is B. C. Goodpasture. For more on Brewer, see Ron Halbrook, "G. C. Brewer: Perennial Protagonist," in *They Being Dead Yet Speak: Florida College Annual Lectures, 1981,* ed. Melvin D. Curry (Temple Terrace, Fla.: Florida College Bookstore, 1981), pp. 198-219.

8. Brewer, *Autobiography of G. C. Brewer* (Murfreesboro, Tenn.: DeHoff Publications, 1957), p. 60.

9. See Perry Mason, "Grover Cleveland Brewer," in *Harding College Lectures: 1967,* ed. W. Joe Hacker (Austin: Firm Foundation Publishing House, 1967), p. 239.

10. Srygley, "G. C. Brewer's Lecture," *GA* 78 (26 November 1936): 1133, 1141. The *Nashville Banner* reported this speech in its 9 November 1936 issue.

11. Brewer, *Communism and Its Four Horsemen: Atheism, Immorality, Class Hatred, Pacifism* (Nashville: Gospel Advocate, 1936). The articles reprinted in the book all ran under the series title "Communism — Its Four Horsemen." The installments appeared in the following issues of volume 78 of the *Gospel Advocate*: 16 July 1936, pp. 686-87; 30 July 1936, pp. 734-35; 6 August 1936, p. 758; 13 August 1936, pp. 782-83; 10 September 1936, pp. 878-79; 24 September 1936, pp. 926-27; and 1 October 1936, pp. 950-51, 959. One additional article appeared in the *Gospel Advocate* series but not in the book: "Questions about Communism," *GA* 78 (22 October 1936): 1010.

12. Brewer, *Communism and Its Four Horsemen,* p. 3.

13. Brewer, *Communism and Its Four Horsemen*, pp. 30-31.

14. Brewer, *Communism and Its Four Horsemen*, p. 10.

15. Brewer, *Communism and Its Four Horsemen*, pp. 12-14.

16. Brewer, *Communism and Its Four Horsemen*, p. 14.

17. Cited by Edwin S. Gaustad in "The Pulpit and the Pews," in *Between the Times: The Travail of the Protestant Establishment in America, 1900-1960*, ed. William R. Hutchinson (Cambridge: Cambridge University Press, 1989), p. 38.

18. On the American peace movement between the two world wars, and Kirby Page in particular, see Charles Chatfield, *For Peace and Justice: Pacifism in America, 1914-1941* (Knoxville: University of Tennessee Press, 1971).

19. Brewer, *Communism and Its Four Horsemen*, p. 10; see further pp. 36-39.

20. Brewer, *Communism and Its Four Horsemen*, pp. 36-37.

21. Fudge, *Can a Christian Kill for His Government?* (Athens, Ala.: C.E.I. Store, 1943). Fudge's son Edward comments on the negative reaction to his father's book from members of Churches of Christ in a letter to the author dated July 1992.

22. See, e.g., Brewer, "Communism or Catholicism: Is This Our Only Choice?" *GA* 91 (24 March 1949): 178.

23. On this point, see David Edwin Harrell Jr., *Quest for a Christian America* (Nashville: Disciples of Christ Historical Society, 1966), pp. 214-21.

24. Brewer, "Our Purpose and Our Method of Attack," *Voice of Freedom* 1 (January 1953): 2.

25. Brewer, "Salutation," *Voice of Freedom* 1 (January 1953): 1.

26. The remaining individuals were Alonzo D. Welch, H. A. Dixon, and J. M. Powell. See Brewer, " 'A Voice Crying in the Wilderness,' " *GA* 97 (15 September 1955): 828.

27. See Bowden, "Perplexity over a Protean Principle: A Response," in *The American Quest for the Primitive Church*, ed. Richard Hughes (Chicago: University of Illinois Press, 1988), p. 176.

28. See Brewer, "Our Purpose and Our Method of Attack," *Voice of Freedom* 1 (January 1953): 2-3.

29. See, e.g., Foy E. Wallace Jr., "The Roman Catholic Syllabus and Vatican Decrees Knights of Columbus Religious Information Bureau," *FF*, 20 September 1960, pp. 600-601; "Matters for Americans to Consider," *20th CC*, October 1960, inside front cover; and Cecil Douthitt, "Arrogance of the Roman Hierarchy," *GG*, 13 October 1950, pp. 6-7.

30. See Mark Silk, "The Rise of the 'New Evangelicalism': Shock and Adjustment," in *Between the Times: The Travail of the Protestant Establishment in America, 1900-1960*, ed. William R. Hutchison (Cambridge: Cambridge University Press, 1989), p. 292.

31. Ellis, "Religion and the Presidency," *GA* 102 (28 July 1960): 465, 474.

32. Goodpasture, "Some Corrections," *GA* 102 (25 August 1960): 530.

33. Goodpasture, "An Unusual Book," *GA* 102 (22 September 1960): 595.

34. Lemmons, "Editorial — Religion and Politics," *FF*, 1 November 1960, p. 690; and "Can a Roman Catholic Be a Good President?" *FF*, 19 April 1960, p. 242.

35. Holley, "Should a Catholic Be Elected President?" *FF*, 5 April 1960, pp. 211, 214.

36. Wilson became editor of the *Voice of Freedom* in July 1956 (Brewer, "Among Ourselves," *Voice of Freedom*, June 1956, p. 82).

37. Wilson, "Let's Keep Politics out of Religion," *Voice of Freedom*, February 1960, p. 21; and "Editorial Comments," *Voice of Freedom*, May 1960, p. 66.

38. Wilson, "Editorial Comments," *Voice of Freedom*, August 1960, p. 114.

39. Wilson, "Editorial Comments," *Voice of Freedom*, May 1960, p. 66.

40. H. W. McClish Jr., "Subtle Propaganda," *FF*, 14 June 1960, p. 382.

41. "Rep. Evins Rebuffs Baxter Sermon," *CC* 18 (21 October 1960): 1.

42. Goodpasture, "Television Network to Air Sermon on Catholicism," *GA* 102 (20 October 1960): n.p.

43. V. E. Howard, "Kennedy Refuses to Deny Doctrine of Mental Reservation on Houston TV Program," *GA* 102 (22 September 1960): 593, 603; and "Kennedy Sidesteps Questions," *Christian Chronicle* 17 (20 September 1960): 1.

44. Lemmons, "The Road Ahead," *FF* 87 (2 June 1970): 338.

45. Lemmons, "The Moral Crisis in America," *FF* 85 (24 September 1968): 610.

46. Hoover, quoted by Goodpasture in "It Happened Here," *GA* 111 (14 August 1969): 518, 527. See further "College Students, Beware," *GA* 110 (31 October 1968): 694.

47. Harless, "The Great Convention," sermon preached at Hillsboro Church of Christ, Nashville, Tennessee, 1 September 1968, and broadcast by radio station WLAC.

48. Hailey, "The Political and Social Attitudes of Church of Christ Ministers," paper presented at the 1988 meeting of the American Political Science Association, Washington, D.C. See also Hailey, "The Political and Social Attitudes of Church of Christ Ministers" (Ph.D. diss., Texas Tech University, 1988).

Notes to Chapter 12

1. Locke, in a letter to Richard T. Hughes dated 1 December 1992.

2. Thomas, *The Travels and Gospel Labors of Joseph Thomas* (Winchester, Va.: n.p., 1812), p. 56.

3. Harrell, *Quest for a Christian America* (Nashville: Disciples of Christ Historical Society, 1966), p. 97.

4. See the letters from S. E. Harris to David Lipscomb and from Lipscomb to Harris in "The Negro in Worship," *GA* 49 (1 August 1907): 489.

5. Lipscomb, "Race Prejudice," *GA* 20 (21 February 1878): 120-21.

6. Elam, in a letter to S. E. Harris in "The Negro in Worship — A Correspondence," *GA* 49 (4 July 1907): 424-25.

7. Lipscomb, "The Negro in the Worship — A Correspondence," *GA* 49 (4 July 1907): 425.

8. Campbell, "Our Position to American Slavery — No. VIII," *MH*, 3d ser., 2 (June 1845): 258-59. Robert O. Fife has produced the two best discussions of the status of slavery in the heritage of Disciples of Christ/Churches of Christ: "Alexander Campbell and the Christian Church in the Slavery Controversy" (Ph.D. diss., Indiana University, 1960) and *Teeth on Edge* (Grand Rapids: Baker Book House, 1971).

9. Alexander Campbell, "Our Position to American Slavery — No. VIII," *MH*, 3d ser., 2 (June 1845): 263.

10. Campbell, "Our Position to American Slavery — No. V," *MH*, 3d ser., 2 (May 1845): 193.

11. Campbell, "Our Position to American Slavery — No. VIII," *MH*, 3d ser., 2 (June 1845): 258.

12. Campbell, "Our Position to American Slavery — No. VIII," *MH*, 3d ser., 2 (June 1845): 259, 262.

13. Scott, "Reply," *The Evangelist* 4 (6 April 1835): 81.

14. See Campbell, *Familiar Lectures on the Pentateuch,* ed. W. T. Moore (St. Louis: Christian Publishing, 1867), pp. 266-304. On Campbell's "canon within a canon," see M. Eugene Boring, "The Formation of a Tradition: Alexander Campbell and the New Testament," *Disciples Theological Digest* 2 (1987): 5-62.

15. Rogers, "The Life and Times of John Rogers," in John Rogers Books, 1800-1859, Book I, p. 163, in Southern Historical Collection, Manuscripts Department, University of North Carolina at Chapel Hill.

16. Franklin, "Our Position Called For," *ACR* 2 (March 1859): 42, cited by James Brooks Major in "The Role of Periodicals in the Development of the Disciples of Christ, 1850-1910" (Ph.D. diss., Vanderbilt University, 1966), p. 97.

17. Lipscomb, *A Commentary on the New Testament Epistles: Ephesians, Philippians, and Colossians*, ed. J. W. Shepherd (Nashville: Gospel Advocate, 1939), p. 121.

18. Rogers, "The Life and Times of John Rogers," John Rogers Books, Book I, pp. 135, 150-51.

19. Lipscomb, "The Negro in the Worship — A Correspondence," *GA* 49 (4 July 1907): 424-25.

20. On Churches of Christ and social concern, see Randall J. Harris, "Current Thought in Churches of Christ about Social Concern in Light of Walter Rauschenbusch and Reinhold Niebuhr" (master's thesis, Harding Graduate School of Religion, 1983). On the fundamentalists' rejection of the social gospel, see George M. Marsden, *Fundamentalism and American Culture: The Shaping of Twentieth-Century Evangelicalism, 1870-1925* (Oxford: Oxford University Press, 1980), pp. 85-93.

21. Sheldon, *In His Steps* (Chicago: Henneberry, 1897).

22. McGary, "What Would Christ Not Do?" *FF* 16 (15 May 1900): 312-13.

23. McGary, "What Would Christ Not Do?" *FF* 16 (19 June 1900): 392.

24. Hardeman, *Hardeman's Tabernacle Sermons*, vol. 2 (Nashville: McQuiddy Publishing, 1932), pp. 207-8.

25. Banowsky, *Mirror of a Movement* (Dallas: Christian Publishing, 1965), p. 330.

26. On the social ministry of the Madison Church of Christ, see Jimmie Moore Mankin, "The Role of Social Service in the Life and Growth of the Madison Church of Christ" (D.Min. diss., Fuller Theological Seminary, 1987). Mankin also chronicles the establishment of a variety of orphans' homes by members of Churches of Christ in both the nineteenth and twentieth centuries (pp. 26-31).

27. "New 'House' Found to Contain Boston Inner City Ministry," *Christian Chronicle* 24 (18 August 1967): 10.

28. People who provided leadership for this ministry between 1963 and 1967 supplied primary information on the history of the House of the Carpenter. Telephone interviews were conducted with Robert M. Randolph (28 December 1994), Patricia Martin (28 December 1994), and William Martin (7 January 1995). Earliest leadership for the House of the Carpenter was provided by William and Patricia Martin, Carl and Jan Haywood, and Rolph and Carol Johnson. Others involved in leadership roles later in the project included Harold and Nathalie Vanderpool, Louis and Harilyn Smith, Harold and Carol Straughn, Warren and Lynne Lewis, Denton and Jackie Crews, Edgar Speer, Milton Gardner, and Robert M. and Jan Randolph.

29. Lemmons, "A Spent Force," *FF* 86 (23 September 1969): 594.

30. Lemmons, "Which Way Are We Going?" *FF* 85 (2 July 1968): 418; and "They Don't Have the Answers Either," *FF* 86 (6 May 1969): 274.

31. Dobbs, "The Social Gospel Is Not the Gospel," *Spiritual Sword* 4 (July 1973): 26.

32. Allen, "Scripture Studies," *GA* 67 (14 May 1925): 457; and J. E. Choate, *Roll, Jordan, Roll: A Biography of Marshall Keeble* (Nashville: Gospel Advocate, 1974), p. 54.

33. Brewer, "Saved By a Moonbeam; or, Facing Death for Saying a Negro Has a Soul," unpublished paper, pp. 2-3.

34. Choate, *Roll, Jordan, Roll*, p. 45; see also Willie Cato, *His Hand and Heart: The Wit and Wisdom of Marshall Keeble* (Winona, Miss.: J. C. Choate Publications, 1990).

35. Wallace, "Negro Meetings for White People," *BB* 3 (March 1941): 7.

36. Keeble, "From M. Keeble," *BB* 3 (April 1941): 5.

37. Wallace, addendum to Keeble, "From M. Keeble," *BB* 3 (April 1941): 5. Other members of Churches of Christ concurred. J. W. Brents wrote of Keeble from Muskogee, Oklahoma, that "the greatest thing about him is that he knows his place and at all times scrupulously keeps in it" (cited by A. M. Burton in "M. Keeble, Colored Evangelist," *GA* 73 [15 October 1931]: 1289).

38. Winrow, statement concerning Marshall Keeble, January 1995, in possession of Richard T. Hughes.

39. Harris, "The Negro in the Worship" (letter), *GA* 49 (1 August 1907): 489. Cf. a letter from J. Hannon of Corinth, Mississippi, *GA* 67 (14 May 1925): 474; and see James Marvin Powell and Mary Nelle Hardeman Powers, *N. B. H.: A Biography of Nicholas Brodie Hardeman* (Nashville: Gospel Advocate, 1964), p. 150.

40. [Lipscomb], "It's Not Keeble, But the Bible Is Right," *CL* 45 (25 August 1931): 6. Lipscomb is identified as the author of this article in *Biography and Sermons of Marshall Keeble, Evangelist,* ed. B. C. Goodpasture (Nashville: Gospel Advocate, 1936), p. 13.

41. Wallace, addendum to Keeble, "From M. Keeble," *BB* 3 (April 1941): 5.

42. Willeford, "Call No Man Common," sermon preached on *Herald of Truth* radio broadcast, 29 January 1955; published in *Churches of Christ Salute You,* a pamphlet containing sermons for January 1956, pp. 25ff.

43. Andrew J. Hairston, "Bold Lines of Division in the Church of Christ," *CE* 58 (December 1963): 1.

44. Hairston, "Color Lines in the Church of Christ," *CE* 59 (April 1964): 3.

45. *Churches of Christ in the United States,* comp. Mac Lynn (Nashville: Gospel Advocate, 1991), p. xi. Brightwell's estimate is cited by Neil Rhoads in "A Study of the Sources of Marshall Keeble's Effectiveness as a Preacher" (Ph.D. diss., Southern Illinois University, 1970), p. 60.

46. V. L. Cathey, "Special," *CE* 60 (June 1965): 7.

47. "The Other Brotherhood," *Christian Chronicle* 25 (8 March 1968): 2.

48. On Bowser, see R. Vernon Boyd, *Undying Dedication: The Story of G. P. Bowser* (Nashville: Gospel Advocate, 1985).

49. James Maxwell, "The Restoration Movement," *GA* 132 (January 1990): 16.

50. Cassius, "Reformation," *GA* 57 (30 December 1915): 1327.

51. Keeble, "The Church among the Colored," *Abilene Christian College Lectures, 1950* (Abilene: ACC Bookstore, 1950), 145-46.

52. Winrow, statement on "Black Churches of Christ," January 1995, in possession of Richard T. Hughes.

53. Church of Christ–related colleges outside the South resisted segregation. George Pepperdine College in Los Angeles and Northeastern Christian Junior College in Villanova, Pennsylvania, were cases in point. Pepperdine had been integrated since its founding in 1937. J. Harold Thomas served as president of Northeastern from 1959-62, when that school was known as Northeastern Institute for Christian Education. Pained that Northeastern's African American graduates could not gain admission to Church of Christ–related senior colleges in the South, Thomas regularly and publicly criticized the policy of those institutions. In a lectureship speech he gave at George Pepperdine College in 1961, for example, Thomas argued strongly that segregation was sinful. Many in the audience walked out. (Thomas spoke of these matters in a telephone interview with the author 22 December 1994.)

54. Locke, "The Church and Civil Rights," *Kerygma* 1 (1965): 3-7.

55. Hairston, "Bold Lines of Division in the Church of Christ," *CE* 58 (December 1963): 1.

56. R. N. Hogan, "The Sin of Being a Respecter of Persons," *CE* 54 (June 1959): 5; and "Brother David Lipscomb Stood with God on Race Prejudice in the Church of Christ," *CE* 55 (June 1960): 2.

57. Spain, "Modern Challenges to Christian Morals," in *Christian Faith in the Modern World: The Abilene Christian College Annual Bible Lectures, 1960* (Abilene: Abilene Christian College Students Exchange, 1960), p. 217.

58. Stevens, in a telephone interview with the author, 8 September 1992.

59. Hogan, "Is It the Law or Down-Right Prejudice?" *CE* 58 (June 1963): 3.

60. Hogan, "Brother David Lipscomb Stood with God on Race Prejudice in the Church of Christ," *CE* 55 (June 1960): 2.

61. Holt, "Tension between the Black and White Church," *CE* 63 (June 1969): 4, 9.

62. Hogan, "The Grab of the Century," *CE* 63 (December 1968): 1-2.

63. Brief for Defendant 5 at 10, *Obie Elie et al. v. Athens Clay Pullias et al.,* case 18,402, (6th Cir., 1967), p. 10.

64. *Elie v. Pullias,* p. 11.

65. *Elie v. Pullias,* p. 12.

66. Keeble, "Nashville Christian Institute to Close," in Annie C. Tuggle, *Another World Wonder* (N.p.: n.p., n.d.), p. 142.

67. Complaint of Plaintiffs in *Obie Elie et al. v. Athens Clay Pullias et al.,* case 4794 (U.S. District Court, Middle District of Tennessee, Nashville Division, 1967), p. 9. On Gray's civil rights work, see Gray, *Bus Ride to Justice: Changing the System by the System* (Montgomery: Black Belt Press, 1995).

68. Hogan, "The Grab of the Century," *CE* 63 (December 1968): 1-2.

69. Holt, "The Tragedy of Complacency," *CE* 63 (December 1968): 3.

70. Evans, "Outreach," *GA* 132 (January 1990): 19-20.

71. One exception was the *Christian Chronicle,* which ran a symposium on the racial issue in 1963. See Richard Baggett and W. P. Jolly, "Two Southern Preachers Discuss Racial Issues," *CC* 20 (20 September 1963): 2; James W. Nichols, "Let's Discuss the Negro Issue," *CC* 20 (27 September 1963): 2; and "Letters Flow from Chronicle Readers with Comments on Negro Issue," *CC* 21 (18 October 1963): 6-7.

72. Pettus, "The Memorial to Marshall Keeble," *GA* 110 (18 July 1968): 449.

73. See Baxter, "The Problem of Prejudice (No. 1)," *GA* 110 (5 September 1968): 565; and "The Problem of Prejudice — No. 2," *GA* 110 (3 October 1968): 628-29.

74. Reuel Lemmons, editor of the *Firm Foundation,* briefly addressed the issue of racial discrimination in 1964 ("The Church and Integration," *FF* 81 [31 March 1964]: 194), but on that occasion he essentially denied that segregation was a problem for the Church of Christ or a suitable topic for discussion.

75. Lemmons, "Marshall Keeble," *FF* 85 (14 May 1968): 306.

76. Adamson, in a letter to Reuel Lemmons dated 29 May 1968, in the John Allen Chalk files in the library of the Harding Graduate School of Religion, Memphis.

77. White, in a letter to Reuel Lemmons dated 10 June 1968.

78. Davis, in a letter to Reuel Lemmons dated 20 May 1968, and Lemmons, in a letter to Jennings Davis, dated 23 May 1968, in John Allen Chalk files.

79. Turner, "The Attitude of a Christian in the Midst of a Race Crisis," March 1965, pp. 1, 4, cited by Lynn Perry in "The Church of Christ and Racial Attitudes," unpublished manuscript.

80. Lemmons, "The Long Hot Summer," *FF* 85 (9 January 1968): 18.

81. Taylor, "The Omission of Jehovah," *FF* 85 (9 July 1968): 439.

82. Lemmons, "The Long Hot Summer," *FF* 85 (9 January 1968): 18.

83. Lemmons, in a letter to Davis dated 23 May 1968, in John Allen Chalk files.

84. Bales, *The Martin Luther King Story* (Tulsa: Christian Crusade Publications, 1967), p. 199.

85. Johnson, in a letter to the elders of the Highland Church of Christ in Abilene, Texas, dated 4 August 1968, in John Allen Chalk files.

86. Patterson, "We Shall Overcome," *Christian Journal,* October 1968, p. 2.

87. Foutz, in a letter to Chalk dated 5 November 1968, in John Allen Chalk files.

88. Willis recalled the reaction to the lecture (which was entitled "Profaning the Sacred Things of the Bible") in a letter to the author dated 16 August 1994.

89. Burch described the event as "underground" in a statement in possession of the author.

90. Burch, in a letter to Bob Douglas dated 6 February 1979, in Walter Burch files.

91. See "Background of Race Relations Workshop," in *Report on Race Relations Workshop: Supplement to Christian Chronicle,* 10 May 1968, p. 3; and Burch, "Statement of Response to Bob Douglas Re: Race Relations in Churches of Christ in 1960s," unpublished manuscript dated 6 February 1979, p. 11, in Walter Burch files.

92. Dwain Evans, "The Meeting at Atlanta," *Milestone* (bulletin of Church of Christ, West Islip, New York), 1 July 1968, n.p.; and interview by the author with Walter Burch, 11 October 1992.

93. "Conference on Race Relations," *Mission* 2 (September 1968): 24-29.

94. Burch, "Statement of Response to Bob Douglas Re: Race Relations in Churches of Christ in 1960s," p. 14.

95. Wallace, "The Atlanta Conference," *FCC* 2 (October 1968): 3.

96. See, e.g., Lemmons, "The Gambling and Liquor Issues," *FF* 80 (12 February 1963): 98; "About to Go by Default," *FF* 86 (5 August 1969): 482; and "The Return of the Saloon," *FF* 86 (16 December 1969): 786.

97. Lemmons, "The Gambling and Liquor Issues," *FF* 80 (12 February 1963): 98.

98. Burch, "Neglecting the Weightier Matters," *FF* 85 (11 June 1968): 372.

99. B. B. Harding, "Neglecting the Weightier Matters," *FF* 85 (9 July 1968): 436; Ron Goodman, "Afterthoughts on 'Neglecting the Weightier Matters,' " *FF* 85 (9 July 1968): 437; and Lemmons, "The Racial Problem," *FF* 85 (9 July 1968): 434.

100. The sermons later were published in book form as *Three American Revolutions* (New York: Carlton Press, 1970).

101. See, e.g., *Three American Revolutions,* pp. 85-86, 105.

102. See "Analysis of Mail Received from Radio for 'Three American Revolutions,' " John Allen Chalk files.

103. Kenneth L. Bray, in a letter to the elders of the Highland Church of Christ (Abilene, Texas) dated 26 August 1968, in John Allen Chalk files.

104. W. R. Craig, in an undated letter to Frank W. Cawyer, an elder of the Highland Church of Christ (Abilene, Texas), in John Allen Chalk files.

105. Carroll Pitts Jr., "A Critical Study of Civil Rights Practices, Attitudes and Responsibilities in Churches of Christ" (master's thesis, Pepperdine University, 1969), p. 104; and interview by the author with Steven Lemley, 8 May 1994.

106. Holt, "Tension between the Black and White Churches," *CE* 63 (June 1969): 4, 9.

107. The text of Wells's speech, originally entitled "Leadership in Facing Inner City Problems (Harlem)," was subsequently published as "The Case for the Black Revolution," *Mission* 4 (July 1970): 4-14.

108. See William C. Martin, "Shepherds versus Flocks," *Atlantic* 220 (December 1967): 55; and Don Haymes, "Churches Begin to Move Back into Cities," *CC* 25 (19 January 1968): 6.

109. McCord, "A Sorry Viewpoint," *GA* 111 (20 March 1969): 190-91.

110. Lawton, "Unity or Union?" *GA* 132 (January 1990): 24.

111. Evans, "Outreach," *GA* 132 (January 1990): 19.

112. Jones, "Growing Their Separate Ways," *GA* 132 (January 1990): 21.

Notes to Chapter 13

1. Lemmons, "Modernism," *FF* 86 (12 August 1969): 498; "Liberalism," *FF* 86 (19 August 1969): 514; and "Traditionalism," *FF* 86 (26 August 1969): 530.

2. Lemmons, "Modernism," *FF* 86 (12 August 1969): 498; "Liberalism," *FF* 86 (19 August 1969): 514; and "Wise Up or Go Under," *FF* 87 (24 February 1970): 114.

3. Lemmons, "Wise Up or Go Under," *FF* 87 (24 February 1970): 114.

4. Lemmons, "Traditionalism," *FF* 86 (26 August 1969): 530; and "The Church and Its Young People," *FF* 87 (8 December 1970): 770.

5. Lemmons, "In Opinions Liberty," *FF* 87 (10 February 1970): 82.

6. See *The Last Things*, ed. Jack P. Lewis (Austin: Sweet Publishing, 1972), pp. 25-29.

7. Don H. Morris and Max Leach, *Like Stars Shining Brightly* (Abilene: Abilene Christian College Press, 1953), p. 229.

8. Haymes, "The Silence of the Scholars," *Mission* 8 (September 1974): 8-9.

9. Malherbe taught at Abilene Christian University from 1963 to 1969, going from there to Dartmouth and then to Yale. Olbricht taught at ACU for nineteen years (1967-1986) before going to Pepperdine University, where he chaired the Religion Division. Ferguson has taught at ACU from 1962 to the present.

10. Garrett, "Christians and Sectarians," *Bible Talk* 6 (October 1957): 4.

11. See, e.g., Garrett, "Gone to the Christian Church," *Restoration Review* 1 (Winter 1959): 63.

12. Ketcherside, *Pilgrimage of Joy: An Autobiography of Carl Ketcherside* (Joplin, Mo.: College Press, 1991), p. 51.

13. Ketcherside, in a letter to William Lee Wilbanks dated 9 February 1965, cited by Wilbanks in "The Contemporary Discussion concerning Fellowship in Light of the Views of Thomas and Alexander Campbell" (master's thesis, Abilene Christian University, 1966), p. 47. Ketcherside also tells this story in *Pilgrimage of Joy,* pp. 208ff.

14. Ketcherside, "Prophet and Priest," *Mission Messenger* 20 (January 1958): 101.

15. Ketcherside, *Pilgrimage of Joy,* p. 117.

16. Concerning Ketcherside, see Wilbanks, "The Contemporary Discussion concerning Fellowship in Light of the Views of Thomas and Alexander Campbell," pp. 15-16, 46; there is evidence of Garrett's consistency in this regard in a letter from Garrett to the author dated 11 June 1993.

17. H. A. Dixon, "Leroy Garrett's Visit to Freed-Hardeman College," *GA* 97 (10 February 1955): 115ff.; and Garrett, "Imprisoned for Truth," *Bible Talk* 3 (February 1955): 69-79.

18. Haymes, "The Silence of the Scholars," *Mission* 8 (September 1974): 18. Malherbe discusses the history of the *Restoration Quarterly* in a statement reproduced by Thomas H. Olbricht in "New Journals for the Sixties: *Restoration Quarterly* and *Mission*," unpublished paper, 1992, in possession of the author.

19. Malherbe statement, in Olbricht, "New Journals for the Sixties," pp. 6-7.

20. Evans, in a letter to Walter Burch dated 9 August 1965 containing a "prospectus" for the new journal.

21. "Statement Outlining Proposed New Christian Journal," 25 June 1966, in files of Walter E. Burch.

22. Statement from Walter Burch, 1993, in possession of Richard Hughes.

23. McRay, "Race or Grace," *Mission* 2 (July 1968): 3; Davis, "Racial Violence," *Mission* 2 (January 1969): 26-28; and Langford, "The Dream Lives On," *Mission* 2 (September 1968): 79.

24. See "Conference on Race Relations," *Mission* 2 (September 1968): 24-29; and David Malone, "A Review of 'Shepherds vs. Flocks,'" *Mission* 2 (October 1968): 24-27. See also William C. Martin, "'Shepherds vs. Flocks' — A Response," *Mission* 2 (November 1968): 22-23.

25. Danner, "The Weightier Matters," *Mission* 5 (July 1971): 17-18. Cf. Alice Boyd, "Today's Children," *Mission* 4 (June 1971): 16.

26. Haymes, "The Christ of the Gospels," *Mission* 2 (December 1968), For a similar concern, see David Graf, "The Scandal of the Incarnation," *Mission* 3 (December 1969): 6-7.

27. Freeman, "Balaam's Friend," *Mission* 3 (January 1970): 30.

28. Pseudo-Amos, "Oracles of a Nonprophet," *Mission* 2 (August 1968): 28-29. On concern for the inner city, see also Hubert Locke, "Discipleship in the Inner City," *Mission* 1 (August 1967): 19-21; and the special May 1968 issue on urban ministry.

27. Jerry E. Hudson, "A Christian View of the Vietnam War," *Mission* 1 (December 1967): 188.

30. On this point, see Randall J. Harris, "Current Thought in Churches of Christ about Social Concern in Light of Walter Rauschenbusch and Reinhold Niebuhr" (master's thesis, Harding Graduate School of Religion, 1983).

31. Ward, "'The Restoration Principle': A Critical Analysis," *RQ* 8 (1965): 208-9.

32. Hunter, "The Three Hundred and One Cubit Ark," *Mission* 5 (December 1971): 7-11. See also Hunter's "Restoration Theology: A Schoolmaster," *Mission* 7 (June 1974): 4-12.

33. Davis, "Is the Restoration Movement on the Wrong Track?" *Mission* 7 (September 1973): 5, 7.

34. Olbricht, "New Journals for the Sixties," p. 21.

35. Lemmons, "We Must Not Forget What the Church Is," *FF* 85 (2 January 1968): 2.

36. Glenn L. Wallace, "A Voice of Concern," *FF* 85 (26 March 1968): 198.

37. Boren, letter to editor, *Mission* 2 (November 1968): 27-28.

38. Woods, letter to editor, *Mission* 6 (September 1972): 27.

39. See Olbricht, "New Journals for the Sixties," pp. 25-26; letter from John Stevens (president of Abilene Christian College) to Don Haymes dated 5 July 1972; and letter from Don Haymes to John Stevens dated 14 July 1972. One of ACU's own trustees, M. I. (Ike) Summerlin, refused to resign from the *Mission* board. J. W. Roberts died 15 April 1973, shortly after the school began to exert pressure on the four *Mission* board members, and so he never resigned. Olbricht resigned, but he did so primarily in order to pursue his own scholarly agenda.

40. Ramsey, "How We Can Save America," *FF* 86 (29 July 1969): 457.

41. Reeves, "War, Peace, Protest and Principle," *SS* 4 (October 1972): 26-29.

42. Shelly confirmed these dates in a telephone interview with the author 20 December 1994.

43. Shelly, "The Present Rebellion against Authority," *SS* 4 (October 1972): 1, 5.

44. An advertisement for the issue appeared in *FF* 85 (3 December 1968): 781.

45. Rob McRay so indicated in a letter to the author dated 4 August 1993.

46. Wallace, "The Perversions of the New Versions," *FCC* 1 (July 1967): 1, 3-4.

47. Warren, "Our Aim," *SS* 1 (October 1969): 2.

48. Rice, *"Restoration Movement Is at the Crossroads: Whither in the '70s?,"* *CF* 1 (January 1970): 1.

49. ". . . Editorial Policy," *Anchor* 1 (Winter 1969): 1.

50. Rice, "Lines Are Drawn for Worldwide Battle for Truth at Freed-Hardeman Lectures," *CF* 1 (February 1970): 8.

51. Rice, *Axe on the Root,* vol. 2 (Nashville: Williams Printing, 1967), p. 8.

52. Adams, "The Bible as Authority," in *The Church Faces Liberalism* (Nashville: Gospel Advocate, n.d.), pp. 109-10.

53. Rice, *Axe on the Root,* vol. 1 (Dallas: n.p., 1966), pp. 8-9, 24.

54. Rice, *Axe on the Root,* 1:72.

55. Rice, *"Restoration Movement Is at the Crossroads: Whither in the '70s?" CF* 1 (January 1970): 2.

56. See Ross W. Dye, "Waybill for Decline," *GA* 110 (30 May 1968): 337; Malcolm L. Hill, "What Breeds Liberalism?" *GA* 112 (12 March 1970): 170; and J. E. Choate, "Rudolph Bultmann: The Demythologizer," *GA* 111 (2 October 1969): 629.

57. Baxter, "The Training of Preachers," *FF* 87 (23 June 1970): 387.

58. Hearn, "Getwell Road School of Preaching," *GA* 110 (1 February 1968): 68-69.

59. Rice, "West Coast Brother Declares Proposed New School Sounds Like 'Old' School!" *CF* 1 (December 1970): 8.

60. Wallace, "A Voice of Concern," *FF* 85 (26 March 1968): 198.

61. See Roszak, *The Making of a Counter Culture: Reflections on the Technocratic Society and Its Youthful Opposition* (Garden City, N.Y.: Doubleday, 1969), p. 8.

62. For more on the exodus movement, see the special February 1966 issue of the *20th CC.*

63. Other exodus movements went to Stamford, Connecticut; Somerville, New Jersey; Burlington, Massachusetts; Rochester, New York; and Toronto, Canada. For a brief history of Exodus Bay Shore and similar movements, see Dwain Evans, "1968 in West Islip," *Milestone* (bulletin of West Islip Church of Christ), 28 December 1967, p. 3. For a record of preparations for the "exodus," including employment preparations, see "Newsletter: Exodus Bay Shore," 23 February 1963, p. 1.

64. "The Campbellites Are Coming," *Time,* 15 February 1963, p. 97. For the perspective within the church, see "Exodus Bay Shore — A Great Undertaking," *CC* 20 (25 January 1963): 2; "Top Story of 1962 Honors Given to Exodus/Bay Shore," *CC* 20 (1 February 1963): 1; and "Bay Shore Congregation Will Begin on August 4," *CC* 20 (26 July 1963): 1. See also Marquita Moss, "Reviewing the Restoration at Abilene," *Christianity Today* 11 (17 March 1967): 45.

65. Evans, "Exodus — With the Bible," *Abilene Christian College Annual Bible Lectures* (Abilene: Abilene Christian College Students Exchange, 1966), pp. 275-78.

66. This according to Evans, in an interview with the author, 25 October 1981.

67. Lemmons, "The Holy Spirit Mania," *FF* 83 (29 March 1966): 194.

68. Lemmons, "The Holy Spirit Again," *FF* 83 (23 August 1966): 530.

69. One notable exception was a series of articles by J. D. Thomas, Bible professor at Abilene Christian College, who essentially supported Evans's position. See, e.g., Thomas, "The Holy Spirit (No. 10)," *FF* 83 (25 October 1966): 679-80; and "The Holy Spirit (No. 11)," *FF* 83 (8 November 1966): 711.

70. Delmar Owens, "Serious Speculations concerning the Spirit," *FF* 83 (28 June 1966): 404.

71. Woods, "The Holy Spirit," *GA* 108 (19 May 1966): 308.

72. Evans, "A Statement of My Convictions," *FF* 83 (15 November 1966): 723.

73. One of my students, Greg Gilliam, has told this story in substantial detail in an unpublished paper entitled "The Church of Christ's View of the Holy Spirit in Light of Pat Boone's View of the Holy Spirit and Speaking in Tongues" (1992).

74. Pat Boone, *A New Song* (Carol Stream, Ill.: Creation House, 1970), pp. 27-47; and interview with Boone by the author and Greg Gilliam, Los Angeles, 13 November 1992.

75. Boone, *A New Song*, pp. 80-83.

76. Interview with Boone by the author and Greg Gilliam, Los Angeles, 13 November 1992.

77. Boone, *A New Song*, pp. 87-89.

78. Boone, *A New Song*, pp. 127-28, 155-58.

79. Smith, "Pat Boone . . . Rex Humbard . . . Oral Roberts," *FCC* 3 (August 1969): 4-5.

80. Lemmons, "On a Letter from Pat Boone," *FF* 86 (2 December 1969): 754.

81. Bales, *Pat Boone and the Gift of Tongues* (Searcy, Ark.: James D. Bales, 1970). For examples of the reaction to Lemmons's statement, see Wayne Jackson, "Reply to Reuel Lemmons," *FCC* 3 (February 1970): 2-3; and James D. Bales, "Pat, the Holy Spirit Is Not a Deceiver," *GA* 112 (27 August 1970): 553-55. Boone finally responded to Bales's book in a book of his own entitled *Dr. Balaam's Talking Mule* (Van Nuys, Calif.: Son-Rise Books, 1974).

82. See Dennis, "From Dead Formality to Living Reality," in *The Acts of the Holy Spirit in the Church of Christ Today* (Los Angeles: Full Gospel Businessmen's Fellowship International, 1971), pp. 11-14.

83. For a review of the *Testimony* articles, see Perry B. Cotham, "Brethren Receive the Holy Spirit (?)," *GA* 112 (28 May 1970): 340-42.

84. Cotham, "Brethren Receive the Holy Spirit (?)," *GA* 112 (28 May 1970): 341-42; and *FCC* 3 (June 1970): 3-4.

85. Jackson, "Pat's New Song," *Christian Courier* 4 (May 1970): 1.

86. Rice, "Now That Pat Boone Is Gone, Will Roy Osborne Be Far Behind? How Long, O Lord, How Long!" *CF* 1 (June 1970): 1-2.

87. Rice, "Will Pat Boone, Ben Franklin and Dean Dennis Succeed in Delivering Churches of Christ to Pentecostals?" *CF* 1 (November 1970): 4-5.

88. On the expulsion, see Boone, *Dr. Balaam's Talking Mule*, pp. 5-6; and Dudley Lynch, "Religion in a New Key," *Mission* 5 (August 1971): 20.

89. For the whole story of Finto and the Belmont Church, see Timothy Roberts, "House of God: The High Drama of Don Finto's Belmont Church," *Nashville Scene*, 26 November 1992, pp. 23-27.

90. "Sweet Company Buys 3 Crown Publications," *CC* 24 (16 June 1967): 1.

91. "What Is Campus Evangelism?" *GO* 3 (February 1970).

92. So Bevis notes in a letter to the Campus Evangelism Steering Committee dated 27 June 1966, in John Allen Chalk files, library, Harding Graduate School of Religion, Memphis.

93. Bevis, in a letter to John Allen Chalk dated 30 June 1966, in John Allen Chalk files.

94. Bevis, in a letter to the Campus Evangelism Steering Committee written in the fall of 1966, in John Allen Chalk files.

95. "Campus Evangelism Seminar Recapped," *GO* 1 (May 1967): 3; and program for Campus Leaders' Seminar, Dallas, 26-27 December 1966.

96. See Richard T. Hughes, "Are Restorationists Evangelicals?" in *The Variety of American Evangelicalism*, ed. Donald Dayton and Robert K. Johnston (Knoxville: University of Tennessee Press, 1991), pp. 109-34.

97. "National Program to Be Launched July 1," *GO* 1 (May 1967): 1.

98. "Campus Evangelism Created to Serve Churches of Christ," *Mission* 4 (October 1970): 13.

99. "Will the Church Survive the 70's," *GO* 3 (January 1970).

100. Evans and Chalk quoted in *GO* 2 (January 1969): 1.

101. Bill England, "Say So," *GO* 2 (January 1969): 1.

102. "Daytona," *GO* 2 (February 1969); see also "Campus Evangelism Created to Serve Churches of Christ," *Mission* 4 (October 1970): 12.

103. See "Banowsky Confronts 'Playboy Philosophy,'" *GO* 1 (November 1967): 1.

Banowsky later took part in debates with Episcopal Bishop James Pike and Joseph Fletcher, author of *Situation Ethics*. See "Banowsky Adds 'Situationist' Fletcher to List as 'Victim,'" *CC* 26 (9 May 1969): 14.

104. "Campus Evangelism Created to Serve Churches of Christ," *Mission* 4 (October 1970): 12.

105. Lemmons, "The Demise of Campus Evangelism," *FF* 87 (26 May 1970): 322. The Broadway congregation relinquished its sponsorship of Campus Evangelism some months before its demise; during the final months it was sponsored by the Burke Road Church of Christ, Pasadena, Texas.

106. Camp, "Campus Evangelism," *FCC* 3 (April 1970): 1.

107. Wallace, "A Permissive Society," *FF* 87 (27 January 1970): 56.

108. Emmons, "Christian Hippies, Indeed," *FCC* 3 (January 1970): 4.

109. Craig, "Campus Advance . . . Where and to What?" *FCC* 3 (August 1969): 3.

110. Brewer, "Campus Evangelism and Daytona," *FCC* 2 (June 1969): 3; and Wallace, "The Beach, Bikinis and Beer," *FCC* 2 (June 1969): 2.

111. "The Feb. 6 'Open Forum,'" *CC* 26 (28 April 1969): 9.

112. Camp, "Campus Evangelism," *FCC* 3 (May 1970): 3.

113. Wallace, "A Peep-Hole Religion," *FF* 87 (6 January 1970): 5.

114. Olbricht, "Is There a Message?" *Mission* 6 (June 1973): 5. For other acknowledgments of the flight of the young from Churches of Christ, see Perry C. Cotham, "Freedom of Expression: Is It Really Necessary in Our Churches?" *Mission* 4 (April 1971): 12-13; and Frank Holden, "The New Children," *Mission* 5 (September 1971): 3-4.

115. Olbricht, "Is There a Message?" *Mission* 6 (June 1973): 7.

116. Abilene Christian College became Abilene Christian University in 1976.

117. Olbricht, "A Time for Doctrine," *FF* 85 (29 October 1968): 691.

118. Olbricht, "Biblical Theology and the Restoration Movement," *Mission Journal* 13 (April 1980): 9.

119. Olbricht, "New Journals for the Sixties," p. 27.

120. Wallace, "Mission — Impossible," *FCC* 1 (October 1967): 2-3.

Notes to Chapter 14

1. See Flavil Yeakley, *Why Churches Grow*, 3d ed. (Broken Arrow, Okla.: Christian Communications, 1979), pp. iv-v. See also *Churches and Church Membership in the United States 1980*, ed. Bernard Quinn et al. (Atlanta: Glenmary Research Center, 1982), p. 2; and Mac Lynn, *Churches of Christ in the United States* (Nashville: Gospel Advocate, 1991), p. xvii.

2. Kelley, *Why Conservative Churches Are Growing: A Study in Sociology of Religion* (New York: Harper & Row, 1972); and "Born Again," *Newsweek*, 25 October 1976, pp. 68-78.

3. Phillip Morrison, "Bringing It All Together," *UpReach* 1 (February 1979): 2.

4. Harold Hazelip, "When We Cease to Be Good," *UpReach* 1 (April 1979): 6-8.

5. Phillip Morrison, "Bringing It All Together," *UpReach* 1 (February 1979): 2.

6. Batsell Barrett Baxter, "What to Do When Your Church Leaves You," *UpReach* 1 (October 1979): 16-19.

7. Joe R. Barnett, "Churches of Christ: Who Are These People," *UpReach* 1 (October 1979): 14.

8. "A Quick Look at Church History," *UpReach* 1 (October 1979): 28-29.

9. The television broadcast was advertised in a series of Herald of Truth mailings to

members of Churches of Christ during the latter part of 1992, and special announcements also appeared in *UpReach* magazine (e.g., an insert entitled "In God We Trust: Moving Forward" in the October-December 1992 issue).

10. A partial transcript of the video was published in "In God We Trust," *UpReach* 15 (January-March 1993): 17-19.

11. See Martin Edward Wooten, "The Boston Movement as a 'Revitalization Movement'" (master's thesis, Harding University Graduate School of Religion, 1990).

12. Some of Lucas's critics have argued that he based his work on Robert Coleman's best-selling book *The Master Plan of Evangelism* (Westwood, N.J.: Fleming H. Revell, 1963). However, Lucas claims that he never saw that book until 1975, seven years after he implemented discipling ministries at the Crossroads Church of Christ. See Lucas, "The Master Plan of Evangelism," *At the Crossroads,* 24 May 1981, pp. 1, 3.

13. Brown, "Cultism in the Church," *GA* 121 (22 February 1979): 114, 121.

14. McKean, "Revolution through Restoration: From Jerusalem to Rome, from Boston to Moscow," *UpsideDown* 1 (April 1992): 13.

15. Wooten, "The Boston Movement as a 'Revitalization Movement,'" pp. 50-51; and McKean, "Revolution through Restoration," p. 12.

16. Richard N. Ostling, "Keepers of the Flock," *Time,* 18 May 1992, p. 62.

17. Ostling, "Keepers of the Flock," p. 62.

18. Michelle Latimer, "Former Members Accuse Church of Mind Control, Manipulation," *U.: The National College Newspaper* 3 (Spring Break 1990): 2; Brian Finnerty, "Students Claim Church Is a Cult," *Daily Trojan* 118 (11 November 1992): 1; and Chris Lebrun, "Church Criticized for High Pressure," *Corsair* 67 (21 April 1993): 1.

19. McKean, "Revolution through Restoration," p. 1.

20. McKean, "Revolution through Restoration," p. 2.

21. McKean, "Revolution through Restoration," p. 2.

22. Yeakley, *Why Churches Grow,* p. v; and Lemmons, "Church Planting," *FF* 99 (9 February 1982): 2.

23. Bob Gempel, "Remnant Theology," *Boston Church of Christ Bulletin* 8 (25 October 1987): 1, 7, cited by Wooten in "The Boston Movement as a 'Revitalization Movement,'" p. 80.

24. McKean, "Revolution through Restoration," p. 10.

25. McKean, "Revolution through Restoration," p. 3.

26. McKean so indicated in a telephone interview with the author, 25 August 1993.

27. McKean, "Revolution through Restoration, pp. 3, 4, 6.

28. See McKean, "Revolution through Restoration," pp. 4, 6.

29. Yeakley, *The Discipling Dilemma* (Nashville: Gospel Advocate, 1988), pp. 1-2.

30. McKean, "Revolution through Restoration," p. 7; and McKean's telephone interview with the author, 25 August 1993.

31. McKean reported that during the mid-1980s, "some of the influential Churches of Christ (Garnett Road [in Tulsa] and Sunset [in Lubbock]), as well as the *Christian Chronicle,* the most prominent Church of Christ publication, stopped considering us a part of the Church of Christ fellowship ("Revolution through Restoration," p. 7).

32. The author was a student in that class and heard and observed these things firsthand. Though they occurred over thirty years ago, they are etched in his memory.

33. Lemmons, "Finis," *FF* 100 (23 August 1983): 2.

34. Information on the establishment of *Image* came from Boultinghouse, in a telephone interview with the author, 20 December 1994. Following Lemmons's death in 1989, Boultinghouse took over as editor of the journal.

35. Lemmons, "The Emergence of IMAGE," *Image* 1 (1 June 1985): 4.

36. These colloquia preceded the annual Christian Scholars' Conferences.

37. Thomas, *We Be Brethren* (Abilene: Biblical Research Press, 1958), p. 6. Thomas Olbricht observed that as far as he had been able to learn, this book was "the first rigorous effort to set forth this tripartite formula in our brotherhood or elsewhere" ("Biblical Interpretation in the Restoration Movement," unpublished paper, p. 10). Thomas elaborated on this approach in a second book, *Heaven's Window* (Abilene: Biblical Research Press, 1974), and finally in a third book, *Harmonizing Hermeneutics* (Nashville: Gospel Advocate, 1991), providing a survey of much of the debate over the hermeneutical question.

38. Olbricht, "Hermeneutics: The Beginning Point (Part I)," *Image* 5 (September 1989): 14-15.

39. Olbricht, "The Bible as Revelation," *RQ* 8 (1965): 229. See also Olbricht, "The Rationalism of the Restoration," *RQ* 11 (1968): 85-88; and "Biblical Theology in the Restoration Movement," *Mission Journal* 13 (April 1980): 4-9.

40. Dudrey, "Restorationist Hermeneutics among the Churches of Christ: Why Are We at an Impasse," *RQ* 30 (1988): 37-42.

41. Collier made this point in "Bringing the Word to Life: An Assessment of the Hermeneutical Impasse in Churches of Christ, Part I: The Rationalist/Inductive School," a paper presented at the Christian Scholars' Conference held at Pepperdine University in 1987. The paper received wide circulation and created substantial conversation. He later published an abbreviated version under the title "Bringing the Word to Life: Biblical Hermeneutics in Churches of Christ" (*Christian Studies* 11 [Fall 1990]: 18-39). He later dealt with many of these same issues at greater length in a book entitled *The Forgotten Treasure: Reading the Bible Like Jesus* (West Monroe, La.: Howard Publishing, 1993).

42. Collier, "Bringing the Word to Life," part 1, p. 29.

43. Olbricht, "Is the Theology of the American Restoration Movement Viable?" paper presented at Restoration Colloquium, Princeton Theological Seminary, December 1991.

44. Shelly confirmed these dates in a telephone interview with the author, 20 December 1994.

45. Shelly and Harris, *The Second Incarnation: A Theology for the Twenty-first Century Church* (West Monroe, La.: Howard Publishing, 1992), p. 76.

46. Shelly and Harris, *The Second Incarnation*, p. 78.

47. Shelly and Harris, *The Second Incarnation*, p. 65. In addition to this book by Shelly and Harris, a whole spate of books appeared in the late 1980s and early 1990s reflecting the paradigm shift that was taking place among Churches of Christ. Among those were Leonard Allen, *The Cruciform Church* (Abilene: ACU Press, 1990); Leonard Allen, *Distant Voices: Discovering a Forgotten Past for a Changing Church* (Abilene: ACU Press, 1993); Leonard Allen, Richard Hughes, and Michael Weed, *The Worldly Church: A Call for Biblical Renewal* (Abilene: ACU Press, 1988); Bill Love, *The Core Gospel: On Restoring the Crux of the Matter* (Abilene: ACU Press, 1992); Mike Cope, *Living in Two Worlds* (Nashville: Christian Communications, 1987); James S. Woodroof, *The Church in Transition* (Searcy, Ark.: Bible House, 1990); Gary D. Collier, *The Forgotten Treasure: Reading the Bible Like Jesus* (West Monroe, La.: Howard Publishing, 1993); Lynn Anderson, *Navigating the Winds of Change: Managing Change in the Church* (West Monroe, La.: Howard Publishing, 1994); and James Thompson, *The Church in Exile: God's Counter Culture in a Non-Christian World* (Abilene: ACU Press, 1990).

48. Shelly, Cope, and Morrison, "Wineskins: A Purpose Statement," *Wineskins* 1 (May 1992): 5.

49. Shelly, "A Passion for Nonsectarian Faith," *Wineskins* 1 (January/February 1993): 4.

50. Shelly, Cope, and Morrison, "Wineskins: A Purpose Statement," *Wineskins* 1 (May 1992): 5.

51. Shelly, "A Passion for Nonsectarian Faith," *Wineskins* 1 (January/February 1993): 4. Shelly originally wrote this confession in the mid-1980s, as part of his preface to *I Just Want to Be a Christian;* it was deleted from that volume at the request of the publisher.

52. Lucado's popular titles include *Six Hours One Friday* (Portland: Multnomah, 1989); *The Applause of Heaven* (Dallas: Word, 1990); *In the Eye of the Storm* (Dallas: Word, 1991); *And the Angels Were Silent* (Portland: Multnomah, 1992); *Everyone Needs a Miracle: He Still Moves Stones* (Dallas: Word, 1993); and *A Gentle Thunder: Hearing God through the Storm* (Dallas: Word, 1995).

53. Casey presented his argument in a paper entitled "Scripture as Narrative and the Church, a Story-Formed Community: A Proposal for a New Restoration Hermeneutic," at the July 1989 Christian Scholars' Conference at Pepperdine University.

54. See Smith, *The Cultural Church: Winds of Change and the Call for a "New Herme-neutic"* (Nashville: 20th Century Christian, 1992), p. 16.

55. Smith, *The Cultural Church,* pp. 82-83.

56. Jones, "The Reformation in Tennessee," cited by J. M. Grant in "A Sketch of the Reformation in Tennessee," manuscript, Center for Restoration Studies, Abilene Christian University, p. 55.

57. Thomas, *The Life of the Pilgrim Joseph Thomas* (Winchester, Va.: n.p., 1817), p. 132.

58. Howard, "The Beginning Corner; or, The Church of Christ Identified," *ACR* 1 (August 1856): 226-35.

59. Jn. T. Jones, Jno. Rigdon, M. Elder, and D. P. Henderson, Committee, "Report," *CM* 9 (November 1835): 251. Cf. J. Stephen Sandifer, *Deacons: Male and Female?* (Houston: Keystone Publishing, 1989).

60. I am indebted to Mary Ellen Lantzer, graduate student at Princeton Theological Seminary, for this suggestion.

61. Lipscomb, cited by Fred Arthur Bailey in "The Status of Women in the Disciples of Christ Movement, 1865-1900" (Ph.D. diss., University of Tennessee, 1979), p. 67. Bailey's work is the standard history of the debate over the role of women in the Stone-Campbell movement from the Civil War to 1900.

62. Bailey tells this story in detail in "The Status of Women in the Disciples of Christ Movement, 1865-1900," pp. 79-122.

63. Lipscomb, "Woman and Her Work," *GA* 34 (13 October 1892): 644.

64. See Lipscomb, "From the Paper," *GA* 39 (19 August 1897): 513; "From the Papers," *GA* 39 (5 August 1897): 481; and "The Vital Point," *GA* 39 (19 August 1897): 514-16.

65. See Bailey, "The Status of Women in the Disciples of Christ Movement, 1865-1900," p. 118. He makes the point more explicitly in "The Cult of True Womanhood and the Disciple Path to Female Preaching," in *Essays on Women in Earliest Christianity,* ed. Carroll Osborne, vol. 2 (Joplin, Mo.: College Press, forthcoming).

66. See Nichol, *God's Woman* (Clifton, Tex.: n.p., 1938), p. 137; and Tant, "Women Preaching," *FF* 6 (25 December 1890): 3.

67. See Thomas E. Kemp, "Putting Woman in Her Place, *Mission* 7 (May 1974): 4-7; Mary Lou Walden, "Church of Christ Women: Up from Traditions of Men," *Mission* 9 (November 1975): 7-10; Walden, "Church of Christ Women: Up from Traditions of Men," *Mission* 9 (December 1975): 5-9; Marquita Moss, "Women in Christ Today — A Seminar," *Mission* 8 (March 1975): 5-7; Bobbie Lee Holley, "God's Design: Woman's Dignity," *Mission* 8 (March 1975): 8-14; and Norman L. Parks, "Set Our Women Free," *Integrity* 4 (January 1973): 114.

68. E.g., the Brookline Church of Christ in the Boston area employed women as leaders of public worship by the late 1970s and in a preaching role by 1983; in 1987 the congregation made Micki Pulley a co-minister with pulpit responsibilities. By the mid-1970s, the Church

of Christ in Chapel Hill, North Carolina, utilized women in every worship capacity other than preaching and serving communion. By 1989, the Bering Drive Church of Christ in Houston involved women in the leadership of public worship, though not in a preaching capacity. By 1994, the Cahaba Valley Church of Christ in Birmingham, Alabama, had opened up all aspects of public worship to women, including preaching; Katie Hays, a recent graduate of the Yale Divinity School, became one of three ministers who regularly filled the pulpit. (This information was drawn from telephone interviews by the author with Robert M. Randolph, Boston; Bobbie Lee Holley, Chapel Hill; Bill Love, Houston; and Lance Pape, Birmingham; and a congregational statement entitled "The Role of Women at Cahaba Valley," January 1990.)

69. See *Gender and Ministry: Freed Hardeman University Preachers' and Church Workers' Forum 1990* (Huntsville, Ala.: Publishing Designs, 1990). The Harding Graduate School forum featured a presentation by Lynn Mitchell entitled "Women's Role in Public Worship of the Church of Christ: A Hermeneutical and Theological Reflection."

Index

435